D0072799

PROGRAMMING FOR ARTIFICIAL INTELLIGENCE

INTERNATIONAL COMPUTER SCIENCE SERIES

Consulting editors **A D McGettrick** University of Strathclyde
J van Leeuwen University of Utrecht

SELECTED TITLES IN THE SERIES

The UNIX System *S R Bourne*

Introduction to Expert Systems *P Jackson*

Modula-2: Discipline & Design *A H J Sale*

PROLOG *F Giannesini, H Kanoui, R Pasero and M van Caneghem*

Data Abstraction in Programming Languages *J M Bishop*

System Simulation: Programming Styles and Languages *W Kreutzer*

PROLOG Programming for Artificial Intelligence *I Bratko*

POP-11 Programming for Artificial Intelligence *A M Burton and N R Shadbolt*

Logic Programming and Knowledge Engineering *T Amble*

Performance Measurement of Computer Systems *P McKerrow*

Syntax Analysis and Software Tools *K J Gough*

Comparative Programming Languages *L B Wilson and R G Clark*

C Programming in a UNIX Environment *J Kay and R Kummerfeld*

Clausal Form Logic: An Introduction to the Logic of Computer Reasoning *T Richards*

Programming in Ada (3rd Edn) *J G P Barnes*

Common Lisp Programming for Artificial Intelligence *T Hasemer and J Domingue*

Program Derivation: The Development of Programs from Specifications *R G Dromey*

Object-Oriented Programming with Simula *B Kirkerud*

Parallel Processing: Principles and Practice *E V Krishnamurthy*

PROGRAMMING FOR ARTIFICIAL INTELLIGENCE

Methods, Tools and Applications

Wolfgang Kreutzer & Bruce McKenzie

University of Canterbury, New Zealand

ADDISON-WESLEY
PUBLISHING
COMPANY

Sydney · Wokingham, England · Reading, Massachusetts
Menlo Park, California · New York · Don Mills, Ontario
Amsterdam · Bonn · Singapore
Tokyo · Madrid · San Juan

Cover designed by Crayon Design of Henley-on-Thames
and printed by The Riverside Printing Co. (Reading) Ltd.
Typeset by Times Graphics, Singapore.
Printed in Singapore.

First printed 1990.

British Library Cataloguing in Publication Data
Kreutzer, Wolfgang, *1946–*
Programming for artificial intelligence: methods, tools and applications. – (International computer science series).
1. Artificial intelligence. Applications of computer systems. Programming
I. Title II. McKenzie, Bruce, *1953–* III. Series
006.3′028′551

ISBN 0–201–41621–2

Library of Congress Cataloging in Publication Data
Kreutzer, Wolfgang.
Programming for artificial intelligence: methods, tools and applications.

(International computer science series)
Bibliography: p.
Includes index.
1. Electronic digital computers—Programming.
2. Artificial intelligence. I. McKenzie, Bruce, 1953– . II. Title. III. Series.
QA76.7.K735 1989 006.3 89–14896
ISBN 0–201–41621–2

Preface

People strive to understand a world by building mental models of structures and events, whose 'recognition' is largely determined by the theories, methodologies and metaphors they subscribe to. Since there is no 'unbiased' problem analysis without some methodological frame being used as a guide, the importance of appropriate frames of reference and structuring tools can hardly be overstated. Programming languages and metaphors provide such a context, and a sufficiently 'deep' understanding of a rich repertoire of tools with different orientations offers the best chance for less biased approaches to problem solving. To lay such a foundation for the development of knowledge-based systems is the purpose of this book.

This book is not about *artificial intelligence* (*AI*) as such, although many examples of typical AI applications will be given. Our central concern lies with artificial intelligence as a practical activity and the many interesting tools, metaphors and styles of program development which have evolved in this area over the last 30 years. Managing complexity is a crucial issue in problem-solving programs and systems. Artificial intelligence has made many contributions to programming technology which have had a significant impact on this endeavour, and tools and metaphors supporting these strategies have now begun to penetrate other, more traditional areas of computing. The authors subscribe to a view of computing as a laboratory subject. In addition to a solid theoretical grounding and descriptive information about prototypical systems and applications, a student or practitioner needs to analyze, write and experiment with actual programs to gain some intuition about the strengths and limitations of a particular approach.

The book falls naturally into three major parts. The first of these will discuss three major programming tools, while the second reviews a number of paradigmatic programming metaphors. The third part then centres on the important issue of the user interfaces in which programming activities may be embedded.

Two research programs, heuristic search and knowledge-based systems, have dominated 30 years of AI's history, and the switch from one to the other occurred sometime in the early to mid 1970s. The *introductory chapter* gives a brief survey of AI's history and folklore, together with some appreciation of the differences between these two paradigms.

Chapter 2 concentrates on a discussion of the languages and environments which have traditionally been used to write AI applications. Managing complexity by concept encapsulation and layers of interpretation, and an exploratory, empirical style of program development, are identified as crucial ingredients of AI programming techniques. The rest of this chapter discusses and demonstrates three main programming metaphors within this context: procedural programming, declarative programming and object-oriented programming.

Scheme is used to provide a procedural perspective of the programming process. The reason we prefer this language to other dialects of **LISP** (LISt Processing) is that it offers a well-structured, highly orthogonal and powerful framework for reasoning about processes. Procedures are treated as 'first class' entities and can be manipulated in the same way as any other data structure. This makes it easy to write procedures returning other procedures and to implement object encapsulation. The notion of continuations also offers an elegant way of defining new control structures, such as co-routines. In recognition of COMMON LISP's practical importance, we will survey differences between Scheme and an appropriate subset of COMMON LISP in Appendix VI.

PROLOG exemplifies a declarative approach to program development. Although we do not emphasize the use of PROLOG throughout the rest of the book, this chapter tries to demonstrate both its strengths and weaknesses.

To promote a wider awareness of the many benefits of object-oriented programming is one of our major objectives. In Section 2.5 we therefore discuss the basic characteristics of this idea in the context of a Scheme-based **flavour system**. Object orientation's main benefits are demonstrated by building a simple system simulator, a task which also requires the use of *concurrency*.

Chapter 3 surveys and analyzes a number of useful and interesting programming metaphors which grew out of the last 25 years of AI research. Our approach uses the Scheme language and is based on a number of so-called **'toolboxes'**, as collections of typical data types and procedures supporting a particular metaphor. Toolboxes for heuristic search, game playing, pattern matching, associative knowledge bases, production systems, associative networks, frame networks and augmented transition network (ATN) grammars are described, discussed and exemplified.

Sophisticated interactive programming environments with graphics support are an important component of AI programming tools.

Apart from being the most paradigmatic of all object-oriented programming systems, the **Smalltalk** language also offers one of the most complete and sophisticated programming environments available today. This makes it an appropriate base from which to investigate the power of user interfaces for exploratory programming, which is the topic of *Chapter 4*. The characteristics of the so-called '*desktop metaphor*' will be demonstrated, and we will show simple uses of graphics and the model–view–controller (MVC) metaphor for building window- and menu-based applications.

The book finishes with some 'crystal ball gazing' about likely developments in AI programming, and programming technology in general. Sets of *Exercises* are presented throughout, and Appendix V offers some sample solutions for starred (*) exercises.

The authors of this book subscribe to the notion that learning to use a programming tool requires much more than learning its syntax. It is also necessary to acquire an appreciation of typical patterns of its application and the contexts in which it is utilized. This book does not stress the description of syntactic conventions or any other information which may easily be obtained from a reference manual. Instead, we shall emphasize issues of style and demonstrate small but typical applications. A large number of examples presents distilled experience, and the reader is invited to browse through them as an introduction to the literature of programs provided by other textbooks and in the relevant journals. To encourage this activity, our programs are often more 'verbose' than is customary, with long names for identifiers and careful indentation. The program examples have been designed to show both positive and negative aspects of a particular programming style and are intended to offer a basis for some intuition about what is easy or difficult. Advantages and disadvantages of each metaphor are of course also explicitly stated and many pointers for further study are given.

All the programs in this book have been run on a variety of machines. Although an **Apple Macintosh** has been used as our main development system, we have also tested most of the programs on a **VAX 750**, a **Sun 3/60** and an **IBM PC**. Apart from the *Concurrent Flavour System* discussed in Section 2.5, we have been very careful to ensure portability. **MacScheme**, **Chez Scheme**, **T**, **XScheme** and **PC Scheme** are the Scheme versions for which the programs have been tested, and for which machine-readable versions of our toolboxes are available. Only standard features of Scheme, as defined by Rees and Clinger (1986), have been used, with the exception of a few convenient 'extensions', whose implementation for a range of Scheme dialects is given in a 'Systems' toolbox. *Standard Edinburgh syntax* and *predicates* are used in the PROLOG chapter, and all the Smalltalk code has been tested under both the Xerox VI2.2 image and Apple's VI1 subset.

The *source code* for the toolbox programs is given in Appendix III. A machine-readable version of these and a number of additional programs (for Apple Macintosh, **UNIX** or IBM PC systems), which are available for a nominal fee, can be obtained directly from the authors by writing to:

Dr W. Kreutzer and Dr B. J. McKenzie,
Re: AI Book,
Computer Science Department,
University of Canterbury,
Christchurch 1,
New Zealand

To order, send your name and address together with money or a money order, stating clearly which of the following versions you require:

Apple Macintosh version (on 3½″ floppies) . . . US$15
IBM PC compatible version (on 5½″ floppies) . . . US$15
Sun version (on 1 cartridge tape) . . . US$50
VAX version (on 1 ½″ 300′ tape) . . . US$25

This book has grown out of a number of lecture courses on AI programming, given by one of the authors. It is suitable for a wide range of readers, including students, computer professionals and hobbyists. The book requires no prior knowledge of artificial intelligence or AI programming. Only some general knowledge of programming, in **Pascal** or a similar language, will be assumed.

The book may therefore be used as the primary textbook in courses on AI programming methodology or programming in Scheme, typically at the upper undergraduate level.

The book is also suitable as a companion to an application or methodology-oriented book on artificial intelligence, and the annotated bibliography of AI textbooks offers some suggestions on this. If it is supplemented by appropriate journal articles, it may even form the basis for a practical course in AI. Another purpose for which it might be used is in a comparative course on programming languages or programming techniques.

Acknowledgements

The authors and publisher wish to thank the following for permission to reproduce their material:

W.H. Freeman and Company for material adapted from *How to Solve Problems* by Wayne A. Wickelgren. Copyright © 1974 W.H. Freeman and Company. Reprinted by permission. ('Lineland' and 'Wanda' problems, Chapter 2)

Professors T. Kaehler and D. Patterson for a quotation from 'A Small Taste of Smalltalk'. *BYTE*, August 1986, p. 145. (Chapter 2)

Professor P. Wegner for a quotation from 'Classification in Object-Oriented Systems' in *SigPlan 1986*, p. 181. (Chapter 2, Section 2.5.4)

F. Rubin (1979) for material adapted from 'The Clocks of Klotz and Klutz' *J. Recreational Mathematics* **12**(1), pp. 53–4. (Exercise 2.27)

Professor A.K. Dewdney (1987) for material from 'Diverse Personalities Search for Social Equilibrium at a Computer Party and Voting Game.' *Scientific American – Computer Recreations*, pp. 104–7. (Exercises 2.10 and 2.28)

R. Smullyan (1984) for material from '*Alice in Puzzle-land*'. Harmondsworth: Penguin. (Exercise 2.12)

Professor H.A. Simon (1982) for material from 'The Architecture of Complexity.' *Proc. American Philosophical Soc.* **106**, pp. 467–82 (Exercise 3.8)

Professor P.H. Winston for material from *Artificial Intelligence* (2nd edn). Copyright © Addison-Wesley 1984. (Exercise 3.44)

Professor E.R. Berlekamp for material adapted from *Winning Ways for Your Mathematical Plays* (2 volumes). Copyright © Academic Press 1982 (Figures 2.28, 3.17, 3.33, 3.34, 3.36, 3.37, 3.41–6)

W. Kreutzer
B. J. McKenzie
Christchurch, 1989

Contents

Table of programs

Chapter 1
Introduction

'There are two quite different starting points to define AI – the dream and the technology. As a dream, there is a unified (if ill-defined) goal of duplicating human intelligence in its entirety. As a technology, there is a fairly coherent body of techniques (such as heuristic search and the use of formal representations) that distinguish the field from others in computer science. In the end, this technological base will continue to be a unified area of study (like numerical analysis or operations research) with its special methodology. We will recognize that it is not coextensive with the dream, but is only one (possibly small) piece . . .'

[*Winograd, in: Bobrow and Hayes, eds (1985), p. 380.*]

1.1 From heuristic search to knowledge-based systems – a brief history of AI

Although the field of artificial intelligence (AI) has had only a short history itself, the dream of building 'mechanical minds' dates back a long time. European literature abounds with stories of people who accomplished this goal (for example, Frankenstein) and, more often than not, met a horrible fate. It has haunted philosophy since the early seventeenth century and René Descartes, whose claim that 'understanding' consists of building appropriate representations, later formed the foundation for highly successful research programs which formalized many commonsense notions in science and everyday life. The first attempt to express such 'laws of thought' on a logical basis was made by the Irish mathematician G. Boole in the nineteenth century. Boole's reduction of logic to a series of 'yes/no decisions' became a cornerstone of twentieth-century philosophy and science. At around the same time, C. Babbage invented his 'difference engine', a device for tabulating arbitrary mathematical functions, which is now generally recognized as the forerunner of today's digital computer systems. Babbage's ideas proved beyond the technological limits of his time and the difference engine was never built. Half a century later, G. Frege, a German mathematician, invented the first formally defined axiomatic logic system ['*Begriffsschrift*' – Frege (1960)], while Whitehead and Russell (1910–1913) wrote their *Principia Mathematica*, whose goal it was to demonstrate that the roots of all of mathematics lie in the basic laws of logic.

All these efforts culminated in one of the most influential intellectual movements of the early twentieth century. 'Logical positivism' [Carnap (1928), Waismann (1967)] tried to define the nature of knowledge with the same formal rigour that was then coming into fashion in the world of mathematics. One very influential work of that time was Wittgenstein's *Tractatus Logico-Philosophicus* (1922), which starts with 'the world is all that is the case' and finishes with 'what we cannot speak about we must pass over in silence.' The rest of the book is a formal argument about the connection between what can be said and what can be thought or known. In some sense, Wittgenstein already forges a link between human thought and computation, in the sense of a formally described sequence of transformations of elementary propositions. The initial enthusiasm and optimism of logical positivism soon proved untenable and Wittgenstein, in his later philosophy, came to reject most of the theses in his *Tractatus*. In 1936, however, A. Turing, an English mathematician, restated the assertion that thought can be reduced to computation. Turing devised a formal definition of computation as programs executed by an automaton, later referred to as a '**Turing machine**'. Since then, Turing machines have served as our predominant model of computation. Turing and the mathematician A. Church, independently, also reframed one of Wittgenstein's key assertions as a hypothesis known as the '**Church – Turing thesis**': *if a problem that could be presented to a Turing machine is not solvable, then it is also not solvable by human thought*. From this assumption, it would follow that if humans can solve problems or behave 'intelligently', then it should ultimately also be possible to build machines to exhibit the same kind of behaviour. This is of course the cornerstone of artificial intelligence. Turing later (1950) also proposed an operational definition of 'intelligence', the so-called '**Turing test**'. Here two parties are allowed to communicate through some impersonal medium (such as a teletype terminal). A program may then be called 'intelligent' if it can fool the human partner into believing that he/she is conversing with another human.

A number of further crucial developments occurred in the late 1940s, when the first digital computer systems were built, following J. von Neumann's (1958) 'stored program' idea. These machines served to demonstrate how logic and arithmetic could work together to describe computational procedures. Cybernetics, the investigation of feedback loops in engineering, science and organisms, was also emerging as a new field, holding much promise for the study of intelligence [Wiener (1948)].

The birth of 'artificial intelligence' as a research program with an identity of its own is often linked to the famous 'Dartmouth Summer School on Artificial Intelligence', where a number of researchers actively engaged in thinking about thinking machines met in 1956 – to discuss their ideas and achievements. Quite a few well-known scientists attended this meeting (for example, C. Shannon), but four of the (later) most influential participants were Herbert Simon, Allan Newell, John McCarthy and Marvin Minsky. While cybernetics centred on the study of essentially 'low level' phenomena, such as feedback control and neural networks, artificial intelligence started with a much more ambitious, 'high level' view of thought as a symbol-processing activity performed by the human problem solver.

The notion of '**intelligence**' is in itself a rather elusive one, although most people would agree that there is some connection with the ability to solve 'hard' problems. One of its best definitions remains the one attributed to M. Minsky, as 'a piece of intellectual behaviour that we admire but don't understand'. Since the Dartmouth conference, the term 'artificial intelligence' (**AI**) has often been used to refer to two quite separate research programs, a state of affairs which is reflected in the quote at the beginning of this chapter. In its narrow interpretation, AI may be seen as an engineering exercise, centring on design and implementation of hardware and software systems, in order to achieve some degree of 'intelligent' performance in a specified task domain. Although the ultimate goal is to create an artificial system which will equal or surpass human performance, much of this work concerns itself with tools to control the intellectual complexity of large computer

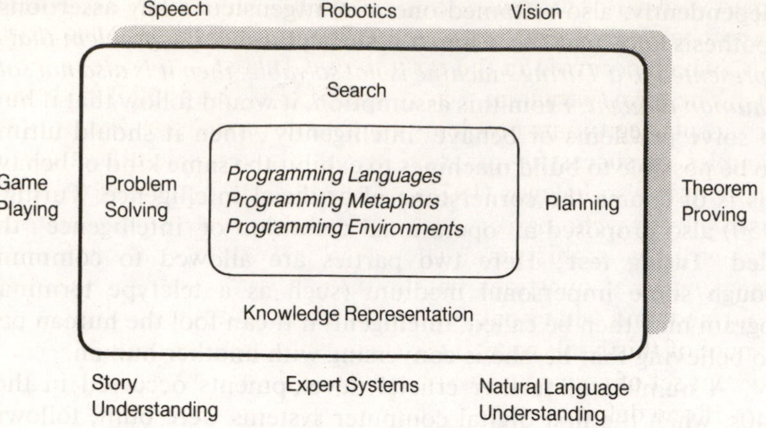

Figure 1.1 Three layers of AI research.

programs (**AI programming**). While this approach is predicated on 'intelligence' as an abstract notion, **cognitive science** [Anderson (1980), Bruner (1983), Gardner (1985)] embarks on the much more ambitious enterprise of defining and explaining *human* performance. This is an interdisciplinary activity, involving psychologists and philosophers as well as computer scientists. Computers are viewed as devices for creation, manipulation and transmission of symbol structures and are therefore used as tools in an attempt to encode human cognition into a formal system. A characterization of 'intelligence' as a software property is tacitly embraced by both these enterprises, although the truth of this assumption is by no means undisputed ['the heart has its reasons that reason does not know' – Dreyfus (1972), Dreyfus and Dreyfus (1986)]. Many prominent researchers in both cognitive science and AI have since further explored the idea of **physical symbol systems** as 'machines that produce through time an evolving collection of symbol structures' and have found reasons to believe that such systems 'have the necessary and sufficient means for intelligent action' [Newell and Simon (1976), p. 116]. In this type of inquiry, AI is concerned with how such symbol systems must be organized in order to behave intelligently. A comprehensive account of the nature of this research program is given by Newell (1980).

Figure 1.1 shows a bird's-eye view of some of AI's many subareas. Research programs are stratified into three levels. The innermost layer contains the methodological heart of **AI programming**, the middle layer lists **theoretical issues** and the outer layer shows some **applications**. Although examples will often be taken from typical AI applications, this book deals primarily with the first two of these levels.

There is currently a considerable amount of interest in AI methodology, fuelled largely by the commercial potential of so-called

'expert systems'. This renaissance can be traced to a fundamental change of approach by wide sections of the AI community; a so-called 'paradigm shift', which occurred in the early to mid 1970s.

The term **'paradigm'** was first used by Kuhn (1970) to define a set of concepts, legitimate problems, acceptable procedures and prototypical examples of successful practice within a given scientific tradition or 'school' [see also Lakatos (1973), Masterman (1970)]. Newtonian physics, behavioural psychology or stochastic queuing theory are good examples for paradigms in this sense, since they provide normative frameworks suggesting what questions will be asked, what experiments should be performed, and what books and articles are published and read. For the purpose of this book we will use the term more generally to refer to any coherent set of concepts and objectives.

If one defines

Intelligence = Knowledge + Reasoning

one may choose to stress either the first or the second of the two components. Since the Dartmouth meeting, AI had for many years been dominated by a search for some powerful universal scheme of deduction, so-called **'weak methods'**, which require little or no knowledge specific to a particular application. As part of this research, various algorithms and programs for **searching** symbolic state spaces were invented and analyzed during the 1960s and early 1970s. By proving theorems from Whitehead and Russell's *Principia Mathematica*, Newell and Simon's (1956, 1957) *Logic Theorist* was the first program which successfully demonstrated the possibility of AI. It was followed by a number of similar programs, many of which were tested on a variety of combinatorial puzzles which have since earned a place in AI folklore (for example, 'river-crossing' problems like 'missionaries and cannibals', the 8-puzzle problem, cryptarithmetic, eight queens, 'ape and banana'; strategic games such as tic-tac-toe, chequers, chess; stacking children's blocks; animal guessing). We will encounter many of these **'microworlds'** in later chapters and exercises. Some methods for 'general problem solving', augmented by so-called 'heuristics', were initially quite successful, causing many to expect their application to real-world problems in the not too distant future. Only a few critics cautioned such enthusiasm [*see*, for example, Dreyfus (1972)], pointing out that all problems which had successfully been solved so far were invariably characterized by highly regular structures and fairly small search spaces. Much of the late 1960s and early 1970s was then spent in largely unsuccessful attempts to adapt weak methods to problems of realistic size and complexity.

Sometime during the 1970s the general disenchantment with the performance of domain-independent, general problem-solving programs had reached a level where most researchers were willing to accept that sole reliance on universal methods of deduction must invariably lead to combinatorial explosions of effort, and that 'weak' methods are therefore ill-suited to problems of realistic size and complexity. Completeness, optimality and efficiency came to be seen as competing, not complementary goals, between which suitable trade-offs had to be made. The lesson to be learned from this 'failure' seemed to be that hardly any practically relevant problems could be solved without some highly specific knowledge about a particular task. A different, less ambitious approach was therefore needed to support practical applications. Many researchers now (re)turned to a study of human problem solving, whose strategies can typically *not* be guaranteed to work under all conceivable circumstances. They are, however, remarkably robust and seem to work surprisingly well in many diverse situations. In order to simulate such styles of information processing we need to turn to constrained rather than strict rationality, and accept memory and reasoning power as limited resources. This new paradigm is largely driven by some rather elusive notion of 'relevance', sacrificing completeness and optimality in return for effectiveness and efficiency. Its successful application strongly depends on personal and traditional knowledge, and is highly dependent on context. A dominance of the *knowledge* component of problem solving can therefore be observed since the late 1970s. So-called '**strong methods**' have moved to the centre of attention, using relatively 'shallow' chains of deduction across large collections of problem-specific facts and rules. Research into efficient structuring and use of such knowledge bases now occupies much of AI methodology, and so-called '**expert systems**' have rapidly gained in popularity over the past few years, as evidenced by a number of ambitious projects in Japan (fifth-generation computer project), the USA (*strategic computer initiative*), England (*Alvey*) and the EEC (*Esprit*).

1.2 Heuristic search – programs as puzzle solvers

Heuristic search methods originated in AI's quest for a universal, domain-independent procedure for reasoning from 'first principles'. Applications of such techniques can be found in programs for tasks as diverse as natural language understanding, combinatorial problem solving, information retrieval, robotics, game playing and mathematical theorem proving. Search techniques solve problems by sequential creation and modification of symbolic expressions, generating potential states and testing them for a solution.

> 'They exercise "intelligence" by extracting information from a problem domain and by using that information to guide their

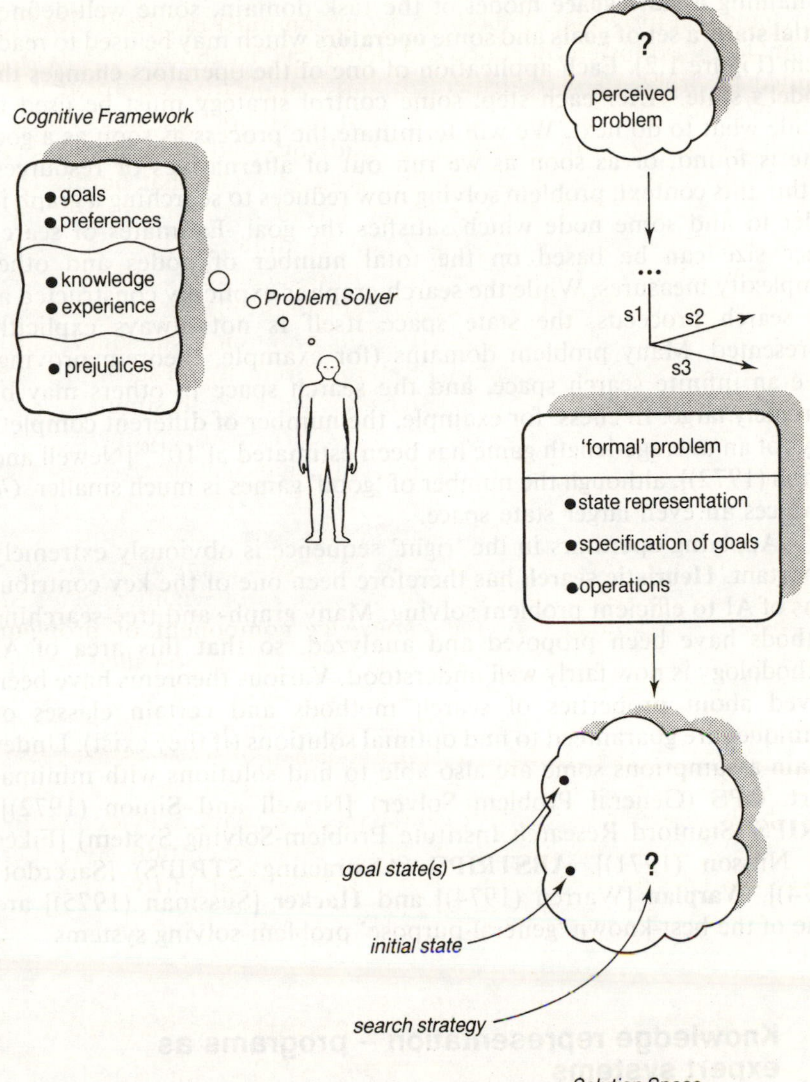

Figure 1.2 The state space paradigm.

> search, avoiding wrong turns and circuitous bypaths. For this to work, a problem domain must contain information, that is some degree of order and structure.'
>
> [*Newell and Simon (1976), p. 126.*]

Within this paradigm, all problem-solving activity may generally be described in terms of five elementary components. There is a data base containing a **state space** model of the task domain, some well-defined **initial state**, a set of **goals** and some **operators** which may be used to reach them (Figure 1.2). Each application of one of the operators changes the model's state. After each step, some control strategy must be used to decide what to do next. We will terminate the process as soon as a goal state is found, or as soon as we run out of alternatives or resources. Within this context, problem solving now reduces to searching a graph in order to find some node which satisfies the goal. Estimates of search space size can be based on the total number of nodes and other complexity measures. While the search graph is explicitly constructed as the search proceeds, the state space itself is not always explicitly represented. Many problem domains (for example, theorem proving) have an infinite search space, and the search space in others may be extremely large. In chess, for example, the number of different complete plays of an average-length game has been estimated at 10^{120} [Newell and Simon (1972)], although the number of 'good' games is much smaller. *Go* produces an even larger state space.

Applying operators in the 'right' sequence is obviously extremely important. **Heuristic search** has therefore been one of the key contributions of AI to efficient problem solving. Many graph- and tree-searching methods have been proposed and analyzed, so that this area of AI methodology is now fairly well understood. Various theorems have been proved about properties of search methods and certain classes of techniques are guaranteed to find optimal solutions (if they exist). Under certain assumptions some are also able to find solutions with minimal effort. **GPS** (General Problem Solver) [Newell and Simon (1972)], **STRIPS** (Stanford Research Institute Problem-Solving System) [Fikes and Nilsson (1971)], **ABSTRIPS** (Abstracting STRIPS) [Sacerdoti (1974)], **Warplan** [Warren (1974)] and **Hacker** [Sussman (1975)] are some of the best-known 'general-purpose' problem-solving systems.

1.3 Knowledge representation – programs as expert systems

The evolution of knowledge bases can be traced to the simpler concepts of discrimination nets and deductive databases, which AI has been experimenting with for at least two decades. Deductive databases contain collections of facts and rules, together with an application-independent deduction program to answer queries about them. Further research has led to **expert systems**, a multitude of which are now being marketed commercially. Most of these are primarily knowledge based, although there are some predominantly algorithmic programs, such as the **MACSYMA** or **Reduce** formula manipulation systems, with a high degree of achievement in their field of expertise. Potential applications for expert systems include areas as diverse as medical diagnosis,

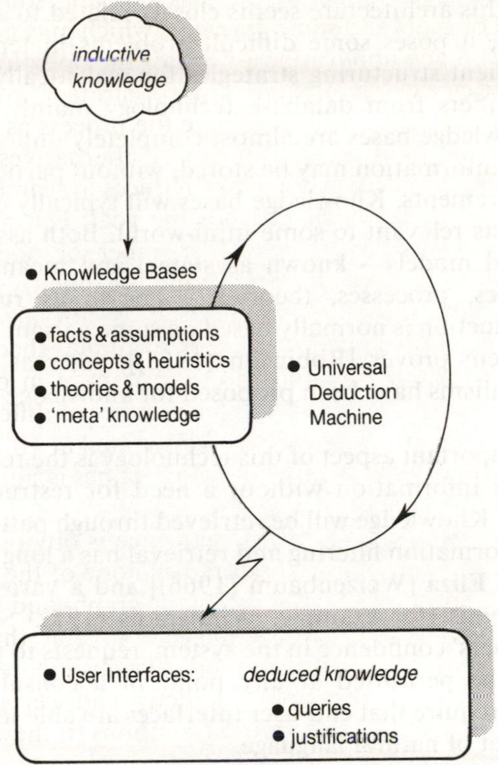

Figure 1.3 Architecture of knowledge-based systems.

statistical data interpretation, financial planning, tax advice, analysis of pollution and plant diseases, automatic transmission of satellite malfunctions, and many others. Most of the earliest and best-known expert systems were developed for tasks involving medical diagnosis. This is certainly no coincidence. Apart from its comparatively generous research funding, medicine, other than for example physics, is not dominated by theories giving strong structure to the field. Casuistic knowledge, encoded in a multitude of specialized rules, is prevalent. This forms a good foundation for knowledge-based systems, which have proved less effective in applications requiring 'deep' reasoning from basic axioms and general laws.

The architecture of a **knowledge-based system**, as shown in Figure 1.3, is fairly simple. There is always an appropriately structured **knowledge base** of facts, beliefs, rules and theories, with some application-independent **deduction machinery** for drawing inferences. Convenient **user interfaces** for problem formulation and knowledge acquisition are also required. These three components, without any specific information loaded into the knowledge bases, are often referred to as an '**expert system shell**'.

Although this architecture seems closely related to a conventional database system, it poses some difficult problems in terms of finding flexible and efficient structuring strategies for realistically sized knowledge bases. It differs from database technology mainly in that usage patterns for knowledge bases are almost completely unpredictable. Any kind of relevant information may be stored, without particular regard to formatting requirements. Knowledge bases will typically contain definitions of all aspects relevant to some mini-world. Both assertions (facts, beliefs, structural models – known as **states**) and means for drawing conclusions (rules, processes, theories – known as **rules**) must be represented. Deduction is normally based on some variant of Robinson's resolution theorem prover [Robinson (1965)], whereas a number of alternative formalisms have been proposed for knowledge-base structuring.

Another important aspect of this technology is the requirement for inclusion of new information without a need for restructuring whole knowledge bases. Knowledge will be retrieved through pattern matching, whose use for information filtering and retrieval has a long history in AI, reaching back to **Eliza** [Weizenbaum (1966)] and a variety of 'natural language' front ends [for example, Winograd's (1972) **SHRDLU**]. In order to assure users' confidence in the system, requests to justify lines of reasoning must be permitted at any point in a consultation. Many systems will also require that end-user interfaces are able to cope with an appropriate subset of natural language.

Knowledge-based systems (KBS) are generally well suited to areas in which decisions are typically made on the basis of large amounts of empirical information, often encoded in case-specific rules, models and analogies. KBSs are less well suited for domains with well-structured deductive knowledge (universal laws), where algorithmic programs should be preferred. **Mycin** [Shortliffe (1976)], **Dendral** [Buchanan and Feigenbaum (1978)], **Prospector** [Duda *et al.* (1979)], **R1** [McDermott (1981)] and **Hearsay-II** [Erman *et al.* (1980)] are some of the best-known and most successful knowledge-based systems.

The true bottlenecks of this technology arise in efficient acquisition, storage and reconstruction of knowledge. Providing some capability to 'learn' inductively has proved much more difficult than originally envisioned and research in this area is still in its infancy. With the current state of technology, we know how to encode definitions and taxonomies, invariants and empirical associations, deductive inferences and simple search heuristics. There are as yet no or only partial solutions for formalization of general problem-solving knowledge, analogies, meta-representations (knowledge about the suitability of representations for different purposes) and elementary world models. By 'elementary world models' we mean common-sense reasoning, which, for example, will tell us that a glass of water, if dropped in mid-air, should fall to the floor and will probably break. It is unclear how one might graft such knowledge on to a symbol processor without letting it gather 'experience' in a relevant environment. Another unsolved problem concerns the optimal compilation and decompilation of knowledge. This refers to the process of translating from some 'higher' (closer to specifications, further away from computations) into some 'lower' (closer to computations, further away from specifications) level of representation. On the one hand, knowledge must be compiled to be efficiently interpretable by computer systems. It must, on the other hand, also be available in symbolic form in order to permit a higher degree of 'understanding' on the part of a user. The optimal levels of binding and redundancy to balance both these objectives are still largely unknown.

1.4 AI folklore – some famous programs

Much of the history of AI has been an account of individual programs and their successful application in small and well-restricted domains.

Mathematics has been a popular domain for early AI research. The **Logic Theorist** was a first successful attempt to demonstrate that programs can, in principle, discover and prove mathematical theorems, an activity long admired as a highly intelligent task [Newell and Simon (1956, 1957)]. **Student** was an early program solving algebra word problems. It worked by translating sentences into equations which could then be analyzed further [Bobrow (1968)]. **Saint** and its successor, **Sin**, two symbolic integration programs, served as forerunners of popular formula manipulation systems such as **MACSYMA** [Slagle (1963), Moses (1967), Martin and Fateman (1971)].

GPS (General Problem Solver) is an important early problem-solving system built around an idea called 'means-ends analysis' [Newell and Simon (1972)]. It was designed to separate general problem-solving techniques from the requirements peculiar to a given task domain. Many of its concepts were derived from analyses of protocols produced by human subjects while thinking aloud. Although its approach was initially successful in solving many traditional micro-world puzzles (for example, cryptarithmetic, 'missionaries and cannibals', 'ape and banana'), it has since, unfortunately, proved unsuitable for real-world applications. **AM** and **Eurisko**, both written by D. Lenat (1976, 1982), were further explorations into the nature of 'heuristics', with an eye towards understanding, efficient acquisition and representation of such mental 'rules of thumb'. **STRIPS** (Stanford Research Institute Problem-Solving System) was part of the ill-fated *Shakey* robotics project at the Stanford Research Institute and is built on GPS's foundations. It contains a depth-first problem solver and later had a profound influence on the design of more modern planning systems [Fikes and Nilsson (1971)].

Samuel's celebrated **checkers** player was the first in a long line of game-playing programs [Samuel (1967)]. Although this field has been extensively researched and is now fairly well understood, with many important theoretical results, we are still waiting for chess programs that perform consistently at the grandmaster level.

Eliza was an exploration of the concept of 'understanding' through pattern matching. It simulated a non-directive psychiatrist and was designed to engage people in conversations through a teletype terminal [Weizenbaum (1966)]. Weizenbaum recalls that it became frighteningly popular with many people; an observation which later caused him to turn into one of the most vocal critics of those aspects of AI research which he sees as infringing upon human dignity [Weizenbaum (1976)].

EPAM (Elementary Perceiver and Memorizer) was the first experimental computer program which 'learned' and 'remembered' things. It was based on the notion of discrimination nets, which are used to categorize and retrieve knowledge about task domains. EPAM has successfully been applied to many aspects of verbal reasoning [Simon and Feigenbaum (1964)]. Later the **SIR** (Semantic Information Retrieval) program implemented an information retrieval system whose knowledge base contained networks of property lists [Raphael (1968)]. Another such program, **Scholar**, also employed semantic networks and pattern matching in an attempt to simulate human memory. It aimed at using the 'socratic method' to teach concepts in a tutorial dialogue. A database of South American geography is often cited as an example [Carbonell (1970)].

So-called 'production systems' have served as a basis for many AI programs. Most notably they set the style in which **Mycin** and other early expert system programs were written [Davis *et al.* (1977)].

Sam [Schank and Colby (1973)] was designed as a question answering system. Researchers at Yale University later used it to explore the idea of 'scripts' in story 'understanding', where it was tested with three famous scenarios: a bus trip script, a pickpocket script and a restaurant script. These contexts have repeatedly been used in the literature to illustrate frame- and script-based programs.

Hearsay is a celebrated speech understanding program with many new and interesting features [Erman *et al.* (1980)]. Its metaphor of autonomous 'knowledge sources' communicating through so-called 'blackboards' has had a major impact on expert system architectures and the emergence of object-oriented design as an important new programming style.

Waltz's procedure for contour labelling probably offers the best-known demonstration of the usefulness of constraints to reduce the large search spaces arising in **visual scene recognition** [Waltz (1975)].

The **SHRDLU** program is one of the most frequently cited AI applications. It was designed as an experiment in language 'understanding' and implements a restricted natural language interface between human operators and a robot manipulating simple geometrical shapes in the so-called 'blocks world' [Winograd (1972)]. Its use of the **MicroPlanner** language with automatic backtracking and so-called 'demon' procedures has later been emulated in many other programs.

Lifer is one of a number of successful tools for building natural language interfaces to database systems [Hendrix *et al.* (1978)].

Finally, learning has always been at the forefront of AI research. Although a few software systems are showing some promise for the future, progress has been much slower than originally hoped for and research in this area is still in its infancy. While early work has concentrated on adaptive learning through pattern classification, **Teiresias, Lex, Induce, Bacon** and Winston's experimental programs deal with learning from analogy and examples [Davis (1979), Mitchell (1982), Winston (1980), Michalski *et al.* (1985)].

AI's theoretical foundations are still weak and we are far from any profound insights which we may claim to be universal. Much further theoretical and empirical research into many aspects of knowledge representation and principles of problem solving is sorely needed. From a practical point of view it may well be true that:

> 'Progress in the next decade will come in discovering those domains in which the assumptions and techniques of AI are appropriate ... the secret of success isn't in building the right program, but in finding the right domain. ... The result may not be "intelligent machines", but intelligent uses of machine capabilities.'
>
> [*T. Winograd, in: Bobrow and Hayes (1985), p. 395.*]

Through discussion and demonstration of basic tools and techniques of AI programming we will try to lay a foundation for such an understanding. Although you will learn of both AI's capabilities and limitations, this book does not claim to be an introduction to 'artificial intelligence' as such. A number of good survey and reference texts already caters for this purpose. Appendix I of this book contains an annotated bibliography of many relevant references. The books by Boden (1977), Raphael (1976), Hofstadter (1979, 1985), Ringle (1979), Sloman (1978) and Dreyfus (1972, 1986) can be recommended for a non-technical survey of AI's philosophical foundations. McCorduck (1979) gives a fascinating account of the field's historical development. Good and very readable introductions to concepts and issues of cognitive science are given by Gardner (1985) and Hayes (1978). Rich (1983) and Winston (1984) are excellent general introductions to AI's major concepts and applications. Rauch-Hindin (1985) gives a more pragmatic overview of the field. Nilsson (1980) and Charniak and McDermott (1985) are good textbooks with emphasis on logic, while Tanimoto (1987) provides a more programming-oriented perspective. Finally, useful as both reference and textbook, Barr *et al.* (1981, 1982) have assembled a three-volume encyclopaedia, which surveys principles and examples of most of AI's major subfields.

Chapter 2
Tools and Environments for AI Programming

> 'Writing about general systems theory is like writing about unicorns. Even after you eliminate all the people who have never heard of them and all the people who have heard of them but are not interested in the subject, you have to contend with the people who do not believe they exist. . . . General systems theory is an attempt to aid the human mind in dealing with a world which is too complex for that mind.'
>
> [*Weinberg (1972), pp. 98 and 99.*]

2.1 AI programming – managing complexity

This book has been motivated by a strong belief that managing complexity is at the heart of AI programming. The notion of 'complexity' [Loefgren (1977)] itself is unfortunately a somewhat ill-defined concept. For our purposes we are interested in the *intellectual complexity* involved in a system's analysis, a concern we share with general systems theory [Klir (1972)], as quoted above. Issues of computational complexity must also be addressed, but they should be treated as a separate issue.

Numerousness of parts is certainly not a decisive or even very relevant complexity measure. We are rather more interested in the diversity and number of links between elements we must 'understand'. There are generally two ways to cope with complexity in programs – simplification and delegation. Simplification requires abstraction, the removal or aggregation of components and/or relationships. To remove complexity, we may factor systems into substructures which are then treated as single elements. In computing we may also wish to define programs through specifications, thereby abstracting from their actual implementation. Hierarchies are a very important concept here, leading to the notion of *layered designs* as a methodological basis for program development. The textbook by Wulf *et al.* (1981) is an excellent demonstration of this technique in the context of a conventional programming language (**Pascal**).

Although simplification should be the preferred approach for the design of well-structured, reliable programs, some tasks will always remain for which complexity cannot be further reduced at the time a problem is formulated. Such tasks are better considered as design rather than implementation problems, and program and specification should therefore evolve together. Most AI applications fall into this category. Since we are often unaware of the nature and implications of many aspects of a problem we wish to explore, insistence on precise specifications may even prove counter-productive. A decision on what exactly it is that we want should typically emerge as a *result* of a programming project and not be 'frozen' in specifications at its start. This leads to an exploratory, experimental style of development, for which it is hard to impose structure. The only way for the programmer to remain in control is through delegation of any but the most important of tasks. *Programming environments* with a wide collection of supporting tools are essential to this approach. Any task which can be performed automatically should be delegated to a program; never mind the expense.

2.1.1 A layered approach to software design

Well-structured programs must be designed in layers, each building on concepts defined in the previous ones [*see* Allen (1978), Wulf *et al.* (1981), Abelson *et al.* (I 985)]. Techniques for encapsulating descriptions

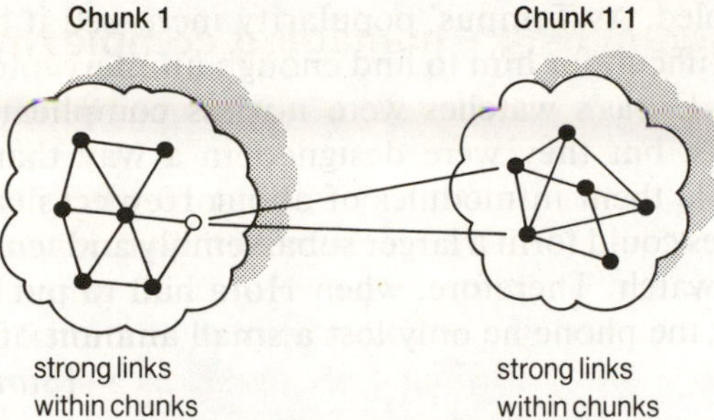

Figure 2.1 'Chunking'.

of both structure and behaviour of objects within modules are used for representation, with hierarchical structures as the predominant means of interconnection. Such hierarchies may greatly simplify a system's description. To reduce complexity we may choose to treat systems as 'nearly decomposable', and aggregate elements into substructures (Figure 2.1). During this process of 'chunking' we need to minimize the number and relevance of links between chunks, so that the resulting modules can be studied independently. This is the essence of modelling as an 'abstraction of reality'.

Minsky, while speculating about the 'essence' of intelligence, stresses the centrality of this idea:

> '. . . replacing an entire conceptualization by a compact symbol. This way we can build up gigantic structures of ideas as easily as our children build great bridges and towers from simple separate blocks. That way we can build new ideas from old ones – and that is what enables us to think. . . . Without this trick of turning symbols on themselves you can't have general intelligence, however excellent your repertoires of other skills may be.'
>
> [*Minsky (1982), p. 134.*]

And Simon, in his image of two watchmakers, Hora and Tempus, gives a beautiful illustration of the advantages of this process:

> 'Hora and Tempus were two watchmakers who built lovely watches and were so highly regarded that the phones in their workshops were always busy with customer enquiries. Although they were equally skilled, Hora prospered while Tempus seemed to grow poorer and poorer. What was the reason for this apparent injustice? The watches made by both of the watchmakers consisted of about 1000 parts each. Tempus' design required assembly as a single, uninterrupted process. If he had to put a watch down – e.g. to answer the phone – it immediately fell to pieces and had to be re-

> assembled. As Tempus' popularity increased it became more and more difficult for him to find enough uninterrupted time to finish a watch. Horas's watches were no less complicated than those of Tempus, but they were designed in a way that allowed him to assemble them in modules of about 10 pieces each. Ten of these modules could form a larger subassembly and ten of these formed a whole watch. Therefore, when Hora had to put down a watch to answer the phone he only lost a small amount of his work.'
>
> [*Simon (1962), p. 91.*]

Simon continues to give a quantitative analysis of the relative difficulty of the two watchmakers' tasks, which shows that Tempus' probability for a successful assembly becomes very small. The probability that Hora will finish a watch, however, is much higher. Assuming a rather conservative estimate of a 1% probability of interruption, it will in fact take Tempus 4000 times longer than Hora to complete a watch.

Hierarchical structures as a 'sequence of higher and lower levels' and the concept of *near decomposability* have been a central part of the intellectual framework of Western culture since Plato [*see*, for example, Whitehead (1925)]. The *reductionist and analytical approach* of splitting wholes into parts, which may then be studied in isolation, has guided many generations of scientists and has only recently been challenged [Berman (1981)].

Figure 2.2 shows a prescriptive framework for program design predicated on this idea. Here the programming process is split into four consecutive phases: problem decomposition, data and process abstraction, module encapsulation and implementation. The Scheme toolboxes presented in Chapter 3 have been written in such a fashion and object-oriented programming methodology is a 'natural' extension of this approach. Figure 2.3 shows how to apply its prescriptions to the design of a simple animation package. The graphical concepts *CoordinateValue, Point, Line, Circle* and *Man* are defined in terms of each other. *Points* are represented as lists of two *CoordinateValues*, with a set of associated functions to **create**, **transform** and **display** such entities, **select** components and **test** whether a given item falls into this category. Both their internal state and an implementation of all applicable operations could be encapsulated under an object-oriented approach (*see* Section 2.5). *Lines* are correspondingly stored as lists of *CoordinateValues*, with appropriate functionality. A line, a point and a shade may represent *Circles* and a 'stick figure' is used to approximate the concept of *Man*. All these entities are thus defined in terms of each other, forming layers of abstraction whose design can proceed in either a 'bottom up' (from *Point* to *Man*) or 'top down' (from *Man* to *Point*) fashion. These layers may of course contain further concepts. For example, at the 'circle layer' we

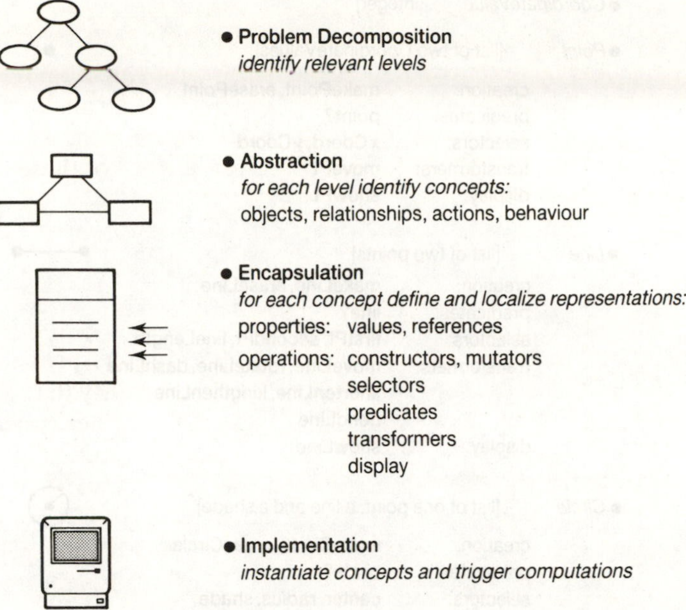

• Problem Decomposition
identify relevant levels
• Abstraction
for each level identify concepts:
objects, relationships, actions, behaviour
• Encapsulation
for each concept define and localize representations:
properties: values, references
operations: constructors, mutators
selectors
predicates
transformers
display
• Implementation
instantiate concepts and trigger computations

Figure 2.2 A layered approach to software design.

might wish to add *Rectangles*. We may also wish to populate the 'Man layer' with 'stick' insects, trees, houses, and so on. At the time of creating new concepts we need to make no commitments regarding their implementation. For example, lists of four lines may be used to encode rectangles, but they may equally well be represented as a list of the two points at their upper left- and lower right-hand corners. Any particular choice of implementation should have absolutely no influence outside a concept's encapsulation. Where exactly a concept should be located in such a hierarchy is often largely a matter of judgement, as long as it is assured that all its components' primitives are located at 'lower' levels. The purpose of such layered designs is 'abstraction'; that is, we wish to separate concepts (specifications) from a particular representation (implementation). For example, we wish to manipulate rectangles without any knowledge of implementation; that is, it should be irrelevant whether they 'really' are lists of lines or lists of points. We may still always 'climb down' to lower levels if we need to deal with such detail. Figure 2.4 demonstrates this idea.

We wish to assemble a *Man*, called Fred, from a head, a body, two arms and two legs. Normally we would just make use of a corresponding set of concepts, defined just below the 'man level'; that is:

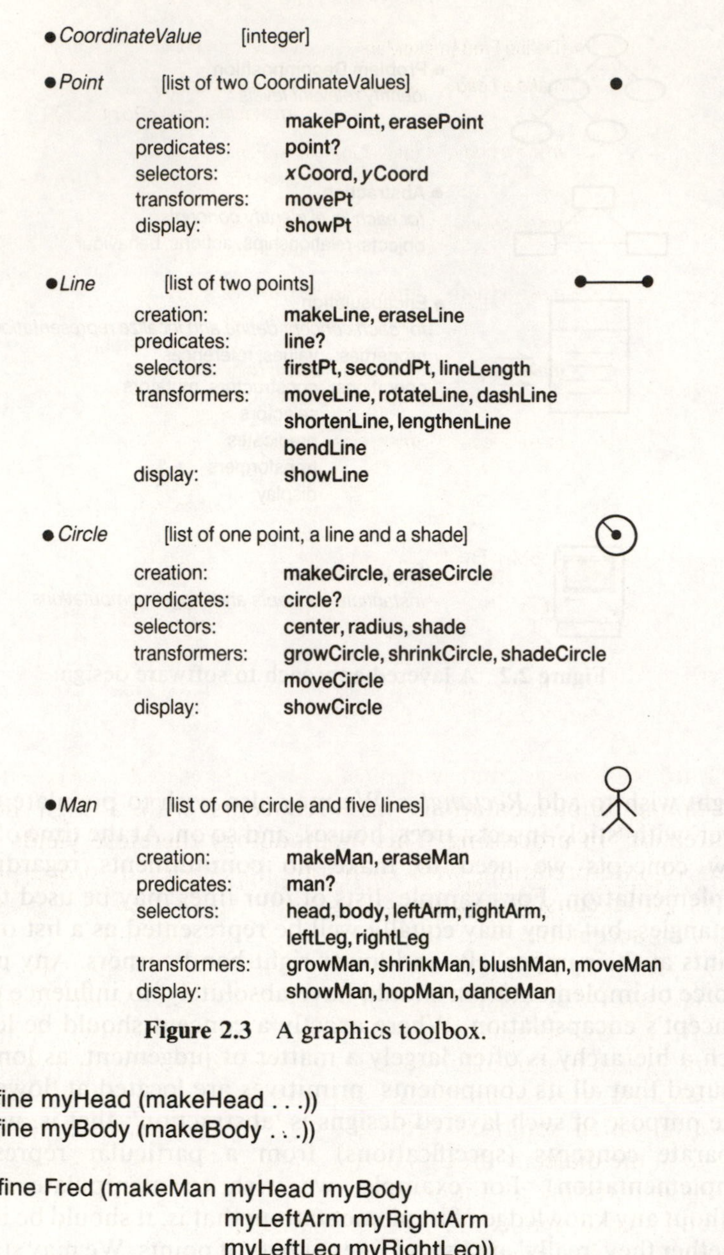

- *CoordinateValue* [integer]
- *Point* [list of two CoordinateValues]

  creation: makePoint, erasePoint
  predicates: point?
  selectors: *x*Coord, *y*Coord
  transformers: movePt
  display: showPt

- *Line* [list of two points]

  creation: makeLine, eraseLine
  predicates: line?
  selectors: firstPt, secondPt, lineLength
  transformers: moveLine, rotateLine, dashLine
  shortenLine, lengthenLine
  bendLine
  display: showLine

- *Circle* [list of one point, a line and a shade]

  creation: makeCircle, eraseCircle
  predicates: circle?
  selectors: center, radius, shade
  transformers: growCircle, shrinkCircle, shadeCircle
  moveCircle
  display: showCircle

- *Man* [list of one circle and five lines]

  creation: makeMan, eraseMan
  predicates: man?
  selectors: head, body, leftArm, rightArm,
  leftLeg, rightLeg
  transformers: growMan, shrinkMan, blushMan, moveMan
  display: showMan, hopMan, danceMan

Figure 2.3 A graphics toolbox.

```
(define myHead (makeHead . . .))
(define myBody (makeBody . . .))
. . .
(Define Fred (makeMan myHead myBody
                      myLeftArm myRightArm
                      myLeftLeg myRightLeg))
```

Figure 2.4, however, shows the complete sequence of such an assembly and the way it crosses from level to level. To make a head, for example, we must first make a circle. Since circles are themselves defined in terms of points and lines, we must make one instance of each of these. To make a line we must first make two points; and so forth. What should

```
• (Define Fred (makeMan
    make a head    (makeCircle (makePoint ... ...)
                               (makeLine (makePoint ... ...)))
    make a body    (makeLine (makePoint ... ...)
                             (makePoint ... ...))
    make an arm    (makeLine (makePoint ... ...)
                             (makePoint ... ...))
    make an arm    (makeLine (makePoint ... ...)
                             (makePoint ... ...))
    make a leg     (makeLine (makePoint ... ...)
                             (makePoint ... ...))
    make a leg     (makeLine (makePoint ... ...)
                             (makePoint ... ...)) ))

• (hopMan Fred)
```

Figure 2.4 Making and moving a *Man*.

become obvious is that we must 'pay' for the benefits earned by decoupling implementations from concepts with a high degree of 'indirection' in processing. This methodology therefore yields multiple levels of interpretation, with corresponding losses in processing efficiencies. Still, considering the advantages in reducing complexity, this seems an acceptable price to pay.

Within the context of AI programming this idea has led to a distinctive style of program development, in which one effectively builds interpreters for special-purpose languages. The basic principle behind this method is first to identify all concepts and transformations relevant to a particular class of problems. This will provide a vocabulary for a language in which solutions become easy to describe, and we can now engage in the dialectic process of designing such a language together with writing and testing an interpreter for it. The LISP family of languages, with its sparse syntax, is particularly well suited as a base for this approach – a fact that will be reiterated in Sections 2.2 and 2.3.

2.1.2 'Classical' versus 'exploratory' programming

AI programs tend to be 'big' and complicated pieces of software, and a tremendous effort has been invested in building tools and environments

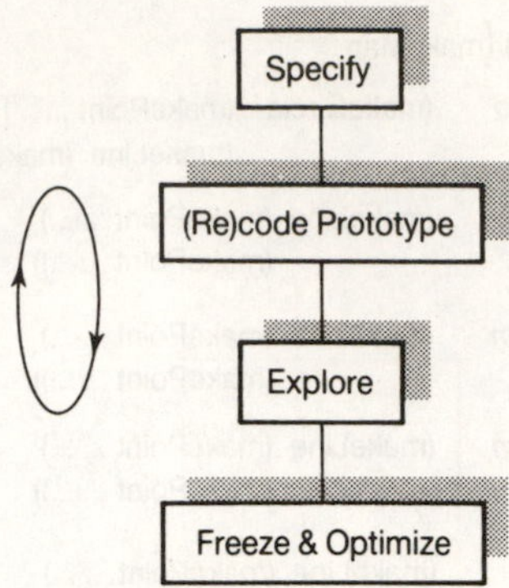

Figure 2.5 'Exploratory' programming.

which help people to 'cope'. Although the methodology of layered design, as discussed in the previous section, should be used wherever possible, there are always some problems for which it fails to provide adequate solutions. Unfortunately such problems abound in artificial intelligence applications, where, by definition, we are forced to operate at or beyond the limits of current technology. This is reflected in another of Minsky's definitions of AI: 'when we know how to program it, it's not AI any more'. How then may we still hope to make any progress at all? The only alternative seems to lie in *experimentation*: exploring and testing ideas. Any context catering for such an *exploratory style* must make it easy to experiment with changes, without incurring undue penalties in terms of intellectual complexity. Building, testing and modification of prototypes must be a fast and painless process. We cannot afford to be slowed down by a tedious '**edit**, **compile**, **link**, **load**, **execute**' cycle. Machine efficiencies are, by comparison, less relevant. It seems only sensible to utilize the computer's potential to reduce a programmer's memory load by freeing him from any essentially 'mechanical' chores. Developing AI applications becomes a process in which models of theories are designed, implemented as prototypes, tested and modified until we converge on a satisfactory solution as illustrated in Figure 2.5. This requires an inductive, rather than a deductive procedure, more closely related to testing of theories in experimental sciences than to theorem proving. Thought experiments have a time-honoured tradition in many disciplines, and under such an approach we are interested in exploring potential implications of our theories, which may as well be generated by a program. We may even throw the program away once we feel that we have reached a sufficiently 'deep' level of understanding. Alternatively it should then also be possible to turn a prototype into a working application, using 'classical' methods of program design, with emphasis

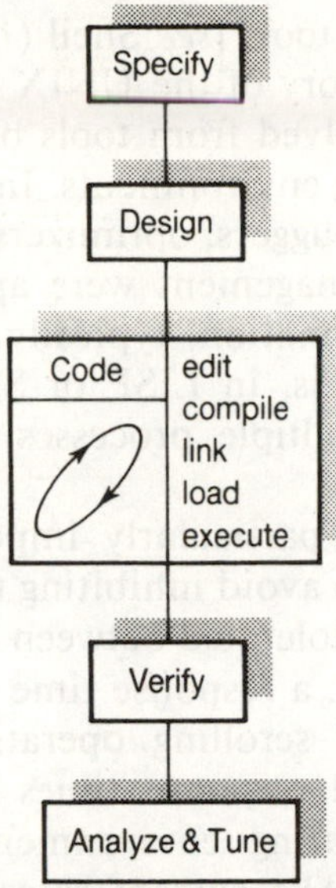

Figure 2.6 'Classical' programming.

on efficiency and verification. In future, much of this process may even be automated through the use of 'intelligent' tools.

This philosophy is different from the style of system development which dominates 'main stream' computer science (Figure 2.6). Here we are asked to start always from precise specifications, using formal deduction to arrive at a working program which should ideally be provably correct: *program development and proof should go hand in hand.* The power of this approach has been very well demonstrated by Wulf *et al.* (1981), with Dijkstra, Hoare and Gries as some of its most vocal proponents. It is appropriate for problems whose properties are well understood at the beginning, and for which invariant, rigorous specifications can therefore be known prior to the coding stage. In keeping with mathematical tradition, it is predominantly concerned with justifying the correctness of implementations and gives little guidance to the process of discovering a workable solution in the first place. (One might suspect that the reason is due to that process's often 'messy' nature and the associated difficulty of formalization.) 'Traditional' methodology advises us to avoid applications with ill-defined specifications, thereby moving many 'interesting' problems beyond our reach. We should first gain a sufficiently precise understanding of a problem and its potential solution, before we try to program it. But how can such an understanding be obtained? Traditional methodology is silent on this issue.

The quest for better support of exploratory programming styles has led to the development of rich interactive environments with a dazzling profusion of programming tools [*see* Sheil (1983), Ramamoorthy *et al.* (1987)]. Similar to the history of the UNIX system [Quarterman *et al.* (1985)], many of these evolved from tools built by individual users to augment their own working environments. Intelligent browsers, editors, interpreters, compilers, debuggers, optimizers, tools for program instrumentation and project management were applied to manipulation of textual and graphical information, typically embedded in a language-centred environment [that is, in LISP or Smalltalk – *see* Dart *et al.* (1987)] which supports multiple processes and some variant of the 'desktop' metaphor.

A rapid response is particularly important in such tool-based environments, if we wish to avoid inhibiting the creative process. While considerable delays can be tolerated between tasks, once some degree of 'closure' has been achieved, a response time of five seconds or more is probably unacceptable for scrolling operations in a text processor. Consistent and guaranteed response times are obviously difficult to ensure in typical time-sharing environments. The use of personal workstations for most of AI's current research, however, has largely solved any problems associated with this requirement.

There are various reasons why exploratory programming and tool-based environments have now also attracted wider attention among software developers outside AI. Firstly, the advent of sufficiently powerful self-contained workstations makes truly interactive programming styles possible and also tempers much of the traditional concern with memory space and processor cycles. The 'desktop metaphor' has become a popular paradigm, supporting a programming style many people find 'natural' and appealing. This approach needs workstations (large memory-mapped screens, pointing devices, plenty of speed and memory) and software architectures (icons, windows, menus, concurrent processes) which were considered far too expensive in the past. The recent dramatic shift in cost ratios among hardware, software and human resources has changed all this. With personal workstations there is no longer any competition for resources. It is therefore not necessary to justify a single user's use of a tool in terms of the overall productivity of a community, and it even becomes reasonable to design tools that operate 'continually' in the background.

Secondly, many of the 'easy' computer applications have already been implemented. Since ambition always seems to expand to tax the limits of technology there is a sore need for more software support for the programming process itself, in order to relieve the programmer from any of the many routine tasks associated with his craft. This will enable him to cope with higher levels of complexity in a more reliable fashion. Program complexity has become the main hurdle for many applications, and AI's programming styles, tools and environments seem a promising way to lighten the programmer's burden and remain in control of a program's evolution. A quote by B. Sheil summarizes this sentiment nicely:

> 'To those accustomed to the precise, structured methods of conventional system development, exploratory development techniques may seem messy, inelegant, and unsatisfying. But it's a question of congruence: precision and inflexibility may be just as disfunctional in novel, uncertain situations as sloppiness and vacillation are in familiar, well-defined ones. Those who admire the massive, rigid bone structures of dinosaurs should remember that jellyfish still enjoy their very secure ecological niche.'
>
> [*Sheil (1983), p. 144.*]

2.2 From IPL to LISP machines – a historical perspective

> 'Adopting a new computer language has the quality of religious conversion, including ferocious bright-eyed conviction and enthusiasm, trances and the invocation of magical requests. Your chosen language also incorporates your vision of the hereafter – or rather what sort of rewards you think are deserved for what sorts of effort and privation. (There are punitive religions and languages, demanding long and painful devotion with little reward; there are pie-in-the-sky religions and languages, promising wonderful rewards for little effort – usually just after some upcoming event, like the next holy war, or in the next version to be implemented.)'
>
> [*Creative Computing (1980), p. 64.*]

AI software technology is characterized by a number of important programming languages, with associated programming environments and a variety of distinctive programming techniques (Figure 2.7). Issues regarding language, environments and techniques (or *metaphors*) are closely intertwined and should not be treated in isolation [*see*, for example, the discussion in Thomas and Carroll (1981)]. In order to gain a proper appreciation of AI programming it is therefore necessary to consider all three of these aspects.

A *programming metaphor* may be defined as '*a way of organizing programs on the basis of some conceptual model of programming*' [Bobrow and Stefik (1986), p. 951]. Different metaphors differ substantially in what can be stated concisely and tend to interact with languages and programming environments that shape the organization of programs using that metaphor. One cannot, for example, expect to gain many

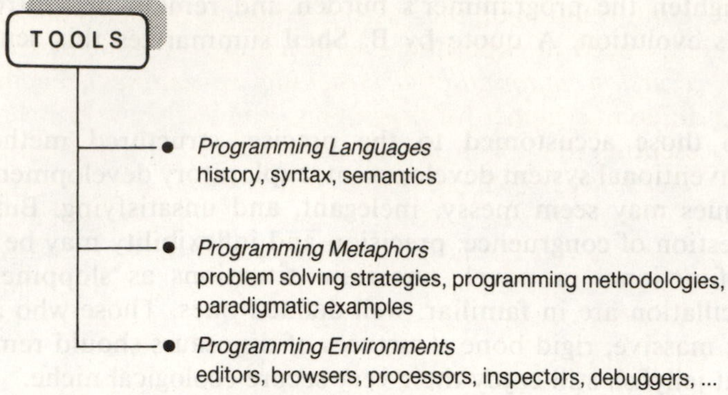

Figure 2.7 AI software technology – some components.

advantages from programming in **Scheme** if one merely acquires some knowledge of its syntax and semantics, but continues to perpetuate 'old' habits. Many programming styles which are appropriate for 'conventional' languages like **FORTRAN** or **Pascal** are clearly inappropriate in the context of an interactive and 'symbolic' language, and vice versa. Also, most of AI's programming environments are not at all language independent. They are often explicitly designed for use with a particular language and will support particular styles of program development. **Smalltalk**, which we discuss in Chapter 4, is a good example of such a context in which knowledge of syntax and functionality of a language is tightly integrated in a sophisticated user interface for object-oriented programming. This chapter will focus on some representative tools, while Chapter 3 will explore more specialized metaphors within the context of the Scheme language.

What are the specific features which make so-called 'AI languages' differ from languages used to write other kinds of programs? We have already discussed the importance of layered design and exploratory programming for implementing complex software systems in general, and AI programs in particular. This calls for convenient facilities to specify *multi-level interpretations* and *late binding*. *Interactive* and *interpretative* program execution is another requirement arising from the desire for exploratory program development. AI applications are 'symbolic' in nature. Different from 'traditional' areas of computing, numeric capabilities are secondary to powerful data structures and operations for symbol processing. *List processing* has historically been predominant, but convenient *text processing* features are also frequently needed. Research in inductive 'learning' requires the means to write programs which may modify themselves on the basis of 'experience'; a kind of 'self-reference' which may well underlie many patterns of 'intelligent' behaviour. *Pattern matching* is often used to 'index' into symbol structures and retrieve information on the basis of 'contents' rather than 'location'. We frequently need to experiment with features to control search (for example, *recursion*, *automatic backtracking*, *co-routines*). Facilities for exploring different schemes for organizing 'knowledge' within a program are also essential (for example, the concepts of *discrimination nets*, *property inheritance*, *production systems*, *frames*, *demon procedures*, *scripts*, *blackboards*, *objects*, *constraints*, and so on), as well as pattern-directed inference, conceptual concurrency, probabilistic and resource-constrained reasoning. In keeping with our previous remarks on programming style, such metaphors often grow to become part of a specialized language.

Some of these features are, of course, also provided by conventional programming languages. No language, however, including so-called AI languages, can reasonably be expected to cater for all of them. What has to be offered as a minimum are an interactive environment with flexible support for symbolic programming, and the means for orthogonal language 'extensions' beyond the power of a simple 'procedure' concept. Any additional features can then be grafted on to that base when desired, a fact we will try to demonstrate in this book, using the Scheme language as a vehicle for this approach.

The ease with which 'new' languages can be implemented in LISP and the perceived needs of individual researchers have caused a proliferation of so-called 'AI languages'. Bobrow and Raphael (1974), Rieger *et al.* (1979), Stoyan (1980), and Bobrow and Stefik (1986) give good surveys of features and historical development of the more important of these. Figure 2.8 shows only the major family lines and tries to classify them according to their base in some theory of computation.

IPL (Information Processing Language) was the first computer language explicitly designed for non-numeric applications. It was very 'low level' in flavour, close to machine language, a fact which should not be surprising in view of its age. First used by Newell *et al.* as a base for their *Logic Theorist* program [Newell and Simon (1956)], it remains of only historical interest today. IPL was first presented at the famous 'Dartmouth Summer School on Artificial Intelligence', and it subsequently had some influence on John McCarthy. At that time, McCarthy had already begun to think about a FORTRAN-based language for writing algebraic formula-manipulation systems. This language, of course, later became **LISP** and has been AI's 'lingua franca' ever since. The LISP family of languages was originally built around the notion of recursive functions as a descriptive formalism. In fact, McCarthy himself first used it as a theoretical device, to demonstrate the equivalence of Turing machines and recursive functions as models of computability [McCarthy (1960)]. In this framework, computation becomes function application. Each such operation creates a new value, so that 'side effects' (that is, changing values associated with variables) become unnecessary.

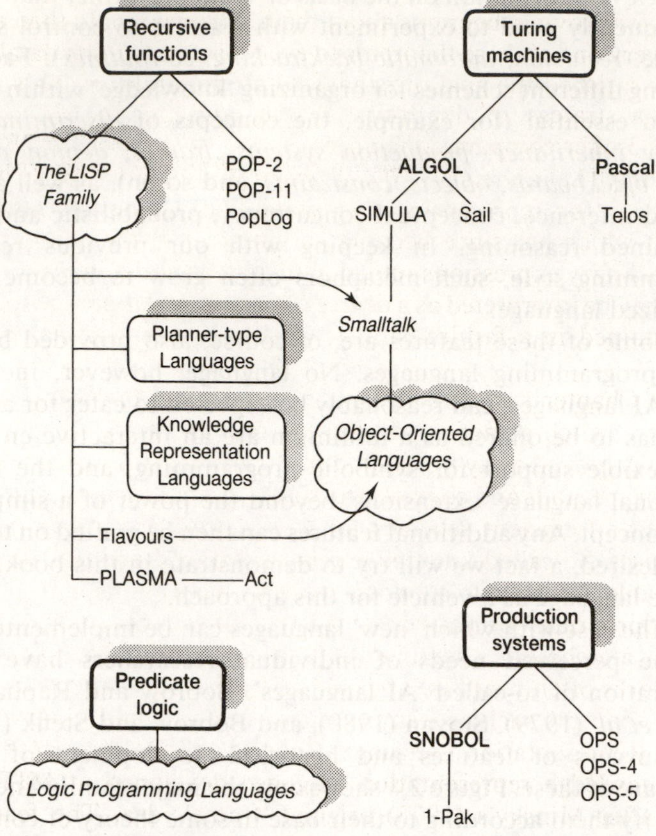

Figure 2.8 Philogeny of some AI programming languages.

Although this view is very beneficial for the mathematical tractability of programs, and has lately resulted in renewed interest in so-called 'functional' programming [Henderson (1980), Michaelson (1989)], LISP is rarely ever used in this 'pure' style any more, since many AI programmers claim that 'purely applicative languages are poorly applicable' [anonymous].

In the 30 years of its history, LISP has sprouted a great number of dialects and 'AI languages', most of which have long been forgotten. The family of so-called **planner-type languages** – for example, **MicroPlanner** [Sussman and Winograd (1970), Hewitt (1972)], **Conniver** [Sussman and McDermott (1972), McDermott and Sussman (1972)], **MLISP** [Smith (1970)], **QA4** [Rulifson (1973)], **QLISP** [Sacerdoti (1976)], and so on – remains largely of historical interest only. Their main features include pattern-matching functions, associative databases, and mechanisms to support the idea of automatic context switching and goal-directed, backwards reasoning in search and problem-solving applications. A program contains a description of a goal, a set of assertions and some procedures for proving theorems about them. **Planner** would then attempt to apply every one of these theorems to every assertion in its database, until it either satisfied the goal or exhausted all possibilities. This procedure implies a strategy of depth-first search, and the *search toolboxes* in Chapter 3 offer comparable features.

Fuzzy [LeFaivre (1974)] was an interesting attempt to implement some ideas for representing and manipulating inexact knowledge, a problem which has since become very topical in the context of expert systems. Fuzzy expressions return both a value and a numeric indicator, which may be interpreted as a degree of certainty. A Fuzzy associative net is maintained in a fashion similar to that in our '*AssociativeNetworks*' toolbox.

In Chapter 1 we already mentioned the fact that AI experienced a paradigm switch sometime during the mid 1970s. Since then research has largely moved away from attempts to automate domain-independent searching methods and control structures, and has focused much more on effective and efficient schemes for storing and processing large knowledge bases. So-called **knowledge representation languages** have become fashionable, designed to support research on reasoning within 'contexts', with appropriate primitives, property inheritance, constraints, procedural attachment, defaults and background assumptions. These frameworks often result in large and complicated software systems built around concepts such as frames, scripts and associative networks. **FRL** (Frame Representation Language [Roberts and Goldstein (1977)]) is an early knowledge representation language developed at MIT and patterned after Minsky's (1975) original 'frame' idea. The features contained in our '*Frame*' toolbox convey some of its flavour. **KRL** (Knowledge Representation Language [Bobrow and Winograd (1977), Bobrow and Winograd (1979)]) was a much more ambitious attempt to experiment with a formalism based on structured descriptions of prototypes and knowledge retrieval by 'recognition' of similarities. The language provides for predefined classes of linkages between concepts, procedural attachment and an agenda-based mechanism for process scheduling and resource allocation. Although it never evolved into a workable tool, its design became influential to other projects. **PEARL** (Package for Efficient Access of Representations in LISP [Deering *et al.* (1981)]) offers a knowledge representation on top of the **FranzLISP** programming system. It combines predicate calculus-like associative databases with frame-based concept descriptions. **KL-ONE** (Knowledge Language One [Brachman (1979)]) is a similar attempt to manipulate objects in a 'structured inheritance network'. Its basic elements are formal structures used to represent objects, attributes and relationships of the domain being modelled. Concepts may be generic, expressing the notion of 'prototype', or they may be treated as individuals. KL-ONE is implemented as a set of primitives for building, accessing and removing such structures. These may be used by higher-level LISP functions for matching, reasoning by analogy, deduction, and so on, to construct and maintain KL-ONE databases. One of the main uses of the language has been the development of natural language understanding programs. **SNePS** (Semantic Network Processing System [Shapiro (1979)]) follows similar ideas. A SNePS 'semantic network' is a labelled, directed graph in which nodes represent concepts and arcs stand for binary relationships between them. A user language for building and reasoning with such networks is provided.

PLASMA (Planner-Like System Modelled on Actors) and its derivatives **Planner-73** [Greif and Hewitt (1975)] and **Act** [Theriault (1982)] were attempts to understand *actor-based programming metaphors* [Hewitt (1977), Creative Computing (1980), Pugh (1984), Agha (1986)]. Their underlying ideas are quite similar to those proposed by a related metaphor, which is now widely referred to as *object orientation*. From both these perspectives, programs are viewed as collections of autonomous agents, classifying and encapsulating both states and behaviour, with communication defined by message-passing operations. A distinction between these two metaphors can, however, be drawn through a difference in focus. Most research into actor systems is concerned with the *communication aspects* of this paradigm, exploring different schemes for task delegation and synchronization among an actor's acquaintances, in order to support genuine parallelism at the hardware level. Such studies are also part of MIT's *Apiary* project [Hewitt (1980)]. Property inheritance is not a major issue here. Object orientation, on the other hand, is dominated by the classification aspect of knowledge representation and the associated problems of property and method encapsulation and inheritance. Parallelism is typically only supported at the software level; through pseudo-concurrent execution of processes.

Flavour systems are particular variants of LISP-based programming languages, supporting object orientation as their main programming metaphor. Their name dates back to the first LISP machines developed at MIT; personal computers with an architecture tailored for efficient execution of LISP programs. The original 'flavour' system (spelt 'flavor' in US contexts) was used to write most of the system software for these machines [Weinreb and Moon (1980)]. The project led to the formation of *Symbolics* as a commercial supplier of such systems and the name 'flavour system' has been adopted by other software with similar features [Stefik and Bobrow (1985)]. Section 2.5 will discuss object-oriented programming in more detail and will also describe a toolbox for flavour-based programming in Scheme.

McCarthy originally intended LISP to be ALGOL-like in flavour. Its 'sparse' syntax came about only as a 'side effect' of easing implementation of the first interpreter. It has, however, since proved to offer so many advantages that the ALGOL-like version, **LISP 2**, never got off the ground and was eventually shelved indefinitely. **Pop** is a British language, developed at the University of Edinburgh in the 1960s [Burstall *et al.* (1971)], which hints at what programming in LISP 2 might have been like. It has also spawned a Planner-like derivative, called **Popler** [Davies and Julian (1973)], at a time when pattern matching and automatic backtracking were in fashion. **PopLog** [Hardy (1984), Burton and Shadbolt (1987)] is a more recent development, offering an integration of Pop with PROLOG and LISP, together with a simple but flexible programming environment both for time-shared and personal computers.

Only very few AI tools have emerged from languages based on the traditional *Turing machine paradigm*, where computations are defined in terms of transformations of memory contents. Most of the few attempts which are known were motivated by a desire to profit from the 'efficiency' of execution associated with a compiled language. This aspect is, of course, particularly essential for time-critical 'real-time' applications, such as robotics. **Sail** [Feldman and Rovner (1969)] grew out of Stanford's ill-fated *Shakey* robotics project. It is an ALGOL-based language with features for associative 'memories' (in software) and multiprocessing. **Telos** [Leblanc (1977)] was a heroic attempt to augment Pascal with some data and control structures which were perceived to be 'basic' to AI programming. **SIMULA** [Dahl and Nygaard (1966)] was not designed as an AI language itself. But its 'class concept' has served as the forerunner of the important ideas of object encapsulation and property inheritance, which form the basis of modern *object-oriented programming languages.* **Smalltalk**, which is the topic of Chapter 4, may claim the honour as the most prototypical of these.

Predicate logic has always been attractive to AI researchers, both as a paradigm for problem solving and knowledge representation. It is a formalism with a long and honourable tradition, and its properties (semantics) are well defined and well understood. Logic assumes a static, 'platonic' universe where assertions remain invariant and 'things' do not change over 'time'. It is therefore a powerful tool for the description of structures, but it must be augmented to cope with the notion of process. The history of logic in AI is therefore characterized by a succession of attempts to offer extensions for tasks like temporal, non-monotonic or 'fuzzy' reasoning. Although some progress has been made, research in these areas has often been inconclusive and remains ongoing. In spite of these problems a large number of logic-based formalisms have been proposed and implemented as programming languages. While **FOL** [Weyrhauch (1980)] and **OMEGA** [Hewitt *et al.* (1980)] have attracted some attention, the best known of these is undoubtedly **PROLOG**, which we will discuss in some detail.

1-Pak and the OPS family have a flavour quite different from any of the other systems mentioned so far. They focus on a notion of computation characterized by pattern matching and textual substitution. *Production systems* are used as a base, comprising a set of rules and some working memory of assertions. The rules are called *productions*, and they consist of patterns guarding a set of commands. Productions are 'fired' whenever their patterns match the assertions held in memory. Computations unfold in this fashion; in a recurring cycle of applying productions and effecting changes in the state of the working memory. OPS [Rychener (1976)] was first developed at Carnegie Mellon University and has served as a base to write AI programs and to experiment with models of human memory organization. Since then it has seen a resurgence in popularity and is now widely used as a programming tool for rule-based expert systems (**OPS-5** [Forgy (1981)]). **1-PAC** [Mylopoulos *et al.* (1973)] is an interesting, 'exotic' attempt to build an AI language as an extension of **SNOBOL**.

This section could only touch on some of the programming systems which have evolved over the more than 30 years of AI's history, but it should have conveyed some idea of the remarkable diversity of approaches and features. Although it has matured substantially, AI programming is still a developing field. A number of metaphors have emerged to dominate current practice, while others remain of didactic and historical interest. Much research is currently devoted to systems that can manipulate complex knowledge representations and generate elaborate inferences. How to harness the potential of massive parallelism at the hardware level is also a particularly topical subject.

Procedural, declarative and object-oriented styles dominate many of today's AI development projects. Scheme, PROLOG and flavour systems are representative of the programming languages supporting these metaphors, and they will be discussed next. Chapter 3 is then devoted to a more detailed study of many of the techniques and representations that have evolved around them, while Chapter 4 addresses the issue of language environments from the Smalltalk perspective.

2.3 Procedural programming – the LISP language

> 'APL is like a diamond. It has a beautiful crystal structure; all of its parts are related in a uniform and elegant way. But if you try to extend this structure in any way – even by adding another diamond – you get an ugly kludge. LISP, on the other hand, is like a ball of mud. You can add any amount of mud to it and it still looks like a ball of mud.'
>
> [*J. Moses* (*MIT*).]

2.3.1 Historical evolution and key concepts

Languages of the LISP family are the oldest and still the most widely used tools for much of the current research in artificial intelligence. Unlike the largely economical motivations which have kept languages like FORTRAN alive for more than a quarter century, LISP has prospered within the AI community because of the superiority of some of its features.

One of the crucial aspects of LISP is its support for the concept of exploratory program development. Any commitment of symbols to values may be deferred until such a decision is unavoidable, and even then it may be reversed at little cost. This allows us rapidly to explore alternative designs and build programs incrementally. LISP's syntax is simple and its programs are naturally represented as data structures, so that it becomes easy to write programs that manipulate other programs.

There are also a number of other factors which have contributed to LISP'S continued popularity [Hayes (1987)]. Unlike FORTRAN or COBOL, LISP proceeds to evolve freely. Until recently, the economic importance of LISP programs was very low, which meant that there was never any pressure to freeze the language definition to a standard set of features. As an AI language, LISP has long been used to attack 'hard' problems, a task which resulted in many new fcatures and powerful tools. The LISP community has always adopted a tool-building culture, a state of affairs greatly aided by the fact that the developers themselves have typically also been the tools' users. LISP is also very easy to extend ('add more mud to') and there is a willingness to 'let the machine do it'. Finally, AI research has always been prepared to expend computer power to better employ human resources, a policy which has frequently resulted in tools that were ahead of their time. Fuelled by the same motivation there was also a very early interest in programming environments and personal workstations.

This spirit of linguistic innovation has been an integral part of LISP's history, which has been chronicled in some detail by McCarthy (1978) and Stoyan (1980). LISP was originally designed as an extension of FORTRAN. John McCarthy, then an assistant professor of mathematics at Dartmouth college, took an early interest in the use of computer systems for symbolic computation, which was further fuelled by Newell and Simon's presentation of IPL during the 'Dartmouth Summer School on Artificial Intelligence', which was organized in 1956 by McCarthy together with Shannon and Minsky. Although at that time none of the participants had any conception of how artificial intelligence might eventually be 'achieved', it seemed evident that numerical computations should be of little importance, while the ability to manipulate symbolic expressions appeared to be crucial. IPL already included ideas such as list processing and recursion, but it was still very 'low level' in flavour. FORTRAN, which had just been celebrated by IBM as the first truly 'high-level' programming language, seemed a step in the right direction. Unfortunately, FORTRAN's design was dominated by the need to cater for efficient execution of numeric computation and the resulting rigidity made it a very poor basis for manipulating the highly dynamic structures required for the kind of applications McCarthy was interested in. A self-contained list-processing language seemed therefore a better solution. By that time McCarthy was also a member of the American delegation to the European ALGOL committee. There he proposed the concept of conditional expressions and was in turn influenced by many of the other members' ideas. McCarthy now envisaged LISP as a compiled language with an ALGOL-like syntax, but its first prototype, **LISP 1**, had quite a different flavour.

LISP's 'sparse' syntactic structure and interpretative nature evolved pretty much by accident. Our discussion of these events will follow the account given by Stoyan (1980). In late 1958, McCarthy was offered an assistant professorship in electrical engineering at MIT. Together with Minsky, then an assistant professor in mathematics, he founded the 'MIT Artificial Intelligence Project', equipped with two programmers, a secretary, a typewriter and six students (with Kleinrock, Bobrow and Slagle among them [Stoyan (1980), p. 165]). This group then embarked on a modest attempt at writing a LISP compiler, but the 30 'man-years' reported for the FORTRAN project made full implementation seem like an unachievable goal. Initially, some simple list-processing functions were hand-coded in assembly language and parenthesized prefix expressions (such as, '(plus 2 2)') were used for testing. This notation was later referred to as '*Cambridge Polish*', in honour of Quine (a renowned Cambridge (Massachusetts) philosopher) and Lukasiewicz (the inventor of the 'Polish notation' prefix form of expressions). Although implementation made reasonable progress and recursion and garbage collection seemed the most difficult obstacles the group would eventually have to tackle, there was still no precise definition of the language. In 1959, McCarthy (1960) was working on a paper to demonstrate LISP's equivalence to Turing machines as an alternative theory of 'computability'. For this he needed a uniform notation in which both LISP expressions and LISP functions could be described by symbolic expressions. This led to the idea of '**quote**' and '**eval**' operators, which were originally solely intended as theoretical vehicles to facilitate such a proof. This paper, however, had a number of unexpected consequences. One of the project's programmers, S. Russell, implemented '**eval**' in assembly language and thereby provided the means for testing the hand-coded functions before the compiler project had even been properly started. In order to run such simple LISP programs in an interpretative style, all expressions now had to be *nested*, so that the program itself became an expression applied to some data. Fortunately, the MIT computing laboratory at that time was also involved in project **MAC** (Multi Access Computing), one of the earliest research efforts into time-shared computer systems, using teletype terminals. The LISP interpreter, together with the use of an interactive teletype terminal (the famous '**read**, **eval**, **execute**' cycle) came to be very popular. The notation recognized by this interpreter was later referred to as '**S-language**' and the first working LISP system was presented at the 1959 annual conference of the Association for Computing Machinery [McCarthy (1959)]. LISP 1 had about 90 predefined functions, and the first example of an application was a simple routine to differentiate elementary functions. This interpreter was soon further refined and extended to become **LISP 1.5** (140 functions [McCarthy (1962)]), which may claim the honour of 'grandmother' to all subsequent LISP systems. LISP 1.5 quickly became an attractive tool to a number of people working on problems of language translation and artificial intelligence within the Boston area. When they left for employment elsewhere, they often took a copy, and this soon led to a wide distribution. McCarthy himself departed for Stanford University in 1962. Since then his research has shifted to more theoretical areas and he has had no major involvement in the further development of the language.

LISP 2, the ALGOL-like compiled version, never did eventuate. There were a number of reasons for this. Firstly, in an interactive context the S-language's 'sparse' syntax (LISP = 'Lots of Irritating, Spurious Parentheses') proved to be an asset rather than a liability. It made parsing expressions extremely easy, thereby allowing rapid development of sublanguages grafted on to a LISP base. Almost all so-called 'AI languages' are implemented in this fashion and many LISP programmers would now fiercely resist the introduction of additional layers of syntactic sugar. Another cause of LISP 2's demise may be connected with 'creeping featuritis' [Clinger (1988a), p. 25]. In the early 1960s, a committee to define LISP 2's features was established at BBN (Bolt, Beranek and Newman), an American research company. This caused the language specification to grow rapidly, as new features were added to keep 'everybody' happy. Implementation was finally scrapped because of financial constraints and has never been revived. **Pop** [Burstall *et al.* (1971), Burton and Shadbolt (1987)], developed at Edinburgh University, possibly comes reasonably close to what LISP 2 might have looked like. The syntax of modern LISP systems, however, has remained identical to the original 'S-notation'. McCarthy himself has always preferred his so-called 'M-notation' [McCarthy *et al.* (1962)], which is also used in Allen's (1978) excellent textbook. Allen refers to 'M-notation' as a specification and to 'S-notation' as a representation language.

Based on LISP 1.5, a number of major dialects have emerged, and

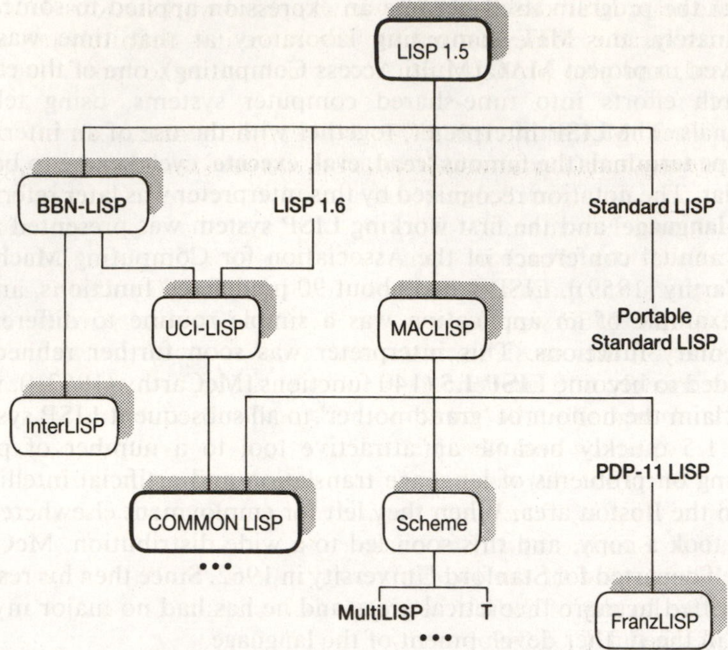

Figure 2.9 A brief genealogy of LISP.

Figure 2.9 surveys the more important ones. All of these, while based on a common ancestor, show remarkable differences in the features and tools they provide. These differences have traditionally been bridged by packages of so-called 'compatibility functions', which interpret the constructs of one language in the context of another. This approach is, of course, computationally expensive and some form of 'manual' translation is usually required to support serious work.

Work on theorem provers (such as **SAINT** and **SIN**) and algebraic formula manipulation systems (such as **MACSYMA**), at MIT's project MAC resulted in **MACLISP** [Moon (1974)]. This dialect is particularly noted for efficiency of numeric computations, a common criticism of many early LISP systems. MACLISP boasts a rich collection of data types (arrays, hunks, and so on), a user-friendly environment for program development and debugging, and a rich repertoire of predefined functions (approximately 300). It has also served as the base for **ZetaLISP**, the LISP version used for MIT's (now *Symbolics*) LISP-machine project [Weinreb and Moon (1981)]. **'Standard' LISP** and its descendant **'Portable' Standard LISP** [Griss and Morrison (1981)] were designed and implemented by Hearn and others at the University of Utah. Originally used as a base for **REDUCE**, another formula-manipulation system, it is now the main LISP dialect for Hewlett-Packard workstations. Unfortunately, its name is somewhat misleading, since it is definitely not a LISP standard, and also probably not that much easier to 'port' than other dialects.

When McCarthy left MIT for Stanford, many of his former graduate students found employment at other universities and research institutions. The two Bobrow brothers, for example, worked at Bolt, Beranek and Newman. D. Bobrow then joined the Xerox Palo Alto Research Center (Parc) in California. For a while a jointly developed LISP system was maintained at both institutions (**InterLISP** [Teitelman (1974)]). InterLISP was also used at Stanford University, where it grew into one of the most sophisticated LISP systems available today (approximately 600 predefined functions), with the largest number of tools and arguably the most user-friendly environment [Sandewall (1978), Teitelman and Masinter (1981)]. A modernized version of this system (**InterLISP-D**) was later implemented on the Xerox line of 'LISP machines' (that is, *Dandelion, Dorado* and *Dolphin*) and it has also been 'ported' to Siemens and IBM equipment.

The second of the two Bobrow brothers, R. Bobrow, eventually joined the faculty of the University of California at Irvine (UCI), where he developed **UCI-LISP** [Meehan (1979)], a popular dialect at many research institutions. For a number of years, UCI-LISP has served as a major programming tool for Carnegie-Mellon University's AI program.

Ever since the donation of the first PDP-6 to MIT's computing laboratory, the DEC range of machines, and the DEC-10 in particular, has been the standard equipment for AI research throughout the world; in the same way that LISP has dominated as a programming tool. This phenomenon can partly be explained by the fact that it was designed as a true time-sharing machine, at a time when most other manufacturers' equipment was still batch oriented; since fast man/machine interaction is mandatory to support AI's typical programming style. Another important explanation for this dominance is the fact that the main AI centres (MIT, Stanford, Carnegie-Mellon, Edinburgh) used these machines for the bulk of their work, making it necessary to have access to one in order to run copies of their software, which was freely distributed. The growing popularity of the UNIX operating system in the late 1970s and 1980s, however, spawned a number of LISP implementations on DEC's range of smaller machines. A **PDP-11 LISP**, again based on MACLISP, was developed at Harvard. It was taken across to the US West Coast when some of their staff went to work for the University of California at Berkeley, where there was already a strong interest in UNIX. **FranzLISP** [Foderaro (1979)] is the name of the dialect which finally emerged. It is UNIX-based and runs on VAXes and other machines popular in university environments (for example, Sun workstations). Much of its continuing popularity is attributable to its low academic price.

Lately there has been a renewed interest in standardization, largely fuelled by commercial use of LISP as an expert system development tool. A number of major computer manufacturers commissioned the design of a 'Standard' LISP variant called **COMMON LISP** [Steele (1984)].

> 'The original goal was to specify a LISP that was close enough to each member of a family of descendants of MACLISP that the guardians of those implementations would be willing to evolve them towards that common definition. A major subgoal of the committee was that programs written in this COMMON LISP would be source-transportable between implementations, regardless of the underlying hardware.'
>
> [*Brooks and Gabriel (1984), p. 1.*]

So far the project seems to have succeeded. Many implementations already exist at this date. However, it remains to be seen whether this attempt to discipline LISP's formerly unchecked growth of 'features' will ultimately be successful [Allen (1987)]. There is still room for doubt, since most LISP programmers are highly individualistic, with strong convictions on questions of style, and because LISP makes implementation of 'new' features so easy. Already there is widespread criticism of the 'size' of COMMON LISP and some of its more arcane features (which were often included to ensure compatibility with the past). There is, however, a good chance that commercial pressures will at least lead to a common base from which more specialized dialects or subsets may sprout, a hope which is also reflected in recent efforts towards an ISO LISP standard.

One of the newer dialects to emerge is **Scheme**, a lexically scoped version of MACLISP (like **NIL**, **T**, and others). Scheme is used at MIT to teach introductory courses in computer programming, and is well documented in an excellent book by Abelson *et al.* (1985). In the authors' opinion, Scheme is an extremely expressive and elegant language, arranged around a small core of simple, orthogonal and very flexible features. Embedded in an appropriate interactive programming environment, it counters practically all of the relevant criticisms usually levelled against LISP. Its only disadvantage is its lack of compatibility with traditional LISP systems and COMMON LISP in particular. Once Scheme is mastered, however, COMMON LISP competence can be achieved relatively quickly. (See Appendix VI for a comparison of the two dialects.)

Software support for parallel processing has become a major research focus in recent years and several language proposals have resulted from this. **MultiLISP** [Halstead (1985)] is an interesting, Scheme-based example.

2.3.2 Programming in Scheme

Posted-Date: Mon, 6 Jul 87 07:46:39 EDT
Date: Mon, 6 Jul 87 07:46:39 EDT
From: Tigger@Hundred-Acre-Woods.Milne.Disney
To: ramsdell@linus.uucp
Subject: Scheme

'The wonderful thing about Scheme is:
Scheme is a wonderful thing.
Complex procedural ideas
Are expressed via simple strings.
Its clear semantics, and lack of pedantics,
Help make programs run, run, RUN!
But the most wonderful thing about Scheme is:
Programming in it is fun,
Programming in it is FUN.'

[*Ramsdell (1987).*]

Overview

Scheme was designed and implemented at MIT by G. J. Sussman and G. L. Steele Jr (1975) as part of an effort to understand the actor model of computation [Hewitt (1977)]. It is a small and compact language, whose concepts can, however, be combined and extended in highly orthogonal ways. Some of the currently available Scheme implementations are listed in Figure 2.10.

C-Scheme [MIT (1984)] is the latest version of the original MIT implementation. **Scheme 311** [Clinger (1984)] was developed at Indiana University and has since evolved into **Chez Scheme** [Dybvig and Smith (1985)]. **Scheme 84** [Friedman *et al.* (1984)], another Scheme project at the University of Indiana, has mainly been used for experimentation with novel control structures – that is, the 'engine' concept. **T** [Slade (1987), Rees *et al.* (1984)] is an extended Scheme system with special emphasis on efficiency of execution. It was developed at Yale University. All these implementations were designed to run on UNIX-based systems, and particularly on VAX and Sun computers. Programming is normally supported by a standard editor, for example **EMACS**, and there are some simple utilities for error tracing and debugging. Implementations for personal workstations usually offer more sophisticated programming environments. **PC Scheme** [Bartley and Jensen (1986), Wong (1987)] was written at Texas Instruments for IBM PCs and DOS-compatible microcomputers. It includes an EMACS-style editor (**Edwin**) and a simple flavours package (**SCOOPS**). **MacScheme** [Semantic Microsystems (1986), Hartheimer (1987)] offers an integrated Scheme environment for the Apple Macintosh. **XScheme**, developed by D. Betz, is another C-based implementation. It has recently become very popular, since it is

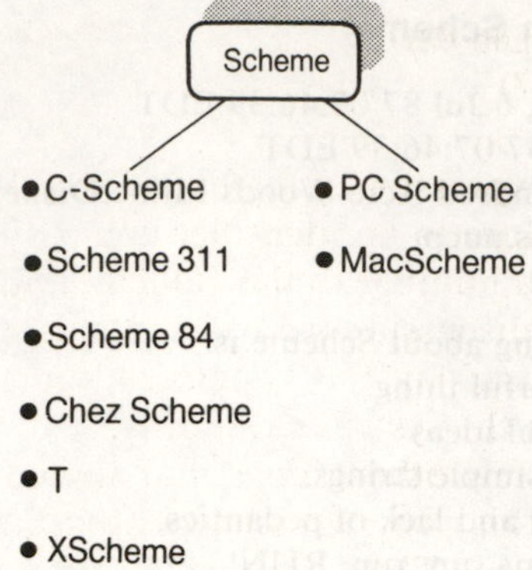

Figure 2.10 Some Scheme implementations.

available as public domain software from many computer bulletin boards.

The 'Revised[3] Report on Scheme' by Rees and Clinger (1986) has served as a standard and can be recommended as an excellent, concise and very readable language definition. Most programs in this book were tested with MacScheme, PC Scheme, Chez Scheme, XScheme and T, although MacScheme was used as the primary development tool. In the interest of portability, non-essential features have been avoided as much as possible.

In contrast to other dialects of LISP, Scheme supports explicit *definition of variables* and *lexical scoping.* The language provides an efficient implementation of '*tail recursion*' and offers '*continuations*' for defining new control structures. All of Scheme's objects are treated as '*first class citizens*', which means that there are no arbitrary restrictions on what an object may do and where it may be used. Any first class object can be assigned as the value of variables, passed as an argument to procedures, returned as a result and stored in a compound data structure. According to this definition, procedures are definitely treated as 'second class citizens' in most other languages, including earlier versions of LISP. Clinger (1988b) offers an excellent in-depth discussion of this concept.

Representation and interpretation – symbols and values

The combination of lexical scope and first class procedures fosters a programming style which emphasizes modularity and data abstraction. A Scheme program may be viewed as a nest of expressions, possibly referring to a number of definitions which will themselves contain further expressions. Each expression is associated with an environment that defines all bindings which are currently 'in scope'. For example, the following:

```
(define MeaningOfLife 42)
(+ MeaningOfLife 7)
```

is a 'program' of two expressions, the first of which applies the system-provided **define** procedure to an identifier and a value as its arguments while the second adds a number to the value bound in this way.

In the following discussion we will use **boldface** to mark all those **identifiers** which are used by the system in some predefined way. A **semicolon** (;) will prefix the system's responses.

There are also a few other things that should be noted before we turn our attention to this program's execution. Scheme has no length restrictions for **identifiers**. They must all begin with a character that cannot be a digit and may contain any number of letters, digits and so-called 'extended alphabetic characters'. * / < = > ! ? : $ % _ & ~ ∧ are categorized as such. Some **identifiers** also serve as syntactic keywords and should therefore not be used as variables. **Comments** begin with a semicolon (;) and extend to the end of a line. They will be ignored by the interpreter. There is also a **syntactic convention** that all procedures that assign values to variables (that is, produce so-called 'side effects') should end with a !, and that all procedures ending in **?** are predicates which return #t or #f (for 'true' and 'false').

The Scheme **interpreter** operates in **LISP**'s classical '**read**, **evaluate**, **print**' cycle; that is, it will read an expression, try to evaluate it and display the result. During execution it will assume that, unless quoted, atoms evaluate to their current bindings, and that list structures denote 'applications' of functions to arguments (hence the term 'applicative language'). According to the conventions of '*Cambridge Polish*' the interpreter will therefore attempt to associate the first element of any (unquoted) list with a procedure, to be applied to all of the following elements as arguments.

Interaction with the interpreter usually takes place through a so-called **transcript**, **workspace** or **listener** window within some supporting programming environment. Expressions may be entered and the interpreter's replies will be printed there. Often, some syntactic support is provided at the editor level – for example, the system will indent definitions appropriately as they are entered and it will 'blink' matching parentheses. These features are absolutely essential for a language with such a sparse syntax. Figure 2.11 shows a transcript window in the MacScheme environment.

Expressions may be entered and evaluated, and the contents of the window may be scrolled to view the results of previous interactions. Figure 2.11 also demonstrates MacScheme's three categories of **menus**. The *File* menu invokes actions for creating, loading, updating and printing of files, as well as for quitting the system. The *Edit* menu

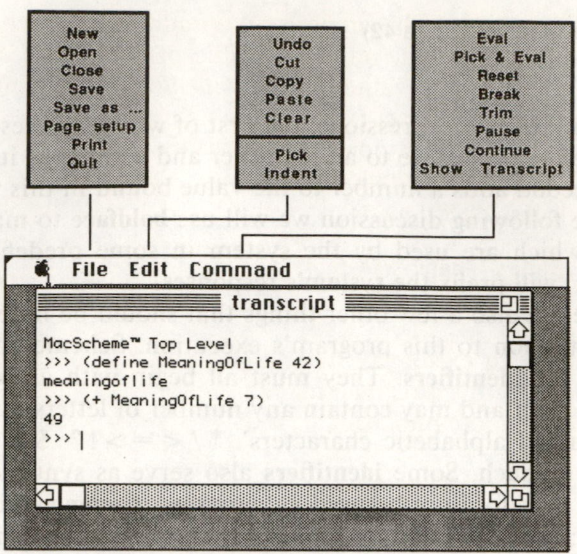

Figure 2.11 A MacScheme transcript.

interacts with a mouse-driven editor. It offers commands for cutting and pasting, as well as for selecting an expression 'up' to a matching left parenthesis ('pick') and to force reindentation (expressions are normally indented as they are typed). The *Command* menu is specific to MacScheme, while the other two menus are similar to the *File* and *Edit* categories of other Macintosh software. There is a command for evaluating expressions once they are selected, for breaking and continuing execution. 'Selection' may use 'pick' (on the *Edit* menu), or it may be accomplished by pushing the 'enter' key after the cursor has been positioned behind the rightmost parenthesis of an expression. Breaking a procedure's execution will invoke a debugger, while 'pause' will simply halt the program. After error conditions have been fixed, 'Reset' may be used to return control to the 'top level' in order to continue a session. MacScheme allows us to open up to four separate windows. One of these will always be the transcript, while others may provide editors on the contents of files. Selection and evaluation of expressions may take place in any window. The expression will then be copied to the transcript and the resulting value will be shown (*see* Figure 2.15). This will often cause the text in the transcript to grow very long, so that its contents should occasionally be 'trimmed'. Finally, since the standard Macintosh screen is fairly small, there is a command to show the transcript if it should become buried below other windows. Other Scheme dialects will offer similar, although often not quite as convenient, programmer interfaces.

When our program is evaluated, it will lead to creation of an environment in which *MeaningOfLife* has been bound (to 42). The subsequent expression will then perform an addition, which, within the scope of this environment, returns a value of '49'. Note also that *all* expressions must yield a value, which will *always* be printed. This is normally the value of the last item to be evaluated. Sometimes, this is of course not the desired behaviour; that is, we may often wish to force the interpreter to accept some data item *literally*. The **quote** function may be used to obtain this effect, as in:

```
(quote (define MeaningOfLife 42))
; (define MeaningOfLife 42)
```

Since quoting is an extremely frequent operation, a shortcut has been provided to reduce the already large number of parentheses. A prime (′) may be used to denote quotation:

```
'(define MeaningOfLife 42)
; (define MeaningOfLife 42)
```

Of course, it should also be possible to negate the effects of quotation. LISP's **eval** serves this purpose. In contrast to LISP, this function is not supported by many Scheme dialects. This is a design decision reflecting the fact that use of **eval** makes selective linking of code difficult or even impossible and therefore requires availability of a 'full' Scheme system to execute stand-alone applications. Most of the time it is also not needed, because the same effect can usually be achieved in a different way. In MacScheme, **eval** is available, but we will refrain from using it. Improper use of quotation and evaluation is an extremely fertile source of programming errors, as will quickly become painfully apparent to any beginner. It is therefore important to appreciate the fundamentals of the model upon which these operations are built. Like assembly language, Scheme draws no syntactic distinction between data and program. The 'meaning' of symbols is only determined within a specific context of interpretation. Symbols denote objects, either literally or through association. During execution a symbol's binding will be obtained, while numbers, Booleans, characters, strings and vectors evaluate to themselves.

Data types and their operations

The types of *literals* provided by Scheme are numbers, Booleans, characters, strings, symbols, lists, vectors and lambda expressions.

Scheme offers some simple procedures for **input/output** operations. Expressions may be **load**ed from files, and evaluation occurs during this process. A **read** function may be employed for programming tasks in which user interaction is necessary. **display** will print the value of any object, and **newline** may be used where line-feeds are required.

```
(define LuckyNumber (read)) ; 7 is entered
; LuckyNumber
LuckyNumber
; 7
(display LuckyNumber)
; 7#t
```

The #t in response to the last expression is the value returned by **display**. The printing of '7' occurs as a side effect.

Although not a standard feature, we will use two additional print procedures in an attempt to reduce the bulk of code associated with our programs' output. Unlike **display**, **DisplayList** and **DisplayLine** accept any number of arguments. **DisplayLine** also performs a line feed at the end. Both these procedures are part of the 'Systems' toolbox.

```
(DisplayList LuckyNumber "is not" 13)
; 7 is not 13 ()
```

Scheme supports three different tests for **equivalence**, which may be applied to any object. **eq?** defines the strongest interpretation of equivalence. It returns *true* where Scheme is completely unable to distinguish between two objects in any way. **eqv?** checks whether two objects are identical under the notion of 'operational equivalence' [Rees and Clinger (1986), p. 13]. In most practically relevant cases the result will be the same as that of **eq?**. **equal?** implements a weaker notion of equivalence, by assuming that objects are equal if 'they print the same'.

```
(eq?    (list 'a) (list 'a)) ; they "look the same", but are
; ()
(eqv?   (list 'a) (list 'a)) ; stored in different memory cells.
; ()
(equal? (list 'a) (list 'a))
; #t
```

Scheme recognizes integer, real and complex **numbers**, written in the conventional way:

```
42
; 42
3.14
; 3.14
1.0e10
; 10000000000
```

There are a multitude of predicates (**number?**, **zero?**, **positive?**, **negative?**, **odd?**, **even?**), comparison (=, <, <=, >, >=), arithmetic (+, −, *, /,

remainder, **exp**, **expt**, **sqrt**, **log**, **floor**, **ceiling**, **round**, **truncate**, and so on), and trigonometric (**sin**, **cos**, and so on) functions, with obvious behaviour.

```
(number? 7)
; #t
(odd? 3.14)
; ERROR: Non-integer argument to function - 3.14
(/ 3 2)
; 1.5
(expt 2 3)
; 8
(floor 3.14)
; 3
(round 7.7)
; 8
(= 7 13)
; ()
```

In most implementations of Scheme the empty list is identical to #f, which explains why the last example above returns it. From now on we will use #f instead of () or '(), wherever this is appropriate. We can also choose **maxima** or **minima**, and there are a number of transformations between forms of representation (**integer->char**, **number->string**, and so on).

```
(number->string (sqrt 3.14))
; "1.772"
```

This example also demonstrates that expressions may be *nested*, in which case evaluation proceeds in the usual way ('inside out' and 'left to right'). Rules of precedence are obviously unnecessary, since *Cambridge Polish* notation forces us always to supply fully parenthesized expressions.

#t and #f are the two 'generic' **Boolean** values. For convenience, any other value can also be used as a Boolean in a conditional test. In this context all values which differ from #f and the empty list count as 'true'. A predicate (**boolean?**) and a number of logical operations are provided (**and**, **or**, **not**).

```
(boolean? #f)
; #t
(or #t #t)
; #t
(and #f (< 7 0))
; #f
```

Characters are objects that represent printed characters, using the notation #\<character> or #\<character name>. For example:

```
#\x
; 120
#\y
; 121
#\space
; 32
```

where the numbers returned are the characters' ASCII code equivalences and '**space**' is a predefined constant. Scheme also provides predicate (**char?**), some comparison (**char=?**, **char->?**, and so on) and some transformation (**char->integer**, **integer->char**) procedures.

Strings are sequences of characters enclosed within double quotes ("). A backslash (\) may be used to include double quotes within a string, for example:

```
(display "the \" character delimits a string")
; the " character delimits a string
```

To include a backslash in strings it must be 'escaped' with another backslash. Scheme provides a variety of creation (**make-string**), predicates (**string?**, **string-null?**), comparison (**string=?**, . . .), selector (**string-length**, **string-ref**, **substring**), mutation (**string-append**, . . .) and transformation (**string->list**, **list->string**) operators.

```
(string-length "mumble")
; 6
(string-append "mumble" "mumble")
; "mumblemumble"
(string-ref "mumble" 4)
; 108
```

The last example shows that string indices stat at 0, since '108' is the ASCII representation of "l".

Symbols other than those mentioned above must be quoted to force a literal interpretation.

```
MeaningOfLife
; 42
(quote MeaningOfLife)
; MeaningOfLife
(quote X)
; X
X
; ERROR: Undefined global variable X
```

In the latter case the interpreter tries to obtain a value for a symbol which has not previously been bound. Since no such value exists, the program is halted and a debugger may be invoked. Scheme uses **define** to introduce variables and bind them to an initial value, which may then be changed (using **set!**) through side effects.

```
(define Capnomancy
        "study of smoke to determine the future")
; Capnomancy
(set! MeaningOfLife Capnomancy)
; MeaningOfLife
MeaningOfLife
; "study of smoke to determine the future"
```

Here we should note how **set!** may rebind a symbol's value, and also that Scheme's 'dynamically typed' nature will allow us to replace a numeric binding (that is, '42' for *MeaningOfLife*) by an instance of a different data type. A predicate (**symbol?**) and a transformation procedure (**string->symbol**) may be used to operate on symbols.

```
(symbol? (string->symbol "Capnomancy"))
; #t
```

Lists are Scheme's most important structure, since they are used for both 'data' and 'programs'. Obviously, they must be quoted to serve as 'inert lumps of LISP-stuff' [Hofstadter (1983)].

```
'(HappyMole LittleBear LittleTiger)
; (HappyMole LittleBear LittleTiger)
```

The above is a (**quoted**) list of three elements. To remove the **quote** would invite disaster.

```
(HappyMole LittleBear LittleTiger)
; ERROR: Undefined global variable Little Tiger
```

Scheme would attempt to process the list as an application of a procedure called 'HappyMole' to the rest of the elements. The resulting error message indicates that MacScheme processes list elements back to front, and therefore fails to find any binding for 'LittleTiger'. Evaluation may fail even if bindings for all components exist:

```
MeaningOfLife
; "study of smoke to determine the future"
('MeaningOfLife)
; ERROR: Bad procedure MeaningOfLife
(MeaningOfLife)
; ERROR: Bad procedure "study of smoke to determine the future"
```

In the first case we ask for a symbol's current binding, while we try to '**execute**' the symbol in the second, and try to do the same to the symbol's

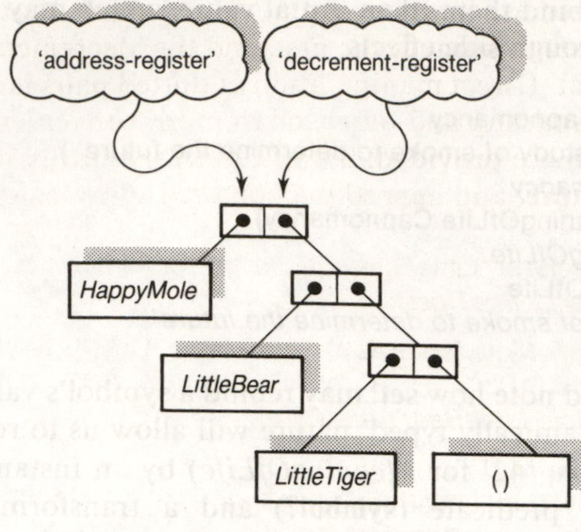

Figure 2.12 'Dotted pairs' and lists.

value in the third case. Remember that, since the list is not **quoted**, Scheme will interpret it as a 'program'. Its first element should denote a procedure, according to the rules of *Cambridge Polish* notation. In the second and third case, however, it actually refers to a symbol or a number, which can of course not be '**executed**'.

Scheme boasts a rich repertoire of procedures for operations on lists. It provides predicates (**pair?**, **null?**), constructors (**cons**, **list**, **append**), selectors (**length**, **car**, **cdr**, . . . , **list-ref**, **list-tail**, **assoc**, **member**, **memq**) and transformers (**list->string**, **list->vector**, . . .).

Internally, lists are stored as tree structures, so-called 'dotted pairs'. This representation dates back to the first LISP interpreter, which was built for an IBM 704, whose 36-bit memory cells could be split into so-called 'decrement' and 'address' parts. One memory cell was therefore used to store either a list element or two pointers. Lists were then (recursively) constructed from elements (the 'contents of address register' – **car**) and references to sublists (the 'contents of decrement register' – **cdr**). Figure 2.12 shows an example of such a representation. **cons** serves as a list constructor. It takes an element and a list as arguments and returns a newly constructed list as the result. Note that the **empty list**, (), serves the same purpose in list-processing operations as 0 does in integer arithmetic. One may enumerate all numbers by adding to zero, and one may likewise build lists by adding to the empty list. This process is often referred to as '**cons**ing up a list'. Even though most implementations treat #f as identical to the empty list, it is good practice to use () and not #f when the empty list is referred to and reserve #f for 'false' values. If **cons** is passed two atoms, it will make a 'dotted pair'; that is, the address pointer will be set to point to the first, and the 'decrement' pointer to the second argument. Direct manipulation of dotted pairs is rarely needed in practical programming and other, often more convenient, operators for list construction are provided. **list** will bind arbitrarily many arguments into a list structure, and **append** may be used to concatenate two lists.

```
(cons 'LittleBear 'LittleTiger) ; make a "dotted pair"
; (LittleBear . LittleTiger)

(cons 'HappyMole (cons 'LittleBear (cons 'LittleTiger ())))
; as in figure 2.12
; (HappyMole LittleBear LittleTiger)

; or, in an easier way:
(list 'HappyMole 'LittleBear 'LittleTiger)
; (HappyMole LittleBear LittleTiger)

(append '(HappyMole LittleBear LittleTiger) '(AuntyGoose))
; (HappyMole LittleBear LittleTiger AuntyGoose)
```

pair? checks whether its argument is a 'dotted pair', and can therefore be used in tests for 'listhood'.

```
(pair? '(LittleTiger))
; #t
```

null? checks whether its argument is the empty list.

```
(null? ())
; #t
```

Implementations which treat #f the same as () will also return #t.

```
(null? #f)
; #t
```

Selecting particular elements in a list is supported by a variety of procedures. **car** and **cdr** are the most important of these. The names have a historical significance which is now completely obsolete, but the LISP community has staunchly resisted any change to more meaningful ones (such as *head* and *tail*, or *first* and *last*). **car** ('contents of address register') refers to the element at the head of a list, while **cdr** ('contents of decrement register') may be used to retrieve a sublist of all the remaining elements. Note that **car** will always return a single element and that **cdr**, when applied to a list, will always return a list (possibly empty)! Trying to take **cars** or **cdrs** of empty lists should result in an error condition, in the same way as attempts to divide by zero do.

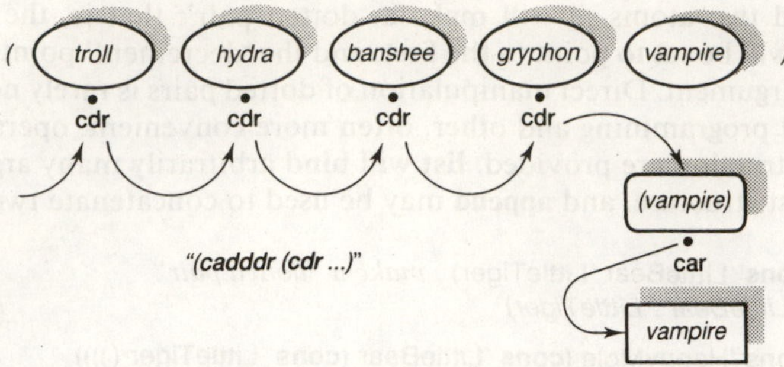

Figure 2.13 **cdr**ing down a list.

Figure 2.13 shows how lists may be processed element by element, using combinations of **car** and **cdr**. When applied to the (quoted!) list (*troll hydra banshee gryphon vampire*), **cdr** will yield the list (*hydra banshee gryphon vampire*) while **car** would return *troll*. To get to the fifth element, we have to invoke **cdr** four times. This will return the list (*vampire*), whose **car** will then yield the desired element. Scheme allows concatenation of these access functions, down to a level of four. **(car (cdr (cdr (cdr (cdr** '(*troll hydra banshee gryphon vampire*)))))) then becomes **(cadddr (cdr** '(*troll hydra banshee gryphon vampire*))). The ease and brevity of pronouncing such 'stutterings' may be one of the reasons for the reluctance to change **car** and **cdr**'s names. There is actually a more convenient way to access the fifth element of a list. **list-ref** could be used for this purpose.

```
(length '(troll banshee vampire))
; 3
(car '(troll banshee vampire))
; troll
(cdr '(troll banshee vampire))
; (banshee vampire)
(car (cdr (cdr '(troll banshee vampire))))
; vampire
(caddr '(troll banshee vampire))
; vampire
(list-tail '(troll banshee vampire) 2)
; (vampire)
(list-ref '(troll banshee vampire) 2)
; vampire
```

Only the last two examples are worth commenting on. **list-tail** obtains a sublist by stripping the first *n* elements, and **list-ref** returns the element at a specified position. Note, however, that these operations start counting at zero!

There are also some procedures for searching lists. **member** and **memq** will return sublists whose **car** is a specified element. They use different procedures (**equal?** and **eq?**) to test for equality and **memq** applies the stricter criterion of 'pointer equivalence'. Note that the fact that they return lists does not prevent us from using them in (Boolean) conditions. This is a case where the convention of treating all non-nil values as 'true' comes in handy. '**Association lists**' are a special class of lists storing 'key–value' bindings. They may be represented as lists of lists of two elements, and Scheme offers an **assoc** procedure to retrieve a value if a key is given as an argument.

```
(member 'vampire '(troll banshee vampire))
; (vampire)
(member 'banshee '(troll banshee vampire))
; (banshee vampire)
(assoc 'LittleBear '((HappyMole vampire)
                     (LittleBear banshee)
                     (LittleTiger troll)))
; (LittleBear banshee)
```

Scheme also provides some functions for conversion between lists and strings. These are of limited usefulness, however, since **list->string** will only accept lists of characters, while **string->list** produces a list of the ASCII equivalent numbers for a string's components.

```
(list->string '(#\b #\e #\a #\r))
; "bear"
(string->list "bear")
; (98 101 97 114)
```

Vectors are heterogeneous structures, whose components may be changed and indexed by integers starting at 0. Their *length* is the number of elements that they may contain, and is fixed at the time a vector is created. Valid index values lie therefore in the range 0 to (length – 1). The # symbol is used to denote vectors.

```
(vector 7 "is one of" '(7 13 42))
; # (7 "is one of" (7 13 42))
```

The above is a vector of three components: a number, a string and a list. To process vectors, Scheme offers creators (**make-vector**, **vector**), predicates (**vector?**), selectors (**vector-length**, **vector-ref**), mutators (**vector-set!**) and transformer (**vector->list**) procedures:

```
(define Friends (make-vector 5))
; #( () () () () () )
(vector-set! Friends 0 'bear)
; #( bear () () () () )
(vector-length Friends)
; 5
(vector-ref Friends 1)
; ()
(vector-ref Friends 0)
; bear
(vector->list Friends)
; ( bear () () () () )
```

Vectors are a useful data structure in applications where access to components must be computed – for example, in the representation of game boards, where moves must be calculated. A chess board, for example, could be stored as a vector of eight vectors. The eight components of each of these would hold 'pieces' or represent empty squares.

Guiding the flow of control

Any programming language needs to provide some facilities to guide the flow of a program's execution. Such **control structures** should traditionally cater for the three categories of *sequence*, *selection* and *repetition*.

Scheme expressions are normally evaluated sequentially – the innermost expressions prior to those at a program's outer layers. **cond, if** and **case** will select some path of execution among a number of alternatives, while **begin** may be used to group expressions into a compound structure.

```
; a "fancy dress" party
(define party '((HappyMole vampire)
                (LittleBear banshee)
                (LittleTiger troll)))
; party
; and some "rules of thumb" for a "guessing game"
(cond
  ((equal? (assoc 'HappyMole party)
           '(HappyMole troll))
   "moles come as trolls")
  ((equal? (assoc 'LittleBear party)
           '(LittleBear banshee))
   "bears come as banshees")
  ((equal? (assoc 'LittleTiger party))
           '(LittleTiger troll))
```

```
"tigers come as trolls")
(else "bad guess ?"))
; an answer for the first match found
; bears come as banshees
```

The **cond** procedure will accept any number of condition–action pairs, where conditions will be evaluated in sequence and, if not false, will then cause evaluation of all expressions associated with that condition. As always, the last of these will produce the value to be returned by the **cond**. In contrast to languages of the ALGOL tradition, evaluation of such conditions is 'lazy'. This means that they will only be elaborated if the previous condition has proved to be false. **cond** exits immediately once a *true* condition is found and its associated expressions have been evaluated. Although the **cond** did contain an appropriate rule in the foregoing example, the correct guess for *LittleTiger*'s role as a 'troll' will therefore never be found, since evaluation of its conditions will stop after the first match. **cond**s may have an optional *else* clause, which will be invoked if everything fails.

cond is sufficiently powerful to describe any conceivable rule of selection. A few additional selection functions, however, are offered for the programmer's convenience, since **cond** seems rather 'baroque' in some circumstances.

```
; looking for tiger as the key of the first pair in 'party'
(if (equal? (caar party) 'LittleTiger)
    (display "tiger is first")
    (display "keep looking"))
; keep looking #t
```

if expects three expressions: a condition, a *then* and an *else* branch. If the condition yields *false*, then the third expression (representing the *else* branch) is executed. Otherwise the second expression (*then* branch) will be evaluated. **begin** may be used to group expressions, since it will often be necessary to associate more than one expression with one of these branches. Our examples assume that 'party' remains as bound by the **define** above.

```
; looking for mole as the key of the first pair in 'party'
(if (equal? (caar party) 'HappyMole)
    (begin (DisplayLine "mole is first")
           (display "who's next ?"))
    (display "keep looking"))
; mole is first
; who's next ? #t
```

case expressions are similar to the corresponding Pascal control structure. An expression is evaluated and the resulting value is used to index into a number of alternatives. Each alternative is described as a list of selectors, which have to be constants, and some associated expressions.

```
(set! age 42)
(case (+ age 1)
      ((6)     'excited)
      ((21)    'rejoicing)
      ((30 40) 'depressed)
      (else 'indifferent))
; indifferent
```

case's values need not be numbers, however.

```
; Owl's birthday party
(set! luckyFellow 'owl)
(DisplayList "an ideal pet for" luckyFellow " would be a ")
(display (case luckyFellow
               ((tiger bear mole) "dog")
               ((owl)             "tortoise")
               ((fox)             "snake")
               ((duck elephant)   "goldfish")
               (else "???")))
; an ideal pet for owl would be a tortoise
```

Recursion is the most elegant and effective way in which we may specify *repetitive evaluations* in Scheme. We will, however, postpone looking at this concept until after a discussion of procedures. Although anything that can be expressed iteratively can also be captured in an equivalent recursive formulation, and in spite of the fact that Scheme optimizes its execution so that there is no associated loss in efficiency, we may sometimes wish to use **do** to describe iterative execution. At first glance, **do** seems a somewhat complicated construction. It takes a number of index variables, starting at some initial value, increments them in the specified way, tests its termination condition, and then evaluates its body if that returns false. If the loop is abandoned, a series of expressions is evaluated and the last of these values is returned. **do**'s structure is exemplified below.

```
(do ((<variable> <init. value> <increment expr.>) . . .); declare variables
    (<test expr.> <expression> . . .)                    ; jump out
    <expression> . . .)                                  ; execute body

(let ((friends '(mole bear tiger)))
  (do ((next friends (cdr next)))
      ((null? next) "all clean now !")
      (DisplayLine "wash " (car next))))
```

```
; wash mole
; wash bear
; wash tiger
; "all clean now !"
```

Note that the binding for *friends* is only available within the scope of the **let**, an appropriately local context for the loop's execution.

Many Scheme dialects (for example, MacScheme) also provide **while** expressions for indefinite iteration. Since this is not a standard feature we will restrict its use to a few situations where it significantly improves the clarity of the code. It can easily be replaced by recursion or **dos**.

Apart from iteration across expressions, Scheme offers iteration across all elements of a list.

```
(for-each display party)
; (HappyMole vampire) (LittleBear banshee) (LittleTiger troll)  ()
(map abs '(1 -2 -3))
; (1 2 3)
```

for-each applies a specified procedure to all elements of a list. Typically, this will be done for the benefits of 'side effects' produced by this procedure. The value returned by **for-each** is unspecified (MacScheme returns an empty list). **map**, on the other hand, will collect the results of each application into a list, which is then returned. In both cases the procedure need not be a predefined one. The programmer can use lambdas or named procedures of his own.

Lambda expressions and environments

Scheme's executable objects are represented by so-called '*lambda expressions*'. This term derives from Church's *lambda calculus*, which served as a model for some of McCarthy's ideas on symbolic computing. Lambda expressions start with the keyword 'lambda', followed by a (possibly empty) list of parameters and a sequence of expressions. Whenever a lambda expression is applied in an appropriate context these expressions will be evaluated in sequence and the last value will be returned.

```
(lambda () "hi there")
; #<PROCEDURE>
(  (lambda () "hi there")  )
; "hi there"
```

The lambda expression in the first example defines a procedure literal. Wrapping an additional pair of brackets around the second lambda expression forces its evaluation (in this example, no arguments were expected). Lambda expressions may take a fixed or variable number of *parameters* and different syntactic conventions are used to indicate which parameter-passing convention is required.

```
((lambda (aFriend)  ; one parameter: aFriend
    (DisplayList "hi there " aFriend))
 'HappyMole) ; invoked with one argument: HappyMole
 ; hi there HappyMole ()
```

Here the procedure represented by the lambda expression is applied to 'HappyMole' as its argument. This spawns a computation in which **DisplayList** puts the requested string on the screen. The empty list is the value returned by the last expression (a *DisplayList*), and it is therefore also the value returned by the whole lambda. If you had written this example on your own, you would almost invariably have forgotten to quote 'HappyMole', causing Scheme to complain about another 'unbound variable'. Getting quotation right will take a bit of practice, but after a while it will, one hopes, become 'second nature'.

Scheme offers two alternative ways of accepting a variable number of arguments.

```
((lambda someFriends   ; no brackets around parameter!
    (DisplayList "hi there " someFriends))
 'mole 'bear 'tiger) ; lambda expression invoked with 3 arguments
; hi there (mole bear tiger) #t

((lambda someFriends
    (DisplayList "hi there" someFriends))) ; invoked with 0 arguments
; hi there () #t
```

Here all arguments are bound into a list (which may be empty) and passed to the lambda expression. Note that we must provide a single parameter without any brackets in order to cause this behaviour. If we do not want all our parameters to be optional, we may use:

```
; one mandatory and some optional parameters
((lambda (aFriend . someMore)
     (DisplayList "hi there " someMore))
 'mole 'bear 'tiger)           ; three arguments
; hi there (bear tiger) #t       ; mole is locally bound to "aFriend"

((lambda (aFriend . someMore)
    (DisplayList "hi there" someMore)))
 ; no arguments
; ERROR: Too few arguments to procedure
; 0 arguments supplied - 1 argument expected
```

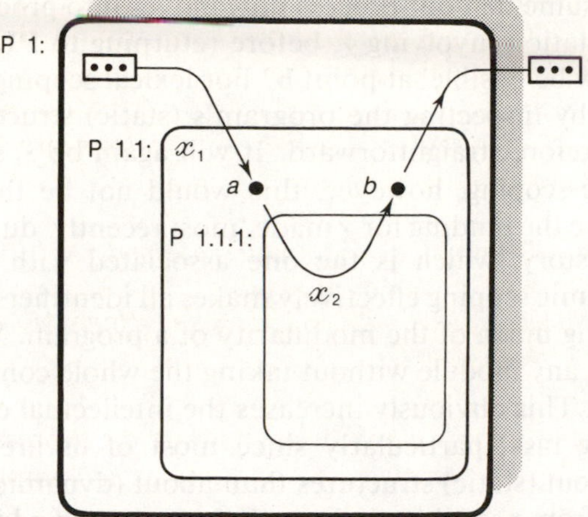

Figure 2.14 A nested context of execution.

Here *aFriend* will be bound to *mole*, while all the remaining arguments will again be assembled into a list and bound to *someMore*. Of course, we will now always have to supply a minimum of one argument.

Scheme offers a predicate (**procedure?**) for testing whether an object is in fact a procedure. **apply**, which forces a procedure's application in the current context, may also be useful in some cases. Note that **apply** expects all arguments of a procedure in a single list (here '(mole)).

```
(procedure? (lambda () (display "hello")))
; #t

(apply (lambda (aFriend)
          (DisplayList "hello" aFriend))
       'mole))
; hello mole #t
```

Lambda expressions may contain their own 'local' definitions for data and procedures. They are therefore the primary building blocks of *environments*, which Scheme arranges hierarchically, according to the notion of '*lexical scoping*'. Such environments are used to define which objects are currently accessible ('in scope') at any point during a computation. Early LISP systems supported 'dynamic scoping' only, a 'feature' which has caused an untold number of extremely hard-to-trace programming errors.

Contour diagrams such as the one in Figure 2.14 were proposed by Organick (1973) to illustrate the context of computations. The one shown here may serve to illustrate the difference between lexical and dynamic scoping. If we were currently executing at point **a** within procedure **P1.1**, any reference to identifier χ would be associated with a binding for χ_1 (defined in procedure **P1.1**). This would hold under both strategies. Let us further assume that our process now moves into procedure **P1.1.1**, for some computation involving χ, before returning to **P1.1**. What binding for χ will now be 'visible' at point **b**? For lexical scoping the answer may be obtained by inspecting the program's (static) structure alone and it becomes therefore straightforward. It will again be χ_1's previous value. For dynamic scoping, however, this would not be the case. Here we would retrieve the binding for χ made 'most recently' during the process's execution history, which is the one associated with χ_2 in procedure **P1.1.1.** Dynamic scoping effectively makes all identifiers globally accessible, destroying much of the modularity of a program. We are unable to reason about any module without taking the whole context of execution into account. This obviously increases the intellectual complexity of the programming task, particularly since most of us are much better at reasoning about (static) structures than about (dynamic) processes.

Apart from nested procedures, Scheme has an additional construct for defining (temporary) environments. So-called **'let** *expressions*' (**let**, **let***, **letrec**) yield a kind of 'block structure' (similar to ALGOL 60). **let** is a special form, which takes bindings and a 'body' as arguments. Within the context defined by these bindings, the expressions contained in the body will then be executed sequentially and the last of their values is returned. **let*** assumes that all bindings will be created sequentially (from first to last), while **let** makes no such assumption. **letrec** is needed for mutually recursive procedures.

```
(let ((seven 7) (thirteen 13))
   (DisplayLine (* seven thirteen)) (+ seven thirteen))
; 91   ; result of multiplication   (displayed)
; 20   ; result of addition   (returned by the 'let')

(let ((aNumber 7)
      (twiceThat (* 2 aNumber)))
  (display twiceThat))
; ERROR: Undefined global variable aNumber

(let* ((aNumber 7)
       (twiceThat (* 2 aNumber)))
  (display twiceThat))
; 14 #t
```

In the second and third example we need to use **let*** to get mutually dependent bindings to work. MacScheme's **let** tries to bind symbols from right to left, thereby encountering *aNumber* before it is defined.

Procedures – definition, testing, debugging

Binding lambda expressions to identifiers yields the concept of 'named procedures'. A typical Scheme program will contain large sets of user-defined procedures, usually grouped into a number of files which must be

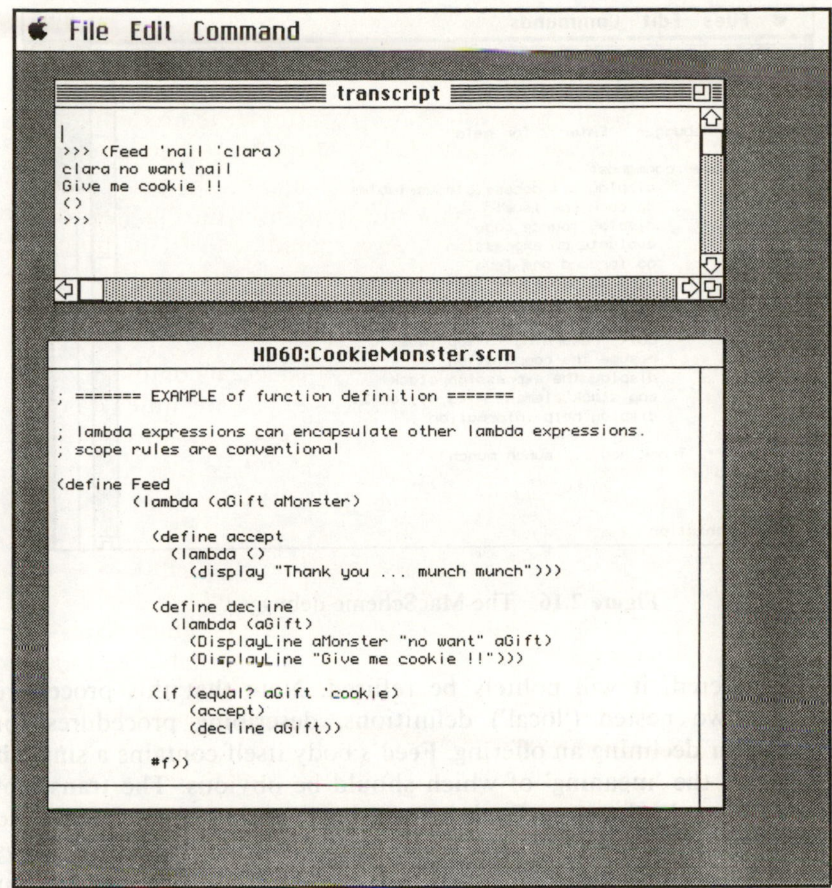

Figure 2.15 Testing a function in MacScheme.

loaded prior to program execution. The **load** procedure will accomplish this.

```
(load "HardDisk:cookieMonster.scm")
```

will attempt to load and evaluate all expressions in file *cookieMonster.scm*, within directory *HardDisk*. Details of file-handling procedures are often specific to a particular Scheme implementation. It is, however, customary to use the suffix '*scm*' for Scheme files. Figure 2.15 shows the *cookieMonster.scm* file after an appropriate window has been opened in order to view its contents (in the MacScheme environment).

Feed implements the well-known notion of a Sesame Street-style cookie monster. It is a procedure of two arguments, which, when confronted with an item, will 'eat cookies' but nothing else. If any other

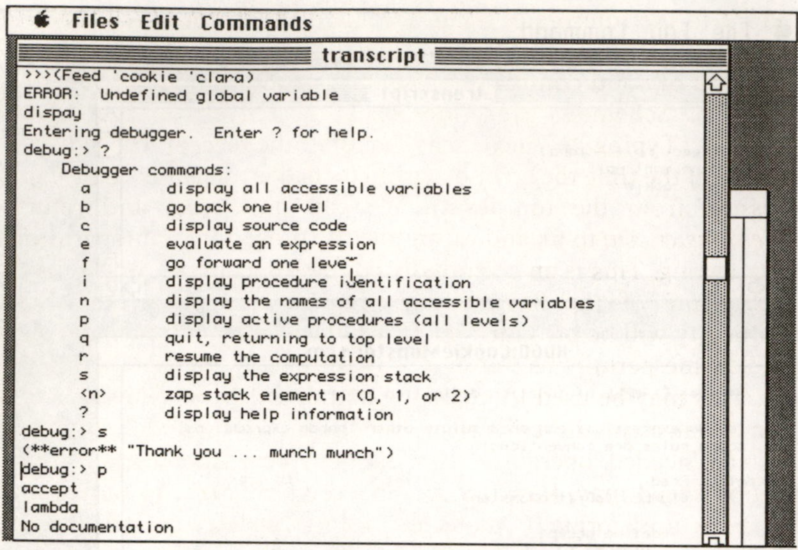

Files Edit Commands
transcript
>>>(Feed 'cookie 'clara)
ERROR: Undefined global variable
dispay
Entering debugger. Enter ? for help.
debug:> ?
Debugger commands:
a display all accessible variables
b go back one level
c display source code
e evaluate an expression
f go forward one level
i display procedure identification
n display the names of all accessible variables
p display active procedures (all levels)
q quit, returning to top level
r resume the computation
s display the expression stack
<n> zap stack element n (0, 1, or 2)
? display help information
debug:> s
(**error** "Thank you ... munch munch")
debug:> p
accept
lambda
No documentation

Figure 2.16 The MacScheme debugger.

item is offered, it will politely be refused. Note that this procedure contains two nested ('local') definitions, describing procedures for accepting or declining an offering. **Feed**'s body itself contains a single **if** expression, the 'meaning' of which should be obvious. The transcript shows the result of testing **Feed**; by offering a *nail* to *clara*. For this to happen we will have to evaluate (**Feed** *'nail 'clara*). Our transcript shows the situation just after this operation, and Clara's reaction to our suggestion is printed.

In this example, nothing went wrong and therefore evaluation terminates normally. Consider, however, what will happen if an error occurs during computation. We could, for example, misspell the second expression in the body of *accept* as (**dispay** "*no want*") and re-evaluate **Feed**'s definition. Initially everything seems to work all right. The procedure will compile properly. If we now try to evaluate (**Feed** *'nail 'clara*) again, however, an error condition will be encountered and the debugger will be invoked (*see* Figure 2.16). The MacScheme debugger is a fairly typical example for the minimum set of features which may be expected from modern LISPs for personal workstations. It will permit us to trace errors back to the start of an evaluation from the point at which they were encountered. During this process we may also browse through the values of all bindings in their corresponding environments. A particularly useful additional feature is the ability to execute any expression within any currently active environment. This should enable us to locate and fix the offending code, after which we must choose **reset** to return to the interpreter's 'top level'. In our example, the error and what caused it is obvious. After entering the debugger we may type a '?' to see a menu of valid commands. We then choose to look at the current contents of Scheme's 'execution stack', which shows the offending expression. Typing '**p**' next tells us that the **accept** procedure was executing at the time the error occurred (called by an anonymous lambda expression from the top level). We can now **reset** and return to *cookieMonster.scm* to fix and recompile the procedure in preparation for further testing. This is an admittedly contrived example, but it may still convey some of the flavour of a typical debugging tool. Similar functionality will be provided by most other Scheme implementations.

Scheme permits us to 'alias' any data structure, including procedures. This may be used to tailor the names of system functions to suit our preferences at the cost of an additional level of indirection. For frequently needed operators (like **car** and **cdr**), the resulting loss in execution speed may, however, be unacceptably high. In our choice of aliases, we are normally protected against accidental redefinition of important system-defined identifiers.

```
(define head car)
; head

(define tail cdr)
; tail

(head (tail '(vampire banshee troll)))
; banshee

(set! + *) ; sneaky: redefine '+' as a multiplication symbol?
; ERROR: Integrable procedures may not be redefined
```

Note that Scheme's model of binding is completely general. There is no distinction between the things we may do to 'passive' objects (data) and those we may do to 'active' objects (procedures). For instance, we can easily write procedures which return other procedures as values.

```
(define GenericMagicLamp
    (lambda (noOfWishes)
        (define count 0) ; local variable
        ; this is the "lambda" we wish to return
        (lambda ()
            (if (< count noOfWishes)
                (begin
                    (set! count (+ 1 count))
                    'Granted)
                "you've had all you're going to get !"))))
; GenericMagicLamp
```

GenericMagicLamp implements the notorious lamp of Aladdin, in which a genie is usually imprisoned and will be freed by the rubbing's vibrations. Being of a grateful nature, she will then proceed to offer the customary three wishes, normally with some protection against meta-circularity (that is, wishes which give you additional wishes are 'out'). Our procedure contains a declaration for a local variable, *count*, which is to be initialized to zero and incremented by one each time a wish is granted. At this point it is important to note that Scheme variables all have 'infinite extent', which means that, other than (for example) local variables in Pascal, they do not lose their values between successive invocations of the procedures in which they are bound. *count* will therefore start with a value of zero, and retain a value of one after the first, two after the second, and three after the third invocation. *GenericMagicLamp*, however, will not grant any wishes itself, but it may be used as a generator, to construct any number of magic lamps with the number of wishes defined at creation time. That is the purpose of the lambda expression, nested inside this procedure. Remember that Scheme functions always return the value of the last expression they encounter. Here this is the inner lambda, and *GenericMagicLamp* is therefore a procedure which returns another procedure as a result of its invocation.

```
(define AladdinsLamp (GenericMagicLamp 3))
; AladdinsLamp
```

may be used to make such a lamp (a procedure) and lets *AladdinsLamp* serve as its identifier. It is important to remember that this procedure will also inherit all bindings visible within the environment it was created in; at the time the creation took place. *count* is therefore accessible to *AladdinsLamp*, and it is still bound to zero. If we now start rubbing, we will produce the behaviour we should expect (the 'shape' of these wishes will be kept private).

```
(AladdinsLamp)
; granted
(AladdinsLamp)
; granted
(AladdinsLamp)
; granted
(AladdinsLamp)
; "you've had all you're going to get!"

(set! count 0)
; ERROR: Undefined global variable count
; hard luck – 'count' is kept private to this lamp object, and can't be accessed!
```

Recursion

Recursion embodies the powerful concept of self-reference, and it is Scheme's most effective tool for specifying repetitive executions of segments of code. A nice example illustrating its general idea is provided by the well-known cartoons of people holding photographs of themselves, in which they are a few years younger. The person in the photograph in turn is holding the same kind of photograph (with a person holding the same kind of photograph, and so on) so that this goes on until it eventually 'bottoms out' with a photograph of a baby.

Recursion can be used to describe both structures and processes in a very elegant fashion [Roberts (1986), Burge (1975)]. The only requirement is some degree of regularity for one to 'recurse' on. This regularity must be contained in both the nature of elements and their interconnections, giving rise to direct or indirect, linear, hierarchical or network structures.

Recursive descriptions of structures are common. Many structures in science and nature are highly recursive, reflecting some regularity in the process by which they are 'grown'. Recursive descriptions also abound in computer science. Think of the specification of binary trees as 'a leaf or a pair of binary trees'; or of lists as an 'empty list or an element followed by a list'. The recursive nature of lists maps very nicely on to the recursive procedures by which they are usually processed. The list shown in Figure 2.13 is a case in point. There we recursively invoked the **cdr** function to 'walk' to an element we were interested in. Recursive descriptions of processes are also prevalent in everyday life. Children's stories are often highly recursive, and such descriptions seem to be perfectly easy to understand and very enjoyable (at that age). We will look at a simple example below. Such stories are also extremely easy to 'generate' (tell) and one therefore tends to get bored rather quickly.

The process of proof by induction in mathematics is closely related to recursive descriptions. More informally we may define recursion as the process of reducing a problem to one or more subproblems which are identical in structure but somewhat easier to solve. This idea can then be applied to each of the subproblems, until the whole process terminates at a level where the subproblems' solutions become obvious. We may then 'recurse up' the chain of subproblems to put things together again, so that a solution to the original problem will be constructed. Hofstadter (1983) gives a silly but revealing example for this process: 'How do you make a pile of 13 stones? Put one stone on a pile of twelve. How do you make a pile of 12 stones? . . .'. We will leave the task's completion as an exercise for the reader. Of course, we must always be careful to offer some way in which such descriptions or processes may be expected to terminate. Imagine what would happen after executing the following program [Dybvig (1987), p. 37] (the name should give it away):

```
(define GoodBye (lambda () (display ".") (GoodBye)))
(GoodBye)
```

Anything that can be expressed iteratively can also be captured in an equivalent recursive formulation. In contrast to other languages, there is often no storage space penalty for using recursion in Scheme, since the interpreter will automatically attempt to translate recursive descriptions into an iterative looping structure. This can always be accomplished for so-called '*tail recursion*'. If the value of a procedure at the point of a recursive call is the value of the recursive call, then the call is 'tail recursive'. Tail recursion does not hold, however, if some operation is first performed on the result before it is passed 'up' the recursive chain of procedure invocations [Dybvig (1987), p. 71]. Tail recursion occurs quite frequently when repetitive application of operations to elements of a list is required, or in many other contexts in which iterative structures (that is, *do*, *for*, *while*) would otherwise be used. Scheme's iteration procedures therefore serve as syntactic sugaring only.

In Scheme, recursion will most often be used for list processing. Consider a program to write a variant of the well-known 'Hairy MacLary' type of children's story [Dodd (1983)]. In one of these stories *Hairy MacLary* (a terrier) goes for a walk and 'accumulates' friends along the way, so that the list of names to be chanted at each door grows longer and longer.

```
(define StoryTeller
  (lambda (mainCharacter . someFriends)
    (define chorus
      (lambda (someFriends caravan)
        ; check for termination
        (if (null? someFriends)
          #f
          (begin
            ; greet a friend
            (DisplayLine (car someFriends))
            ; and "walk down" all the ones who have already joined
            (display "with ")
            (map (lambda (aFriend)
                   (DisplayLine aFriend)
                   (display "and "))
                 caravan)
            (DisplayLine "...")
            ; recurse on another friend (and let this one join the
            ; "caravan")
            (chorus (cdr someFriends)
                    (append
                      caravan
```

```
                                    ; needs a list here !
                                    (list (car someFriends))))))))

    ; body of "StoryTeller" function
    (DisplayLine "out of the gate and off for a walk went")
    (DisplayLine mainCharacter ". . .")
    (newline)

    (chorus someFriends (list mainCharacter))

    ; we will skip some more friends here, and also their encounter with
    ; Scareface Claw (the toughest Tom in town)

    (newline)
    (display "straight back home to bed")))
    ; StoryTeller
```

When invoked with the data below, this tail recursive procedure produces the following familiar story:

```
(StoryTeller
 "Hairy MacLary from Donaldson's Dairy"
 '("Hercules Morse, as big as a horse"
   "Bottomley Potts, covered in spots"
   "Muffin McLay, like a bundle of hay"))
; out of the gate and off for a walk went
; Hairy MacLary from Donaldson's Dairy . . .

; Hercules Morse, as big as a horse
; with Hairy MacLary from Donaldson's Dairy
; and . . .
; Bottomley Potts, covered in spots
; with Hercules Morse, as big as a horse
; and Hairy MacLary from Donaldson's Dairy
; and . . .
; Muffin McLay, like a bundle of hay
; with Bottomley Potts, covered in spots
; and Hercules Morse, as big as a horse
; and Hairy MacLary from Donaldson's Dairy
; and . . .

; straight back home to bed#t
```

The above program is tail recursive, because we make no attempt to modify any of the data generated by successive calls to *chorus* after these calls return.

It may also be instructive to show a non-tail recursive procedure. This time some friends are saving up for a new sofa, and they periodically wish to count all their money to see whether they can yet afford it. The following procedure should do the trick, assuming that we list friends and their wealth as associations of the form (<name> <amount>).

```
(define HowMuchMoneyDoWeHave
  (lambda (someFriends)
    (define count
      (lambda (aFriend) (cadr aFriend)))

    (trace count)
    ; body of "HowMuchMoneyDoWeHave" procedure
    (if (null? someFriends) ; termination condition
        0
        ; else add it all up
        (+ (count (car someFriends))                    ; this much
           (HowMuchMoneyDoWeHave (cdr someFriends)))    ; and more
    )))
; HowMuchMoneyDoWeHave

(trace HowMuchMoneyDoWeHave)
; #t
```

Figure 2.17 shows how the recursion unfolds while the program is executing. Note the use of the *trace* function for tracking all calls on the *count* and *HowMuchMoneyDoWeHave* procedures. It is not a standard Scheme feature, but some such utility is provided by most dialects.

```
(HowMuchMoneyDoWeHave
  '((HappyMole 3) (LittleBear 1) (LittleTiger 0)))
```

will print:

```
; recurse "into" the list
Computing (#<PROCEDURE howmuchmoneydowehave>
                ((happymole 3) (littlebear 1) (littletiger 0)))
    Computing (#<PROCEDURE howmuchmoneydowehave>
                    ((littlebear 1) (littletiger 0)))
        Computing (#<PROCEDURE howmuchmoneydowehave>
                        ((littletiger 0)))

            Computing (#<PROCEDURE
                              howmuchmoneydowehave>
                              ())
            ; termination condition is met, "unwind" the recursion
            ; (counting as we go)
            (#<PROCEDURE howmuchmoneydowehave> ()) --> 0

        Computing (#<PROCEDURE count> (littletiger 0))
            (#<PROCEDURE count> (littletiger 0)) --> 0
                (#<PROCEDURE howmuchmoneydowehave>
                    ((littletiger 0))) --> 0
```

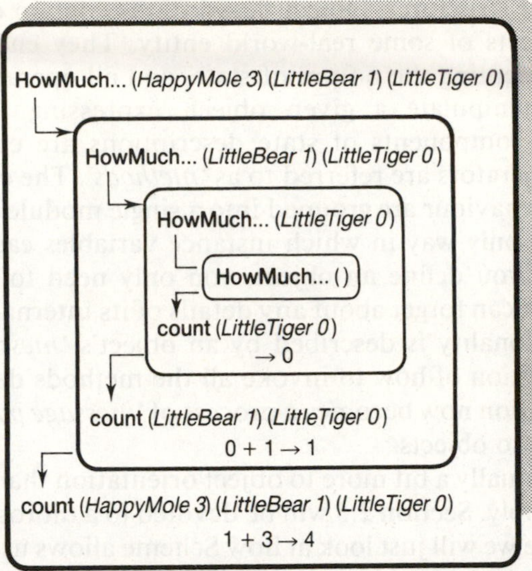

Figure 2.17 Tracing *HowMuchMoneyDoWeHave*'s invocation.

```
        Computing (#<PROCEDURE count> (littlebear 1))
          (#<PROCEDURE count> (littlebear 1)) --> 1
              (#<PROCEDURE howmuchmoneydowehave>
                  ((littlebear 1) (littletiger 0))) --> 1
    Computing (#<PROCEDURE count> (happymole 3))
        (#<PROCEDURE count> (happymole 3)) --> 3
            (#<PROCEDURE howmuchmoneydowehave>
                ((happymole 3) (littlebear 1) (littletiger 0)))
                --> 4
; 4
```

Bad luck, the sofa costs ten gold pieces, and so they will not be able to afford it yet. As expected, one should not rely too much on *tiger*. He has just no mind for money.

Objects and continuations

Scheme makes it easy to write functions which produce other functions as a result. We have already demonstrated the utility of this feature in the *MagicLamp* example, and it may also be employed to emulate so-called **'object-oriented' programming**. Object orientation offers many advantages over other programming styles with regard to understandability and maintainability of programs. A reason for this can be found in the way in which it encourages the description of processes in terms of strongly modular structures. Object descriptions contain definitions for **all** relevant aspects of some real-world entity. They encapsulate data structures, representing the notion of state, and all operators which are permitted to manipulate a given object, expressing the notion of behaviour. The components of state descriptions are called '*instance variables*' and operators are referred to as '*methods*'. The crucial point is that states and behaviour are grouped into a single module and that these methods are the only way in which instance variables can be accessed. Therefore, once you define an object, you only need to remember its functionality and can forget about any details of its internal implementation. This functionality is described by an object's '*message protocol*'; that is, the definition of how to invoke all the methods defined for that object. Computation now becomes a process of '*message passing*'; that is, sending requests to objects.

There is actually a bit more to object orientation than this brief description may imply. Section 2.5 will be devoted to a thorough discussion of this idea. Here we will just look at how Scheme allows us to implement objects quite elegantly, making use of a combination of lexical scoping and procedures which may return other procedures [Shalit (1986)].

Consider the idea of a *magic wand*, whose use for the casting of spells has been reported for centuries, by more or less reliable sources. The following implements a wand-making procedure, similar to the one for making magic lamps. As in that case, there may be variables (implemented as arguments to *lambda* or via local *define*s) with persistent state, bound in the procedure's 'private' environment. They are therefore only accessible to that procedure's own local functions – that is, procedures defined in the same environment. This is exactly what we need to implement the concept of *instance variables*. The procedure to be returned is now a *dispatch* on the names of all defined messages, which will 'really' be passed as arguments to this procedure. In this way *dispatch* implements the idea of a *message protocol*, since it will invoke the relevant internal procedure (method) if a request can be granted and will print an appropriate error message if it cannot. Since *dispatch* is defined within the procedure's 'private' environment, it will, of course, have free access to all instance variables.

```
(define WandGenerator
   (lambda (aCharge)

        ; instance variables in addition to "aCharge" may be defined here
        ; methods:
        (define charge (lambda () aCharge))

        (define spellOfSlimyExile
            (lambda (aVictim) (list 'toad aVictim)))

        (define spellOfBedazzlement
            (lambda (aVictim) (list 'pretty aVictim)))
```

```
; dispatch defines the message protocol
(define dispatch
    (lambda (anAction . someArgs)
        (if (equal? anAction 'charge)
            (charge)
            ; check which spell and decrement aCharge
            (begin
              (if (<=? aCharge 0)
                "..."
                (begin
                  ; spells always take "spellenergy" (even if they fail !)
                  (set! aCharge (- aCharge 1))
                  (cond
                    ((equal? anAction 'toad)
                     (apply spellOfSlimyExile someArgs))
                    ((equal? anAction 'pretty)
                     (apply spellOfBedazzlement someArgs))
                    (else 'poof))))))))
; the "value" (body) of dispatch will be returned by WandGenerator
dispatch))
; WandGenerator
```

The notable thing about this procedure is the way in which *dispatch* is set up to take a variable number of arguments. The dot between *anAction* and *someArgs* causes it to expect at least one argument, which is bound to *anAction*. There may also, however, be any number of further arguments, which will be stored in a list referred to by *someArgs* ! This enables us to dissect a message into its identifier (*anAction*) and zero or more arguments (*someArgs*). After a valid message is recognized, we want to apply the corresponding method to its arguments. For this to happen we use **apply** instead of invoking the procedure directly, because it saves us the trouble of 'un-listing' the argument list; remember that **apply** always expects a procedure and a list (possibly empty) of arguments. Note also how the nesting of this procedure tends to 'creep to the right'. This is a common problem with all schemes of indentation.

We can now make a wand, good for a certain number of spells.

```
(define CheapWand (WandGenerator 3))
; CheapWand
```

The 'value' returned by *WandGenerator* is the body of the *dispatch* procedure, together with the environment in which it was created (that is, with 'instance variable' *aCharge* bound to 3). We can now start to test it.

```
(CheapWand 'charge)
; 3
(CheapWand 'curse 'cugel)
```

```
; poof
(Cheapwand 'toad 'cugel)
; (toad cugel)
(CheapWand 'pretty 'cugel)
; (pretty cugel)
(Cheapwand 'toad 'kermit)
; "..."
(Cheapwand 'charge)
; 0
```

Since we are able to turn *cugel* 'literally' (that is, in quoted form) into a toad, the wand seems to work. Unfortunately, this cheap model soon runs out of 'spell energy'. Note how invocation does indeed appear as though we had passed messages (that is, *'toad*) with arguments (that is, *'cugel*) to objects (that is, *CheapWand*). The fact that these are 'really' procedure calls (that is, call procedure *CheapWand* with arguments *'toad* and *'cugel*) can be completely hidden from the user.

Another very powerful feature of Scheme is its ability to capture and freely manipulate a program's so-called '**continuation**'. The concept of a *continuation* [Hayes and Friedman (1987), Clinger (1987), Felleisen *et al.* (1986), Hayes *et al.* (1986), Wand (1980)] is a fairly old notion, dating back to ideas by Strachey, Landin and Reynolds in the late 1960s, who hypothesized that any expression in a program may be understood as being evaluated with respect to an implicit default continuation representing the program context that awaits the result of the expression. In this sense a continuation stores the future of a program's execution.

In Scheme we may think of continuations in terms of an environment and some pointer to a piece of code which will be evaluated next in this environment. Such continuations exist at any point within a program, although they are normally invisible to the programmer. Scheme's **call-with-current-continuation** procedure allows such continuations to be captured. The procedure created by call-with-current-continuation is a 'first class object', like any other Scheme entity. This means that it may be stored in a variable and later invoked from different parts of the program, and it gives us the power to implement new control structures elegantly and in a transparent fashion.

Continuations in Scheme look like procedures of one argument, which accept the result of a subcomputation and then continue to compute the result of an entire program [Clinger (1987), p. 23]. A simple example of how to capture a continuation is given below.

```
(define StoredContinuation #f)
; StoredContinuation

(define SayHiTo
   (lambda (aFriend)
   ; capture and store this program's continuation
```

```
        (call-with-current-continuation
            (lambda (aContinuation)
            (set! StoredContinuation aContinuation)))
        (DisplayLine "hi " aFriend)))
    ; SayHiTo
    (SayHiTo 'spot)
    ; hi spot #t
```

This example should make it apparent that **call-with-current-continuation** is a one-argument procedure, which must itself be a procedure of one parameter. This parameter provides a 'value' to be returned by the captured continuation whenever it is invoked, and can therefore be used for passing 'messages' to the point where the computation is meant to continue. In this example, we captured a continuation just prior to the printing of 'hi spot' and bound it to a global variable called *Stored-Continuation.*

```
(StoredContinuation #f)
```

will now 'throw' execution to the point where the process captured by this continuation was about to continue.

```
; hi spot #t
```

Here the continuation's parameter was ignored (that is, *StoredContinuation* was invoked with #f). The following example shows how we may use it to pass information.

```
(define SayHiAgain
  (lambda (aFriend)
    (display
      (list 'hi
            ; now capture the continuation within an "unfinished" evaluation
            (call-with-current-continuation
              (lambda (aContinuation)
                (set! StoredContinuation aContinuation)
                ; this is the value returned from "call-with ...". Note: when
                ; the captured continuation is invoked, it will return the
                ; value of its argument ! (so this one will be 'listed' instead)
                aFriend))))
    (display ",")))
; sayHiAgain

(SayHiAgain 'spot)
; (hi spot), #t
(StoredContinuation 'sally)
; (hi sally), #t
```

This process shows clearly how the outer **list** statement will accept *aFriend* at the time the continuation is captured, but thereafter it will use any argument supplied by the parameter of the continuation's invocation.

It must further be stressed that the 'continued' process will not only remember the point of execution at which it was 'captured'. It will also proceed to execute in the same environment in which that capture occurred. For example, if *greeting* were a 'private' variable, encapsulated within a procedure:

```
(define HilnContext
  (lambda (aFriend)
    ; define a "private" greeting
    (define greeting "lovely to see you ")

    ; and a procedure body which captures a continuation during a
    ; "greeting"
    (display
      (string-append greeting
        (call-with-current-continuation
          (lambda (aContinuation)
            (set! StoredContinuation aContinuation)
            aFriend))))))
; HilnContext
```

and if we now call that procedure to capture the 'greeting's' continuation:

```
(HilnContext "spot")
; lovely to see you spot #t
```

and if we then defined a new *greeting* at the level at which we invoke this continuation:

```
(define greeting "how very kind of you to come ")
; greeting
(StoredContinuation "spot")
; lovely to see you spot #t
```

then the continuation is still executed within the environment in which it was originally captured; that is, the greeting we get is the one defined in *HiInContext*, not the one we would get if we evaluated any other expression at this level:

```
(display (string-append greeting "sally"))
; how very kind of you to come sally #t
(StoredContinuation "sally")
; lovely to see you sally
```

Continuations may be used quite elegantly to implement 'unusual' control structures. For example, so-called 'non-local' exits can easily be defined. Non-local exits are sometimes required when a procedure 'gets into trouble' and wishes to leave some context immediately (that is, to 'jump' to a central error-handling routine) in order to avoid any further damage. The Scheme toolboxes in Chapter 3 use such a scheme for error reporting, which also offers hooks for user-defined error recovery routines. In the following example, we apply this idea to the problem of escaping from a procedure once it has been found that some operation on an 'illegal' argument (here a concatenation of a string and a non-string value) has been requested. This prevents a break in the computation, but the example is of course somewhat contrived. The same effect could be achieved by an explicit test of that argument at the time the procedure is entered.

```
(define SpellOfEuphoria
  (lambda (aVictim)
    (call-with-current-continuation
      ; capture a continuation prior to entering the "protected" code
      (lambda (aContinuation)
        (string-append
          "Be ecstatic"
          ; test whether it's "do-able" first
          (if (string? aVictim)
            ; then: ok, go ahead
            aVictim
            ; else: oops . . . hop out of this evaluation before (!!) any
            ; "damage" is done
            (aContinuation "victim unsuitable")))))))

; SpellOfEuphoria

(SpellOfEuphoria "cugel")
; "Be ecstatic cugel"
(SpellOfEuphoria 'bruce)
; "victim unsuitable"
```

What should be noted is that the non-local exit has been achieved by invoking the continuation inside the same invocation of **call-with-current-continuation** that captured it. This is equivalent to the use of **catch** and **throw** in some LISP dialects (for example, MACLISP or FranzLISP). The capture of the continuation corresponds to the **catch**, and its invocation to the **throw** operation.

As a final example of the usefulness of this concept we will demonstrate how **co-routines** may be implemented. Co-routines [Conway (1963)] are procedures with symmetrical threads of execution, which means that they can simulate concurrency by passing control (in 'ping pong' fashion) among themselves. Such a co-routine could, for example, invoke a procedure and later be reactivated at the point where it last suspended itself (!), instead of starting at its beginning again. Consider two girls, *Mary* and *Jane*, playing ball. *Mary* will throw the ball to *Jane* and *Jane* will return it. During this process they may also chat to each other. The structure of a program for such a scenario may be abstracted into a definition for the *ball* and two *player* objects, one for *Mary* and one for *Jane*. This maps nicely into a formulation as a set of procedures passing control (the 'ball') back and forth. To reinforce the way in which Scheme implements this notion we will write this example in an object-oriented style.

Let us define the *Ball* object first. This entity acts as an intermediary between the two players. Its message protocol includes *dropped?*, *pickup!* and *stuffContinuation!*. When 'caught' it will randomly decide whether it has been dropped, whereupon it terminates the current round of play.

```
(define Ball
 ; holds a random "number-generator" to decide whether it is "dropped", or
 ; in some other state
 ; also stores a continuation to escape from the current play, once it is
 ; dropped.
 (lambda (dropProb)
    (define state #f)    ; "dropped", if dropped, #f otherwise
    (define exitFromPlay #f)
    ; a continuation returning to the point of the program immediately
    ; after the game was started (put here by the first player)

    ; body of "Ball" procedure
    (lambda (aMessage . anArgument)
     (cond
       (; ball dropped?
        (equal? aMessage 'dropped?)
          (if (eq? state "dropped")
              #t
              (if ; return #t in "dropProb" % of all cases
                (<= (MyRandom 99)  (* dropProb 99))
                (begin (set! state "dropped")
                       (DisplayLine "oops . . .")
                       (exitFromPlay #f))
                #f)))
       (; pick it up again
        (equal? aMessage 'pickUp!) (set! state #f))
       (; stuff continuation to be used at a game's termination
        ; into "exitFromPlay" slot
        (equal! aMessage 'stuffContinuation!)
        (set! exitFromPlay (car anArgument)))
       (else ; reject any other requests
              "Sorry, I don't know how to do this !")))))
```

A few things about this procedure are worth noting. The '.' in the lambda's parameter list indicates that it will accept one mandatory and any additional number of optional parameters, since we want some messages (for example, *dropped?*) to take none and others (for example, *stuffContinuation*) to take one argument. The **MyRandom** procedure (again not part of the standard, with a default definition given in the 'Systems' toolbox) produces randomly distributed integer numbers from 0 up to its argument.

Let us now turn our attention to the definition of the ball players themselves. Upon invocation *Player* will 'make' player objects which respond to *playWith*, *whoAreYou* and *playBall* 'messages'. This is accomplished by returning the *dispatch* procedure together with an environment encapsulating the three 'instance variables' (*aName*, *aPartner*, *aBall*). This object contains a **while** loop. While this is not a standard Scheme feature (as mentioned above), we use it here because the alternative (**do** or recursion) would look tedious and distract from the essence of this example. In case **while** is not supported on your system, we have put a version of it in the 'Systems' toolbox. Unfortunately, both condition and body must be given as quoted lists in our implementation, since we cannot assume that macros will always be available.

```
(define Player
 ; make a player object with 3 attributes: name & partner & ball
   (lambda (aName aPartner aBall)
     ; and one more for "sequence" control
     (define nextContinuation nil)
    ; and a "playBall" method
    (define playBall
      (lambda ()
        ; introduce yourself!
        (DisplayLine "hi " (aPartner 'whoAreYou))
        ; now play until the ball is dropped (should happen eventually) !
         (while #t
           (call-with-current-continuation
          ; capture the state before the ball is gone and "throw" control
          ; to your partner
            (lambda (aContinuation)
               (set! nextContinuation aContinuation)
               (aPartner 'continue)))
          ; Reactivation point #1: continue to throw the ball
          (if (not (aBall 'dropped?))
             (DisplayLine aName
                          " throws the ball to "
                          (aPartner 'whoAreYou)))
          ; if the ball has been dropped we will never get here, since
          ; the program will "escape" from the ball (to the instruction
          ; following the start of the game)
```

```
        (call-with-current-continuation
        ; capture the state before the "chattering" starts and "throw"
        ; control to your partner
         (lambda (aContinuation)
            (set! nextContinuation aContinuation)
            (aPartner 'continue)))
        ; Reactivation point #2: continue to "chatter"
        (DisplayLine "       " aName ": chitter chatter"))))

(define dispatch
 ; the "message protocol" of Player
  (lambda (a MessageSelector . args)
    (cond ((equal? a MessageSelector 'playWith )
           (set! aPartner (car args)) 'ok)
          ((equal? aMessageSelector 'whoAreYou) aName)
          ((equal? aMessageSelector 'playBall )
            (call-with-current-continuation
           (lambda (aContinuation)
            ; save continuation for exit
            (aBall 'stuffContinuation! aContinuation)
            (playBall))))
         ((equal? aMessageSelector 'continue )
          (if (null? nextContinuation)
              (playBall)
              (nextContinuation #f)))
        (else "sorry, I don't know how to do that"))))

  ; return the dispatch procedure (with environment) as the
  ; "value" of Player
  dispatch))
; Player
```

The following script creates a *Ball* and two players, *Jane* and *Mary*, and then proceeds to test the procedure. Some comments on the co-routine's sequence of execution are included.

```
; creates a Ball with a drop-probability of 10%
(define ourBall (Ball 0.1))
; and two Player entities
(define Mary (Player "Mary" #f    ourBall))
(define Jane (Player "Jane" Mary ourBall))
(Mary 'playWith Jane)
(Mary 'playBall)
```

Note that we can't set the partner of *Mary* immediately, because at the time *Mary* is created *Jane* does not yet exist. Therefore we tell her later that *Jane* is the one she must play with. After convincing us that message passing seems to work (the response to *whoAreYou* is satisfactory and *goHome* is properly rejected), we initiate a brief play.

```
(Mary 'whoAreYou)
; "Mary"
(Mary 'goHome)
; "sorry, I don't know how to do that"
(Mary 'playBall)
; hi Jane
; hi Mary
; Mary throws the ball to Jane ; Mary "continues" Jane
; Jane throws the ball to Mary ; Jane "continues" Mary's chattering
;           Mary: chitter chatter ; Mary "continues" Jane's chattering
;           Jane: chitter chatter ; Jane "continues" Mary.
; Mary throws the ball to Jane
; Jane throws the ball to Mary
;           Mary: chitter chatter
;           Jane: chitter chatter
;
;
; oops . . .
; ()
```

In Section 2.5 we will return to a discussion of concurrency and will demonstrate how the essential features of co-routine synchronization may be encapsulated and implemented as part of a so-called flavour system.

Additional features

This section concludes our brief introduction to Scheme. Although most of Scheme's major features have been covered, we have deliberately confined our treatment to those aspects of Scheme which we believe to be essential and portable. Rees and Clinger (1986) give a complete definition of the language. There are additional standard features, particularly in areas such as numeric and input/output operations. Concepts like *engines* [Dybvig (1987), Hayes and Friedman (1984)], *macros* and *syntactic extensions* [Dybvig (1987)] have not been mentioned; mainly because standard implementations of these concepts are still lacking, although many dialects provide some such facility. Note that this book is not intended to serve as a substitute for a language manual. We would therefore strongly encourage you to use such a reference for the particular dialect you are working with, and that you continue exploration on your own. A number of interesting exercises are included at the end of this and other sections.

Programming is a skill which needs practise, particularly for the development of 'good' style. Reading programs written by others is certainly important, but writing your own and learning from your mistakes is vital. In Section 2.5.2 we will encounter Scheme again, where we talk about object orientation in the context of *flavour* systems. Scheme will also be used as the programming tool for a demonstration of various styles and metaphors of AI programming in Chapter 3. This will provide ample examples for a more specific discussion of programming styles.

Scheme is a powerful programming tool which invites its users not only to code a solution to some problem, but also to look for particularly elegant formulations. Friedman comments that a good computer language:

> '... should provide an environment in which the programmer can creatively produce good computational models or paradigms for the problems at hand. The programmer's ability to construct paradigms should not be restricted. I call the ease of constructing paradigms the language's "paradigmicity". Languages with low paradigmicity are boring ... How do we create languages with high paradigmicity? We introduce a few fundamental concepts, a few ways of combining these concepts, and in doing so we take advantage of years of experience in solving problems. No programming language in existence today has more paradigmicity than Scheme. Its fundamental concepts are procedures, continuations, engines, conditionals, and assignment statements. Everything is closed under composition and recursion, and there is provision for both syntactic and semantic extension. ... The more experience and practice one gets with using its fundamental concepts, the quicker new paradigms emerge.'
>
> [*Friedman, in: Dybvig (1987), Preface.*]

This section has surveyed and illustrated Scheme's fundamental concepts. Chapter 3 will attempt to prove the language's elegance and power in forging new programming paradigms.

2.3.3 Some comments on style

Scheme is a highly interactive language, a feature which encourages exploratory styles of problem solving and eases the learning process. New ideas can be experimented with immediately, which serves to demystify difficult concepts much more effectively than any 'static' form of description. List structures are used to represent both data and programs. Since they also emphasize hierarchical nesting and recursion, this encourages the application of 'chunking' and the creation of layered designs.

There are a few basic rules for writing well-structured Scheme programs, and most of these are similar to the guidelines given in any typical LISP textbook. Abelson *et al.* (1985) and the toolbox programs discussed in this book may serve as representative examples.

Procedure definitions should be brief, and they should be oriented towards a single, well-defined purpose. If they extend over more than a single page, a task should probably be split into a number of subtasks which are delegated to other procedures. Procedures should also be grouped around concepts, which are in turn reflected in appropriate data structures. This requirement derives from the methodology of layered design, the use of which we strongly encourage. The notion of *creation*, *query*, *selection*, *display* and *mutation* procedures gives some guidance as to which kinds of procedures are normally needed.

Programs should be readable and easy to understand. This principle has obvious implications for the naming of identifiers and for the way in which programs are structured. **Identifiers** should be descriptive, and should build mnemonic associations with the denoted concepts. You may also wish to follow certain stylistic conventions in categorizing identifiers. For example, we use an upper-case letter to start names of toolbox procedures, while lower-case letters are used for system-defined ones. Scheme uses special suffixes: '?' for predicates (that is, functions returning #t or #f) and '!' for any procedure with 'side effects' (that is, changes of bindings for non-local variables). Since Scheme is a dynamically typed language, the names of parameters should reflect their value. Use *aNumber* or *anAList* instead of just *n* or *l*. Although you may initially hate typing long names and may feel that your programs are too verbose, the additional effort will pay off later.

Imposing a clean structure on your programs will require some judgement, and you will eventually develop a **style** of your own. The only way to achieve this goal is by reading and criticising other people's code, and to adopt what you like in writing your own. Since such decisions require a sense of aesthetics, no general rules can be given other than that consistency be maintained. Don't be afraid to experiment. Throw an old program away and start again if you feel that an improved understanding will now enable you to do a better job.

Recursion and list structures are just as common in symbolic applications as iteration and arrays are in numeric ones. Even though you may need to make a conscious effort to overcome any Pascal or FORTRAN conditioning, you should use them to their full advantage. Recursion is a 'natural' and elegant way to define and process repetitive and regular structures, and such structures are easily represented as lists.

The *set!* procedure may generate 'non-local' **side effects** and it is therefore often detrimental to a program's understandability. This has caused some people to discourage its use completely and advocate 'purely' functional programming, free of all side effects. Since such a style is often not very practical in situations where processes are to be described in terms of state transformations, the authors do not fully agree with this line of reasoning. The ability to change the binding of variables is an extremely useful tool, whose effects cannot always conveniently be achieved in any other way. One should however be very careful to keep the scope of such bindings as local as possible, and to document them properly. In many cases **let** expressions, nested procedures and recursion will result in a cleaner structure.

Deeply nested **cars** and **cdrs** are often difficult to understand, and should therefore be avoided. A better way of dealing with deeply nested structures uses layers of interpretation, so that long chains of **car** and **cdr** become unnecessary. For example, *(GetXCoordinate (GetFirstPoint (GetBottomEdge (aTriangle))))* is greatly preferred to (**car** (**caddr** *aTriangle*)). The use of appropriate selector functions will lead to more flexible programs, which are also easier to maintain. The substantial benefits of object encapsulation should also be explored, since use of this metaphor may help in making your programs more robust and secure.

Like many other powerful features, **continuations** can be a dangerous tool. Although they are somewhat 'safer' than the related idea of '**go to**' statements (*see* [Computing Surveys (1974)] for a summary of the 'go to' controversy), their proper use requires considerable self-discipline on the part of the programmer. Appropriate documentation of 'why', 'what', 'where' and 'how' is also essential, much more so than for simpler structures. Continuations should therefore be used only sparingly, to fulfil objectives which cannot be achieved in any other way. Even then you should not use them in their 'raw' form, but should view them as building blocks for assembling suitable higher-level structures (for example, non-local escapes, co-routines, and so on).

Scheme's interactive nature permits you to **test procedures immediately**, as they are written. You should take full advantage of this possibility and run a selection of test cases, both valid and invalid ones.

Most general guidelines on programming style also apply to Scheme programs. Kernighan and Plauger (1974), and Ledgard (1975) give good summaries of these. Programs should be suitably indented and commented, although the use of appropriate identifiers and the possibility of testing procedures 'on the fly' reduces the bulk of the **comments** which are still required. Procedure definitions should often start with a brief explanation of their purpose, if this is not already obvious from their name. In complex applications there should also be a description of type, structure and purpose of identifiers. Apart from these considerations, comments should be used to highlight important aspects of a piece of code. They should often be explanatory (that is, 'what' is being done) rather than purely descriptive (that is, 'how' it is achieved). **Indentation** should be consistent and should emphasize a program's structure. Since listings of nested procedures have an unfortunate tendency to 'creep' to the right of the page under any scheme of indentation, it will often be necessary to exercise some judgement in order to achieve a reasonable trade-off between consistency and aesthetics.

All information should be **modularized and localized** as strongly as possible. Globals should only be used very sparingly! Scheme supports local variables and local procedures, and you should employ these facilities to chunk information into appropriate modules. Any procedure, for example, which is only ever invoked from within another procedure should be nested inside the latter one. In its logical conclusion this leads to object-oriented structures, although there are cases where procedures are simple and in which the additional 'scaffolding' associated with object orientation may not be justified.

Since we will use Scheme as a tool for discussing a number of important programming metaphors, the following sections will provide ample opportunities to see these recommendations applied.

2.3.4 Summary and perspective

LISP is built around the idea of symbol manipulation. Atoms and lists are its basic structural building blocks. Every object is either a list or an atom. Lists are recursively defined, so that we can have lists of lists of lists . . . , forming arbitrarily complicated tree structures. Lists and atoms can be evaluated, either as data or so-called lambda expressions. In fact, LISP interpreters will evaluate anything they encounter, unless it is explicitly quoted.

LISP is an applicative and expression-based language, which means that the main unit of interpretation is a parenthesized expression. 'Pure' LISP forbids 'side effects'. This restriction can often prove too limiting and has largely been abandoned in practical programming. LISP can therefore not normally be considered a *functional language*. Functional programming [Henderson (1980), Michaelson (1989)] is an active area of research, which has spawned its own language culture, for example *ML* [Reade (1989)], *HOPE* [Field and Harrison (1988)] and **Miranda** [Turner (1989)]. In such languages, assignments are not permitted. The state of a computation must be uniquely defined by the program's 'value' independent of 'context'. For example, 25 would be printed upon encountering the expression ((lambda (x) (/ (+ (*xx) (* x x)) 2)) 5), applying the 'lambda expression' to its argument of 5. The subexpression (* x x) would need to be evaluated twice. This 'inefficiency' could be prevented by introducing assignment – that is, ((lambda (x) (define temp (* x x)) (/ (+ temp temp) 2)) 5). The price we must pay is that it now becomes more difficult to 'reason' about the program. The example given above, however, may not be a particularly convincing one, since we could use **let** to save the intermediate result. A proper justification of the need to introduce assignment must deal with the problem of modularity and is beyond the scope of this chapter. Chapter

3 of Abelson *et al.* (1985) is a good source for a detailed analysis. LISP expressions may refer to other expressions, either directly or through applying some function to arguments. Every object, including functions, can be constructed and manipulated dynamically; so that we can have function-returning functions, functions which change a function's definition and so forth. Storage management is performed automatically. There are no type restrictions on objects, but the programmer may care to introduce structure through appropriate choice of identifiers. Although associating data types with variable declarations is generally recognized as an important aspect of compiled programming languages, it is less essential in interpretative environments. Its main benefit is that it enables compilers to optimize storage and execution, and to perform consistency checks of a program. Interpreters create data structures dynamically, and optimization is therefore less important. Automatic consistency checks might be desirable, but since the programmer has access to the source and values of all bindings at the time a program fails, error prevention is often not as crucial as in a compiled environment. It may be replaced by superior error detection and correction features. To verify and optimize a program once its design has stabilized, such information would, of course, still be highly desirable but it should not be obtained at the expense of flexibility at the exploratory stage.

Recursion is LISP's main control structure, together with conditional expressions. This is appropriate, since it permits easy and elegant definition of repetitive, regular structures. The inefficiency of recursion on conventional computer architectures has always been one of the main criticisms of LISP. While this argument had merit until some years ago, it has now largely been overcome by new implementation techniques and the advent of special-purpose 'LISP machines' which support lists and recursion at the microprogram level. It is, however, still fair to say that use of LISP will often result in 'memory hungry' programs.

LISP is an interactive language, supporting an exploratory style of program development. Structure editors and sophisticated debugging tools are usually provided as part of the programming environment in which it is embedded. This makes the task of writing LISP functions much easier, in spite of the proverbial jungle of parentheses. Structure editors can help parenthophobics to overcome most of the drawbacks of LISP's sparse syntax.

Many other frequently cited disadvantages (such as dynamic scoping, lack of 'block structure', single data type, inefficient numerical operations and computational inefficiency) have been removed in various ways by newer dialects.

Although even five years ago there were only a few textbooks for teaching programming in LISP, this situation has recently changed quite dramatically. Now there is a wide range of texts for different dialects and for readers with different backgrounds. The book by Siklossy (1976) is one of the oldest of these. It largely restricts itself to features which were already introduced by LISP 1.5. Allen (1978) is still an excellent technical introduction. Its use of 'M-notation' makes it largely independent of any specific dialect, and it also contains a solid discussion on implementation issues. While Allen's text will probably be inaccessible to students without prior programming experience, the books by Touretzki (1984), Hasemer (1984), Steele (1989) and Hasemer and Domingue (1989) were explicitly written for such 'beginners'. Wilensky (1984) is another interesting textbook with a more technical orientation. The book is available in two versions, one based on FranzLISP and the other on COMMON LISP. Winston and Horn (1984) emphasize AI applications. Their book is meant as a companion to Winston (1984) and has now been rewritten to offer COMMON LISP compatibility. Tanimoto (1987) is a recent textbook on AI methodology. As with many other such texts it contains a good, although necessarily brief introduction to LISP. Finally, for an advanced treatment of AI programming techniques, based on UCI-LISP, there is the text by Charniak *et al.* (1980), of which a new edition is scheduled to appear in the near future. Abelson *et al.* (1985) is still the most important textbook on Scheme while Friedman and Felleisen (1986), and Eisenberg (1987) offer a less demanding introduction. Dybvig (1987), the developer of Chez Scheme, has written a text with some more substantial examples, in which he also covers such features as engines and semantic extensions. The new scheme introduction by Springer and Friedman (1989) places more emphasis on examples taken from computer science and may serve as an alternative to Abelson *et al.* (1985). There is an active Scheme users' group which communicates through a mailing list at MIT (Scheme@mc.lcs.mit.edu).

EXERCISES

> '"Well," said Owl, "the customary procedure in such cases is as follows." "What does custimoney proseedcake mean?" said Pooh. "For I am a bear of very little brain, and long words bother me." "It means the thing to do." "As long as it means that, I don't mind," said Pooh humbly.'
>
> [*A.A. Milne, **'Winnie the Pooh'**, quoted in Roberts (1986), p. 47.*]

Write Scheme procedures for the following problems. Solutions to **starred * exercises** are listed in Appendix V. Many of the PROLOG problems in Section 2.4 also provide good, and sometimes quite challenging exercises. Section 2.5 contains some suggestions for writing flavour-based programs, and Chapter 3 offers a wealth of further material.

2.1 Write procedures for drawing geometric figures of your choice (that is, triangles, squares, circles). This can easily be accomplished by using character graphics.

2.2 'This is Spot.
See Spot run.
Run, Spot, run.'

Many children's stories try to develop reading skills through the repetition of simple sentence patterns. Such primers use a very limited vocabulary and a highly restricted sentence structure. Presumably, this makes them easier to understand by those who are just learning to read and, of course, it should also make this sort of text easier to write. Use your favourite story as a template for a program that generates simple English sentences.

2.3* Design a simple *maze* for playing adventure games. An appropriate structure should consist of some interconnected rooms, with monsters and objects lurking or stored within them. Association lists may be an appropriate representation for such a structure. Once your maze is defined, write and test some simple procedures for processing it. For example,

(a) Print a description of the maze.
(b) Assuming an object called *adventurer*, report on her current position.
(c) Look into a room and return a list of treasure, monsters and possible exits.
(d) Accept a room and a direction, and return a destination.
(e) Accept a direction and change the adventurer's location accordingly.
Note: It is illegal to walk through walls!

2.4 The *Little Monster's Counting Book* [Mayer (1978)] contains a nice example of a recursive 'song':

'Ten little Weedles
Sitting in a row;
If one falls down,
How many to go?

Nine little Weedles
Sitting in a row;
If one falls down . . .
. . .
One little Weedle

Sitting with a frown
'Cause he's all alone –
The rest are on the ground.'

[*Mayer (1978), p. 12.*]

Teach a procedure to 'sing' that song. (Alternatively you might wish to use the widely known '*25 bottles of beer on the wall* . . .').

2.5 Write a recursive procedure to solve the following puzzle:

Three Yogis – a host, an elder and a younger guest – participate in a tea ceremony. They have to perform four different tasks, listed in ascending order of importance: feeding the fire, serving cakes, serving tea, reading poetry.

The host performs all tasks at the start of the ceremony, and the tasks are then transferred back and forth among the participants until the eldest guest performs all the tasks. The tea ceremony is completed as soon as this state is reached.

There are two constraints on the one-at-a-time transfer of tasks:

- only the least important task he is performing may be taken from a person;
- no person may accept a task unless it is less important than any task he is performing at the time.

In case you have not already noticed, we should mention that this is an isomorph of the well-known 'Towers of Hanoi' puzzle.

2.6 A *tour* of a chessboard by a given chess piece is a sequence of moves by that piece, such that each square of the chessboard is occupied once and only once during the journey. The tour is said to be re-entrant if the chess piece can move from the last square of the tour directly back to the first square of the tour. Tours are possible by the king, queen, rook and knight, but not by a bishop. Write a procedure to generate such a tour for the piece of your choice.

Note: When the occupied squares are successively numbered 1,2,3,4 . . . , the tour is known as a *magic tour* if the resulting numbered array is a magic square (that is, rows, columns and both diagonals add to the same 'magic' number). The tour is a *semi-magic tour* if the result is only a semi-magic square (rows and columns add up to the magic constant, but the two diagonals do not both add up to the magic constant). On the standard 8×8 chessboard, a re-entrant magic king's tour is known. There is also a re-entrant magic queen's tour. No fully magic knight's tour is known. Write a program to generate such tours through systematic experimentation.

2.7 Write a procedure for interpreting programs stored as quoted lists of expressions. Assume that such programs do not use mapping functions (such as **for-each** or **map**) or **eval**. For example:

```
(execute '( (define result nil)
            (set! result (+ 2 2))
            (display result) ) )
```

might produce:

```
; 4 #t
```

Initially you may want to restrict yourself to a subset of 'simple' expressions (that is, no lambdas or **lets**). For testing purposes it may also be wise to restrict the depth to which expressions may be nested, although this could be relaxed as you grow more confident. Such a procedure may easily grow into an interpreter for a substantial subset of LISP or some application-specific sub-language. LISP's **eval** procedure is actually implemented in a similar fashion [Allen (1978)].

2.8 (Note that this exercise requires access to some simple graphics primitives.) Write an object-oriented program to represent simple faces, each composed of a circular frame, two eyes, a nose and a mouth. The frame, eyes, nose and mouth should themselves be defined as objects. You may then choose to represent these as 'primitives', using the concepts of circles (eye), filled-circles (nose) and three-segment-lines (mouth). The face's frame should also be drawn as a circle. Experiment with some facial transformations (such as 'smile' or 'wink' (close and open an eye a number of times)).

2.9 The game of 'Krock' may be played by a group of four students, each of whom owns a tiny green alligator and a small 36-step ladder. The game proceeds in a clockwise direction, with players rolling a dice whose six faces are painted in red (labelled 1 to 2) and green (labelled 1 to 4). If a green number is rolled, the player will chase his alligator up the ladder for the relevant number of steps. Conversely, the beastie will have to climb down one or two tiers if a red number shows (it need not crawl lower than the table top). The winner's alligator will be the first to reach the lofty height of the last step on the ladder.

Assuming well-behaved alligators and honest play, write a Scheme version for playing 'Krock'. You should report the winner and his score. A *MyRandom* function is available from the 'Systems' toolbox, if such a feature should not be provided by your dialect. Elegant solutions will use co-routines, implemented through **call-with-current-continuation.**

2.10 The notion of an ideal distance is not a complete mathematical fiction; behavioural scientists use a similar concept called social distance. In daily interactions with others there is a distance we naturally tend to adopt depending on our relative mobility and our relation to the other person. Social distances are determined in part by culture, role and sex. New Zealanders, for example, may sometimes feel a bit crowded in conversation with people from a country where social distances are smaller.

Dewdney (1987) reports a nice problem in 'party dynamics'. His fictional party is attended by eight guests, who have quite distinct personalities and occupations. For example, there is Walter (the weight lifter). Walter harbours a hopeless passion for another guest, Princess Penelope, a refined and sensitive woman of aristocratic pretensions. Throughout the party he will therefore continually edge closer to her, while she will just as continually move away from him. In quantitative terms Walter would like to spend the entire evening just three feet away from Penelope; to be any closer would be socially unacceptable. Penelope, on the other hand, is not comfortable unless fifteen feet separate her from her admirer. But if Walter strays any further, Penelope will begin some edging of her own. Perhaps she enjoys remaining in his view.

Write a Scheme program to simulate such a party. The guests may be represented as 'screen-characters': Walter may appear as a 'W' and Penelope as a 'P', for example. As the party proceeds, the eight guests may drift about the room in a seemingly endless search for 'social equilibrium'. Occasional clusters of closely interacting people will form, only to be dispelled by the arrival of a new individual who upsets the delicate balance in some subtle way. Each guest has an ideal distance from each of the others and will always move in the direction in which unhappiness will be minimized. In the context of such an admittedly stereotyped party, the unhappiness of a given guest may be measured by the sum of the differences between the ideal and the actual distances from all other guests.

Let us assume that the guests are all confined to a single rectangular room, dominated by a table spread with tempting refreshments. Each person has an ideal distance from the table as well as from each of the other guests. Dieters prefer a distance of five feet, whereas others are not completely happy unless they are just a foot from the table.

As an extension to the basic scenario one could allow some

guests to be completely indifferent towards certain other guests. When that is the case, an appropriate symbol might be used as an indication. When the program comes to consider the attraction of that guest for others, it could skip the calculation, since this one contributes nothing to their happiness or unhappiness. Richard Goldstein, the game's original inventor, has even suggested holding what he calls 'irrational parties': guests are invited in 'off the street'. In other words, the ideal distance is determined by random integers chosen from an appropriate range of numbers.

It can be quite interesting to experiment with various predetermined guest lists. Sometimes the results are predictable. For example, if all the ideal distances are greater than the room size the partygoers will all become wallflowers, skirting walls in a vain attempt to avoid everyone else. If, on the other hand, the ideal distances are small, guests will form a single, tight conversational knot near the refreshments table. Curious results can be caused by an endless cycle of one-way attractions: A loves B, but B hates A. At the same time, B loves C, but C hates B. The chain continues until it closes in on itself at A again. Depending on how the guests are distributed initially, one may witness an endless chase with occasional romantic or tragic endings.

2.4 Declarative programming – the PROLOG language

'"I know what you're thinking about," said Tweedledum; "but it isn't so, nohow." "Contrariwise," continued Tweedledee, "if it was so, it might be; and if it were so, it would be; but as it isn't, it ain't. That's logic."'

[*L. Carroll*, '***Through the Looking Glass***'.]

2.4.1 Programming in logic – historical evolution and key concepts

Since the early days of AI there has been a continuing debate on the relative merits of procedural or declarative schemes for knowledge representation [Bobrow and Collins, eds (1975)].

The **procedural view** asserts that human knowledge is characterized mainly by 'knowing how'; that is, knowing how to perform some sequence of operations in problem solving. Scheme and conventional programming languages should be viewed as procedural in this sense. At the lowest level there is not even any clear distinction between programs and data, independent of some specific context of execution. The programmer is in direct control of which operations to apply and how they interact with other components within and outside a procedure. This is a very powerful representational metaphor, allowing for almost unlimited flexibility. As a recipe for building intelligent artifacts, it has been associated with a group of researchers at MIT (Minsky, Papert, Hewitt and Winograd [*see* Winograd (1975), p. 186, Hewitt (1985)]).

By choosing a **declarative viewpoint**, on the other hand, one may conceive of the interpreter as the only 'active' process in the system, with anything else, programs or data, delegated to the status of 'passive' entities. Proponents of this approach view the foundations of 'intelligence' as a general, domain-independent set of procedures for manipulating such tokens, which will be augmented by a collection of specific concepts and their relationships when applied to a particular task. This view has long been subscribed to by McCarthy, Hayes, Nilsson and others at the Universities of Stanford and Edinburgh [Winograd (1975), p. 187, Genesereth and Nilsson (1987)].

Declarative representations are usually based on an axiomatic model of mathematical logic and attempt to draw clear distinctions between axioms, rules of deduction and logical inference. The notion of proof is central to this paradigm. Proof may be defined as reduction of well-formed formulas to axioms, using only 'valid' sequences of transformation. Axioms are therefore the ultimate primitives for defining a 'world' to such systems, and great care is taken to ensure their logical independence.

Logic has a long and respected history in science and Western culture in general. Malpas (1987) gives an excellent overview of its development and we will largely follow his line of argument.

Like many other fundamental ideas, logic dates back to Hellenistic Greece, and Aristotle in particular. To establish a standard for judging the correctness of rational debate, Aristotle developed the notion of *syllogisms*, as a set of rules governing what conclusions may rationally be reached from a statement. The basic laws on which this traditional, 'philosophical' logic was founded asserted the 'self-evident' principles of:

(1) *identity* (things are always equal to themselves),
(2) *contradiction* (nothing can be both true and false), and
(3) *excluded middle* (anything has to be either true or false).

[*Malpas (1987), p. 7.*]

Logical inference now becomes the process of reaching conclusions from premisses, where each step in a 'valid' argument can be defined, forming a so-called syllogism. Arguments are *consistent* if it is impossible to derive a contradiction from a given set of axioms. On the other hand, a set of axioms is considered to be *complete* if any true argument can also be proven.

Generations of students were schooled in Aristotelian lôgic and it took many centuries before the next major step in the development of logic occurred.

In the mid nineteenth century, the mathematicians de Morgan and Boole criticized the fact that Aristotelian logic was formulated in terms of natural language with all its inherent imprecision, and they proceeded to design more formal and rigorous notations. Many other excellent mathematicians later continued these efforts at formalization, and the modern history of symbolic logic begins with Frege's *Begriffsschrift*, a symbolic calculus for representation and manipulation of logical forms which later formed the foundation of predicate calculus.

Predicate logic has greater expressive power than propositional logic. While propositional logic permits no variables of any kind, atomic formulas, composed of a *predicate* symbol and some arguments (called *terms*), are the basic objects in predicate logic. Such predicates may define arbitrary relations between arguments, which may themselves be represented by constants, variables or functions. A well-formed formula (wff) results from combining atomic formulas with logical connectives like *not*, *and*, *or*, *implication*, *there exists* and *for all*. Variables must be quantified (by *there exists* or *for all*) before a truth value can be assigned to a well-formed formula. *Existential quantification* (*there exists*) requires that there must be at least one member of a domain which, when bound to the variable, will make the formula true. *Universal quantification* (*for all*) requires the same of all the members of the domain. First-order predicate logic only permits variables which represent objects, while second-order predicate logic also allows the predicates themselves to serve as a variable's value.

First-order predicate logic has undoubtedly been the most popular formal system within AI. For a given domain, entities will map into appropriately named constants, while relations and functions are mapped to the corresponding logical concepts. A list of all such correspondences is regarded as an interpretation. Predicate logic offers a set of techniques for proving whether a well-formed formula can be derived as a consequence of a set of axioms, and it seems a 'natural' next step to computerize such a process. This idea is closely related to Hilbert's program to base all mathematical knowledge on purely logical foundations, and to provide mechanical proofs for its theorems. Of course, Hilbert's program was doomed to fail, due to incompleteness and undecidability, as demonstrated by Gödel and Turing.

Because full predicate logic is a very expressive language whose generality leads to combinatorial explosion, a group of researchers in the early 1960s continued to search for computationally more efficient proof procedures in order to implement some appropriate subset. In 1965, Robinson proposed the idea of *resolution*, a technique which was later refined by Kowalski and Kuehner (1971). The PROLOG programming system is a direct result of these efforts.

Logic is devoted to the formal study of the relationship between beliefs and 'rational' conclusions. It is one of only a small number of formal systems whose semantics are well understood. Its greatest advantages lie in its *precision* and its guarantees for *consistency*. Its inherent *modularity* allows assertions to be added incrementally, without the necessity for considering interactions with other assertions within a given context. Unfortunately, these benefits do not come free and there are also a number of disadvantages. Logical reasoning is more constrained than other forms of knowledge representation. Although there is general agreement on the desirability of some general-purpose mechanism for writing declarative specifications, there are a number of difficulties associated with logic which have caused many people to deny its suitability for the task of building 'intelligent' programs. Other researchers have persevered and are engaged in an effort to overcome some of these deficiencies [*see* Turner (1984)].

Logic takes a simplistic 'static' view of a world to be modelled. Descriptions can't 'change'; they may only be augmented by new assertions. It is invalid to withdraw assertions once they are made. This property of '*monotonicity*' is incompatible with human thought patterns, where we are continually forced to modify and reassemble our conceptual frameworks in order to cope with 'exceptions' to previously held beliefs. Solving this problem requires a new category of logic, so-called non-monotonic logic [McDermott (1980, 1982)]. Research in this area currently commands a prominent position on the agenda of many researchers and institutions. Logic also, rather 'idealistically', assumes that one 'automatically' knows all the consequences implied by a set of assertions. There is therefore no room for the notions of *limited rationality* and *resource-constrained reasoning*. Although logic will guarantee that no false conclusions can be derived, it may well lead in practical situations to a large number (even infinitely many) of 'irrelevant' ones. Unfortunately, logic makes it difficult to describe 'heuristics' in order to provide more efficient guidance to a reasoning process, accepting the possibility of incompleteness or even occasional inconsistencies in return. 'Classical' logic offers a powerful formalism for the definition of structures, but its static nature makes it ill-suited for describing processes. Some so-called 'temporal logics' have been proposed [Winograd (1980), McDermott (l982a), Ladkin (1987)], but as yet this research has not produced any practically useful systems. In trying to reason about change, one still has to resort to 'snapshots' of some state of affairs before and after some transformation was made. This quickly tends to become very cumbersome, since there is also no way of asserting which aspects of a situation will remain unchanged. One must therefore restate all of a world's properties again, including the ones which remain unchanged. This dilemma is known as the 'frame problem' [Brown (1987)], and so far no satisfactory solution within the confines of logic has been found.

The very precision which is the hallmark of logic may also sometimes be undesirable. There are situations – for example, in so-called expert systems – where a state of affairs cannot be described precisely, but only with some degree of imperfection (that is, something may 'sometimes', 'often' or 'usually' be true). However, there are many attempts to define probabilistic or 'fuzzy logics' [Zadeh (1979)] to deal with this problem.

Although many researchers would be quite satisfied with an augmented logical system in which these problems had been 'fixed', there are still a number of applications in which there is a need for a representation in which the 'meaning' of entities would depend on more than just what is currently asserted. This leads to the concept of so-called intensional logics – that is, *modal logic*. 'Classical' logic is 'extensional' in the sense that the 'meaning' of propositions is given by the set of all objects for which these propositions are true. *Intensions* are a more elusive concept, associated with the notion of 'possible worlds'. *Modal logics* [McDermott (l982b), Charniak and McDermott (1985)], for example, provide connectives like 'possibly' or 'entails', so that we may reason about whether a false statement could possibly, if true, entail a true one.

2.4.2 Programming in PROLOG

> 'PROLOG may be seen as an effort to simplify a theorem prover down to a point where it is as efficient as a programming language.'
>
> [*McDermott (1980), p. 19.*]

Historical development

The basic idea of logic programming stresses a separation of specification and execution of programs. Logic programs may therefore act as specifications, executed by some application-independent inference procedure. A more precise definition of this metaphor is given by Kowalski, who writes that:

> 'Logic programming shares with mechanical theorem proving the use of logic to represent knowledge and the use of deduction to solve problems by deriving logical consequences. However, it differs from mechanical theorem proving in two distinct but complementary ways: (1) it exploits the fact that logic can be used to express definitions of computable functions and procedures;

> and (2) it exploits the use of proof procedures that perform deductions in a goal-directed manner, to run such definitions as programs. . . . The most straightforward case of logic programming is when information is expressed by means of Horn clauses and deduction is performed by backwards reasoning embedded in resolution.'
>
> [*Kowalski (1988), p. 38.*]

PROLOG is the best-known attempt to define a logic programming language. Since its invention in the early 1970s it has enjoyed a rapid growth in popularity. Although the name PROLOG stands for 'Programming in Logic', it must be stressed that many claims made for logic programming do not automatically hold for PROLOG, and vice versa.

PROLOG is based on the Horn clause form of first-order predicate logic [Kowalski (1979)], which can be shown to have the same expressive power as any of the more standard logical notations. Programming in PROLOG is related to theorem proving: the existence of a solution to a problem is proven (if one exists), a process during which the solution(s) itself will be constructed as a side effect.

The first PROLOG interpreter was written in 1972 by A. Colmerauer at the University of Marseilles, based on discussions with R. Kowalski (then at the University of Edinburgh). It was initially used as a tool for writing a substantial natural language understanding system and was later also employed for a variety of projects in the University of Edinburgh's AI laboratory. The initial interpreter was implemented in ALGOL-W, followed by versions in FORTRAN and Pascal. These systems proved to be slow, and in 1977 Warren wrote a compiler for the DEC-10/20 line of computers which, at that time, were almost universally used in all of the major AI laboratories. This compiler convincingly demonstrated that PROLOG programs could achieve acceptable speeds of execution and it also popularized a notation that still acts as a *de facto* standard today: the so-called 'Edinburgh Syntax', as described by Clocksin and Mellish (1981). In 1974, Kowalski left Edinburgh for London's Imperial College, where he established a centre of research into logic programming. In 1980, Clark and McCabe completed a PROLOG version for microcomputers (Micro-PROLOG) that has since been used to teach programming to high school students. A portable, C-based PROLOG interpreter was written at Edinburgh, and today we may choose from a wide range of PROLOG systems, with particular variety in a UNIX-based environment.

In spite of some early interest from theoretical computer scientists and people engaged in projects involving natural language understanding, PROLOG might have remained a fairly esoteric intellectual curiosity, if the Japanese had not boosted it to sudden prominence in the early 1980s. Late in 1978 the Japanese Ministry of International Trade and Industry (MITI) commissioned a project to develop a so-called 'fifth-generation' computer architecture for the 1990s [Brooking (1984), Feigenbaum and McCorduck (1984)]. The project formally started in 1982 and was intended to address such diverse topics as machine translation, speech understanding, image understanding, knowledge-based systems, relational databases, data flow machines, VLSI, distributed hardware and software, computer networks, man/machine communication, automatic programming, functional programming and logic programming. The important point, however, was that the Japanese intended to design new programming tools on the basis of logic programming, using PROLOG as their initial model. The goals of this research were very ambitious and the building of systems with speeds approaching 1 GigaLips was envisaged, using VLSI and large-scale parallelism. The term *GigaLips* stands for 1,000,000,000 logical inferences per second (*Lips*). To put these goals into perspective: the original DEC-10 compiler produced code running at 10K Lips and interpreted C-PROLOG typically runs at about 1.5K Lips on a VAX 11/780 [Malpas (1987), p. 50].

The announcement of the Japanese fifth-generation project caused a flurry of activity around the world, and it also brought PROLOG into many people's consciousness. Research in logic programming became fashionable, and many university and industrial laboratories explored the use of PROLOG for their particular applications. On a practical level, this development led to the availability of a wide range of PROLOG implementations on practically all major computer systems. Figure 2.18 shows some of the more important family lines. The fifth-generation project has also caused a number of funding initiatives for AI research in the USA (*Strategic Computer Initiative*), Great Britain (*Alvey*) and the EEC (*Esprit*). These were intended to provide sponsorship to major joint projects among industrial research laboratories and universities, aimed at the development or application of new technologies. At this time, no specific results from such projects, including the fifth-generation initiative, are known to the authors.

UNIX PROLOG was originally developed at the University of Edinburgh for PDP-11s running under UNIX V7. It is a simple interpreter, implemented in assembly language, which may be obtained for a nominal fee. **C-PROLOG**'s easy availability and low price has made it attractive to many universities in Britain, the USA and Europe. It is also an interpretative system, designed at the University of Edinburgh, for larger UNIX- and VMS-based computers. C-PROLOG is now distributed by both Edinburgh and Stanford University. Australian universities have long been at the forefront of PROLOG development, and there are active research groups in Melbourne and Sydney. **MU-PROLOG**, written in C for VAXes and Motorola 68000-based systems, and **NSW-PROLOG** [Sammut and Sammut (1983)], for a similar range

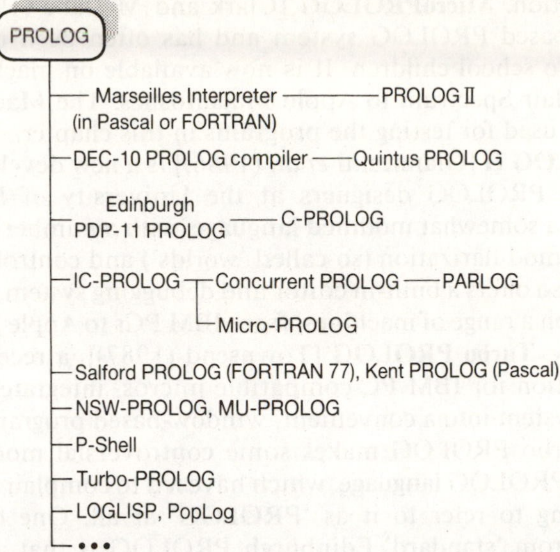

Figure 2.18 Some PROLOG implementations.

of machines, have been developed there. **Quintus PROLOG** is renowned as a particularly efficient implementation. It features an incremental compiler and a fairly complete development environment. D. Warren, the architect of the famous DEC-10 PROLOG implementation, was among its developers. Quintus PROLOG is distributed by a Californian software house for VAXes and various types of CAD workstations (Sun, Apollo, etc.). Unfortunately, it is also fairly expensive. **P-shell** is a VAX-based system, developed at Bell Laboratories. Its features include special support for AI programming. This system is now distributed commercially.

There are also a number of interpreter-based PROLOG systems written in FORTRAN or Pascal. **Salford PROLOG** (University of Salford – FORTRAN 77), **York PROLOG** (University of York – Pascal) and **IC PROLOG** (Imperial College – Pascal) [Clark and McCabe (1979)] are three of the better known versions. IC PROLOG is also noteworthy as an early attempt to augment PROLOG with additional control features, and it has later served as a model for modern concurrent logic programming languages like **Concurrent PROLOG**, **PARLOG** [Ringwood (1988)] and **EPILOG** [Wise (1986)]. Some attempts to integrate PROLOG as a subsystem into environments hosting other programming languages have also been reported. **LOGLISP** and **PopLog** [Hardy (1984)] are two well-known examples.

The wide range of micro-based PROLOG implementations is far too numerous to survey in detail. Three of them, however, deserve special mention. **MicroPROLOG** [Clark and McCabe (1984)] was the first micro-based PROLOG system and has often been used to teach computing to school children. It is now available on machines ranging from a Sinclair Spectrum to Apple Macintoshes. The Macintosh-based version was used for testing the programs in this chapter.

PROLOG II [Giannesini *et al.* (1986)] is a new development from the original PROLOG designers at the University of Marseilles. It implements a somewhat modified language, with a number of additional features for modularization (so-called 'worlds') and control flow manipulation. It also offers a built-in editor and debugging system. PROLOG II is available on a range of machines, from IBM PCs to Apple Macintoshes.

Finally, **Turbo PROLOG** [Townsend (1987)], a recently released implementation for IBM PC-compatible micros, integrates a compiled PROLOG system into a convenient, window-based programming environment. Turbo PROLOG makes some controversial modifications to the original PROLOG language, which have led to complaints that it may be misleading to refer to it as 'PROLOG' at all. One of the major deviations from 'standard' Edinburgh PROLOG is that all predicates have to be declared before they may be referred to, giving the compiler a chance to use this information for code optimization and type checking. A consequence of this requirement is that one now loses the ability to handle objects from different type domains within a single predicate. Also, only facts but not clauses can be asserted and retracted from databases at execution time. This makes it difficult to write programs which modify their behaviour in the light of 'experience', a not uncommon metaphor in AI programming. Some other so-called 'metalinguistic' predicates, which are important to many AI applications, are also unsupported. All these restrictions combine to make Turbo PROLOG more suitable for deductive information retrieval than for AI programming. On the positive side, Turbo PROLOG offers a rich set of predefined predicates, with text and graphics support, as well as the possibility of linking programs written in other languages. A further attraction lies in its modest memory requirements, its impressive performance and its remarkably low price.

Defining a world – facts and rules

Programming in PROLOG is different from programming in more conventional languages. Instead of prescribing a step-by-step plan for a problem's solution, one must define a problem's structural properties in terms of what may be 'true' and how further conclusions based on these facts may be obtained. A PROLOG program is therefore a formal description of some possible 'world' in terms of 'relevant' objects and relationships. Execution will then result in a computational process of logical deduction across this database, establishing whether our 'informal' assumptions are consistent with our formal description. During the course of this process, rules will be applied and variables may be instantiated.

Kowalski (l979b) defines a **logic program** as:

Program = Logic + Control

and we will therefore now look at each of these two components in turn.

Terms and **clauses** form the lowest level of PROLOG programs. Terms refer to classes of individuals, which may denote constants or variables. Valid PROLOG *constants* may include both integer and floating-point *numbers*, *symbols*, *structures* and *lists*. Many PROLOG extensions to the Edinburgh Syntax will also offer a *string* data type. *Numbers* are written in the conventional way – for example, 7, 3.14 or 1.23E-3. *Symbols* are *identifiers* chosen from the set of letters, digits and special characters other than ( ) | [ ],' " { } %. It is important to note that symbols representing *individuals* (that is, symbols which are not variables) must start with a lower-case letter, whereas *variable* names must begin with an upper-case one. *Structures* are collections of entities, representing relationships between objects. The first element of a structure is usually referred to as a *functor*, which names the relationship. For example:

```
friends (mole, bear).
friends (bear, tiger).
```

defines the binary relationship *friends* and asserts two instances of it. We will use the term '**arity**' to refer to the number of arguments of a functor. *Friends* has therefore an arity of 2. Note that we are normally not allowed to insert spaces between a functor and its argument list.

Variables denote classes of objects, and only during interpretation will they be instantiated to a particular individual of that class. As already mentioned, PROLOG will treat all identifiers starting with an upper-case letter as variables.

Terms are the building blocks of *clauses*, a collection of which forms a program. Clauses are separated by periods, and are interpreted as either facts or rules. *Comments*, enclosed by /* and */ or preceded by % (not supported by some systems !), may be included among clauses and will be ignored during interpretation. Facts are defined through predicates or functors of higher arity. *Predicates* and *n-place functors* express properties and *n*-place relationships. *Lists* describe classification.

```
happy (mole).
% prescribe property 'happy' to individual 'mole', meaning:
% there exists a 'mole' with predicate 'happy', ergo a "happy mole"
likes (bear, tiger).
% prescribe binary relation 'likes' among individuals 'bear' and 'tiger',
% meaning: there exists a 'bear' and a 'tiger' and they 'like' each other;
% ergo: "bear likes tiger"
washes (bear, tiger, soap).
% ternary relation: . . . "bear washes tiger with soap"
creatures ([mole, bear, tiger]).
% 'mole', 'bear' and 'tiger' belong to class (list) 'creatures', meaning:
% there exists . . . and they are all members of class 'creatures'
```

All these clauses assert individual facts, and existential quantification (there exists . . .) is implied. The sum of all such assertions forms the PROLOG database, defining the state of the world we wish to describe. It is important to note that PROLOG subscribes to a strict '*closed world*' assumption. Only what is 'provable' from the facts ('axioms') stored in this database, according to the rules provided, is accepted as 'true'. Anything else must be 'false', the 'law of the excluded middle' leaves no other logical alternative. We can therefore trust PROLOG's conclusions only insofar as our descriptions are *complete.* They must, of course, also be *consistent.* It is even impossible to express inconsistencies in PROLOG directly.

```
happy (mole).
sad (mole).
```

will not do the trick, since PROLOG itself associates absolutely no 'meaning' with *primitives* like 'happy' or 'sad'. The fact that these assertions may contradict each other exists only in the mind of the programmer. We may wish to state somehow that 'happy' and 'sad' are two mutually exclusive (?) states, but this notion turns out to be difficult to define. We will return to this topic when we discuss PROLOG's (and logic's) problem with 'negation'.

Facts may also include variables.

```
likes (tiger, Anybody).
```

would assert that *tiger* is not very choosy in bestowing his affections. Here *Anybody* is the name of a variable which PROLOG may instantiate to any of the individual objects in the database. Since we often do not really care about such an object's specific identity, PROLOG also provides a special '*anonymous*' *variable*, represented as an underscore character.

likes (tiger, _).

may therefore be used to express the same notion.

We could now proceed to define a query language to enter and retrieve information about the state of some possible world. Since we can define properties of objects as well as relationships, this will result in a tool with an expressive power similar to a simple relational database system. However, we may also wish to 'reason' about a world's properties, deducing new facts from those we have already asserted. After all, to be able to frame and test theorems is a prime motivation behind our use of logic as a knowledge representation, and we must therefore have some means of conditional and recursive inference. PROLOG rules are designed to specify such chains of deduction, leading from *premisses* to *conclusions*. A rule has two parts, separated by the ':-' symbol. The left-hand side specifies a pattern for a concept, and the right-hand side elaborates on its composition.

conclusion :- conjunction of premisses to reach that conclusion

There are two different ways in which we may understand the execution of logic programs: the so-called *declarative* and *procedural* views. Under a purely **declarative interpretation**, we view rules as descriptions of some possible state of affairs, ultimately framed in terms of some elementary concepts. We could, for instance, state that a *house*, from a somewhat simplistic point of view, is composed of four *walls* and a *roof*. This may simply be taken as a description of a structure, representable directly by the relation '*house(fourWalls, roof)*' or as a potential deduction '*house-hood implies fourWalls and roof*'. This is a purely static description, and in both cases there would be absolutely no commitment to any kind of 'action'. After all there may be a whole class of different processes by which houses may come about. We simply declare how a new concept may be 'recognized' in terms of more primitive ones. On the other hand, we may opt for a **procedural interpretation** and view rules as prescriptive recipes for 'action'. In order to '*make a house by making fourWalls and then a roof*' we would expect to prescribe an appropriate process. This perspective explicitly recognizes the fact that 'execution' is dynamic and will lead to sequential transformations of state.

Declarative programming has advantages in terms of the intellectual complexity we have to face. After all, one of the most important qualities of a tool is that it automatically performs many tasks we need not think about any further. Declarative specifications require no commitment to specific step-by-step procedural descriptions. In order to express a problem we just need to define a set of concepts and their 'logical' constraints. PROLOG's theorem-proving machinery will then awaken behind the scenes and attempt to prove constructively any relevant hypothesis within the context of this framework. Appropriate 'solutions' will be produced as 'side effects'. Since understanding a 'structure' can be much easier than understanding a 'process', we gain much by such a procedure. '*Logic clears the mind*' [Sterling and Shapiro (1986)]. However, in many cases we cannot completely shield ourselves from all consideration of process dynamics. In line with much of Greek philosophy, logic implies a 'platonic' vision of an immutable world, composed of eternal truths. Since our programs will eventually have to be executed in a resource-constrained environment, there are some purposes for which the dynamic nature of computational processes cannot safely be ignored. We will return to this problem when we discuss how to 'control' a program's execution.

All PROLOG rules are implicitly universally quantified.

```
clean (Friend) :- washed (Friend).
washed (Friend) :- soaped (Friend), rinsed (Friend).
```

Here we define two rules, one to define the concept of '*clean*' and another for '*washed*'. Both rules have an 'arity' of 1, since they both own a single argument. The first rule states that 'for all possible instantiations of *Friend*: the assertion that someone is "washed" implies that he is also "clean"'. At least this will now be inferred in our micro-world; the 'extra-logical' truth of the corresponding statement 'all washed objects are also clean objects' need not concern us here. The fact that someone is '*washed*' may, of course, be asserted directly or inferred through a different rule, for example:

```
washed (mole).
washed (Friend, When) :- saturday (When).
```

states that *mole* is a very clean creature and that on Saturday all entities are always washed. Note the use of the **variable** '*Friend*' (starts with an upper-case letter!). It will act as a 'place holder' for various individuals the PROLOG interpreter will try to bind to the premiss in order to infer the conclusion. Its scope is restricted to the clause in which it occurs! The *Friend* in the second rule is unrelated to any of those occurring in any other rule; that is, there is no sharing of bindings.

One of the rules just given contains two premisses on its right-hand side. The *comma* which separates the two indicates a *conjunction*. A *Friend* must be shown to be both *soaped* and *rinsed* in order to qualify. Some PROLOG systems will also recognize a semicolon as an '**or**' operator. However, without any loss of generality, the same effect can always be achieved by writing separate clauses, as for the one-place *washed* predicate: either a *Friend* is soaped and rinsed OR we are dealing with *mole*.

The notion of all clauses with the same name and arity is similar to the concept of a '*procedure*' in conventional programming languages. Together, they define all the possible ways in which some concept (property or relationship) can be established. For example, there are three different ways in which the property '*washed*' is defined (one fact and two rules). One fact and one of the rules have the same arity and will therefore correspond to the idea of a one-argument procedure for '*washed*', with the second rule forming an alternative line of definition (a separate procedure), requiring two arguments. When testing the truth of some relevant hypothesis the PROLOG interpreter will try each of these in turn.

No more than one item may ever occur on the left-hand side of a rule. If a premiss may lead to more than one conclusion, we may again state this through separate clauses.

```
gentry (Creature) :- offspring (Creature, Father), gentry (Father).
gentry (Creature) :- done (Creature, Deed),
                         noble (Deed),
                         daring (Deed).
admirable (Creature) :- done (Creature, Deed),
                         noble (Deed),
                         daring (Deed).
```

Here we see that the concept of 'gentry' can be derived in two different ways: either by having a gentry father OR by some remarkably noble deed, which can be classed as daring. Also, such a deed may lead to both formal (*gentry*) and social (*admirable*) recognition.

Rules may involve self-reference, either directly or indirectly (referring to another rule, which refers to . . . and back to this one). This allows *recursive descriptions* of structures or processes. The first rule in the above example demonstrates this. One way to establish the nobility of a candidate is to establish her male ancestry and her male ancestry's nobility. Of course, this will eventually have to 'bottom out' in some non-recursive fashion; for example, this could be a direct assertion of nobility, such as:

```
gentry (bigBear).
```

or the fact that one of the male ancestors performed some marvellous deed. Recursion is both a powerful and potentially dangerous tool, which should have become apparent from our discussion of Scheme. PROLOG, like Scheme, uses recursion as its primary means of describing repetitive patterns. In the above example it may generate chains of relationships: father, father of father, father of (father of father), ... Such chains must of course eventually be terminated by a stopping condition, and it must be stressed that PROLOG will *not* be able to find it unless it is asserted before the recursive rule is applied! If it occurs after the recursive rule, the interpreter will be caught in an infinite cycle before the stopping rule can ever be reached. This is a good example of a situation where some understanding of both the declarative and procedural semantics of PROLOG are needed for a working program. Putting the recursive predicate at the tail of a rule is another advisable strategy. As in Scheme procedures, this will constrain processes to the narrower path of tail recursion, which may be optimized to execute in constant space.

Functors describing conclusions may have arbitrary arity. The rule:

```
travels (Friend, NewPlace, Vehicle) :-
        location (Friend, OldPlace),
        connected (OldPlace, NewPlace),
        OldPlace \= NewPlace,
        location (Vehicle, OldPlace).
```

for example, has an arity of 3. It states that in order to travel to a new place by use of some vehicle one must first be in some location other than the new place, and these two locations must somehow be connected, and the vehicle must be at one's current location. As is always the case in formulating such rules, we have to ignore many possibly relevant aspects (for example, the vehicle must be in working order, it must be able to use the connection, . . .). The logical assumption is that we only need to include 'relevant' features and that such relevance is determined by a particular purpose.

Searching a world – queries and bindings

Once a database of facts and rules has been asserted, we can frame and explore hypotheses within this framework. For this purpose, PROLOG offers two ways of formulating a search procedure, whose execution will generate computations, deducing new facts from old. The first possibility is to specify queries through fully or partially instantiated patterns. Depending on the presence of variables in a question, this will produce either yes/no answers or a sequence of possible bindings. The syntax for such queries is:

```
?- a pattern.
```

and a brief demonstration is given below. Figure 2.19 shows how a query is posed and processed in the context of the MACPROLOG [Logic Programming Associates (1986)] programming environment. Three windows are visible on the screen. One, called *clean-friends*, shows a view

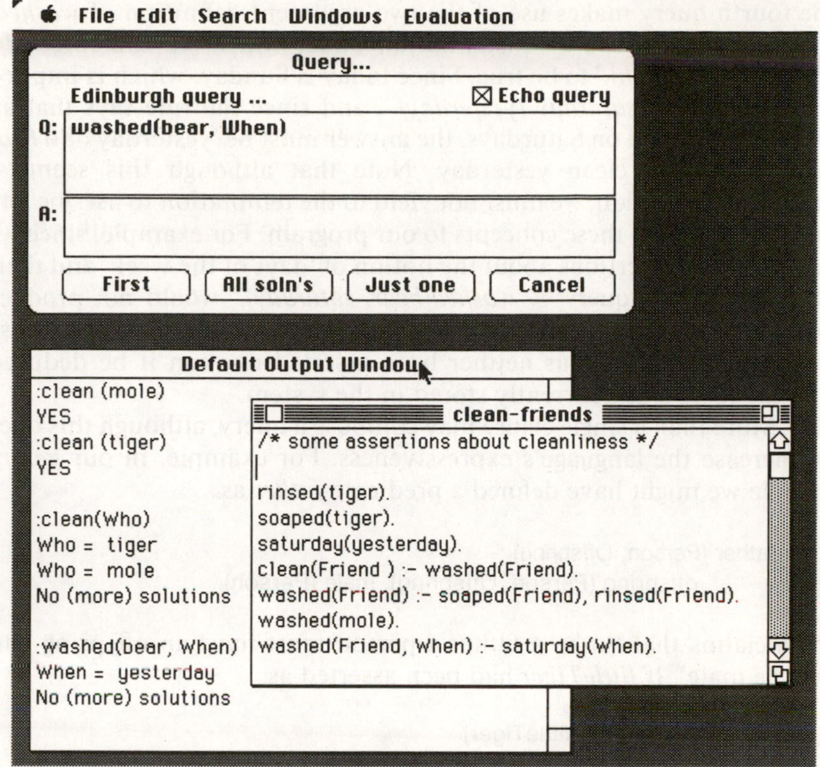

Figure 2.19 A PROLOG query.

into a file where a number of facts and rules about cleanliness have been asserted. There is also a *query* window, and an *output* window similar to Scheme's transcript, where the results of some queries are shown.

The first two queries require no variables. PROLOG is simply asked to verify the truth of the two statements. The first statement is trivially true, since the fact that *mole is clean* is directly asserted. The second statement prompts PROLOG to search for the cleanliness of *tiger*, which is not stated directly. However, since *clean* is also defined in terms of *washed*, which requires an object to be both *soaped* and *rinsed*, and since *tiger* has both of these properties, this query also succeeds. The third query shows the use of a variable as part of a hypothesis. We are effectively asking for all possible interpretations under which *Who* may be instantiated to let this query succeed. Two bindings for *Who* are returned as a result: for *mole* and *tiger*, as expected. PROLOG first returns a single result (*tiger*) and will have to be forced to backtrack to provide any further solutions. Most systems will accept a semicolon (; - read: '*or*') followed by a carriage return as a prompt for the next solution.

The fourth query makes use of the two-argument definition of *washed.* Here we wish to find an instantiation under which we can force '*? - washed(bear, When).*' to be true. Since today is Sunday, which is implied by the assertion '*saturday (yesterday).*', and since the rule says that all objects are washed on Saturdays, the answer must be 'yesterday'. So *bear* must have been clean yesterday. Note that although this seems a reasonable deduction, we must not yield to the temptation to ascribe any 'understanding' of these concepts to our program. For example, since we have made no assertions about the notion of 'days of the week' and their relationships, the query '*?- washed(bear, saturday).*' would not produce the expected result. Although this may appear silly, it would fail because '*saturday (saturday).*' has neither been asserted nor can it be deduced from the knowledge currently stored in the system.

More than a single clause may compose a query, although this does not increase the language's expressiveness. For example, in our *gentry* example we might have defined a predicate *father* as:

```
father (Person, Offspring) :-
        offspring (Person, Offspring), male (Person).
```

which claims that 'to be a father a person must have an offspring and must be male'. If *littleTiger* had been asserted as:

```
offspring(bigTiger, littleTiger).
```

and *bigTiger* as:

```
male (bigTiger).
```

then both queries

```
?- father (Who, littleTiger).
?- offspring (Who, littleTiger), male (Who).
```

would produce the same effect. Whether they have the same 'meaning' is in the eye of the beholder.

Before we continue our discussion, two important aspects of PROLOG's query facility should again be stressed. Firstly, all queries are implicitly existentially quantified and should be read as 'find a state (possible world) in which there exists . . . (for example, a clean mole)'. Also, from a declarative point of view, there is no syntactic distinction between input and output variables. Output will be produced for whatever 'slot' a variable occurs in, so that we can write queries with zero (provable versus not provable), one, or more output variables without making any modification to our database ('program'). Once a query has been completed all variables are again uninstantiated.

There is a different form of search, in which replies by the system are not directly required. This is indicated by using the :- symbol with an 'empty' left-hand side. The effect of this is that PROLOG will try to satisfy any goals listed on the right-hand side. Results may be announced through 'side effects' caused by output statements encountered during this process.

```
:- initialize(Problem), solve(Problem, Answer), report(Answer).
```

A procedural view of this directive might state that an appropriate problem representation should first be created, then a solution should be obtained and instantiated to *Answer*, and that this solution should finally be reported. We will further discuss this style of deduction when we look at the way in which PROLOG may be employed to solve combinatorial puzzles.

Search control and the PROLOG interpreter

PROLOG implements a theorem prover, based on depth-first search with backtracking. The strategy of *resolution* is used to implement this process, and Robinson (1979) gives a detailed description. PROLOG searches its database from top to bottom and from left to right. Whenever it finds a clause with a matching predicate it will check for matches in the argument positions, with eventual instantiation to appropriate constants. There is no assignment statement and pattern matching is the only way variables and constants may ever be associated. Such matches are usually referred to as '**unification**'. Unification may later be rejected if failure of other clauses leads to backtracking. Backtracking causes a search to go backwards to the 'historically' preceding goal, whenever the system fails to find valid instances of a goal and an alternative must be sought. Such situations may occur if there is no solution in a given part of the search tree, or if all solutions have already been explored and there is nothing remaining. While processing a query PROLOG will therefore attempt to apply resolution until a proof is constructed ('success'), or until this process ends in a failure. Selection of alternative choices and repetition is also accomplished through failure, backtracking and recursion.

The trace shown in Figure 2.20 exemplifies this strategy for a simple query's execution. It also shows how a trace may be set up in the MACPROLOG environment. Most other PROLOG systems offer similar features, although multiple windows will often not be available. Here we assert a simple database, defining the concept of *admirable* in terms of the deeds performed by some creature. To be considered *admirable* a creature must have performed at least one noble and daring deed. In this world only *bigMole* will qualify, because, even though *bigTiger* has certainly done something noble, this deed has not been classed as particularly daring. The query '*?- admirable(Who).*' will therefore return

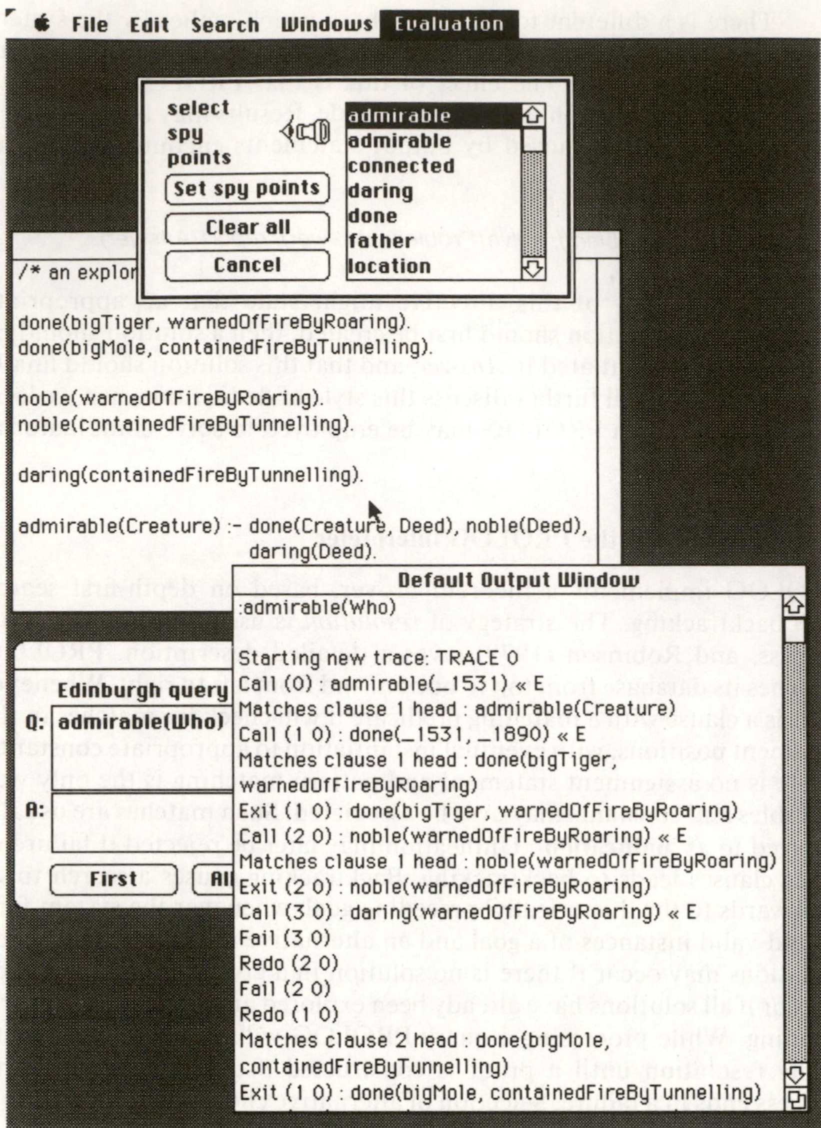

Figure 2.20 Some assertions, a query and a trace of its execution.

bigMole as the only successful match. To trace its execution we may use a PROLOG feature, called *spypoints*. *Spypoints* are similar to the switches controlling MacScheme's tracing facility. In PROLOG they refer to 'procedures', in the above-mentioned sense. Here we set a spypoint on the procedure used for deducing whether a creature may be *admirable* (for which there is only one rule). The interpreter will now print information on each of its 'calls', and (after querying the user) also on each call to a relevant subgoal. The full trace produced by this query is listed below.

```
Starting new trace: TRACE 0
Call (0) : admirable(_1552) ≪ E
% goal: find admirable creature
Matches clause 1 head : admirable(Creature)

   % instantiate Who to bigTiger
   Call (1 0) : done(_1552, _1911) ≪ E
   % must have done some deed
   Matches clause 1 head : done(bigTiger, warnedOfFireByRoaring)
   % ok, bigTiger has - instantiate Deed to warnedOfFireByRoaring
   Exit (1 0) : done(bigTiger, warnedOfFireByRoaring)

   Call (2 0) : noble(warnedOfFireByRoaring) ≪ E
   % but was it noble ?
   Matches clause 1 head : noble(warnedOfFireByRoaring)
   % ok, it was
   Exit (2 0) : noble(warnedOfFireByRoaring)

   Call (3 0) : daring(warnedOfFireByRoaring) ≪ E
   % but was it also daring ? - No, backtrack to previous goal
   % (to bigTiger's deeds - undoing the binding of Deed)
   Fail (3 0)

   Redo (2 0)
   % any more of bigTiger's deeds we can instantiate Deed to
   % (and check for noble) ?
   % No, backtrack one level further - undoing the binding for Who
   Fail (2 0)

   % instantiate Who to bigMole
   Redo (1 0)
   % must have done some deed
   Matches clause 2 head : done(bigMole, containedFireByTunnelling)
   % ok, bigMole has - instantiate Deed to containedFireByTunnelling
   Exit (1 0) : done(bigMole, containedFireByTunnelling)

   Call (2 0) : noble(containedFireByTunnelling) ≪ E
   % but was it noble ?
   Matches clause 2 head : noble(containedFireByTunnelling)
   % ok, it was
   Exit (2 0) : noble(containedFireByTunnelling)

   Call (3 0) : daring(containedFireByTunnelling) ≪ E
   % but was it also daring ? -
   Matches clause 1 head : daring(containedFireByTunnelling)
   % yes, it was indeed ! - no more things to try,
   % backtrack to announce success !
   Exit (3 0) : daring(containedFireByTunnelling)
```

```
Exit (0) : admirable(bigMole)
% search with binding of Who to bigMole and Deed to
% containedFireByTunnelling was successful
Leaving: TRACE 0
% announce the result
Who = bigMole

Continuing: TRACE 0
% try to find more . . .

   Redo (3 0)
   % no more deeds or individuals left to try - "pop up" all the way to the top
   Fail (3 0)

   Redo (2 0)
   Fail (2 0)

  Redo (1 0)
  Fail (1 0)

Redo (0)
Fail (0)

% announce the result
No (more) solutions
```

The comments should be sufficient to follow the path of deduction, as PROLOG tentatively instantiates *Who* to the two known individuals in turn and then checks all their deeds, backtracking whenever there are no more alternatives to explore, or if a feasible solution is found. Figure 2.21 gives a complementary view of this process as a walk through a decision tree, whose edges represent alternative bindings for variables. Some nodes represent alternative choices of clauses (so-called 'or nodes'), whereas others (indicated by arcs) are so-called 'and nodes'. 'And nodes' define how goals may be split into a conjunction of subgoals – for example, a deed must be both noble and daring to qualify.

In principle, such knowledge of the interpreter's operation may be transparent to a PROLOG programmer, who may choose to remain unaware of the exact sequence of operations occurring behind the scene. A knowledge of the purely logical relationships of the task domain should suffice to understand the declarative semantics of a PROLOG program. In practice, of course, knowledge of PROLOG's search strategy may turn out to be crucial, since the order in which clauses were asserted may have an order of magnitude effect on machine efficiencies. Also, some programs, namely those involving recursion, may not even terminate if the order of declaration is injudiciously chosen. The PROLOG environment will provide some *interrupt* feature (usually a control-key combination, such as **CTRL .** or **CTRL C**) to terminate a chain of deductions if the interpreter may be caught in an infinite loop.

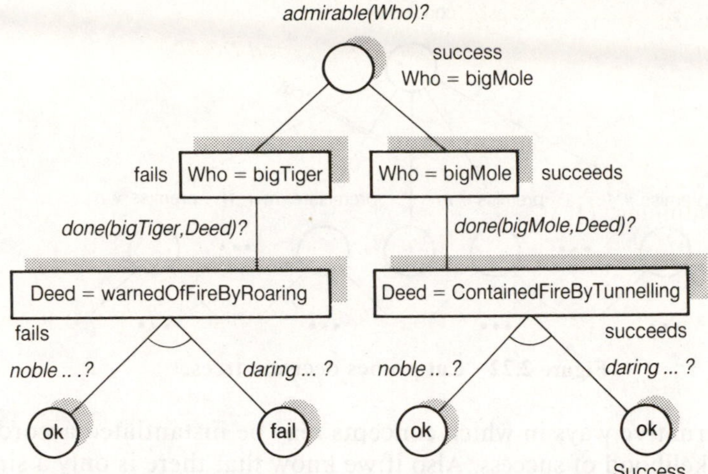

Figure 2.21 The trace as a decision tree.

Since programs for any but the simplest of tasks are always plagued by efficiency constraints, primitives to guide the flow of interpretation (the infamous '**cut**') are part of any PROLOG system.

The **cut** predicate, symbolized by an exclamation mark (**!**), is an 'extra-logical' operator, which will always succeed when it is first encountered. Thereafter it will always fail, and block any alternative instantiations for the 'father goal' and all the subgoals preceding it in the current clause. The effect of this behaviour is that all choices down to the point where the **cut** was encountered will now be frozen, together with all the current bindings for relevant variables – that is, the search tree will be 'pruned' below the **cut**. In the following rule:

conclusion :- premiss # 1, . . . premiss # m, !,
premiss # $(m+1)$, . . . premiss # n.

PROLOG will perform deductions and backtrack as necessary between all the premisses before the **cut**. Once the truth of all these has been established it will encounter the **cut**, which will succeed. All the succeeding premisses are then processed, but backtracking cannot proceed beyond premiss # $(m+1)$. If all of these failed, the rule as a whole would fail. Alternative ways of satisfying premisses #1 to #m will not be explored. Figure 2.22 shows the corresponding tree structure.

One of the purposes of **cuts** in a program is to eliminate 'unprofitable' search. If some decisive evidence for an answer to a query or a solution to a problem is encountered, we may wish to discard any further exploration of alternative possibilities, which might otherwise be generated through backtracking. This strategy works particularly well if we can

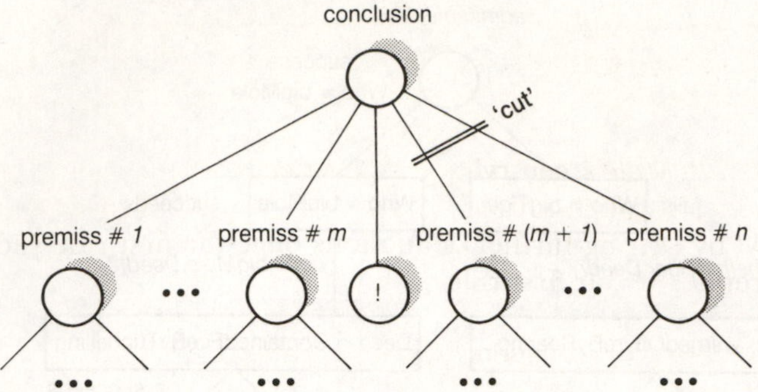

Figure 2.22 **Cut** prunes decision trees.

order alternative ways in which concepts may be instantiated according to their likelihood of success. Also if we know that there is only a single way in which a clause may be satisfied, or if we don't care for further alternatives, we may cut exploration as soon as the goal is accomplished.

Let us return to a slightly embellished version of our previous example in which we asserted a creature's gentryhood.

```
offspring (littleMole, bigMole).
offspring (littleBear, bigBear).
done (littleMole, savedFoxFromDrowning).
done (fastHare, toldOfBigFlood).
noble (savedFoxFromDrowning).
daring (savedFoxFromDrowning).
daring (toldOfBigFlood).
gentry (bigMole).
gentry (Creature) :- offspring (Creature, Father), gentry (Father).
gentry (Creature) :- done (Creature, Deed),
                     noble (Deed),
                     daring (Deed).
gentry (bigBear).
```

Here we define the *gentry* concept in terms of a 'procedure' of two direct assertions and two alternative rules of deduction. The first rule specifies that all offspring of gentry will inherit the honour, while the second one states that it may be bestowed in recognition of noble and daring deeds. One could argue that the second eventuality is much more remote than the first, so that it should always be tested last. If we now frame a query:

```
?- gentry (Who).
   Who = bigMole
   Who = littleMole
   Who = littleBear
```

```
    Who = littleMole
    Who = fastHare
    Who = bigBear
```

we see that *littleMole*'s gentryhood is deduced twice, once through his father and once through a deed of his own. We could prevent such an 'inefficiency' by cutting further deductions once the first rule succeeds – that is, by replacing our first rule with:

```
gentry (Creature) :- offspring (Creature, Father),
                     gentry (Father), !.
```

The above query now would return only one instance of *littleMole*:

```
?- gentry (Who).
   Who = bigMole
   Who = littleMole
```

but at considerable cost in terms of the predicate's generality. Since any further exploration of *gentry* is now pruned as soon as a gentryhood has been established through ancestry, we will be unable find any other members of the gentry. This holds regardless of whether they might have been confirmed by the same rule (gentryhood through ancestry), as in the case of *littleBear*, or by any of its alternatives (gentryhood through deed), as in the cases of *fastHare* and *bigBear*. This restriction would of course not matter if we never wanted to use *gentry* to generate qualifying individuals, but only for testing, as in:

```
?- gentry (littleMole).
yes
?- gentry (fastHare).
yes
```

For this purpose the '**cut**' version will still work, and much more efficiently. We have turned *gentry* into a *determinate* procedure; that is, one which will yield at most one answer. The occurrence of 'bigMole' in the previous example is due to the fact that a *gentry(bigMole)* assertion had been found before the rule was tried. The important point is, however, that we had to trade flexibility and generality in return for efficiency. We now have to observe this predicate's usage very carefully. There is no 'free lunch' in this world.

Misunderstandings of the effects produced by some **cut** in a program haunt both novices and experts and are a major source of 'mysterious' programming errors. Sterling and Shapiro (1986, Chapter 11) offer a comprehensive survey of **cut**'s many uses. From a declarative viewpoint all **cuts** are undesirable, since they destroy the context independence of assertions and thereby reduce the generality of our programs. Logic is only concerned with a solution's *existence*, not with the practicalities of its *discovery*. From a procedural point of view, however, **cuts** are often unavoidable in order to turn a theoretically solvable problem into a practically solvable one. In many circumstances the use of the **cut** operator is therefore appropriate. This includes the removal of duplicates as well as the case where there are several mutually exclusive rules that define different criteria to reach the same conclusion. It also applies to the stopping conditions of recursive rules, and to so-called *generators*, such as procedures proposing moves in a game-playing program.

Cuts may also be used in conjunction with facts [Malpas (1987), p. 141].

```
age (mole, 13) :- !.
age (bear,   5) :- !.
age (tiger,   5) :- !.
```

makes use of the knowledge that, by definition, there is only a single age for a creature, and that we may therefore wish to tell PROLOG that it should stop 'looking' once a relevant assertion is found. Again, this works well as long as we are careful to use *age* only this way, since this procedure has now become unsuitable for other purposes (for example to search for all creatures with a given age).

```
? age (Who, 5).
Who = bear
```

We see that *tiger* has been 'cut' from consideration. As a matter of style, one should try to localize any **cuts** as tightly as possible. Here this may be achieved through use of the **once** predicate, as defined by Malpas (1987, p. 144).

```
once (Predicate) :- Predicate, !.
?- once (age (Who, 5)).
Who = bear
```

'once' offers a much more satisfactory solution to the problem of restricting an individual's 'age' to a single number, since it now leaves 'age' in its full generality. So far we have encountered only constants as arguments to a functor. 'once' is also an example where use of a predicate as an argument is required. Although it will have the same effect as a direct **cut**, its use will (we hope) more clearly signal the intended purpose of this operation.

There is another use of **cut** in which it combines with the **fail** predicate to eliminate certain instantiations of a predicate from further consideration. **fail** is a predefined goal which will always fail, and will therefore cause immediate backtracking. If we know, for example, that *fox* is a shady character who could not possibly qualify as gentry under any conceivable circumstances, we might wish to put the assertion:

```
gentry (fox) :- !, fail.
```

at the very start of our database. This will guard against any eventuality that he may very sneakily somehow get his name on the king's birthday honours list. Declaratively this might read as: 'but, whatever happens, *fox* need never be put forward !'. As before, this will restrict the application of the *gentry* predicate to the testing of proposals and prevent its use as a generator for alternative candidates.

The **cut/fail** combination used in our previous example might also have been expressed as: 'but **not** fox'. The term 'negative' information refers to facts which are false, or relationships which do not hold. The **cut** and **fail** combination is the only way by means of which negative information may be expressed directly in PROLOG. Logically the common sense meaning of **not** is difficult to formalize. As with logic, PROLOG observes a strict '*closed world*' assumption; that is, whatever facts are not asserted or implied are deduced to be false. 'If' becomes 'if and only if'. If a fact cannot be proven, PROLOG also assumes its negation, true to the 'law of the excluded middle'. The meaning of rules in PROLOG is therefore somewhat tighter than that which is normally intended in natural language statements.

PROLOG's **not** predicate is itself defined in terms of **cut** and **fail**. To stress its differences from **not**'s 'normal' interpretation, the symbol '\+' is sometimes used. **not** reverses the truth value of its argument, a strategy which has been referred to as '*negation as failure*'. The implications of this concept can be somewhat subtle. For example, in:

```
creature (bear).
likes (mole, Who) :- creature (Who), not Who == fox.
?- likes (mole, bear).
yes
?- likes (mole, fox).
no
?- likes (mole, snake).
no
?- not likes (mole, snake).
yes
?- likes (mole, Who).
Who = bear
?- not likes (mole, Who).
No (more) solutions
```

everything seems to work as it should. *snake* is assumed to be 'false', since no other assertion has been made about it (that is, it has not been asserted as a *creature*). The variable *Who* in '*?- likes(mole, Who).*' is existentially quantified; that is, is there a single instance of *Who* who *mole* likes? The *Who* in '*?-* **not** *likes(mole, Who).*', however, is universally quantified; that is, for all possible values of *Who*, is there one which mole doesn't like? Only a single such value suffices to let this query fail and the use of **cut** in **not**'s implementation therefore again prevents us from finding all the things which *mole* doesn't like. This is not unreasonable, however, since these would include *snake* and the infinity of objects about which no assertions have been made. The only way in which PROLOG could be forced to answer such queries would require definition of a new predicate *notLiked* and appropriate declarations explicitly asserting all those things which are 'not liked' as a complement to the 'likes' relation.

In this way **not** may also be used in an attempt to introduce contradictory information.

```
likes (mole, snake).
likes (mole, poetry).
likes (Who, What) :- not hates (Who, What).
hates (mole, snake).
```

asserts that *mole* both likes and hates *snake* (something which is not unheard of), but also that to like somebody implies not to hate that same creature. At first glance these assertions seem incompatible. Let's see what happens if we offer them to PROLOG.

```
?- likes (mole, snake).
yes
?- hates (mole, snake).
yes
?- likes (mole, billard).
no
?- likes (mole, What).
What = snake   What = poetry
```

This is different from what we might have intended. The **not** apparently just causes PROLOG to fail and abandon the third clause. Other than that it seems to have no global effect at all. In particular, it will not invalidate any of the predicates which are directly asserted.

To force PROLOG to approximate our intention we again have to put a 'guard' such as '*likes (Who, What) :- hates(Who, What), !,* **fail**' at the start of our database. This will now screen all potential instantiations for *likes* before anything 'hated' can be retrieved.

```
likes (Who, What) :- not hates (Who, What).
likes (mole, snake).
likes (mole, poetry).
hates (mole, snake).
?- likes (mole, snake).
no
?- likes (mole, poetry).
yes
?-likes (Who, poetry).
Who = mole
?- likes (Who, snake).
No (more) solutions
?- likes (mole, What).
No (more) solutions
```

As before, this strategy will only 'almost' achieve what we intend to express, since it will unfortunately prevent us from using the *likes* predicate to find **all** the non-snake things a person who both likes and hates snakes might like (for example, poetry). This is the price we must pay for using such a procedural interpretation. The 'logical' way to deal with this problem would have been simply not to assert that *mole* likes *snake*, in which case any such query would fail. But then it is still difficult to express the notion that one may either like or hate something, but not both!

Van Emden (1982) introduced a distinction between so-called 'green' and 'red' **cuts**. **Green cuts** are restricted to those uses of the **!** operator which have no logical effect on the declarative interpretation of a program. This category includes programs in which **cuts** force a binding to be retained, once the only, and therefore necessarily correct, possible conclusion has been reached. **Red cuts**, on the other hand, often invalidate a declarative interpretation of a program for the sake of efficiency. The detailed sequence of goal execution (its 'use') must then be known to deduce its behaviour. In such cases the **not** predicate should often be used instead.

As for members of the LISP family, recursion is PROLOG's main control structure for defining repetition. Although the use of tail recursion is frequent and most PROLOG systems will optimize it for execution in constant space, iteration is still often perceived as a useful feature. PROLOG offers **repeat** as a building block for failure-driven loops. When first encountered **repeat** will succeed, but when the predicate is again backtracked, it will 'repeat' the previous cycle. Backtracking must therefore somehow be terminated to stop this process. The following example uses such a loop for reading some input from the user until the term 'bye' is encountered.

```
chomp :- repeat, acquire (Answer),
                 echo (Answer),
                 finished (Answer).
% "read" is implementation dependent -
% for MACPROLOG use "prompt_read".
acquire (Answer) :- read (Answer).
echo (Answer) :- display (Answer), nl.
finished (bye) :- !.
finished (Term) :- fail.

?- chomp.
hello
here
bye
yes
```

Note the use of **cut** and **fail** to trigger and terminate the loop's execution. The **fail** predicate is used to force backtracking until 'bye' can be unified with the user's keyboard input. Once that happens the **cut** will terminate backtracking and the *chomp* loop will fail (and therefore terminate). Until then, control will 'ping pong' back and forth between **repeat** and **fail**. In this example we have used a number of predefined predicates (shown in boldface) for input and output operations. **read** will read from the current input device, **display** will write to the current output device and **nl** will generate linefeeds after each token. The next section will look at some further such predicates which are part of a typical PROLOG environment.

Built-in predicates

PROLOG offers a large number of predefined predicates, similar to the concept of procedure libraries in conventional languages. We will only discuss the more interesting ones, grouped around the classes of objects they are defined to operate on.

Objects may be tested for **equality**. The relevant symbols denote *infix* operators, like =, ==, =:= as well as \=, \==, =\=, @>, @>=, @<, @=<. = and \= are the weakest of these, used to test equality between objects of arbitrary type. In trying to establish equality PROLOG will attempt to find appropriate bindings for any uninstantiated variables.

```
nice (bear).
nice (tiger).
?- nice (bear) = nice (tiger).
no
?- nice (bear) = nice (Who).
Who = bear
```

Notice that PROLOG unifies *bear* with *Who* to force the query to succeed. == and \== are used to test for literal equality; that is, two terms must be exactly alike in their textual representation. No variables are instantiated and uninstantiated variables will only be considered as equal in this sense if they have previously been explicitly designated as such.

```
?- likes (bear, mole) == likes (bear, mole).
yes
```

=:= and =\= may only be used to test for equality between numeric objects. It must be possible to evaluate the two expressions completely; that is, there must be no uninstantiated variables.

```
?- 2+2 =:= 4.
yes
```

The above-mentioned comparison operators can be applied to numbers.

```
?- 2 < 3.
yes
```

< is the *infix* form of @<.

```
?- (@< 2 3)
yes
```

PROLOG also offers a wide range of other predicates for numbers. This is the only place where something similar to 'assignment' occurs. The special symbol **is** binds a variable whose name appears on its left-hand side to the value of the expression on its right. Valid expressions are sequences of symbols representing *arithmetic* operations and values. To make arithmetic determinate, there is a restriction that this expression must not contain any uninstantiated variables. The standard *infix* operators are used to describe computations.

```
?- Result is 2 + 2 * 3 / 4.
Result = 3.5
?- Result = 2 + 2 * 3 / 4.
Result = 2 + 2 * 3 / 4
```

In the first case we should note that standard rules of precedence (multiplication and division prior to addition and subtraction, left to right) apply. The second case demonstrates that = is not an assignment symbol. PROLOG will rather instantiate *Result* to the right-hand expression, so that the match for equality can succeed.

Other than the four standard arithmetic infix operators there are functors for **abs**, **sqrt**, **int**, **sign**, **ln**, **pwr**, **mod** and a rich repertoire of trigonometric operations.

```
?- int (3.14, Result).
Result = 3
```

A large number of predefined predicates deal with *file handling* and *input* and *output*. PROLOG's model of I/O is stream oriented, with terminal screen and keyboard assigned as default devices. **consult** or **reconsult** are used to read programs from files. **consult** will add the contents of files to PROLOG's database, while **reconsult** will also replace old assertions by new ones with the same functor and arity. **save** will write PROLOG's database into a specified file. Individual assertions can also be added and retracted. In the section on deductive databases we will look at this more closely. **see** can be used to switch to a different input stream, while **tell** performs the same function for output streams. **seen** and **told** will close those files. **read** is used to read *terms* from the current input stream, while **write** and **display** (in a form which may be read into PROLOG again) will write terms to an output stream. **nl** creates new-line characters and there is also a collection of functors for character I/O (**get**, **skip**, **put**, **tab**). The previous example on the use of **repeat** should give some indications of how terms may be read and written.

PROLOG also offers some facilities to add information to its database of assertions (facts and rules). As seen above, this will occur each time the user declares a new relationship or a new predicate. It may, however, also occur under program control, using the **assert** (or **assertz**) or **asserta** predicates. Both will accept an assertion (fact or rule) as their argument and will add that assertion to the database. The difference is that **asserta** will enter the new assertion before and **assert** after any others with the same predicate (name and arity).

```
asserta (blind (mole)).
assert ((understands (mole, Who) :- mole (Who))).
?- blind (Who).
Who = mole
?- understands (mole, mole).
no
```

The last case again highlights an important 'feature' of logic. We can only reason about concepts which have been asserted. Although naming often seems to suggest a correspondence between 'reality' and some tokens in a PROLOG program, this is not the case at all. In Wittgensteinian terms PROLOG is just playing 'games' with symbolic tokens according to purely formal rules. The 'meaning' of these 'games' is solely in the mind of the programmer. Here we forgot to assert that *mole* is a *mole*. But shouldn't that be obvious? Not to PROLOG, since it is unable to derive any 'meaning' from an identifier other than that which has been explicitly formalized and programmed into its database.

From a purely declarative viewpoint, PROLOG's database should be immutable. Knowledge should only be asserted in a cumulative, 'monotonic' fashion, and new facts or rules should never invalidate any already asserted ones. In practice, however, there is often a need for programs to retract previously made assertions – for example, in order to change the state of a dynamic process (world) or to reflect 'learning' from experience. Since this may well lead to 'side effects' for other relations or predicates, the program's meaning can now only be established in the light of its execution history, thereby forcing us to adopt a procedural point of view. **retract** and **abolish** offer such tools. **retract** removes a specified assertion, while **abolish** removes all assertions with a predicate and arity that match the description.

```
understands (mole, mole).
understands (mole, mouse).
understands (mole, digging).
?- understands (mole, Which).
Which = mole   Which = mouse   Which = digging

retract (understands (mole, mouse)).
?- understands (mole, Which).
Which = mole   Which = digging
abolish (understands, 2).
?- understands (mole, Which).
No definition for relation understands (mole, _)
```

The **listing** predicate may be used to view the current contents of the database.

```
% before the retract and abolish to the above database
:- assert (understands (mole, poetry)).
yes
:- listing.
understands (mole, mole).
understands (mole, mouse).
understands (mole, digging).
understands (mole, poetry).
```

PROLOG offers a number of other so-called *meta-logical predicates*, whose name already indicates that, in common with all input and output operations, these are outside the scope of first-order logic. The following functors are concerned with the form rather than the contents of terms and clauses in PROLOG's database. **var** will succeed if its argument is a variable. Similar definitions hold for **nonvar**, **atom**, **number**, **atomic** (constant or number), **integer** and **float. arg** is more interesting. It takes three arguments, the argument (its index) of the clause we are interested in, the clause itself and the value of that argument. For example:

```
?- arg (3, travels (littleBear, balloon, panama), Where).
Where = panama
```

The **functor** predicate can be used to analyze and build functors. Its arguments denote a clause, a functor and an arity.

```
?- functor (Hate, hates, 2).
Hate = hates (_1, _2)
```

creates a new functor, *hates*, with two anonymous argument slots.

```
?- functor (Hate, hates, 2),
    arg (1, Hate, mole),
    arg (2, Hate, snake),
    assert (Hate).
Hate = hates (mole, snake)
?- hates (Who, snake).
Who = mole
```

assembles a *hates* relationship between *mole* and *snake* and also **asserts** it into the database.

=.. is a useful infix operator for converting a clause to a list or vice versa.

```
?- Clause =.. [respects, snake, mole].
Clause = respects (snake, mole)
?- cantStand (papaBear, noise) =.. List.
List = [cantStand, papaBear, noise]
```

Finally, **call** may be used to force a goal's execution (similar to **eval**).

```
?- Clause =.. [respects, snake, mole], assert (Clause).
Clause =.. [respects, snake, mole]
?- Query =.. [respects, snake, Who], call (Query).
Who = mole
```

shows how it may be employed.

Sometimes it is convenient to attach special symbols to a collection of concepts. PROLOG supports this idea through the definition of *operators*.

```
op (500, xfy, =>).
X=>Y :- creature(X), creature(Y), X \== Y,
        write(X), tab(1), write(washes), tab(1), write(Y), nl.
```

```
creature (bear).
creature (tiger).
?- bear => tiger.
bear washes tiger
yes
?- bear => bear.
% fails the "identity test": X \== Y
no
?- bear => snake.
% snake is not asserted to be a creature
no
```

Here we declare a new binary operator, =>, to symbolize the notion of *washing*. It has an overall precedence level of 500 and the order of *x* and *y* defines their relative precedences. We then define the details of *washing* through a corresponding functor. Note that **tab** writes spaces and **nl** forces a line feed. The test for identity is necessary to prevent infinite recursion if *bear* should try to wash himself. *xfx*, *yfx*, *xf*, *yf*, *fx* and *fy* would have been other possible patterns for operator specifications.

Another built-in feature of some PROLOG systems is a facility for defining so-called '*definite clause grammars*' (DCGs), a variant of context-free grammars. This feature traces back to Colmerauer's original natural language parser, one of the very first PROLOG applications. We will not cover this subject here, but we will return to parsing in a Scheme context, when we discuss 'augmented transition networks' (ATNs) in Chapter 3.

List processing

Lists are an extremely useful concept in symbol-processing applications. They may, for instance, support both structural and procedural abstraction via the process of chunking and classification. PROLOG's list-processing features are very similar to those offered by LISP. Lists are composed of some head element and a tail of successors. Both the building and processing of lists are recursive activities, terminating with the empty list, [ ]. The vertical bar (|) plays a role similar to that of **car** and **cdr**, with *head* and *tail* written as [Head | Tail].

```
friends ([mole, bear, tiger]).
% take car and cdr
?- friends ([Head | Tail]).
Head = mole
Tail = [bear, tiger]

% take (car (cdr ..))
?- friends ([_ | [SecondElement | _]])
_1 = mole
```

```
SecondElement = bear
_2 = [tiger]
```

Remember that the anonymous variable, _, is used to denote objects whose identity we are not particularly interested in. One may easily define additional selectors, membership and append predicates, for example, to access the first, third or last elements of a list.

```
first (Element, [Element | _]).
?- first (BestFriend, [mole, bear, tiger]).
BestFriend = mole
third (Element, [_, _, Element | _]).
?- third (ThirdBestFriend, [mole, bear, tiger]).
ThirdBestFriend = tiger
last (Element, [Element]).
last (Element, [_| Tail]) :- last (Element, Tail]).
?- last (LeastBestFriend, [mole, bear, tiger]).
LeastBestFriend = tiger
```

The last predicate is more interesting than the other two. It uses an obviously recursive definition, with the first clause as the termination condition. Whenever we encounter a single element list, then the single element is obviously the last one. Remember that we must always put the terminating case first, so that the interpreter won't be caught in any infinite loop. The second clause describes the recursive case, applicable where the list has both a head and a tail. In that case the last element is defined in terms of the tail of that list, the tail of the tail of that one, and so on – a description which must eventually terminate in a single element list (where the recursion stops).

We can define a similar pattern as a criterion for list membership.

```
inList (Who, [Who | __]).
inList (Who, [_| Tail]) :- inList (Who, Tail).
?- inList (tiger, [mole, bear, tiger]).
yes
```

This pattern can also be applied to uninstantiated variables, such as

```
?- inList (Who, [mole, bear, tiger]).
Who = mole
Who = bear
Who = tiger
```

and as a predicate to test for list membership.

```
friend (Who) :- friends (List), inList (Who, List).
```

makes use of the *friends* list we asserted at the start of this section and declares membership in that list as a criterion for friendship. We can now test (and only test) candidates accordingly, for example:

```
?- friend (bear).
yes
?- friend (fox).
no
```

The order of the two premisses is important. *List* must obviously be bound before we may test for membership.

One of the most frequently required list operations is that of appending a list to another one. Note the ('natural' ?) slip into a procedural perspective; alternatively one may just as well view **append** as a definition of the way in which lists may be composed in terms of each other. The following definition of **append** is more 'liberal' than the membership predicates we described above, since it may be used both to find components and to construct the combined list.

```
% a list appended to an empty list yields the same list (stopping case)
append ([ ], List, List).
% two non-empty lists appended to each other have all the elements of the
% first list appended to the second list. This can be recursively defined:
% element by element.
append ([Element | List1], List2, [Element | List3])
        :- append (List1, List2, List3).

?- append ([goose, frog], [mole, bear, tiger], Friends).
Friends = [goose, frog, mole, bear, tiger]
?- append ([goose, frog, mole],
           WhichList,
           [goose, frog, mole, bear, tiger]).
WhichList = [bear, tiger]
```

append will most likely be a predefined predicate in most PROLOG implementations, and we will therefore not be permitted to redefine it. However, choosing a different name for our implementation (for example, *myAppend*) will still allow us to experiment.

sort is a predefined predicate for sorting lists in lexical order.

```
?- sort ([mole, bear, tiger], Result).
Result = [bear, mole, tiger]
```

Two useful predicates (**bagof** and **setof**) are provided for collecting alternative bindings (multiple solutions) into a list structure.

```
lives (mole, hole).
lives (bear, littleHouseByTheRiver).
lives (tiger, littleHouseByTheRiver).
lives (Guest, Place) :- frequentVisitor (Guest, Host),
                        lives (Host, Place).
frequentVisitor (mole, bear).
frequentVisitor (mole, tiger).

?- bagof (Where, lives (mole, Where), Places).
Where = hole
Places = [hole]
Where = littleHouseByTheRiver
Places = [littleHouseByTheRiver,
          littleHouseByTheRiver]
No (more) solutions
```

Here we collect the result of applying the '*somebody practically lives in a place if he's a frequent visitor there*' predicate to *mole* into a list. Since *mole* is a frequent visitor of both *bear* and *tiger*, the list contains two duplicate references to their home. Note that *hole* is contained in a separate list, since it was returned by a different 'knowledge source' (predicate). The **setof** predicate sorts the resulting list and will also get rid of the duplicates.

```
?- setof (Where, lives (mole, Where), Places).
Where = hole
Places = [hole]
Where = littleHouseByTheRiver
Places = [littleHouseByTheRiver]
No (more) solutions
```

findall provides an alternative to **bagof**, where this is not provided. It takes a term, a relationship and a list as arguments. It will then return the list bound to a collection of all valid instantiations of the term in the relationship.

```
?- findall (Where, lives (mole, Where), Solutions).
Solutions = [hole, littleHouseByTheRiver,
             littleHouseByTheRiver]
?- findall (Who, lives (Who, littleHouseByTheRiver), Solutions),
   sort (Solutions, SortedSolutions).
Solutions = [bear, tiger, mole, mole]
SortedSolutions = [bear, mole, mole, tiger]
```

We could now apply **setof** to remove *mole*'s second incarnation.

List processing is a prominent feature in many PROLOG programs. For example, it may be desirable to collect all of a problem's solutions produced by a backtracking program and print them in order of importance, or to manipulate them in some other way. Lists also permit us to let procedures act as filters to other procedures. We will use lists in the following section, where we discuss how PROLOG may be used to solve a simple combinatorial puzzle.

Deductive databases – a dungeon master

Writing patterns of inquiry for simple deductive databases offers an excellent demonstration of the advantages of a declarative programming style. This class of applications focuses on the description of a 'world' in terms of all its relevant entities and relationships. Appropriate instantiations of such entities and relationships are then asserted as *facts* into a PROLOG database. Additionally we may also provide a number of *rules* for deductions which are assumed to be valid within that world, hence the term 'deductive databases'. These deductions allow logical inference to proceed from 'primitive' facts to 'higher-level' concepts.

To demonstrate this style of usage we will look at the task of writing an advisory system for a simple adventure game. Adventure games have been a popular pastime of computer science students for many years, and recently they have also caught on to a wider audience. Symbolic programming languages make it quite simple to write simulators for such games, although the first computerized adventure games were considered experiments in artificial intelligence. Their continuing popularity as paradigmatic programming examples in courses and textbooks is due to the fact that they offer a conveniently constrained context to explore different strategies of symbolic inference, natural language parsing and graphical interaction. Paroli (1983) gives an intriguing account of 'personal' experiences in playing such a game, while Townsend (1987, Chapter 20), and Cuadrado and Cuadrado (1985) discuss simple PROLOG programs for this task.

Although the basic metaphor offers ample scope for individual creativity, such games often involve some '*maze*' of locations (enchanted forests, castles, inns, caves, dungeons, and so on) in which some 'agents' (adventurers, innkeepers, witches, demons, monsters, beautiful princesses, . . .) reside and interact. There are usually also various '*items*' (food, jewellery, weapons, scrolls, . . .) with mundane, magical or mysterious properties. As in real life, a typical '*scenario*' commands some adventurer to maximize his or her goal (collect treasure while alive, reach an exit, solve a theorem, . . .) within the constraints provided by a generally hostile environment. Figure 2.23 shows a very simple example of such a framework.

There are three *caves*, labelled *first*, *second* and *third*, connected as shown. The first cave is the start of the maze and our *adventurer*, called *cugel*, is currently located there. Otherwise this cave proves to be empty. The second cave is inhabited by *herman*, a fierce and vicious *monster* who owns a *goldBar*. The third cave is the most dangerous of all. *sadlark*

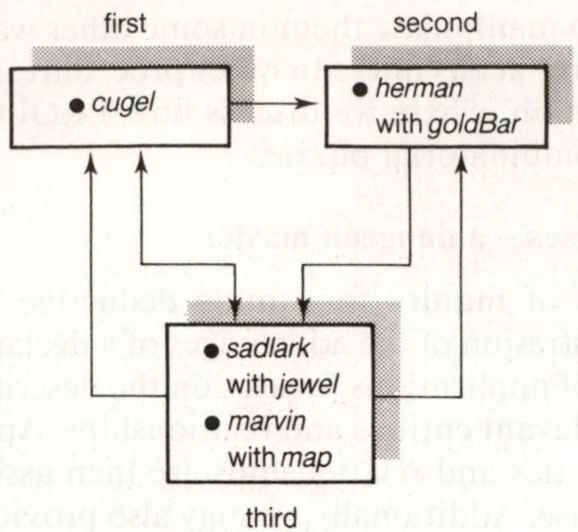

Figure 2.23 A simple adventure game (*maze*, *agents*, *items*).

and *marvin* dwell there. *sadlark*, a particularly nasty creature, owns a precious *jewel*, while *marvin* will jealously fight any attempt to separate him from his *map* of treasure island, a prized and cherished family heirloom. The objective of our game is for *cugel* to navigate this maze, eventually returning to the first cave with as many valuables as he can acquire (we assume infinite greed and carrying capacity). Since the three monsters are obviously reluctant to part with their treasure, this may result in some unpleasant encounters. In addition, a tendency on the part of the monsters to act in an acquisitive fashion, stealing among themselves, is introduced to make the game more interesting. To facilitate some prediction of the likely result of a venture we will also assert that *cugel* is *stronger* than both *herman* and *marvin*, *marvin* is *stronger* than *herman* and *sadlark* is *stronger* than both other monsters. Whether *cugel* or *sadlark* are stronger is currently unknown.

Figure 2.24 summarizes these concepts and relationships. We will only look at five of many possible deductions: *rich*, *riches*, *acquire*, *go*, *grab*. Further caves, characters, properties and patterns of reasoning may be explored by the reader.

In order to implement this framework as a PROLOG database we may now wish to enter the following assertions.

```
/* FACTS: elementary concepts, relationships and their instantiations */
adventurer (cugel).
monster (herman).
monster (sadlark).
monster (marvin).

dungeon (first).
dungeon (second).
dungeon (third).
```

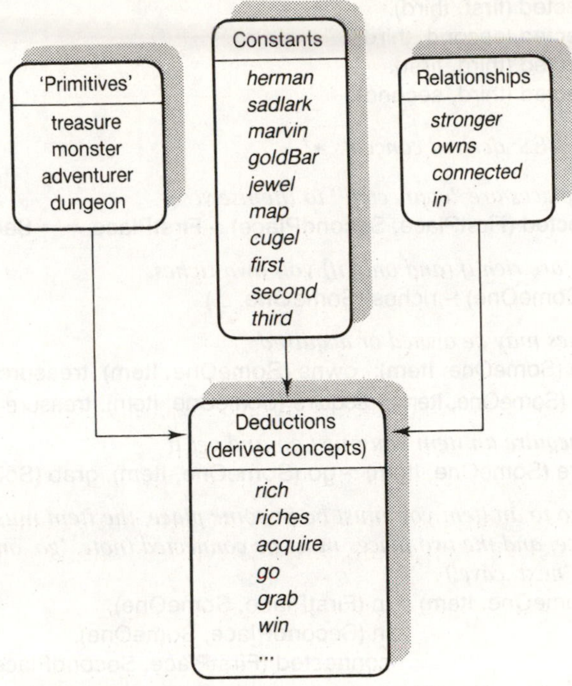

Figure 2.24 Concepts, constants and relationships.

```
treasure (gold).
treasure (jewel).
% we don't class marvin's map as a treasure -
% it's most likely it's a forgery anyway

owns (herman, gold).
owns (sadlark, jewel).
owns (marvin, map).

in (first, cugel).
in (second, herman).
in (third, sadlark).
in (third, marvin).
in (second, gold).
in (third, jewel).
in (third, map).

stronger (cugel, herman).
stronger (cugel, marvin).
stronger (sadlark, herman).
stronger (sadlark, marvin).
stronger (marvin, herman).

connected (first, second).
```

```
connected (first, third).
connected (second, third).
connected (third, first).
connected (third, second).

/* RULES: derived concepts */

% all places are "connected" to themselves
connected (FirstPlace, SecondPlace) :- FirstPlace == SecondPlace.

% you are rich if (and only if) you own riches
rich (SomeOne) :- riches (SomeOne, _).

% riches may be owned or acquired
riches (SomeOne, Item):- owns (SomeOne, Item), treasure (Item).
riches (SomeOne, Item):- acquire (SomeOne, Item), treasure (Item).

% to acquire an item you must go and get it
acquire (SomeOne, Item) :- go (SomeOne, Item), grab (SomeOne, Item).

% to go to an item you must be in some place, the item must be in some
% place, and the two places must be connected (note: 'go' only reaches
% the 'next' cave!)
go (SomeOne, Item) :- in (FirstPlace, SomeOne),
                      in (SecondPlace, SomeOne),
                      connected (FirstPlace, SecondPlace).

% to grab an item from a monster you must take it away,
% which will only succeed if you win the resulting "fight"
grab (SomeOne, Item) :- owns (Owner, Item),
                        monster (Owner),
                        win (SomeOne, Owner).

% to win a fight you must be stronger than your opponent
win (SomeOne, Opponent) :- stronger (SomeOne, Opponent).
```

We can now 'play' by framing some queries.

```
?- monster (Who).
Who = herman   Who = sadlark   Who = marvin

?- rich (sadlark).
yes
?- rich (marvin).
no   % the map doesn't count (not a treasure),
     % but he can acquire the goldBar from herman

?- acquire (marvin, What).
What = goldBar

?- go (cugel, herman).
yes  % first and third cave are directly connected
?- go (herman, cugel).
no   % second and first cave are not directly connected
```

```
?- acquire (sadlark, What).
What = gold   What = map
?- acquire (Who, jewel).
no more solutions    % sadlark has got it and she is too strong
?- acquire (Who, goldBar).
Who = cugel   Who = sadlark   Who = marvin
% herman is just too weak to defend it

?- owns (cugel, What).
no more solutions
?- grab (cugel, goldBar).
yes   % he may take it from herman
?- acquire (cugel, sword).
no    % can't go to sword (not asserted to be 'in' anywhere)
?- acquire (cugel, What).
What = goldBar   What = map
?- rich (cugel).
yes
?- riches (cugel, What).
What = goldBar

?- riches (Who, What).
% any treasure that anybody can own or acquire
% remember that the map is not classed as "treasure" !
Who = cugel      What = goldBar    % they can all rob poor herman
Who = sadlark    What = goldBar
Who = marvin     What = goldBar
Who = herman     What = goldBar    % herman owns it
Who = sadlark    What = jewel
% nobody ever takes anything from sadlark!
```

and we shall leave it at that. The above advisory problem is particularly well suited to PROLOG's declarative style of system description. Most definitions refer to the game's structure and we needed to declare only a few simple deductive patterns. The program is easily understood just by looking at these definitions. So-called **'expert systems'** use a similar programming metaphor; and Chapter 3 will return to this idea in more detail. Here it should just be noted that we have restricted ourselves to a purely declarative style; queries did not result in any actual changes to the state of the game. This meant in particular that the program may only be used as an advisor which explores potentialities; that is, for example, to deduce all the things that *cugel* may possibly acquire (*'?-acquire(cugel, What')*, but not as a tool to actually play a game. On the positive side, all patterns of deduction are perfectly general and may be used with any combination of instantiated and uninstantiated constants and variables.

Playing a game would require that the state of the world be changed. If *cugel* acquires a *goldBar* from *herman*, it must be removed from *herman*'s possession and given to *cugel*. It is of course possible for PROLOG to reflect such changes, namely by execution of '*assert(owns (cugel,goldBar)).*' and '*retract(owns(herman,goldBar)).*', but such use of **assert** and **retract** will force a procedural perspective and prohibit the use of any predicates using such side effects in other than definite queries – for example, '*acquire(cugel,X)*' would get caught in a non-terminating loop.

Combinatorial problem solving – the Lineland puzzle

Our next example shows the use of PROLOG as a tool for solving combinatorial problems. Consider the following typical puzzle:

In the far away one-dimensional world of Lineland there are a small number of excellent universities, whose faculties are devoted to teaching the arts, law and a few of the occult sciences. Every Wednesday, seminars for staff and graduate students are held in each department. At these occasions, as in our three-dimensional world, lecturers have for a long time been discriminated against. In Lineland, however, they are finally making some progress and major concessions have been won. For example, while lecturers have always sat in the front of seminar rooms in the past, the emperor has now ordered that, starting immediately, students must all sit in the front and lecturers may sit in the back.

Assume that this order is taking effect while a seminar at Miskatonic University is currently in progress, with a five-seat seminar room already filled with two students in the last two seats, two lecturers in the next two seats and the front seat remaining empty. For the purpose of our discussion we may safely ignore the speaker, since she must always stand at the front. In order to comply with the new regulation, students and lecturers must now switch places. Let us further assume that people in Lineland can easily move to adjacent spots in their linear world, so a person can move to an empty adjacent seat in the room, and, that a special device will allow them to pass through two-dimensional space for a very limited distance, hopping over any intervening objects in either direction. In the seminar room this hopping ability has a limit of two seats. Thus either a lecturer or a student could hop into the first or second adjacent seat, provided the target was empty. For example, in the above scenario, the first lecturer could move into the front seat, or the second lecturer could hop over his colleague into the front seat. The students, on the other hand, can currently not move at all. Using these patterns of movement, we may now try to solve the problem of reversing positions of the two lecturers and two students, so that all students end up in front of all the lecturers. Note that it is irrelevant where empty seats occur, as long as this condition is met.

[*Problem adapted from Wickelgren (1974).*]

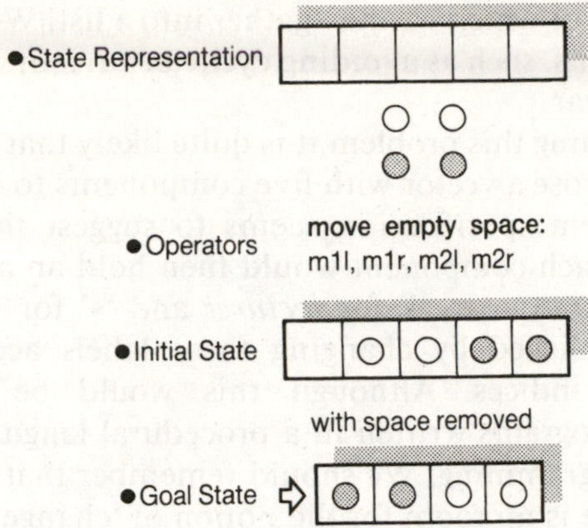

Figure 2.25 Lineland – a combinatorial search problem.

Puzzles like this one are very useful for studying problem-solving strategies in an idealized setting. They allow us to explore ideas without the need to worry about the many complicating details of 'world representation'. Figure 2.25 suggests a state space representation as an appropriate structure for our program. Chapter 3 will discuss this concept in more detail. At this stage it will be sufficient to note that within this framework we need some way to express the states of the 'world' in a prudently chosen representation, the valid transformations applicable to such states and a strategy for finding a solution. The four basic modules of our program therefore become: a description of the *initial state*, a description of legal *operators*, a means of detecting a *goal state* and some *strategy* to deduce a solution.

For the above problem all relevant state information can be encoded in a structure of five elements (the *room*), each of which may be labelled as *empty*, holding a *lecturer* (white token) or *student* (grey token). The *initial state* follows trivially from our description. *Patterns of movement* within the room can be mapped into 'hops' of the empty seat, without any loss of generality (that is, moving a token into an empty space to the left corresponds to a 'hop' of the empty seat one space to the right, . . .). Since any state where all students are placed in front of all the lecturers fulfils our requirements, it would simplify testing for goal satisfaction if the empty seat was first removed.

PROLOG itself will provide a search strategy for our program. Remember that the PROLOG interpreter implements a depth-first, backtracking theorem prover. We can make use of this knowledge to solve the Lineland problem, as long as we are not too concerned about computational efficiency. What remains to be done is to assert the problem's structure and prompt PROLOG to find an appropriate solution, the path of which we may gather into a list. We may still expect a few complications, such as avoiding cyclic behaviour, but our principle strategy seems clear.

In approaching this problem it is quite likely that one may initially be tempted to choose a vector with five components to encode room and seats. The problem specification seems to suggest this as a 'natural' representation. Each component would then hold an appropriate label, such as '**e**' for *empty* seat, '**l**' for *lecturer* and '**s**' for *student. Hopping* could be accomplished by changing these labels according to some calculations on indices. Although this would be an appropriate framework for programs written in a procedural language, it is inapplicable to logic programming. We should remember that logic 'inhabits' a static world; there is no room for the notion of 'change'. This is also the reason for the absence of an assignment statement from PROLOG. This view does not match well with the way we 'normally' tend to think about combinatorial problems. Here we do expect things to change, since a problem and its solution are usually defined in terms of some sequence of state transformations. We could still opt for a procedural approach and use PROLOG's extralogical features destructively to change states in response to a move – that is, via **assert** and **retract**. It is, however, much more instructive and in keeping with the spirit of logic programming if we subscribe to the notion of 'possible worlds' instead. Using this metaphor we will deduce 'possible' states from actual ones, causing entities to be copied when necessary. Tentative new states (possible worlds) will be generated, tested, remembered or discarded, but no information is ever explicitly altered. From a pragmatic point of view (outside the realm of logic programming!), states will eventually become irrelevant to the reasoning process and will be reclaimed by PROLOG's garbage collector. Under most circumstances we will not even wish to define a new entity's creation explicitly, since this will automatically follow from PROLOG's strategy of goal instantiation.

To solve the *Lineland* problem we will therefore instruct PROLOG to construct, test and expand possible sequences of states in some systematic fashion (namely depth-first with backtracking). In a finite search space such as the one under consideration this chain of reasoning will eventually find an acceptable candidate, if one exists. Since vectors are not a particularly appropriate data structure for PROLOG programs, we will still have to make a decision on how to store states. Either structures or lists may be chosen; unfortunately both share the same difficulty concerning indexing by position. In this program we have opted for structures, but the reader may well consider changing this to lists as an exercise.

States are therefore represented as instances of a five-place *state* predicate, with each component referring to one of the room's seats – that is, *state(e,l,l,s,s)* is our initial state. 'Seats' will be accessed through pattern matches and their contents will be modified by selective copying, constructing new instances of this functor in the process.

Following a top-down design strategy, we will first identify:

```
SolveLineland (InitState) :-
   solution (InitState,      % from an initial state
             NewState,       % (via other states) to a goal
             [InitState],    % path initialization
             Solution),      % (via other paths) to a solution
   show (Solution).
```

as a *top-level assertion*, stating that to solve *Lineland* for a given initial state we will have to find a solution and then we must show it. A solution in turn is defined as a deduction of the existence of a goal state. A path of intermediary states will be constructed as a 'side effect' of this proof, and at the beginning it must be initialized to hold only the start-up state. This path will be built as a list of states and their successors. At the conclusion it will hold the order of hops by which our goal may be achieved, without showing the whole sequence of deductions (many of them dead ends) which were necessary to reach this result. Defining the predicate to **show** a *Solution* is easy.

```
show(Path) :- display (solution), nl, showSteps (Path).
showSteps ([ ]).
showSteps ([Head | Tail]) :- display (Head), nl, showSteps (Tail).
```

showSteps will recursively step through the list and print each state on a separate line. What remains to be decided is how the solution itself may be obtained. Towards this end we define the *stopping conditions* first.

```
solution (state (e, s, s, l, l), done, OldPath, OldPath).
solution (state (s, e, s, l, l), done, OldPath, OldPath).
solution (state (s, s, e, l, l), done, OldPath, OldPath).
solution (state (s, s, l, e, l), done, OldPath, OldPath).
solution (state (s, s, l, l, e), done, OldPath, OldPath).
```

will serve this purpose, although admittedly not very elegantly. Note that in the goal state we wish to return the resultant binding for *OldPath* as the solution. *OldPath* must therefore appear in both the two rightmost slots. It would no doubt be better to make use of the above-mentioned 'trick' of removing the empty seat before comparing the room with '*state(s,s,l,l)*'. This strategy would adapt much more easily to different room sizes. In PROLOG this is, however, not an altogether simple operation. We will either have to build a new functor (removing the 'e' in the process), or we may use the =.. operator to turn *state* into a list, from which we may then remove the empty seat. This seems the more obvious strategy and we recommend its implementation as an exercise.

The structure of alternative *paths to solutions* will have to be defined next. A potential solution, or at least some progress towards it, may be derived from a state by applying one of the four alternative moves (hop 1 right, hop 2 right, hop 1 left, hop 2 left). Parameterizing this pattern into a single rule would require more effort than it is worth, since it would involve a decision on 'hop width' incrementation or decrementation as well as the treatment of 0 (no move) as a special case. The four moves are therefore defined by four different rules, and PROLOG will try to apply them in order of their declaration.

```
solution (OldState, NewState, OldPath, NewPath) :-
        hop (+1, OldState, NextState, OldPath, NextPath),
        solution (NextState, NewState, NextPath, NewPath).

solution (OldState, NewState, OldPath, NewPath) :-
        hop (+2, OldState, NextState, OldPath, NextPath),
        solution (NextState, NewState, NextPath, NewPath).

solution (OldState, NewState, OldPath, NewPath) :-
        hop (-1, OldState, NextState, OldPath, NextPath),
        solution (NextState, NewState, NextPath, NewPath).

solution (OldState, NewState, OldPath, NewPath) :-
        hop (-2, OldState, NextState, OldPath, NextPath),
        solution (NextState, NewState, NextPath, NewPath).
```

Each of the *moves* themselves follows a similar pattern. Remember that we have chosen to express moves in terms of the empty seat 'hopping' about. We therefore have to obtain the empty seat's current position and compute a move's destination by adding the relevant *Places* (+1, +2, −1 or −2). This number is then tested to ensure that we stay within the room's bounds. If this is not the case, the predicate will simply fail, causing PROLOG to backtrack and look for an alternative move instead. If the move stays within bounds, *hopSpace* will create a new state (*NewState*). After testing whether we have seen this state on the current path before, so as to avoid being trapped in any cycle of oscillating moves, it is finally appended to the current solution and *NewPath* is instantiated accordingly. Note that the **write** and **nl** predicates serve to trace the search's progress. This information is useful for debugging purposes, but should probably be deleted once correctness of any modified version of the program has been established.

```
hop (Places, OldState, NewState, OldPath, NewPath) :-
        position (e, OldState, From),
        To is From + Places,
```

```
          To > 0, To =< 5,
          hopSpace (From, To, OldState, NewState),
          not cyclic (NewState, OldPath),
          NewPath = [NewState | OldPath],
          write (NewPath), nl.
```

To simplify the program's explanation we use a somewhat inelegant procedure to obtain the empty seat's *position*, by matching against all the possible places where it could occur. Since generalization to a different number of seats (which would also require the '5' in *hop* to be changed!) is again somewhat tedious under this scheme, you may wish to rewrite it. A possible strategy would turn *state* into a list (using =..) and count predecessors to compute the e's position.

```
position (Symbol, state (e, _, _, _, _), 1).
position (Symbol, state (_, e, _, _, _), 2).
position (Symbol, state (_, _, e, _, _), 3).
position (Symbol, state (_, _, _, e, _), 4).
position (Symbol, state (_, _, _, _, e), 5).
```

Since *OldPath* already holds all the previous states for the partial solution currently under investigation, *cycles* are easily detected by (recursively) searching this list.

```
cyclic (State, Path) :- onPath (State, Path).

onPath (State, [State |_ ]).
onPath (State, [_ | Tail]) :- onPath (State, Tail).
```

onPath will either detect the relevant *State* at the head of this list or one of its component lists, or the list will reduce to the empty list and the search will fail. *Reflecting the move* of the empty seat turns out to be somewhat more complicated. The following strategy builds a copy of the *state* functor, replacing the empty seat's origin and destination (*To*) by the appropriate symbols. *hopSpace* drives this replacement process, using *moveSymbol* to fill first the empty seat's destination (*To*) with 'e', and then its origin (*From*) with the symbol replaced at that destination.

```
hopSpace (From, To, OldState, NewState)
          :- % get the 'e' into place
             moveSymbol (e, To, OldState, BufferState, ReplacedSymbol),
             % now put the replaced symbol where the 'e' came from
             moveSymbol (ReplacedSymbol, From, BufferState, NewState,
                         Dummy).
```

moveSymbol is used to build the new functor's shell, while *build* fills in the details.

```
moveSymbol (Symbol, To, Old, New, ReplacedSymbol)
        :- functor (Old, State, Arity), % bind the old State and Arity
           functor (New, State, Arity),% build a new one with these values
           build (Arity, Symbol, To, Old, New, ReplacedSymbol).
```

build starts with the highest numbered (rightmost) slot in the structure. It uses recursion to step through all of the new functor's slots and fills them with either the corresponding old value, or the 'e' *Symbol* (*To*-index), or the symbol replaced by the empty seat's move (*From*-index). Remember that it is necessary to declare the stopping case (*index* becomes 0) first.

```
build (0, Symbol, To, Old, New, ReplacedSymbol).

build (Index, Symbol, To, Old, New, ReplacedSymbol)
    :- Index > 0, not Index =:= To,          % no change
       arg (Index, Old, Value),              % get and
       arg (Index, New, Value),              % copy the old slot's value
       Next is Index - 1,                    % recurse to the next slot
       build (Next, Symbol, To, Old, New, ReplacedSymbol).
build (Index, Symbol, To, Old, New, ReplacedSymbol)
    :- Index > 0, Index =:= To,              % destination of 'e'
       arg (Index, New, Symbol),             % put 'e' in slot
       arg (Index, Old, ReplacedSymbol),     % remember what was there
       Next is Index - 1,                    % recurse to the next slot
       build (Next, Symbol, To, Old, New, ReplacedSymbol).
```

When this program is now executed with the directive:

```
:- solveLineland (state (e, l, l, s, s)).
```

it will produce the following answer (assuming that *hop*'s **write** statement has been deleted).

```
solution
state (s, e, s, l, l)
state (s, l, s, e, l)
state (s, l, e, s, l)
state (e, l, s, s, l)
state (l, e, s, s, l)
state (l, s, s, e, l)
state (l, s, e, s, l)
state (l, s, l, s, e)
state (l, s, l, e, s)
state (l, s, e, l, s)
state (l, e, s, l, s)
state (l, l, s, e, s)
state (l, l, e, s, s)
state (l, e, l, s, s)
state (e, l, l, s, s)
yes
```

You should note that the solution is given 'back to front'; that is, with the goal state first, followed by all the intermediary states required to reach it. This deficiency could easily be remedied by **show**, reversing the list before it is printed. It should also be noted that PROLOG's depth-first search does not find a particularly 'good' solution to this puzzle. Here it required 14 moves to fulfil the court's order. There are in fact shorter sequences, which may be found under a different search strategy. We will give a more thorough discussion of such methods in Chapter 3, and the Scheme-based 'Search' toolbox presented there may be used as a means for further experimentation. Figure 2.26 shows part of the search tree generated by our program. In this graphical representation, nodes correspond to states and edges correspond to moves.

The solutions to exercises in Appendix V also include a Scheme program solving this problem. From this, we deduce that only seven steps are minimally necessary to swap students and lecturers. This solution will therefore eventually be found if we restrict PROLOG's search to a maximum depth of seven. This will require only some minor changes to our program, which we again recommend as an exercise. After these modifications the optimal solution will now be generated by the call:

```
:- solveLineland (state (e, l, l, s, s,), 7).

solution
state (s, s, l, e, l)
state (s, e, l, s, l)
state (e, s, l, s, l)
state (l, s, e, s, l)
state (l, s, l, s, e)
state (l, s, l, e, s)
state (l, e, l, s, s)
state (e, l, l, s, s)
yes
```

This concludes our discussion of PROLOG as a programming tool for combinatorial problems. This class of applications does not seem to map as easily into the logic-based programming metaphor as the field of deductive databases. For a programmer brought up in the procedural tradition it is often difficult to avoid 'slipping' into a procedural interpretation of the problem. It should, however, be appreciated that 'ease of representation' and 'naturalness of expression' are relative concepts, strongly connected with a specific intellectual and social context. Proponents of logic-based languages will claim that PROLOG is perfectly suitable for such types of problems and one must merely be prepared to escape from the straitjacket of traditional programming methodology and be willing to 'relearn' a view of things from a different perspective. In the meantime it is probably fair to say that PROLOG's (and logic's) benefits for describing structure – for example, as a tool for

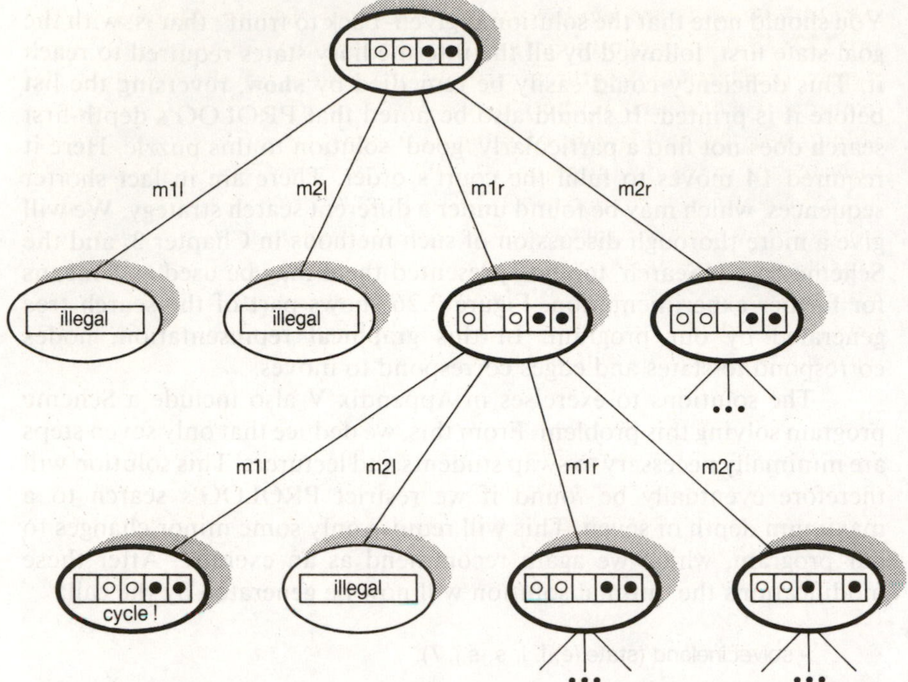

Figure 2.26 Part of the search tree for the Lineland problem.

deductive databases – will be immediately obvious to most of us. This is also the reason for PROLOG's popularity for writing so-called expert systems, a task domain we will return to in Chapter 3. Appreciating the more sophisticated uses of logic programming for the description of process dynamics, however, may require a more substantial intellectual investment.

The infamous '*missionaries and cannibals*', '*wolf, goat and cabbage*' and various other so-called 'river-crossing' problems have a structure very similar to *Lineland.* Coelho (1980) offers a PROLOG program for solving the '*missionaries and cannibals*' puzzle. Dahl (1983), Clark and McCabe (1984, pp. 342–346), Conlon (1985, pp. 158–166), and Stirling and Shapiro (1986, pp. 286–287) describe PROLOG solutions for the related, but simpler, '*wolf, goat and cabbage*' problem. Stirling and Shapiro (1986, pp. 287–290), finally, give a thorough discussion of *water jugs* (problems).

2.4.3 Some comments on style

While it is true that PROLOG is often described as a 'declarative' language, most practical applications will require a mixture of both *declarative* and *procedural* styles. We will follow Malpas (1987, pp. 322–323) in recommending to beginners that they initially write purely declarative programs without using any of the features (for example, **cuts**, **assert**, retract) that cause side effects. The programmer should also be well aware of **not**'s sometimes surprising implications. Subsequent to the development of such basic coding skills, one will then have to learn how to harness side effects for the definition of more complicated control structures. As a general rule we should always strive to separate the declarative part of a program from its procedural aspects. This will improve a program's potential reliability and modularity. The logic of the declarative component can be checked and its correctness ensured, while testing will still be required to establish the validity of any procedural parts. In line with an exploratory style of program development this approach will also permit us to defer commitment of general goals to specific implementation as long as possible. Great care should therefore be taken to avoid blurring the separation between descriptive and prescriptive information any more than is absolutely necessary for a particular application.

Most specifications should proceed in a '*top-down*' fashion, where relevant entities, relationships and patterns of deduction for a particular task domain are defined first. These specifications may then be mapped into appropriate assertions. This process should, of course, require none of PROLOG's extra-logical features.

Logic has a 'flat' structure, making no provision for *modularization*. However, all PROLOG systems offer some means for separating parts of a problem description. In the simplest case, different files may be used to store different groups of assertions. More modern dialects (such as PROLOG II) may offer 'worlds' as separate knowledge bases.

In line with generally accepted guidelines of good coding practice in other programming languages both clauses and procedures should be short, and clustered around a well-defined set of concepts to which they apply. *Naming* should be mnemonic, so that it can convey the extra-logical 'meaning' of objects. *Layout* and adequate *comments* are also important. Indentation and spaces should be used to illuminate the program's overall structure and thereby improve its readability. Details of such stylistic conventions may differ on an individual basis, but it is important that *consistency* be maintained. Bratko (1986) gives a good summary of more detailed recommendations.

As in Scheme, *testing* should proceed incrementally, clause by clause. The concepts of tracing and spypoints may often be used to good effect. Once a program's correctness has been established, its efficiency may be improved by judicious ordering of clauses, so that those assertions which have the highest likelihood of success will occur first. Using **cuts** to prevent backtracking is a more drastic step, which should only be considered once both the problem's and the program's properties and behaviour are thoroughly understood. **Cuts**, and in particular 'red cuts' which invalidate a program's declarative interpretation, should be used sparingly. Use of **cuts** may also imply some commitment on which arguments will be used in input and which will be used in output patterns.

2.4.4 Summary and perspective

Logic programming is currently a topical programming paradigm, with rapidly increasing popularity. Its applications include such diverse tasks as deductive databases, expert systems, combinatorial problem solving, theorem proving, symbolic formula manipulation, natural language understanding, architectural design, chemical analysis and various domains of artificial intelligence. Logic programming has even been applied to robotics, although unsatisfactory run-time performance may still make it unsuitable for most real-time applications.

Logic programming's intellectual roots reach back to the late 1960s and early 1970s. PROLOG was the first and is still the most widely used language subscribing to this idea, although it remains a continuing challenge for active research programs working on different logic programming systems to overcome PROLOG's various weaknesses.

Although most PROLOG implementations are still interpretative, there are now a number of products which offer compiled execution. The main disadvantages of an interpreter lie in its slow speed and high memory requirements. Also, the user must own a copy of the interpreter in order to execute customized applications. On the positive side we gain more control over the system. Programs can be stopped, examined, edited and restarted at any point during their execution. This contrasts well with compiled execution, which has the advantage of being fast, but the program's source will often not be directly available. The classical DEC-10 implementation and Turbo PROLOG are examples of compiled PROLOG systems. Like Scheme, many modern PROLOGs have also opted for the compromise of incremental compilation, sometimes augmented by optimizing 'back-ends'.

Proponents and adversaries of PROLOG and other logic programming languages have claimed many **advantages** and disadvantages for logic programming. It is certainly true that logic is a well-understood formal system, with a long history and well-formed semantics. Practical logic programming languages, like PROLOG, encourage clear separation of the declarative and procedural aspects of a task domain. Logical specifications are independent of context. A program's declarative parts are therefore easy to understand, maintain, prove and re-use. Apart from reducing the cognitive load of the programmer, this property of context independence also permits multiple uses of programs; no prior commitment to input and output is necessary. As a base for writing programs for highly parallel hardware, however, PROLOG's backtracking features need to be somewhat constrained. Languages like PARLOG and Concurrent PROLOG offer some relevant suggestions on how this may be achieved. There are of course also a number of **disadvantages**. PROLOG is 'incomplete' in that it offers only an approximation to logic programming. Most of the time PROLOG will produce a correct program from correct specifications, but there are some cases (such as infinite recursion) where termination cannot be assured outside a specific procedural context. Logic itself subscribes to a static view of a world. This has been called the 'closed world' assumption, a name which reflects the hypothesis that the locally available knowledge is always complete; that is, anything not directly asserted is assumed to be 'false'. The logical view is also characterized by monotonicity and non-fuzzyness, and process specifications are plagued by the 'frame problem'. These restrictions have caused many researchers to reject logic (and therefore 'pure' PROLOG) as a viable tool for building 'intelligent' entities. According to this school of thought 'meaning' is fundamentally interactional and open-ended, and logical proof is therefore inadequate as a reasoning mechanism. This leads to the conclusion that we need some more flexible form of 'due process reasoning' [Hewitt (1985)], which investigates beliefs, goals and hypotheses instead. For problems of practical size and complexity we are often unable to constrain ourselves to 'pure' PROLOG, just as 'pure' LISP may not be a particularly practical programming language. Efficiency of execution must eventually be a concern, the resolution of which requires an understanding of processes. Another disturbing feature of PROLOG is its lack of support for 'chunking' knowledge into contexts. As in logic, PROLOG's database of assertions is globally accessible and has a 'flat' name space, a fact which causes considerable problems for larger programs and programming teams in particular. Many modern PROLOG implementations attempt to resolve this difficulty by offering some kind of extra-logical module facility (for example, the 'worlds' of PROLOG II). Finally, the lack of a generally accepted standard has often been cited as a serious shortcoming. There are now attempts (for example, the 'BSI' draft standard) to achieve some 'official' standardization, although the Edinburgh Syntax and the set of predefined predicates supported by this dialect have for a number of years continued to provide a reliable core for a *de facto* standard.

In the authors' opinion PROLOG will not replace LISP as the main AI programming language, although it will enjoy further growth in popularity. In response to the efficiency problem we will most likely see the emergence of dialects which combine some of the advantages of procedural programming with logic programming. While features like coroutines and 'intelligent' backtracking can still be accommodated within the metaphor of logic programming itself (as demonstrated by IC-PROLOG, PROLOG II, MU-PROLOG), there are also many proposals on how PROLOG may be augmented with more imperative control structures to define loops, indexing into arrays and other such facilities [Munakata (1986), Vasak (1986)]. Many of PROLOG's practical applications have already become more procedural in outlook.

On the other side of the fence, subsystems for logic programming have also been grafted on to procedural languages. It is not too difficult to implement PROLOG in Scheme [for instance, *see* Abelson *et al.* (1985)] or LISP and a number of such systems have been reported in the literature (for example, LOGLISP). POPLOG [Hardy (1984)] offers an interesting integration of PROLOG and an ALGOL-like symbol processing language (Pop). Many so-called expert system development tools (KEE, KnowledgeCraft, Babylon, . . .) also provide logic subsystems in a LISP-based environment. Smalltalk V offers logic programming as one of its library classes.

Exploitation of parallel hardware may ultimately present a viable alternative for elevating PROLOG's status to that of a practical tool for large-scale software development. Concurrent PROLOG [Shapiro (1986)] and PARLOG [Ringwood (1988)] as well as the Japanese fifth-generation project continue to offer some hope in this area.

In view of the subject's maturity it should not be surprising that there is a substantial body of literature on logic and its application in mathematics and philosophy. Logic programming, however, is still very young, and there are only a few relevant textbooks. Robinson (1979) gives a thorough and detailed discussion of logic programming's bases in resolution theorem proving. Kowalski (1979) is another excellent introductory text on this topic, while Hogger (1984) and Lloyd (1984) offer more recent surveys.

Even two or three years ago there were only a few books for learning and teaching about PROLOG. The 'classical' textbook by Clocksin and Mellish (1981) was in fact the only easily available introduction for quite some time. This book may take much of the credit for causing the 'Edinburgh Syntax' to be so widely accepted. Over the last two years, however, many new texts have been published and there is now no scarcity of introductions to PROLOG programming. Burnham and Hall (1985), and particularly the excellent text by Rogers (1986), offer 'gentle' introductions to beginners, while Conlon (1985) is aimed at the level of high-school students. Other books focus on particular implementations. Clark and McCabe (1984) cater for Micro-PROLOG, Giannesini *et al.* (1986) introduce PROLOG II, and Townsend (1987) discusses Turbo PROLOG in detail. There are of course also a number of texts which address themselves to the more experienced programmers. Among these, Sterling and Shapiro (1986) can be particularly recommended. Malpas (1987) gives an excellent discussion of PROLOG's relation to logic, and Bratko (1986) places special emphasis on AI applications. After the initial learning phase has ended, it is often particularly instructive to attempt more difficult programming problems and to analyze other people's solutions. Walker *et al.* (1987) employ IBM-PROLOG and provide a comprehensive perspective on the state of the art in natural language processing, while Coelho (1980) offers a large, but unfortunately only inadequately documented collection of interesting and sometimes challenging programming problems with PROLOG solutions.

Logic programming's declarative framework treats computation as 'logical' deduction, a perspective which is complementary to that of classical procedural languages. In fact, Planner, an early AI language, proposed just the opposite notion of viewing logical implication (deduction) as a procedure. From this idea, Planner and its descendants Conniver, MLISP, and others derived a framework for automatic deduction. This framework turned out to be surprisingly similar to the one offered by PROLOG, since it was also based on depth-first search with backtracking. The inherent inefficiency of this technique, coupled with a general disillusionment with search-oriented problem-solving paradigms at that time, led to its downfall. PROLOG's current popularity has largely profited from recent advances in hardware.

Each of the two perspectives, procedural as well as declarative programming, yields certain advantages. Procedural programming offers a high degree of flexibility, particularly for the description of processes with temporal extension. 'Change' as a concept is easy to represent. The price we must pay is in terms of intellectual complexity, since we are often forced to consider a process's history in order to understand its behaviour. Procedures are context dependent and may yield different results from different sequences of execution. The declarative viewpoint, on the other hand, offers consistency, completeness and context independence of descriptions. It is particularly effective for the definition of structures, under the notion of 'composition'. Here the price will be paid in terms of immutability of entities and assertions. Change must be described by copying and reassertion of every relevant fact, even those which have not been changed by a transformation (the 'frame problem'). In response to this viewpoint's various shortcomings a number of special logics have been designed – for example, temporal logics, fuzzy logics, modal logics, and so on – but so far each of these has produced problems of its own. It seems that we need both representations, under a dual approach, each for a different purpose. If we aim at reducing the intellectual complexity of the programming task, then we should use declarative frames for the description of structures and procedural schemes for the prescription of processes. PROLOG supports this by offering 'extra-logical' features, and many further extensions have been proposed. Conversely, in order to provide some of the advantages of declarative styles of system description, procedural languages like Scheme should be extended by frameworks for classification. Object orientation is a particularly appropriate metaphor in this context and the next section will therefore discuss it in more detail.

EXERCISES

The following list of projects offers you a chance to develop and practise your PROLOG programming skills. Many of the exercises given for Scheme, the flavours system and Smalltalk will also be suitable for this purpose. For slightly more challenging tasks you may wish to turn to the puzzles, games, pattern matches, production systems, and so on in Chapter 3.

2.11 *Bear likes tiger, fox likes snake, snake likes mole, mole hates snake, tiger likes bear, mole likes everyone who likes her (but not fox), nobody likes fox.*

Write a PROLOG program to determine who likes somebody and is liked in return. You may then wish to extend this description to define predicates for cases of mutual affection (creatures who like each other), divided affections (a creature who likes two or more other ones) and rivalries (two or more creatures like the same). Lists offer an appropriate structure to store such information.

2.12* The following problem is taken from Smullyan, who has assembled a delightful collection of further such 'brain teasers'.

'SomeOne has stolen the jam! When confronted with this nefarious deed the March Hare said he didn't do it (naturally!). The Mad Hatter proclaimed one of them (the March Hare, the Hatter, the Dormouse) stole the jam, but he of course didn't. Asked whether the Mad Hatter and the March Hare spoke the truth, the Dormouse said that at least one of them must have done it (including herself). Employing the (very expensive) services of Dr. Himmelheber, the famous psychiatrist, we were eventually able to discover that not both of the Dormouse and the March Hare spoke the truth. Assuming, as we do, that fairy tale characters are always either straight liars or straight truthtellers it remains to discover who "really" did it.'

[*Smullyan (1984).*]

Write a PROLOG program to solve this logical puzzle. It should be as brief and well structured as you can manage and built around declarations for relevant concepts and relationships. Do not include any information which is clearly irrelevant. It is most likely that one of the three characters is the culprit, but there is always the possibility of blaming it on an outsider. This 'cop out' should only be taken if there is in fact insufficient information to solve the problem in any other way. To encode the statements you will have to use PROLOG's **not** predicate. But be aware of its sometimes peculiar implications. Casimir (1987) offers a solution.

2.13 Write a PROLOG specification for the following restrictions on dungeon design in a simple adventure game and use it to instantiate all possible variants of a maze:

- All dungeons have two rectangular caves.
- A wall can hold at most one door or a monster.
- Caves must be connected by interior doors.
- Each room must hold exactly one monster and one interior door.
- There is exactly one entrance to each dungeon, which is always in an east wall.
- Monsters abhor south walls.

You may also wish your program to draw these mazes.

2.14 Write a PROLOG program for colouring any planar map with at most four colours, so that no two adjacent regions will be painted in the same colour. *Hint*: Assume a map of six regions and map it on to pairs of adjacency relationships; for instance, (draw a proper map first) r1 and r2, r1 and r3, r1 and r5, . . , r5 and r6. The program may consist of a complete list of pairs of different colours (select any four). These represent the admissible pairs of colours for regions next to each other. The deduction made by the program will draw a conclusion about all the pairs of regions that are next to each other. The premisses may pair region 1 with a higher numbered one next to it, . . . and so on, then on to region 2, . . . and so forth. Coelho (1980) gives a solution.

2.15 Studies of family relationships often figure prominently as examples in introductory PROLOG textbooks. Assert the family relationships, shown in Figure 2.27, among a clan of well-known poultry celebrities and write (recursive) predicates to define the concepts of *father, mother, brothers* and *grandfather*. We recom-

Facts:

Male:	dicky Duck, dacky Duck, ducky Duck, donald Duck, gustaf Goose, uncle Scrooge, swindolar Swan dufflecoat Duck, primus van Quack
Female:	daisy Duck, granny Duck, sally Swan, yezebelle Duck

Relationships: **(descendent)**

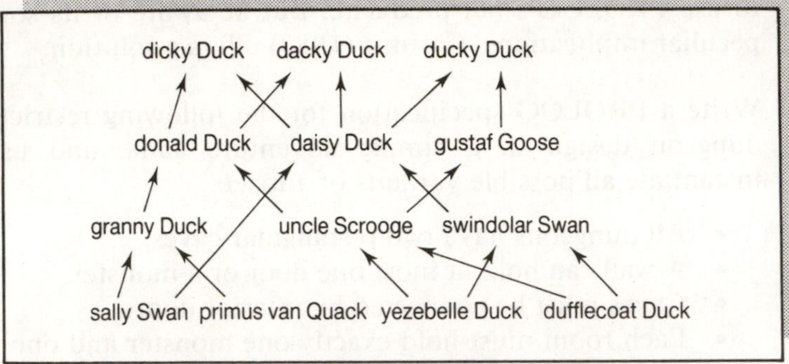

Figure 2.27 Family relations among 'Birds'.

mend Gans (1972) as an excellent reference for further studies into this clan's origins, traditions and habitats.

2.16 The 'Eight Queens' problem has haunted computer science textbooks for many years. Solutions to this puzzle require 'one' to place eight chess queens in such a way that they will not attack each other. In PROLOG we may, for example, represent chess boards by a collection of two-place predicates, defining relationships of x and y coordinates for each square. A queen's threats may then be encoded in rules and the puzzle's solution will be generated by searching and backtracking in a way similar to that given in our *Lineland* example. During development of this program you may wish to restrict yourself to a smaller board. Coelho (1980) and Bratko (1986, p. 108) give a solution.

2.17 The following interesting exercise was adapted from Walker *et al.* (1980, p. 104). Many of us will remember a popular children's puzzle where arbitrary permutations of upper and lower parts of some poor creatures' bodies were created by flipping the pages of a book or rotating the bricks of a rod. In order to refrain from ruthless genetic tampering we will simulate this process of creating hybrid creatures. Our PROLOG program will accept the names of any pairs of creatures with an overlap of two or more letters between the end of the first and the beginning of the second name.

It will then print the name of the relevant hybrid in the following form:

> *cross a kangaroo with a rooster to get a kangarooster.*
> *cross a hippopotamus with a mussel to get a hippopotamussel.*

For a real challenge to 'intelligent' programs you may wish to draw the resulting creature. Your lecturer will probably be prepared to give you extra marks for any successful attempt.

2.18 Augment the adventure game program with additional cast, treasure and places. You may then consider rules for deducing *cugel*'s life expectancy, possible dungeon traversals, and so on. A graphical representation of this scenario would also be interesting, if your PROLOG implementation permits this.

2.19 Modify the *Lineland* program to handle rooms of arbitrary size. This will require a generalization of our method of goal detection and the way in which we obtain the position of the empty seat. Some hints on how to achieve this have already been given in the program's description. If you are more ambitious you may wish to consider how the program may be extended to accept moves in terms of additional 'characters' (such as a professor who will always sit behind all of the lecturers).

2.20 The following combinatorial puzzle has been discussed by Wickelgren. It is representative for a whole class of so-called 'water jug' problems, which require sequences of exchanges between two or more objects in order to reach some objective. The structure of a program for their solution may thus show some similarity to the strategy used in the *Lineland* problem.

'Wanda the witch agrees to trade one of her magic broom-sticks to Gaspar the ghost in exchange for one of his gold chains. Gaspar is somewhat sceptical that the broomstick is in working order and insists on a guarantee equal to the number of links in the chain. Specifically, he insists on paying in daily instalments, one link per day until the end of the 63-day warranty period, with the balance to be forfeit if the broomstick malfunctions during this period. Wanda agrees to this arrangement, but insists that the instalments are to be made by cutting no more than three links in the chain. Can this be done, and if so, what links should be cut? The chain initially consists of 63 closed gold links arranged in a simple linear order (not closed into a circle).'

[*Wickelgren (1974).*]

Hint: Assume that it is indeed possible to solve this problem by making only three cuts. It is obviously impossible to make only three cuts and separate the chain into individual pieces. Any solution will therefore clearly require Gaspar and Wanda to exchange chains on various days during the warranty period. Having three individual links would permit payment of one link per day. As the first subproblem we may therefore wish to determine the longest link of chain that can be used in order to permit payment of an additional link on the fourth day. The solution is obviously a segment of length four, since Wanda could then return the three individual links in exchange. The exchange of links that are known to be part of a solution becomes a subgoal until all of these have been paid to Wanda and a longer chain is required. Formulate a PROLOG program for this strategy to continue.

2.21 PROLOG has also been successfully used as a language to write game playing programs. Section 3.2 contains a more detailed discussion of this area, and Sterling and Shapiro (1986, Chapter 20) offer interesting programs for *Nim*, *Kalah* and *Mastermind*. Berlekamp *et al.* (1982) offer a wealth of other suitable candidates, some of which are included as exercises to Section 3.2.

The game of 'Hare and Hounds', sometimes also referred to as 'French Military Hunt', features a hunter whose three dogs try to trap a poor rabbit on the board shown in Figure 2.28. The name is attributed to its popularity among French military officers in the nineteenth century, who, like computer scientists, possibly did not have anything better to do. The rules of this game are simple. At each turn the hunter moves a dog to a neighbouring space, provided it is empty, and the rabbit responds with a similar move. However, the dogs, starting from the top, are never allowed to

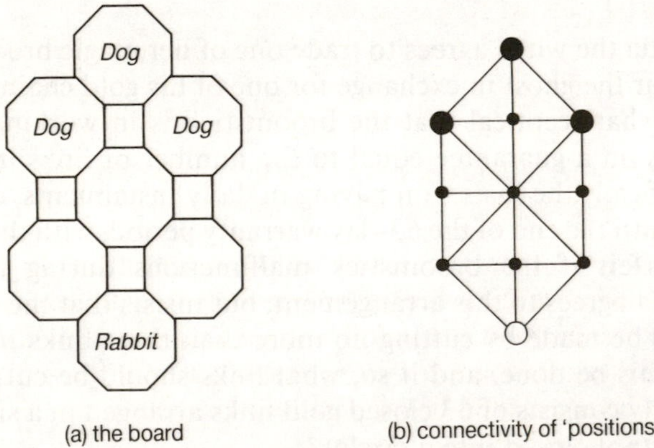

Figure 2.28 The game of 'Hare and Hounds' on a small board.

retreat, although they may move forwards and go back and forth horizontally. The rabbit is completely unconstrained in his patterns of movement. The goal of the game is achieved whenever the rabbit is trapped, so that there is no valid action remaining when it is his turn to move. Hopping over the dogs is not a valid manoeuvre. The rabbit wins if he gets past the dogs, or if they fail to advance downwards for ten consecutive moves.

If you can't persuade the right animals to make these manoeuvres, you may wish to use more conventional tokens. Although this game is mathematically 'solved' and there is an optimal strategy [*see* Berlekamp *et al.* (1982), pp. 647–65], you may wish to consider writing a PROLOG program to play it. The game becomes more interesting on a larger board (for example, use 13 hexagons (and 10 squares) instead of the seven (and four squares) shown in Figure 2.28).

2.5 Object-oriented programming with flavours

'Newcomers to object-oriented languages often have difficulty phrasing their programming problems in terms of objects. They struggle with how to divide a new programming problem into objects. A good starting place is to imagine that every fragment of program and every piece of data are floating together in space. Now imagine pieces of string between code and the data it uses, and between segments of code that are used together or that perform a similar function. Then imagine moving everything around until the total length of string is the shortest. Clustered around each data structure would be the routines that use it, and natural divisions in the code become apparent. Dividing a problem into objects is just a process of putting things where they belong.'

[*Kaehler and Patterson (1986).*]

2.5.1 Object encapsulation, classification and communication – historical evolution and key concepts

Over the last few years the term 'object orientation' has become a fashionable 'buzz word', which has been applied to a wide range of concepts. For the purpose of the following discussion we will restrict it to a particular style of program development and the programming languages which have evolved to support this metaphor.

A large class of applications parallel some physical or conceptual process, and objects are a 'natural' metaphor for model building

[Kreutzer (1986)]. Object orientation has therefore proved to be an elegant and powerful way to organize our knowledge about many important task domains. An early appreciation of the concept of 'objects' within the computing community can be traced back to the SIMULA language [Dahl and Nygaard (1966), Birtwistle *et al.* (1973)], where we find the notion of 'classes' which encapsulates both the state and behaviour of entities. Smalltalk [Goldberg and Robson (1983)] was the first and is still the most prototypical object-oriented language, but now there are probably more than 50 different object-oriented programming tools. Many of these, however, will enjoy only a very limited distribution.

There has lately been some controversy regarding the question of exactly which properties an 'object-oriented' program should have. We are inclined to follow Wegner (1987), who claims that:

Object orientation = *Objects* + *Classes* + *Inheritance*

In this formula the idea of '**objects**' is coextensive with what has elsewhere been referred to as 'data abstraction', 'information hiding' or 'data encapsulation'. It means that descriptions of the state and behaviour of a conceptual entity are clustered into a single textual module. Figure 2.29 exemplifies this idea. 'Chip' is the name of a dog, owned by one of the authors. As a data structure employed by a domestic simulation program, he could, for example, be represented by a number of attributes asserting his *state* (for example, *age*, *race*, *size*, *looks*, *temper*) and *behaviour* (for example, *show*, *bark*, *cutHair*, *growOlder*). The crucial thing to note is, however, that such an entity can be completely 'encapsulated'. Locally defined functions will then become the only means of altering its state, an activity which may be viewed as a form of 'message passing'. Only by reference to *show* may state information be obtained, and only *cutHair* and *growOlder* may change the bindings of *looks* and *age*. From outside the object none of the other attributes' values may be changed at all. Almost all modern object languages support the idea of data encapsulation. One of the most important characteristics of this type of program organization is the fact that it allows objects to 'defend' themselves against invalid or unwelcome requests, since it is up to the receiver of messages to decide whether and how to respond. This encourages construction of highly modular and reliable programs, in which complexity ceases to escalate exponentially with the number of components. Hewitt from MIT has coined the term 'actors' for this idea, since programming can now be likened to directing performances of such objects on a 'stage'. Some 'older' programming languages support only this and none of the other two aspects of object orientation. Wegner therefore refers to them as 'object based'. Ada, Modula, CLU and Hewitt's 'actor' languages fall into this category.

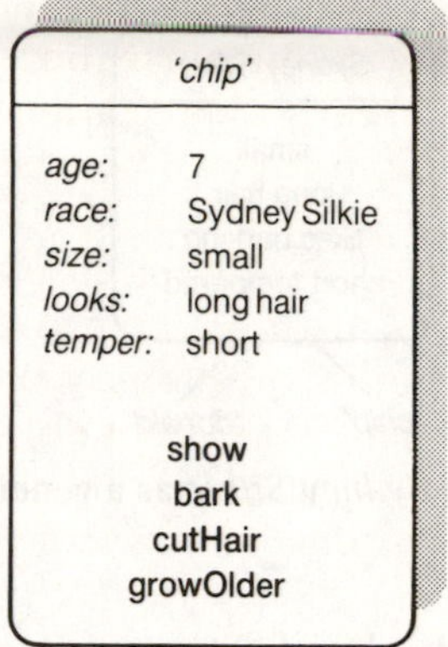

Figure 2.29 A *Chip* object.

The notion of *classification* carries this idea one step further. Entities may now be grouped into categories which share similar structure and behaviour. A '*class*' describes such commonalities in the form of a template from which *new* objects can be produced. In this way classes will act as *generators* of dynamically created objects, describing interfaces and implementations for *instances* of a particular class. This is SIMULA's original idea, and dynamic binding is essential for its realization. CLU, various versions of flavours, Smalltalk, Objective C, C++ and others implement this concept, while Ada and Modula insist on compile-time binding of package or module instances.

To continue our previous example, we could factor aspects relevant to all entities of race *Sydney Silkie* into a class (Figure 2.30). At execution time a program could then use this definition as a template to generate instances of such dogs on demand; thus *chip* ← *SydneySilkie new.* and *donald* ← *SydneySilkie new.* would create two such creatures with appropriate attributes and behaviour.

Classification is often associated with the idea of **inheritance**. This concept revolves around the notion of sharing properties and behaviour among trees or networks of 'superclasses'. Inheritance is a common concept in everyday experience. For example, when we learn that 'this dog is a Sydney Silkie terrier' it is very likely that we will immediately make a number of background assumptions – for example, that the creature is small, has long hair, barks a lot and is often short-tempered. Our assumptions will furthermore extend to characteristics shared by all 'dogs' as a class of creatures (they have four legs, are usually loyal towards their owners, like bones, and so on) and indeed to properties of creatures as a group (for example, have a parent, a limited life span, a soul, and so on) and physical objects in general (for example, have an age, a weight, a

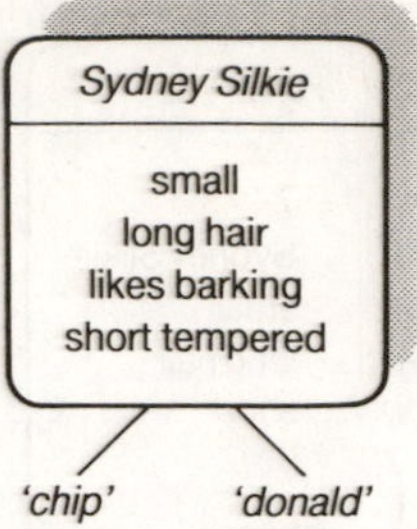

Figure 2.30 Class *Sydney Silkie* as a generator for 'objects'.

colour, and so on). Such classifications serve to activate contexts of 'expectations' and enable us to respond quickly to novel situations. We are rarely forced to reason from 'first principles', and it seems only rational to provide tools to organize programs according to the same kind of strategy. Figure 2.31 shows this generalization hierarchy as a tree structure, where each node adds additional detail to the description in its superclass. If we now instantiate *chip* as a *Sydney Silkie*, he will automatically inherit all of that race's attributes plus those of all *dogs* plus those of all *creatures* plus those of all *physical objects*. Here the term 'attributes' is used to refer to both properties and patterns of behaviour. In fact, outside an object it need not even be known whether the response to a method is generated by returning assertions (stored values) or executing procedures (computed values). This is a detail of implementation which should properly be 'hidden' within the relevant class definition. At creation time some of *chip*'s attributes will initially be unbound, and the term *instance variables* is usually applied to those. *age* and *owner*, whose values are particular to each individual and may often change over time, are two typical examples. The values of other attributes may be fixed for all members of a class, and they are therefore referred to as *class variables. LifeSpan*, a property inherited by dogs through creaturehood, exemplifies this idea. One must, however, be careful of 'pathological' cases. Although one might be tempted to bind '4' to the value of *legs* as a class variable for dogs, there may be unfortunate counter-examples.

Based on these concepts of object, class and inheritance, the process of design and implementation of object-oriented programs is summarized in Figure 2.32. It will be illustrated by examples in the rest of this section, and it will also be reiterated in our discussion of Smalltalk in Chapter 4.

Not all object languages subscribe to inheritance. Ada, Modula and CLU, along with actor languages, do not support this idea. It is therefore proper that they should not be classed as 'object oriented'. There are, however, quite a large number of programming systems which feature

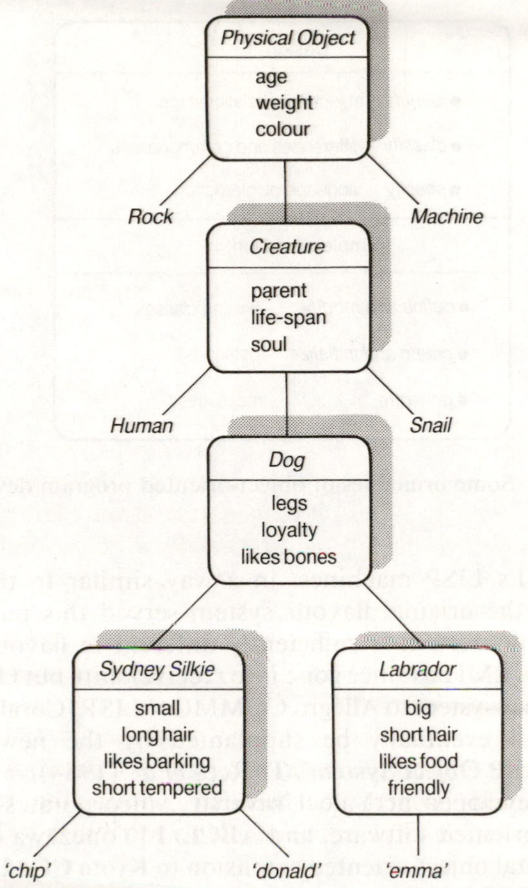

Figure 2.31 An inheritance tree.

objects + classes + inheritance. Figure 2.33 summarizes the most popular representatives. **Smalltalk** [Goldberg and Robson (1983)] is the oldest of these and Chapter 4 will discuss it in detail.

Many systems have evolved in the LISP tradition, with influences from both Smalltalk and so-called 'knowledge representation languages' (such as **FRL, KRL, Pearl**). **UNITS** [Stefik (1979)], **GLISP** [Novak (1983)], **OBJTALK** [Rathke (1984)] and **XLISP** [Betz (1985)] are early attempts to graft object-oriented features on to a LISP base. The original **flavours** system [Weinreb and Moon (1980)] is a by-product of MIT's LISP machine project. It proved highly successful for writing system software and graphical interfaces in particular and has since spawned a great number of direct and indirect descendants. **SCOOPS** [Texas Instruments (1985), McGregor (1987)] is a recent Scheme-based variation of this idea. **Object LISP** [Drescher (1985)] was designed as the main

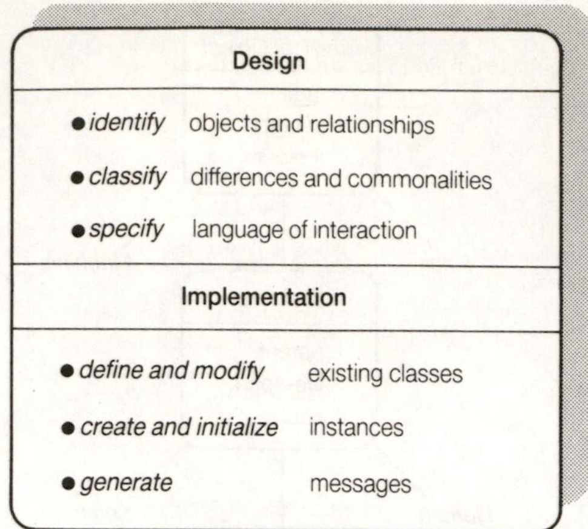

Figure 2.32 Some principles of object-oriented program development.

dialect for LMI's LISP machines, in a way similar to that in which **ZetaLISP** and the original flavour system served this purpose for its Symbolics competitors. It is sufficiently different in flavour to deserve special mention. LMI has since gone into receivership, but Object LISP is still 'alive' as a subsystem to Allegro COMMON LISP [Coral Inc. (1987)], although it will eventually be supplanted by the newly emerging '**COMMON LISP Object System**'. **T** [Rees *et al.* (1984)], a Scheme-like LISP dialect developed at Yale University, incorporates features for writing object-oriented software, and **ABCL/1** [Yonezawa *et al.* (1986)] is an experimental object-oriented extension to **Kyoto COMMON LISP**. **COMMON LOOPS** [Bobrow *et al.* (1985)], **KEE** [Intellicorp (1984)], **Knowledge Craft** [Pepper and Kohn (1986)] and **Babylon** [GMD (1987)] are just some of the better-known so-called 'expert system development tools', which cater for a variety of different programming styles, with particular emphasis on object orientation. Finally, within the context of COMMON LISP there are ongoing efforts to provide an object-oriented subsystem as part of the standard [DeMichiel and Gabriel (1987)].

C is another well-known language whose suitability as a base for object-oriented programming tools has repeatedly been explored. **Objective C** [Cox (1986)], the first of these attempts, was modelled after Smalltalk. **C+** and **C++** [Stroustrup (1985)] pursue an alternative philosophy rooted more in the SIMULA tradition. C+ extends C with provision for classes, while C++ adds inheritance. Since truly dynamic binding is not supported, these two languages fall short of 'genuine' object orientation.

Neon [Schmucker (1986)] and **Actor** [Duff (1986)] are object-oriented extensions of Forth, while **Lore** [Marcoussis Lab. (1986)] and

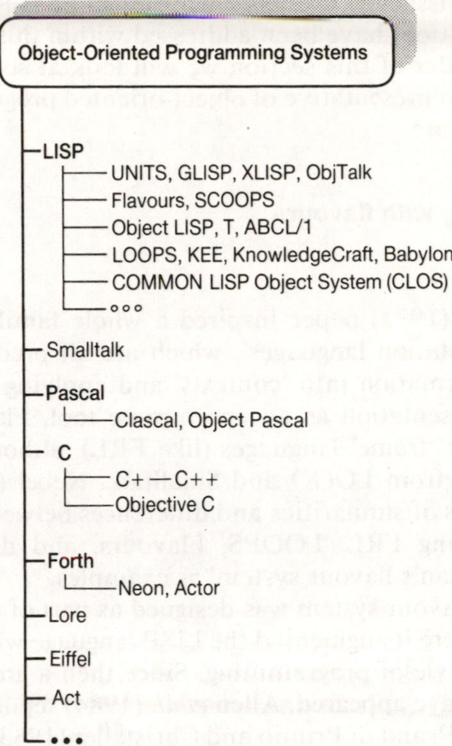

Figure 2.33 Some object-oriented programming systems.

Eiffel [Meyer (1987)] are two self-contained developments which also offer an integrated programming environment.

Clascal and **Object Pascal** [Doyle (1986)] are Pascal extensions of particular relevance to the Macintosh community. Clascal was used by Apple computers to write most of the system software for the *Lisa* toolkit. Its descendant, Object Pascal, was later designed in consultation with Wirth and formed the base of Apple's MacApp application development system for the Macintosh [Schmucker (l986a and b)]. The evolution of these two languages is a reflection of a firm belief, held by most of the original members of the *Lisa* and *Macintosh* projects, that object orientation can play an essential role in constraining the complexities inherent in the development of highly interactive and graphical user interfaces. This conviction has grown out of prior experience with the Smalltalk user interface.

Finally, the **Act** family of languages was developed at MIT and has largely been used for research on large-scale concurrency in software and hardware [Hewitt (1977), Theriault (1983), Agha (1986)]. These languages stress the use of delegation for structuring the sharing of code between actors, and issues of process synchronization (such as deadlock detection and resolution) have been addressed within this framework.

In the remainder of this section we will look at so-called flavour systems as a typical representative of object-oriented programming tools within the LISP culture.

2.5.2 Programming with flavours

History

Minsky's landmark (1975) paper inspired a whole family of so-called 'knowledge representation languages', which are all predicated on the idea of placing information into 'contexts' and applying some kind of object-centred representation as an appropriate tool. Flavour systems evolved from earlier 'frame' languages (like FRL), although there was also some influence from LOGO and Smalltalk. Nebel (1985) gives a comparative analysis of similarities and differences between frames and flavour systems, using FRL, LOOPS, Flavours, and di Primio and Christaller's 'poor man's flavour system' as examples.

The original flavour system was designed as part of the MIT LISP machine project, where it augmented the LISP language with a frame for an object-oriented style of programming. Since then a great number of derivative systems have appeared. Allen *et al.* (1984) report on a flavour system for FranzLISP, and di Primio and Christaller (1983) have written a nice tutorial on how to build your own flavour system in LISP.

In line with the basic requirements for all object-oriented software, flavour systems share the notions of objects, classification and inheritance. The terminology used for these concepts differs from languages in the SIMULA/Smalltalk tradition. Objects are partitioned into generic and individual flavours, corresponding to the notions of classes and instances. Often there is no distinction between these two categories, other than through the way in which they are used. *Individual flavours* appear at the fringe of an inheritance network and represent real-world entities. *Generic flavours*, on the other hand, may be employed to capture some common structure or functionality within a group of individuals. Sometimes 'meta-objects' (such as the flavour 'Flavour'), describing sets of generic objects, are also involved.

Flavour systems often support the idea of '*multiple inheritance*', where flavours may be attached to more than one superclass. This stresses the fact that an object may play different 'roles', in each of which different properties and functionalities may become relevant. To elaborate on our previous example, depending on a specific context, a *dog* may be viewed as a pet, as a means of transportation (for example, by an Eskimo) or as a story character. Multiple inheritance provides a useful way of separating the descriptions of aspects relevant to different perspectives, if more than one of these views is requested within the same program. Unfortunately it can also lead to problems in interpretation of cycles and to other conflicts which may occur in such tangled hierarchies. In contrast to strictly hierarchical inheritance, multiple perspectives often do not provide orthogonal but overlapping views, and the semantics of some of their aspects is not well defined. What should happen, for example, if a characteristic with the same 'name' is inherited from more than one source? Questions like these are still unresolved and remain a challenge to formal investigation [Touretzky (1984)]. In practice there is usually a top-level object, often referred to as the 'Vanilla' flavour, and languages differ in the degree of control over 'mix-ins'. Cycles and consistency problems are all too frequently resolved in idiosyncratic and *ad hoc* fashion.

The roots of the name 'flavour system' should be obvious from the foregoing discussion. In line with a lack of distinction between classes and instances, the notions of *class variables* and *class methods* are often also unsupported.

The Canterbury Flavour System (C-Flavours)

In Section 2.3 we have already discussed how Scheme may be used in an object-oriented style. The technique we proposed there made use of Scheme's static scoping, as well as of its procedures' persistent state and first class nature. It relies on a view of objects as functions. From this perspective the role of instance variables may be played by parameters or local definitions, and message passing becomes a procedure call. The expression '*(chip'say "woof")*' may be interpreted as either 'send message *'say* to object *chip*', with argument *"woof"* or as 'call the *chip* procedure with arguments *'say and "woof"*'. Both readings are equivalent and it is a matter of choice or convenience which we prefer. This strategy gives us an elegant implementation for objects, which may be extended to offer the notion of class as well. For this we can make use of the fact that Scheme procedures will always return the last value of the last expression they encounter. Since this may be a procedure or lambda expression, we can easily write procedures which return other procedures. This leads to the concept of functions as *generators* of objects; that is, in response to a call they will return instances of procedures whose environments may be initialized as requested. (*MakeDog 'labrador*) may be a call on such a generator (a 'class'), returning an anonymous function (an 'instance'), with *breed* bound to *labrador*. We can now use *MakeDog* to create any number of individual 'dogs', for example:

```
(define emma (MakeDog 'labrador))
(define chip (MakeDog 'sydneySilkie))
```

Although this idea gives us *data encapsulation* and *classification*, it is not yet sufficient justification for labelling Scheme as 'object oriented' according to our definition. Although there is no direct way in which *inheritance* can be provided, it is not very difficult to define a special processor to handle such dependencies among objects. A further useful property of typical flavour systems is the ability to add and modify things 'on the fly'; that is, without any need to recompile objects. Debugging large objects in 'pure' Scheme can be a tedious and time-consuming exercise, since even for small changes the whole object's definition will have to be re-evaluated. Logically there is no reason why superclasses and methods may not be added, changed or deleted dynamically, although any changes to instance variables will still require recompilation.

The **Canterbury Flavour System** (C-Flavours [Kreutzer and Stairmand (1989)] was developed as a tool for teaching the principles of object-oriented programming. It runs under MacScheme on the Macintosh family of personal workstations and is included on the toolbox disk for that line of machines. Since it is intended to be used for small, didactically motivated examples, implementation efficiencies were not a primary concern. The system is 'memory hungry', since it trades space for gains in speed of execution.

Different from many other flavour systems, C-Flavours draws a syntactic distinction between *flavours* and *instances*. While flavours provide templates for structure and functionality of classes of objects, instances are used for the representation of objects themselves. A *Monster*, for example, might be defined as a creature which possesses *horns* and some *treasure*. It may also respond to commands for *growling* and *grabbing*. *Marvin*, on the other hand, may be the name of a particular monster, to whom such requests may be sent. C-Flavours offers the means for defining these concepts, along with inheritance and a number of other generally useful features.

C-Flavours may be used at two different levels. The lower of these (called *level 1*, since level 0 is provided by the underlying Scheme implementation itself) is purely object oriented. This means that *every* action must be triggered through message passing. A strategy for multiple inheritance is supported, whereby new concepts inherit structure (instance variables) and functionality (methods) from all of their superclasses. *Vanilla* serves as the root of this inheritance network for flavour instances, while flavour *Flavour* encapsulates the commonalities of all flavours. Messages to flavour *Flavour* create concepts by adding methods and instance variables, as well as catering for any new instances' creation. The *Monster* concept, for example, may be defined as:

```
(define Monster (Flavour 'newFlavour))
    (Monster 'name! 'monster)
    (Monster 'addSuper Vanilla)
    (Monster 'addIvars '(horns treasure))
```

```
(Monster 'addMethod 'growl ( ) '((DisplayLine "grrr . . .")))
(Monster 'addMethod 'grab '(someTreasure)
         '((+ treasure someTreasure)))
```

This message sequence will first create a 'generic' *Monster* flavour and then add relevant super-flavours, instance variables and methods. Note that all messages and arguments must be quoted to prevent their evaluation. We can now create *marvin* by:

```
(define marvin (Monster 'new '((horns 4) (treasure 0))))
```

To illustrate the idea of inheritance we will extend this example further. Assume that we also define some flavour of *Dog*:

```
(define Dog (Flavour 'newFlavour))
    (Dog 'name! 'dog)
    (Dog 'addSuper Vanilla)
    (Dog 'addIvars '(tail))
    (Dog 'addMethod 'bark ( ) '((display "woof!")))
```

and may now wish to combine these two concepts:

```
(define BaskervilleMonster (Flavour 'newFlavour))
    (BaskervilleMonster 'name! 'baskervilleMonster)
    (BaskervilleMonster 'addSuper (list Monster Dog))
```

It is the programmer's responsibility to ensure that such inheritance networks contain no cycles. *marvin*, in a new incarnation as a *Baskerville-Monster*, could now own a tail:

```
(define marvin
    (BaskervilleMonster 'new '((horns 4) (treasure 0) (tail #t))))
```

Note that although *marvin* may be instructed to both growl (inherited from *Monster*) and bark (inherited from *Dog*), these messages would make no sense to the *BaskervilleMonster* flavour itself. Only its instances may respond, that is:

```
(marvin 'growl)
grrr . . .
(marvin 'bark)
woof!
(BaskervilleMonster 'growl)
Sorry, I do not know how to growl
```

Level 2 offers some syntactic sugaring for flavour, method and instance definitions. Four macros are available to ease flavour and method definition and removal, as well as instance creation. For further convenience three optional keywords (*getivars*, *setivars*, *testivars*) may be used to toggle the automatic creation of access, modifier and predicate functions for instance variables. Defining the notion of *CircusDog*, for example, may be short-circuited by:

```
(defFlavour CircusDog (ako Dog) (ivars bones)
     getivars setivars testivars)
     (defMethod (bark CircusDog) ( ) (self 'deepBark 0))
     (defMethod (deepBark CircusDog) (previousBarks)
                    (if (=? previousBarks bones)
                         (display " ")
                         (begin (self 'sendToSuperFlavours '(bark Dog))
                                   (self 'deepBark (+ 1 previousBarks)))))
```

Any *CircusDog* instance will now be able to bark according to the number of bones she currently owns. Note that *self* is a so-called 'pseudo variable', bound to the currently executing process (that is, an instance of procedure *CircusDog*). It is used to facilitate message passing within an object. The message *sendToSuperFlavours* is sent to access flavour *Dog*'s implementation of *bark*, which would otherwise be hidden by the local version.

The keywords *getivars*, *setivars*, *testivars* will cause automatic creation of a number of functions for accessing (**bones**), modifying (**bones!**) and querying (**bones?**) instance variables. A new *CircusDog*, *fifi*, may demonstrate this newly acquired behaviour.

```
(makeInstance (fifi CircusDog) ((tail #t)))
(fifi 'bones?)
()                        ; fifi owns no bones yet
(fifi 'bark)
                          ; and will therefore refuse to bark
(fifi 'bones! 4)
 4
(fifi 'bark)
woof ! woof ! woof ! woof !
(fifi 'tail! #f)
Sorry, I don't know how to tail!
```

Note that, although *fifi* has access to a *tail*, which she inherits from *Dog*, we have failed to provide any means for changing or even obtaining its value. Access to it outside the scope of her own methods is therefore illegal, a protection which saves it from an unhappy fate. We can, however, easily patch this:

```
(defMethod (showTail Dog) ( ) tail)
#t
(defMethod (chopTail Dog) ( ) (set! tail #f))
#t
(fifi 'chopTail)
()
(fifi 'showTail)
()
```

but it would, of course, be irresponsible to leave her in such a state:

```
(defMethod (growTail Dog) ( ) (set! tail #t))
#t
(fifi 'growTail)
#t
```

Figure 2.34 lists most of the basic functions provided by the C-Flavours package.

Figure 2.35 shows a typical session with C-Flavours. Four windows are visible on the screen; three of these show definitions for the concepts of *Dog*, *Monster* and *BaskervilleMonster*, according to the previous discussion. To avoid cluttering the presentation with unnecessary detail, we have used the macros provided by level 2. The *transcript* window traces a sequence of declarations and message expressions.

marvin, an instance of *BaskervilleMonster*, is created first. From the system' s response we can deduce that 'behind the scenes', *marvin* is 'really' a procedure, in the style we have used to simulate objects before. Messages may now be sent to *marvin*. *flavour* and *flavourName* allow access to *marvin*'s class (its 'flavour') and the name of that class. Note that *marvin*'s internal state is completely encapsulated. His only accessible instance variable is his *tail*. This attribute is inherited from *Dog*, where we set switches to create the relevant access functions (*tail?*, *tail* and *tail!*) automatically. Any attempts to access his horns, however, are bound to fail and terminate in error. Of course we may explicitly define an appropriate selector 'on the fly', after which this information will become accessible. Note that we need not worry about naming conflict between instance variables and methods (what *horns* refers to depends on the context of use) and that adding the *horns* method requires no recompilation of any flavours. Also, before we test our newly defined method we set a *trace flag* on *marvin*. This will cause the system to print an explanatory message each time a message is received by this object. Tracing chains of messages often provides very useful debugging information. In the remainder of the transcript the effects of the *akoTree* and *describe* messages can be observed. Both may only be sent to

```
LEVEL 2: Macros

; new flavour definition (classes of objects)
; testivars, getivars, setivars are optional and may be given in any order. They control the
; automatic creation of test (...?), access (...) and change (...!) methods for instance
; variables.
(defFlavour aName (ako super-flavour ...) (ivars aName ...)
        testivars getivars setivars)

; definition of methods
; this can occur 'on the fly' without recompilation of the corresponding flavour – if instance
; variables are changed, however, then that flavour and all its relatives (via ako ...)
; must be recompiled !!!
(defMethod (aName aFlavour) (arguments) expressions ...)

; instance creation
(makeInstance (aName aFlavour) (list of (aName aValue ) pairs
  for all instance variables which should not be initialized to nil ))

; message passing
(anInstance 'aMessageName 'someArgument ...)

LEVEL 1: messages to flavours and instances

A.  (to flavours – inherited from 'Flavour')

addSuper     'aName ...  ; adds new superclasses
addIvars     '(aName ...) ; adds new instance variables
addMethod 'aName '(arguments) expressions ...
describe                 ; lists ivars and methods (including inherited ones)
akoTree                  ; shows class/subclass relationships
new '((aName aValue) ...) ;  creates a new instance of the receiver
(initialized as given)

B.  (to instances – inherited from 'Vanilla')

flavour  ; returns an instance's flavour
sendToSuperFlavours 'aMethod 'anArgument
     or: '(aMethodName aFlavourName) 'anArgument ...
; permits access to hidden methods in a flavour's superflavours
```

Figure 2.34 C-Flavours – basic functionality.

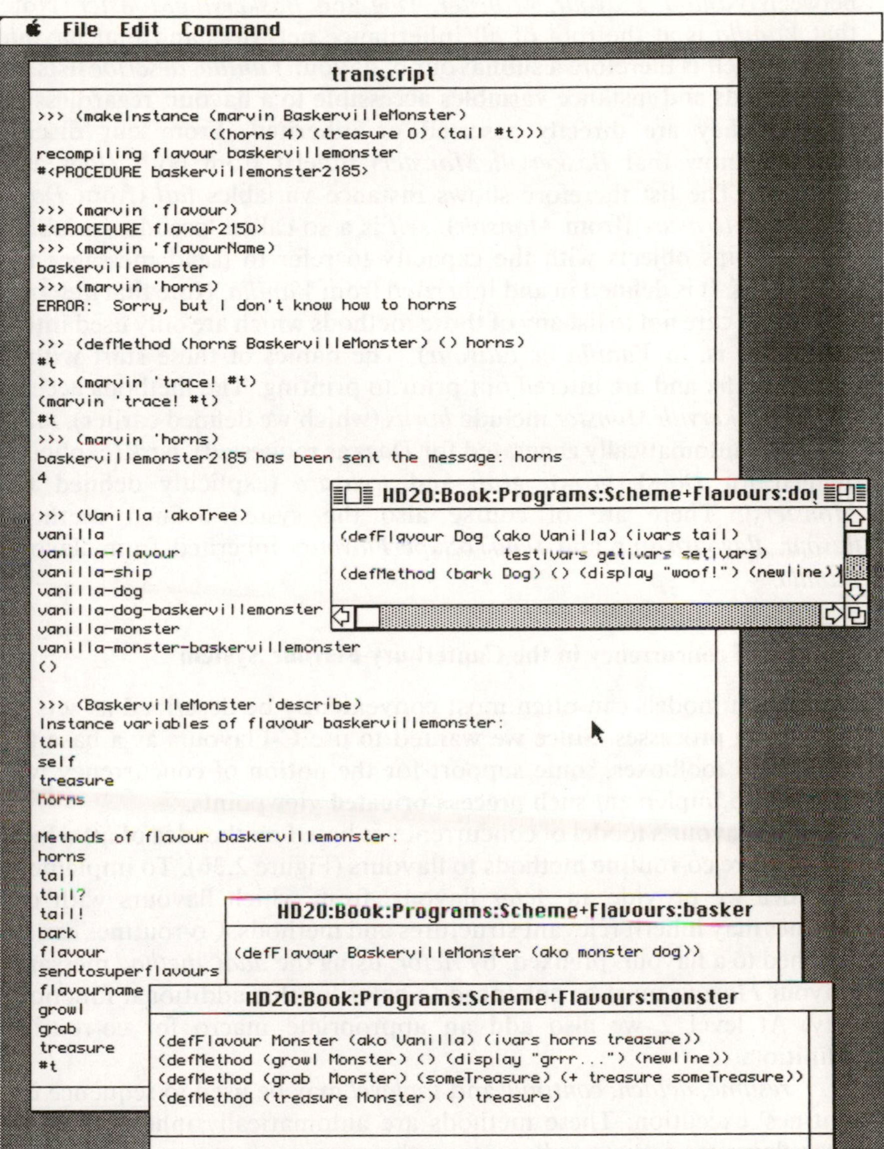

File Edit Command
transcript
>>> (makeInstance (marvin BaskervilleMonster)
((horns 4) (treasure 0) (tail #t)))
recompiling flavour baskervillemonster
#<PROCEDURE baskervillemonster2185>
>>> (marvin 'flavour)
#<PROCEDURE flavour2150>
>>> (marvin 'flavourName)
baskervillemonster
>>> (marvin 'horns)
ERROR: Sorry, but I don't know how to horns
>>> (defMethod (horns BaskervilleMonster) () horns)
#t
>>> (marvin 'trace! #t)
(marvin 'trace! #t)
#t
>>> (marvin 'horns)
baskervillemonster2185 has been sent the message: horns
4
>>> (Vanilla 'akoTree)
vanilla
vanilla-flavour
vanilla-ship
vanilla-dog
vanilla-dog-baskervillemonster
vanilla-monster
vanilla-monster-baskervillemonster
()
>>> (BaskervilleMonster 'describe)
Instance variables of flavour baskervillemonster:
tail
self
treasure
horns
Methods of flavour baskervillemonster:
horns
tail
tail?
tail!
bark
flavour
sendtosuperflavours
flavourname
growl
grab
treasure
#t
HD20:Book:Programs:Scheme+Flavours:do
(defFlavour Dog (ako Vanilla) (ivars tail)
testIvars getivars setivars)
(defMethod (bark Dog) () (display "woof!") (newline))
HD20:Book:Programs:Scheme+Flavours:basker
(defFlavour BaskervilleMonster (ako monster dog))
HD20:Book:Programs:Scheme+Flavours:monster
(defFlavour Monster (ako Vanilla) (ivars horns treasure))
(defMethod (growl Monster) () (display "grrr...") (newline))
(defMethod (grab Monster) (someTreasure) (+ treasure someTreasure))
(defMethod (treasure Monster) () treasure)

Figure 2.35 A session with C-Flavours.

flavours, not to instances! *akoTree* will prompt a flavour to show all its links to subclasses. Sending it to *Vanilla* will therefore cause the whole inheritance network to be printed. Here we see all inheritance paths between *Vanilla*, *Flavour*, *Monster*, *Dog* and *BaskervilleMonster*. Note that *Vanilla* is at the root of all inheritance networks and that flavour *Flavour* itself is therefore a subflavour of flavour *Vanilla. describe* lists all the methods and instance variables accessible to a flavour, regardless of whether they are directly asserted or inherited. From our discussion we know that *BaskervilleMonsters* inherit from both *Dogs* and *Monsters*. The list therefore shows instance variables *tail* (from *Dog*), *horns* and *treasure* (from *Monster*). *self* is a so-called 'pseudo variable', which equips objects with the capacity to refer to (send messages to) themselves. It is defined in and inherited from *Vanilla*. Note that *describe* takes great care not to list any of those methods which are only used internally (that is, in *Vanilla* or *Flavour*). The names of these start with a special prefix and are filtered out prior to printing. The methods accessible to *BaskervilleMonster* include *horns* (which we defined earlier), *tail?*, *tail*, *tail!* (automatically generated for *Dogs* as requested), *bark* (explicitly defined for *Dogs*), *growl*, *grab* and *treasure* (explicitly defined for *Monsters*). There are of course also the system-defined methods *flavour, flavourName* and *sendToSuperFlavours* inherited from flavour *Vanilla*.

The role of concurrency in the Canterbury Flavour System

Simulation models can often most conveniently be described as sets of interacting processes. Since we wanted to use C-Flavours as a base for simulation toolboxes, some support for the notion of concurrency was required to implement such **process-oriented** viewpoints.

C-Flavour's model of concurrency is based on the idea of attaching one or more co-routine methods to flavours (Figure 2.36). To implement this idea we provide an *Actor* flavour, from which flavours with co-routines may inherit relevant structures and methods. Co-routines can be attached to a flavour 'prefixed' by *Actor*, using the *addCmethod* message. Flavour *Flavour* must be enhanced to cater for this additional functionality. At level 2 we also add an appropriate macro for co-routine definition.

resume, *detach*, *continue* and *toplevel* may be used to sequence co-routines' execution. These methods are automatically inherited by all *actor* flavours. *resume* will capture the current context and locus of execution (as a 'continuation') and store it, so that the co-routine can later be 'continued' or 'resumed' again. It then 'continues' the relevant co-routine and actor. *detach* is used to return control to whoever last invoked the currently active co-routine, saving its continuation. The *continue* method 'continues' a co-routine from its current entry point

LEVEL 2: Macros

(defCoroutine (*aName aFlavour*) (*arguments*) *expressions* ...)

LEVEL 1: messages to flavours and instances

A. (to flavours – inherited from 'Flavour')

addCMethod (*aName anActorFlavour*) (*arguments*) *expressions*) ...
; *defines a coroutine method*

B. (to instances – inherited from flavour 'Actor')

detach ; *may only be sent to self*
resume *anActorFlavour 'aCoroutine ; may only be sent to self*
continue *'aCoroutine arguments ...*
topLevel
reset
terminated? *'aCoroutine*

Figure 2.36 C-Flavours – co-routine support.

(where it relinquished control the last time), but it will not remember its own continuation. If a co-routine has not previously been invoked, it will start at its first expression. *topLevel* throws control from a co-routine immediately up to the 'top level' (that is, the system's 'read, eval, print' loop). The continuation that is used to do this is captured and stored by a ***x*** procedure, so that it must be assured that that function is invoked at the time the flavours package is loaded.

In order to resume a co-routine method from where it last relinquished control any co-routine may send *resume* to itself. This will capture a point of return and the context of the current computation. It will then transfer control to the specified co-routine within the specified object.

```
(self 'resume jonathan 'tasks pub)
```

for example, will restart the *tasks* method of object *jonathan* (with argument *pub*) at the point where it was last interrupted. *resume*s may be sent to 'ping pong' control among a group of objects. Game programs and simulation models are typical applications where such a strategy is required. The following program models a 'Pub' scenario, where two processes, *beth* and *jonathan*, interact.

```
; . . . a "drinker-driven" Pub model . . .
(defFlavour Pub (ako Vanilla) (ivars barstaff)
```

```
                    setivars getivars testivars)
    (defFlavour Drinker (ako Actor) (ivars nickname thirst)
                        setivars getivars testivars)
      ; these flags are set to create access methods and predicates
      ; automatically
      (defMethod (askForDrink Drinker) ( ) (DisplayLine ''Beer thanks''))
      (defMethod (drink Drinker) ( )
          (DisplayLine ''glug, glug'')
          (set! thirst (- thirst 1)))
      (defCoroutine (tasks Drinker) (aPub)
          ; this represents the life cycle of drinkers
          (DisplayLine ''Howdy !'')
          ((aPub 'barstaff) 'greetCustomer nickname)
          (while (>? thirst 0)
              (self 'askForDrink)
              ; now activate the 'serve' method
              ; of the Pub's barstaff
              (self 'resume (aPub 'barstaff) 'serve self)
              ; invoke the drinker's 'drink' method
              (self 'drink)
              ; prompt the barstaff to offer another beer
              ((aPub 'barstaff) 'offerMore))
          ; full - go home now
          (DisplayLine ''No thanks – wife's waiting''))
  (defFlavour BarStaff (ako Actor) (ivars pub)
                        setivars getivars testivars)
     (defMethod (greetCustomer BarStaff) (aName)
         (DisplayLine ''what will you have'' aName ''?''))
     (defMethod (offerMore BarStaff) ( )
         (DisplayLine ''want another ?''))
     (defCoroutine (serve BarStaff) (aDrinker)
           ; pass control back and forth, between staff and customer
          (while #t
           (DisplayLine ''here you are'' (aDrinker 'nickname))
           (self 'resume aDrinker 'tasks pub)))

    ; --- an instantiation ---

    (makeInstance (roversReturn Pub))
    (makeInstance (beth Barstaff) ((pub roversReturn)))
    ; We can't associate beth and the pub immediately –
    ; one has to be created before the other one may be linked to it!
    (RoversReturn 'barStaff! beth)
    (makeInstance (jonathan Drinker) ((thirst 3) (nickname 'joe)))
```

We may now start an 'episode' by sending the message *tasks* to *jonathan*.

+++ jonathan's responses +++	+++ beth's responses +++
Howdy!	
	what will you have joe?
Beer thanks	
	here you are joe
glug, glug	
	want another?
Beer thanks	
	here you are joe
glug, glug	
	want another?
Beer thanks	
	here you are joe
glug, glug	
	want another?
No thanks – wife's waiting	

Figure 2.37 A trace of the *Pub* model.

```
(jonathan 'tasks roversReturn)
```

This will produce the dialogue printed in Figure 2.37.

Co-routine methods need not be associated with instances of different flavours, or even different instances of a given flavour. They may equally well reside within the same flavour instance, as the following example demonstrates. Here we may want to model the process of *juggling* a ball. Assuming a somewhat clumsy right-handed person, the relevant code becomes:

```
(defFlavour Juggler (ako actor))

    (defCoroutine rightHand Juggler) ()
        (while (<? 1 (MyRandom 4))    ; 20% chance of dropping the ball
            (DisplayLine "right catches and throws back")
            (self 'detach))
        (DisplayLine "oops . . ."))
    (defCoroutine leftHand Juggler) ()
        (display "left throws ball to right       ")
        (self 'resume self 'rightHand)
        (while (and (<? 0 (MyRandom 3))    ; 25% chance of dropping ball
                    (not (self 'terminated? 'rightHand)))
            (display "left catches and returns to right ")
            (self 'resume self 'rightHand))
        (DisplayLine "oops . . ."))
(makeInstance (me Juggler))
(me 'leftHand)
```

```
+++ left's responses +++              +++ right's responses +++

left throws ball to right             right catches and throws back
left catches and returns to right     right catches and throws back
oops ...
```

Figure 2.38 The dialogue produced by the *Juggler* model.

Figure 2.38 shows this 'left-handed' episode.

Some remarks on implementation

C-Flavours was implemented on an Apple Macintosh using the MacScheme programming system [Semantic Microsystems (1986)]. It requires a minimum of 1 MB of storage in order to function effectively. C-Flavours uses **eval** and makes certain assumptions on how environments are handled. This may make it more difficult to port to other Scheme implementations, although all the implementation-dependent code has been localized (in procedure *CallWithEnvironment*).

Procedure '*CallWithEnvironment*' (also known as '**call/we**') is the backbone of the flavours system. It permits a procedure (a method) to be called within any given environment (an instance). For example:

```
(define instantEnvironment
    (let ((x "mumble")) (make-environment)))
```

Here an environment, containing a binding for *x*, is returned. *printStuff*, defined as:

```
(define printStuff
    (let ((x "grumble")) (lambda ( ) (display x))))
```

would normally 'grumble' whenever it is invoked, since the function is compiled within the environment created by **let**. We may, however, choose to execute it within *instantEnvironment*, causing it to 'mumble' instead.

```
(call/we instantEnvironment printStuff)
; mumble
```

A flavour *instance* is represented as an environment and a pointer to an association list of valid methods for that instance. At the implementation level it is a procedure which accepts a *message* and some *arguments*, which means that it must know its environment and what messages it should understand. An *instantiate* procedure is used to create such instances. It expects three arguments: the environment of the new instance, a pointer to a methods list and the instance's name. In return it creates a procedure of two parameters: a message name and an optional list of arguments. This newly created instance will automatically have access to all arguments of this particular invocation of *instantiate*, since it has been compiled within its scope. Messages can now be sent to this object. Methods attached to instances may change whenever their flavours are modified. This requires no recompilation, since they are accessed through pointers rather than being stored locally.

A simple flavour-based simulation package

The following example demonstrates how flavour systems may be employed to build layers of software in an elegant fashion.

Let us assume that we wish to design programs for simulation, where the term '*simulation*' is used to refer to any experimental exploration of symbolic models. A number of programming metaphors have evolved around this concept and a detailed discussion of their characteristics is offered by Kreutzer (1986). Simulation is an inherently experimental activity and some kind of monitor entity and facilities for *data collection* and analysis are therefore always required. The *monitor* will be responsible for supervising experiments; that is, to start, control and terminate a model's execution. Simulations may either be deterministic or stochastic. *Stochastic simulation* requires procedures for sampling from *distributions*, while a *time-slicing approach* to model evaluation is often sufficient for simple deterministic models. As an illustration of a stochastic process you may imagine the path of an intoxicated friend on his way home, while the well-known '*game of life*' [Gardner (1984)] is one of the better-known examples of a deterministic model with time-slicing. In 'pure' sampling and time-slicing models the monitor's control activity can adequately be implemented by a simple loop, incrementing some counter (such as for the number of samples or ticks of a 'clock'). It will terminate execution whenever it reaches a predefined value or state. There are of course also more complex models in which the behaviour of entities can be quite complicated, and where decomposition of a time dimension into fixed increments may not be productive. Some classes of models, for example, suggest 'natural' representations in terms of differential equations, whose evaluation may require integration with variable step sizes. A controller for the flight path of a plane or rocket offers a good example. These models are usually referred to as *continuous* simulations. One may also combine discrete models with stochastic components. Some models of this kind are discontinuous in the sense that for a long time nothing relevant may happen, followed by a sudden burst of activity. Imagine a simulation of the life of a desert flower, which may lie dormant for many months and will suddenly burst into bloom after the rare event of a rainstorm. With a small time slice, a time-slicing model would have to perform many unprofitable iterations, while it may miss relevant activities completely if a large time slice was used. Simple time-slicing techniques are not effective in such cases, and a *next-event* approach to model evaluation should be employed. A *next-event monitor* keeps an *agenda* of things to do in the future. This agenda is usually ordered on time and contains references to tasks which should be performed next. As soon as the current task is finished the one following it may start, which is always the first on the agenda. In this way long periods of inactivity will not result in wasteful iterations within some 'polling' cycle, and the 'clock' will immediately (and asynchronously) jump from its current value to the time of the *next* imminent *event*.

Figure 2.39 shows some building blocks for simulation from a programming point of view. Let us briefly investigate the components involved in a simple framework for discrete event simulation.

Discrete event simulation views models as structured collections of objects, bound into webs of relationships and transformations. Although a wide variety of systems can be studied by using discrete simulation techniques, the **queuing network paradigm** is the most popular. Here we try to explore the effects of capacity limitations and routing strategies on the flow of some class of transactions. The objects of interest are different kinds of resources, queues and workload items. Analytical queuing theory can be used to analyze such models, but only if they have a relatively simple structure. Inventory models are an example of another well-established class of simulation studies.

Tools for discrete event simulation must provide facilities for model structuring and execution. Object-oriented programming languages are eminently well suited to this task. The idea of object orientation even originated in SIMULA, a language for building discrete event simulation models. Statistical instrumentation, the representation of random processes, and time and event management facilities are minimally required to support this programming metaphor.

Data collection devices are used to monitor a model's execution and gather appropriate statistics about its behaviour. Since simulation is an experimental technique in which we can never guarantee that solutions will eventually be found, obtaining statistical data about a model's behaviour is often the main purpose of the whole exercise. This data will have to be presented in a meaningful way, so that it can be analyzed at the end of a simulation run. A flavour system makes it easy to define data collection entities. To demonstrate the basic principle, *count* and *tally* objects shall suffice.

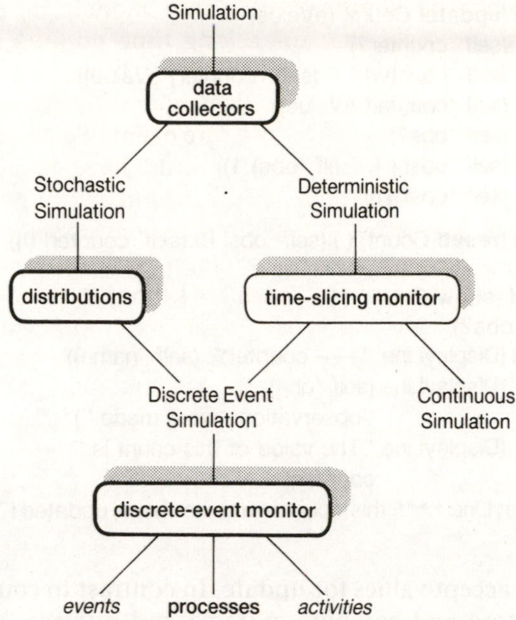

Figure 2.39 Building blocks for various classes of simulation.

All data collection entities share the common properties of an identifying *name* (for labelling their output) and the number of times they have been updated; this number is incremented after each observation. These attributes may therefore be factored into a root flavour and inherited from there.

```
(defFlavour DataCollector (ako Vanilla)
    (ivars name obs) testivars getivars setivars)
```

Remember that *testivars, getivars* and *setivars* will cause automatic creation of methods for accessing the *name* (*name? name, name!*) and *obs* (*obs?, obs, obs!*) instance variables. **Counts** are employed to record the number of occurrences of different kinds of events. They therefore need to contain a counter, which may be incremented by a specified number.

```
(defFlavour Count (ako DataCollector)
    (ivars counter) setivars getivars testivars)
```

The protocol for all data collectors includes methods for updating, resetting and displaying their values. Although they will all respond to such messages, individual implementations may differ. This possibility for separation of functionality from specific implementations is one of the strengths of the object-oriented approach. The relevant specifications for *Count* are as follows:

```
(defMethod (update! Count) (aValue)
    (if      (self 'counter?)
             (self 'counter! (+ (self 'counter) aValue))
             (self 'counter! aValue))
    (if      (self 'obs?)
             (self 'obs! (+ (self 'obs) 1))
             (self 'obs! 1)))

(defMethod (reset! Count) ( ) (self 'obs! 0) (self 'counter! 0))

(defMethod (show Count) ( )
    (if (self 'obs?)
        (begin (DisplayLine "--- counter:" (self 'name))
               (DisplayLine (self 'obs)
                            "observations were made.")
               (DisplayLine "The value of this count is:"
                            counter))
        (DisplayLine "*** this counter has not been updated !")))
```

Tallies will also accept values for update. In contrast to counts, however, they will also store and compute maxima and minima, as well as the mean (sum divided by number of observations) of a series of observations. This makes them suitable for finding aggregate measures of performance; that is, the average of the score of a number of students sitting a test. Since their structure is very similar to that of counts we will leave their definition as an exercise. Note that **update!**, **reset!** and **show** will need to be redefined appropriately. Some of the functionality required by both tallies and counts (for example, incrementation of the number of observations) may even be factored out and attached to the *DataCollector* level. Appendix II suggests a solution.

Counts and tallies provide only a bare frame for a more comprehensive toolbox of data collection facilities. There are many other useful entities for model instrumentation, such as frequency tables, accumulators, scatter plots and chronological graphs. Kreutzer (1986) discusses a number of these, as do many other textbooks on simulation. The **show** methods may also be redefined to produce graphical output, if access to graphics primitives is available.

Data collectors form the bottom layer of a simulation toolkit. Sampling from distributions, as defined at the next level, provides for stochastic behaviour. Since practically all interesting phenomena are too complex to be modelled in all their details, random processes will often be used to represent less essential aspects of a system under study. Inputs to so-called *trace-driven* models may be deterministic, using externally determined events, but more often models are internally driven by samples taken from stored probability or frequency distributions and are therefore referred to as *sample-driven* scenarios.

As in the case of data collectors, all **distribution objects** also share a number of properties and common operations. To illustrate the flavour of a more complete collection of classes of distributions we will show only a uniform integer (distributing numbers between *lower* and *upper*) distribution here, and provide a Boolean (*true/false*) distribution as part of the toolbox in Appendix III. Entities to encode continuously uniform, exponential, normal and other distributions can easily be defined in a similar fashion. It must be noted, however, that the 'quality' of the results of any stochastic simulation is strongly dependent on the quality of the so-called '*pseudo-random*' *numbers* which were used in the sampling process. The simulation toolkit we discuss in this chapter is suitable only for pedagogical purposes and we cannot take any responsibility for a model's validity. The 'Systems' toolbox's *MyRandom* function is based on a simple multiplicative congruential random drawing procedure. Although it has not been extensively tested, it may not provide the required degree of 'randomness' for serious applications. We will not mention this problem further and you should again refer to an appropriate textbook for a thorough discussion of this aspect of simulation methodology [*see*, for example, Knuth (1969), pp. 1–161].

All distributions own a tally object, for collecting and reporting statistics. This is, however, not visible to the user. What is visible at the user level is a number of methods to **reset!**, **show** and **sample** distributions. The implementations of **reset!** and **show** are identical across all distribution objects, and they are therefore attached to and inherited from **Distribution. sample** is specific to a particular class of distributions, and its definition for **RandInt** distributions is as follows:

```
; --- note: the 'MyRandom' function in the 'Systems' toolbox is used ---

(defFlavour Distribution (ako Vanilla) (ivars name sampleTally)
                          setivars getivars testivars)

(defMethod (reset! Distribution) ( )
   (sampleTally 'reset!))

(defMethod (show Distribution) ( )
   (DisplayLine "===" (self 'flavourName ":" name))
   (if (self 'sampleTally?)
      (sampleTally 'show)
      (DisplayLine "No samples were taken !")))

(defMethod (updateTally! Distribution) (aValue)
    (if (not (self 'sampleTally?))
       (set! sampleTally (Tally 'new)))
   (sampleTally 'update! aValue))

; --- an integer uniform distribution ---
(defFlavour RandIntDist (ako Distribution) (ivars lower upper)
                          setivars getivars testivars)
```

```
(defMethod (sample RandIntDist) ( )
    (define sampleInt 0)
    (define range (− upper lower))
    (set! sampleInt (+ lower (MyRandom (+ 1 range))))
    (self 'updateTally! sampleInt)
    sampleInt)
```

The method used for sampling a uniformly distributed integer should be apparent from the code. First we obtain the range of the relevant interval, we then randomly draw an integer from within this range (using *MyRandom*), and we finally convert this to an appropriate sample by adding the random number to the interval's lower bound. The '(+ *1 range*)' is necessary because *MyRandom* will generate numbers from 0 to $n-1$.

The final step towards a working discrete event simulator will be the construction of an appropriate 'next event' *monitor*. Since this is a slightly more complex task we will discuss it in somewhat more detail. A complete definition is again given in Appendix II.

Sequencing state transitions in models is the responsibility of an execution monitor, often also referred to as a *run-time control system*, *scheduler* or *simulation executive*. Various kinds of 'next event' monitors have been proposed and are described in the literature. A number of prototypical components are required in any such object. All dynamic models need a *clock* for time management. Discrete event models typically use an asynchronous, next-event strategy for advancing model time. Here the clock's value jumps to the time of the next relevant event once it has been established that no further actions can be performed at the current time instant. This method should be contrasted with the synchronous time-slicing technique often used for simpler models. To select the next relevant event we need an *agenda* of future tasks. This is sometimes called a *sequencing set*, *event list*, *noticeboard* or *scheduling list*. Since it eases the scheduling of multiple events involving the same entity, special objects called *event notices* are often used as members. These store the time of occurrence and a reference to the object involved, thereby representing changes of model state planned to occur in the future. Most event list implementations are designed so that the next imminent event can very quickly be determined and removed from the head of the sequencing set. Finding the place where newly scheduled events should be inserted usually takes more time, involving a search for the appropriate position. Simple linked lists are the most common data representation, although trees, heaps and other sophisticated data structures have also been experimented with [Vaucher and Duval (1975)].

The principal difference between various categories of discrete event simulators concerns the way in which changes of state are encapsulated. Event scheduling binds actions associated with individual events into single-entry modules, called *event routines*. To model a shopping trip, for example, the arrival in and departure from shops, the start and end of periods of deliberation about what items to buy, as well as the start and end of any buying and paying activities will have to be defined as a separate event and stored as a separate piece of code. Each of these will define a synchronous cluster of changes of state. An *activity-oriented* approach, on the other hand, would view such a trip as a nest of activities reflecting the shopping, choosing, buying and paying. Such activities are inherently time consuming and are guarded by sets of conditions under which they may occur and finish. The event-oriented approach has the advantage of being easily implemented in conventional languages, but the programmer must explicitly deal with all the complexities involved in event interaction, through scheduling statements. The activity-oriented strategy offers a more declarative view, under which we only need to assert some conditions for activities to start and finish. It is then up to the monitor to invoke relevant activities at the right point in time. The relative advantages and disadvantages of these two methods are similar to those we have mentioned for other procedural and declarative approaches before. Activity-based methods tend to be slow and inefficient, while event-based strategies lose in terms of programming convenience. *Process-based* descriptions offer an alternative viewpoint, whose spirit is similar to object orientation. Here we chunk all relevant aspects of an entity's description into a single module and let entities communicate via message passing. For our shopping trip example this would lead to a description of processes *shopper* and *store*, with interactions occurring between instances of the two. At the programming level this implies data encapsulation and multi-entry modules in the form of co-routines. In terms of descriptive convenience, robustness and maintainability, process orientation is superior to the other two approaches. Unfortunately its realization requires object-oriented features which make it difficult to implement in traditional languages like FORTRAN or Pascal, a fact which until recently has seriously impeded its acceptance as a modelling style. Special-purpose languages like SIMULA or SIMSCRIPT support process orientation, but since a majority of modelling applications are still written with FORTRAN-based tools it will take some time for this style to be generally adopted.

Fortunately, our flavour system offers all the required functionality to implement process orientation in an elegant way. In fact, it was originally designed for exactly this purpose. Figure 2.40 shows the components of a process-oriented monitor.

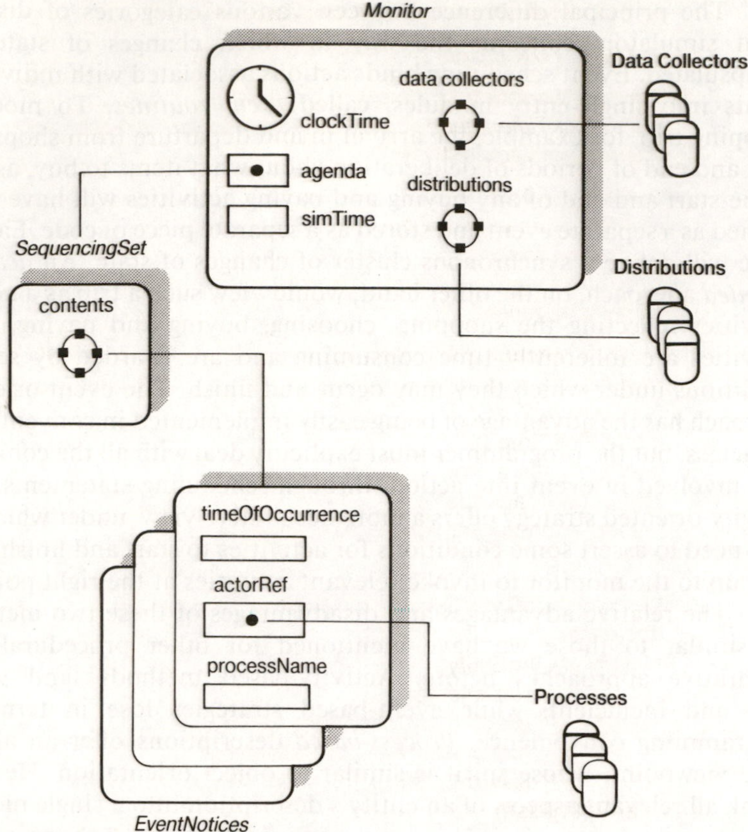

Figure 2.40 A process-oriented monitor for discrete event simulation.

Under the proposed architecture, a **model** is a collection of data collectors, distributions, processes and a monitor. All these are defined by flavours with appropriate instance variables and message protocols.

The *monitor* has five instance variables: *clockTime*, *agenda*, *simTime*, *dataCollectors* and *distributions*. *clockTime* represents the model's clock. *agenda* stores a *SequencingSet* entity. *simTime* defines a simulation's duration in terms of 'ticks' of the model clock. *dataCollectors* and *distributions* are lists of such objects known to the monitor, so that they can collectively be shown or reset. A *SequencingSet* flavour owns a list of *EventNotices*, ordered on ascending values of time, which are in turn implemented as flavours with *timeOfOccurrence*, *actorRef* and *processName* slots. *actorRef* and *processName* serve to identify *processes*, which are implemented through co-routine methods attached to 'actor' flavours. By changing the state of other entities these processes describe a model's behaviour. The following listing shows the monitor's definition. A description of flavours *SequencingSet* and *EventNotice* is again given in Appendix II.

```
; === a simple Discrete Event Simulator ===

; --- a MONITOR flavour ---

(defFlavour Monitor (ako Actor)
   (ivars clockTime agenda simTime dataCollectors distributions)
   setivars getivars testivars)

; <clockTime> holds the model's current clock time (a real number)
; <agenda> is an object of flavour "SequencingSet"
; <simTime> limits a simulation's duration
; <dataCollectors> and <distributions> are lists of entities -
; for reset! and report!

(defMethod (simulate! Monitor) (aTimeLimit)
 ; initializes the monitor and gives a time limit for simulation runs
    (set! tracing? #f)
    (set! clockTime 0)
    (set! simTime aTimeLimit)
    (if (not (self 'agenda?))
       (set! agenda (SequencingSet 'new)))
    #t)

(defMethod (addDataCollectors! Monitor) anEntityList
    (for-each
       (lambda (anEntity)
         (self 'dataCollectors!
               (if (pair? dataCollectors)
                  (cons anEntity dataCollectors)
                  (list anEntity))))
       anEntityList))

(defMethod (addDistributions! Monitor) anEntityList
   . . . similar to addDataCollectors

(defMethod (startUp! Monitor) ( )
; starts the monitor's processing of events on the agenda
   (if (>? simTime clockTime)
      (self 'continue 'resumeProcesses)
      (DisplayLine ''time limit too low -''
                   ''no simulation started !!!'')))

(defMethod (schedule! Monitor) (anObject aMethodName aTime)
; places a new event on the agenda
   (if (<? aTime clockTime)
      (error ''clocks can't run backwards !!!'' aClockTime)
      (agenda 'noteEvent! aTime anObject aMethodName)))

(defCoroutine (resumeProcesses Monitor) ( )
; cycles through the agenda, triggers processes and updates the clock
; - until it is time to stop
   (let ((next nil))
     (while (not (self 'finished?))
          ; get first event on the agenda
          (set! next (agenda 'nextEvent!))
```

```
            ; update the clock to this event
            (set! clockTime (next 'timeOfOccurrence))
            ; execute event
            (if (<=? clockTime simTime)
            ; transfer control to the appropriate process (coroutine) of
            ; the relevant actor
            (self 'resume
                  (next 'actorRef)
                  (next 'processName))))
      (DisplayLine "*** simulation stops at:" clockTime)))

(defMethod (finished? Monitor) ()
; a simulation finishes once there is nothing more to do (agenda
; empty), or once the time limit has been reached
   (or (agenda 'empty?) (>? clockTime simTime)))

(defMethod (reset! Monitor) ()
; resets the monitor and cycles through the lists of data collectors
; and distributions to reset their statistics in preparation for a new,
; "clean" simulation run
   (set! tracing? #f)
   (set! clockTime 0)
   (agenda 'clear!)
   (for-each (lambda (anEntity) (anEntity 'reset!))
             dataCollectors)
   (for-each (lambda (anEntity) (anEntity 'reset!))
             distributions) #t)

(defMethod (show Monitor) ()
; prints the monitor's state
   (define toGo (if (or (<=? simTime 0) (<=? clockTime 0))
                    0
                    (- simTime clockTime)))
   (DisplayLine "+++++ Monitor STATE +++++")
   (DisplayLine "... Clock Time:" clockTime "...")
   (DisplayLine "->" (if (>? toGo 0) toGo 0) "to go !")
   (agenda 'show))

(defMethod (report Monitor) ()
; reports the results of a simulation -
; after showing the state of the monitor, "show" cycles through the
; lists of all data collectors and distributions in the model to show
; their statistics -
   (self 'show) (newline)
   (DisplayLine "+++ data collectors:")
   (for-each (lambda (anEntity) (anEntity 'show) (newline))
             dataCollectors)
   (DisplayLine "+++ distributions:")
   (for-each (lambda (anEntity) (anEntity 'show) (newline))
             distributions))
```

The **schedule!** and **resumeProcesses** methods are at the heart of the monitor's operation, **schedule!**'s implementation simply delegates the task of planning for a process's future reactivation by sending a message to the *agenda* flavour, which will then create, initialize and file an event notice object at the appropriate place in its scheduling list. **resumeProcesses** will prompt the *agenda* for a new event, updating *simTime*'s value accordingly. The relevant action is deduced from this event notice through a reference to the actor flavour and co-routine method involved. This process will then be reactivated and the monitor therefore relinquishes control. The active process will now effect changes in its own and other entity's state, triggered by messages sent to acquaintances; that is, those flavours it 'knows' about. This may involve sampling some distribution in order to model activities stochastically. 'Interesting' changes may also be recorded by data collection devices. Delays in a process's progress are modelled by **hold** messages sent to the process. In response to this, the relevant monitor's **resumeProcesses** method will re-awaken and continue its cycle, activating the process next on its agenda. In this way a simulation is 'moved' through the specified segment of model time. Execution stops whenever the time limit is reached or the agenda is empty.

In this system *processes* are represented in a very simple fashion. They are attached to a monitor and are given just enough functionality to **hold** execution (passing control back to the monitor) and respond to simple queries. In a specific model, 'active' entities will be attached as subclasses and will therefore inherit from this flavour. They will also typically add further detail to an entity's functionality, by adding co-routine methods for any relevant processes. We will soon give an example to illustrate this point.

```
; --- flavour Process --- Processes define objects with life cycles
(defFlavour Process (ako Actor) (ivars name monitor)
                    setivars getivars testivars)

(defMethod (hold Process) (aMethodName aDuration)
; models time delays -
; by passing control to the monitor, to be re-awakened at the appropriate
; time
   (monitor 'schedule!
            self
            aMethodName
            (+ (monitor 'clockTime) aDuration))
   (self 'resume monitor 'resumeProcesses))
(defMethod (show Process) ( )
   (DisplayLine "+" name ", a Process of flavour"
                (self 'flavourName)))
```

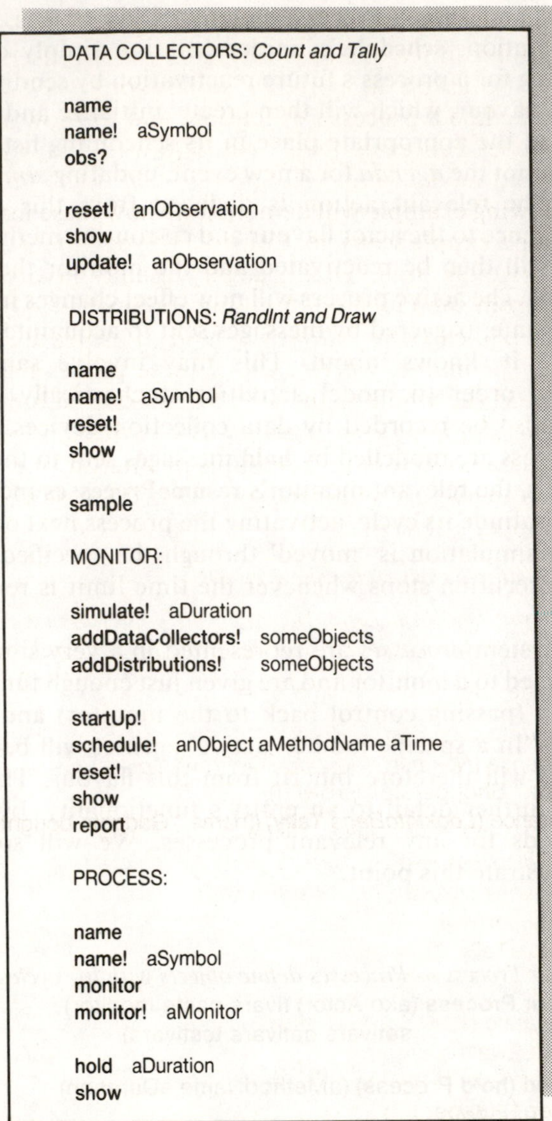

DATA COLLECTORS: *Count and Tally*
name
name! aSymbol
obs?
reset! anObservation
show
update! anObservation
DISTRIBUTIONS: *RandInt and Draw*
name
name! aSymbol
reset!
show
sample
MONITOR:
simulate! aDuration
addDataCollectors! someObjects
addDistributions! someObjects
startUp!
schedule! anObject aMethodName aTime
reset!
show
report
PROCESS:
name
name! aSymbol
monitor
monitor! aMonitor
hold aDuration
show

Figure 2.41 The 'Simulation' toolkit – message protocols.

This concludes our discussion of the simulator's architecture. Before we demonstrate how it may be used, we will briefly look at a summary of its functions, as reflected in the message protocols in Figure 2.41.

Figure 2.41 only shows those messages which are relevant to a user of the system. You will note that many of them end with '!', which indicates that they will produce side effects – that is, a change in bindings of state variables. All data collectors and distribution objects can be displayed and reset. Data collectors may also be updated, while distributions must be sampled. Although specific implementations for these methods may differ in flavour, this need not concern users in any way. Monitors may be asked to perform simulations (via **simulate!** and **startUp!**), to schedule a process's execution, and to show and report on the state of a model. Processes, finally, know how to delay their execution for some specified model time period.

The following example will demonstrate how these features may be used to simulate a simple scenario. Consider the perennial task of buying presents at Christmas time. This drudgery usually involves driving to town, walking from shop to shop, thinking about what to buy, acting on such a decision and carrying the stuff around. It can easily be simulated as a discrete event model, where each of these phases may be defined stochastically and the whole sequence of tasks can be lumped into the description of a 'shoppingTrip' process. The corresponding model will contain a few data collectors for measures of interest (for example, the items bought by an average shopper), some distributions and a definition of a typical shopper's activities.

```
; === a simple christmas-time scenario ===

; the Systems, DataCollectors, Distributions, and Simulator toolbox
; definitions must be loaded before this program will work!

(DisplayLine "Jingle bells, jingle bells . . .")

; --- some data collectors ---
(makeInstance (NumberOfShoppersOnProwl Count)
    ((name "Shoppers on prowl")))
(makeInstance (LookIntoBags Tally) ((name "Gadgets bought")))

; --- some distributions ---
(makeInstance (ArrivalDelay RandIntDist)
    ((name "arrival delays")
     (sampleTally (Tally 'new))
     (lower 1) (upper 7)))

(makeInstance (WalkToShop RandIntDist)
    ((name "walk to shop")
     (sampleTally (Tally 'new))
     (lower 1) (upper 5)))

(makeInstance (TimeToChoose RandIntDist)
    ((name "time to choose")
     (sampleTally (Tally 'new))
     (lower 0) (upper 10)))

(makeInstance (GadgetsBought RandIntDist)
    ((name "gadgets bought")
     (sampleTally (Tally 'new))
     (lower 0) (upper 3)))

(makeInstance (Stressed? DrawDist)
    ((name "stressed ?")
     (sampleTally (Tally 'new)) (%true 0.2)))
```

```
; --- a monitor entity ---
(makeInstance (ShoppingTrip Monitor))
    (ShoppingTrip 'addDataCollectors!
                        NumberOfShoppersOnProwl
                        LookIntoBags)
    (ShoppingTrip 'addDistributions!
                        ArrivalDelay WalkToShop TimeToChoose
                        GadgetsBought Stressed?)
; --- a shopper process ---
(defFlavour Shopper (ako Process) (ivars pouch)
                    setivars getivars testivars)
(defMethod (buy Shopper) ()
    (define loot (GadgetsBought 'sample))
    (DisplayLine "--> at:" ((self 'monitor) 'clockTime)
                 (self 'name) "buys" loot "gadgets !")
    (self 'pouch! (+ (self 'pouch) loot)))
(defCoroutine (shoppingSpree Shopper) ()
    (NumberOfShoppersOnProwl 'update! +1)
    (while (not (Stressed? 'sample))
        ; walk to next shop
        (self 'hold 'shoppingSpree (WalkToShop 'sample))
        ; now take your time to make a wise choice
        (self 'hold 'shoppingSpree (TimeToChoose 'sample))
        ; now buy it quickly (before anybody else snatches it up)!
        ; NOTE: we may use the same distribution again - i.e. it takes the
        ; same span of time for a typical "buy", as for a typical
        ; "choose" activity
        (self 'hold 'shoppingSpree (TimeToChoose 'sample))
        (self 'buy))
    ; stressed! - go home and back to bed
    (NumberOfShoppersOnProwl 'update! -1)
    (DisplayLine name
                 "feels stressed and leaves at"
                 (monitor 'clockTime))
    (LookIntoBags 'update! (self 'pouch)))
```

We may now illustrate this model's operation by sending a few friends on a shopping trip. Since we do not wish to appear unkind we will limit it to one hour's duration.

```
; --- organize a shopping trip ---
(define sendFriendsShopping
    (lambda someFriends
        (for-each
            (lambda (aFriend)
                (define doodleTime (ArrivalDelay 'sample))
                (define friend (Shopper 'new))
                (friend 'monitor! ShoppingTrip)
```

```
            (friend 'name! aFriend)
            (friend 'pouch! 0)
            (ShoppingTrip 'schedule!
                          friend
                          'shoppingSpree
                          (+ (ShoppingTrip 'clockTime)
                             doodleTime))
           (DisplayLine aFriend ''leaves at''
                        (+ (ShoppingTrip 'clockTime)
                           doodleTime)))
    someFriends)))

; --- and send some friends on it ---
(ShoppingTrip 'simulate! 60)
(sendFriendsShopping 'bruce 'wanda 'cugel)
(ShoppingTrip 'startUp!)
```

This scenario will produce the simulation shown in Figures 2.42 to 2.44.

Figure 2.42 shows our three friends leaving. Appropriate instances of flavour *Shopper* are created and placed on the monitor's agenda. The sampling of *ArrivalDelay* produces some 'doodle' time, so that they will not leave all at once. Before starting a simulation we ask for a snapshot of the monitor's state, which tells us that the simulation is set up for 60 'ticks' (read 'minutes') and our three shoppers are scheduled as requested. (*ShoppingTrip 'simulate! 60*) and (*ShoppingTrip 'startUp!*) then trigger the simulation itself. Note that we could choose to 'break' its execution at any time to inspect the state of the model (for example, to see events on the agenda, statistics), possibly make some changes and ask the simulation to resume from that state. This is the advantage of interactive execution in an interpretative environment. In a compiled system the user will have to wait for the simulation to terminate before he can interact with the model again. Scheme's flexibility, however, does not come for nothing. We will have to accept some penalty in terms of execution time. For many predominantly numerical models this may be too high a price to pay.

The bottom of the transcript in Figure 2.42 shows the model in execution. We learn that *cugel* is not very resilient to crowds and leaves right away. *bruce* and *wanda* are more robust and continue shopping until the simulation terminates at time 62. The fact that the model does not 'shut down' exactly at 60 is due to the way in which the test for termination is implemented in the monitor's **resumeProcesses** method. Here it is only performed whenever a new item is taken from the agenda. Since it is in the nature of the next event strategy that the clock 'jumps' from event to event, this may be well after the prescribed time. However, no harm is done by this, since nothing relevant (no other event) could have occurred in the meantime. If we wished to avoid such 'time overruns' we could choose to schedule the termination as a special event of its own.

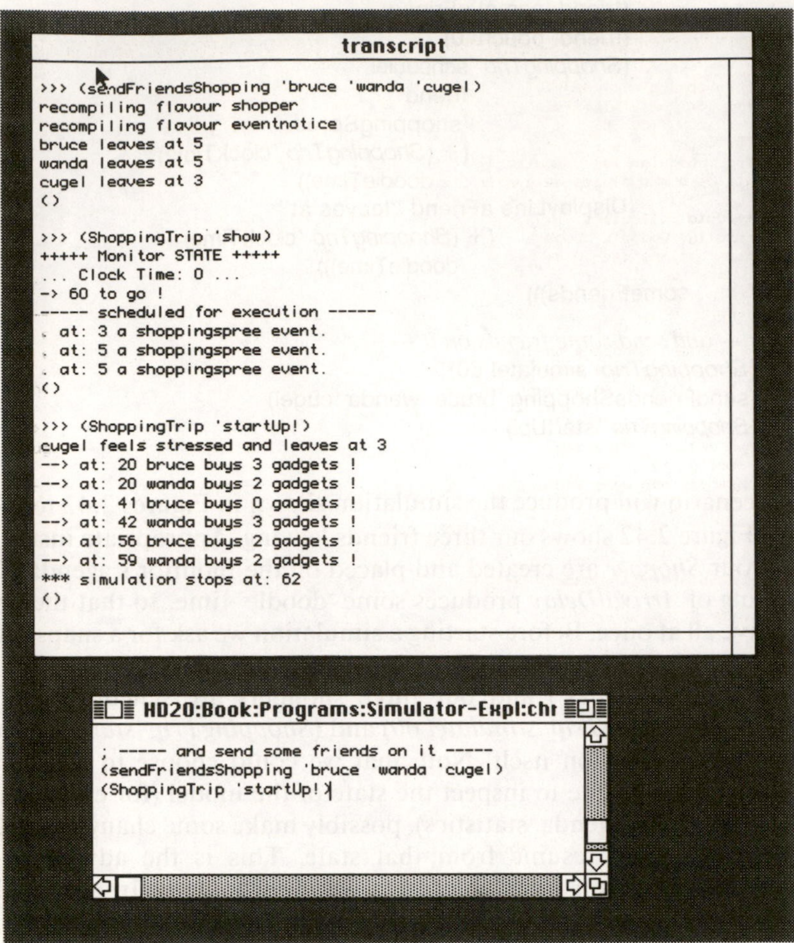

Figure 2.42 *bruce*, *wanda* and *cugel* go on a *ShoppingTrip*.

Figure 2.43 shows some statistics for our shopping trip. Details about data collectors are given first. Since only *cugel* was finished with shopping at the time our simulation was terminated, the 'Gadgets bought' statistics are not very telling. Since he left straightaway, *cugel* naturally didn't ever get any chance to make purchases. The statistics on 'Shoppers on prowl' seem to be accurate. Both *bruce* and *wanda* are still 'loose' in the model. The rest of the report offers information on the behaviour of our various distributions. Although from looking at these statistics we might be tempted to suspect that the random number generator does not seem to function particularly well, it should be borne in mind that the sample sizes are far too small for such a conclusion. We

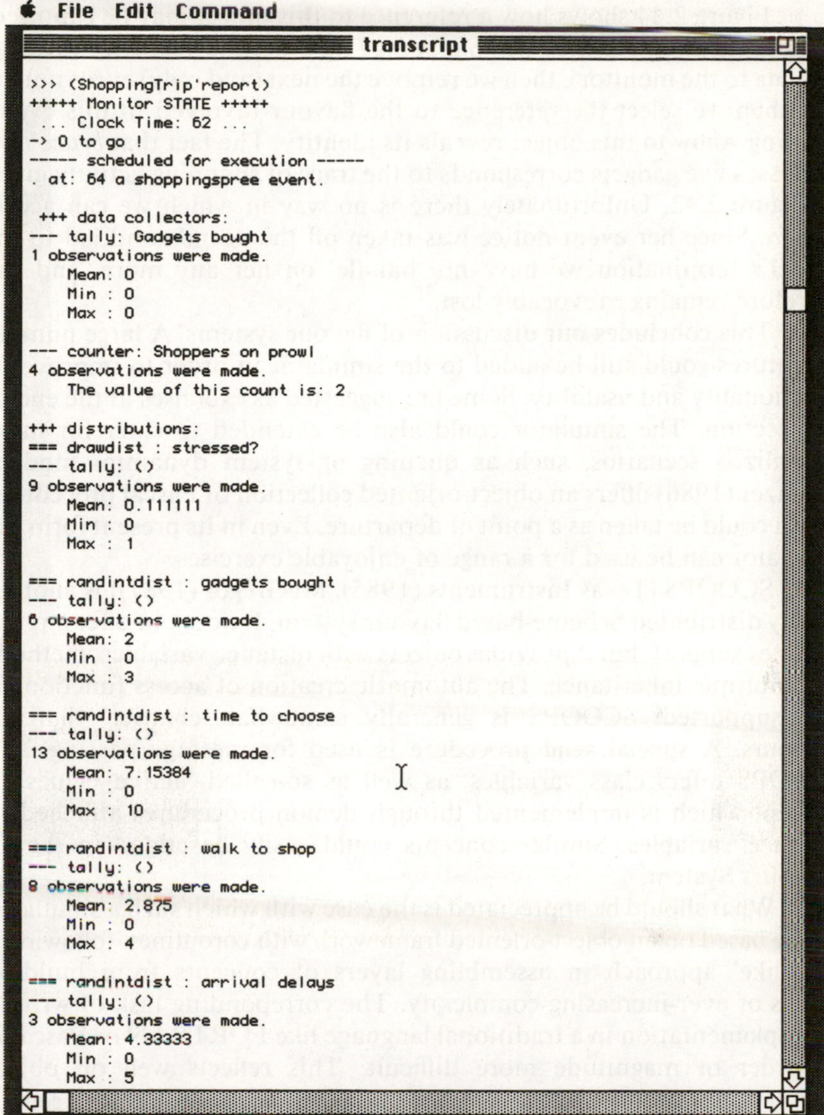

File Edit Command
transcript
>>> (ShoppingTrip'report)
+++++ Monitor STATE +++++
... Clock Time: 62 ...
-> 0 to go !
----- scheduled for execution -----
. at: 64 a shoppingspree event.
+++ data collectors:
--- tally: Gadgets bought
1 observations were made.
Mean: 0
Min : 0
Max : 0
--- counter: Shoppers on prowl
4 observations were made.
The value of this count is: 2
+++ distributions:
=== drawdist : stressed?
--- tally: ()
9 observations were made.
Mean: 0.111111
Min : 0
Max : 1
=== randintdist : gadgets bought
--- tally: ()
6 observations were made.
Mean: 2
Min : 0
Max : 3
=== randintdist : time to choose
--- tally: ()
13 observations were made.
Mean: 7.15384
Min : 0
Max : 10
=== randintdist : walk to shop
--- tally: ()
8 observations were made.
Mean: 2.875
Min : 0
Max : 4
=== randintdist : arrival delays
--- tally: ()
3 observations were made.
Mean: 4.33333
Min : 0
Max : 5

Figure 2.43 The *ShoppingTrip*'s statistics.

may wonder whatever happened to *bruce* and *wanda*. From the trace in Figure 2.42 we would deduce that by now they must have accumulated quite a sizeable number of gadgets. A glance at the agenda at termination (top of the transcript window) tells us that one of them is still scheduled for execution (at 64) and we may wish to take a closer look.

Figure 2.44 shows how a reference to this object may be captured. We first get the state of the *ShoppingTrip*'s agenda (sending message '**agenda** to the monitor), then we remove the next (and only) event notice, and then we select the reference to the flavour involved in this event. Sending '**show** to this object reveals its identity. The fact that *bruce* now possesses five gadgets corresponds to the trace of shopping activity given in Figure 2.42. Unfortunately there is no way in which we can access *wanda*. Since her event notice was taken off the agenda and led to the model's termination we have no 'handle' on her any more, and she therefore remains irrevocably lost.

This concludes our discussion of flavour systems. A large number of features could still be added to the simulator in order to improve its functionality and usability. Some are suggested as exercises at the end of this section. The simulator could also be extended to cater for more specialized scenarios, such as queuing or system dynamics models. Kreutzer (1986) offers an object-oriented collection of Pascal procedures which could be taken as a point of departure. Even in its present form the simulator can be used for a range of enjoyable exercises.

SCOOPS [Texas Instruments (1985), McGregor (1987)] is another widely distributed Scheme-based flavour system. It does not offer any coroutines support, but it provides objects with instance variables, methods and multiple inheritance. The automatic creation of access functions is also supported. SCOOPS is generally somewhat 'chattier' than C-Flavours. A special **send** procedure is used for message passing, and SCOOPS offers class variables, as well as so-called 'active values', a concept which is implemented through demon procedures attached to instance variables. Similar concepts could easily be added to the C-Flavours System.

What should be appreciated is the ease with which such a simulator can be based on an object-oriented framework with coroutines, following a 'lego-like' approach in assembling layers of concepts from building blocks of ever-increasing complexity. The correponding task of writing an implementation in a traditional language like FORTRAN or Pascal is an order of magnitude more difficult. This reflects well on object orientation's frequently advertised benefits for complexity reduction. Since flavours are used to encapsulate closely related information, the complexity of the programming task does indeed fail to increase exponentially with the number of interacting components. For example, once the *event notices* are defined and their functionality is tested, they may be used as building blocks for the *sequencing set*. Since we know that communication can only occur through the well-tested interfaces of those messages we choose to make available, we do not need to worry at all about possible interactions with the rest of our toolkit. Only the functionality (message protocol) of a building block needs to be known in order to use it. The *monitor* flavour can therefore use a

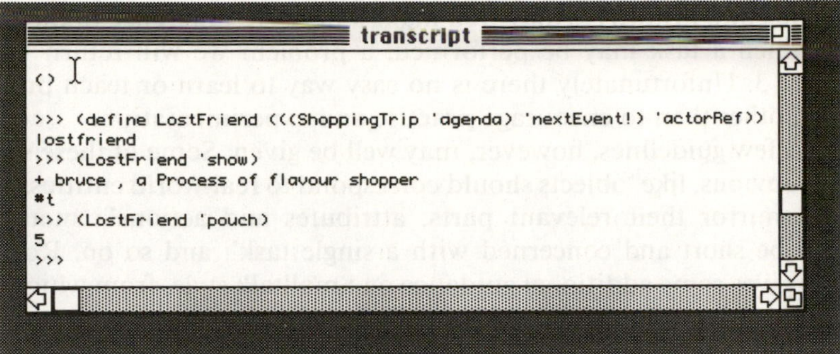

Figure 2.44 Checking *bruce*'s progress.

sequencing set as one of its elements, without any concern about its internal implementation, which remains 'closed'. At the level of the model itself we could then use the monitor, data collector and distribution entities. Extensions to ever higher-level structures (such as transactions, queues, resources) follow naturally from this concept of 'closure'. Naming of messages can be meaningful and short. All distributions respond to **sample** and all data collectors to **update!**. Although implementations for these methods may differ widely among different classes of entities, this need not concern the user in any way. Inheritance of structure and behaviour also helps in keeping modules easy to define and understand. It enables us to import functionality from superclasses. Class *distribution* provides an example for this. Here many aspects of individual distributions (they all have a name, they all own a tally, they all show themselves in the same way, and so on) are similar and can be factored out. This means that all these aspects need to be defined only once and it has the nice 'side effect' that checks on consistency become much easier, since information is localized in a single place.

We will further elaborate on this model of program development and its advantages and disadvantages when we discuss Smalltalk in Chapter 4.

2.5.3 Some comments on style

Object orientation views programming as *simulation*, reflecting some part of the world as a collection of interacting entities. From this perspective a program becomes a description of such entities in terms of their structural and behavioural characteristics. Proper classification is important, since it involves putting things 'where they belong', by sharing common attributes and operations. The 'right' way to decompose problems into primitives may well make a decisive difference to the ease with which a task may be performed, a problem we will return to in Chapter 3. Unfortunately there is no easy way to learn or teach proper design, other than to encourage practise and experimentation.

A few guidelines, however, may well be given. Some of these seem rather obvious, like 'objects should correspond to real-world entities, and should mirror their relevant parts, attributes and actions', 'methods should be short and concerned with a single task', and so on. Rochat (1986) gives some additional guidance on Smalltalk style, from which we will borrow some insights.

The general principles of classification and re-usable code should be applied to any program. Object orientation provides excellent support for such a programming style. You should therefore always design your flavours so that they may become re-usable for future applications. The simulator gives an example for this strategy. In this fashion we may 'grow' fairly complex conceptual structures in a reliable, enjoyable and painless fashion. It is tempting for a beginner always to attach flavours to *Vanilla*, and then to proceed to start his descriptions from scratch. One should resist this impulse and should instead make a conscious effort to use the system's existing functionality and factor common aspects into inheritance structures. Subclasses share structure and functionality with their superclasses and may respond to additional messages, restrict the use of certain messages, or implement some messages differently. If a system supports the notion of *class variables*, then these should be used to store constants, to avoid distributing such values throughout a set of methods. This recommendation is similar to the use of named constants in conventional languages like Pascal. A method should have a single purpose. If it performs more than a single function, these should probably be split into separate methods. Its placement should be carefully scrutinized. It may be better to attach it to a different flavour, if *self*, instance or class variables are never accessed and no new instances are ever created. The textual layout of a method should reflect its flow of control and proper indentation should be used to highlight this. There should be a comment describing its general purpose, if this is not already obvious from the choice of names. Before the next layer of objects is built, the message protocol of all classes or flavours at the current level should have been thoroughly tested. This may be accomplished by exercising all messages with parameters reflecting the typical cases as well as all boundary values.

2.5.4 Summary and perspective

Object-oriented programming may become to the 1990s what structured programming was in the 1970s. It has already proved itself as a valuable way of organizing programs in certain task domains. Its essence is built on a very simple metaphor: that similar things can be grouped into more general classes. As is the case with many other important ideas, this notion leads back to fundamental issues in mathematics and philosophy. Object orientation offers an integrated viewpoint of both the classification and communication paradigms. Wegner compares this duality to God and Plato.

> 'The "classification" view of systems can be likened to that of the creator of a domain of discourse who must know all interfaces, be omniscient, and have a global perspective. In contrast, the "communication" view can be likened to that of Plato's cave dwellers who can interact with the universe in which they live only in terms of observable communications, represented by reflections on the wall of their cave.
>
> The classification perspective is that of God the creator while the communication perspective is that of Plato the cave dweller. A system for programming in the large must support both the viewpoint of the creator/designer and the viewpoint of individuals who will populate the system after its creation. It must support the viewpoint of both God and Plato. In addition, Platonic cave dwellers must be allowed to play God with respect to the subsystems they create and the God of any given domain of discourse may be a Platonic cave dweller in some larger universe.'
>
> [*Wegner (1986).*]

Object orientation's principal assumptions state that every entity may be represented as an *object*, every object encapsulates its own *state* and *behaviour*, objects communicate with each other by sending *messages*, and every object can be generalized in terms of some *class* of which it is an instance. Writing a program now becomes the task of defining such classes in terms of enumerating their properties, the valid messages they may receive and the appropriate action or response to each of those.

Object orientation aims at reducing a task's complexity through chunking and layering. Essential concepts at each layer are highlighted, and the details of their elaboration are delegated to lower levels. The advantage of programming systems subscribing to this approach is that once a user masters a few very general concepts, he can learn more by experimentation and digging deeper and deeper into the system. The general concepts provide a base for an intuition of overall layout, and there are no barriers to exploration, modification and expansion of new ideas. This building-block approach leads to a programming style which views program design as an empirical activity, involved with model building and experimentation. In some sense every message is a *simulation* of an idea. This is the cave dweller's perspective, who is also allowed to play God in building his own shacks or cathedrals.

As for any other programming style, a large number of advantages and disadvantages can be attributed to object orientation. We have already mentioned that *classification* offers considerable benefits in terms of economy of description and a reduction of the bulk of code. The *closeness* in representation of real-world models and programs is also a considerable advantage, since it leads to programs which are easy to understand and communicate, and whose 'correctness' is easier to justify. Data encapsulation results in highly modular program structures, which offer a whole range of advantages. *Strong modularity* improves a program's reliability, since objects may now guard against invalid requests. It also decouples specification from implementation through 'information hiding', leading to easily re-usable, modifiable and maintainable code. Overloading identifiers follows as a side effect. All names are local to a class of objects, and there is therefore no need to consider possible conflicts with names used in other parts of a program. The message protocols of objects can be designed and tested independently from any other aspect of the systems in which they will be embedded. Finally, strong modularity offers good potential for exploitation of parallel hardware, and *dynamic binding* provides the required flexibility for exploratory styles of program development.

The semantic gap between object-oriented systems and the classical von Neumann style of computer architecture is considerably larger than for more conventional languages, and there are therefore a number of performance penalties to pay.

Apart from the SIMULA language, whose technical advantages were for a long time largely ignored outside the field of simulation, object-oriented programming is a relatively recent development. For this reason there is still a shortage of literature describing the principles of the field. Good introductions to the philosophy of object-oriented programming are provided in articles by Robson (1981), Stefik and Bobrow (1985), Cardelli and Wegener (1986), Diederich and Milton (1987), as well as by browsing through the proceedings of the ACM conferences on Object-Oriented Programming Languages and Systems (OOPSLA) [SIGPLAN (1986)–(1988)]. Tesler (1986) has surveyed a number of programmers who have used object-oriented programming in large programming projects. Apart from a newsletter published by *ParcPlace* Systems, *HOOPLA* ('Hooray for object-oriented programming') and the *Journal of Object-Oriented Programming* are currently the only periodicals dedicated to a discussion of this programming metaphor, but there is also a fairly active Smalltalk newsgroup on UseNet (*comp.lang.smalltalk*). Unfortunately, there are no good sources for the different kinds of object-oriented LISP dialects and flavour systems other than their reference manuals and some conference papers. Cox (1986) is a text on object-oriented programming in Objective C. Stroustrup (1986), and Wiener and Pinson (1988b) describe the use of object orientation in the context of the C++ programming language, while Schmucker (1986a and b) discusses a number of object-oriented programming systems, including MacApp, Clascal, Neon, Smalltalk, ExperCommonLisp flavours, Object-LOGO and Objective C.

EXERCISES

Many of these exercises can be attempted in any object-oriented language, although a few require access to a good graphics system. Further to the ones listed here, many of those given for Scheme, PROLOG, Smalltalk and the toolboxes in Chapter 3 are also suitable material for a flavour-based perspective.

A Flavours

2.22 Hayes (1986) describes a Scheme implementation for a simple children's game, called '*Scissors, paper, stone*'. In this game two players select moves from these three alternatives, and the winner is the one whose move 'breaks' the object represented by the other player's move. A conventional interpretation is that scissors *cut* paper, paper *wraps* stone and stone *breaks* scissors. Write flavour descriptions for a program to play such a game. You will need to create a *player* flavour with two instances, and possibly also an *umpire* object. McGregor (1987) discusses a SCOOPS implementation.

2.23 The following proposal for a simple *adventure game* is due to Jennifer Cant. This game, '*Getting a degree*', requires a heroine to ascend from the lowly depths of stage 1 to the pinnacle of stage 4 computer science, and finally to the roof of the computer building, where she may then graduate and spend the rest of her life sipping Campari in the sunshine. During her ascent, the heroine may encounter monsters, who will attempt to divest her of her sanity. She may ignore them, or resort to violence; but violence itself of course reduces one's sanity. The monsters are either awake or asleep, and the active ones will walk about the building looking for poor students. The heroine also moves about rooms, but every second spent in the building saps her sanity. Fortunately there are literary works of art (books) which she may read to replenish it, always provided the books concerned are artistically or educationally worthwhile.

Heroine, monsters, rooms and books therefore form the basic flavours used in the game. In contrast to many other adventure games, the 'treasure' (literary works) is also the 'food' (sanity value), and so the heroine may be forced to trade some of the hard-earned treasure against her continued sanity. She may do this by reading a book and thus she gains sanity equal to its 'nutritional value' (brain food!), but if she does this, its 'treasure value' is lost to her. Of course it is the aim of the game not merely to reach the top of the building, but to get there with as much 'treasure' as possible. A certain amount of artistic licence may be applied to the actual layout of rooms and building. Your monsters may encode local personalities: students, staff and lecturers. The books' value must be judged by the heroine; beware, however, since some books are actually harmful to mental health and will reduce the heroine's sanity, if read.

Each object in the adventure should be represented as a flavour instance. Some suggestions for possible commands are:

(a) Move in a given direction.
(b) Take some object (book).
(c) Drop some object.
(d) Fight some monster.
(e) Read some book.
(f) Display the heroine's treasure.
(g) Introspect – *examines the sanity of the heroine, as well as the contents of her library.*
(h) Pray – *To be used in panic situations – gives a 5% chance of deliverance from the department. (To prevent its use as a 'soft' option, you may wish to make her 'pay' for each prayer.)*

B Flavours and co-routines

2.24* Model a typical *party* held in the embassy of an anonymous country. As is customary at such events, ambassadors will continue to talk until there's no caviar left. After each ambassador's talk there is always a 20% probability that this contingency will occur. Once it does happen they will all go home and the program stops. Individual ambassadors may leave whenever they are 'full'.

You will first need to represent ambassadors as flavours with *talk* co-routine methods, and then instantiate, link and loop across all of them, giving each a chance to say something profound. This loop will be guarded by the above-mentioned caviar criterion. Each ambassador is to be *resumed* by the main loop whenever it is his turn for some pearl of wisdom – unless, of course, he is full and has already left.

2.25 The McVitie and Wilson algorithm (1969) to find *stable marriages* among a group of people of either sex describes a very effective style of courtship. To perform this ceremony we must first partition a group into males and females. Each male then proposes in order of his preferences, until he is eventually accepted. If he is jilted, he continues with his next-best choice. Females are selective: each will continue to accept a more greatly preferred suitor. The first proposal is always accepted, but a fiancé may later be jilted if a better offer is received. The sequence of events in such a 'marriage tournament' therefore starts with the first male proposing to his first choice, and being accepted. Each subsequent male either proposes to an unengaged female, who will always accept, or to an already engaged one. In the latter case she may reject him, or, if she prefers him to her current fiancé, break her current engagement. In either case, the rejected male proposes to his next-best choice.

This algorithm is quite naturally expressed in terms of co-routines. It will, incidentally, lead to a male optimal solution, in which each male is at least as well off as in any other solution. Reversing roles will produce a female optimal solution. Write a flavour-based implementation. Kreutzer (1986) gives a SIMULA program set in a 'Muppetland' scenario.

C Flavours and simulator

2.26 Write a program to simulate the movement of an *intoxicated and silly beetle*, who has foolishly made a bet that he can crawl randomly around a ten-by-ten grid without falling off its edge. Each crawl he makes is one unit in the direction of one of the principal points of the compass. He starts off in the centre of the grid, and keeps crawling for a total of ten steps. He wins his bet if he is still on the grid after this. Use the *Distributions* flavours defined in the text to simulate the expected outcome. To make sure that he is indeed foolish, replicate the experiment a number of times.

2.27 The remote and inaccessible *mountain villages* of *Tick* and *Tock* are jealously proud of their ancient clockmaking traditions. The master clockmakers, of whom there are exactly 100 in each town, are so proud that each wears one of his own clocks on a gold chain around his neck. They are also equally skilled, their clocks running from one minute slow to one minute fast per day, with uniform and independent probabilities. Whenever two masters meet in the town square, which happens frequently, they perform the 'masters Matching Ceremony'. In *Tick*, each master sets his clock to the mean of their two clocks; in *Tock*, each sets his clock to the time shown on the other's clock.

On New Year's Eve, all of the clockmasters meet in the town square to compare their clocks with the clock in the Town Hall Tower, which is always exactly correct. Any master whose clock is more than one hour in error is dropped from the guild, sent into exile, and his place is taken by an aspiring young apprentice. Then the new year starts with everyone setting his clock to the correct time.

Design and implement a model for 100 clocks (masters), whose rates are evenly distributed from -0.99 to $+0.99$ minutes per day. At the time of each meeting all clocks are updated and then two of them are selected at random. Either the *Tick* or the *Tock* transformation is performed. Assume that meetings occur equally spaced throughout a year. At the end of the year the number of clocks with errors greater than one hour should be printed. Assume that you are an anthropologist who wishes to perform a comparative study of this strategy's impact on both the *Tick* and the *Tock* Society, with 150, 300 and 600 meetings respectively. In which town can we expect the most tragedies?

Note: You will need to sample from two streams of random numbers: a continuously uniform distribution from -0.99 to $+0.99$ representing the daily rate of deviation from the correct time, and an integer uniform distribution from 1 to 100 for the selection of clocks. The required continuously uniform distribution should easily be derived from the integer one. Avoid comparing a clock with itself!

The problem is a modified version of that given by Rubin (1979). Kreutzer (1986) gives a SIMULA solution.

2.28 The following scenario has been proposed as a particularly simple-minded model for the *political process in a democracy* [Dewdney (1987), p. 14]. Assume that we may represent a country's population by a grid of randomly coloured squares, that there are only two parties, *black* and *white*, and that each square symbolizes the current political persuasion of its inhabitant. We may now simulate how voters' allegiances change under social pressure. At each tick of a clock a square is randomly selected and its inhabitant's opinion may be changed by persuasion. In order to accomplish this, one of the voter's eight neighbours is selected at random and the voter's political conviction becomes that of his neighbour, regardless of earlier belief. To ensure that there are always eight neighbours we will postulate that our country's topology is such that it wraps around itself; therefore its top edge borders on its bottom and its left edge on its right. As this model is run, strange things may happen. First, large blocks of votes will develop within the grid, geographic areas where everyone has the same opinion. These blocks will migrate around the grid, and for a while two blocks may struggle for dominance. Finally the two-party system collapses and everyone ends up voting the same way.

This problem is a nice example for a simulation for which a simple time-slicing monitor is perfectly adequate. It is somewhat similar in flavour to the well-known '*game of life*' [Gardner (1984)]. Hofstadter (1985, pp. 49–69) discusses the related notion of self-replicating ideas. To implement the '*Voters*' problem we should select three random integers that give a random row index, a random column index and a random neighbour code for each tick of the clock. Our program will then replace the array value at this index position with the one found at its neighbour. To keep some statistics we may wish to record the changes that voters undergo – for example, using a *tally* flavour. A graphic display of the grid makes patterns strikingly visible. Donnelly and Welsh who invented this game also propose a variation they call the 'anti-voting game'. Just out of spite, randomly selected voters adopt an opinion opposite to that of their randomly selected neighbour. Will democracy survive in this setting?

2.29 Extend the simulator toolbox by defining some additional data collection and distribution flavours. You may also wish to consider extending the monitor to deal with simple quasi-continuous models. *System Dynamics*, which is easy to implement [Roberts *et al.* (1983)], offers a framework and a large collection of examples for such an approach. You may also experiment with the effectiveness of alternative schemes for organizing the next-event monitor's agenda (for example, as a binary tree).

A further worthwhile extension of the simulator involves adding some building blocks for modelling *queuing networks*. Flavours for queues, resources and transactions would be adequate for many modelling purposes. Kreutzer (1986) gives some suggestions and many examples of how such toolboxes may be used.

Chapter 3
Programming Metaphors

> 'The debate was between the "scruffies", led by Roger Schank and Ed Feigenbaum, and the "neats", led by Nils Nilsson. The neats argued that no education in AI was complete without a strong theoretical component, containing, for instance, courses on predicate logic and automata theory. The scruffies maintained that such a theoretical component was not only unnecessary, but harmful. . . The end product of the scruffy researcher is a working computer program, whereas the neat researcher is not satisfied until he has abstracted a theory from the program.'
>
> [*Bundy (1982).*]

3.1 From heuristic search to knowledge representation

One may describe a *knowledge representation* as a set of syntactic and semantic conventions 'to describe things', where 'things' may be objects, relations, actions, events or processes. This definition stresses the fact that representation and interpretation are closely intertwined. Whatever media and processes are used for encoding and interpretation, they must share a common set of conventions referring to the *form* ('recognizable' symbols, valid rules of combination) and *meaning* ('primitive' concepts, valid rules of deduction) of tokens. 'Without a reader a book is just ink on paper' [Wittgenstein (1956)]. Even worse, the concepts of 'ink' and 'paper' wouldn't even exist outside some kind of conceptual framework. A representation must be chosen to be 'appropriate' to the task at hand. Rather elusive notions of 'quality' may apply (such as completeness, conciseness, relevance, familiarity, ease of computation, and so on). There is no 'good' representation independent of use (Figure 3.1)!

Finding 'appropriate' representations for classes of problems is a very important aspect of the problem-solving process. Good representational frameworks may explicate and highlight 'important' aspects and expose 'natural' structures and constraints. A change in representation may well change our perception of a problem from an apparently unsolvable one to a trivial exercise. A classical demonstration of this may be given by the following problem:

Suppose two diagonally opposite corner squares are removed from a square of 16 by 16 cells. Can 31 rectangles, each the size of 4 by 2 of the squares, be so placed that they cover the remaining board completely (Figure 3.2)?

If one tries to approach this problem from a *search* perspective, with states as configurations of tiles and operators corresponding to the tiles'

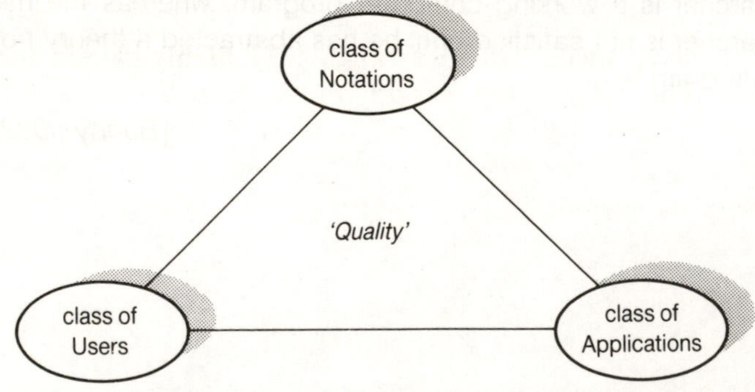

Figure 3.1 There is no 'good' representation independent of use!

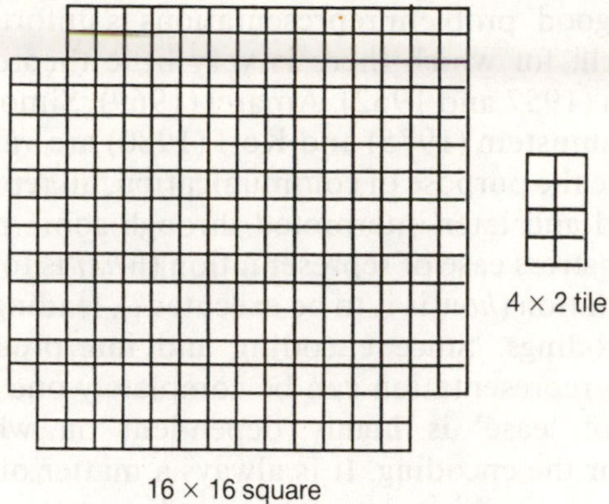

Figure 3.2 The mutilated square.

placing, the search space becomes very large. If, however, one maps it into a simpler representation, one may solve the problem through *reasoning*. While preserving all relevant geometric properties, and therefore without loss of generality, it is obviously possible to reduce the square to 8 by 8 and the tile to 2 by 1. One may now recognize the similarity to a chessboard. If one further notices the fact that every tile must necessarily cover both a white and a black square on such a board, and that the removed squares are both of the same colour, the answer becomes simple. Any representation attaching binary labels to squares allows this conclusion to be drawn easily, while it is unlikely to be noticed when this aspect of the square is seen as irrelevant. The shift into the more familiar domain of game boards helps one to recognize its significance. There is an even more 'suggestive' isomorphous specification, in which the solution becomes trivial.

> 'In a small but very proper Russian village, there were 32 bachelors and 32 unmarried women. Through tireless efforts, the village matchmaker succeeded in arranging 32 highly satisfactory marriages. The village was proud and happy. Then one drunken Saturday night, two bachelors, in a test of strength, stuffed each other with pirogies and died. Can the matchmaker, through some quick rearrangements, come up with 31 satisfactory marriages among the 62 survivors?'
>
> [*Hayes (1978), p. 180.*]

Here the problem is shifted into a highly 'familiar' frame, about which we all share considerable experience. The answer will therefore immediately be 'recognized' as obvious.

Finding 'good' problem representations is unfortunately a difficult problem in itself, for which there is very little theoretical or practical guidance. Polya (1957 and 1962), Amarel (1969), Simon (1969), Wickelgren (1974), Rubinstein (1975) and Korf (1980) are valuable sources for insight. To serve the purpose of communication, all representations must first be encoded and later interpreted through some process. One may therefore either stress ease of representation (*what* is to be described?) or ease of interpretation (*how* is it to be executed?), leading to declarative or procedural encodings. Since encoding and interpretation are always intertwined, no representation can be completely one or the other, and any measure of 'ease' is highly dependent on who performs the interpretation or the encoding. It is always a matter of degree, although logic and Turing machines may be cited as extreme examples for declarative and procedural viewpoints. In the early days of computing, the computer component was the 'expensive' partner in man/machine dialogues. This led to the notion of low-level languages, in which problems were easy to execute, but difficult to encode for the programmer. Lately this perception has changed in favour of the human component, and so-called 'declarative' problem specifications (for example, 'fourth-generation' languages, such as PROLOG) have become popular. *Declarative specifications* share the properties of finiteness and a high degree of context independence, which make them attractive for representing structural knowledge. *Procedural encodings*, on the other hand, are better suited to representing knowledge about processes, a task which is open ended and context sensitive by nature. The question of whether declarative representations are in any sense 'better' than procedural ones is essentially unsolvable. It always depends on one's specific purpose. Artificial intelligence has unsuccessfully grappled with this problem for many years [Winograd (1975)]. Although it has by no means been resolved, there now seems to be a consensus that a whole range of representational metaphors are necessary, for a variety of problems and purposes. Figure 3.3 summarizes some programming aspects of a number of the historically most popular schemes.

In the remainder of this chapter we will illustrate the use of some of the most typical representational tools which have evolved to support different AI programming metaphors. Our discussion will be based on '**toolboxes**', built around a set of prototypical data structures and their operations. In line with our earlier recommendations these toolboxes were built in a layered fashion. Although we have not chosen to encapsulate toolboxes as objects, a decision which was largely made with regard to their portability to other dialects of LISP, this may easily be accomplished by attaching their procedures to an appropriate 'top level' data structure. We recommend this task as an exercise. The relevant programming techniques for such encapsulation were discussed in

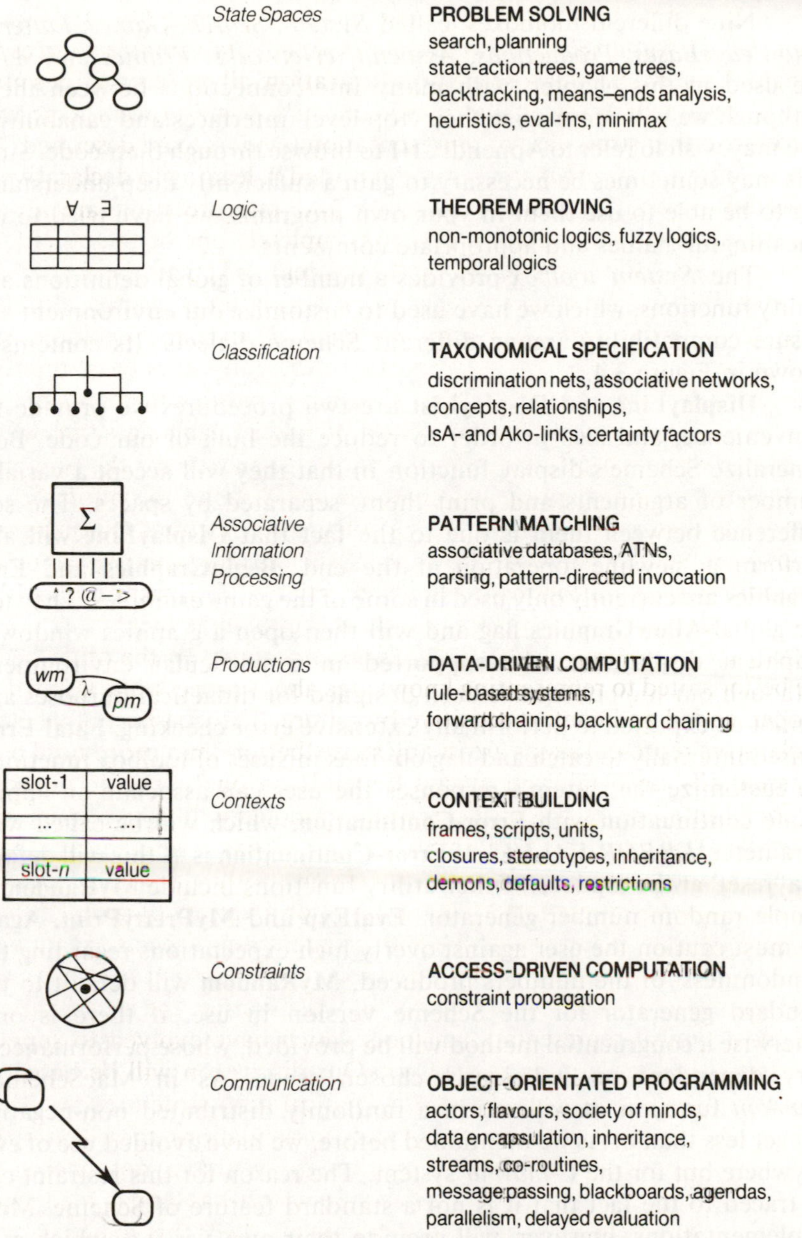

Figure 3.3 AI programming – some common metaphors.

Section 2.3, where we have also commented on the many advantages of this approach.

Nine different toolboxes, called *System*, *Search*, *Games*, *Patterns*, *KnowledgeBases*, *Productions*, *AssociativeNetworks*, *Frames* and *ATN*, are used in this chapter, with many interconnections between them. Although we will summarize their 'top level' interfaces and capabilities, you may wish to refer to Appendix III to browse through their code. Since this may sometimes be necessary to gain a sufficiently deep understanding to be able to use them in your own programs, we have tried to use 'meaningful' names and appropriate comments.

The '*System*' *toolbox* provides a number of global definitions and utility functions, which we have used to customize our environment and ensure compatibility among different Scheme dialects. Its contents is shown in Figure 3.4.

DisplayLine and **DisplayList** are two procedures we provide for convenience, and also in order to reduce the bulk of our code. Both generalize Scheme's display function in that they will accept a variable number of arguments and print them, separated by spaces. The sole difference between them is due to the fact that **DisplayLine** will also perform a 'newline' operation at the end. **BeginGraphics** and **EndGraphics** are currently only used in some of the game examples. They test the global **AllowGraphics** flag and will then open a graphics window if graphical displays can be supported in a particular environment. Although our toolboxes have been designed for didactical purposes and cannot be expected to perform any extensive error checking, **Fatal-Error** is used internally to catch and flag obvious misuses of toolbox functions. To customize the system's responses the user can associate an appropriate continuation with **Error-Continuation**, which will be called with parameter '*ERROR-VALUE*'. If **Error-Continuation** is **#f** this will default to a 'reset' at the top level. Other utility functions include **MyRandom**, a simple random number generator, **EvalExp** and **MyPrettyPrint**. Again we must caution the user against overly high expectations regarding the 'randomness' of the numbers produced. **MyRandom** will default to the standard generator for the Scheme version in use, if there is one; otherwise a congruential method will be provided, whose performance is very dependent on judiciously chosen seeds. As in MacScheme's *Random* function, it will return a randomly distributed non-negative integer less than *n*. As we mentioned before, we have avoided use of **eval** anywhere but for the *C-Flavour* system. The reason for this restraint can be traced to the fact that it is not a standard feature of Scheme. Most implementations, however, will provide their own version, which may differ with regard to the exact nature of the environment in which evaluation will occur. MacScheme, for example, uses the top-level environment, unless a different one is explicitly specified. **EvalExp** has

Global Variable	Meaning
Scheme Version	currently used version (for example, MacScheme)
INFINITY	largest positive fixnum
NEG-INFINITY	smallest negative fixnum
Error-Continuation	can store a continuation to be used if 'Fatal-Error' is called (see below)
AllowGraphics	flag which is tested before any attempts at producing graphical output are made
Routine Name	**Parameters**
	Display functions
DisplayLine	any number of items
DisplayList	any number of items
BeginGraphics	
EndGraphics	
	Error-handling functions
Fatal-Error	any number of items
	Utility functions
MyRandom	an integer as an upper bound
EvalExp	an expression
MyPrettyPrint	an expression

Figure 3.4 The global variables and functions contained in the 'System' toolbox.

therefore only been used in order to 'automate' toolbox testing. **MyPrettyPrint** uses a particularly 'neat' scheme of indentation to display expressions. Most Scheme implementations will again provide their own version.

The hierarchy illustrated in Figure 3.5 shows the dependencies between toolboxes. To use any of these toolboxes you will have to load all the dependent toolbox files, which will always include the 'System' one. For example, the *Systems.scm*, *Patterns.scm*, *KnowledgeBases.scm* and *Productions.scm* files will first have to be loaded in order to use the features offered by the 'Productions' toolbox. The suffix '*.scm*' is used to indicate code files. Alternatively, if you acquire the toolbox disk for the Macintosh, you can start any particular toolbox directly from the toolbox's *heap* image.

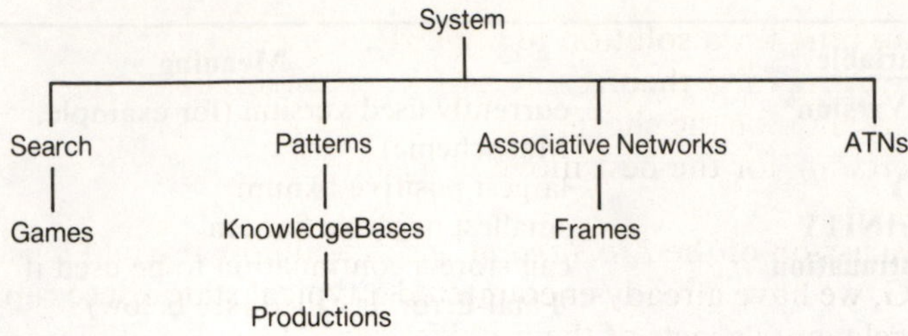

Figure 3.5 Hierarchy of dependencies between toolboxes.

3.2 The state space metaphor

'Search is centrally concerned with discovery, reasoning with proof.'

[*Simon (1983), p. 9.*]

3.2.1 Search, planning and problem solving

Problem solving and planning are central concerns of AI. As we have seen in Section 3.1, these tasks will always require both an appropriate structural representation, and a process for finding solutions. Search is one of a number of possible perspectives from which the problem-solving process may be analyzed. Deductive reasoning and constraint satisfaction offer alternative viewpoints. According to Simon, we may describe the 'world', or rather some relevant part of it, as a kind of 'space' in which treasures are hidden. The *state space metaphor* is a helpful way of visualizing a large class of such problems.

State space representations regard each valid configuration of entities, their values and relationships, as a *state* in some *state space.* One of these is designated as an *initial state* and represents the starting configuration, while solutions are known as *goal states.* Valid changes to a given configuration are encoded by *actions* or *operations,* which will act on a state to produce a new one. Problem solving now maps on to the process of searching this state space for a sequence of actions that produce a path from the initial state to a goal.

This idea of searching in state spaces played a central role in the early years of AI. In fact, at some point early workers in the field felt that search 'was' AI, but this is no longer a common view. As a research program, 'heuristic' search is built around a core of related ideas dealing with deduction, inference, planning, reasoning and proof procedures. A good summary is given by Nilsson (1971) and Pearl (1984). Some typical problems which are well suited to this paradigm are:

- Searching for a solution to a puzzle.
- Searching for a theorem in logic or mathematics.
- Searching for the shortest path in a graph.
- Searching for the best move in a game.

In our discussion of the *Lineland* program and how it could be solved in PROLOG, we have already encountered a typical state space representation. All relevant aspects of the problem could be encoded by a vector of five elements (the room), each of which was labelled as either empty, holding a lecturer (white token), or a student (grey token). The initial state was obvious from the problem specification, patterns of movement were encoded as 'hops' of the empty seat, and any state in which all students were placed in front of all the lecturers fulfilled our goal criterion.

Efficiently searching such state spaces hinges on strategies for 'pruning' unpromising paths of deduction, so that we always make just enough of the search space explicit to retain a solution. Newell and Simon [Hayes (1978), pp. 145–146] have coined the term *'British Museum Algorithm'* for any strategy involving exhaustive search, which is rarely feasible for other than trivial problems. The name dates back to the time of their work on the *Logic Theorist* program, when they tentatively hypothesized and immediately rejected such an exhaustive proof procedure. They illustrated their proposal by describing the lively scenario of 1000 monkeys with 1000 typewriters, locked into the cellar of the British Museum. Given even some modest degree of 'academic' curiosity in typewriters, they would surely eventually have to produce all the volumes held in that prestigious institution. Of course, the problem is that 'eventually' may take quite a while. Examining all possible sequences of n moves would lead to a search space in which the number of nodes grows exponentially with n, a phenomenon which is often referred to as '*combinatorial explosion*'. If we allow 26 letters and a space as valid symbols, there are then 27^{100} possible strings of length 100 [Hayes (1978), p. 146]. Even if we ignore any possible repetitions, this number is obviously much larger than we should reasonably expect our monkeys to produce in a million years of typing. Fortunately there are a number of alternative problem-solving strategies, some of which we will explore in this section.

There are basically two directions in which state spaces may be searched. '*Forward chaining*' proceeds to modify the initial state until a goal is reached, while '*backward chaining*' requires operators to reduce goals to subgoals, which may then be easier to solve. This is a recursive process, which terminates as soon as only solved or trivial problems remain. A more complex kind of backward reasoning ('*problem reduction*') occurs if a problem may be divided into a conjunction of

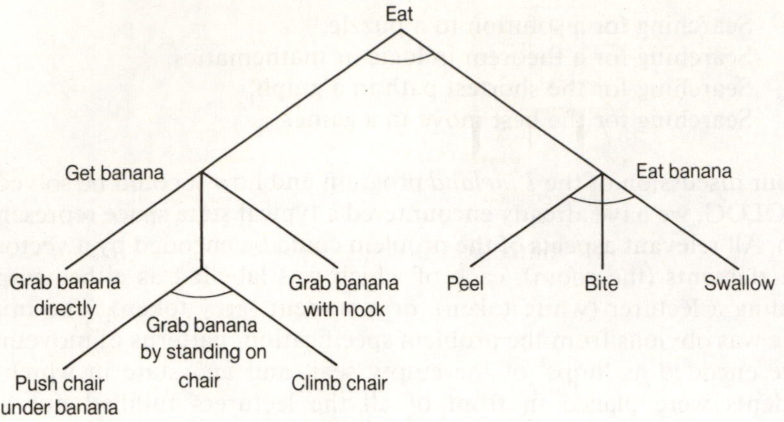

Figure 3.6 A problem decomposition.

subproblems, each significantly easier than the original one. There may or may not be constraints on the order in which we are to solve the subproblems. A variation on the notorious 'monkey and banana' puzzle may serve to illustrate this. Let us picture a monkey standing at the door into a room in which a banana is suspended on a string from the ceiling. The monkey is hungry and would like to eat the banana (goal). Although it is too high for him to reach, there are a number of actions (moves) he may still try to explore. Figure 3.6 shows a partial decomposition of the problem into subtasks, using a so-called 'AND/OR tree'. 'And' nodes, *all* subproblems of which must be solved in order to satisfy the goal, are symbolized by an arc (that is, the monkey must *peel* and *bite* and *swallow* the banana in order to eat it). Subgoals for 'or' nodes, however, are disjunctive (that is, *grab* the banana directly, or *grab* the banana by standing on a chair, or *grab* the banana with a hook).

Another important technique involves a combination of forward and backward reasoning, and is called '*means/ends analysis*'. The current situation is compared with the current goal and some measure of 'difference' (distance) between the two is computed. This number is then used to find the best operator to reduce this difference. This strategy was used by the famous General Problem Solver (GPS) program [Newell and Simon (1972)].

Game-playing problems must account for an opponent's as well as the player's own moves. The usual game-tree representations therefore share many features with problem reduction.

The 8-puzzle problem

This problem is set in the context of a 3×3 grid of 8 tiles, numbered as one to eight. These are initially located in the positions shown in Figure

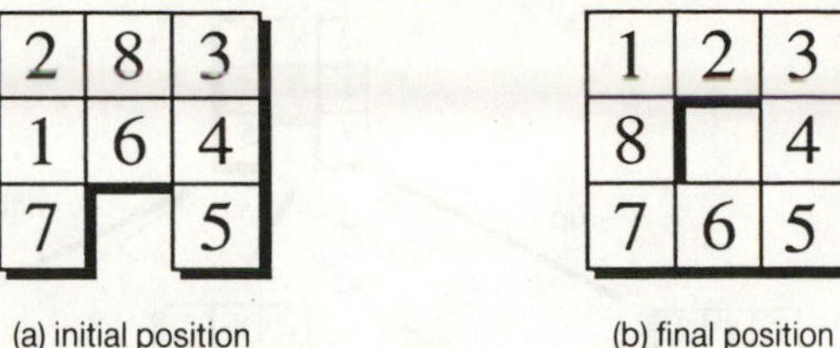

Figure 3.7 Initial and final positions for 8-puzzle problem.

3.7(a) and may only be moved by one space up, down, left or right, within the confines of the grid, and into the empty position. The problem asks for a sequence of moves that will yield the final configuration as shown in Figure 3.7(b).

The first step in mapping a problem into the state space metaphor is to identify its relevant states. In this problem we may use the tiles' relative positions. Valid actions are transformations between states – for example, whenever a tile may move to an empty position. It is easier to visualize this in terms of swapping the empty position with a tile, one place up, down, left or right. There is also the restriction that no tile may move outside the 3 × 3 grid, yielding four different actions or operators:

- Up – move the empty position one place up.
- Down – move the empty position one place down.
- Left – move the empty position one place to the left.
- Right – move the empty position one place to the right.

The solution to this puzzle has now been reduced to the problem of finding a sequence of applying these operators, so that we will eventually reach a goal from the given initial state. One such sequence, for example, is represented by: *up, up, left, down, right.*

State space graphs

A graphical view of the state space can serve to picture the effect of applying all valid actions to each of the states. This is called a *state space graph* or *state/action tree.* The initial state forms its root, and the daughters of any node are produced by applying valid actions to the state which is represented by it. Such transformations are shown as arcs, which may be labelled by the action involved. States that do not result in any further valid states form the leaves of this tree, while the number of actions (arcs), which may 'in principle' be applied to each state (node), determines the *branching factor*, four in this case. We shall limit our attention to pure tree structures and deal with repeating states (cycles) in

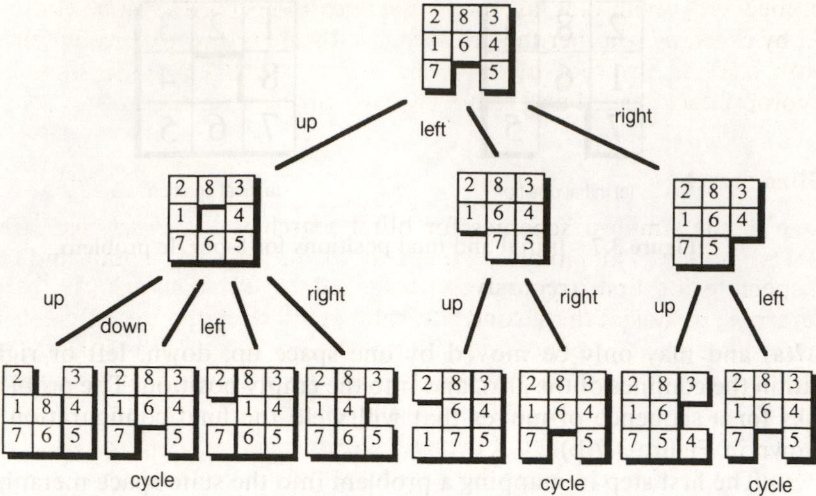

Figure 3.8 A portion of a state space graph for the 8-puzzle problem.

other ways. A portion of the corresponding graph for the 8-puzzle problem is shown in Figure 3.8, pruned of all arcs leading to invalid states (that is, those 'outside' the 3 × 3 square).

Search strategies

Solving a search problem within the state space metaphor now reduces to a search for goal states in the corresponding state/action tree. This requires inspection of states in some order, until a goal is found. In practice the computational effort of inspecting states and the generation of the tree will of course be done in parallel. We can formulate a large number of strategies for deciding in which order states should be generated and inspected. In the following sections we shall consider a few of the more common forms. Such strategies can usefully be divided into two classes: *blind* search strategies and *heuristic* search strategies. Blind search methods stick to a predetermined order of inspection, without using any information about previously inspected states to guide future search. Heuristic search methods, on the other hand, attempt to derive estimates of a state's likely distance from a goal state at each stage of the search; a measure which can then be used to focus the search on a particular branch.

It is necessary to carefully avoid potential *cycles* in the tree. For example, in the 8-puzzle problem's state space graph of Figure 3.8 the initial state reappears after the actions *up* and *down* have been performed. It would be possible to avoid trivial cycles by storing the last move that generated a given state and then not generating moves that immediately undo that last move. More complex cycles can be eliminated by checking whether the last generated state is already present on the path back to the root of the tree; if it is, then that node should be appropriately flagged and removed from further consideration.

Blind search

One of the simplest schemes for blind search is the *depth-first search* (**DFS**) strategy. This involves generating all daughters of a node and then inspecting the first, (recursively) followed by all its daughters, before returning to look at the second and subsequent daughter nodes. Since the state space graph may not be finite, or because it may be very deep, it is usually necessary to limit the search to some maximum depth. A solution will of course only be found if a goal state exists within the depth to which the tree has been searched. Furthermore, no valid path from root to goal found by this method can be guaranteed to have the fewest possible moves.

Figure 3.9 again shows the 8-puzzle's state space graph, drawn to a depth of three, with labels indicating the order in which nodes would be inspected during a depth-first search. While the search is in progress, only that part of the tree which includes all nodes on the current path and their elder (those to the right) sisters need to be stored, rather than the whole tree. Thus when the node labelled 12 is about to be inspected, only the part of the tree containing nodes 1, 10 and 12 needs to be stored.

Breadth-first search (**BFS**) offers an alternative strategy. *All* nodes at a given level of the search tree will be investigated before those at the next deeper level are examined. Under this strategy it is unnecessary to limit the depth of the search (assuming there is a solution or the tree is finite), and any solution found will be one with the shortest possible path from the root node. However, since the whole of the tree down to the current depth must be stored, considerably more memory is needed, particularly for trees with a large branching factor.

Figure 3.10 shows the order in which the nodes of the 8-puzzle problem's state space graph will be inspected during the first stages of a breadth-first search.

Heuristic search

In an attempt to improve the search's effectiveness, heuristic techniques will attempt to use (typically approximate) information obtained from states which have already been visited. At each stage they will try to focus a search in a particularly 'promising' direction, so that fewer states need to be generated and inspected. For example, if it were known, at every node of the tree, exactly which of the possible actions are on the path to

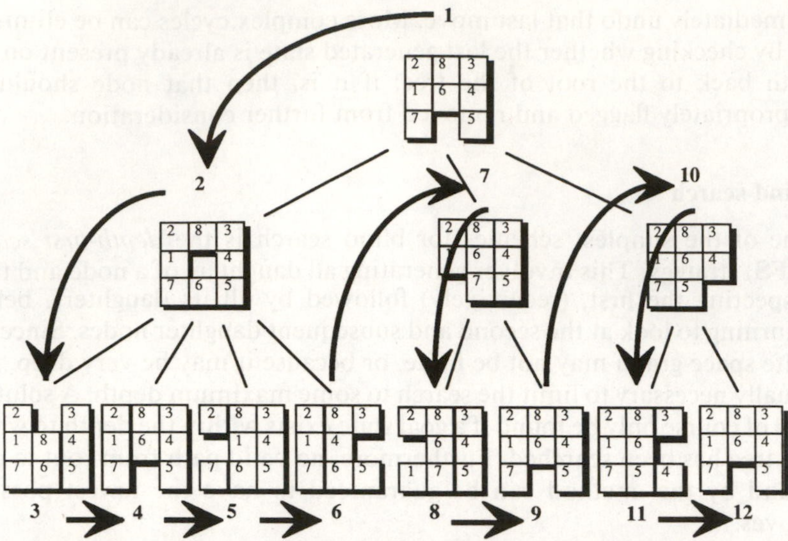

Figure 3.9 The order in which the nodes of the 8-puzzle problem state space graph are inspected by a depth-first search to level 3.

the shallowest goal state, then only states on the solution path would ever need to be generated. In practice this is usually far too much to hope for, but if we were somehow in a position to compare the likelihood for this property across a given set of candidates, then the cost of finding a goal state could be significantly reduced.

Another important consideration is whether we are content with *any* solution to a problem or whether we require one that satisfies some further criteria. For example, we may be interested in finding the solution which is at the shallowest depth in the tree. Or there may be costs involved in each action, and we want the solution which lies on a path for which the sum of the costs is minimized. If the cost of each move is 'one', then the second case includes the first. In the rest of this section we shall assume that any solution is acceptable, since minimal cost solutions typically require more sophisticated techniques [*see*, for example, McMillan (1975)].

The most common method of evaluating the suitability of any state for further expansion is to attempt to find an *evaluation function* that may be applied to a state and will yield a 'score' which measures the likely 'distance' to a goal state. Let us assume that this function yields larger values for states that are closer to a goal state, and smaller values for those that are further away. In practice the function used need not give strictly monotonically increasing values, but if this can be ensured, then the following heuristics are more likely to be effective.

For example, in the 8-puzzle problem we might choose an evaluation function that involves the sum, over all tiles, of the number of steps which are required to move that tile into its proper position. Such

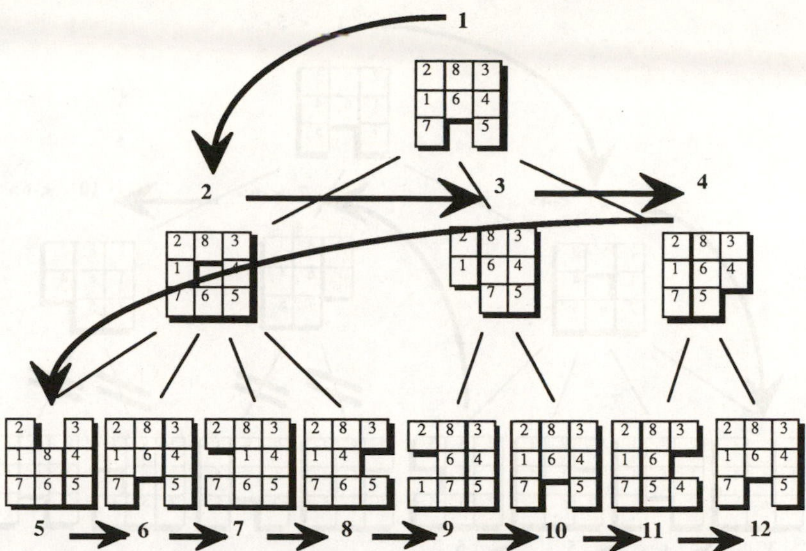

Figure 3.10 The order in which the first few nodes of the 8-puzzle problem state space graph are inspected in breadth-first search.

a measure is often referred to as the *Manhattan distance.* As we require our evaluation function to yield larger values for better states we would need to take the negative of this sum.

The *hill climbing search* (**HCS**) strategy generates all successors of a state and then prunes all those daughter states which have a lower score than their parent. During this pruning process the strategy generates and inspects states in a depth-first manner. If a state has no successors, or if some predetermined depth in the tree is reached, the search 'backs up' for one level and other nodes with non-decreasing scores are considered. This heuristic of only investigating paths that have states with non-decreasing scores can be quite effective in reducing the number of states that need to be generated and inspected. If a goal state exists within the specified depth of the search, and if it lies on a path from the root of the tree where all states have non-decreasing scores, then this method guarantees that a solution will be found. Hill climbing can easily be 'misled' by bad terrain, however. If all goal states within this depth of the tree lie on paths where the score decreases at some point, then no solution will be found at all. The so-called 'foothill' problem occurs when there are secondary maxima, and the procedure will 'peak' at a suboptimal solution. It is prone to miss a solution completely if the search space is mostly 'flat' (leaving the score unchanged), with small, steeply rising 'plateaux'. Both the DFS and BFS methods would eventually find such solutions.

Figure 3.11 shows the order in which nodes will be inspected during the early part of a hill climbing search in the 8-puzzle problem. The scores for each state are shown in angle brackets.

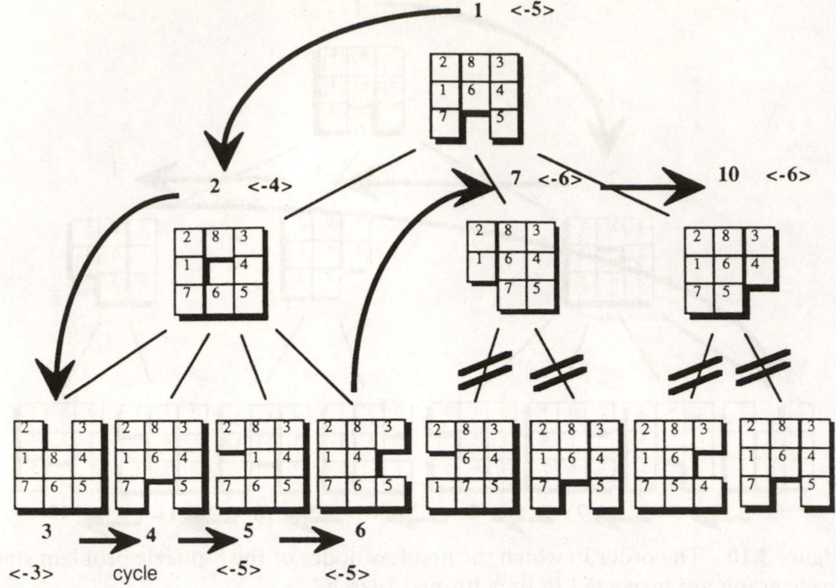

Figure 3.11 Order in which the nodes of the 8-puzzle state space graph are inspected in a hill climbing search to level 3. The score for each state is given in angle brackets.

The *steepest search* (SS) strategy generates all successors of a state and then chooses the state with the highest score for further inspection. If several states have an equally high score, one is arbitrarily chosen – for example, the rightmost one. Thus at any point in the search only a single node at each level of the tree is retained and only a single path is investigated. If both evaluation function and state space are 'well behaved', this method finds a solution with very little effort. If, however, the path 'dies' at a node with no successors, then no solution is found at all. Therefore a solution is often found quickly, but only if it lies on a path where the states' scores rise the fastest.

Figure 3.12 shows the order in which nodes will be inspected during the early part of a steepest search in the 8-puzzle problem. Scores for each state are shown in angle brackets.

Toolbox outline

Appendix III contains a '*Search*' *toolbox* which allows experimentation with different styles of search method and problems. Like all the toolboxes described in this chapter it is built in layers, where subsequent layers make use of concepts defined in earlier ones. Its top-level functions are summarized in Figure 3.13. The following brief outline should be completed by browsing through the comments and the code in Appendix III.

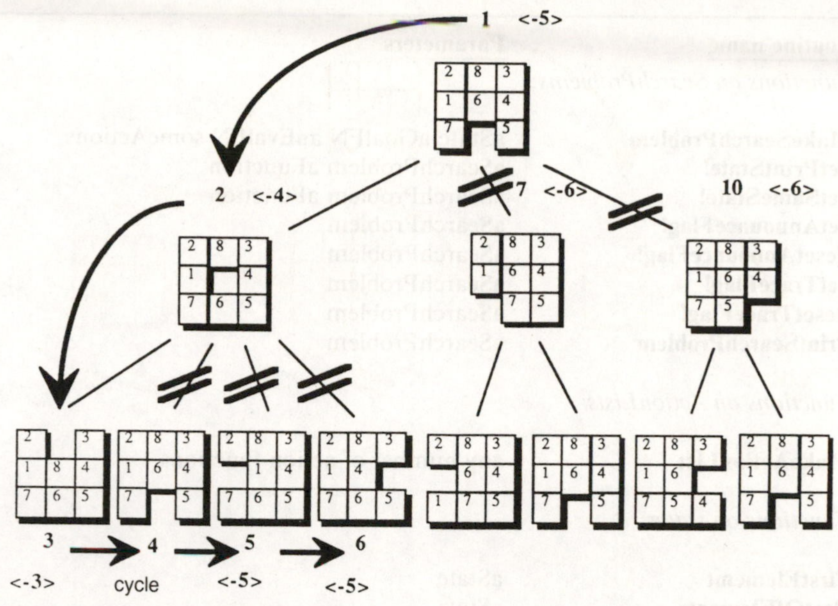

Figure 3.12 Order in which the nodes of the 8-puzzle state space graph are inspected in a steepest search to level 3. The score for each state is given in angle brackets.

A *SearchProblem* may be constructed by using **MakeSearchProblem**, a toolbox routine which expects four parameters: an initial state, two functions and a list. Each of the two functions themselves will expect a state as a parameter. The first will return **#t** for goal states and **#f** for non-goal states, while the second is an evaluation function to score states according to some heuristic. The final parameter is an *ActionList*. It may be constructed through the toolbox routine **MakeActionList**, taking any number of functions as parameters. Each permissible action is implemented by such a function, which takes a state as a parameter and yields a new state as a result. It returns **#f** if the move is invalid for that state. A *SearchProblem* will therefore contain all relevant global information and may then be supplied as a parameter to the functions performing various types of search.

SetPrintState! can be used optionally to add a function to a *SearchProblem*. This function will print the state representation in a more readable form, rather than using the standard **display** procedure. It will accept the state description as a parameter. Fairly complicated tests may sometimes be necessary to detect cycles in a state space graph. **SetSameState!** can modify the function used to compare two states for equality (**equal?** by default). The comparison function will expect both states as parameters. It is also possible to control the output of tracing information (which takes the form of dumps of the current state space)

Routine name	Parameters
Functions on SearchProblems:	
MakeSearchProblem	aState aGoalFN anEvalFN someActions
SetPrintState!	aSearchProblem aFunction
SetSameState!	aSearchProblem aFunction
SetAnnounceFlag!	aSearchProblem
ResetAnnounceFlag!	aSearchProblem
SetTraceFlag!	aSearchProblem
ResetTraceFlag!	aSearchProblem
PrintSearchProblem	aSearchProblem
Functions on ActionLists:	
MakeActionList	any number of action functions
Functions on states:	
FirstElememt	aState
RestOfElements	aState
EmptyState?	aState
FindSymbolInSlot	aSlotNumber aState
FindFirstSlotOfSymbol	aSymbol aState
FillSlot	aSlotNumber aSymbol aState
Functions to perform searches:	
DFSearch	aSearchProblem aMaxDepth
BFSearch	aSearchProblem
HillSearch	aSearchProblem aMaxDepth
SteepestSearch	aSearchProblem

Figure 3.13 Summary of the 'Search' toolbox interface routines.

while the search is in progress (routines **SetTraceFlag!** and **ResetTrace Flag!**). The routines **SetAnnounceFlag!** and **ResetAnnounceFlag!** are provided to toggle the display of information about the final solution (if any) of the search and the number of actions applied. If the problem uses a list structure as its state representation, then the following routines for state manipulation may prove useful. **FirstElement**, **RestOfElements** and **EmptyState?** correspond to *car, cdr* and *empty*? respectively. The routine **FindSymbolInSlot** yields the element stored in a particular slot of the list (numbered from zero for the first element), while **FindFirstSlotOfSymbol** yields the slot number of the first element matching (in the sense of **eq?**) a particular symbol. Finally, **FillSlot** yields a new state, with a particular slot value replaced by a new one.

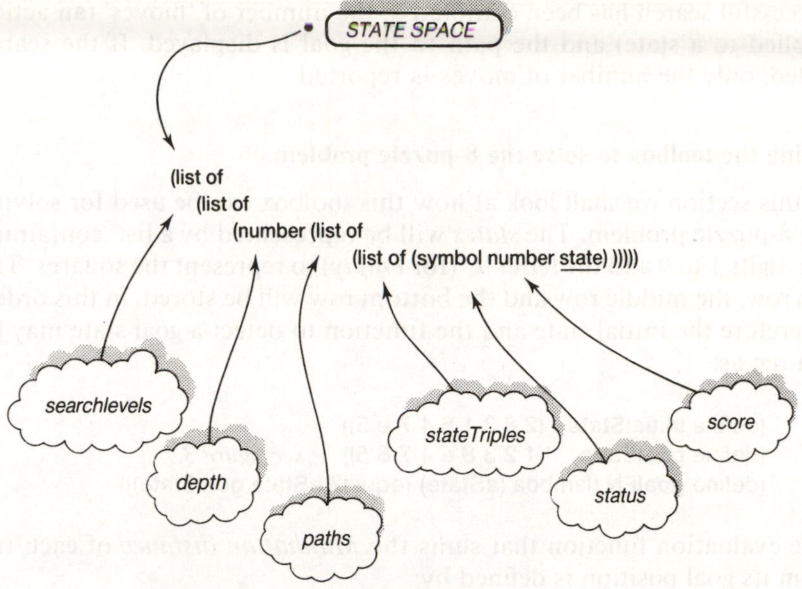

Figure 3.14 Toolbox representation of state spaces.

Internally the toolbox stores a *StateSpace* as a list of *SearchLevels*, which in turn consist of a list whose first element defines its depth, and the remaining elements are *Paths* of that depth in the state space graph.

Procedures **DFSearch**, **BFSearch**, **HillSearch** and **SteepestSearch** are provided as examples of search functions. For any particular *Search-Problem* they allow us to search for a single goal. These routines are implemented by supplying an appropriate argument to the **Search** routine. These functions also determine what the current *StateSpace* contains after the current state is inspected. Each *path* is a list of states, ordered from the deepest state on the path to the initial one. The first state of the first *Path* of the first *SearchLevel* is always the state which is currently inspected. For example, the **DFSearch** method applies each of the actions to the current state if its depth is less than the *MaxDepth* to which it is expected to search. Any resulting new states are appended to the current path to form a new set of paths at a depth one greater than this one. These are then combined to form a new search level, which is added to the front of the *StateSpace* after the current path is deleted. Each time a new *StateSpace* is constructed, the current state is tested with *GoalFN* to see if a goal has been reached and the search has succeeded, or if the *StateSpace* is empty, which indicates that the search has failed.

After a successful search the **Search** routines return a list of the form (*depth-of-path number-of-moves solution-path*). They return **#f** upon failure. If **SetAnnounceFlag!** has previously been called, then after a successful search has been completed, the number of 'moves' (an action applied to a state) and the path to the goal is displayed. If the search failed, only the number of moves is reported.

Using the toolbox to solve the 8-puzzle problem

In this section we shall look at how this toolbox can be used for solving the 8-puzzle problem. The *states* will be represented by a list, containing the digits 1 to 9 and the letter 'e' (for *empty*) to represent the squares. The top row, the middle row and the bottom row will be stored, in this order. Therefore the initial state and the function to detect a goal state may be written as:

```
(define initialState  '(2 8 3 1 6 4 7 e 5))
(define goalState     '(1 2 3 8 e 4 7 6 5))   ; see figure 3.7
(define goalFN (lambda (aState) (equal? aState goalState)))
```

The evaluation function that sums the *Manhattan distance* of each tile from its goal position is defined by:

```
(define evalFN
 (lambda (aState)

  (define movesRequired
   (lambda (source dest)

  ; how many moves does it take to get from 'source' to 'dest'?
  (vector-ref
   (vector-ref
    (vector
     ; dest 1 2 3 4 5 6 7 8 9
     ;      _ _ _ _ _ _ _ _ _
     (vector 0 1 2 1 2 3 2 3 4)  ; source 1 to others
     (vector 1 0 1 2 1 2 3 2 3)  ; source 2 to others
     (vector 2 1 0 3 2 1 4 3 2)  ; source 3 to others
     (vector 1 2 3 0 1 2 1 2 3)  ; source 4 to others
     (vector 2 1 2 1 0 1 2 1 2)  ; source 5 to others
     (vector 3 2 1 2 1 0 3 2 1)  ; source 6 to others
     (vector 2 3 4 1 2 3 0 1 2)  ; source 7 to others
     (vector 3 2 3 2 1 2 1 0 1)  ; source 8 to others
     (vector 4 3 2 3 2 1 2 1 0)  ; source 9 to others
     )
   (- source 1) )   ; vector indices start at 0 !
  (- dest 1))) )    ; vector indices start at 0 !

  ; accumulate for each of tiles 1 thru to 8
  (do   ((tile 1 (+ 1 tile))  ; start and increment
         (moves 0))
        ((> tile 8) moves)    ; termination and val. returned
```

```
(let ((source (FindFirstSlotOfSymbol tile aState))
      (dest (FindFirstSlotOfSymbol tile goalState)))
  (set! moves
        ; Manhattan dist. is negative (!) of sum
        (- moves (movesRequired source dest)))))))
```

Action routines are generated by the following function, which, for each cell (*emptyTo*), requires a list of positions the empty cell can move to; that is, **(#f #f #f 1 2 3 4 5 6)** for all moves in the 'upwards' direction. **#f** is encoded to indicate it would move off the edge of the 3 × 3 grid (invalid).

```
(define makeMove
  (lambda (emptyTo)
    ; returns a function to move the empty cell as
    ; indicated by the list of moves in emptyTo
    (lambda (aState)
      (let* ((emptyCell (FindFirstSlotOfSymbol 'e aState))
             (newCell (FindSymbolInSlot emptyCell emptyTo)))
        (if (not newCell)
            #f ; would move empty cell off frame
            (FillSlot
              newCell   ; empty the vacated spot
              'e
              (FillSlot emptyCell   ; fill the destination
                        (FindSymbolInSlot newCell aState)
                        aState)))))))
```

A routine to print states laid out on a 3 × 3 grid is defined by:

```
(define 8-printState
  (lambda (aState)
    (define printIn3s
      (lambda (aList)
        (if (null? aList)
            #f
            (begin (display (list (car aList)
                                  (cadr aList)
                                  (caddr aList)))
                   (printIn3s (cdddr aList) ) ) ) ) )
    (display "[")
    (printIn3s aState)
    (display "]")))
```

Finally the *SearchProblem* itself is constructed:

```
(set! 8-SearchProblem
  (MakeSearchProblem
    initialState
```

```
        goalFN
        evalFN
        (MakeActionList
          (makeMove '(#f #f #f 1 2 3 4 5 6))   ; up
          (makeMove '(4 5 6 7 8 9 #f #f #f))   ; down
          (makeMove '(#f 1 2 #f 4 5 #f 7 8))   ; left
          (makeMove '(2 3 #f 5 6 #f 8 9 #f))   ; right
        )))
(SetPrintState! 8-SearchProblem 8-printState)
```

This can now be used for experimentation. Figure 3.15 is an (edited) transcript of output from the toolbox routines, when various search methods are used on this problem. It starts with a *depth-first search* to a level of three, with the *trace* flag set. Each state space is shown as it is constructed, and it can be observed that deeper (longer) paths are investigated prior to those at shallower levels. When a path reaches the maximum depth (three), it is pruned from the state space and the search is continued with the remainder. A search level is itself pruned from consideration if it turns out to be empty. Eventually there are no levels remaining and the search terminates with failure; a fact indicated by returning a null list (equivalent to **#f**). Note that each state's *score* is bound to a large negative number ('infinity' as defined by the toolbox; here shown as *–INF*), since this class of search uses no evaluation function.

Subsequent searches are performed with the *announce* flag set, so that the number of moves made during the search is displayed, and the successful path (if any) is also shown. This time the *trace* flag is turned off, to reduce the amount of output. The depth-first search to depth three is repeated; it fails again, and we learn that 16 actions were applied to states during the search. A depth-first search to a depth of ten, however, reports success after 52 moves. This solution is shown as a trace from the goal back to the initial state. It is found at a depth of six (after five transformations). The solution is identical to the one mentioned earlier: *up*, *up*, *left*, *down*, *right*.

A *breadth-first search* is performed next. It finds exactly the same solution, but only after 136 moves have been tried. This result should not be interpreted as any indication that this form of searching is less efficient than the depth-first strategy. Such a judgement would have to be qualified by the location of the goal states, the order in which actions are applied and the depth limit of the search. For example, if the only goal state is 'to the right' at the second level of a tree, then a breadth-first search will locate it as soon as it has applied each of the valid actions to its initial state – that is, after only four moves. On the other hand, a depth-first search may then have to investigate large sections of the tree if its limiting depth was set to a large number. To emphasize this in the context of the current problem, consider what happens if the order in which the

```
>>> (SetTraceFlag! 8-SearchProblem)

>>> (DFSearch 8-SearchProblem 3)
*** After 0 moves the state space is:
Level at depth 1 contains 1 path(s):
. . . . #<ok –INF [(2 8 3) (1 6 4) (7 e 5)]>

*** After 4 moves the state space is:
Level at depth 2 contains 4 path(s):
. . . . #<ok –INF [(2 8 3) (1 e 4) (7 6 5)]>
        #<ok –INF [(2 8 3) (1 6 4) (7 e 5)]>
. . . . Invalid path: #< invalid-state –INF [ ]>
                           #<ok –INF [(2 8 3) (1 6 4) (7 e 5)]>
. . . . #<ok –INF [(2 8 3) (1 6 4) (e 7 5)]>
        #<ok –INF [(2 8 3) (1 6 4) (7 e 5)]>
. . . . #<ok –INF [(2 8 3) (1 6 4) (7 5 e)]>
        #<ok –INF [(2 8 3) (1 6 4) (7 e 5)]>
Empty search level

*** After 8 moves the state space is:
Level at depth 3 contains 4 path(s):
. . . . #<ok –INF [(2 e 3) (1 8 4) (7 6 5)]>
        #<ok –INF [(2 8 3) (1 e 4) (7 6 5)]>
        #<ok –INF [(2 8 3) (1 6 4) (7 e 5)]>
. . . . Invalid path: #<cycle –INF [(2 8 3) (1 6 4) (7 e 5)]>
                           #<ok –INF [(2 8 3) (1 e 4) (7 6 5)]>
                           #<ok –INF [(2 8 3) (1 6 4) (7 e 5)]>
. . . . #<ok –INF [(2 8 3) (e 1 4) (7 6 5)]>
        #<ok –INF [(2 8 3) (1 e 4) (7 6 5)]>
        #<ok –INF [(2 8 3) (1 6 4) (7 e 5)]>
. . . . #<ok –INF [(2 8 3) (1 4 e) (7 6 5)]>
        #<ok –INF [(2 8 3) (1 e 4) (7 6 5)]>
        #<ok –INF [(2 8 3) (1 6 4) (7 e 5)]>
Level at depth 2 contains 3 path(s):
. . . . Invalid path: #<invalid-state –INF [ ]>
                           #<ok –INF [(2 8 3) (1 6 4) (7 e 5)]>
. . . . #<ok –INF [(2 8 3) (1 6 4) (e 7 5)]>
        #<ok –INF [(2 8 3) (1 6 4) (7 e 5)]>
. . . . #<ok –INF [(2 8 3) (1 6 4) (7 5 e)]>
        #<ok –INF [(2 8 3) (1 6 4) (7 e 5)]>
Empty search level
. and so on . . .

*** After 16 moves the state space is:
Empty search level
PruneTopLevel pruning empty level in state space!!
*** After 16 moves the state space is:
()
```

Figure 3.15 Edited transcript of output from the 'Search' toolbox as applied to the 8-puzzle problem.

```
>>> (SetAnnounceFlag! 8-SearchProblem)
>>> (ResetTraceFlag! 8-SearchProblem)
>>> (DFSearch 8-SearchProblem 3)
Search failed after 16 move(s)
()
>>> (DFSearch 8-SearchProblem 10)
Solution found after 52 move(s) at depth 6
Successful path (length 6) is:
#<ok -INF [(1 2 3) (8 e 4) (7 6 5)]>
#<ok -INF [(1 2 3) (e 8 4) (7 6 5)]>
#<ok -INF [(e 2 3) (1 8 4) (7 6 5)]>
#<ok -INF [(2 e 3) (1 8 4) (7 6 5)]>
#<ok -INF [(2 8 3) (1 e 4) (7 6 5)]>
#<ok -INF [(2 8 3) (1 6 4) (7 e 5)]>
(6 52 (#(ok -536870911 (1 2 3 8 e 4 7 6 5)) . . . )
>>> (BFSearch 8-SearchProblem)
Solution found after 136 move(s) at depth 6
Successful path (length 6) is:
#<ok -INF [(1 2 3) (8 e 4) (7 6 5)]>
#<ok -INF [(1 2 3) (e 8 4) (7 6 5)]>
#<ok -INF [(e 2 3) (1 8 4) (7 6 5)]>
#<ok -INF [(2 e 3) (1 8 4) (7 6 5)]>
#<ok -INF [(2 8 3) (1 e 4) (7 6 5)]>
#<ok -INF [(2 8 3) (1 6 4) (7 e 5)]>
(6 136 (#(ok -536870911 (1 2 3 8 e 4 7 6 5)) . . . . )
>>> (HillSearch 8-SearchProblem 10)
Solution found after 20 move(s) at depth 6
Successful path (length 6) is:
#<ok 0 [(1 2 3) (8 e 4) (7 6 5)]>
#<ok -1 [(1 2 3) (e 8 4) (7 6 5)]>
#<ok -2 [(e 2 3) (1 8 4) (7 6 5)]>
#<ok -3 [(2 e 3) (1 8 4) (7 6 5)]>
#<ok -4 [(2 8 3) (1 e 4) (7 6 5)]>
#<ok -5 [(2 8 3) (1 6 4) (7 e 5)]>
(6 20 (#(ok 0 (1 2 3 8 e 4 7 6 5)) . . . . )
>>> (SteepestSearch 8-SearchProblem)
Solution found after 20 move(s) at depth 6
Successful path (length 6) is:
#<ok 0 [(1 2 3) (8 e 4) (7 6 5)]>
#<ok -1 [(1 2 3) (e 8 4) (7 6 5)]>
#<ok -2 [ (e 2 3) (1 8 4) (7 6 5)]>
#<ok -3 [(2 e 3) (1 8 4) (7 6 5)]>
#<ok -4 [(2 8 3) (1 e 4) (7 6 5)]>
#<ok -5 [(2 8 3) (1 6 4) (7 e 5)]> . . . . )
```

Figure 3.15 (cont.)

actions are applied is reversed to '*right, left, down and up*'. Now the same depth-first search takes 1052 moves and finds a solution at depth ten, while a breadth-first search again finds the solution after 236 moves at depth six.

Heuristic search has been a very active research area for a relatively long time, and a great number of alternative techniques are therefore available. Some of these make use of powerful and sophisticated ideas, which are beyond the scope of this book. Pearl (1984) gives an excellent summary of the state of the art and Korf (1985) analyzes a variation of the 8-puzzle using a number of further search techniques. The last two search strategies we will investigate are *hill climbing* to depth ten and a *steepest search*. Both of these locate the solution at depth six, after only 20 moves. These search heuristics therefore do in fact find a shortest path solution, since we know there can be no path shorter than length six or it would have been located during the breadth-first search. They also expand only the minimum number of states. This can largely be credited to the accuracy of the evaluation function used for this problem, whose scores increase monotonically along a solution path, and will immediately show a decrease once one moves off it. These scores, therefore, conveniently guide these methods to the optimal solution in the minimum number of moves. Even when the order of actions is reversed, as described above, the number of moves required remains at this minimum value.

A further experiment was performed, in order to illustrate the importance of an appropriate choice of evaluation function. For this scenario the evaluation function was changed so that it now simply counts the number of tiles in their 'correct' final position, and the order of actions was reversed. This new evaluation function will not discriminate between any changes which keep tiles in a non-final position, and it is therefore often unable to focus the search on the path to the nearest goal. Although the steepest search still locates a solution at depth six in 20 moves, the hill climbing search now gets trapped by a suboptimal path of 36 moves and finds a solution at depth ten.

A final example may serve to illustrate that for some problems it may often prove difficult to find any successful evaluation function at all. The '*missionaries and cannibals*' expedition has continued to haunt AI textbooks for decades. This problem is the best-known example of so-called 'river-crossing' scenarios, and Jeffries *et al.* (1977) gives a comprehensive discussion of this class of puzzles. Isomorphic problems have been described as '*monsters and globes*', '*hobbits and orcs*', '*elves and men*', and so on. '*Wolf, farmer and cabbage*' is a somewhat simplified version.

The objective is to enable a party of three missionaries and three cannibals to cross a river, somewhere in a remote wilderness. The usual formulation of this puzzle states that cannibals will eat missionaries as soon as they outnumber them on either of the two riverbanks. If you object to this racist perspective you may alternatively assume that missionaries will try to convert the poor cannibals to Christianity, once they get the upper hand. Both states of affairs are considered as invalid, and we must look for a strategy to allow a 'safe' (that is, no cannibalism or conversion) crossing. To enable the party to reach the opposite bank of the river at all, there is a boat with two seats only. 'Moves' may therefore represent the boat's crossings, from left to right or right to left. Any combination of missionaries and cannibals in the boat is allowed.

The problem is interesting, since there are no 'greedy' evaluation functions which permit 'linear' progress. We may have to be prepared to 'move away' from the goal first, in order to reach it eventually. In an attempt to find a suitable evaluation function for this problem it should be noted that such a function must *encourage* the missionaries and cannibals to move from one side of the river to the other. At first glance the difference between the number of people at the destination and the number on the original bank suggests itself as a candidate. However, under this heuristic all attempts to solve the problem through hill climbing will fail, because it is necessary to row the boat back to the original side after each crossing. Any such return journey will result in a decreasing score, and hence no path with non-decreasing scores can possibly lead to a goal state. It should also be noted that the reason the steepest search heuristic still finds a solution is due to the fact that the score of the steepest path is allowed to decrease, as long as the path that decreases the least is chosen.

3.2.2 Game playing, minimaxing and tree pruning

Game playing has long been a popular and fruitful area of investigation for AI. Early workers believed that such studies should yield valuable information about how computer programs could employ strategies similar to those observed in human problem solvers. Although AI has been quite successful in terms of producing game-playing programs that play a large class of games extremely well, and in some cases better than human experts, the techniques they applied have largely turned out to be quite different from those which are typically employed by human players. Judged as an attempt to obtain insight into human reasoning, these studies have therefore been somewhat disappointing. In spite of any such disappointment, this area remains a focus for active research and has yielded a number of interesting programming metaphors that are applicable to large classes of game-playing problems. Bramer (1983) gives a good summary of the state of the art in this field during the early 1980s.

In the rest of this section we will use a simple game to illustrate our discussion.

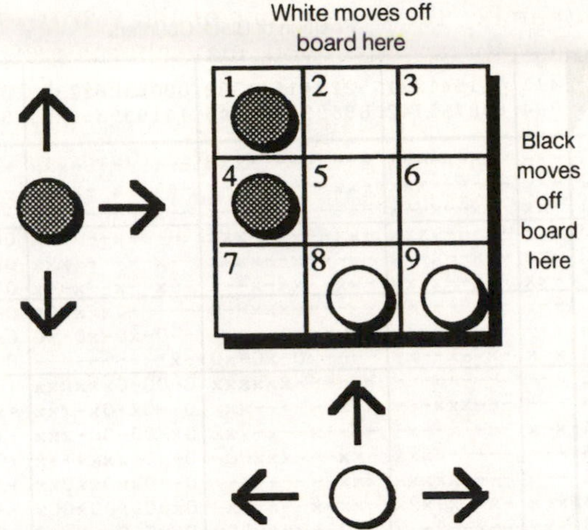

Figure 3.16 Initial board position and moves for 'Dodgem'. The numbers will be used to refer to positions occupied by the counters, with zero indicating that a counter is off the board.

The 'Dodgem' game problem

'Dodgem' is an interesting little game with a conveniently small branching factor. It was invented by Colin Vout [Berlekamp *et al.* (1982)] and is played with two black and two white counters on a 3 × 3 board. These counters' initial positions are shown in Figure 3.16. Only a single counter is allowed to occupy a particular board position at a time. Counters are constrained to the nine squares, except that the black counters will try to move off the board from the right-hand column (and cannot return to the board) while the white ones may move off the board from the top row. One of the players is in charge of the black counters and can, in a single move, guide one of them one step up, right or down. The opponent controls the white counters, which may move left, up or right. The goal of the game is to be the first to move both counters off the board. One may also win if the opponent creates a situation where the currently active player is left with no possible move remaining.

This game is quite interesting, in spite of the small board and the few pieces. Initially it is not at all obvious which playing strategies are likely to prove successful. However, the size of the game tree is small enough to enable every board position to be generated and analyzed. In the following discussion we shall assume that the machine plays the black counters and moves first. For each position we may determine which player should win under the best possible strategy. The table in Figure 3.17 gives the results of such an analysis [Berlekamp *et al.* (1982)], with rows referring to the position of the white, and columns to those of the black counters. The initial position corresponds to row 89 and column 14, and the '0' entry indicates that the first player who moves should win; always assuming that he follows a flawless strategy.

Position of Black Counters

Position of White Counters	411 774	741541221 888755742	522741641331 885999766743	000852652332 741999866853	000 852	633 996	000 963
03	---	---------	---------xxx	---------xxx	---	-xx	00x
02	---	------xxx	-xx---------	-----x--x--x	--x	---	000
01	-xx	--x--x--x	-----x--x--x	--x---------	---	---	000
23	---	------xxx	-xx------xxx	-----x--xxxx	00x	0xx	++x
13	-xx	--x--x--x	-----x--xxxx	--x------xxx	00-	0xx	++x
12	-xx	--x--xxxx	-xx--x--x--x	--x--x--x--x	00x	000	+++
06	---	---------	------xxx--0	-----0xxx00*	0-0	x+x	+x+
05	---	---xxx---	x-x---------	--0-x0-x0-x0	0x+	000	+++
04	x-x	-x--x--x-	----x0-x0-x0	-x*---------	000	000	+++
36	---	---------	------xxxxxx	0-00-0xxxxxx	+0*	xxx	+xx
35	---	---xxx---	x-x------xxx	0--0x-0x-xxx	+x0	+xx	++x
34	x-x	-x--x--x-	----x--x-xxx	0x-00-00-xxx	++0	+xx	++x
26	---	------xxx	-xx---xxx00-	0--0-xxxx++x	+0x	x+x	+x+
25	---	---xxxxxx	xxx---------	0--0xx0xx0xx	+xx	+++	+++
23	x-x	-x--x-xxx	-xx-x--x--x-	0x000x00x00x	++x	+++	+++
16	-xx	--x--x--x	-00--xxxx00x	0-x0-0xxx++0	+00	x+x	+x+
15	-xx	--xxxx--x	x0x--x--x--x	0-x0x+0x+0x+	+x+	+++	+++
14	xxx	-xx-xx-xx	----xx-xx-xx	0xx000000000	+++	+++	+++
09	---	----00--0	-00xxx0++00+	0-0xxx0++++0	*0+	xx+	x++
08	--0	xxx0++-00	xx0-00-00-00	-0+x++x++x++	x++	+++	+++
07	xx+	x-0x+0x+0	---x++x++x++	x+0000000000	+++	+++	+++
39	---	----0----	0-0xxx0+0xxx	-0-xxx+++xxx	0+0	xxx	x+x
38	---	xxx------	xx--0--0-xxx	-00x+0x+0xxx	x++	+xx	++x
37	xx-	x0-x0-x--	0--x+0x+0xxx	x+0++0++0xxx	+++	+xx	++x
29	---	----0-xxx	0xxxxx0+00+0	-0-xxx++x++x	0+x	xx+	x++
28	---	xxx---xxx	xxx-0--0--0-	-0-x+xx+xx+x	x+x	+++	+++
27	xx-	x0-x0-xxx	0xxx+0x+0x+0	x+0++x++x++x	++x	+++	+++
19	-xx	--x-0x00x	0++xxx0+x0+x	-0xxxx++++++	0++	xx+	x++
18	-xx	xxx--x-0x	xx+-0x-0x-0x	-0xx++x++x++	x++	+++	+++
17	xxx	x0xx0xx+x	000x+xx+xx+x	x+x+++++++++	+++	+++	+++
56	---	---xxx00-	x0x0--xxx++0	+00+x0xxx+x+	+x+	x+x	+x+
46	x-x	-x--x-0x0	-000x-xxx+x+	+x0+00xxx+++	+++	x+x	+x+
45	x-x	-x0xxx0x*	x+x0x00x00x0	+x++x++x++x+	+x+	+++	+++
69	---	-0-0-0000	*0+xxxxxx+++	000xxxxxx+++	+++	xxx	xx+
68	---	xxx---000	xx0-00xxx+++	-0+x++xxxx++	x++	x+x	+x+
67	xx-	x+0x0-x00	000x+0xxxx++	x++++xxx+++	+++	x+x	+x+
59	-00	--0xxx++0	x+xxxx++++++	0-0xxx+x++x+	+x+	xx+	x++
58	--0	xxxxxx0++	xxx0+00+00+0	--0xx+xx+xx+	xx+	+++	+++
57	xx0	x+0xxxx+0	x+xx++x++x++	x0++x++x++x+	+x+	+++	+++
49	x-x	-x00x00x+	0++xxx+x++x+	0x+xxx++++++	+++	xx+	x++
48	x-x	xxx-x+-x0	xx+0x+0x+0x+	+x+x++x++x++	x++	+++	+++
47	xxx	xx+xx+xx+	+++xx+xx+xx+	xx++++++++++	+++	+++	+++
89	-00	xxx000+++	xx+xxx++++++	-0+xxxx++x++	x++	xx+	x++
79	xx0	x++x+0x++	+++xxxx++x++	x++xxx++++++	+++	xx+	x++
78	xx+	xxxx++x++	xx+x++x++x++	x++x++x++x++	x++	+++	+++

Figure 3.17 Analysis of all possible board positions for 'Dodgem'. Entries are: + is a win for black, – is a win for white, 0 is a win for the player who moves first, * is a win for the player who moves second and x is an illegal position.

AND/OR trees and the role of an adversary

Many of the concepts used in game problems are identical or similar to those encountered in search problems. There is typically some sort of environment, such as a board with pieces, whose *configuration* corresponds to the concept of states. The set of legal *moves* describes how to transform a given state into a new one and corresponds to what we have previously called 'actions'. There is an *initial configuration*, and the *goal states* correspond to 'win' positions for the player in question. The process of applying moves to configurations can therefore again be pictured as a state space traversal.

The major contrast with the puzzle-solving examples, however, is that there is now at least one active *adversary* or opponent whom the game is played against. If we restrict ourselves to *two-person games*, actions must be divided into those which are available to the first and those which are available to the second player. 'Win' positions for one are 'loss' positions for the other. Our programs must therefore assume that an adversary moves in an attempt to force such a 'loss' position. The concept of a 'draw' position may also be applicable to many games; such a position will be preferred to a loss, but is clearly not as attractive as a win.

The presence of the adversary imposes a quite different view on the state space graph. It is no longer sufficient just to find a move that lies on a path to a goal or win, as any such move may give the opponent an opportunity to force (either directly or eventually) a loss position in return, a situation we clearly must strive to avoid. The state space graph must therefore now contain two different types of node: one corresponding to states where the next move is made by our program, and the other to states where the next move is made by an opponent. At the first type, referred to as *OR* nodes, the program may choose a move from a number of alternatives. This selection should be made in such a way that the best overall result will eventually be achieved. The opponent's decisions, however, must be encoded as *AND* nodes, where we need to consider all of an opponent's possible responses. An alternative way of thinking about these two types of nodes is that the problem consists of finding a win position, and the choice of which move to make at each node is equivalent to dividing the problem into a number of subproblems. At *AND* nodes the solution of the problem requires *all* the subproblems to be solved before any decision can be propagated upwards in the tree, while at *OR* nodes *only one* of the subproblems needs to be solved. A comparison with the state graphs used in the puzzle-solving examples shows that these consist of *OR* nodes only.

Figure 3.18 shows part of 'Dodgem's' state space graph. *AND* nodes are labelled by arcs connecting all subtasks.

Evaluation functions and goals

Another major distinction between search and game-playing problems is that in many interesting games the number of possible moves at any given state is so high, and the depth at which a goal may be found is so

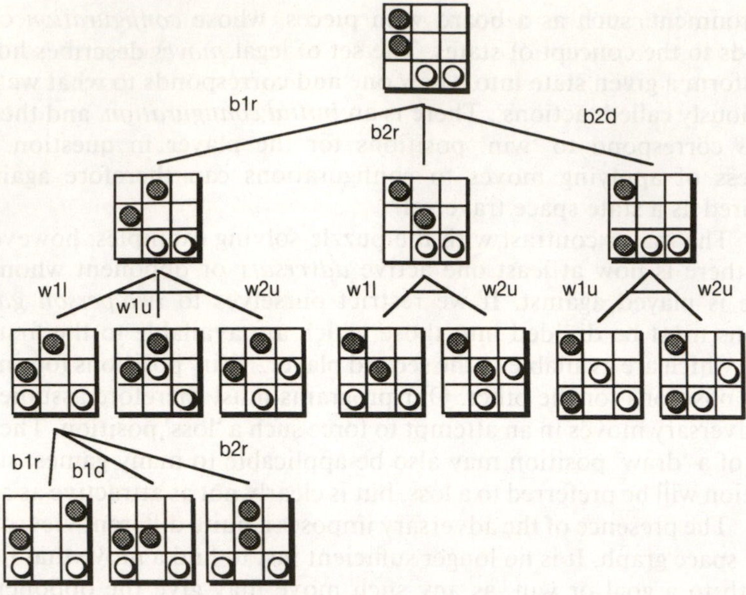

Figure 3.18 A portion of 'Dodgem's' state space graph. The arcs joining actions indicate *AND* nodes. The moves are labelled with colour (b or w), counter (1 or 2) and direction (u, d, r or l).

great, that it is completely unfeasible to select a move by exhaustive investigation. For example, in the game of chess it has been estimated that the state space graph for a 40-move game contains about 10^{120} non-terminal nodes [Newell and Simon (1972)]. This is larger than the estimated number of atoms in the universe. For this reason move selection will have to be made after considering only a small subset of the total state space. It is therefore most likely that no goal states can be found immediately. In practice this usually means that each time it is the program's turn to select a move, only states to some limited depth below the current state will be generated and analyzed. This depth is often referred to as the *ply* of the search. A 'one-ply' search only considers the immediate successor states of the program's move, whereas a 'two-ply' search will also look at all possible replies by its opponent, and so on. For a complex game in which a large number of moves are applicable at each state, like chess, many programs will limit their search to between one and ten ply.

For most interesting games it is most unlikely (especially early in the game) that the part of the tree to which the search is limited will contain any win, loss or draw positions. This means that it is not always possible to choose a move that will guarantee a win; we must instead attempt to find the 'best' move, the one most likely to result in a win later.

This also seems to be the strategy pursued by human experts. The concept of a goal state is thus somewhat weaker than that in the search problems we considered in Section 3.2.1. There the search failed if no goal state was found in the searched section of the state space graph. In the context of game playing, however, we want to choose a move that guarantees a win if it is possible to do so after searching some subset of the tree. If this is not possible, however, we still wish to select the move giving us the 'best' position towards that goal.

To achieve this objective it is again necessary to use an *evaluation function* to order states, so that it can be decided which are more likely to lead to win positions. Such a function, sometimes referred to as a *static evaluation function*, will analyze positions from the program's viewpoint and will return a higher score for those positions which are regarded as 'better' than for ones which are less likely to result in a win. The more accurately this function is able to assess a position, the more successful the game played by our program will be. In deciding what should be included in an evaluation function we must also consider that any additional effort needed to compute a 'best' move for a given depth increases the overall computational expense of the search. Within reasonable constraints on response time this will, in practice, result in a trade-off between the acceptable complexity of an evaluation function and the feasible depth of a search.

Taking 'Dodgem' as an example for the kind of information we may wish to include in an evaluation function, it would seem that, since it is the aim of the game to move our own counters off the board as quickly as possible, a state's score should increase as the black counters move further to the right and off the board. It should correspondingly decrease as the white counters move up and off the board. After playing a few games, we may conclude that the top right-hand square suggests itself as a good one to occupy. From these observations we may then deduce an evaluation function which sums a given score for each square (such as the values in Figure 3.19) over all counters. This would, for example, assign a value of $10 + 5 - 5 - 10 = 0$ to the initial board state. After a few more games have been played it should become clear that it is quite an advantage to block an opponent by positioning a counter between him and that edge of the board which his counters must reach to leave it. This suggests that we add an additional component to the evaluation function that adds some value (such as 40) for each black counter that blocks a white one directly (so it is unable to move upwards at all), and a lower score (such as 30) for any indirect blocks. An 'indirect block' may occur wherever there is still a one-square distance between counters, but the black counter is already in a direct line above the white one (*see* Figure 3.19). Similar values should be subtracted for white counters blocking black ones.

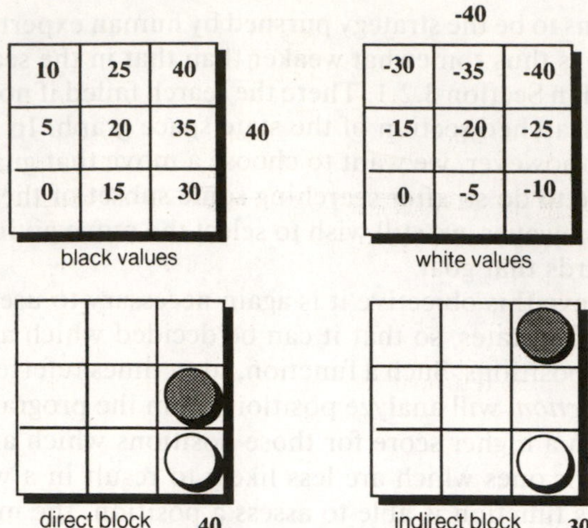

Figure 3.19 Contributions to the evaluation function for black and white counters in 'Dodgem' (program plays 'black').

Figure 3.20 shows the graph of this state space, drawn to a one-ply level. The scores are computed from this evaluation function, with the initial constellation at the root. As the evaluation is designed to indicate which states are more likely to lead to a win, even though there are no win or loss positions in this part of the tree, our program should choose the move with the highest score. This is '*move the second black counter to the right*', leading to a score of 55. In practice no evaluation function is likely to be perfect – in fact, according to the table in Figure 3.17, the move chosen above is actually one that may eventually lead to a loss position. Such inaccuracies in evaluation are often due to a lack of information about the dynamic context of a position (that is, how it will develop) and what is likely to happen to improve or worsen the score during the next few moves made by each player. For this reason it is important to look at the state space graph to as deep a ply level as we can afford, so that more information becomes available on which a 'good' choice can be based.

The 'minimax' strategy

As soon as a choice of move is made by a search at more than a single-ply level, it becomes important to include factors other than just whether it lies on the path to the leaf state which has the highest score. This is necessary because our adversaries are always trying to make the best possible moves for themselves, and because the program controls only every second move. For example, consider the two-ply search graph given in

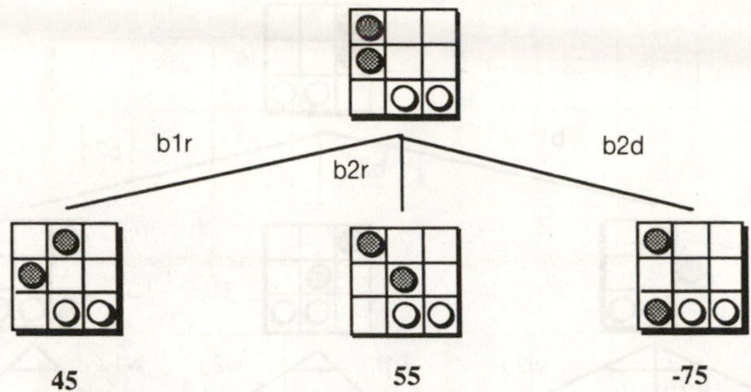

Figure 3.20 Scores returned by evaluating states in a one-ply search of 'Dodgem's' state space.

Figure 3.21. Here the best move would initially appear to be 'b1r', as this lies on the path to the state with the highest score of 60. However, after our program has made this move an opponent will be able to select his best move. Assuming that both players are using the same evaluation function, it is most unlikely that the state with value 60 will eventually result. The opponent will instead choose either of the moves 'w1u' or 'w2u', leading to a score of 0. Similarly, if the program had initially chosen 'b2r', the opponent's best play (using only the part of the tree shown and the same evaluation function) would be 'w2u', again yielding a state with value 0. At the two-ply level both of the initial moves 'b1r' and 'b2r' are of equal 'value' as far as the program is concerned, and either of them could be chosen.

The idea that a game-playing program attempts to choose states which maximize the scores returned by its evaluation function, and that the opponent is likewise attempting to choose states that minimize his scores, is known as the *minimax* concept. To choose a move using an n-ply state space graph, the value of minimax(s, $n-1$) for each of the successor states s generated by all one-ply moves is calculated, using the recursive *minimax* function defined in Figure 3.22. The move with the maximum value is then chosen. Random selection applies if there are a number of moves with the same maximum. For example, using the two-ply search graph of Figure 3.21, the *minimax* function would return values of 0 for the state generated by the move 'b1r', 0 for 'b2r' and -60 for 'b2d'. The maximum of these is 0 and so choice of either of the moves 'b1r' or 'b2r' would be in agreement with our previous analysis. Figure 3.23 gives an outline for the equivalent three-ply search, where the values for terminal nodes are those produced by our evaluation function, and the values for interior nodes are recursively computed by minimax. The best moves (moves on the best paths are 'emboldened') are again 'b1r' or 'b2r', with a maximum value of 45 for both of them.

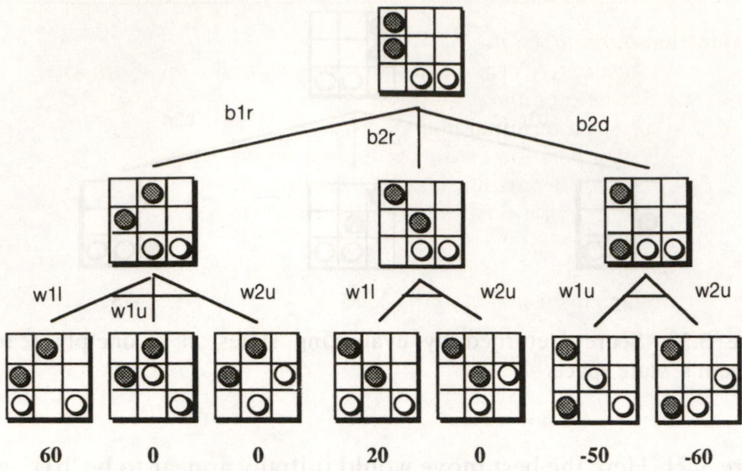

Figure 3.21 Scores returned after evaluating states in a two-ply state space graph rooted at the initial state of 'Dodgem'.

After the program has made this move and the opponent has made his move in reply, an *n*-ply state space graph rooted in the resulting state is computed and used to choose the following move. This continues until a win position for one of the players, or a draw is detected. Won, lost or drawn positions encountered while building the state space graph will become terminal nodes.

Tree pruning and the alpha-beta method

The *minimax* function of Figure 3.22 requires the complete tree to the given ply level to be constructed, and the evaluation function to be applied to every one of its terminal nodes. It would result in major savings if it were possible to find some method that reduced the number of nodes that needed to be generated and evaluated. These savings could then be employed to either reduce the time taken to select a move, or to search to a greater ply level. One such method for selectively pruning 'unpromising' parts of a graph is known as *alpha-beta pruning*.

As an indication that such a pruning should be possible, consider Figure 3.23. It shows the values obtained during a three-ply *minimax* evaluation in 'Dodgem'. When the part of the tree corresponding to move 'b2d' from the initial position is considered, it is already clear that the best moves available will have a value of at least 45, since both of the first two moves ('b1r' and 'b2r') return that value. Therefore, as soon as it is discovered that the subsequent move 'w1u' returns only a value of 5, we can safely assume that the move 'b2d' 's score cannot be greater than 5 and will never be chosen by our program. Hence the opponent's

```
function minimax(s, n):
    ;; recursively evaluate a score for a state s using evaluation
    ;; function f and an n-ply state space graph
if n=0 or s is a terminal node then {
    if won position for machine then return +∞
    else if lost position for machine then return −∞
    else if drawn position then return 0
    else return f(s) }
else { let bestScore = if machine's move then −∞ else +∞
    for each successor state s' of s do {
        let v = minimax(s', n−1)
        if program's move then
            bestScore = max(v, bestScore)
        else
            bestScore = min(v, bestScore)
    }
    return bestScore }
```

Figure 3.22 Recursive *minimax* procedure.

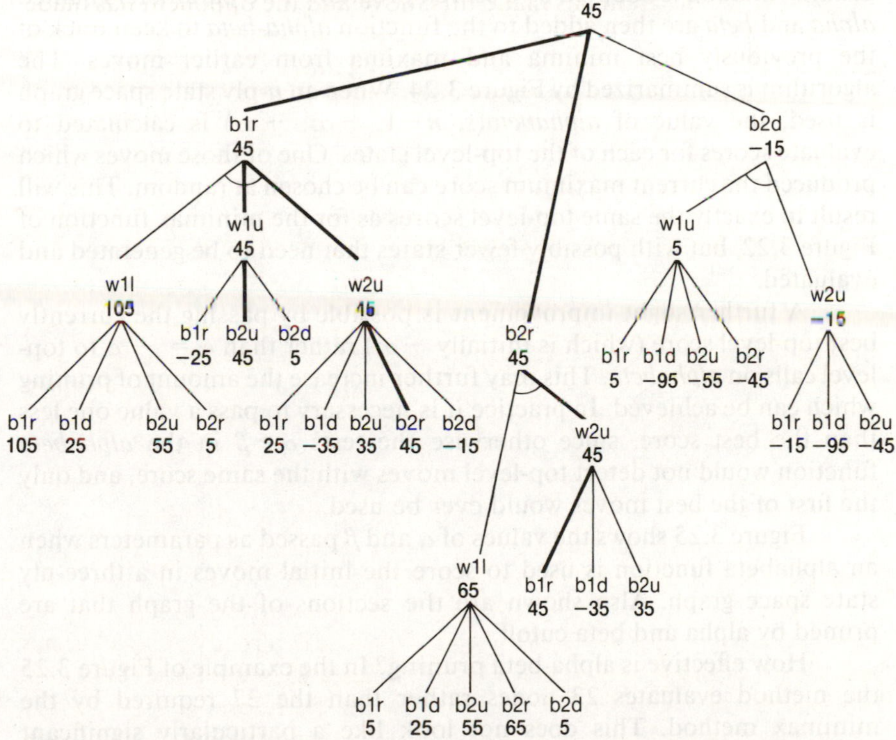

Figure 3.23 Scores returned by evaluating terminal nodes and values with a minimax strategy.

responding move 'w2u' (and, if there were any, any other of his moves possible at that stage) need never be considered.

This pruning of the part of the graph rooted at move 'w2u' is an example of an *alpha cutoff*, where the value after an opponent's move is less than or equal to a previously found move by the program. The other form of pruning, a *beta cutoff*, occurs when the value after one of the program's moves exceeds or equals a previously found better move by the opponent. In Figure 3.23 an example of this occurs in that section of the tree rooted in the state we encounter after moves 'b1r' and 'w2u' have been made. At this point it is already known that the initial move 'b1r' followed by 'w1u' yields a value of 45, so that when the second state in the subtree generated by 'b2r' is also labelled with a value of 45, it becomes clear that the value of the whole subtree will have 45 as its lower bound. The move 'w2u' will therefore return a value of at least 45 and it becomes unnecessary to generate and evaluate any further moves in its subtree, as this value is at least that of the best move for white which we have so far been able to find.

The names *alpha* and *beta* refer to the way in which the *minimax* strategy is improved by the use of an alpha-beta function, when this pruning method is adopted by a search program. Two parameters named *alpha* and *beta* are then added to the function *alpha-beta* to keep track of the previously best minima and maxima from earlier moves. The algorithm is summarized by Figure 3.24. When an n-ply state space graph is used, the value of $alphabeta(s, n-1, -\infty, +\infty)$ is calculated to evaluate scores for each of the top-level states. One of those moves which produced the current maximum score can be chosen at random. This will result in exactly the same top-level scores as for the minimax function of Figure 3.22, but with possibly fewer states that need to be generated and evaluated.

A further slight improvement is possible by passing the currently best top-level score (which is initially $-\infty$) rather than $\alpha = -\infty$ to top-level calls on *alphabeta*. This may further increase the amount of pruning which can be achieved. In practice it is necessary to pass a value one less than the best score, since otherwise the tests $\alpha \geq \beta$ in the *alphabeta* function would not detect top-level moves with the same score, and only the first of the best moves would ever be used.

Figure 3.25 shows the values of α and β passed as parameters when an alphabeta function is used to score the initial moves in a three-ply state space graph. Also shown are the sections of the graph that are pruned by alpha and beta cutoff.

How effective is alpha-beta pruning? In the example of Figure 3.25 the method evaluates 23 nodes rather than the 27 required by the minimax method. This does not look like a particularly significant improvement. However, the order in which the nodes are generated and inspected has obviously quite a large impact on the savings which can

```
function alphabeta(s, n, α, β):
        ;; recursively score a state s using evaluation
        ;; function f and an n-ply state space graph
if n=0 or s is a terminal node then {
        if win position for machine then return +∞
        else if loss position for machine then return −∞
        else if draw position then return 0
        else return f(s) }
else { let bestScore = if program's move then α else β
      for each successor state s' of s do {
            let v = alphabeta(s', n−1, α, β)
            if program's move then {
                    bestScore = max(v, bestScore)
                    α = bestScore
                    if α ≥ β then {
                            bestScore = β
                            prune any more successors of s }
            }
            else { bestScore = min(v, bestScore)
                   β = bestScore
                   if α ≥ β then {
                            bestScore = α
                            prune any more successors of s }
            }
      }
      return bestScore }
```

Figure 3.24 Recursive function for scoring states with alpha-beta pruning.

be expected. If a state space graph with exactly b moves at every node is constructed to n-ply depth, there will be b^n terminal nodes. The minimax method will need to evaluate every single one of these nodes, whereas, in the best case, the alpha-beta method needs to evaluate only $b^{\lfloor n/2 \rfloor} + b^{\lceil n/2 \rceil} - 1$ nodes† which is a substantially smaller number [Pearl (1984), pp. 235 – 239]. A comparison of these two functions with a branching factor of $b = 2$ can be seen in Figure 3.26.

Although it can be shown that it is 'in principle' always possible to reorder terminal nodes in such a way that the best case is always achieved, this is rarely possible 'in practice'. It would effectively require prior knowledge of all the best moves before the search is started, thereby defeating the purpose of the whole process. In the next section we will investigate by how much alpha-beta pruning can reduce the number of evaluations needed for the 'Dodgem' game problem.

† The function $\lfloor n \rfloor$ is the floor function which yields the largest integer not greater than n and $\lceil n \rceil$ is the ceiling function which yields the smallest integer not less than n.

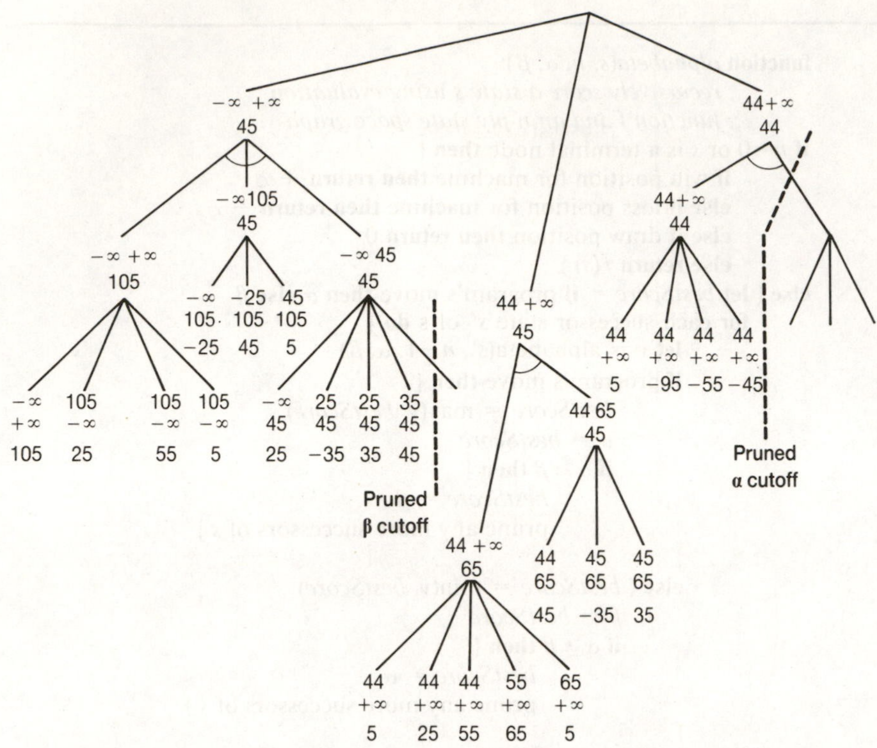

Figure 3.25 *Alphabeta* scores in a three-ply search graph rooted at the initial state of 'Dodgem'. The values of parameters α and β, and the pruned parts of the graph, are also shown.

Toolbox outline

A '*Games*' *toolbox* of useful Scheme functions has been provided by the authors. It allows easy experimentation with various games and evaluation functions. The lower levels of the search toolbox were used in its construction, and, in addition, both minimax and alpha-beta strategies are supported. A summary of the major routines visible at its user interface is given in Figure 3.27. A brief outline of how to use these routines follows, while the source code listings in Appendix III will provide additional information.

A *GameProblem* is constructed by the toolbox routine **MakeGameProblem**, which must be called with five parameters: the initial state of the game, a function to test for special (that is, goal) states, an evaluation function, an *ActionList* describing the program's moves and another *ActionList* for the opponent's moves. Arguments to the function to test for a 'special state' must provide both a state and a Boolean flag. This flag is set to **#t** if it is the program's turn to move. The function looks for goal states and

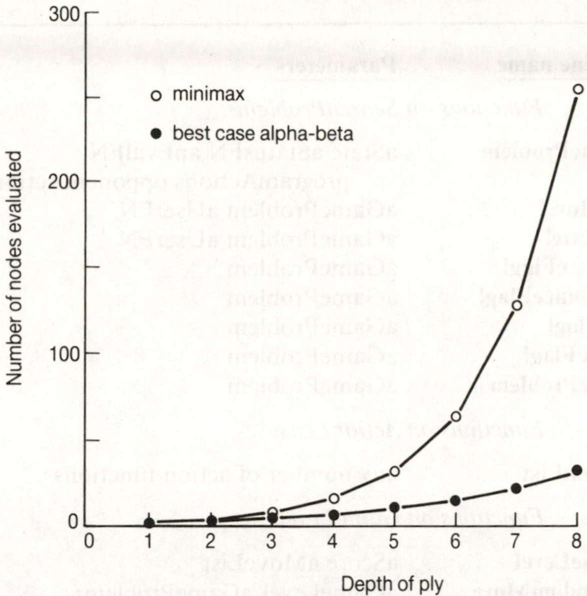

Figure 3.26 Graph showing how the number of nodes which must be evaluated grows with increasing ply (branching factor $b=2$).

returns '*machine*' if the state corresponds to a winning position for the program, '*opponent*' for a winning position for the opponent, '*draw*' for a drawn position and **#f** for any other state. The evaluation function also expects a state and a Boolean as parameters and will return a score, where higher values are regarded as *better* for the program. The *ActionLists* for the program's and opponent's moves can be built with **MakeActionList** from the search toolbox. Remember that each of the action functions in such a list expects a single state as a parameter, and it will return the new state resulting from the move (or #f if the move is invalid). The resulting *GameProblem* consists of all the global information relevant to a particular game (which is also just an extension of a *SearchProblem*'s representation). It can now be provided as a parameter to whatever function is used to start playing a game or select program moves by the program.

The **SetPrintState!** routine allows printing of game states with a user-provided function; *display* is normally used as the default. **SetAnnounceFlag!**, **ResetAnnounceFlag!**, **SetTraceFlag!** and **ResetTraceFlag!** offer capabilities similar to their namesakes provided by the '*Search*' toolbox; namely, to activate or suppress the announcement of solutions and the printing of tracing information. **PrintGameProblem** displays all relevant information about *GameProblems*, including the current status of the *announcing* and *tracing* flags.

Routine name	Parameters
Functions on SearchProblems:	
MakeGameProblem	aState aStatusFN anEvalFN programActions opponentActions
SetGetAMove!	aGameProblem aUserFN
SetPrintState!	aGameProblem aUserFN
SetAnnounceFlag!	aGameProblem
ResetAnnounceFlag!	aGameProblem
SetTraceFlag!	aGameProblem
ResetTraceFlag!	aGameProblem
PrintGameProblem	aGameProblem
Functions on ActionLists:	
MakeActionList	any number of action functions
Functions on GameLevels:	
MakeGameLevel	aScore aMoveList
ChooseRandomMove	aGameLevel aGameProblem
Functions to control a game:	
FindBestMachineMove	aState aGameProblem alphabeta? aPly
PlayGame	aGameProblem

Figure 3.27 Summary of the 'Games' toolbox interface routines.

SetGetAMove! allows use of a custom-written routine for requesting moves from an opponent. If this is not provided, a simple default routine asks a player to enter the state of the game after each move has been made. **#f** may be entered if he wishes to resign, and, if he wishes to pass (allowed in some games), an unaltered state can be given. Any replacement for this default should accept the current state and should return a new one (or **#f** for resignation, or the same state for a pass). Such a routine could allow the player to make moves in a manner that is more appropriate to some particular game. It could also perform some domain-dependent validity checking of moves.

The routine **FindBestMachineMove** accepts a current state, the *GameProblem*, whether alpha-beta pruning should be used (a Boolean) and the search's ply level. It returns the best move available to the program at a given state. If there is more than one best move, then all of them are returned in the form of a *GameLevel*. This data structure consists of a score and a list of all states with that score. The function **ChooseRandomMove** can be used to choose from among these at random.

From a user's point of view, **PlayGame** is the most important toolbox function. It expects a *GameProblem* as a parameter, and, after querying for the search's ply level, it asks whether alpha-beta pruning should be applied and whether the program or the opponent is to move first. After this it will cause a complete game to be played, if this is possible. Moves are requested from the user and the state of the game is displayed after each move. At the end of the game a winner (if any) is announced and the final state is shown.

Using the toolbox to play 'Dodgem'

This section will apply the 'Games' toolbox to 'Dodgem', the game introduced earlier. This should serve as an example of the way the various routines may be used.

To represent states in 'Dodgem' we shall use a list of four integers. The first two will give the position of the black (machine) counters and the final two the positions of the white (opponent) counters, in terms of the values in Figure 3.16. A zero value is used to symbolize a counter that has been moved off the board. Thus the initial state is defined by:

```
(define initial '(1 4 8 9) )
```

An appropriate evaluation function is encoded in the following procedure. It uses the table of scores shown in Figure 3.19 and the function *getPos* to find the square occupied by a given counter. The counters are labelled as *Black1, Black2, White1* and *White2* with values 0, 1, 2 and 3.

```
(define evalFN
  (lambda (aState machineMove?)
    ; Encourage black to move right and up and white to move up and right,
    ; by assigning appropriate values to each board position. Also encourage
    ; blocking an opponent by positioning a counter between one of his and
    ; the row from which they must move off the board.
    ; Value of squares:        0   1   2   3 . . . etc.
    (define blackValues '(    40  10  25  40
                                   5  20  35
                                   0  15  30))
    (define whiteValues '(   -40 -30 -35 -40
                                 -15 -20 -25
                                   0  -5 -10))
    (define blockingFactor
      (lambda (whitePos blackPos)
        ; White is blocking black if its number is one greater
        ; White is (partially) blocking black if its number is two greater
        ; Black is blocking white if its number is three less
```

```
; Black is (partially) blocking white if its number is six less
; (Must ignore pieces off the board)
    (cond ((or (= whitePos 0)
               (= blackPos 0)) 0)
          ((= whitePos (+ blackPos 1)) -40)
          ((= whitePos (+ blackPos 2)) -30)
          ((= blackPos (- whitePos 3)) +40)
          ((= blackPos (- whitePos 6)) +30)
          (else 0))))

; sum across all counter positions and poss. blocks
(+ (list-ref blackValues (getPos aState Black1))
 (+ (list-ref blackValues (getPos aState Black2))
  (+ (list-ref whiteValues (getPos aState White1))
   (+ (list-ref whiteValues (getPos aState White2))
    (+ (blockingFactor (getPos aState White1)
                       (getPos aState Black1))
     (+ (blockingFactor (getPos aState White1)
                        (getPos aState Black2))
      (+ (blockingFactor (getPos aState White2)
                         (getPos aState Black1))
         (blockingFactor (getPos aState White2)
                         (getPos aState Black2)))))))))))
```

The program's and the opponent's moves are defined below:

```
; Moves from: 0 1 2 3 4 5 6 7 8 9
(define left   '(#f #f 1 2 #f 4 5 #f 7 8))
(define right  '(#f 2 3 b 5 6 b 8 9 b))
(define up     '(#f w w w 1 2 3 4 5 6))
(define down   '(#f 4 5 6 7 8 9 #f #f #f))

(define moveCounter
  (lambda (which moves)
   ; Return a function which moves the counter in the 'which' position of
   ; the state according to the "coded instructions" in 'moves'. It is
   ; assumed that the program always plays black. The moves consist of a
   ; list accessed by a counter's current position. This list specifies a new
   ; state if legal, #f if not, and 'b' or 'w' if the state is only legal for a
   ; black or white counter. It is also necessary to ensure that the target
   ; position is free.
   (lambda (aState)
     (let* ((currPos (getPos aState which))
            (newPos (list-ref moves currPos))
            (newState #f))
       (cond ((not newPos) #f)
             ((eq? newPos 'b)
              (if (blackPos? which)
                  (setPos aState which 0)
```

```
                    #f))
                  ((eq? newPos 'w)
                   (if (blackPos? which)
                       #f
                       (setPos aState which 0)))
                  (else (setPos aState which newPos)))))))

(define b1u  (moveCounter Black1 up))
(define b1r  (moveCounter Black1 right))
(define b1d  (moveCounter Black1 down))
(define b2u  (moveCounter Black2 up))
(define b2r  (moveCounter Black2 right))
(define b2d  (moveCounter Black2 down))
(define w1l  (moveCounter White1 left))
(define w1u  (moveCounter White1 up))
(define w1r  (moveCounter White1 right))
(define w2l  (moveCounter White2 left))
(define w2u  (moveCounter White2 up))
(define w2r  (moveCounter White2 right))
```

The test for final positions is given next. **specialStatus** uses the Boolean function *offBoard?* to check whether a counter has moved off the board:

```
(define specialStatus
  (lambda (aState machineMove?)

    (define noBlackMove?
      ; returns true if no black move can be made
      (lambda (aState)
        (not (or (b1u aState)
                 (b1r aState)
                 (b1d aState)
                 (b2u aState)
                 (b2r aState)
                 (b2d aState)))))

    (define noWhiteMove?
      ; returns true if no white move can be made
      (lambda (aState)
        (not (or (w1l aState)
                 (w1u aState)
                 (w1r aState)
                 (w2l aState)
                 (w2u aState)
                 (w2r aState)))))

    (cond ( ; black wins if both its counters are off
           (and (offBoard? (getPos aState Black1))
                (offBoard? (getPos aState Black2))) "machine")
          ( ; white wins if both its counters are off
           (and (offBoard? (getPos aState White1))
```

```
                (offBoard? (getPos aState White2))) ''opponent'')
        ( ; black wins if white can't move
          (and machineMove?
                (noBlackMove? aState)) ''machine'')
        ( ; white wins if black can't move
          (and (not machineMove?)
                (noWhiteMove? aState)) ''opponent'')
        (else #f))))
```

A *GameProblem* can now be constructed by:

```
(define DodgemGameProblem
        (MakeGameProblem initial
                         specialStatus
                         evalFN
                         (MakeActionList
                              b1u b1r b1d b2u b2r b2d)
                         (MakeActionList
                              w1l w1u w1r w2l w2u w2r)))
```

and a special routine to display board positions as 3×3 grids may be encoded as:

```
(define printDodgem
  (lambda (aState)
   ; Build a vector and then print in rows of three
    (define in3
      (lambda (list)
       (if (null? list)
           (newline)
           (begin (newline)
                  (display (car list))
                  (display (cadr list))
                  (display (caddr list))
                  (in3 (cdddr list))))))
    (if (null? aState)
       (display ''Invalid board state'')
       (begin
        (let ((board (make-vector 10 ''.'')))
          (vector-set! board (getPos aState Black1) ''b'')
          (vector-set! board (getPos aState Black2) ''b'')
          (vector-set! board (getPos aState White1) ''w'')
          (vector-set! board (getPos aState White2) ''w'')
          (in3 (cdr (vector->list board)))
          (newline))))))
(SetPrintState! DodgemGameProblem printDodgem)
```

A customized interface may be used to prompt for, validate and initiate moves:

```
(define getMove
  (lambda (aState)
   (let* ((which
          (do ((ok #f)
               (pos 0))
              (ok pos) ; return pos once it is "ok"
              (newline)
              (display "Give position (1-9): ")
              (set! pos (read))
              (cond ((not (number? pos))
                     (display "invalid number"))
                    ((or (< pos 0)
                         (> pos 9))
                     (display "invalid position "))
                    ((= pos (getPos aState White1))
                     (set! pos White1)
                     (set! ok #t))
                    ((= pos (getPos aState White2))
                     (set! pos White2)
                     (set! ok #t))
                    (else
                     (display "Not a white counter")))))
         (direction
          (do ((ok #f)
               (dir #f))
              (ok dir) ; return direction once it is "ok"
              (newline)
              (display "Give direction ")
              (display "(u(p), (l)eft, (r)ight) : ")
              (set! dir (read))
              (set! ok #t)
              (cond
               ((eq? dir 'u) (set! dir up))
               ((eq? dir 'l ) (set! dir left))
               ((leg? dir 'r) (set! dir right))
               (else (display "Invalid direction! ") (set! ok #f))))))
      ; make the move !
      ((moveCounter which direction) aState))))

(SetGetAMove! DodgemGameProblem getMove)
```

We can now use this program to conduct a number of experiments, such as testing the effectiveness of alpha-beta pruning. Figure 3.28 is an (edited) transcript of a play's output.

```
>>> (SetTraceFlag! DodgemGameProblem)
>>> (SetAnnounceFlag! DodgemGameProblem)
>>> (FindBestMachineMove '(1 4 8 9) DodgemGameProblem #t 3)
Enter scoreState (MIN) state=(2 4 8 9) depth=2 alpha=-INF beta=+INF
Enter scoreState (MAX) state=(2 4 7 9) depth=1 alpha=-INF beta=+INF
Enter scoreState (MIN) state=(3 4 7 9) depth=0 alpha=-INF beta=+INF
Exit scoreState (MIN) state=(3 4 7 9) depth=0 -> 105
Enter scoreState (MIN) state=(5 4 7 9) depth=0 alpha=105 beta=+INF
Exit scoreState (MIN) state=(5 4 7 9) depth=0 -> 25
Enter scoreState (MIN) state=(2 1 7 9) depth=0 alpha=105 beta=+INF
Exit scoreState (MIN) state=(2 1 7 9) depth=0 -> 55
Enter scoreState (MIN) state=(2 5 7 9) depth=0 alpha=105 beta=+INF
Exit scoreState (MIN) state=(2 5 7 9) depth=0 -> 5
Exit scoreState (MAX) state=(2 4 7 9) depth=1 -> 105
Enter scoreState (MAX) state=(2 4 5 9) depth=1 alpha=-INF beta=105
.
.
Exit scoreState (MAX) state=(2 4 5 9) depth=1 -> 45
Enter scoreState (MAX) state=(2 4 8 6) depth=1 alpha=-INF beta=45
Enter scoreState (MIN) state=(3 4 8 6) depth=0 alpha=-INF beta=45
Exit scoreState (MIN) state=(3 4 8 6) depth=0 -> 25
Enter scoreState (MIN) state=(5 4 8 6) depth=0 alpha=25 beta=45
Exit scoreState (MIN) state=(5 4 8 6) depth=0 -> 35
Enter scoreState (MIN) state=(2 1 8 6) depth=0 alpha=25 beta=45
Exit scoreState (MIN) state=(2 1 8 6) depth=0 -> 35
Enter scoreState (MIN) state=(2 5 8 6) depth=0 alpha=35 beta=45
Exit scoreState (MIN) state=(2 5 8 6) depth=0 -> 45
Exit scoreState (MAX) (PRUNED) state=(2 4 8 6) depth=1 -> 45
Exit scoreState (MIN) state=(2 4 8 9) depth=2 -> 45
Enter scoreState (MIN) state=(1 5 8 9) depth=2 alpha=44 beta=+INF
Enter scoreState (MAX) state=(1 5 7 9) depth=1 alpha=44 beta=+INF
Enter scoreState (MIN) state=(2 5 7 9) depth=0 alpha=44 beta=+INF
Exit scoreState (MIN) state=(2 5 7 9) depth=0 -> 5
.
.
Exit scoreState (MIN) state=(1 8 5 9) depth=0 -> -45
Exit scoreState (MAX) state=(1 7 5 9) depth=1 -> 44
Exit scoreState (MIN) (PRUNED) state=(1 7 8 9) depth=2 -> 44
Best moves for machine from state:
b..
b..
.ww
 found after trying 34 moves at 3 ply.
Best score: 45 Best moves:
b..
.b.
.ww
```

Figure 3.28 Edited transcript of some experiments.

```
.b.
b..
.ww
(45 ( 1 5 8 9) (2 4 8 9))
>>> (ResetTraceFlag! DodgemGameProblem)
>>> (ResetAnnounceFlag! DodgemGameProblem)
>>> (FindBestMachineMove '(1 4 8 9) DodgemGameProblem #f 3)
(45 (1 5 8 9) (2 4 8 9))
>>> (GetCount DodgemGameProblem)
37
>>> (PlayGame DodgemGameProblem)
Is machine to move first? (y/n) : y
Use alpha-beta pruning? (y/n : y
Give ply level (>0) : 6
Current game state (Machine's move):
b..
b..
.ww
Move chosen from among 1 of value -25 after generating 605
Current game state (Your move):
.b.
b..
.ww
Give position (1-9) : 8
Give direction (u(p), (l)eft, (r)ight) : u
Current game state (Machine's move):
.b.
bw.
..w
Move chosen from among 1 of value -35 after generating 813
Current game state (Your move):
..b
bw.
..w
Give position (1-9) : 9
Give direction (u(p), (l)eft, (r)ight) : u
Current game state (Machine's move):
..b
bww
...
~~~~~~~~~~~~~ etc ~~~~
Current game state (Machine's move):
```

Figure 3.28 (cont.)

```
.w.
...
..b
Move chosen from among 1 of value +INF after generating 10
Machine wins. Bad luck!
Final state of game is:
.w.
...
...
```

Figure 3.28 (cont.)

After setting both the *trace* and *announce* flags, the first section of Figure 3.28 shows how the leftmost subtree is searched, looking for the best moves from the initial position at the three-ply level with alpha-beta pruning. This is exactly the same example as was used to construct Figure 3.25. It gives the values of α and β at entry and a score returned from *ScoreState* after applying the recursive alpha-beta function of Figure 3.24. *ScoreState* actually uses a combination of both the alpha-beta and minimax strategies, with a parameter to decide whether alpha-beta pruning should be applied. The next section of the transcript traces the search at the stage where pruning occurs. The subsequent experiment repeats this without alpha-beta pruning, returning the higher move value of 37. Four states were pruned. Note that these counts include interior nodes as well as terminal ones. The final trace in the transcript shows a game of 'Dodgem', giving the first move to the program. A six-ply search with alpha-beta pruning was employed.

The toolbox was also used for finding the best machine move from the initial state, at various ply levels, both with and without alpha-beta pruning. The values in the table below give both the number of moves made and the approximate time in seconds to find the best move on a Macintosh SE running *MacScheme + ToolSmith 1.0.*

	Minimax		*Alpha-Beta*	
Ply	*moves*	*seconds*	*moves*	*seconds*
1	3	0.3	3	0.3
2	10	0.9	10	0.8
3	37	2.9	34	2.5
4	138	10.6	105	6.9
5	417	33.4	273	18.3

EXERCISES

The following exercises may serve to explore the capabilities of both the '*Search*' and the '*Games*' toolboxes. Many of these problems were inspired by the mathematical analyses of puzzle solving and game playing in Berlekamp *et al.* (1982), which is a genuine treasure trove for anyone who is at all interested in this topic. The well-known collections of M. Gardner's *Scientific American* columns (1956, 1961, 1969, 1984) are also good sources, as is Smullyan's (1984) delightful book. These texts are completely independent of any particular considerations of computer-based implementation. Banerji (1980) and Pearl (1984) can be recommended for an AI perspective.

All problems are also suitable as test-beds for logic-based or object-oriented approaches, and many offer nice frameworks for experimenting with interactive and graphical environments.

If you should get bored with these exercises you may wish to try your skills on 'harder' games and puzzles – for example, old favourites like the *Rubik cube*, *Reversi*, *Backgammon*, *Checkers*, *Chess*, *Go* and others.

Combinatorial puzzles

3.1* In Section 2.4 we discussed the *Lineland* puzzle and also gave its solution in PROLOG. Due to the nature of PROLOG's inference engine we restricted ourselves to simple depth first search with backtracking. Implement *Lineland* as a Scheme program and use it for a comparative analysis of alternative search strategies. The number of moves needed to reach a goal might be an appropriate measure. Any gains will most likely be strongly dependent on the 'quality' of your evaluation function, a comment which will equally well apply to any of the other problems in this section. Reorder the sequence in which your program tries moves and experiment with some alternative scoring methods.

3.2 Section 3.4 uses the notorious *monkey and bananas* problem to illustrate some properties of production system interpreters. Find a search-based formulation for this puzzle.

3.3 Write a Scheme program for solving the *Missionaries and Cannibals* puzzle described in Section 3.2.1.

3.4 Augment the toolbox with facilities to specify a 'best first' search. Under this strategy we will need to remember all partially explored paths and sort them according to their 'value'. The 'best' of these will always be deepened next. Note that this strategy differs substantially from the 'steepest' search procedure which is currently supported by the toolbox.

3.5 Twenty-four matches are arranged in three piles, initially containing 11, 7 and 6 matches respectively (*see* Figure 3.29). A move consists of a transferral of matches from one pile to another, in such a way that the number of matches on the second pile doubles. Write a program which finds a way to create three equal piles of matches in three moves at the most.

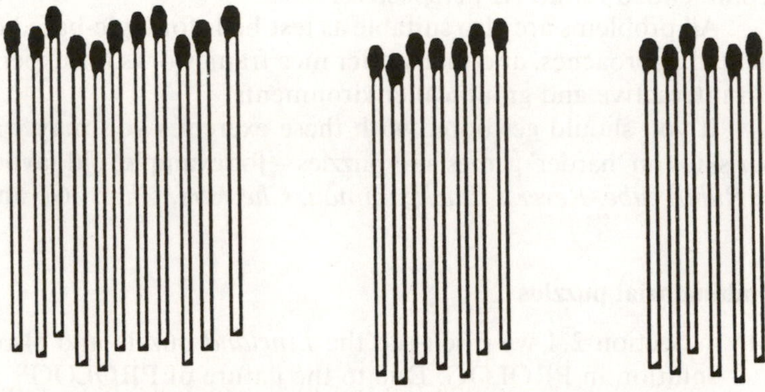

Figure 3.29 Exercise 3.5.

3.6 Three black and three white coins are laid out on a grid containing ten squares, as shown in Figure 3.30 (a). A move consists of sliding any *pair* of adjacent coins to free squares (the coins may not be rotated or separated). For example, Figure 3.30 (b) shows the arrangement of coins which would result from one possible choice of first move. The aim is to arrive at the state shown in (c) with no more than three moves. Berlekamp *et al.* (1982, p. 807) give some guidance on how to deduce a solution.

Write a Scheme program to solve this puzzle. You will need to define a state representation, a set of valid moves, an initial state and a goal state in analogy to our *8-puzzle* program. All of the search strategies are applicable and may be compared.

3.7 *Solitaire* has at times been a popular pastime of the 'leisure classes'. The board for such a peg-jumping puzzle consists of an array of holes in the shape of a cross, and all but the center one are filled

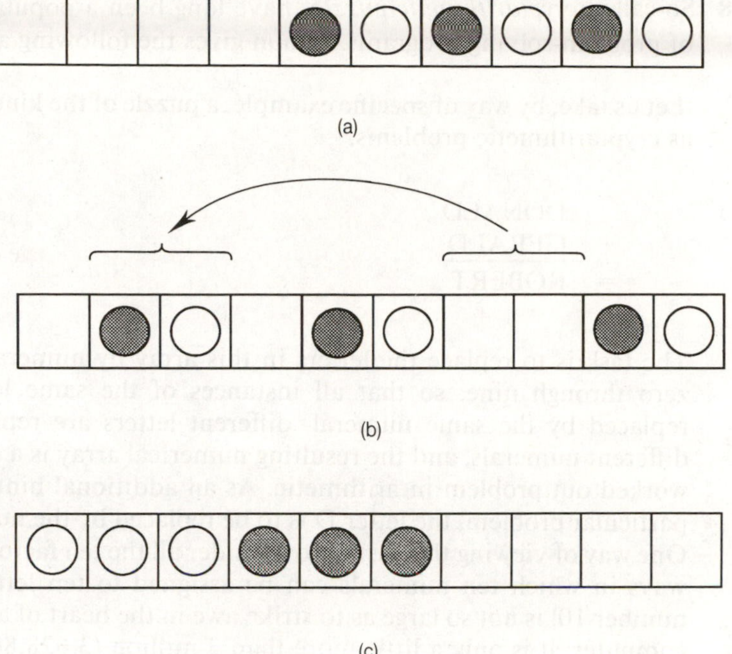

(a)

(b)

(c)

Figure 3.30 Exercise 3.6.

with a peg. Valid moves jump a peg over an adjacent one into an empty hole, removing the peg over which we have jumped. The goal of the puzzle is to find a sequence of 'hops' which will eventually leave only a single peg on the board. Figure 3.31 shows the initial state of the board. Find an appropriate representation and write a Scheme program to solve the puzzle.

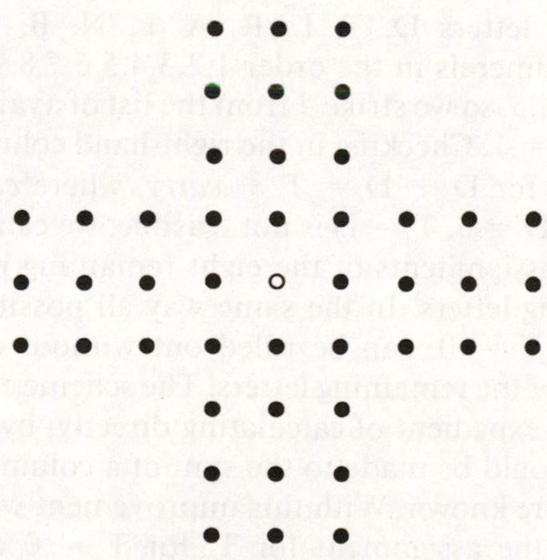

Figure 3.31 Exercise 3.7.

3.8 So-called *cryptarithmetic puzzles* have long been a popular target of problem-solving programs. Simon gives the following account:

'Let us take, by way of specific example, a puzzle of the kind known as cryptarithmetic problems.

```
    DONALD
 +  GERALD
 =  ROBERT
```

The task is to replace the letters in this array by numerals, from zero through nine, so that all instances of the same letter are replaced by the same numeral, different letters are replaced by different numerals, and the resulting numerical array is a correctly worked out problem in arithmetic. As an additional hint for this particular problem, the letter D is to be replaced by the numeral 5. One way of viewing this task is to consider all the ten factorial (10!) ways in which ten numerals can be assigned to ten letters. The number 10! is not so large as to strike awe in the heart of a modern computer; it is only a little more than 3 million (3,628,800, to be exact). A program designed to generate all possible assignments systematically, and requiring a tenth of a second to generate and test each, would require at most about ten hours to do the job. One way to cut down the search drastically is to make the assignments systematically, as before, but to assign numerals to the letters one by one so that inconsistencies can be detected before an assignment is complete, and hence whole classes of possible assignments can be ruled out at one step. Let me illustrate how this works.

Suppose we start from the right, trying assignments successively for the letters D, T, L, R, A, E, N, B, O and G, and substituting numerals in the order 1,2,3,4,5,6,7,8,9,0. We already know that D = 5, so we strike 5 from the list of available numerals. We now try T = 1. Checking in the right-hand column, we detect a contradiction, for D + D = T + *carry*, where *carry* is 10 or 0. Hence, since (D = 5, T = 1) is not feasible, we can rule out all the remaining 8! assignments of the eight remaining numerals to the eight remaining letters. In the same way all possible assignments for T, except T = 0, can be ruled out without considering the assignments for the remaining letters. The scheme can be improved further by the expedient of calculating directly, by addition, what assignment should be made to the sum of a column whenever the two addends are known. With this improvement we shall not need to search for the assignment for T, for T = 0 can be inferred directly from D = 5. Using this scheme, the DONALD + GERALD = ROBERT problem can be solved quite readily, with paper and pencil. Ten minutes should suffice!'

[*Simon (1969), second edition (1981), pp. 68–72.*]

Design such an 'intelligent' strategy and encode it as an evaluation function for a search program. Bratko (1986, pp. 159–162) and Walker *et al.* (1987, pp. 93–98) offer PROLOG solutions if you should get 'stuck'. If you should get 'hooked', many more such 'brain-teasers' are offered by Kahan (1987).

3.9 The following interesting and challenging problem has been referred to as the 'domino puzzle' and is described by Hodgson (1986). It consists of *two* 3 × 3 layers of blocks each labelled with one to nine dots. There is one white and one black block for each number of dots. In the goal state all the blocks on the top layer are white and the numberings run from one to nine as read from left to right, top to bottom. The bottom layer is similar except that all the blocks are black. Figure 3.32 shows a view of the goal state on one face.

The puzzle has some similarity to the infamous *Rubik cube*, since its top and bottom layers can be independently rotated through 90 degrees about the central block of the layer. Let us denote these moves as T and B, under the assumption that rotation is clockwise as seen from the face being rotated. Each set of six side blocks can be rotated through 180 degrees about the axis that passes through the centre of the puzzle between the two centre blocks on the side. We denote these moves by N, E, S, W as shown in Figure 3.32.

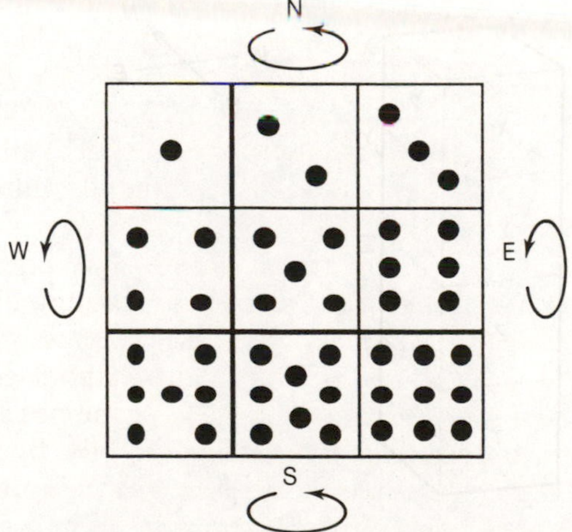

Figure 3.32 Exercise 3.9.

Hodgson continues to give an insightful analysis of the puzzle. Your task is to design an effective search program for its solution.

3.10 *Instant Insanity* surfaces every now and then under a new name. Berlekamp *et al.* (1982) report on an early American version as the '*Katzenjammer*' puzzle. The problem is to assemble its four cubes into a vertical 1×1×4 tower in which each wall displays the four 'colours': *A*, *B*, *C*, *D*.

In Figure 3.33 the outer letters describe the hidden faces. If you don't go instantly insane playing with the cubes, you'll probably be greatly tantalized by them, which is the reason that Berlekamp *et al.* (1982) also refer to them as the *great tantalizer*.

Berlekamp *et al.* (1982) and Godran (1983) give an analysis of the solution. Find an appropriately formal representation and write a Scheme program.

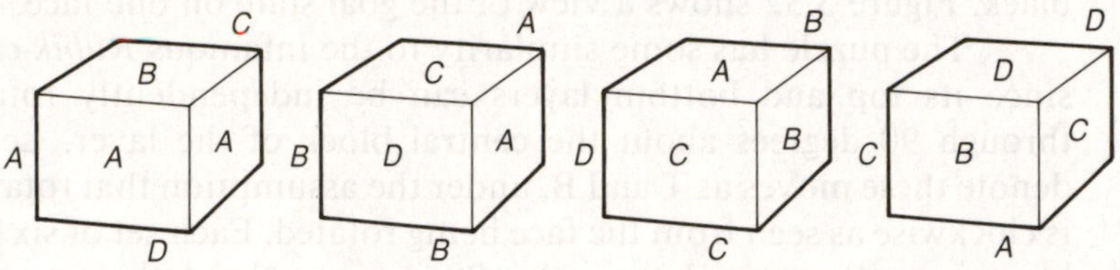

Figure 3.33 Exercise 3.10: The four pieces of insanity.

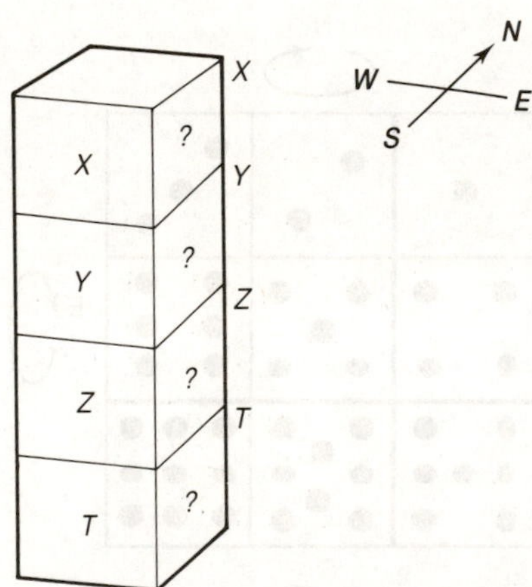

Figure 3.34 Exercise 3.10: A solution?

3.11 *Mastermind* is a popular two-person game, although it is really more like a combinatorial puzzle in nature. There are a number of variations. Our description is taken from a discussion of strategy given by Flood (1986).

One player, the 'coder', selects a sequence of four integers from among the digits 1 to 6. The other player, hereafter called the 'guesser', attempts to guess this sequence. After each guess the coder informs the guesser about the number of guessed digits that are exactly correct in both value and position; and the number of guessed digits that appear in both the guess and the code, but in different positions. The guesser will try to minimize the number of guesses required to arrive at a completely correct guess.

Stirling and Shapiro (1986) discuss a PROLOG implementation and Norvig (1984) describes an algorithm implemented in LISP.

Games

3.12 *Tic-Tac-Toe* is a traditional, simple board game, also often referred to as *noughts and crosses*. Two players alternate their moves, one placing an X and the other an O, on some empty square of the board shown in Figure 3.35.

The first player to complete a horizontal, vertical or diagonal straight line is the winner. In the position shown, X will make a winning move, unless O plays wisely.

Rosenholtz (1984) describes a winning strategy.

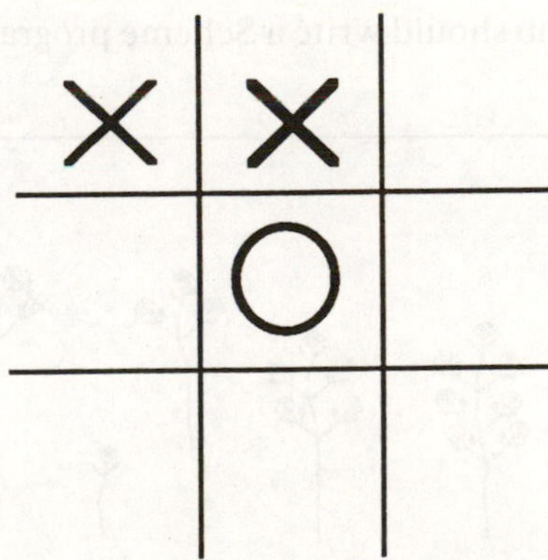

Figure 3.35 Exercise 3.12.

Figure 3.36 Exercise 3.13.

3.13 In Berlekamp *et al.* (1982, p. 430) the Walrus and the Carpenter are playing the rather cruel game of *Turtle Turning*. At each move one of them must put a turtle on its back, and he may also turn over any single turtle to the left of it. This second turtle, unlike the first, may be turned either on to its feet or on to its back. The player who turns the last turtle upsidedown wins the game.

Figure 3.36 shows an intermediate game position. As you may already suspect, an appropriate strategy for playing this game is similar to the ones used for '*Nim*' (see Exercise 3.15).

3.14 Another of the many games surveyed in Berlekamp *et al.* (1982, p. 490) revolves around a fictional beauty, hereafter referred to as Princess Romantica. The princess is known to have two persistent suitors, Handsome Hans and Charming Charles, whom she instructs to take turns to visit the castle's rose garden (shown in Figure 3.37) to pick exactly one or two roses from different bushes. Naturally this ceremony is meant to fathom the depth of their true love, so that she may later decide to whom she wants to award her hand in marriage.

In the figure Princess Romantica is just about to smell a beautiful rose that Charming Charles has picked from the largest bush. This 'game' will continue until eventually one of the suitors will be unable to pick a rose, because there are none left; upon which event he will despondently creep away to let the winner live happily ever after. Assuming the roses shown are the only ones in the country, you should write a Scheme program to win the heart of the princess.

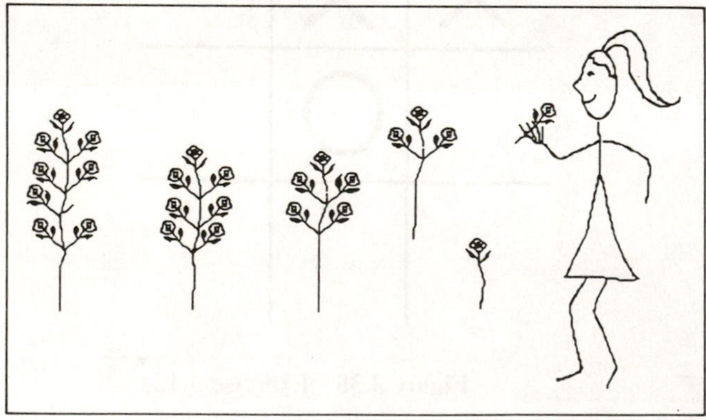

Figure 3.37 Exercise 3.14.

3.15 *Nim* is also a very simple game for two players. There are *n* piles of matches and the players take turns in removing some of them from a pile. There is even the option of removing a pile completely, should they so wish. The player who takes the last match will win the game. A common starting position initially provides four piles, with 1, 3, 5 and 7 matches respectively. Use our *Games* toolbox to write a Scheme program for playing a fierce game of *Nim*. Stirling and Shapiro (1986) give a PROLOG implementation.

3.16* The ancient game of *Kalah* is played on a board with two rows of six holes facing each other. Each player owns a row of six holes, plus a *kalah* to the right of the holes. In the initial state there are six stones in each hole and the two *kalahs* are empty. A player begins a move by picking up the stones in one of his holes. Proceeding counterclockwise around the board, he puts one of the picked-up stones in each hole and in his own *kalah*, skipping the opponent's *kalah*, until no stones remain to be distributed. There are three possible outcomes. If the last stone lands on the *kalah*, the player earns another move. If the last stone lands on an empty hole owned by the player, and the opponent's hole directly across the board contains at least one stone, then the player takes all the stones in this hole plus his last landed stone and puts them all in his *kalah*. Otherwise the player's turn ends and his opponent will move.

The bottom *kalah* board in Figure 3.38 (b) represents a move following from the constellation at the top board (a), by the owner of the top holes. He took the six stones in the rightmost hole and

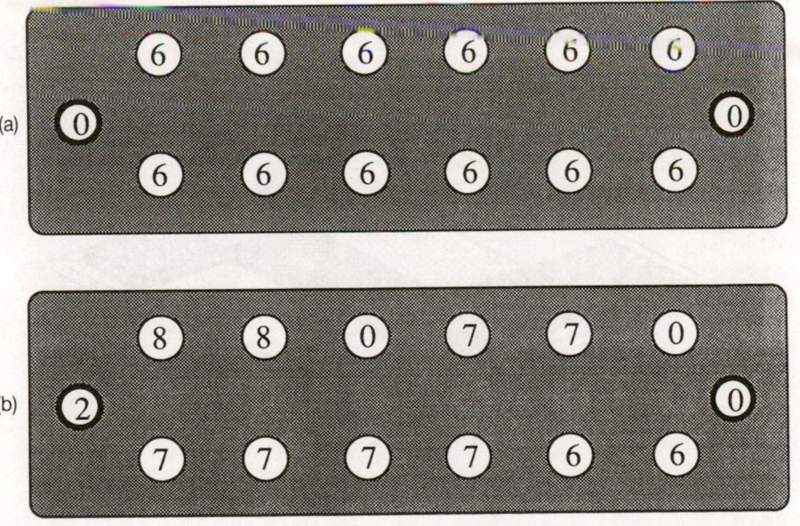

Figure 3.38 Exercise 3.16.

distributed them, the last one landing in the *kalah*, allowing another move. The stones in the fourth hole from the right were then distributed.

If all the holes of a player become empty (even if it's not his turn to play), the stones remaining in holes owned by an opponent are put in the opponent's *kalah* and the game ends. The winner of the game is the first player to get more than half of the stones in his *kalah*.

You are to write a Scheme program which plays a good game of *kalah* against a human opponent. You should at least implement heuristic search with alpha-beta pruning, using some simple evaluation function (such as the difference between the number of stones in the two *kalahs*).

3.17 The *L-game* is described by E. de Bono in his book '*The Five-Day Course in Thinking*'. It is played on the 4 × 4 board shown in Figure 3.39, and its rules are deceptively simple.

Each player has his own L-shaped piece which may be turned in any direction or flipped around, and there are also two neutral 1 × 1 squares. A move has two parts: (1) the player lifts his own L-piece and places it at a different position; (2) if he wishes, he may then change the position of one of the two neutral pieces. The player who can't move, because there is only one place for his L-piece, loses the game.

Berlekamp *et al.* (1982, p. 364) give an analysis of this game, which has a reasonably small search space. It is, however, an interesting challenge to devise a convenient move representation for a computer-based implementation.

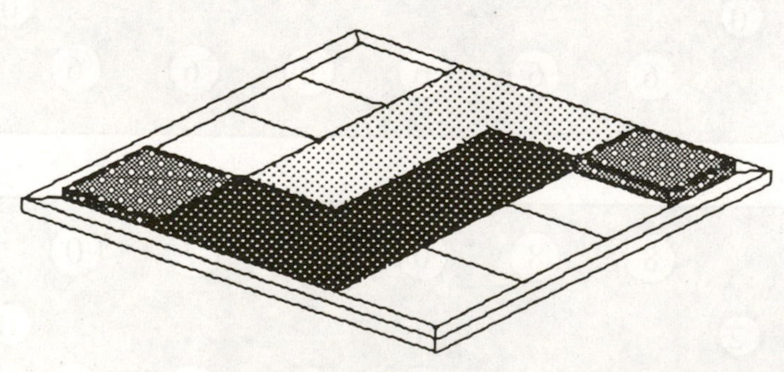

Figure 3.39 Exercise 3.17.

3.18 The following little game simulates a frequently recurring event at a children's birthday party. We will assume two players, let us call them *Left* and *Right*. *Left* will seat all the boys and *Right* all the girls around a circular table with 15 seats. Assuming an unlimited supply of children of both sexes, both players will alternate in their 'moves' (seatings). To preserve decorum no child may be seated next to another of the opposite sex. Whoever is first unable to seat a child loses and will be left to cope with the angry parents.

3.19 In the game of *Biominoes* a 4 × 4 square is covered alternately by the two players, using a domino, until no more moves can be made (that is, the board is full or there are some isolated empty squares with no square empty at the four edges). The last player to move wins. [Banerji (1980), pp. 99–104] discusses its solution.

3.20 *Nine Men's Morris* is played with nine counters for each player on a square or rectangular board designed as shown in Figure 3.40. Each player may place one of his counters in turn. After all counters have been placed, players must move them along the board's lines, but only by one position.

When a player forms a mill (gets three in a row) he removes an opposing counter, but is not allowed to take one from an opposing mill. After a player has only three counters left, he is allowed to jump into any unoccupied positions. A player with fewer than three counters has lost.

This is an interesting game and a number of variations are known under different names: Merrilees, Morelles, Mill, Muehle. Write a Scheme program.

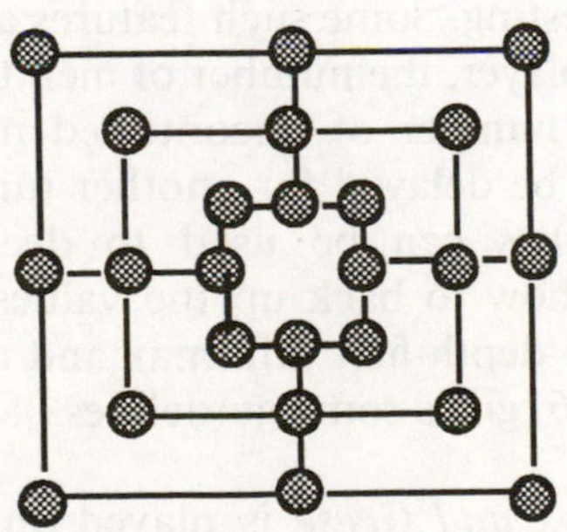

Figure 3.40 Exercise 3.20.

3.21 *Konane* ('Hawaiian checkers') is a native Hawaiian game, reported by Gyllenskog (1976). Its rules are simple enough to permit the creation of reasonably good computer programs. The game is played on a board called *Papa* or *Papamu*, with indentations called 'pits'. The total number of pits varies from 64 to 260. The strategies for winning seem to be independent of the board's size. For obvious computational reasons we will restrict ourselves to a small board (8×8). Alternate dark and light stones are placed in the pits, requiring 32 pieces of each colour. We will make an essentially arbitrary decision on numbering the board, as shown below.

```
8 ● ○ ● ○ ● ○ ● ○
7 ○ ● ○ ● ○ ● ○ ●
6 ● ○ ● ○ ● ○ ● ○
5 ○ ● ○ ● ○ ● ○ ●
4 ● ○ ● ○ ● ○ ● ○
3 ○ ● ○ ● ○ ● ○ ●
2 ● ○ ● ○ ● ○ ● ○
1 ○ ● ○ ● ○ ● ○ ●
  1 2 3 4 5 6 7 8
```

After deciding which colour each player will have, the dark player removes a dark piece either from the centre or one of the corners. The light player may then remove any adjacent man. With two empty spaces the first player now jumps over one of the light men and removes it. Jumps can be made horizontally or vertically. If a player wants (!), he can make a multiple jump (hyperjump, metajump?) as long as successive jumps are in the same direction with the same man. The first player unable to make a move is the loser.

There are sufficient features on the board to make a static evaluation interesting. Some such features are the number of legal moves for each player, the number of men that can move for each player and the number of uncontested moves for each player (moves that can be delayed for another turn without being lost). Various techniques can be used to decide which moves to investigate and how to back up the values of tip nodes. Useful methods include depth-first minimax and alpha-beta procedures. Gyllenskog (1976) gives some guidelines.

3.22 The game of *Fox and Geese* is played on an ordinary checkerboard, between the *Fox*, who owns a single black or red piece, and the *Geese*, who have four white ones. As in checkers the players use only the squares of one colour, and the Geese are initially placed on

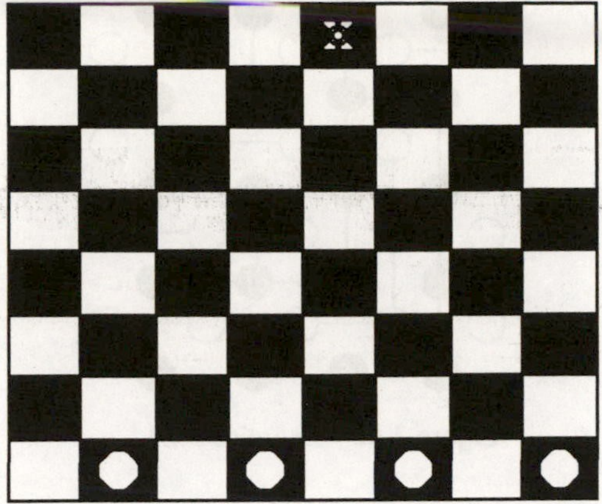

Figure 3.41 Exercise 3.22: The usual starting positions.

the squares marked O. The Fox starts at X, but since the Geese seem to have an advantage, it is perhaps wiser to allow the Fox to choose his own starting square (provided this has the correct colour), and then let the Geese have the first move.

The Geese move diagonally one place forward – like ordinary checkers they are not allowed to retreat. The Fox also moves diagonally and only one place, but like a King in checkers, he may move in any one of the four diagonal directions. There is no taking or jumping. Braver than in real life, the Geese aim to trap the Fox so that he has no legal move left, while conversely the Fox tries to break through the barrier of Geese in order to escape. The first player unable to move is therefore the loser. Write an appropriate Scheme program.

Berlekamp *et al.* (1982) report a generally held opinion that between expert players the Geese should win, but even against most moderately competent players a wily Fox can usually win a game every now and then, and if we let him choose his starting position, he should be able to defeat most novices for quite some time.

3.23 Figure 3.42 shows the board of an interesting game, called *BridgeIt* (also sometimes referred to as *Gale*). Imagine a swamp: its north and south shores are called Black's shores and the east and west are White's shores. Black and White have built white and black piers in a regular pattern in the swamp (represented by dots) with the ultimate plan of building a bridge between their shores.

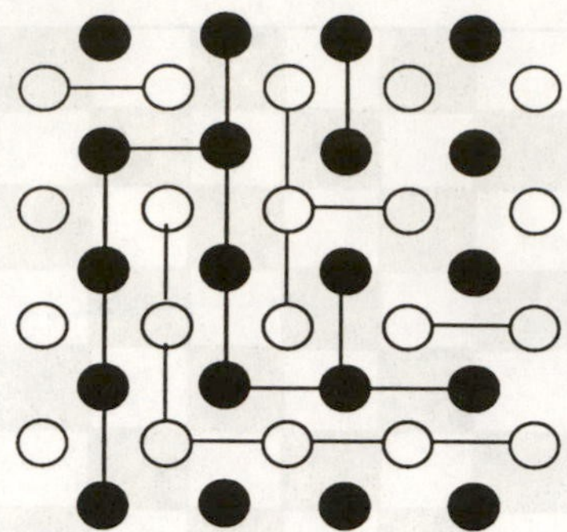

Figure 3.42 Exercise 3.23.

Bridges are not allowed to cross each other. When it is his turn, each player can throw a bridge of his own colour between piers of his own colour. Whoever completes the first bridge wins. In the figure, Black has just won.

3.24 *Officers and Recruits* is the name of another game taken from Berlekamp *et al.* (1982). Their description reads as follows:

'The army has been in disarray and the General has reduced all officers to the ranks and made everyone directly responsible to him. He now intends, on the advice of his military advisers, Left and Right, to recruit, from inside the army, a new hierarchy of officers. Left and Right will alternately advise that some officer currently in direct charge of four or more officers and men should recruit a new subordinate. This new officer will be directly responsible to the one who appointed him, and will, until further notice, take direct responsibility for three or more, but not all, of those officers and the men previously directly responsible to his appointer. Of course, the game must end when every officer has either two or three direct subordinates, and whichever of Left and Right gave the last advice retains the confidence of the General. We can play the game with pencil and paper by drawing the men with a circle round them all to represent the General, as in Figure 3.43. As each officer is recruited we draw a circle round all his subordinates. Figure 3.43 shows four different ways in which the first officer can be recruited for the seven-man army.

For administrative purposes officers are classified, not according to rank, but according to their number of direct subordinates. A class n officer is directly responsible for just $n + 2$ officers and men. So the General for the army in Figure 3.43 is initially a class 5 officer, but after the first move his class will be reduced.'

[*Berlekamp* et al. *(1982).*]

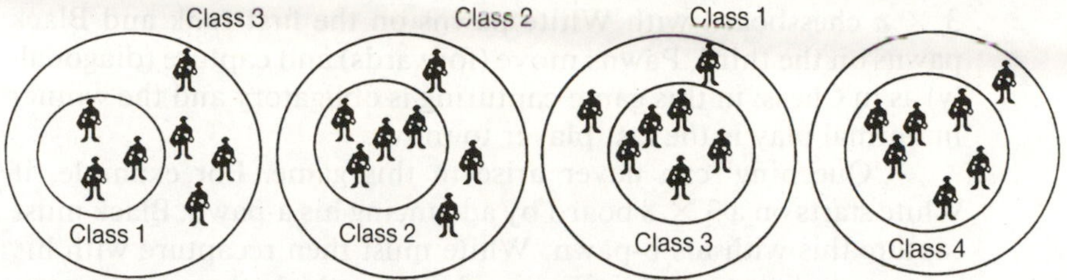

Figure 3.43 Exercise 3.24: The first recruit takes command of his men.

3.25 As a first step towards a *Go*-playing program you may wish to explore a similar but simpler game, often called *Go-Moku* or *Five in a Row*. In this game two players take turns to place stones on a rectangular grid of squares. Whoever first gets five of his stones in an orthogonal or diagonal row wins the game. Mathematicians may prefer to play on an infinite board.

3.26 Before you embark on a project to hone your newly acquired programming skills at writing *GrandMaster 0.1*, your ultimate challenge to chess programming, it may be appropriate to try something a bit simpler first. T.R. Dawson invented a game, which Berlekamp *et al.* (1982) call *Dawson's Chess*. It is played on a

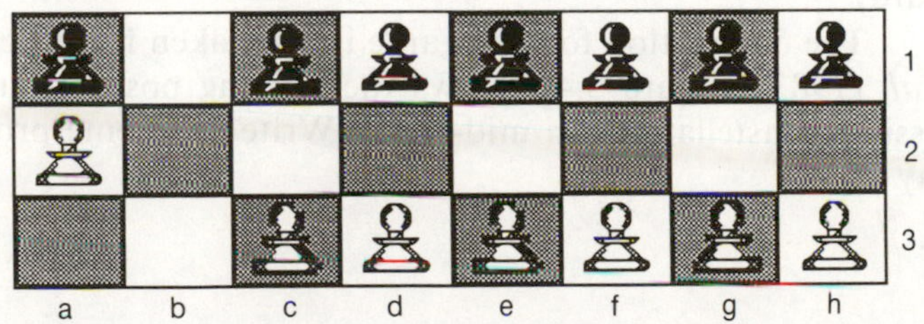

Figure 3.44 Exercise 3.26.

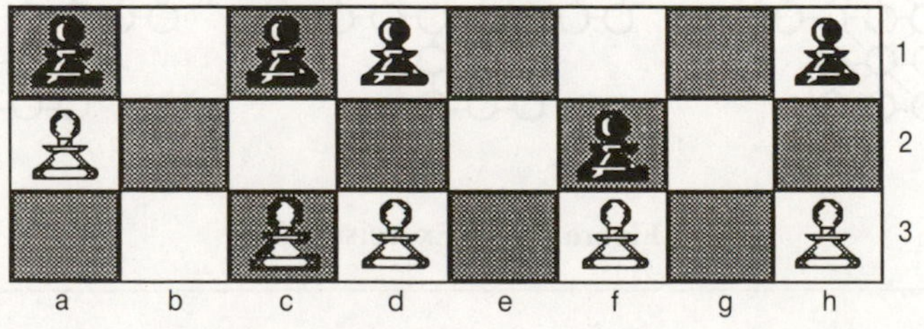

Figure 3.45 Exercise 3.26.

$3 \times n$ chessboard with White pawns on the first rank and Black pawns on the third. Pawns move (forwards) and capture (diagonally) as in Chess; in this game capturing is obligatory and the winner in normal play is the last player to move.

'Queening' can never arise in this game. For example, if White starts on a 3×8 board by advancing his a-pawn, Black must capture this with his b-pawn. White must then recapture with his b-pawn and the result is Figure 3.44 in which the a-pawns are immobilized and it is Black's turn to move. If Black now advances his f-pawn, White must capture with his e- or g-pawn, which Black will recapture, and after two further recaptures we reach the situation shown in Figure 3.45. Once again a pair of pawns is blocked and the player to move has changed. White may pass the turn back to Black by advancing his h-pawn, and so immobilizing yet another pair.

3.27 In the game of *Wolves and Sheep* the player known as the shepherd has 20 sheep, which have the first move. They may only move one place forward or sideways, and only on to unoccupied places. The two wolves can move similarly, but on any of the indicated lines and can capture in these directions by jumping, as in checkers. They may also make the same kind of multiple captures. A wolf failing to make a possible capture may be removed by the shepherd, so that the sheep may be used as decoys. The shepherd wins if he gets nine sheep into the *fold* (top nine positions of the board).

The description for this game is also taken from Berlekamp *et al.* (1982). Figure 3.46 shows the starting position and some possible constellations in mid-game. Write a Scheme program to play it.

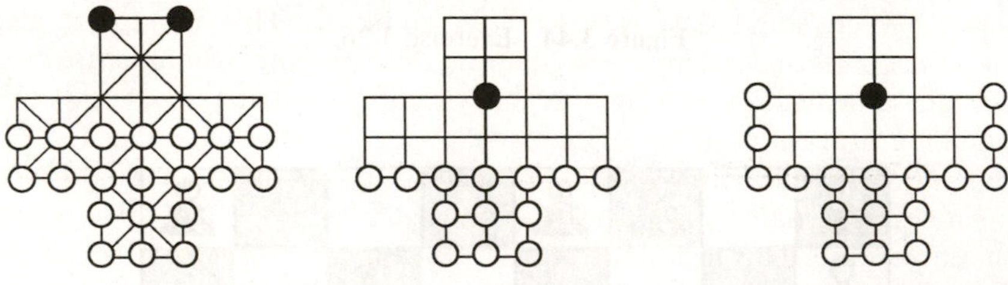

Figure 3.46 Exercise 3.27.

3.3 Pattern matching and associative databases

'My mumble bzzz grumble grumble.
That's very interesting.
Ugh, you izzle flerp me.
What makes you think that I izzle flerp You?
Gorch.
Does that have anything to do with the fact that
your mumble bzzz grumble grumble?
. . .'

[*From a dialogue with* Eliza, *reported in Hayes (1978), p. 161. The user's inputs are italicized*.]

3.3.1 A historical perspective

Since problem solvers must often look for patterns in problems in order to decide on a promising strategy for their solution, pattern matching is one of the most fundamental techniques underlying AI programs. Although the term has been used for a large and only weakly connected body of procedures, their common philosophy seeks to discover regularities in a domain. This may either be accomplished in a holistic fashion, or by sequential testing against some familiar frame of reference.

In the simplest case the input to a pattern-matching procedure may consist of a string of symbols, and the reference frame may be a partially instantiated template, whose elements are to be compared for identity. This is the realm of *syntactic pattern matching*, an area which achieved early prominence in Weizenbaum's *Eliza* program. The same set of techniques may also be ported to other contexts – for example, to the retrieval of information from data or knowledge bases. In traditional computing, information is accessed through 'names' bound to an address in some storage space. An alternative approach, sometimes referred to as '*associative memory*', seeks to retrieve information by 'value', given some description of its contents. This metaphor also suggests a pattern-matching activity, this time ranging over all entities in a database instead of ranging over all symbols in a string. The result of a matching process may be a Boolean answer, or, if we wish to force a match to succeed, it may consist of a set of bindings to uninstantiated variables. Alternatively we may wish to trigger a computation, by calling on a procedure. This technique of '*pattern-directed procedure invocation*' [Kornman (1983)] became popular in the early 1960s, and it is closely associated with **Planner**, **QA4**, **Conniver**, **QLISP**, **Popler** and other AI languages of that period. It was a basic notion of these systems that knowledge should reside in procedures rather than propositions, and

Routine name	Parameters
	functions on associations
MakeAssoc	aSymbol aValue
GetSymbol	anAssociation
GetValue	anAssociation
	functions on ALists
MakeAList	any number of associations
GetAssociation	aPatternVariable anAlist
GetAssociationValue	aPatternVariable anAlist
	functions on patterns
PATTERN	any number of **pattern elements** (*see Figure 3.48 below*)
PrintPattern	aPattern
MakeVariableSubst	aPattern anAList
	functions for pattern matches
Match	aPattern aList [optionalAList]

Figure 3.47 Some of the procedures in the 'Patterns' toolbox.

pattern-directed invocation, associative databases, automatic backtracking and goal orientation were among their central features. The term 'demon procedures' is often used in this context. One such language, **Planner** [Hewitt (1972)], in its incarnation as **MicroPlanner** [Sussman *et al.* (1981)], was used to implement **SHRDLU**, which became an extremely influential AI program.

3.3.2 The 'Patterns' toolbox

Pattern-matching techniques are a basic building block for a wide range of programming metaphors, and many of our other toolboxes rely on them. The *Patterns* toolbox therefore contains a representative collection of simple pattern-matching functions, which are listed in Figure 3.47.

MakeAssoc, **GetSymbol** and **GetValue** are grouped around a data structure called '*associations*'. Such *associations* are used to store pairs of <symbol, value> bindings and are collected into list structures called *AList*s. **MakeAList**, **GetAssociation** and **GetAssociationValue** process such *AList*s. **GetAssociationValue** is in fact equivalent to '**(GetValue (GetAssociation anAList))**', with the additional effect that '*Fatal-Error*' will be called if there is no binding for the requested pattern variable.

Form	Meaning
?	match any single basic element.
(? var)	match any single basic element and bind it to var in the returned AList.
?+	match any sequence of one or more basic elements.
(?+ var)	match any sequence of one or more basic elements and bind var in the returned AList to this value.
(<-? var)	match against the basic element bound to var by a previous match.
(? var predicate . . . .) (?+ var predicate . . . .) (<-? var predicate . . . .)	these functions are similar to the equivalent definitions above, but they will additionally require that the predicate functions succeed when the current AList is passed to them as a parameter.

Figure 3.48 Valid pattern elements.

PATTERN, PrintPattern and **MakeVariableSubst** process a range of patterns, the interpretation of which we will describe further later. **PATTERN** forms a pattern out of descriptions of individual pattern elements, **PrintPattern** just shows such patterns in a more readable format and **MakeVariableSubst** replaces all references to previous bindings, which may be requested by **(<-? var)** pattern elements, with the associated values stored in its *AList*.

Match is the main driver function, triggering syntactic pattern matches at the user level. It expects a list and a pattern as arguments, and may return **#t** for a successful match, or **#f**. If a pattern contains variables, it will return an *AList* of bindings instead. An optional parameter can also be offered to **Match**, containing an initial *AList*. In this case its bindings will be taken for **(<-? var)** during the matching process. This feature is useful since the initial *AList* may have been constructed by a previous match, to which we wish to add further elaborations. An outline of the matching algorithm used by **Match** is shown in Figure 3.49.

Patterns are lists of *basic elements* and *matching elements*. Basic elements may include strings, numbers, symbols, lists and others. The eight forms of valid *matching elements* are listed in Figure 3.48. Note that our notion of pattern is recursive, since patterns may include other patterns as elements.

```
function Match ( pattern, list, AList )
  if both pattern and list are empty then
      if AList ≠ #f then return AList                          ; success
      else return #t                                           ; success
  else if either pattern or list are empty then
      return #f                                                ; fail
  else case car(pattern) of
      ?:      return Match( cdr(pattern), cdr(list), AList )
      ?+:     { let try = Match( cdr(pattern), cdr(list), AList )
                if try ≠ #f then return try
                else return Match( pattern, cdr(list), AList )
              }
      (? var predicates) :
              let newAList = bind var to car(list) in AList
              if predicates are satisfied using newAList then
                   return Match( cdr(pattern), cdr(list), newAList )
              else return #f                                   ; fail
      (?+ var predicates) :
              let newAList = add car(list) to end of list bound to
                                        var using AList
              if predicates are satisfied using newAList then
                  { let try = Match( cdr(pattern), cdr(list), newAList )
                    if try ≠ #f then return try
                    else return Match( pattern cdr(list), newAList )
                  }
              else return #f                                   ; fail
      (<-? var predicates) :
              if predicates are satisfied using AList then
                { let binding = value bound to var in AList
                  let newPattern = concatenate( binding, cdr(pattern) )
                  return Match( newPattern, list, AList )
                }
              else return #f                                   ; fail
      ( . . . . ) :
              ; match sub-list recursively
              let newAList = Match ( car(pattern), car(list), AList )
              if newAList = #f then return #f                  ; fail
              else return Match ( cdr(pattern), cdr(list), newAList )
      otherwise :
              ; simple basic element
              if equal( car(pattern), cdr(list) ) then
                    return Match ( cdr(pattern), cdr(list), AList )
              else return #f                                   ; fail
```

Figure 3.49 Algorithm used by recursive *Match* function.

Let us look now at some simple examples.

```
(Match (PATTERN ''unlucky number'' 13 '!)
       '(''unlucky number'' 13 !))
   returns:    #t
(Match (PATTERN ''unlucky number'' 42 '!)
       '(''unlucky number'' 13 !))
   returns:    #f
(Match (PATTERN ''unlucky number'' ? '!)
       '(''unlucky number'' 13 !))
   returns:    #t
(Match (PATTERN ''unlucky number'' ?+)
       '(''unlucky number'' 13 !))
   returns:    #t
```

The reason why these matches succeed or fail should be rather obvious. Patterns must be constructed by use of the **PATTERN** function, which takes any number of symbols and matching elements. If **PATTERN** is not used, no pattern elements will be expanded and a list will be matched 'literally'.

```
(Match '(''unlucky number'' ?)
       '(''unlucky number'' 13))
   returns:    #f
(Match '(''unlucky number'' ?)
       '(''unlucky number'' ?))
   returns:    #t
```

The following group of matches will bind some variables:

```
(Match (PATTERN ''unlucky number'' (? 'x) '!)
       '(''unlucky number'' 13 !))
   returns:    ((x 13))
(Match (PATTERN ''unlucky number'' (? 'x) (? 'y))
       '(''unlucky number'' 13 !))
   returns:    ((x 13) (y !))
(Match (PATTERN ''unlucky number'' (?+ 'x))
       '(''unlucky number'' 13 !))
   returns:    ((x (13 !)))
```

We can also match against bindings obtained in previous matches:

```
(Match (PATTERN ''unlucky number'' (? 'x) (<-? 'x)
       '(''unlucky number'' 13 13))
   returns:    ((x 13))
(Match (PATTERN ''unlucky numbers'' (?+ 'x) (<-? 'x))
       '(''unlucky numbers'' 7 13 7 13))
   returns:    ((x (7 13)))
```

If predicate functions are supplied, these will be invoked before any matches are allowed to succeed. Note, however, that tentative bindings will have already been made, and that these functions will also be applied to the current *AList* as a whole. It is therefore the responsibility of each predicate to retrieve any current bindings for the pattern variables it is interested in.

```
(Match (PATTERN "unlucky number"
                 (? 'x
                    (lambda (anAList)
                    ; predicate for checking if x is "positive"
                     (positive?
                       ; get current binding for x (just made !)
                       (GetAssociationValue 'x anAlist)))))
       '("unlucky number" 13))
    returns:    ((x 13))
(Match (PATTERN "unlucky number"
                 (? 'x
                    (lambda (anAList)  ; test for positiveness
                     (positive?
                       (GetAssociationValue 'x anAlist)))
                    (lambda (anAList)  ; test for evenness
                     (even?
                       (GetAssociationValue 'x anAlist)))))
       '("unlucky number" 13))
    returns:    #f
```

In the first case we test the second string element for positiveness, which succeeds. An appropriate *AList* is therefore returned. The match in the second example fails when the second predicate is applied, since '13' is certainly not 'even'.

If we wish to match against properties of substructures we may make use of the fact that patterns may contain patterns themselves.

```
(Match (PATTERN "secret of success:"
                 (PATTERN (? 'x) 'attitude) (? 'y))
       '("secret of success:" (positive attitude) !))
    returns:    ((x positive) (y !))
```

It should be stressed that the list (*positive attitude*) serves as a substructure here.

Since none of these matches took account of any previous bindings for pattern variables, we will show the use of an *AList* as a third argument to **Match** as a final example.

```
(Match (PATTERN "unlucky number" (<-? 'x))  ; a pattern
       '("unlucky number" 13)               ; a list
       '((x 13)))                           ; an Alist
    returns:    ((x 13))
```

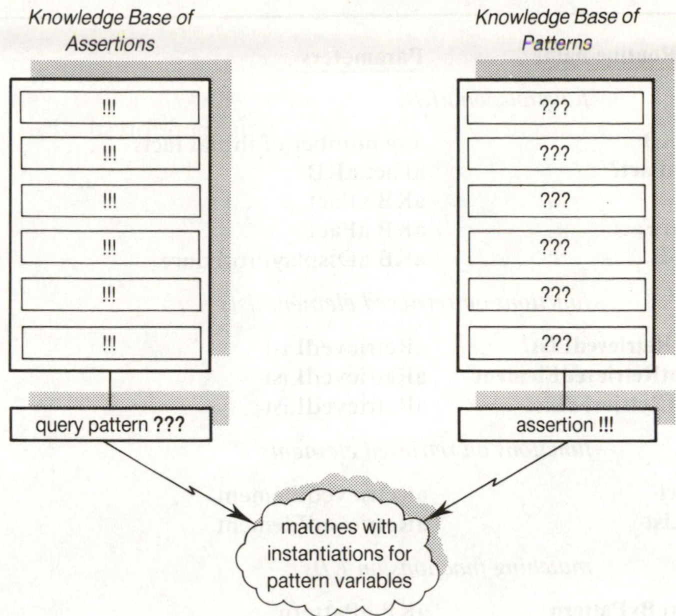

Figure 3.50 Two types of knowledge bases.

These functions provide only a kernel of features for a fully fledged pattern-matching language. They do, however, offer sufficient flexibility for our purposes. Since their commented source is given in Appendix III, you may wish to browse these definitions in order to gain a clearer understanding of their detailed operation.

3.3.3 The 'KnowledgeBases' toolbox

Many typical applications will require repeated matches of patterns against a collection of items stored in some knowledge base. Alternatively we may also wish to test a given item against a whole collection of patterns. Recursive or iterative constructs may be built to serve this purpose, but it is often more convenient to group items into an entity we will refer to as a '*knowledge base*'. At this stage we will leave the specific contents of the knowledge bases undefined, although we deem it appropriate to refer to such individual items as '*facts*'. If we view facts as lists of assertions, then the idea of such knowledge bases corresponds to the notion of *associative databases*, whose contents are retrieved through a matching process rather than by location. If patterns are stored in the knowledge base, we obtain the concept of *pattern bases*, against which assertions may sequentially be matched.

Routine name	Parameters
functions on aKBs	
MakeKB	any number of initial facts
KnownFact?	aFact aKB
AddFact	aKB aFact
RemoveFact	aKB aFact
PrintKB	aKB aDisplayProcedure
functions on retrieved element lists	
EmptyRetrievedList?	aRetrievedList
CurrentRetrievedElement	aRetrievedList
RestOfRetrievedList	aRetrievedList
functions on retrieved elements	
GetFact	aRetrievedElement
GetAList	aRetrievedElement
matching functions on KBs	
RetrieveByPattern	aKB aPattern [optional: aSelectorFN anAList]
RetrieveByString	aKB aPattern [optional: aSelectorFN anAList]
RetrieveAllByPattern	aKB aPattern [optional: aSelectorFN anAList]
RetrieveAllByString	aKB aPattern [optional: aSelectorFN anAList]

Figure 3.51 Summary of the *KnowledgeBases* toolbox interface routines.

Figure 3.50 shows these two types of knowledge bases, both of which are supported by our *KnowledgeBases toolbox.* This toolbox builds on the pattern-matching facilities mentioned, and adds a collection of functions for making and printing knowledge bases. Addition and removal of *facts* is supported, and the presence of *facts* can of course also be tested for, either by explicit assertion, or through a description in terms of appropriate patterns. Figure 3.51 lists this toolbox's protocol.

The purpose of the first group of procedures should be self-explanatory. A *RetrievedElement* is a data structure describing the components of *RetrievedList*s, which are returned by our retrieval functions. The cluster of functions on lists of retrieved elements allows the sequential processing of such *RetrievedList*s. Any *RetrievedElement* is itself a list of two elements: a *fact* and the *AList* of bindings for pattern variables which were established by the matching process. **GetFact** and **GetAList** are used to select these two components.

The 'top-level' functions of this toolbox permit retrieval of appropriate elements by either matching a pattern against a knowledge base of facts, or by matching a fact against a knowledge base of patterns. **RetrieveByPattern** and **RetrieveAllByPattern** will both process a given pattern against the contents of the knowledge base. Again, an optional *AList* may be provided to pre-instantiate pattern variables. Since we refrain from making any assumptions about a fact's structure, the user may also wish to supply *aSelectorFN* (the whole fact is otherwise used by default), which is a procedure for selecting that part of a fact the matching process should be addressed to. We will give an example below.

The difference between the two functions is that **RetrieveAllByPattern** returns a list of all matching elements in the database, while **RetrieveByPattern** stops after the first match has been found. **RetrieveByString** and **RetrieveAllByString** are the corresponding operations for matching items against pattern bases. All the stored patterns will be tried in sequence, and a list of matching elements and their *AList*s will again be returned.

```
(define RiverWorld (MakeKB '(little bear)
                           '(little tiger)
                           '(big tiger)
                           '(happy mole)))
; riverworld
```

defines a small database of facts about story characters, which we may wish to process. A simple query language for such an associative database can easily be assembled from the above pattern-matching functions. Here we will just show how to retrieve names by property. One way to achieve this for a given property name is just to make a pattern whose first element refers to the property and whose second element's value we do not care about for the moment. This will return a list of all those facts in which the property appears in the first slot. This list can then be processed to yield all the associated second elements; that is, the story characters to which the property applies.

```
(define whoIs
  (lambda (aWorld aProperty)
    (map (lambda (anElement)
            (cadr (GetFact anElement)))  ; get second element of match
         (RetrieveAllByPattern aWorld (PATTERN aProperty ?)))))
; whois
(whoIs RiverWorld 'little)
; (bear tiger)
```

The basic idea is of course fairly similar to Scheme's association lists. Our pattern-matching functions, however, are much more flexible and powerful.

Instead of having a list of facts against which a query pattern is to be matched, we can also store a list of patterns and match them against a list of items which represent facts. For example:

```
(define OwlsMemory (MakeKB
                        (PATTERN ?+ 'little  (? 'smallOne) ?+)
                        (PATTERN ?+ 'brave (? 'braveOne) ?+)
                        (PATTERN ?+ 'happy (? 'happyOne) ?+)))
; owlsmemory
```

Each of the patterns will be independently applied to the list representing the fact. If any dependencies between 'passes' must be encoded, this can be done by attaching *AList*s to patterns; that is, the bindings in such an *AList* will be determined by the processing of the *AList* returned by a previous match. Here we assume that all three passes are made independently, checking for *little*, *brave* and *happy* creatures respectively. Note that the use of *?+* assumes that those keywords are surrounded by other text. We will not find them if they occur at the start or end of a string.

```
(RetrieveAllByString
   OwlsMemory
   '(there is little bear,
     who is also a brave bear,
     and then there is happy mole, of course))
; (((#<PROCEDURE ?+> little
     (#<PROCEDURE ?> smallone ( ))  #<PROCEDURE ?+>)
   ((smallone bear)))
   ((#<PROCEDURE ?+> brave
     (#<PROCEDURE ?> braveone ( ))   #<PROCEDURE ?+>)
   ((braveone bear)))
   ((#<PROCEDURE ?+> happy
     (#<PROCEDURE ?> happyone ( ))  #<PROCEDURE ?+>)
   ((happyone mole))))
```

We should carefully observe the structure of what is returned by **RetrieveAllByString**. As stated earlier this *RetrievedList* consists of three *RetrievedElements*, each of which is a list of a pattern and its associated *AList*. The first of these *AList*s shows an association between *bear* and *smallOne*, and the rest bind the other relevant creatures. This list also makes it apparent that our toolbox implements pattern elements as procedures.

We have already mentioned that our retrieval procedures' optional arguments may include a selector function as well as an initial *AList*. This facility is an important prerequisite for employing this toolbox as the base for the 'production systems' idea we discuss in the next section. We will also soon use it to implement a *Tiny-Eliza* program, but it may be instructive to review the basic idea first. Let us therefore assume that we wish to associate a procedure with each of our patterns. The patterns will still act as triggers for what should be retrieved, but apart from the pattern itself any knowledge base item will now also contain such a procedure. It might be the purpose of the procedure to announce what match has been made, or it may produce some other relevant side effects.

```
(define OwlsMemory
    (MakeKB
     (cons (PATTERN ?+ 'little (? 'x) ?+)
           ; a procedure
           (lambda (aFriend)
               (DisplayLine ''I'm little'' aFriend)))
     (cons (PATTERN ?+ 'hasty (? 'x) ?+)
           ; a procedure
           (lambda (aFriend)
               (DisplayLine ''I'm hasty'' aFriend)))
     (cons (PATTERN ?+ 'lazy (? 'x) ?+)
           ; a procedure
           (lambda (aFriend)
               (DisplayLine ''I'm lazy'' aFriend)))))
; owlsmemory
```

The '*cons*' makes a fact as a (dotted) pair of a pattern and a procedure, which we then store in the knowledge base. Invoking **RetrieveByString** will now return a *RetrievedList*, which we will bind to *element*, so that we may examine it further. For this scheme to work we also need a means to constrain matches to parts of a fact only, and this is what our selector procedure is meant to provide.

```
(define element
    (RetrieveByString
     ; the knowledge base
     OwlsMemory
     ; the "string" (a list !)
     '(there is little bear, who is also a brave bear
       , and there is happy mole, of course)
     ; and the selection procedure
     car))
; element
```

Selection procedures will always operate on facts as their arguments. Here we chose the *car* of the fact (the pattern) as the part on which matching should be attempted. Since we have also changed our patterns so that there is now only a single match, the returned *AList* looks like this:

```
(GetAList element)
  ; ((x bear))
```

and the relevant fact is the pair of a matched pattern and its associated procedure.

```
(GetFact element)
  ; ( ; this is the "successful" pattern
     (#<PROCEDURE ?+> little (#<PROCEDURE ?> x ())
      #<PROCEDURE?+>)
     ; and this is the associated procedure
      #<PROCEDURE>)
```

We may now choose to execute this procedure, with the retrieved *AList* element (*bear*) as its argument:

```
( ; apply the procedure
 (cdr (GetFact element))
 ; to the AList binding for 'x
 (GetAssociationValue 'x (GetAlist element)))
 ; I'm little bear
```

3.3.4 'InnKeeper' – a crude example of a counselling program

To summarize the main features of both the *Patterns* and *KnowledgeBases* toolboxes, we will now show a crude example of programs which simulate language 'understanding' in man/computer dialogues. **SHRDLU** was one of the first systems to demonstrate that computer-based language understanding is possible, as long as we restrict ourselves to a closed and well-defined domain. SHRDLU's domain was the so-called 'blocks world', a scenario which also served as a setting for many other AI programs. The tasks in this microworld revolve around a tabletop of children's coloured blocks and other geometric objects, and SHRDLU's 'understanding' is limited to the physical properties of such blocks and their relationships with each other. **Eliza** [Weizenbaum (1966)] is a much less sophisticated program, which simulates the therapeutic conversation of a non-directive psychiatrist. Unlike SHRDLU it is almost contentless, since its responses to keywords are merely reflexive and draw no conclusions at all about 'semantic' connections between symbols and any part of 'reality'. **Racter** is the name of another well-known program in which pattern matching plays a dominant role. Its name is derived from the French *'raconteur'* (story teller), abbreviated to the six-character limit imposed on identifiers in the FORTRAN and BASIC traditions. Unlike Eliza and many of its variants, Racter has grown into a stimulating program, whose conversations revolve around Italian music, wine and food. A number of the more outrageous of these are recorded in a book called *The Policeman's Beard Is Half-Constructed* [Racter (1984)]. Finally, Carbonnell's (1981) **Mixed-Initiative Conversational System (MICS)** is an example of a much more sophisticated program, which combines pattern matching with schemata and conceptual graphs. MICS forms internal models of a speaker and uses goals and subgoals to direct the flow of a conversation.

Our design for this example was influenced by features found in many similar systems, like **Eliza**, **Doctor** and **Shrink** [Tanimoto (1987)]. It must be stressed that ascribing any degree of 'understanding' to such a program is totally unwarranted. What is offered is only a shallow screening of input strings with regard to certain 'stimuli' (keywords), for which a 'canned' response is produced.

InnKeeper's task domain is the counselling of patrons in a restaurant microworld. All its functionality is embedded in a single parameterless procedure, which may be invoked by evaluating the expression (*InnKeeper*). We assume that all user input is given as a list. The pattern base and some additional variables are defined at the procedure's top level. These variables are used as intermediate storage, to set certain background modes (for example, *desire*, *evicted*, *allDone*) and as indices to select sequentially from a repertoire of 'canned' phrases and answers (such as '*? is never on our menu*' or '*indeed?*'). One of these phrases is always used when *InnKeeper* has no better response to give.

```
; ===== InnKeeper =====

(define InnKeeper
  (lambda ()

  ; the knowledge base and other global variables
   (let ((InnKeeper-KB #f)
         (guestName     #f)
         (sentence      #f)  ; guest's reply
         (desire        'food) ; food or drink
         (selectionNo   0)   ; index into lists of alternatives
         (evicted       #f)
         (allDone       #f))
```

The menus of currently available food and drink items are also stored globally.

```
(define mealList
    '("gooey gruel" "mouldy mushrooms"
     "leathery leg of lamb"))
(define drinkList
    '("stale beer" "sour wine" "murky water"))
```

A number of predicates for testing for a pattern variable's membership in certain word categories need to be defined.

```
(define orderWord?
  (lambda (anAList)
    ; does the pattern variable 'order' express a wish to order ?
    (member (GetAssociationValue 'order anAList)
            '(have want like about))))

(define eatWord?
  (lambda (anAList)
    ; does the pattern variable 'eat' express a wish to eat ?
    (member (GetAssociationValue 'eat anAList)
            '(eat hungry starving))))

(define drinkWord?
  (lambda (anAList)
    ; does the pattern variable 'drink' express a wish to drink ?
    (member (GetAssociationValue 'drink anAList)
            '(drink thirsty dry))))

(define possessionWord?
  (lambda (anAList)
    ; does the pattern variable 'possession' denote something valuable ?
    (member (GetAssociationValue 'possession anAList)
            '(money gold silver))))

(define pleasureWord?
  (lambda (anAList)
    ; does the pattern variable 'pleasure' express pleasure ?
    (member (GetAssociationValue 'pleasure anAList)
            '(lovely yummy excellent great))))

(define displeasureWord?
  (lambda (anAList)
    ; does the pattern variable 'displeasure' express displeasure ?
    (member (GetAssociationValue 'displeasure anAList)
            '(filthy yacky awful terrible inedible))))
```

The next two functions are used to select food or drink items from the menu. This is done according to the value of a global index variable (*selectionNo*), so as to offer the guest some variety.

```
(define meal
  (lambda ()
    (set! selectionNo (+ 1 selectionNo))
    (if (= selectionNo (length mealList))
        (set! selectionNo 0)
        #f)
    (list-ref mealList selectionNo)))

(define drink
  (lambda ()
    (set! selectionNo (+ 1 selectionNo))
    (if (= selectionNo (length drinkList))
        (set! selectionNo 0)
        #f)
    (list-ref drinkList selectionNo)))
```

The following procedures use the same index to select sequentially from a number of 'hollow' phrases, offering stereotyped replies.

```
(define evasiveAnswer
  (lambda ()
    (define repertoire '("is off today"
                         "is never on our menu"
                         "is not popular around here"))
    (set! selectionNo (+ 1 selectionNo))
    (if (= selectionNo (length repertoire))
        (set! selectionNo 0)
        #f)
    (list-ref repertoire selectionNo)))

(define disinterestedComment
  (lambda ()
    (define repertoire '("Indeed ?"
                         "Amazing"
                         "That's fairly interesting"))
    (set! selectionNo (+ 1 selectionNo))
    (if (= selectionNo (length repertoire))
        (set! selectionNo 0)
        #f)
    (list-ref repertoire selectionNo)))
```

Any other reply should be generated by a procedure attached to the relevant pattern for which this reply is fitting. The next procedure turns a list representing such a reply into a string.

```
(define reply
  (lambda aList
    ; remove any outer brackets or sublists and show the resulting list
```

```
(define replyAux
  (lambda (aList)
    (do ((rest aList (cdr rest)))
        ((null? rest))
        (if (pair? (car rest))
            (replyAux (car rest))
            (display (car rest)))
        (display   " "))))

  (replyAux aList)))
```

We need two further utility functions: to check whether a patron can actually pay before we serve him, and to remove him from our inn if he cannot. Note that *serve* uses the pattern matcher directly.

```
(define serve
  (lambda ()
    (reply "You are a man of means, I assume ?")
    (set! answer (readAnswer))
    (if (Match (PATTERN ?+ (? 'possession possessionWord?))
               answer)
       (begin
         ; serve
         (reply "Nissifer will bring your order in a minute.")
         (reply "Stay as long as you like"))
       (begin
         ; evict
         (reply "Much as it embarrasses me, I"
                "must urge you to take your business elsewhere")
       evict)))))

(define evict
  (lambda () (set! evicted #t)))
```

All of *InnKeeper*'s conversational patterns are stored as a pair of the pattern against which the user's replies are matched, and a procedure which will be called once a match has succeeded. *makeFact* creates such pairs, and *selectPattern* and *selectProc* act as selector functions.

```
(define makeFact
  (lambda (aPattern aProcedure) (cons aPattern aProcedure)))

(define selectPattern car)        ; select the pattern part of a fact
(define selectProc    cdr)        ; select the procedure part of a fact
```

The following procedure fills the knowledge base with some exemplary facts (pattern–procedure pairs).

```
(define initializeKB
  (lambda ()
    (set!
      innKeeper-KB
      (MakeKB
       ; guest wants to eat
       (makeFact (PATTERN ?+ (? 'eat eatWord?))
                 (lambda (al) (set! desire 'food)
                              (reply ''May I suggest the'' (meal) ''?'')))
       ; guest wants to drink
       (makeFact (PATTERN ?+ (? 'drink drinkWord?))
                 (lambda (al) (set! desire 'drink)
                              (reply ''May I suggest'' (drink) ''?'')))
       ; guest wants to order an item
       (makeFact (PATTERN ?+ (? 'order orderWord?) (?+ 'what))
                 (lambda (al)
                  (if (or (member (GetAssociationValue 'what al)
                                  mealList)
                          (member (GetAssociationValue 'what al)
                                  drinkList))
                      ; ordered item is on menu
                      (serve)
                      ; ordered item is not on menu
                      (reply ''Sorry, but''
                             (GetAssociationValue 'what al)
                             (evasiveAnswer))) ))
       ; guest accepts
       (makeFact (PATTERN 'yes ?+) (lambda (al) (serve)))
       ; guest declines
       (makeFact (PATTERN 'no ?+)
                 (lambda (al)
                  (reply ''Would you care for some''
                         (if (eq? desire 'food) (meal) (drink))
                         ''then ?'')))
       ; guest wants to pay a compliment
       (makeFact (PATTERN ?+ (? 'pleasure pleasureWord?))
                 (lambda (al) (reply ''Thank you.'')))
       ; guest didn't like it
       (makeFact (PATTERN ?+ (? 'displeasure displeasureWord?))
                 (lambda (al) (reply ''This is preposterous !''
                                     ''I must ask you to leave'')
                              (evict)))
       ; guest leaves
       (makeFact (PATTERN 'Bye) (lambda (al)
```

```
                                    (set! allDone #t)
                                    (if (not evicted)
                                        (reply "Come back soon"))
                                    (newline)))
        ; guest just wants to chat
    (makeFact (PATTERN ?+ (lambda (al)
                                (reply (disInterestedComment))))
    ))))
```

The final procedure is concerned with reading the user's answers,

```
(define readAnswer
  ; get a response from the guest
  (lambda ()
    (newline)
    (display "...> ")
    (set! answer (read))
    (newline)
    (if (not (pair? answer))
        (begin (reply "Please give your replies as a list")
               (readAnswer))
        answer)))
```

and the body of the *InnKeeper* procedure will now need to initialize the pattern base and cycle through a conversation. This loop is terminated whenever the user types (*bye*).

```
(initializeKB)
(set! allDone #f)
(DisplayLine "Welcome to the Blue Unicorn"
             "I am Weamish, the owner.")
(display "How may I address you ?")
(set! guestName (readAnswer))
(reply "How may we be of service" guestName "?")
(do ((answer #f)
     (element #f))
    (allDone #f)
    (set! answer (readAnswer))
    (set! element
          (RetrieveByString innKeeper-KB
                            answer
                            selectPattern))
    ((selectProc (GetFact element)) (GetAList element))))))
```

The last four lines warrant a closer analysis. After the user's reply has been stored in *answer*, the **RetrieveByString** procedure is invoked to search for the first matching pattern in the knowledge base. The returned

RetrievedElement is then locally stored in *element*. Remember that *selectPattern* selects the first component of the <pattern procedure> pairs which are stored in the knowledge base, and this pattern is then used for the match. **GetFact** will return the matched <pattern procedure> pair, the procedure component of which is then obtained by *selectProc*. This procedure is now applied to the match's association list. This whole structure, while possibly somewhat confusing to a novice Scheme programmer, is almost identical to the one we already discussed in the context of a simpler example earlier.

To keep the program from growing too long we have refrained from including too much variety in response patterns, but it should now be obvious how this repertoire can easily be extended by just adding additional facts to the pattern base. Such facts must of course be pairs of relevant patterns found in the input string and procedures describing appropriate responses. We may also extend the range of the various word categories and 'canned' replies. Let us now pay the 'Blue Unicorn' a visit. Figure 3.52 shows the resulting conversation.

In this example the user's answers are of course carefully chosen, in order to maintain the illusion of at least some limited degree of 'understanding'. As the dialogue progresses, however, it becomes painfully apparent that the level of conversation quickly starts to deteriorate. Somewhat more 'creative' responses would quickly reveal how such programs will patiently continue totally 'meaningless' exchanges of platitudes, like the one quoted at the start of this chapter.

Programs like SHRDLU, MICS and Racter are relatively 'brittle', since they convey a shallow illusion of 'understanding', whose quality tends to deteriorate quickly as soon as they move out of the relatively narrow range of their model's competence. Eliza-like systems avoid that problem by building on a simple stimulus-response metaphor, but this also makes them completely unsuited to any 'deeper' understanding at all. The section on parsing natural language expressions will later return to this topic.

EXERCISES

Since the *Patterns* toolbox is used in a number of other toolboxes and also for a number of our demonstration programs, there will be ample opportunities for exercises on how to write patterns and knowledge bases.

3.28 Use the *Patterns* toolbox to write a *CookieMonster* procedure. You will need to supply patterns which test offerings for the

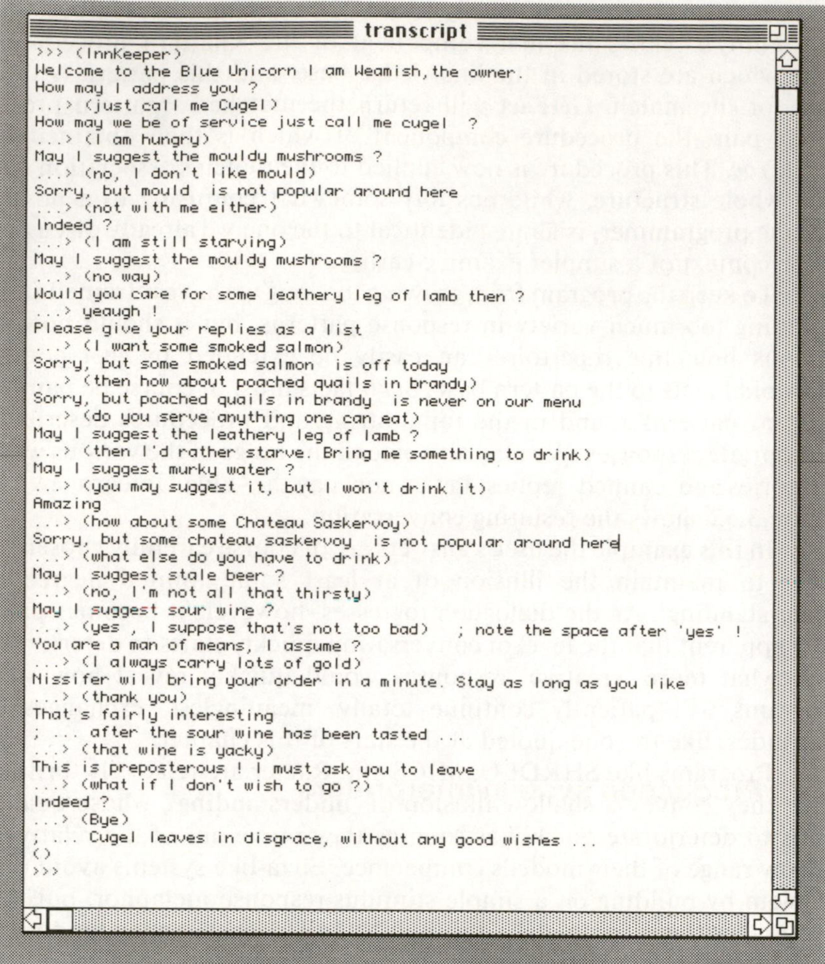

Figure 3.52 A session with *InnKeeper.*

presence of cookies or any other acceptable substitutes. Make sure that cookies are always accepted, regardless of their position in an input list. The procedure should terminate once the monster is 'full'. It may be made more interesting if you also check and penalize for swear words.

3.29 Design and implement a simple database query language, built on the features of the *KnowledgeBases* toolbox. You may assume fixed formats for database entries (that is, various classes of entities and relationships) and offer retrieval by properties, as well as facilities for compound queries, using the standard logical connectives (and, or, not). How would you define a corresponding 'data definition language'?

3.30* Write a *Tiny Eliza* program. Your program should offer a stimulating conversation partner, but you may wish to restrict dialogues to task domains in which you are particularly interested (for example, mythological creatures, world politics or the state of the economy). Try to coax your program into saying something 'profound'.

3.31 Extend the *Patterns* toolbox by implementing a **?* pattern**, which will match zero or more occurrences of a token. (?* 'unicorns), for example, should match all of the strings: (*there are no unicorns*), (*unicorns are extinct*) and (*winged unicorns may ride to the moon*). *Warning*: This is not an easy exercise.

3.32 Some early LISP interpreters running on conventional time-sharing systems provided a pattern-based list editing function as a primitive utility for interactive program editing. This typically included operations like: **display**, **find sublist**, **search and replace**, **delete**, **insert**, and so on. Design your own set of commands and implement such a facility as a pattern base, with associated 'action' procedures.

3.4 Production system interpreters

> 'A production system has two main parts – a communication area, called the workspace, and a set of condition–action pairs, called productions. If the condition side of a production is satisfied by the current contents of the workspace, then that production is said to be evoked, and the action on its action side is carried out. The workspace resembles a public bulletin board, with the productions resembling simple-minded bureaucrats who do little except look at the bulletin board. Each bureaucrat, however, is looking for a certain pattern of "notices" on the board. When it finds that pattern, the "bureaucrat" performs whatever its action is – usually merely posting a notice of its own.'
>
> [*Pylyshyn (1984), p. 82.*]

3.4.1 A historical perspective

Decision-making expertise in many types of problem-solving tasks can often be expressed quite succinctly in terms of <pattern, action> rules. One type of pattern-invoked deduction which has been of particular interest to AI is the so-called 'production system'. Production rules may be viewed as 'degenerate' procedures of the form:

condition ⟶ *a sequence of actions*

where the condition on the left-hand side defines a pattern (that is, a constellation of facts) under which the rule will be invoked, and the right-hand side is used to describe an appropriate response. Since such a 'procedure' does not respond to explicit requests, but will rather react to changing patterns in data, this concept has also been referred to as 'pattern-directed invocation'. A '*production system*' is a collection of such production rules, bound into a knowledge base called a *production memory* (**PM**), whose left-hand side patterns will be tested against the contents of another knowledge base called a *working memory* (**WM**). The working memory therefore encodes the conditions under which rules may 'fire', and its contents may be changed by assertion and retraction of facts. Such changes may occur as a consequence of a rule's application.

Using production systems for computation requires a monitor, or 'interpreter', which continually cycles through all the rules in the production memory and invokes any whose patterns will match the working memory's current state. This so-called 'recognize–act' cycle is representative of a '*forward chaining*' strategy, which deduces all implications which may follow from a given state. Such a style of inference should be contrasted with the '*backward chaining*' strategy we encountered in PROLOG, and which is also used by many other goal-directed problem solvers and planning systems. Both strategies search for some sequence (path) of 'actions', 'moves' or 'transformations' which map initial states into goal states, but they differ in the direction in which the search will proceed. **Backward chaining** reasons from goals to preconditions, as symbolized by the state/action tree shown in Figure 3.53(a). In this figure '?' is used to label goal nodes and '!' refers to an initial state. Deductions will flow 'upwards' (or 'backwards') in the problem's state/action tree. For example, in PROLOG we may write a deduction as "*friendly(bruce) :- lecturer(bruce), mood(bruce,chirpy).*" to state that: '*One way in which we may deduce whether bruce is friendly is to observe whether he is a lecturer and whether the* "*value*" *of his mood is chirpy*'. In reading this procedurally, we can view "*friendly(bruce)*" as a goal, a proof path which must be guided by the constraints (subgoals) asserted on its right. Reasoning therefore proceeds from goals to assertions.

In a **forward chaining** system, on the other hand, reasoning flows 'downwards' (or 'forwards'), from some current state to all of its implications, as shown in Figure 3.53(b). We must jump from assertions to conclusions, and may wish to continue this process until we have established a goal. The above example would need to be restated as: "*(lecturer bruce) and (mood bruce chirpy)* → *(assert (friendly bruce))*", interpreted as: '*If assertions for bruce's lecturerhood and bruce's chirpiness should appear in our workspace, then this pattern also implies the*

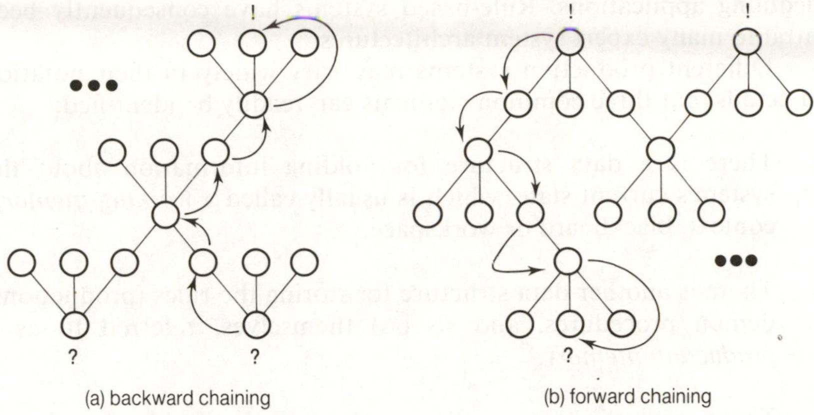

Figure 3.53 Forward and backward chaining.

assertion that he is friendly'. Both strategies' advantages and disadvantages depend very much on the topology of a particular search space. Backward chaining is superior if there are few goal states and only a few paths by which they may be reached. The state/action tree as a whole should also have a high branching factor (number of arcs leaving a node). In this case forward chaining would be forced to explore many dead ends. If, on the other hand, there are many goals, reached by many different paths, and if the state/action tree shows a low branching factor overall, then forward chaining may be superior. In such a case the backward chaining process would find it more difficult not to get trapped in dead ends. The first situation possibly arises more often in analysis problems, while the second one may be more typical in a design context. Many planning and problem-solving systems support both styles of deduction.

The original idea of production systems traces back to a computational formalism proposed by Post (1943). The notion of Markov algorithms and the stimulus–response models underlying many theories of animal behaviour are also related to this concept, while decision tables are probably its closest correspondence within the narrower realm of computer science.

The use of production systems within AI was explored by Newell and Simon (1972), and it has since become a very popular metaphor, applied under names such as *production systems*, *blackboard systems*, *pattern-directed inference systems* or *rule-based systems*. Davis and King (1977) and Hayes-Roth (1985) offer excellent surveys of the underlying principles, and Waterman and Hayes-Roth (1978) give many examples of their practical application.

Production rules seem a natural way to express many heuristics inherent in expert knowledge for diagnosis, design, planning and scheduling applications. Rule-based systems have consequently been central to many expert system architectures.

Different production systems may vary widely in their notation and details, but three common elements can readily be identified:

(1) There is a data structure for holding information about the system's current state, which is usually called a *working memory*, context, blackboard or workspace.

(2) There is another data structure for storing the rules (productions, demon procedures, and so on) themselves, referred to as a *production memory*.

(3) There is a monitor procedure, often called a *production system interpreter*, which cycles over all rules, testing their conditions against the current contents of the working memory. If a given pattern matches, it will 'fire' an associated procedure, which will often lead to changes in the working memory's state. This has been referred to as the '*recognize–act*' *cycle*, which will terminate as soon as there are no more productions to fire, or if a rule explicitly forces this cycle to be abandoned.

Figure 3.54 shows these three components in a context we will use again to demonstrate our toolbox routines. Various systems differ in the strategies they use for resolving conflicts among rules which may all wish to fire in a given state. These schemes may range from simple 'first in, first out' disciplines to some quite elaborate algorithms. Davis and King (1977) give a good summary of the most important of these.

Over the last 15 years a large number of production system interpreters have been designed, implemented and used. Their range of application includes such diverse areas as equipment maintenance, component selection, computer operation, process control and quality assurance. During the last five to seven years they have also been used very successfully for expert system development. This is due to the ease with which heuristics may be formulated to capture an expert's large body of empirical knowledge.

OPS5 [Forgy (1981)] is probably the most well-known production system 'language'. Although originally written in LISP, there are now also BLISS and C implementations. Since its origin as a tool for a PhD thesis [Rychener (1976)] it has seen extensive use in many research projects at Carnegie-Mellon University, and it is now available for many main-frames and microcomputers. OPS5 is particularly noted for its efficiency, since it encodes partially matched patterns in a discrimination net which it then uses to avoid unnecessary matches. **YAPS** [Allen (1983)] is another LISP-based production system. It offers a more flexible

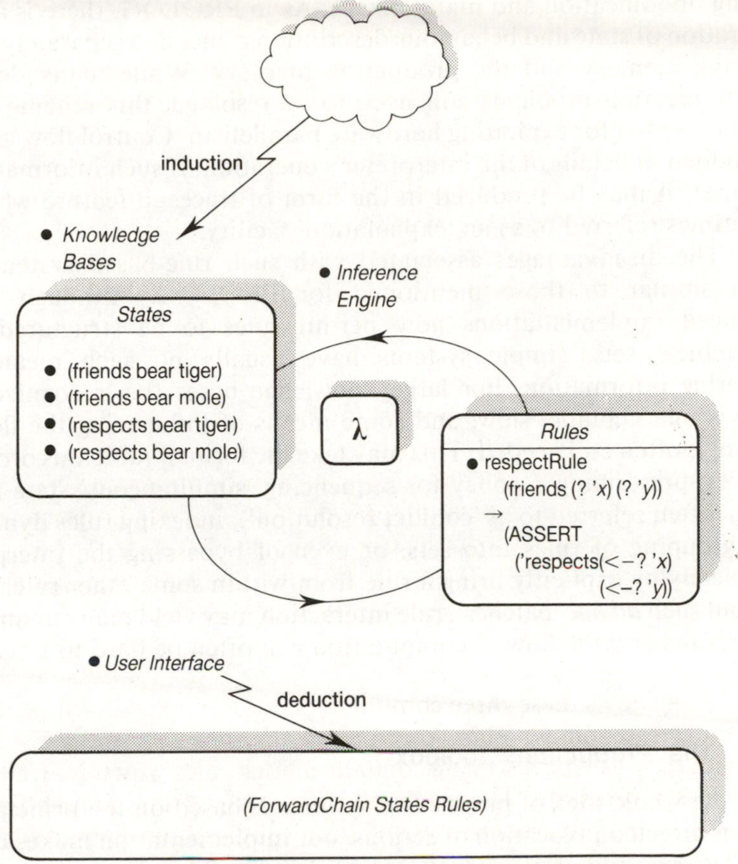

Figure 3.54 A typical production system architecture.

framework, in that objects may be directly stored in its working memory. **Opus** [Laursen and Atkinson (1987)] is a recently developed production system based on Smalltalk. Most of the so-called expert system 'shells', like **Kee**, **KnowledgeCraft**, **LOOPS** and **Humble**, are either rule-based themselves or offer some rule-based subsystem.

Production systems can claim a number of advantages which make them a good metaphor for knowledge representation. The formulation of domain knowledge in the form of rules often enhances a program's understandability and ease of modification. Since rules may in principle be written independently of each other, they provide very modular definitions. This property is similar to that of PROLOG, with which they share the associated performance penalties. Modularity allows incremental acquisition of knowledge, with the resulting ease of program testing, modification and maintenance. As in PROLOG, there is a clear separation of state and behaviour descriptions, encoded separately in the working memory and the production memory. While many detailed communication problems still need to be resolved, this scheme offers some potential for exploiting hardware parallelism. Control flow aspects are hidden in details of the interpreter's operation. If such information is required, it may be produced in the form of traces, a feature which is sometimes referred to as an 'explanation' facility.

The disadvantages associated with such rule-based systems are again similar to those mentioned for PROLOG. Although many advanced implementations now permit rules to be structured into hierarchical sets, simple systems have usually no such means for clustering information. For large knowledge bases the 'recognize–act' cycle is unacceptably slow, and some means of influencing the flow of control is often still needed. This may take the form of judicious ordering of rules, prescribing a policy for sequencing 'simultaneous' state transitions (often referred to as 'conflict resolution'), indexing rules dynamically, grouping of rules into sets, or even of bypassing the interpreter completely by explicitly firing a rule from within some other rule. Even without such *ad hoc* 'patches', rule interaction may yield many unanticipated results and the flow of computation will often be hard to trace.

3.4.2 The 'Productions' toolbox

Since the whole idea of production systems is based on the principle of pattern-directed invocation of actions, our implementation makes use of the *Patterns* and *KnowledgeBases* toolboxes. The *Productions* toolbox follows the architecture shown in Figure 3.54. There are two database entities, for storing facts (the *working memory*) and for storing rules (the *production memory*). These are implemented as knowledge bases in terms of the terminology of the *KnowledgeBases* toolbox. The interpreter itself is encapsulated by the **ForwardChainer** procedure, which implements a production system's 'recognize–act' cycle. *Facts*, stored in a working memory, may again be arbitrary lists of items, whose structure will only be reflected in the *Rules*' patterns. *Rules*, stored in a production memory, must have a left- and a right-hand side. Their left-hand side encodes a condition, in terms of an implied conjunction of patterns or their negations. A logical 'or' is not supported, but, as in PROLOG, this can easily be catered for by multiple rules with identical right-hand sides. The right-hand side of a rule specifies an arbitrary number of actions, which may assert or retract facts from a working memory, trigger procedures or terminate a production system's execution. Figure 3.55 summarizes the toolbox interface.

Routine name	Parameters
	functions on Memories
MakeWM	any number of initial facts
PrintWM	aWM
MakePM	any number of initial rules
PrintPM	aPM
	functions on Rules
RULE	aName aConditionList aConclusionList
Fire	aRule aWM
PrintRule	aRule
	functions on Conditions
CONDITIONS	any number of Patterns or Negated Patterns
~	aPattern ; *negation operator*
	functions on Conclusions
CONCLUSIONS	any number of Assertions, Retractions, Executions, or Returns
ASSERT	aFact
RETRACT	aFact
EXECUTE	aProc followed by any number of parameters
RETURN	aProc followed by any number of parameters
	control functions on production systems
ForwardChainer	aPM aWM [optional: aVerboseFlag]

Figure 3.55 Summary of the *Productions* toolbox's interface routines.

MakeWM and **PrintWM** are used to create and display knowledge bases used as a working memory.

```
(define RiverWorld (MakeWM '(friends bear tiger)
                           '(friends bear mole)))
; riverworld
(PrintWM RiverWorld)
; Fact: (friends bear tiger)
  Fact: (friends bear mole)
  ()
```

defines a *RiverWorld* working memory which we will use in our examples. Note that a fact may be any list, containing any kind of object.

To define and show a new rule we may use the **RULE** and **PrintRule** functions.

```
(define RespectRule
        (RULE 'friendshipImpliesRespect
            (CONDITIONS
                (PATTERN 'friends (? 'x) (? 'y)))
            (CONCLUSIONS
                (ASSERT (PATTERN 'respects (<-? 'x) (<-? 'y))))))
; respectrule
(PrintRule RespectRule)
; +++ Rule: friendshipimpliesrespect
  Conditions : (friends (? x) (? y))
  Conclusions: (ASSERT (respects (<-? x) (<-? y)))
  #t
```

From this definition you should observe that *Rules* have a structure of three components: a *name*, a *Conditions* part and a *Conclusions* part. This *Rule* asserts that if two people are friends then one will also respect the other. Note that we refrain from making the obvious symmetric assertion. Procedurally this means that if we should happen to find a working memory element with three 'slots' and the symbol '*friends*' as its first element, then we will bind the second element to pattern variable *x*, and the third element to pattern variable *y*, and then we should fire the conclusions. All the conditions in the *Conditions* part of a *Rule* must be patterns, as defined for the **PATTERN** procedure from the *Patterns* toolbox function (see Figure 3.48). Conditions may also include negated patterns, which will return #*t* if the match fails. The ~ symbol is used to name the relevant function. The *Conclusions* part of a *Rule* may include any number of **ASSERT**ions and **RETRACT**ions, and calls on the **EXECUTE** and **RETURN** procedures. Our example only asserts that the *AList* bindings made for the two *friends* should be substituted into the last two slots of a newly made *respects* fact, and then this fact should be asserted. We use **PATTERN** to build this assertion. This does not, however, mean that the facts themselves are patterns. They are simply lists and no pattern elements are allowed in a fact! In making the assertion, however, **PATTERN** must be used to force substitution of the values of the two pattern variables into the appropriate slots.

We may now wish to define a second rule, stating that if two creatures quarrel with each other they cease to be friends. In response to a *quarrels* fact this rule will therefore remove the two friendship assertions. Whether this is in fact empirically true is irrelevant in this context.

```
(define QuarrelRule
        (RULE 'breakFriendship
            (CONDITIONS (PATTERN 'quarrels (? 'x) (? 'y)))
            (CONCLUSIONS
```

```
            (RETRACT (PATTERN 'friends (<-? 'x) (<-? 'y)))
            (RETRACT (PATTERN 'friends (<-? 'y) (<-? 'x))))))
; quarrelrule
```

Note that **ASSERT** will never assert a fact which is already known, and that conversely **RETRACT** will simply ignore any request to remove facts that are not there. We can now enter our two rules into a newly made production memory and then print it.

```
(define Deductions (MakePM RespectRule QuarrelRule))
; deductions

(PrintPM Deductions)
 ; +++ Rule: friendshipimpliesrespect
        Conditions : (friends (? x) (? y))
        Conclusions: (ASSERT (respects (<-? x) (<-? y)))
   +++ Rule: breakfriendship
        Conditions : (quarrels (? x) (? y))
        Conclusions: (RETRACT (friends (<-? x) (<-? y)))
                     (RETRACT (friends (<-? y) (<-? x)))
   ()
```

To update the state of our *RiverWorld* according to these rules we will need to start the production system with the two memories as arguments. Note that we 'set' the optional trace flag to observe the sequence in which the rules fire.

```
(set! RiverWorld
      (ForwardChainer Deductions RiverWorld #t))
; Rule friendshipimpliesrespect
 (ASSERT (respects (<-? x) (<-? y)))
 . . . . adds fact (respects bear tiger )
 Rule friendshipimpliesrespect
 (ASSERT (respects (<-? x) (<-? y)))
 . . . . adds fact (respects bear mole )
 ((friends bear tiger) (friends bear mole)
  (respects bear tiger) (respects bear mole))
```

As expected, the '*friendshipImpliesRespect*' rule fires twice, on two different facts. This leads to two new facts being asserted: (*respects bear mole*) and (*respects bear tiger*). Since there are no more rules to fire, the 'recognize–act' cycle terminates and the **ForwardChainer** procedure returns with the new state of the working memory. Since there was no hint of a quarrel the second rule has never been tried. Let us now 'manually' insert a fact which will test it. Since the working memory and the production memory are both knowledge bases, we may use the *KnowledgeBase* functions to add new facts.

```
(set! RiverWorld
      (AddFact RiverWorld (PATTERN 'quarrels 'bear 'mole)))
; ((friends bear tiger) (friends bear mole)
   (respects bear tiger) (respects bear mole)
   (quarrels bear mole))
```

Invoking the forward chainer again will now break *bear*'s and *mole*'s friendship, as may be seen from the listing of *RiverWorld*'s state. Their mutual respect remains unchanged.

```
(set! RiverWorld
      (ForwardChainer Deductions RiverWorld #t))
; Rule breakfriendship
  (RETRACT (friends (<-? x) (<-? y)))
  . . . . removes fact (friends bear mole )
  ((friends bear tiger) (respects bear tiger)
   (respects bear mole) (quarrels bear mole))
(PrintWM RiverWorld)
; Fact: (friends bear tiger)
  Fact: (respects bear tiger)
  Fact: (respects bear mole)
  Fact: (quarrels bear mole)
  ()
```

To show the use of the 'not' function, let us assume that we wish to prescribe the rule that a creature 'respects' some other creature if there is no quarrel between them. Again we will leave that assertion's validity outside the scope of this book.

```
(define LikesRule
        (RULE 'likes
           (CONDITIONS
              (PATTERN 'respects (? 'x) (? 'y))
              (~ (PATTERN 'quarrels (<-? 'x) (<-? 'y))))
           (CONCLUSIONS
              (EXECUTE
                 (lambda (message) (DisplayLine message))
                 (PATTERN (<-? 'x) ''likes'' (<-? 'y))))))
; likesrule
```

This time the rule's conclusions also contain an **EXECUTE** element. Such elements may refer to procedures with an arbitrary number of arguments. Here the procedure triggered by **EXECUTE** is used to print the respecting pair and announce that they like each other (which is not directly asserted!).

```
; we can add to PM as any other knowledge base
(set! Deductions (AddFact Deductions LikesRule))
; . . . {a new PM is returned} . . .
(PrintRule LikesRule)
; +++ Rule: likes
  Conditions : (respects (? x) (? y))
               (~ (quarrels (<-? x) (<-? y)))
  Conclusions: (EXECUTE #<PROCEDURE>
                 (((#<PROCEDURE <-?> x ())
                 likes
                 (((#<PROCEDURE <-?> y ())))))
```

If we do not yet wish to add this rule to our production memory we can use the **FireRule** procedure to test it against the current contents of the *RiverWorld.* This will again return a new *RiverWorld* instance.

```
(FireRule LikesRule RiverWorld)
; the "side effect" (printed by the procedure invoked by Execute)
; (bear likes tiger)
; the returned working memory (unchanged)
  ((friends bear tiger) (respects bear tiger)
   (respects bear mole) (quarrels bear mole))
```

These simple examples demonstrate all of the toolbox's features other than the function of **RETURN** elements, whose invocation will terminate a forward chainer's cycle after triggering the associated procedure. Both the working memory and any additionally specified parameters will be passed to this procedure as arguments. Thereafter **RETURN** will return with the procedure's result. We will see how it is used in the examples that follow.

It may also be helpful to comment on **ForwardChainer**'s algorithm which is outlined in Figure 3.56. In line with what we earlier observed about production systems in general, this procedure will cycle through rules looking for a pattern which matches. For each successful match it will 'fire' the elements given as the conclusion, using the accumulated *AList*s of all the left-hand patterns to instantiate any pattern variables occurring on the relevant rule's right-hand side. This cycle will continue until none of the rules has made any further changes to the working memory's contents throughout a whole cycle, or until **RETURN** forces its execution to be terminated (for example, because a goal has been found).

```
function ForwardChainer ( PM, WM)
;; apply rules in production memory PM to the facts in working
;; memory WM and return the new working memory
{     let returnContinuation = save current continuation
      while WM keeps changing do {
            for each rule R in PM do
                  if the conditions of R are satisfied then
                  { let rList = retrieved list of pairs of: (facts from WM
                                that matched conditions of R, and the
                                AList of any bindings made during match)
                    for each conclusion C of rule R do
                        case C of {
                        (ASSERT fact):
                              for each element E in rList do
                                let newFact=substitute for (<- ...) type
                                      patterns in fact using AList of E
                                if newFact not known in WM then
                                      add newFact to WM and note that
                                      WM has changed
                        (RETRACT fact):
                              for each element E in rList do
                                let newFact=substitute for (<- ...) type
                                      patterns in fact using AList of E
                                if newFact is known in WM then
                                      remove newFact from WM and note
                                      that WM has changed
                        (EXECUTE proc parameters):
                              for each element E in rList do
                                let newParams=substitute for (<- ...)
                                      type patterns in parameters using
                                      AList of E
                                call proc( newParams)
                        (RETURN proc parameters):
                              let E = first element in rList
                              let newParams = substitute for (<- ...)
                                    type patterns in parameters using
                                    AList of E
                              let result = proc( WM newParameters)
                              use saved returnedContinuation to exit
                                    ForwardChainer returning result
                        }
                  }
      }
      return WM
}
```

Figure 3.56 Outline of the *ForwardChainer* algorithm.

Our implementation does not accept any rules for tiebreaking (that is, rules are always fired in textual order) and the strategy outlined may cause the same rule to be fired twice on the same working memory. However, since an already known fact will never be reasserted, this will eventually terminate and it makes no difference to the final working memory's contents.

3.4.3 Some simple examples

As our first example let us recall a childhood trauma which is probably shared by many of us. When going to bed at night kids are often worried about the exact nature of the occupants of the glaring dark space under their beds. Even as grown ups we may not completely lose some degree of reluctance about venturing into dark spaces. This natural apprehension paired with a healthy degree of curiosity may be encoded in a guessing game, called '*GuessWhosHidingUnderYourBed*', which is easily implemented as a production system. In this game the program will prompt the 'guesser' for a number of clues about the suspected beastie and will then pass this information as a collection of facts to a production system which will draw a comforting (?) conclusion. The global variables **WM** and **PM** will serve to label our working and production memories. Let us define the 'driver function' and the user interface first.

```
(define GuessWhosHidingUnderYourBed
  (lambda ()
    (define result #f)
    (define ask!
       (lambda (aString yesFact noFact)
         ; ask question and get their reply
         ; if the answer is yes, then add the yesFact to *WM*
         ; if the answer is no, then add the noFact to *WM*
         (define addRealFact!
           (lambda (aFact)
             ; add aFact to *WM* if not null
               (if (not aFact)
                   #f
                   (set! *WM* (AddFact *WM* aFact)))))

         (let ((reply #f)
               (yesReplies '(Yes yes y yep YES))
               (noReplies   '(No no n nope NO)))
              (newline)
              (DisplayLine aString)
              (set! reply (read))
              (cond ((member reply yesReplies)
```

```
                    (addRealFact! yesFact))
                    ((member reply noReplies)
                    (addRealFact! noFact))
                    (else
                    (newline)
                    (DisplayLine "I don't understand your answer")
                    (ask! aString yesFact noFact))))))

; setting the scene – the 'main' program's body
(set! *WM* (MakeWM))
(DisplayLine "Oh oh, I think there is a monster under your bed !")
(DisplayLine "Take a careful peek and tell me what it looks like")
(DisplayLine "Don't take chances, just guess if you can't see it properly")
; start asking for properties and make appropriate assertions into the
; *WM*
(ask! "Can you see it at all ?" #f '(thingy is invisible))
(ask! "Can you see it grin ?" '(thingy is friendly) #f)
(ask! "Is it green all over ?" '(thingy is green) #f)
(ask! "Does it wail a lot ?" '(thingy is loud) #f)
(ask! "Does it look sad ?" '(thingy is sad) #f)
(ask! "Are you scared of it ?" '(thingy is scary) #f)
(newline)
; now invoke the forward chainer to deduce the thingy's nature
; based on these answers and the rules in the *PM*
(set! result (ForwardChainer *PM* *WM*))
(newline)
; if RETURN has returned a conclusion, then it will already have
; been announced by the associated procedure then do nothing.
; Otherwise conclude that it must be a "hide behind", which one can
; never see (since it is always behind one; by definition)
(if (and (pair? result) (equal? (car result) 'ItsA))
    #f
    (DisplayLine "Must be a hidebehind then"))))
```

From this procedure you can already deduce that there are only six characteristics of monsters which our program is interested in: invisibility, friendliness, greenness, loudness, sadness and scariness. Other properties are of course easy to add. Next we will define the two memories as global variables and bind them to appropriate initial values. Since we haven't got a clue about what the creepy thing might be, the working memory is initially empty.

```
(define *WM* (MakeWM))
```

ask! will fill it with observations so that we can draw a reasonable conclusion. The production memory contains a number of rules for characterizing the monsters the system knows about, in terms of the above-mentioned six properties. For the purpose of this example we have 'borrowed' from Borges (1969), a highly recommendable book of monster lore. The working memory contains rules for recognizing four fairly common kinds of monsters, not including the evasive 'Hide-Behind'. To improve the program's powers of discrimination, many additional rules may easily be added by any bright kid. Our four monster classes are *banshees*, *cheshireCats*, *squonks* and *alligators*. *alligators* will no doubt be perfectly familiar to all of us, and the fact that they are green, scary and definitely not friendly will be common knowledge. Perhaps some clarifying remarks about the other four categories are in order (this time including the notorious 'hideBehind').

banshees are a type of monster one should avoid keeping under children's beds. Borges reports that according to his sources few people seem to have laid eyes on this 'woman of the fairies'. She is less a shape than a mournful screaming that haunts the Irish night and (according to Sir Walter Scott's *Demonology and Witchcraft*) the Scottish highlands. Within the current context it is probably sufficient to class her as loud and scary.

Everyone is familiar with the phrase 'grin like a Cheshire cat'. According to Borges, many explanations of its origins have been attempted. In *Alice in Wonderland*, published in 1865, Lewis Carroll endowed the *cheshireCat* with the faculty of slowly disappearing to the point of leaving only its grin – without teeth and without a mouth. For our purposes Cheshire cats are characterized by the fact that they are invisible, friendly and completely harmless (not scary).

The *squonk* is a quaint beast few people outside of Pennsylvania have ever set eyes on, although it is said to be fairly common in the hemlock forests of that state. Borges notes that the *squonk* is of a very retiring disposition, generally travelling about at twilight and dusk. Because of its misfitting skin, which is covered with warts and moles, it is always unhappy; in fact it is said by people who are best able to judge to be the most morbid of beasts. Hunters who are good at tracking are able to follow a *squonk* by its tear-stained trail, for the animal weeps constantly. When cornered and escape seems impossible, or when surprised and frightened, it may even dissolve itself in tears. Green, friendly and sad should be sufficient information to recognize it in an emergency.

The *hideBehind* is part of American folklore. It is always hiding behind something. No matter how many times or whichever way one turns, it is always behind, and that's why nobody has yet been able to describe it. It therefore serves nicely as a default for our monster-guessing program.

```
(define
 *PM*
 (MakePM
  (RULE 'bansheeRule
```

```
(CONDITIONS (PATTERN (? 'who) 'is 'loud)
            (PATTERN (<-? 'who) 'is 'scary))
(CONCLUSIONS (ASSERT (PATTERN (<-? 'who) 'is 'a 'banshee))
             (EXECUTE Wail 3) ; just for its weird effect
             (RETURN ItsA 'banshee)))
(RULE 'cheshireCatRule
(CONDITIONS (PATTERN (? 'who) 'is 'invisible)
            (PATTERN (<-? 'who) 'is 'friendly)
            (~ (PATTERN (<-? 'who) 'is 'scary)))
(CONCLUSIONS (ASSERT (PATTERN (<-? 'who) 'is 'a 'cheshire-cat))
             (RETURN ItsA 'cheshire-cat)))
(RULE 'squonkRule
(CONDITIONS (PATTERN (? 'who) 'is 'green)
            (PATTERN (<-? 'who) 'is 'friendly)
            (PATTERN (<-? 'who) 'is 'sad))
(CONCLUSIONS (ASSERT (PATTERN (<-? 'who) 'is 'a 'squonk))
             (EXECUTE Honk)
             (RETURN ItsA 'squonk)))
(RULE 'alligatorRule
(CONDITIONS (PATTERN (? 'who) 'is 'green)
            (~(PATTERN (<-? 'who) 'is 'friendly))
            (PATTERN (<-? 'who) 'is 'scary))
(CONCLUSIONS (ASSERT (PATTERN (<-? 'who) 'is 'an 'alligator))
             (RETURN ItsA 'alligator))) ))
```

Note that a **RETURN** procedure called *ItsA* is used to terminate further speculation once a monster has been unmasked. Purely to demonstrate use of this feature we have attached **EXECUTE** procedures to two of the monsters. When detected *banshees* will *Wail* and *squonks* will *Honk*. Before our program is complete we must therefore show these three definitions.

```
; two 'sound' procedures
(define Wail
  (lambda (aNumber)
    (do ((i aNumber (-1+ i)))
        ((zero? i))
        (DisplayLine "Whaiiiiiilll . . ."))))

(define Honk
  (lambda ( ) (DisplayLine "Honk honk . . .")))

; announce the monster after the forward chainer's return

(define ItsA
  (lambda (aWM monster)
    (DisplayLine "Don't worry it's only a" monster)
    (list 'ItsA monster)))
```

As a **RETURN** procedure, *ItsA* expects a working memory and a second parameter which at the time of its invocation signalled the right type of monster. It will announce the monster and will also return this fact as a list, since the *GuessWhosHidingUnderYourBed* procedure uses this return value to decide whether invoking of the *hideBehind* is called for.

Our program is now complete and we may proceed to test it. If you have no child handy you may look under your desk and give the answers yourself. Figure 3.57 shows some example scenarios the first of which also has the 'trace flag' set, so that all knowledge-base operations are shown.

This program could of course also have been written by using **if** statements to build a simple decision-tree structure. A comparable flexibility in recognition patterns, however, would be hard to achieve. Most importantly, the logic and sequence of testing would be 'hard wired' into the program, and would therefore be difficult to change and extend. The production system-based approach offers much more flexibility. We can easily cater for new monsters by changing existing rules and adding new ones, which we may in principle define and test independently from any of the others. This modularity and context independence of rules is the main attraction of production systems as a program-structuring device.

Forward chaining production systems are both easy to write and easy to use. They have therefore been successfully applied to a whole range of problems. There are however some classes of applications for which 'blind' forward chaining is not very effective. Such problems will usually be characterized by a large search space in which only few goal states are hidden. Effective solutions to these types of problems require some goal-directed planning procedure, to which backward chaining is much better suited than a pure forward chaining approach.

Our final example will demonstrate this. It is set in the context of the notorious '*monkey and bananas*' microworld, which is frequently used to show characteristics of different problem-reduction and planning procedures. The salient features of this scenario are as follows. There is a monkey, initially positioned at the door to a room. The room contains a bunch of bananas, hanging from the ceiling, as well as a number of other objects. The monkey is hungry and wants to eat the bananas, but he can't reach them. The other objects include a box (or a chair), which, when climbed on, will give him sufficient height to reach the bananas. The goal of this problem is to design a procedure which allows the monkey to formulate a plan to get to the bananas, in terms of the operators available to him (*reach*, *walk*, *climb*, *push*). The puzzle can in principle be solved by stating it in terms of a production system, where rules encode possible actions and all the objects' states and locations are stored in the working memory. It is, however, not easy to persuade such a system to exhibit any

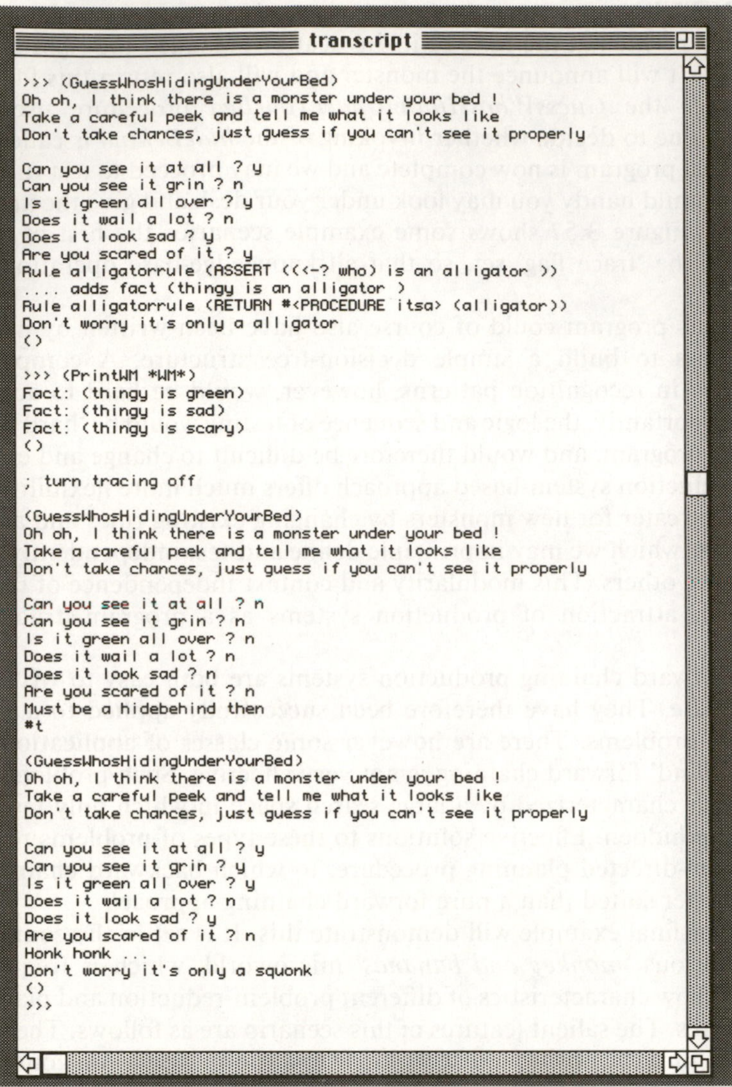

transcript
>>> (GuessWhosHidingUnderYourBed)
Oh oh, I think there is a monster under your bed !
Take a careful peek and tell me what it looks like
Don't take chances, just guess if you can't see it properly
Can you see it at all ? y
Can you see it grin ? n
Is it green all over ? y
Does it wail a lot ? n
Does it look sad ? y
Are you scared of it ? y
Rule alligatorrule (ASSERT ((<-? who) is an alligator))
.... adds fact (thingy is an alligator)
Rule alligatorrule (RETURN #<PROCEDURE itsa> (alligator))
Don't worry it's only a alligator
()
>>> (PrintWM *WM*)
Fact: (thingy is green)
Fact: (thingy is sad)
Fact: (thingy is scary)
()
; turn tracing off
(GuessWhosHidingUnderYourBed)
Oh oh, I think there is a monster under your bed !
Take a careful peek and tell me what it looks like
Don't take chances, just guess if you can't see it properly
Can you see it at all ? n
Can you see it grin ? n
Is it green all over ? n
Does it wail a lot ? n
Does it look sad ? n
Are you scared of it ? n
Must be a hidebehind then
#t
(GuessWhosHidingUnderYourBed)
Oh oh, I think there is a monster under your bed !
Take a careful peek and tell me what it looks like
Don't take chances, just guess if you can't see it properly
Can you see it at all ? y
Can you see it grin ? y
Is it green all over ? y
Does it wail a lot ? n
Does it look sad ? y
Are you scared of it ? n
Honk honk ...
Don't worry it's only a squonk
()
>>>

Figure 3.57 Guess who's hiding under your bed?

degree of 'goal directedness'. Unless we order our rules very carefully the monkey will have a tendency to wander about aimlessly and actions will be prone to get caught in cycles. To give more 'guidance' to the monkey we will have to introduce some measure of control. One way in which this can be accomplished is by using some 'flags' in the working memory to signal the monkey's state of mind, in the sense that their value defines which 'goal' he should attend to next. Initially, for example, he will focus on 'eat', which should then be replaced by the intention to 'move' something climbable (such as the box) under the bananas. What we are giving here is effectively a prescription of an appropriate goal structure for the monkey, which determines which subset of all the production rules will become eligible to fire next. To a certain extent this runs against the grain of the simple forward chaining idea, where we just generate all of a fact's implications sequentially. But to avoid 'blind' searches some such guidance is needed.

Our working memory will therefore contain a 'goal' fact, initially bound to eat (bananas) and later instantiated to 'climb', 'move' and 'find' (box) in turn. Other facts will refer to the position of objects in the room.

```
; To introduce a measure of 'control' into the monkey the Working
; Memory (WM) will contain a fact giving its current 'goal', which will
; move among the following states:
; (goal eat) eat the bananas
; (goal climb) climb on to the box
; (goal move) move the box to the position of the bananas
; (goal find) move to the position of the box in the room

; Other facts in the WM will give the positions of the objects monkey,
; box and bananas: (object at position) with object = monkey, box,
; bananas and position = door, middle, window and whether the monkey is
; on the box or the floor: (monkey on box) (monkey on floor);
```

These considerations suggest the following state for the working memory at the start of the monkey's adventure:

```
(define *MonkeyWM* (MakeWM '(monkey at door)
                           '(bananas at middle)
                           '(box at window)
                           '(monkey on floor)))
```

The production memory (PM), on the other hand, will contain eleven rules about how and under what conditions the monkey can move about:

```
(define *MonkeyPM*
  (MakePM
   ; #1. If monkey has no goal then start with eating
   (RULE "1-GiveGoal"
     (CONDITIONS (~ (PATTERN 'goal?)))
     (CONCLUSIONS (ASSERT '(goal eat))))
   ; #2. If the goal is to eat, and the monkey is on the box,
```

```
; then eat the bananas and leave
(RULE "2-Eat"
   (CONDITIONS '(goal eat)
               '(monkey on box))
   (CONCLUSIONS
      (EXECUTE
        DisplayLine "Eating banana. . .delicious!")
      (RETURN
        (lambda (aWM) "Hunger satisfied"))))

; #3. If the goal is to eat, but the monkey is not on the box,
; then change the goal to climb
(RULE "3-Eat"
      (CONDITIONS '(goal eat)
                  '(monkey on floor))
      (CONCLUSIONS (RETRACT '(goal eat))
                   (ASSERT '(goal climb))))

; #4. If the goal is climb, and the monkey is on the box,
; then change the goal to eat
(RULE "4-Climb"
      (CONDITIONS '(goal climb)
                  '(monkey on box))
      (CONCLUSIONS (RETRACT '(goal climb))
                   (ASSERT '(goal eat))))

; #5. If the goal is climb, and the monkey is on the floor with the box
; under the bananas, then climb the box
(RULE "5-Climb"
      (CONDITIONS '(goal climb)
                  '(monkey on floor)
                  (PATTERN 'monkey   'at (? 'x))
                  (PATTERN 'box      'at (<-? 'x))
                  (PATTERN 'bananas  'at (<-? 'x)))
      (CONCLUSIONS (RETRACT '(monkey on floor))
                   ; climb box
                   (ASSERT '(monkey on box))))

; #6. If the goal is climb, but the box is not under the bananas,
; then change the goal to move
(RULE "6-Climb"
      (CONDITIONS '(goal climb)
                  '(monkey on floor)
                  (PATTERN 'box   'at (? 'x))
                  ; box and bananas must be in different places
                  (PATTERN 'bananas 'at (? 'y x<>y?)))
      (CONCLUSIONS (RETRACT '(goal climb))
                   (ASSERT '(goal move))))

; #7. If the goal is move and the monkey and box are under the bananas,
; then change the goal to climb
```

```
(RULE "7-Move"
      (CONDITIONS '(goal move)
                  (PATTERN 'monkey   'at (? 'x))
                  (PATTERN 'box      'at (<-? 'x))
                  (PATTERN 'bananas  'at (<-? 'x)))
      (CONCLUSIONS (RETRACT '(goal move))
                   (ASSERT '(goal climb))))

; #8. If the goal is move, and the monkey is with the box, but not
; under the bananas, then push the box to under the bananas
(RULE "8-Move"
      (CONDITIONS '(goal move)
                  (PATTERN 'monkey   'at (? 'x))
                  (PATTERN 'box      'at (<-? 'x))
                  (PATTERN 'bananas  'at (? 'y x<>y?)))
      (CONCLUSIONS (RETRACT ; move box
                     (PATTERN 'box      'at (<-? 'x)))
                   (ASSERT (PATTERN 'box   'at (<-? 'y)))
                   (RETRACT ; and also move monkey
                     (PATTERN 'monkey      'at (<-? 'x)))
                   (ASSERT (PATTERN 'monkey   'at (<-? 'y))))

; #9. If the goal is move, and the monkey is not with the box,
; then change the goal to find
(RULE "9-Move"
      (CONDITIONS '(goal move)
                  (PATTERN 'monkey   'at (? 'x))
                  (PATTERN 'box      'at (? 'y x<>y?)))
      (CONCLUSIONS (RETRACT '(goal move))
                   (ASSERT '(goal find))))

; #10. If the goal is find, and the monkey is with the box,
; then change the goal to move
(RULE "10-Find"
      (CONDITIONS '(goal find)
                  (PATTERN 'monkey   'at (? 'x))
                  (PATTERN 'box'     'at (<-? 'x)))
      (CONCLUSIONS (RETRACT '(goal find))
                   (ASSERT '(goal move))))

; #11. If the goal is find, and the monkey is not with the box,
; then move the monkey to the box
(RULE "11-Find"
      (CONDITIONS '(goal find)
                  (PATTERN 'monkey   'at (? 'x))
                  (PATTERN 'box      'at (? 'y x<>y?)))
      (CONCLUSIONS (RETRACT ; move the monkey
                     (PATTERN 'monkey   'at (<-? 'x)))
                   (ASSERT
                     (PATTERN 'monkey   'at (<-? 'y))))))
```

Next we need to define procedure *x<>y?*, which tests whether the objects bound to *x* and *y* in the match's *AList* are in different places:

```
(define x<>y?
; return #t if x and y are bound to different values
   (lambda (anAList)
    (not (equal? (GetAssociationValue 'x anAList)
                 (GetAssociationValue 'y anAList)))))
```

Finally, our monkey is ready to go.

```
(define SolveMonkey
  (lambda ()
    (let ((result (ForwardChainer *MonkeyPM* *MonkeyWM* #t)))
     (if (equal? result "Hunger satisfied")
         #f
         (DisplayLine "Monkey is still hungry")))))
```

Figure 3.58 traces our monkey's progress.

You will remember that the monkey is initially positioned at the door, the bananas are suspended in the middle of the room and the box is at the window. Using the 'intelligence' implied by the program's goal structure he knows immediately that the bananas are too high and that he must look for something to climb on, a box in this case. Rule 3 fires and his goal therefore changes from 'eat' to 'climb'. At this stage it might have been more realistic to wander over to the bananas first and let him try to grab them. After this unsuccessful attempt he might then 'look' around the room to find any object which may serve as a hook, or which he may climb on (*see* Figure 3.6). Since such deliberations would have made the program even longer we decide to let him look for a box (or chair) straight away. It should soon become obvious that rules may be added to provide less tightly constrained ('purposeful') 'exploratory' behaviour. In the above scenario, since the monkey can't climb on to the box immediately because he isn't in the right position, the next goal is to move to the box. This is of course followed by the urge to move to where the box currently is (the window). Rule 11 therefore asserts this change in the world's physical state. Thereafter we focus on the task of moving both box and monkey under the bananas. Once that is accomplished the appropriate goal becomes climbing on to the box. Rule 5 asserts the new state of affairs after this action has taken place. Finally the monkey's goal will change to 'eat' again, and, since all relevant preconditions are met, he will now succeed. Rule 2 announces success and returns from the forward chainer.

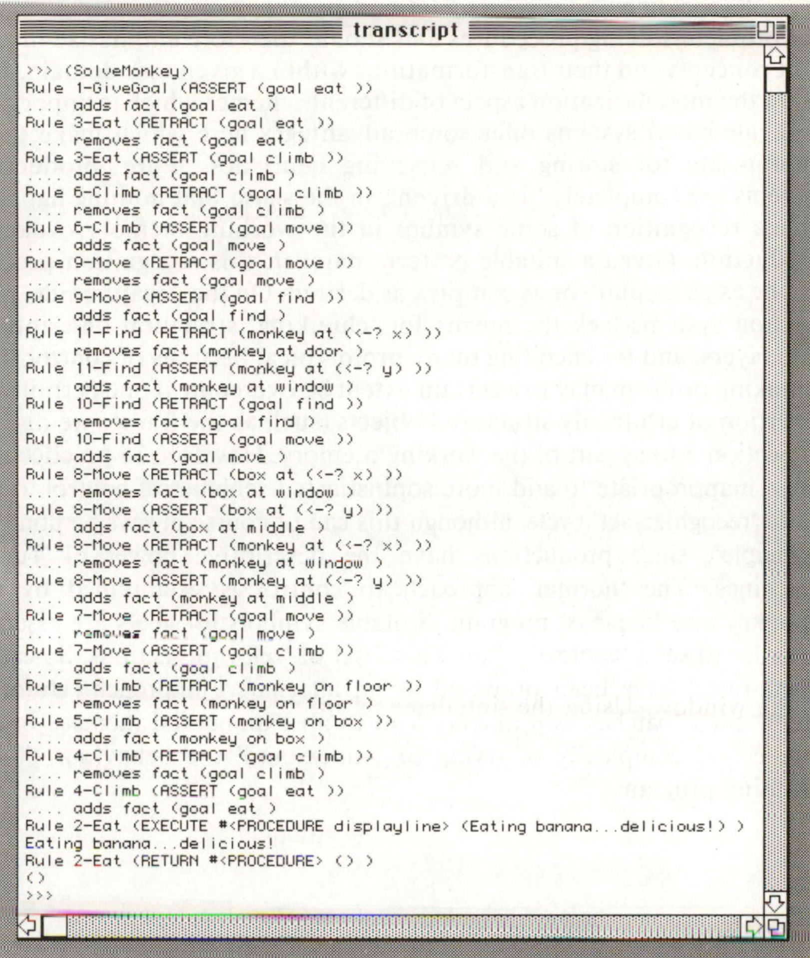

```
transcript
>>> (SolveMonkey)
Rule 1-GiveGoal (ASSERT (goal eat ))
.... adds fact (goal eat )
Rule 3-Eat (RETRACT (goal eat ))
.... removes fact (goal eat )
Rule 3-Eat (ASSERT (goal climb ))
.... adds fact (goal climb )
Rule 6-Climb (RETRACT (goal climb ))
.... removes fact (goal climb )
Rule 6-Climb (ASSERT (goal move ))
.... adds fact (goal move )
Rule 9-Move (RETRACT (goal move ))
.... removes fact (goal move )
Rule 9-Move (ASSERT (goal find ))
.... adds fact (goal find )
Rule 11-Find (RETRACT (monkey at (<-? x) ))
.... removes fact (monkey at door )
Rule 11-Find (ASSERT (monkey at (<-? y) ))
.... adds fact (monkey at window )
Rule 10-Find (RETRACT (goal find ))
.... removes fact(goal find )
Rule 10-Find (ASSERT (goal move ))
.... adds fact (goal move )
Rule 8-Move (RETRACT (box at (<-? x) ))
.... removes fact (box at window )
Rule 8-Move (ASSERT (box at (<-? y) ))
.... adds fact (box at middle )
Rule 8-Move (RETRACT (monkey at (<-? x) ))
.... removes fact (monkey at window )
Rule 8-Move (ASSERT (monkey at (<-? y) ))
.... adds fact (monkey at middle )
Rule 7-Move (RETRACT (goal move ))
.... removes fact (goal move )
Rule 7-Move (ASSERT (goal climb ))
.... adds fact (goal climb )
Rule 5-Climb (RETRACT (monkey on floor ))
.... removes fact (monkey on floor )
Rule 5-Climb (ASSERT (monkey on box ))
.... adds fact (monkey on box )
Rule 4-Climb (RETRACT (goal climb ))
.... removes fact (goal climb )
Rule 4-Climb (ASSERT (goal eat ))
.... adds fact (goal eat )
Rule 2-Eat (EXECUTE #<PROCEDURE displayline> (Eating banana...delicious!) )
Eating banana...delicious!
Rule 2-Eat (RETURN #<PROCEDURE> () )
()
>>>
```

Figure 3.58 How the monkey ate the bananas.

The production system metaphor gives a new perspective to the 'search' problem. The specific strategy in which a search space will be traversed is of course highly dependent on the way in which rules have been ordered, and what changes are made to the production memory. Production systems are also quite similar to procedurally interpreted PROLOG programs, with which they share many advantages and disadvantages. These similarities should serve to emphasize the fact that procedural and declarative approaches to knowledge representation are always closely intertwined.

'Good' knowledge representations must serve as structuring devices for problem-solving procedures and should therefore emphasize important concepts and their transformations within a given task domain. It is often the modularization aspect of different schemes which is important, and rule-based systems offer some advantages here which make them appropriate for storing and retrieving heuristics. 'Pure' production systems are completely 'data driven', in the sense that nothing happens unless recognition of some symbol in the working memory evokes a production. Given a suitable pattern matcher, this recognition process can be as elementary or as complex as desired. On the negative side, production systems lack the means for 'chunking' structural descriptions into layers, and for encoding many prototypical patterns of control. The chunking problem may to a certain extent be overcome if one permits the assertion of arbitrarily structured objects (such as the frames we discuss in Section 3.6) as part of the working memory. However, in practice it is often inappropriate to add more sophisticated schemes of control to the basic 'recognize-act' cycle, although this can of course always be done 'in principle', since productions have the descriptive power of Turing machines. The 'normal' approach to control is exemplified by the 'monkey and bananas' program. Suitable symbols for goals are asserted in order to set a 'context' of only a subset of 'relevant' actions. So-called 'meta-rules' have been proposed as an alternative approach. Unfortunately such 'patches' can quickly lead to an exponential increase in the intellectual complexity of trying to 'understand' the behaviour of the resulting programs.

EXERCISES

Many of the exercises we described for PROLOG and the *Search* toolbox are also applicable here. Any task which is readily characterized in terms of collections of 'rules of thumb' or 'heuristics' is a good candidate for a production-based approach, and there is a wide variety of problems which we encounter almost every day and which fall into this category.

3.33 Add some additional monsters to the *GuessWhosHidingUnderYourBed* program. The aforementioned book by Borges (1969) is a good source for 'inspiration'.

3.34 Explore further implications of the 'planning' metaphor by enriching the monkey's environment and goal structure. Some additional climbable furniture, positions and other means of obtaining the banana (for example, a stick with a hook) may be considered. You will need to strike a balance between the extremes of 'wiring' too much 'preknowledge' in terms of constraints into the monkey's behaviour (as encoded by anticipated interactions between his goal structure and the rules in the working memory) and letting him wander 'aimlessly' about.

3.35 Add a backward chaining facility to the toolbox. This will involve reasoning from conclusions to premisses. For example, we would start with the goal that the monkey eats the banana and try to find a path of valid assertions back to the starting state. From a programming point of view we need to permit arbitrary patterns in the working memory and implement a device similar to PROLOG's unification algorithm. Clocksin and Mellish (1981) or Kowalski (1979 a and b) give good accounts of this strategy. *Note*: This is not a simple exercise.

3.36 Write a production system program for solving the well-known 'Towers of Hanoi' puzzle. Exercise 2.5 in Section 2.3.5 describes an isomorphous problem. Hasemer (1984) offers a Lisp-based production system as a solution.

3.37 Write a production system encoding the knowledge required to translate 'number words' from one language to another (use English to: German, French, Latin, Japanese, for example). You may wish to restrict yourself to a suitable subset (such as the numbers 1 to 100).

3.38 Write a production system program to translate roman numerals into decimal representation. Again, you may wish to restrict yourself to a suitable subset (for example, 1 to 39). Tanimoto (1987) offers a Lisp-based solution.

3.39 Write a production system representation of the rules governing symbolic differentiation of algebraic expressions. Again, Tanimoto (1987) provides a solution in Lisp.

3.40 Write a production system program which acts as an adviser for filling in tax returns. This program could also serve as a basis for exploring other areas of legal reasoning.

3.41 Write a production system program for dream analysis. If you feel that you lack the necessary psychoanalytical skills, you may wish to consult Drege (1981), who refers to a book on the interpretation of the Duke of Zhou's (Chou's) dreams in which over 300 production rules of the form: '*dream that you are falling into water: worries with your wife or the tax man*' are given.

3.42 Write a production system program to counsel students at your university with regard to which courses they should take. This task will require some knowledge of a degree's structure, the courses offered, who is teaching them, time constraints, empirical assertions about certain courses and lecturers, and so on.

3.43 Guessing games, similar to the one we used as an example, have often been employed to demonstrate the basic ideas of production system interpreters. A paradigmatic program of this kind is Winston's (1984) implementation for guessing an animal's nature from a number of its characteristics. Write a similar program to deduce the name of a person from her recreations. To achieve this goal your program may carry on an 'intelligent' conversation about leisure time activities. Since it is often rude to ask directly which sports one feels competent in, your program will have to circumscribe its intentions. It could 'sneak' queries on important characteristics of such sports into a seemingly innocent conversation about weather, health, well-being of relatives, and so on. Needless to say, your program should strive for a minimum number of questions before unmasking the person.

The necessary domain knowledge could be encoded in some rules, such as:

- IF ball game, NOT two teams with more than two players per team, ball solid, NOT played indoors, ball round, mallet NOT used THEN 'is golf'.
- IF NOT ball game, NOT played sitting down, played indoors, NOT racquet used THEN 'is darts'.

You may wish to test your program on some of your acquaintances.

3.44 Winston (1984, p. 465) describes a 'bartender' program in terms of production rules. Such a program will need to store knowledge about drinks, wines and moods, and it will also need to employ heuristics as to what drink is appropriate for a particular meal in a particular situation. You may wish to make such decisions on the basis of the meal's components (such as meat, fowl, fish, greens), the wine's properties (red, white, dry, sweet, expensive, cheap,

French label) and the situation's characteristics (someone you like is invited, a pain in the neck, romantic mood, business lunch). An interactive interface could drive a conversation to gather the relevant information.

3.45 Write production rules which can serve as the basis for a flood-warning system. The knowledge base would need to store information about townships (near a river, for example), rivers (water level, state of floodbanks) and relevant properties of the terrain (snow). Information about the weather (rainfall, temperature) could then trigger a forward chainer to give flood warnings automatically.

3.5 Associative and semantic networks

'To discover the logical relations of a concept is to discover the nature of that concept. For concepts are, in this respect, like points: they have no quality except position. Just as the identity of a point is given by its coordinates, that is, its position relative to other points and ultimately to a set of axes, so the identity of a concept is given by its position relative to other concepts and ultimately to the kind of material to which it is ostensively applicable ...'

[*White (1975), as quoted in Sowa (1984), p. 76.*]

3.5.1 General principles and historical perspective

A 'concept' is a basic unit for representing chunks of knowledge. Abstract concepts acquire 'meaning' through their position in a vast network of relationships which ultimately link them to concrete concepts. We will use the term '*associative network*' for the collection of all such relationships, although names like *conceptual networks*, *propositional networks* or *semantic networks* have also been used in this context. The origins of the ideas underlying the use of graphical representations to encode associative networks have a long history, reaching back as far as the time of Aristotle. Their basic ingredients are *nodes* which represent concepts and *arcs* which denote links between them. Such structures can conveniently be used to represent associations in webs of ideas, either for structural description (for example, a 'chair' has a back, a seat, four legs, a colour, and so on), taxonomies (for example, 'my chair' is a chair, which is a piece of furniture, which is a physical object), situations ('my chair' is in my office and I am sitting on it), events (such as: I fell off my chair) or even sentences (such as: 'yesterday bruce offered me a chair'). These 'associative networks' may then be used to document, build or recognize instances of such structures.

Knowledge representations based on associative networks have long been attractive to psychologists, linguists and computer scientists. In psychology they have served as a metaphor used to explain the structure of human memory. For example, the notion of 'semantic distance' may be defined in terms of the number of intermediary links between two concepts. In linguistic research so-called 'semantic networks' have been employed as a means of mapping language on to ideas and ideas on to language, since they provide a convenient formalism for representing notions such as 'semantic structure' or 'deep structure' of sentences. In a computational context, semantic networks have been applied as a data structure, together with a set of recognition or query procedures which define some operational 'meaning' for the concepts encoded in a net. *Arcs* in such associative networks mix two ideas, the notion of class/subclass relationships via *isa* or *AKO* ('a kind of') links, and the graphical representation of attribute/value links as labelled binary relationships. When we compare them to logic, networks will result in a more 'visual' and therefore faster access to a set of assertions. On the negative side we lose logic's independence of assertions from each other, and the associated flexibility in adding or removing items without any need explicitly to consider their connections.

Although the original ideas proved very attractive to early AI research, it soon became apparent that large network systems tend to become 'cludgy' when used to store non-binary concepts, events or propositions. This led to the proposal of additional scaffolding such as different classes of nodes and 'predicate structures'. While these augmentations give networks a descriptive power equivalent to that of first-order predicate logic [Kowalski (1979b)], they remove much of the initial attraction associated with their simplicity.

The advent of 'semantic networks' within AI is usually associated with Quillian's (1968) proposal to represent the meaning of English sentences in terms of objects and relationships, although Raphael's (1968) SIR (Semantic Information Retrieval) question-answering program had already employed a similar data structure before that date. The authors believe that the term 'semantic network' is an unfortunate one, since it somehow implies that 'meaning' resides in the network itself. Since this is not really the case and the semantics of network structures can only be established by interaction with an associated set of interpretation procedures, we will adopt Findler's (1971) usage of the term 'associative network' instead.

3.5.2 The 'AssociativeNetworks' toolbox

To demonstrate the facilities provided by our *AssociativeNetworks* toolbox we will again look at some simple examples first. Figure 3.59

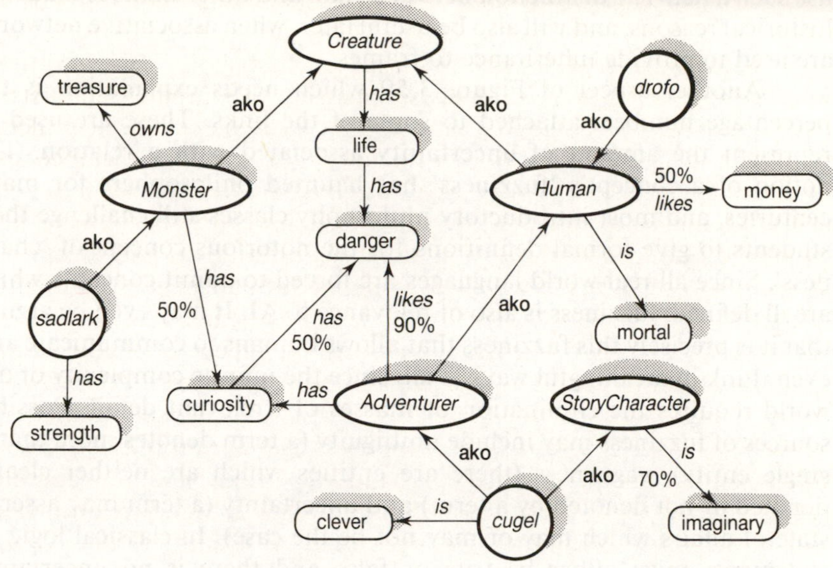

Figure 3.59 *CugelsSaga* – some concepts and their relationships.

shows a simple associative network for a small subset of a microworld we will hereafter refer to as *CugelsSaga*. You may remember that we have encountered Cugel before, and to put this into perspective, we should mention that he is a literary character who roams the imaginary landscape of J. Vance's (1972, 1983) 'Dying Earth' series of fantasy novels. We have, however, taken a certain amount of liberty in describing his adventures.

Note that Figure 3.59 uses different shapes for nodes. The circular nodes refer to individual objects, whereas the elliptical and oval ones are used to denote generic concepts. The distinction between elliptical and oval nodes is made because there is an intuitive temptation to associate the elliptical ones with object categories and to ascribe the notion of properties to the oval ones. It is important to stress that this convention is solely employed to clarify the nature of the ideas shown in this figure. Our toolbox makes no such distinctions! Any node in an associative network (**AN**) denotes a **CONCEPT**, which is linked to other concepts. The system, however, does recognize two different categories of **Links**. **AKOLinks** define class/subclass relationships, while ordinary **LINK** structures are used to denote any other kind of binary association. Any distinction between individual and generic concepts is therefore purely in the mind of the beholder or must be encoded in the procedures which use such a net. The distinction between **Ako-** and other **Links** is made for historical reasons, and will also be useful later, when associative networks are used to provide inheritance to frames.

Another aspect of Figure 3.59 which needs explanation is the percentage numbers attached to some of the links. These are used to represent the amount of uncertainty associated with a relation. The notion of a concept's 'fuzziness' has haunted philosophers for many centuries, and most introductory philosophy classes still challenge their students to give formal definitions for the notorious concept of 'chairness'. Since all real-world languages are forced to admit concepts which are ill defined, fuzziness is also of relevance to AI. It may even be argued that it is precisely this fuzziness that allows humans to communicate and even think in meaningful ways at all, since the infinite complexity of our world requires the elimination of masses of irrelevant detail. Possible sources of fuzziness may include ambiguity (a term denotes more than a single entity), vagueness (there are entities which are neither clearly denoted or not denoted by a term) and uncertainty (a term may assert a state of affairs which may or may not be the case). In classical logic all statements must either be true or false and there is no uncertainty associated with propositions. For reasons of analytical tractability most formal languages cannot admit fuzzy concepts, but this is only a poor reflection of real 'life'. This sentiment is nicely expressed by Bertrand Russell, who writes:

> 'All traditional logic habitually assumes that precise symbols are being employed. It is therefore not applicable to this terrestrial life, but only to an imagined celestial existence.'
>
> [*Russell (1923), p. 88.*]

Exact deduction and plausible inference are at two ends of a spectrum. Depending on the resources available we may wish to choose any appropriate degree of rigour and certainty. To reflect this in our system we introduce a so-called '*certainty factor*', which may optionally be attached to a link. A value of zero will indicate that a relationship definitely does not hold (identical to a situation in which the link does not exist) and '1' means absolute certainty. These certainty factors are only expected to reflect some subjective judgement about the 'strength' of evidence for a link's existence, and the procedures which combine them will simply multiply these numbers. As an additional restriction we will not allow them to be attached to **AKOLinks**.

There are a number of proposals for more sophisticated probability-based schemes in reasoning procedures. The so-called '*Dempster–Shafer calculus*' [Zadeh (1986)], for example, has lately attracted considerable attention as a promising method for combining incomplete evidence and fusing uncertain data. However, since adequate understanding of such methods requires a considerable background in probability theory, they are beyond the scope of this book.

Figure 3.60 summarizes the features provided by the user interface in the 'AssociativeNetworks' toolbox.

Routine name	Parameters
	functions on Links
AKO	any number of concept names
LINK	aLinkName aConceptName [aCertaintyFactor]
AddAKOLink	anAN aSubclassName aSuperclassName
RemoveAKOLink	anAN aSubclassName aSuperclassName
AddLink	anAN aConceptName aLink
RemoveLink	anAN aConceptName aLinkName
	functions on Concepts
CONCEPT	aConceptName, followed by any number of links
	maintenance functions on ANs
MakeAN	any number of concepts
PrintAN	anAN
AddConcept	anAN aConcept
RemoveConcept	anAN aConceptSymbol
	query functions on ANs
FindAllConcepts	anAN
FindAllLinkNames	anAN
FindConcept	anAN aConceptSymbol
GetAKOSlot	anAN aConceptSymbol
GetAKOLinks	anAN aConceptSymbol
GetAKOChain	anAN aConceptSymbol
GetLinkSymbolSlots	anAN aConceptSymbol aLinkSymbol
FindAllLinkedConcepts	anAN aConceptSymbol aLinkSymbol optional: aThresholdValue
FindAllLinks	anAN a firstConceptSymbol a secondConceptSymbol optional: aThresholdValue
Linked?	anAN a firstConceptSymbol a secondConceptSymbol optional: aThresholdValue

Figure 3.60 Summary of the *AssociativeNetworks* toolbox routines.

An associative network (**AN**) is stored as a web of **CONCEPTS**. **CONCEPTS** are linked by two types of relationships: **AKO** and **LINK**. In addition to those directly attached to a concept, relationships can be inherited. This may occur either through **AKOLinks** (for example, Cugel is *clever* and an *Adventurer*, and therefore *Human* and therefore *mortal*, and . . .) or by recursion along chains of the same class of relationship (for example, Cugel *has* curiosity, which *has* danger).

MakeAN is used to build an associative network, to which concepts may then be added using **AddConcept**. **CONCEPT** makes new concepts from a list of links. **LINK** will return link objects, which consist of a label (*LinkName*), a source concept (the concept to which the link is attached), the target concept and optionally a real number between zero and one. This 'certainty factor' denotes the 'strength' of a relationship and may be used to quantify some queries. It defaults to a value of 1.0. **RemoveConcept** will remove a concept from the network and **PrintConcept** will display its state. Note that as in previous toolboxes **CONCEPT** and **LINK** are implemented as procedures, which means that all symbols supplied as arguments will need to be **quoted**!

```
(define
  CugelsSaga
   (MakeAN
     (CONCEPT 'Creature
              (LINK 'has 'life))
     (CONCEPT 'Monster (AKO 'Creature)
              (LINK 'has   'curiosity 0.5)
              (LINK 'owns 'treasure))
     (CONCEPT 'sadlark (AKO 'Monster)       ; an 'individual'
              (LINK 'has 'strength))
     (CONCEPT 'Human (AKO 'Creature)
              (LINK 'likes 'money 0.5)
              (LINK 'is    'mortal))
     (CONCEPT 'drofo (AKO 'Human))          ; an 'individual'
     (CONCEPT 'Adventurer (AKO 'Human)
              (LINK 'has   'curiosity)
              (LINK 'likes 'danger 0.9))
     (CONCEPT 'StoryCharacter
              (LINK 'is 'imaginary 0.7))
     (CONCEPT 'cugel                        ; an 'individual'
              (AKO 'Adventurer 'StoryCharacter)
              (LINK 'is 'clever))
     (CONCEPT 'life (LINK 'has 'danger))
     (CONCEPT 'treasure)
     (CONCEPT 'money)
     (CONCEPT 'strength)
     (CONCEPT 'danger)
     (CONCEPT 'mortal)
```

```
        (CONCEPT 'curiosity (LINK 'has 'danger 0.5))
        (CONCEPT 'clever)
        (CONCEPT 'imaginary)))
; cugelssaga
(PrintAN CugelsSaga)
 ; *** Associative Network ***
 creature: (LINK has life)
 monster: (AKO (creature)) (LINK has curiosity 0.5 )
 sadlark: (AKO (monster)) (LINK has strength )
 human: (AKO (creature)) (LINK likes money 0.5 ) (LINK is mortal)
 drofo: (AKO (human))
 adventurer: (AKO (human)) (LINK has curiosity )
                (LINK likes danger 0.9 )
 storycharacter: (LINK is imaginary 0.7 )
 cugel: (AKO (adventurer storycharacter)) (LINK is clever )
 life: (LINK has danger )
 treasure:
 money:
 strength:
 danger:
 mortal:
 curiosity: (LINK has danger 0.5 )
 clever:
 imaginary:
 #t
```

AddConcept and **RemoveConcept** link concepts into a net and remove them again. Both procedures will return new networks, which must be bound to an appropriate variable if the change should be remembered.

```
(set! bunderwalConcept (CONCEPT 'bunderwal (AKO 'adventurer)))
; (bunderwal ((ako (adventurer))))
(set! CugelsSaga (AddConcept CugelsSaga bunderwalConcept))
; ((creature . . .
(imaginary ()) (bunderwal ((ako (adventurer)))))
```

The returned value (a new network) shows that *bunderwal* was indeed added as a new *adventurer*. We will now remove him again.

```
(set! CugelsSaga (RemoveConcept CugelsSaga 'bunderwal))
; ((creature . . . (imaginary ()))
```

Both **AKO** links and ordinary links can easily be added to or removed from a concept's definition. Our implementation requires a *unique name for each of the links owned by a concept*, so that, for example, there may not be more than one 'likes' link emanating from Cugel. If it is believed that Cugel likes both wine and beer, there are various ways in which this may still be asserted. We may call the two links '*likesWine*' and '*likesBeer*', or we may associate one of them with a superclass (for example, so that all adventurers like wine). This convention may seem unduly restrictive, but its disadvantages will disappear as soon as frames (whose slots can hold any combination of values) are used as components of networks. **AddLink** adds links to the network. Note, however, that the 'source' concept to which the link should be attached and the 'target' to which it refers must exist, although the system will not complain about non-existent targets and will just create a 'dangling' reference. You may wish to modify this behaviour as an exercise. **RemoveLink** can be used to remove links again.

```
(set! CugelsSaga
      (AddLink CugelsSaga 'sadlark (LINK 'can 'fly)))
; ((creature . . . (sadlark ((ako (monster))
  (has strength) (can fly))))

(set! CugelsSaga
      (RemoveLink CugelsSaga 'sadlark 'can))
; ((creature . . . (sadlark ((ako (monster))
  (has strength))))
```

The **Linked?** query function tests whether a connection between two concepts exists. As with many other queries it may be quantified by a so-called 'threshold' value (between 0 and 1), which represents the likelihood ('truth') of the value returned. This likelihood is computed by multiplying the certainty factors of all the links along a given path. If there is more than one path, all of those above the threshold will be returned.

```
(set! CugelsSaga (AddAKOLink CugelsSaga 'cugel 'monster))
; ((creature . . . (ako (adventurer storycharacter monster)))))

(Linked? CugelsSaga 'cugel 'treasure 0.9)
; #t

(set! CugelsSaga (RemoveAKOLink CugelsSaga 'cugel 'monster))
; ((creature . . . (ako (adventurer storycharacter)))))
(Linked? CugelsSaga 'cugel 'treasure 0.9)
; #f
```

Here we wish to test for links between *cugel* and *treasure*, but any such link must show a likelihood of at least 90%. This conjecture is confirmed, since *cugel* has just added *monster* to his superclasses, and since in our network *monsters* are believed to *own treasure* with certainty (remember that 100% is used as a link's default). After that link is removed, again the same query is doomed to fail.

Addition and deletion of 'non-AKO' links follows the same principles. **GetLinkSymbolSlots** is a query function. It may be employed to ask for all non-AKO links emanating from a given node. The next few examples will demonstrate such queries.

```
(set! CugelsSaga (AddLink CugelsSaga 'sadlark (LINK 'is 'vicious)))
; NOTE: the concept 'vicious' has not been defined in the net
; ((creature . . . (has strength) (is vicious))))

(GetLinkSymbolSlots CugelsSaga 'sadlark 'is)
; ((is vicious))

(set! CugelsSaga (RemoveLink CugelsSaga 'sadlark 'is)
; ((creature . . . (has strength))))
(GetLinkSymbolSlots CugelsSaga 'sadlark 'is)
; ()
```

FindAllConcepts will return a list of all concepts the network 'knows' about and **FindAllLinkNames** performs the same task for all the links' labels.

```
(FindAllConcepts CugelsSaga)
; (creature monster human drofo adventurer
  storycharacter life treasure money strength danger
  mortal curiosity clever imaginary cugel sadlark)

(FindAllLinkNames CugelsSaga)
; (is likes owns has)
```

We may search for a specific concept – *adventurer*, for example.

```
(FindConcept CugelsSaga 'adventurer)
; (adventurer ((ako (human)) (has curiosity) (likes danger 0.9)))
```

We may also request various kinds of information about concepts' AKO relationships. **GetAKOSlot** produces the relevant slot itself, **GetAKO-Links** will return only a list of superclasses and **GetAKOChain** will 'run' along a given concept's AKO links to collect all the superconcepts with which the given one is directly or indirectly connected.

```
(GetAKOSlot CugelsSaga 'cugel)
; (ako (adventurer storycharacter))

(GetAKOLinks CugelsSaga 'cugel)
; (adventurer storycharacter)

(GetAKOChain CugelsSaga 'cugel)
; (cugel adventurer storycharacter human creature)

(GetAKOChain CugelsSaga 'sadlark)
; (sadlark monster creature)
```

Here we note that *cugel* is an *adventurer* and a *storycharacter*. Since *adventurers* are *humans*, and since *humans* are *creatures*, *cugel* is also a *human* and a *creature*. We may also explore the implications of non-AKO links. We have already encountered **GetLinkSymbolSlots**. We can apply it to *cugel* and learn that an 'is' link to concept 'clever' is directly attached to him. Further 'is'-type relationships are inherited from concept *human* (is mortal), as returned by **FindAllLinkedConcepts**.

```
(GetLinkSymbolSlots CugelsSaga 'cugel 'is)
; ((is clever))

(FindAllLinkedConcepts CugelsSaga 'cugel 'is)
; ((is clever) (is mortal))
```

Queries which are not quantified by a threshold value will only search for connections which are 100% certain. You may already have noted that *cugel* should also inherit a link to *imaginary* from *storycharacter*, but since this connection has only a strength of 70%, it was ignored by the previous query. Most query procedures will accept a threshold value. For example we may state that we wish to be at least 50% certain of any 'is' relationships. This time **FindAllLinkedConcepts** includes the 70% link to *imaginary* in its response. **FindAllLinks** is another useful query procedure. It will return a list of alternative connections between two given concepts.

```
(FindAllLinkedConcepts CugelsSaga 'cugel 'is 0.5)
; ((is clever) (is imaginary 0.7) (is mortal))

(FindAllLinks CugelsSaga 'adventurer 'danger)
; ((has danger))

(FindAllLinks CugelsSaga 'adventurer 'danger 0.5)
; ((likes danger 0.9) (has danger 0.5) (has danger))
```

The only certain connection between *Adventurer* and *danger* is established via the fact that adventurers are *human*, humans are *creatures*, creatures have *life* and life certainly *has* its dangers. This chain of relationships shows that query procedures will recursively follow links with the same name (that is, *has life*, *has danger*). The rationale for this is that if creatures have life, then they should also have anything which life has. On the other hand, there are alternative connections between an *Adventurer* and *danger*. Adventurers are curious, which is a dangerous character trait, and they also like danger anyway. The connection between curiosity and danger carries a likelihood of 50%. If we set our threshold to this number, this link will therefore be found. The algorithm used by **FindAllLinkedConcepts** is outlined in Figure 3.61.

```
function FindAllLinkedConcepts( AN, ConceptSymbol,
                                 LinkSymbol, Threshold)

;; The lists of nodes held by the variables nodesToSearch and nodesSeen each
;; consist of a pair of: (an element, a weight). These are constructed with the
;; function MakeNode and the parts of the pair retrieved with GetElement
;; and GetWeight. The element is either a ConceptName (derived from an
;; AKO link) or a LINK slot

let nodesToSearch = list containing item MakeNode( ConceptSymbol, 1.0 )
let nodesSeen = empty list
while nodesToSearch not empty do {
      let node = first node of nodesToSearch
      let nodesToSearch = rest of nodesToSearch
      let element = GetElement( node )
      let symbol = if element is a ConceptName then element
                   else get concept name of element
      let weight = GetWeight( node )
      for each symbol akoSym connected by an AKO link from
                                 symbol in AN do {
            let newNode = MakeNode( akoSym weight )
            if newNode is not on list nodesSeen then
                  append newNode to nodesToSearch
            }
      for each slot linkSlot connected from symbol labelled with
                                 LinkSymbol in AN do {
            let newWeight = weight * certainty factor of linkSlot
            let newNode = MakeNode(linkSlot, newWeight)
            if newWeight >= Threshold then
                  if newNode not on list nodesSeen then
                        append newNode to nodesToSearch
            }
      }
remove all nodes from nodesSeen whose element part is not a LINK slot
return nodesSeen
```

Figure 3.61 Outline of the algorithm used by *FindAllLinkedConcepts*.

Normally the toolbox functions will just ignore cycles in the network, since they keep a list of all symbols they have already seen. If we attach certainty values to links, however, these will be recursively multiplied, leading to links with different 'strengths' at each pass through the cycle. Unless we set our threshold to 0.0, this process will terminate

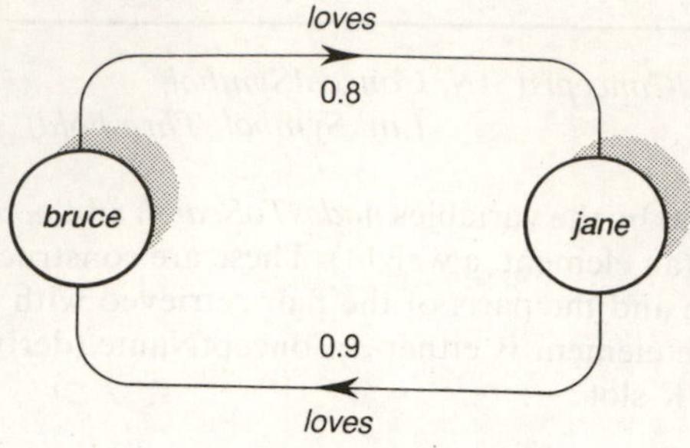

Figure 3.62 How *bruce* and *jane* (recursively) love one another.

whenever the compound likelihood drops below it. What we will see in such a case is a sequence of links with ever-decreasing certainty. Consider the example in Figure 3.62.

'*bruce loves jane with 80% and jane also loves bruce*' (with a bit more conviction). If we now ask for all *loves* links between these two, we will get a nice 'daisy chain'.

```
(define Love (MakeAN
  (CONCEPT 'bruce (LINK 'loves 'jane 0.8))
  (CONCEPT 'jane (LINK 'loves 'bruce 0.9))))
; love

(FindAllLinks Love 'bruce 'jane 0.2)
; ((loves jane 0.8) (loves jane 0.576) (loves jane 0.41472)
  (loves jane 0.298598) (loves jane 0.214991))
```

This example shows how certainty values of all the links in a path will be recursively multiplied. Of course, should we attempt this with a threshold of 0.0 the program will never terminate. To give a more straightforward example, we remove *life*'s link to *danger* (in *CugelsSaga*!); if we then ask whether *sadlark* is linked to *danger*, we would only find such a connection if we dropped our threshold to 25%. The reason for this is that *sadlark* is a *monster*, a *monster* has a 50% *curiosity*, and *curiosity* has a 50% chance of being dangerous. The compound link between *sadlark* and *danger* has therefore a strength of only 25% ($0.5 \times 0.5 = 0.25$).

```
(Linked? CugelsSaga 'sadlark 'danger)
; #f

(Linked? CugelsSaga 'sadlark 'danger 0.25)
; #t
```

3.5.3 The 'Bestiary' microworld

Our next example illustrates how to use a combination of the *KnowledgeBases* and *AssociativeNetworks* toolboxes to build networks interactively, and how to answer queries about concepts and their connections. Simple statements and questions are recognized through patterns stored in a knowledge base, and an associative network is created and maintained in response. Statements assert links between concepts: for example, *(a lecturer is a creature)* or *(all types of animal like to roll in the mud)* and questions must be of the form: *(show me what you know)*, *(what is an animal)*, *(what does an animal like to do)*, *(is a lecturer an animal)*. '*Bestiary*', a global network of facts about beasts, is used to illustrate this idea.

Only a few facts are initially known.

```
(define Bestiary (MakeAN (CONCEPT 'Creature)
                         (CONCEPT 'Human (AKO 'Creature))
                         (CONCEPT 'Beast (AKO  'Creature))
                         (CONCEPT 'Stuff )))
; bestiary
```

'*QueryPatternsKB*' defines a pattern base, similar to the one used by the *InnKeeper* program. Facts in this knowledge base are lists of the form: (*pattern-to-match procedure-to-invoke*). **MakeFact** builds such lists, and **GetPattern** and **GetProc** act as selector functions.

```
(define MakeFact
   (lambda (aPattern aProcedure) (list aPattern aProcedure)))
; makefact
(define GetPattern car)
; getpattern
(define GetProc cadr)
; getproc
```

The pattern base is defined next. Note that assertions and deductions are made on the global *Bestiary*, a variable which refers to the changing associative network itself. The order in which the patterns are stored is important, since we wish more specific patterns to be tested before the more general one. Six types of request are recognized, as described in the associated comments.

```
(define QueryPatternsKB
; NOTE: Uses the global 'Bestiary' for assertions and deductions !!!
; the order in which the patterns are tried IS important!
      (MakeKB
```

```
; #1: show the state of the network
(MakeFact (PATTERN ?+ 'you 'know)
          (lambda (aDummy) (PrintAN Bestiary)))

; #2: accept questions of the form: (what is an X)
(MakeFact
   (PATTERN 'What 'is (? 'xArticle) (? 'x))
   (lambda (anAL)
     (let ((superClass
              ; get and list all of x's superclasses
              (GetAKOChain Bestiary
                  (GetAssociationValue 'x anAL))))
        (if superClass
           (begin
              (DisplayLine
                 (GetAssociationValue 'xArticle anAL)
                 (GetAssociationValue 'x anAL))
              (for-each
               (lambda (super)
                 (DisplayLine " is a subclass of " super))
               superClass))
           (display "I don't know - you tell me")))))

; #3: accept questions of the form: (what does an X Y)
(MakeFact
   (PATTERN 'What ? (? 'xArticle) (? 'x) (? 'y))
   (lambda (anAL)
    (let ((linkedConcepts
               ; get and list all concepts linked to x under label y
               (FindAllLinkedConcepts
                  Bestiary
                  (GetAssociationValue 'x anAL)
                  (GetAssociationValue 'y anAL)))
          (getConceptNameOfLink cadr))
      (if linkedConcepts
        (DisplayList
             (GetAssociationValue 'xArticle anAL)
             (GetAssociationValue 'x anAL)
             (GetAssociationValue 'y anAL)
             (map (lambda (aLink)
                     (getConceptNameOfLink aLink))
                  linkedConcepts))
        (display "I wouldn't have a clue")))))

; #4: accept questions of the form: (is an X a Y)
(MakeFact
   (PATTERN 'Is (? 'xArticle) (? 'x) (? 'yArticle) (? 'y))
   (lambda (anAL)
    (let ((subclass (GetAssociationValue 'x anAL))
          (superClass (GetAssociationValue 'y anAL)))
```

```
        (if (member superClass
                          ; test whether y is on z's AKO chain
                          (GetAKOChain Bestiary subclass))
            (display "Yes it is")
            (display "No it is not")))))

  ; #5: accept assertions of the form: (. . X is . . Y)
  (MakeFact
     (PATTERN ?+ (? 'x) 'is ?+ (? 'y))
     (lambda (anAL)
       (let ((subclass (GetAssociationValue 'x anAL))
             (superClass (GetAssociationValue 'y anAL)))
            (display "ok")
            (set! Bestiary
                    ; make a new concept x and make it AKO y
                    (AddConcept Bestiary
                                (CONCEPT subclass
                                    (AKO superClass)))))))

  ; #6: accept assertions of the form: (all . . X Y Z)
  (MakeFact
     (PATTERN ?+ (? 'x) (? 'y) (? 'z))
     (lambda (anAL)
       (let ((firstConcept (GetAssociationValue 'x anAL))
             (linkSymbol (GetAssociationValue 'y anAL))
             (secondConcept (GetAssociationValue 'z anAL)))
            (if (and (FindConcept Bestiary firstConcept)
                     (FindConcept Bestiary secondConcept))
                (begin
                  (display "if you say so.")
                  (set! Bestiary
                        ; establish a new link labelled y between
                        ; x and z (replace it if it already exists)
                        (AddLink Bestiary
                                 firstConcept
                                 (LINK linkSymbol
                                       secondConcept))))
                (DisplayList "Invalid request ->"
                             "you haven't defined one of them")
            ))))))
```

The following 'driver' function chats with a user until (*bye*) is entered. During this dialogue a reply is read and tested against the patterns stored in *QueryPatternsKB*. The first match which succeeds will return a retrieved element, consisting of the matched element and its *AList*. The element will have a pattern and a procedure part. Triggering the appropriate response requires execution of the procedure part of the matched element, with the *AList* as its argument. This is accomplished by: ((*GetProc fact*) *anAL*). The reply 'Sentence not understood' is printed if none of the patterns will match.

```
(define Dialogue
  ; NOTE: 'fiddles' the global 'QueryPatternsKB' !!!
  (lambda ()
   (DisplayLine "Please supply your input as a list "
               "(use (bye) to terminate)")
   (display " >> ")
   (do ((sentence (read))
        (aRE #f))
       ((equal? sentence '(bye)) #f)
       (newline)
       ; (aRE -> a RetrievedElement) stores the retrieved list
       ; returned from the matching process
       (set! aRE (RetrieveByString QueryPatternsKB
                                   sentence
                                   GetPattern))
       (if (not aRE)
          (display "Sentence not understood")
          (let ((fact  (GetFact aRE))
                (anAL (GetAList aRE)))
               ; now invoke the relevant procedure on the bindings
               ; we made in matching this query
            ((GetProc fact) anAL)))
       (newline)
       (display " >> ")
       (set! sentence (read)))))
```

Figure 3.63 shows the program in execution. The user's input and its responses should be self-explanatory. You should draw the network built by these assertions and use it to follow the chains of deduction. What should be noted is that these patterns will allow many wildly different sentences to match, as long as only a few keywords ('clues') are in the right position. It is instructive to refer to the listing of the pattern base in order to see how particular matches occur. One problem with such an interface is that it is very easy to make the system accept implausible statements and to respond in surprising ways. The more specific the patterns are, the less likelihood there is that such things will occur. The patterns we supplied for the *InnKeeper* example were fairly tightly constrained. However, this also prevents us from catering for more variety in responses, since we must limit the vocabulary and structure of those replies we anticipate. To design a pattern-driven interface for a particular application will always require skilful trade-offs between the two extremes.

Although many forms of associative networks are used in AI, many of the underlying logical and philosophical questions have largely been

```
transcript
>>> (dialogue)
Please supply your input as a list (use (bye) to terminate)
 >> (hello)
Sentence not understood
 >> (the concept of beer is an example of the notion called stuff)
ok
 >> (a piece of chalk is made of the same stuff)
ok
 >> (a fire is another good example of stuff)
ok
 >> (any material is in fact made of the same stuff)
ok
 >> (all stuff isMadeOf material)
if you say so.
 >> (a lecturer is a human)
ok
 >> (all of a lecturer isMadeOf chalk)
if you say so.
 >> (a student is another type of human)
ok
 >> (all of a student isMadeOf beer)
if you say so.

>> (show me what you know)
*** Associative Network ***
 creature:
 human: (ako (creature))
 beast: (ako (creature))
 beer: (ako (stuff))
 chalk: (ako (stuff))
 fire: (ako (stuff))
 material: (ako (stuff))
 stuff: (ismadeof material)
 lecturer: (ako (human)) (ismadeof chalk)
 student: (ako (human)) (ismadeof beer)

>> (What is a lecturer isMadeOf)
a lecturer ismadeof (chalk material)

 >> (a Jinn is a beast)
ok
 >> (a Jinn isMadeOf Fire)
if you say so.
 >> (What is a Jinn)
a jinn
 is a subclass of jinn
 is a subclass of beast
 is a subclass of creature
 >> (What is a Jinn isMadeOf)
a jinn ismadeof (fire material)
 >> (Is a lecturer a Beast)
No it is not
 >> (What is the truth)
I don't know - you tell me
>> (What will a lecturer like)
I wouldn't have a clue
>> (bye)
>>>
```

Figure 3.63 Building a '*Bestiary*'.

ignored. Findler (1971) and Brachman (1979) are good references to a wider discussion of this framework, as is the book by Sowa (1984). Most of the early work on associative networks involved problems associated with machine translation and later with representation of the semantics of natural language statements. Since then they have evolved into fairly complete and substantial systems for structure generation, storage and recognition. Raphael's **SIR** and Carbonnell's **Scholar** programs used semantic networks as a base for information retrieval. Heidorn's (1975) '**augmented phrase structure grammar**' is a versatile notation for mapping conceptual graphs from and into natural language. Hendrix's (1979) 'partitioned networks' have been used for the **Ladder** natural language query system [Hendrix *et al.* (1979)] and the **Prospector** expert system for mineral exploration [Duda *et al.* (1979)]. The **KL-ONE** knowledge representation language is based on Brachman's (1979) 'structured inheritance networks'. Shapiro's (1979) **SNEPS** has evolved into a general system for logic on graphs. **NETL** [Fahlman (1979)] and **OWL** [Martin (1979)] are other systems in which associative networks play a major part. Rosenfeld (1979) used them to describe the 'grammar' of pictures and Winston (1980) employed them for his experiments in concept learning.

Conceptual networks have also been used as the base for the so-called '**conceptual dependency theory**', developed by Schank, Abelson and others (1977) at Yale University. Conceptual dependency theory seeks to determine the most primitive ideas that every proposition may eventually be mapped into, and one of these proposals reduces the number of such elementary concepts to around fifteen. The **MARGIE** system and many other 'story-understanding' programs have been built on that basis [Schank *et al.* (1981)].

Within AI, associative networks are considered an important means for knowledge representation, although there has been an ongoing argument between the 'neats' and the 'scruffies' regarding their usefulness [Sowa (1984), p. 136]. The 'scruffies' dismiss symbolic logic as psychologically unrealistic and much of the work on formal systems as irrelevant. They wish to concentrate on topics like common-sense reasoning and advocate the use of prototypical programs to test their theories. The 'neats', on the other hand, place these 'network hackers' on a level with wizards' apprentices, developing, at best, trivial variants of first-order logic, and confused notations in the worst case.

The main attraction of associative networks as a representational tool lies in the guidance they give to the task of model and program structuring. The notion of 'relevance', which is missing from logic, is well supported, and this is what is effectively encoded by links and the kinds of labels one may wish to attach to them. As always there is of course also a number of disadvantages. Quantifiers (that is, 'for all', 'there exists') are not easily expressed and, in contrast to logic, there is no canonical and well-established body of deduction procedures. Special-purpose interpreters without clear semantics abound. Since the notion of links is related to the idea of a 'pointer', associative networks tend to become messy tangles when applied to large knowledge bases. By analogy to the notorious debate about the pitfalls of using '**go to**' statements in programming languages (*see* [Computing Surveys (1974)]), chunking into higher level, more tightly restricted and well-behaved concepts must be applied to constrain their complexity. Combining them with the frame-based approach we discuss next is a step in this direction.

EXERCISES

Although associative networks have in the past often been applied to language 'understanding' problems, our main interest has been in their use as a base for giving inheritance to frames. Many of the *Frames* examples are therefore also relevant for demonstrating the features provided by the *AssociativeNetworks* toolbox.

3.46 Describe the room you are sitting in. What are the relevant concepts and relationships, and how are they linked? Draw up an associative network.

3.47* Extend the 'bestiary' example by adding an 'explanation' facility. This would involve inclusion of a 'special' link each time an assertion is made, where the 'concept' the link refers to denotes the source of some information (for example, *was originally known*, *was told*). The query system should then be able to answer questions like '*Why is a lecturer made of chalk*?' or '*Why is a Jinn a Beast*?' There are a few problems with this approach (for instance, you can't attach links to links) and various ways in which they may be overcome.

3.48 The notion of 'semantic distance' has been explored by psychologists to explain differences in people's response times, when trying to remember things. Extend the toolbox by writing a 'distance' function. When applied to two concepts it should return the minimum number of links between them, or #f if there is no connection.

3.49 Define a taxonomy for a university microworld (people, courses, departments, degrees, buildings, equipment, and so on) and provide a simple query interface for it.

3.50 Define and implement a network which may serve as a base for a program to recognize flying objects. Based on this structure your program should at least be able to distinguish between birds and planes, but you may also wish to extend its capabilities to the differences between various types of planes.

3.51 Use associative networks to store the 'meaning' of sentences. You will need to draw nodes for word categories and links which denote grammatical structures. Can you employ such networks for sentence generation and parsing? What are the problems? Patch the toolbox to make it more suitable for this class of applications.

3.6 Frames and scripts

'The fact is that our pure sensuous concepts do not depend on images of objects, but on schemata. No image of a triangle in general could ever be adequate to its concept. It would never attain that generality of the concept, which makes it applicable to all triangles, whether right-angled, or acute-angled, or anything else, but would always be restricted to one portion only of the sphere of the concept.'

[*Immanuel Kant (1781), as quoted by Sowa (1984), p. 2.*]

3.6.1 General principles and historical perspective

All complex behaviour has a need for strategies that organize elementary units into larger patterns, and such schemata therefore pervade every aspect of our society and culture. Once schemata are selected and activated they serve as a guide to the thinking process until some state of *closure* is achieved.

Early attempts at building intelligent programs used procedures or first-order predicate calculus to encode reasoning strategies. Neither of these two representations offers adequate facilities for encapsulating complexity in structures. Procedures lack clarity of denotation and the generality of predicate logic prevents efficient deduction procedures for large task domains. The paradigm shift caused by these difficulties with both approaches has already been referred to in Chapter 1. It occurred in the mid 1970s and accelerated investigations of alternative schemes for knowledge representation. Semantic networks and frames were two of the metaphors which emerged.

The original *frame* idea was first introduced to AI in a landmark paper by Marvin Minsky (1975). Minsky's primary interest in frame structures was to direct the reasoning of scene analysis programs in computer vision systems. He defined *frames* as 'chunks' of situation-specific knowledge, such as a collection of questions to be asked about a hypothetical situation. Frames can also be used to encapsulate all the properties of a single object or a whole class of related objects. Each frame will have pointers to other frames, representing relationships. Using such frames for reasoning implies a matching process in order to fill the 'slots' of any frame which is currently activated. If the match fails, and an alternative frame must be considered, we do not wish to start from 'first principles' again. If we can find a new frame that shares enough terminals with the old one, then we may continue from there. Although Minsky's proposal emphasized structure 'recognition', most of the subsequent work within this paradigm has instead focused on using frames for 'representation' of objects and their properties.

The concept of frames is a precursor to an object-oriented programming style. Frames offer structured representations of objects or classes of objects. Special facilities are available to define prototypes, and taxonomical classification and inheritance is supported. Most practical implementations also provide demon procedures which maintain integrity constraints and they perform automatic inferences all the way up an 'AKO' chain, although such facilities are to some degree orthogonal to the original frame idea. **FRL** [Roberts and Goldstein (1977)], **KRL** [Bobrow and Winograd (1977)], **Units** [Stefik (1979)], **PEARL** [Deering *et al.* (1981)], **LOOPS** [Bobrow and Stefik (1983)] and **KEE** [Intellicorp (1984)] are some of the more well-known programming systems offering support for the frame metaphor. Our toolbox routines are patterned after the facilities provided by FRL.

In FRL a *frame* consists of a number of *slots*, which may be filled with various classes of values (*see* Figure 3.64). There are two kinds of *slots*, **AKO** slots and others. AKO slots are special because they define paths along which slots are inherited when frames are linked into networks. In our system, AKO slots contain lists of a frame's 'superclasses', providing for multiple inheritance, and no other information may be attached to them. 'Ordinary' slots, on the other hand, may be composed of a whole range of so-called *facets*, which store different types of information about properties. *Value* facets are used to store a property's value, while *default* facets provide background assumptions in cases where a specific value may be unknown. Each ordinary slot may also include a number of 'demon' procedures which are activated by attempts to access its value in a specified manner. In some sense these were precursors of the concept of 'methods' in flavour systems. **IF-NEEDED** demons will be invoked when neither a value nor a default is present. They will provide values of slots on demand; that is, by querying

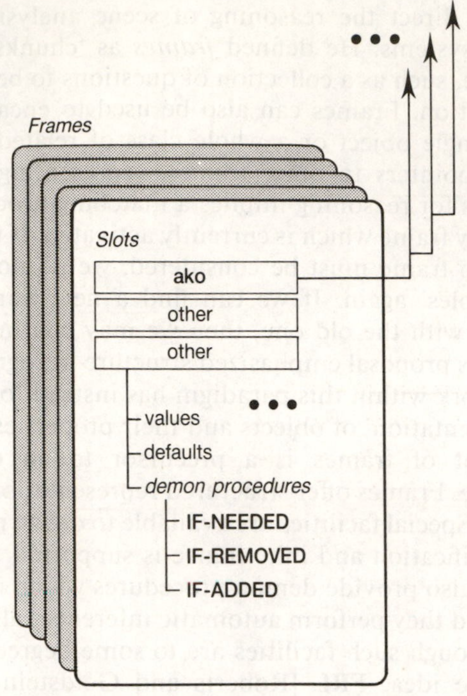

Figure 3.64 A frame structure.

the user or by computing them on the basis of some other information. **IF-ADDED** demons are triggered by attempts to add to (that is, change) the value of a slot. Their execution may, for example, serve to enforce integrity checks on the new value. Finally, an **IF-REMOVED** demon will be awakened whenever its slot's value is removed. This suggests an elegant solution to the updating problem, since we may thus propagate related changes to other parts of the system. The idea of demon procedures has lately also been used to update automatically graphical representations of objects in user interfaces, and has been referred to as 'data-driven programming', 'access-oriented programming' or 'active values'. As in object-oriented programming, its main attraction is the possibility it offers for localizing the sources of all changes to a variable's value in a single place.

3.6.2 The 'Frames' toolbox

Appendix III contains the source code for a *Frames* toolbox, in order to facilitate experimentation with frame-based knowledge representations.

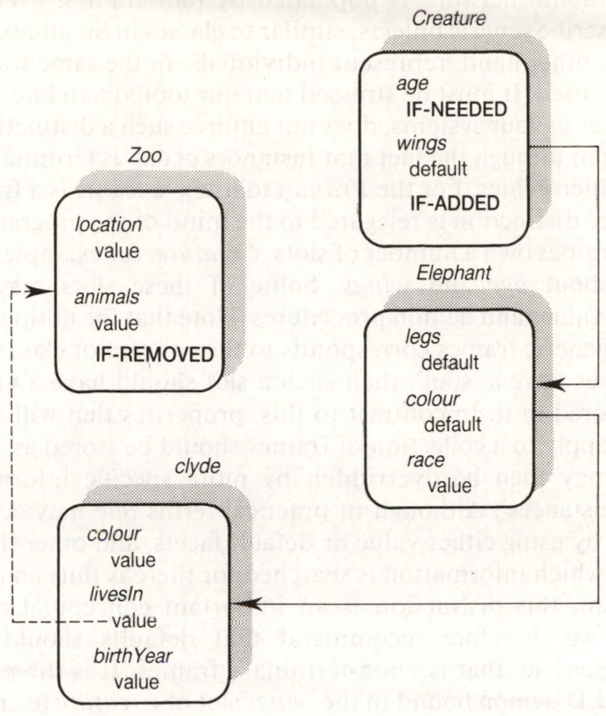

Figure 3.65 The *Habitat* microworld.

This toolbox is built on top of the one for *AssociativeNetworks* and provides additional support for attaching slots to concepts, as well as for the three types of demon procedures. In this context, frames are structured as shown in Figure 3.64, and they are bound into structures called '*FrameNetworks*'. A given slot's values may therefore be obtained by indexing into a network, a frame and the relevant slot. During its search the system will first attempt to access the value facet of a slot. If none exists it will query for a default, followed by an invocation of any **IF-NEEDED** demon procedure. This process is continued 'up' the whole length of any inheritance chains, until a value is eventually found or until all alternatives have been exhausted. The string "NOTKNOWN" will be returned in the latter case. If any **IF-ADDED** or **IF-REMOVED** demons are encountered they will also be executed, with arguments we will explain further in the following.

To facilitate our discussion of the toolbox's features we will refer to the simple microworld shown in Figure 3.65.

The *Habitat* network is populated by four frames. *Creature* and *Elephant* describe generic objects, similar to classes in Smalltalk. *Zoo* and *clyde*, on the other hand, represent individuals, in the same way as class instances are used. It must be stressed that our toolbox, in line with most other frame or flavour systems, does not enforce such a distinction in any way other than through the fact that instances occur as terminal nodes in inheritance hierarchies. For the *Frames* toolbox 'a frame is a frame'; any class/instance distinction is relegated to the mind of the programmer. All four of our frames own a number of slots. *Creature*, for example, holds information about *age* and *wings*. Some of these slots may contain appropriate values and demon procedures. Note that the notion of values attached to generic frames corresponds to the concept of class variables. If all creatures have a 'soul', then such a slot should have a value facet with 'yes' stored in it. In contrast to this, properties that will often, but not always, apply to a collection of frames should be stored as 'defaults', since they may then be overridden by more specific information in particular 'instances'. Although in practical terms one may achieve the same effects by using either value or default facets, and other than in the sequence in which information is searched for there is thus no difference in our system, this distinction is an important conceptual one. As a convention we therefore recommend that defaults should only be attached to generic (that is, 'non-terminal') frames. It is the purpose of the **IF-ADDED** demon bound in the *wings* slot of *Creature* to ensure that only birds (that is, frames whose 'race' slot contains the symbol '*bird*) can own them. Note that there is never any explicit value stored for a creature's age. The **IF-NEEDED** procedure associated with this slot will compute such a value on demand, since it can easily be established as the difference between the *birthYear* and the current date, which the user is queried for.

Elephant is a subframe of *Creature*. It is usually 'grey' in *colour*, will have four *legs* and is a 'mammal' by *race*.

clyde is a notoriously overworked example of a particular elephant, who has traditionally been employed in papers and textbooks to exemplify issues related to frames and conceptual networks. Our incarnation will be pink, was born in 1946 and lives in a zoo.

The *Zoo* frame is the final component of our *Habitat* example. It has only two slots, *location* and *animals*. There is an **IF-REMOVED** demon associated with *animals*. This procedure will ensure that the value of the *livesIn* slot of an animal, if it has any, is properly updated (that is, to 'homeless') whenever it is removed from the zoo. We could also provide a symmetric **IF-ADDED** demon, which might even be prodded to watch that no non-animal is ever admitted.

We will now discuss and demonstrate this toolbox's main functions, as listed in Figure 3.66.

Routine name	Parameters
	functions on Facets
VALUE	aValue
DEFAULT	aValue
IF-NEEDED	aDemonProcedure *; must accept anFN, aFrameName, aSlotName as* *; arguments and returns a new FN*
IF-ADDED	aDemonProcedure *; must accept anFN, aFrameName, aSlotName and* *; aValue as arguments and returns a new FN or #f (operation* *; refused) will be returned*
IF-REMOVED	aDemonProcedure *; must accept anFN, aFrameName, aSlotName and* *; aValue as arguments and returns a new FN or #f (operation* *; refused) will be returned*
	functions on Slots and Frames
AKO	any number of frame names
SLOT	aSlotName followed by any number of facets
AddAKOLink	(*as for associative networks*)
RemoveAKOLink	(*as for associative networks*)
FRAME	aFrameName followed by any number of slots
	functions on FNs (Frame Networks)
MakeFN	any number of frames
AddFrame	anFN aFrame
RemoveFrame	anFN aFrameName
PrintFN	anFN
	FN (Frame Network) maintenance functions
AddSlot	anFN aFrameName aSlot
RemoveSlot	anFN aFrameName aSlotName
AddFacet	anFN aFrameName aSlotName aFacet
RemoveFacet	anFN aFrameName aSlotName aFacetName
AddAValue	anFN aFrameName aSlotName aValue
RemoveAValue	anFN aFrameName aSlotName
	FN (Frame Network) query functions
FindAllFrame Names	anFN
FindAllSlotNames	anFN
FindFrame	anFN aFrameName
FindSlot	aFrame aSlotName
GetAValue	anFN aFrameName aSlotName
GetAKOSlot	anFN aFrameName
GetAKOLink	anFN aFrameName
GetAKOChain	anFN aFrameName

Figure 3.66 Summary of the *Frames* toolbox – functions on frame networks (FNs), slots and facets.

VALUE, **DEFAULT**, **IF-NEEDED**, **IF-ADDED** and **IF-REMOVED** are again functions which create these respective slots, as are **AKO, SLOT** and **FRAME**. **MakeFN** will create a new frame network (FN) and **PrintFN** may be used to print it.

```
(define Habitat
  (MakeFN
   (FRAME 'Creature (SLOT 'wings (DEFAULT 'none)))
   (FRAME 'Elephant (AKO 'Creature)
                    (SLOT 'legs (DEFAULT 4))
                    (SLOT 'colour (DEFAULT 'grey))
                    (SLOT 'race (VALUE 'mammal)))
   (FRAME 'clyde    (AKO 'Elephant)
                    (SLOT 'livesIn (VALUE 'zoo))
                    (SLOT 'colour (VALUE 'pink))
                    (SLOT 'birthYear (VALUE 1946)))))
; habitat
(PrintFN Habitat)
  ; *** FRAME Network ***
    creature :
           (SLOT wings (DEFAULT none))
    elephant :
           (AKO ((creature)))
           (SLOT legs (DEFAULT 4))
           (SLOT colour (DEFAULT grey))
           (SLOT race (VALUE mammal))
    clyde:
           (AKO ((elephant)))
           (SLOT livesin (VALUE zoo))
           (SLOT colour (VALUE pink))
           (SLOT birthyear (VALUE 1946))
```

Note that we have not yet added the *Zoo* frame or any slots with demon procedures. The procedures **FindAllFrameNames** and **FindAllSlotNames** can be employed to list all concepts defined in our network:

```
(FindAllFrameNames Habitat)
; (creature elephant clyde)
(FindAllSlotNames Habitat)
;(birthyear livesin race colour legs wings)
```

while **FindFrame** and **FindSlot** may be used to obtain a specific frame or slot item.

```
(FindFrame Habitat 'clyde)
  ; (clyde ((ako (elephant))
            (livesin ((value zoo)))
            (colour ((value pink)))
            (birthyear ((value 1946)))))

(FindSlot (FindFrame Habitat 'clyde) 'colour)
  ; (colour ((value pink)))
```

The inheritance structure for 'Frames' is based on the corresponding concepts provided by the 'AssociativeNetworks' toolbox. The same procedures can therefore be used to explore it.

```
(GetAKOSlot Habitat 'clyde)
  ; (ako (elephant))

(GetAKOLinks Habitat 'clyde)
  ; (elephant)

(GetAKOChain Habitat 'clyde)
  ; (clyde elephant creature)
```

GetAValue is probably the most important of all the toolbox functions. It will accept a frame network as well as the name of a frame and slot, and in return it will produce the relevant value. To achieve this, it will locate the frame and search for a *value* facet attached to the specified slot. If there is no such information, it will then look for a *default*, followed by an attempt to awaken an **IF-NEEDED** demon. If all these endeavours fail, it will recursively repeat the same sequence of actions along all the inheritance links listed in the frame's **AKO** slot, until a value is found. If no such value can be established, it will eventually fail and return "NOTKNOWN".

Note that, as always, proper quotes are important. We need to provide an FN object, and frame and slot names.

```
(GetAValue Habitat 'clyde 'colour)
  ; pink

(GetAValue Habitat 'clyde 'politicalPersuasion)
  ; "NOTKNOWN"
```

AddAValue should be used to add new values to a slot. If there is no such slot the function will proceed to create it. Since there may only be a single value per slot, adding a new one will remove the old value! This means that any **IF-ADDED** and **IF-REMOVED** demons (searched for all the way up the **AKO** chain, until the first one is found) will both be run. If either returns **#f**, the operation is not performed! **AddAValue** will build and return a new frame network. If we wish this to replace the old one we will have to bind it (for instance, to *Habitat*). Here we refrain from doing so.

```
(AddAValue Habitat 'clyde 'colour 'striped)
; ((creature . . . (livesin ((value zoo))) (colour ((value striped))))))
```

RemoveAValue complements **AddAValue**. It will run any **IF-REMOVED** demons it encounters. If they return any value other than **#f**, the value facet is removed (if there is one). Here we remove clyde's *colour*. Note that this time we make the change permanent (by using **set!**). Checking for his *colour* reveals that poor clyde has turned grey. Since this is the default inherited from *Elephant*, everything is as it should be.

```
(set! Habitat
      (RemoveAValue Habitat 'clyde 'colour))
; ((creature . . . ((value zoo))) (colour ())))))

(GetAValue Habitat 'clyde 'colour)
; grey
```

AddFacet will add a new facet, and it will also create a new slot if one does not already exist. Here we show how to add an **IF-NEEDED** demon to clyde's *colour* slot. Since we have just removed it before, a new one will be created, and the procedure will be attached. Since no value or default is explicitly stored in the slot, **GetAValue** will now execute the demon.

```
(set! Habitat
      (AddFacet Habitat 'clyde 'colour
                'IF-NEEDED
                 (lambda (aNetwork aFrame aSlot)
                   ; IF-NEEDED demons always expect 3 parameters!
                   (display "you tell me!")
                   "NOTKNOWN")))
; ((creature . . . ((if-needed #<procedure>))))))

(GetAValue Habitat 'clyde 'colour)
; you tell me! "NOTKNOWN"
```

Note that we always need to declare network, frame and slot parameters for **IF-NEEDED** demons, even though they may not use this information. Like any other Scheme function they will return the value of the last expression to be evaluated.

Facets may be removed in the same way as they are created. **RemoveFacet** provides this functionality and an outline of its algorithm is given in Figure 3.67.

```
function RemoveFacet ( FN, FrameName, SlotName, FacetName )
let frame = find frame labelled FrameName in network FN
if no such frame then
    return FN
let slot = find slot labelled SlotName in frame
if no such slot then
    return FN
let facet = find facet labelled FacetName in slot
if no such facet then
    return FN
if FacetName is VALUE then {
    let superFrames = list of all Frames linked (recursively) from frame
                              FrameName by AKO links
    let value = value list of facet
    for each frame F in superFrames and while FN ≠ #f do {
        let demon = IF-REMOVED demon in FrameName slot of F
        if demon exists then
            FN = value returned from demon when invoked with
                    parameters FN FrameName SlotName and value
        }
    }
return FN
```

Figure 3.67 Outline of the algorithm used by *RemoveFacet*.

To relieve clyde of any recurring queries about his colour we therefore only need to execute:

```
(set! Habitat (RemoveFacet Habitat 'clyde 'colour 'IF-NEEDED))
; ((creature . . . ((value zoo))) (colour ())))
(GetAValue Habitat 'clyde 'colour)
; grey again !
; grey
```

You will remember that we have not defined any *Zoo* frame yet. Let us use **AddFrame** to add such an entity to the network. This procedure accepts the name of the new frame, together with any slots we wish to define, and it will return a new network in response. To convince ourselves that the addition was successful we can now ask for a listing of names of all the frames known to the network. **FindAllFrameNames** will accomplish this.

```
(set! Habitat (AddFrame Habitat
                (FRAME 'Zoo
```

```
                    (SLOT 'location
                              (VALUE ''out of town and down by the river''))
                    (SLOT 'animals (VALUE ()))))))
; ((creature . . . (animals ((value )))))))

(FindAllFrameNames Habitat)
; (creature elephant clyde zoo)
```

We can now add *clyde* to the *zoo*. Note that although *clyde* is the only animal there right now, we may later wish to store more than one creature as the zoo's inhabitants. Slots can only have a single *value* facet, but this facet may of course be a list. The value of our zoo's *animals* slot should therefore become a list with *clyde* added to it. Again we should convince ourselves that the addition was successful.

```
(set! Habitat (AddAValue Habitat 'zoo 'animals
                         (cons 'clyde
                               (GetAValue Habitat 'zoo 'animals))))
; (creature . . . (animals ((value (clyde)))))))
(GetAValue Habitat 'zoo 'animals)
; (clyde)
```

IF-NEEDED demons can be used for purposes other than printing some flippant remark. For example, we may employ them to compute the value of a slot when required. In our scenario we want to know about *age*, but we have already stored information about every creature's *birthYear*. If in response to an *age* query we wish to enquire about the current year, we can easily compute the ages of all our creatures. The main advantage of such a scheme is that now we need not remember to update ages each year. **IF-NEEDED** demons provide the means for implementing this concept.

```
(set! Habitat
      (AddSlot Habitat
               'Creature
               (SLOT 'age
                     (IF-NEEDED
                      (lambda (aNetwork aFrameName
                               aSlotName)
                        (let ((year 0))
                          (display ''What year is it?'')
                          (set! year (read))
                          (newline)
                          (- year
```

```
                             (GetAValue aNetwork
                                        aFrameName
                                        'birthYear))))))))
  ; (creature . . . (age ((if-needed #<procedure> )))))))

 (GetAValue Habitat 'clyde 'age)
  ; What year is it ? 1988
  ; 42
```

To demonstrate a possible use for **IF-ADDED** demons we will now attach such a procedure to a *Creature's wings* slot, and entrust it with the task of ensuring that only birds are allowed to change this value. In implementing such a guardian we make use of the fact that **IF-ADDED** and **IF-REMOVED** procedures will have to return a value other than #f for any value-changing operation to succeed. This will often be the modified 'value' (state) of the network, whose original state is passed to them as their first argument. Note that the value to be added or removed must be made available as a fourth parameter to these procedures.

```
(set! Habitat
     (AddFacet Habitat 'Creature 'wings
       (IF-ADDED
         (lambda (aNetwork aFrameName aSlotName aValue)
           (if (not (eq? (GetAValue aNetwork aFrameName 'race)
                         'bird))
               (begin
                 (DisplayLine "only birds may have wings !"
                              "since you're not a bird"
                              "you can't have" aValue)

                 #f
               aNetwork)))))
  ; (creature . . . (((default none) ((if-added #<procedure>)))))))
```

Note that we also use the value of the attempted addition in our reply. We can now test this function.

```
(AddAValue Habitat 'clyde 'wings 2)
 ; only birds may have wings! since you're not a bird you can't have 2
 ; ((creature . . . (((default none) ((if-added #<procedure>)))))))
```

Our final demonstration uses an **IF-REMOVED** demon to maintain the network's consistency in the case where an animal is removed from the zoo. Since all animals are *creatures*, which may have a *'livesIn'* slot, the associated value must be changed to reflect the fact that the creature is now 'homeless'. Since the *animals* slot of *Zoo* already exists we just add the demon as a new facet.

```
(set! Habitat
    (AddFacet Habitat 'Zoo 'animals
      (IF-REMOVED
        (lambda (aNetwork aFrameName aSlotName aValue)
          ; make all animals homeless
          (for-each
            (lambda (anAnimal)
              (set! aNetwork
                    (AddAValue aNetwork anAnimal livesIn 'homeless)))
            aValue)
          aNetwork))))
; ((creature . . . ((value (clyde)) (if-removed #<procedure> ))))))
```

This demon will be activated whenever a removal of the zoo's *animals* slot is attempted. It will cycle through the list of all the animals in the zoo and set their *livesIn* slot to 'homeless'. Note, however, that there is now a slight problem with adding new animals, since the *RemoveAValue* procedure will first be called, before any new value can be entered. This means that our demon will also be run in that case and make all of the newcomers homeless as soon as they arrive. The way to overcome this difficulty should be obvious. We will need to attach an **IF-ADDED** demon to the slot, which puts all animals into the zoo – that is, it sets their *livesIn* slot to 'zoo' if they have any. This would be necessary for all the 'new' animals anyway, and this way of handling the update offers a clean solution. The following expression shows that our procedure works and *clyde* is indeed removed from the zoo and tossed into homelessness.

```
(GetAValue Habitat 'clyde 'livesIn)
 ; zoo
(set! Habitat (RemoveAValue Habitat 'zoo 'animals))
 ; ((creature . . . (animals ((if-removed #<procedure>))))))
(GetAValue Habitat 'clyde 'livesIn)
 ; homeless
```

3.6.3 The 'Toyland' microworld

While we have so far explored the frame metaphor's potential for storing structured data, our next example will demonstrate how it may be applied to the problem of scene recognition, its original purpose in terms of Minsky's proposal. The example is set in a microworld pioneered by Winograd's (1972) famous SHRDLU program. Our much simpler version uses frames to store properties of a collection of blocks, some of

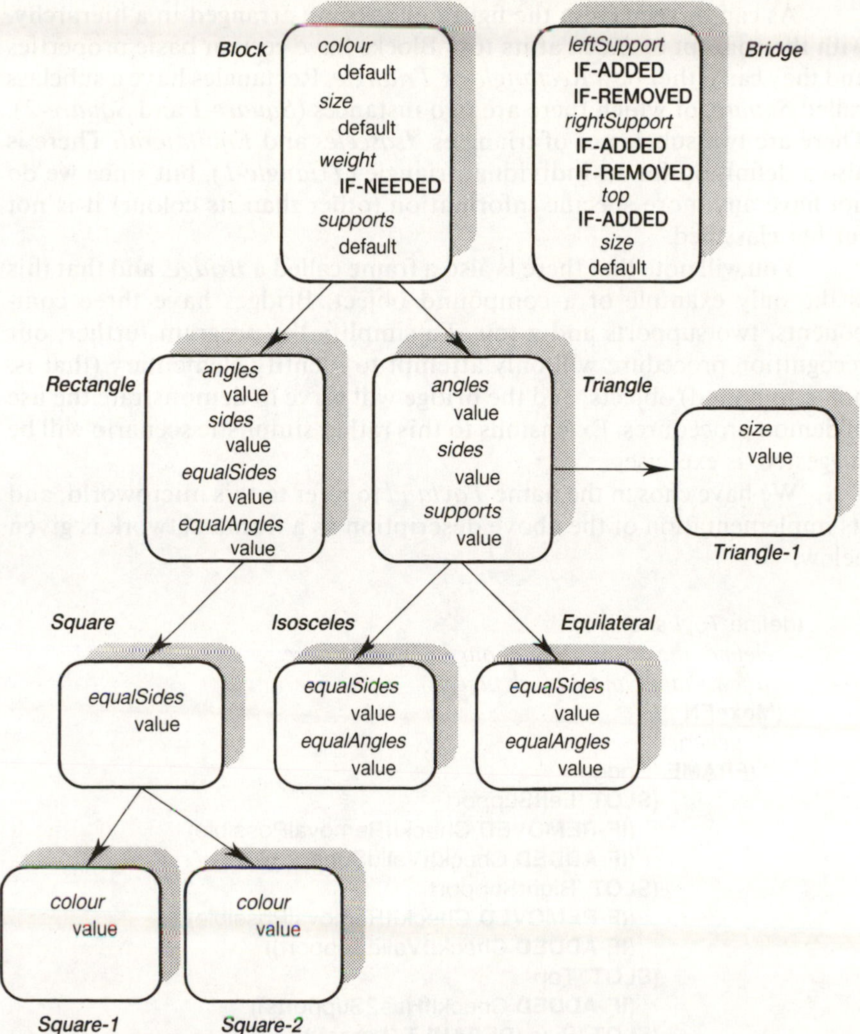

Figure 3.68 The *Toyland* microworld.

which can be stacked on top of each other. To simplify our program we will allow only two-dimensional side views of the shapes of such blocks. Our database encodes knowledge of various properties of different shapes, such as squares and various types of triangles. The program itself includes a recognizer function, which tries to establish a block's nature from clues we provide. When a new block is described it tries to decide how to classify it to the best of its knowledge. If necessary, it will ask for further information from the user. Figure 3.68 shows the frames we want to define.

As can be seen from the figure, blocks are arranged in a hierarchy, with the concept of *Block* at its top. Blocks have certain basic properties and they can either be a *Rectangle* or *Triangle*. Rectangles have a subclass called *Square*, of which there are two instances (*Square-1* and *Square-2*). There are two subclasses of triangles, *Isosceles* and *Equilateral*. There is also a definition for an individual triangle (*Triangle-1*), but since we do not have any more specific information (other than its colour) it is not further classified.

You will note that there is also a frame called a *Bridge*, and that this is the only example of a compound object. Bridges have three components, two supports and a top. To simplify the program further, our recognition procedure will only attempt to identify elementary (that is, non-compound) objects, and the bridge will serve to demonstrate the use of demon procedures. Extensions to this rather simplistic scenario will be suggested as exercises.

We have chosen the name *Toyland* to refer to this microworld, and its implementation of the above description as a frame network is given below.

```
(define ToyLand
  ; defines the initial state of our knowledge base:
  ; a few shapes and 2 block objects
  (MakeFN
    ; generics
    (FRAME 'Bridge
              (SLOT 'LeftSupport
                (IF-REMOVED CheckIfRemovalPossible)
                (IF-ADDED CheckIfValidSupport))
              (SLOT 'RightSupport
                (IF-REMOVED CheckIfRemovalPossible)
                (IF-ADDED CheckIfValidSupport))
              (SLOT 'Top
                (IF-ADDED CheckIfHas2Supports))
              (SLOT 'Size (DEFAULT 'Large)))
    (FRAME 'Block
              (SLOT 'Colour (DEFAULT 'White))
              (SLOT 'Size   (DEFAULT 'Small))
              (SLOT 'Weight (IF-NEEDED CharacterizeWeight))
              (SLOT 'Supports (DEFAULT 'CanDo)))
    (FRAME 'Rectangle (AKO 'Block)
              (SLOT 'Angles (VALUE 4))
              (SLOT 'Sides (VALUE 4))
              (SLOT 'EqualSides (VALUE 2))
              (SLOT 'EqualAngles (VALUE 4)))
    (FRAME 'Triangle (AKO 'Block)
              (SLOT 'Angles (VALUE 3))
              (SLOT 'Sides (VALUE 3))
```

```
                (SLOT 'Supports (VALUE 'Nothing)))
      (FRAME 'Square (AKO 'Rectangle)
                (SLOT 'EqualSides (VALUE 4)))
      (FRAME 'Isosceles (AKO 'Triangle)
                (SLOT 'EqualSides (VALUE 2))
                (SLOT 'EqualAngles (VALUE 4)))
      (FRAME 'Equilateral (AKO 'Triangle)
                (SLOT 'EqualSides (VALUE 3))
                (SLOT 'EqualAngles (VALUE 3)))
   ; individuals
      (FRAME 'Square-1 (AKO 'Square)
                (SLOT 'Colour (VALUE 'Blue)))
      (FRAME 'Triangle-1 (AKO 'Triangle)
                (SLOT 'Size (VALUE 'Big)))))
```

CharacterizeWeight is the name of an **IF-NEEDED** procedure which will produce a qualitative value for the *weight* slot of blocks on demand. The algorithm for this is rather elementary: all little and tiny blocks are 'light', and all big and huge ones are 'heavy'.

```
(define CharacterizeWeight
  (lambda (aNetwork aFrameName aSlotName)
   (case (GetAValue ToyLand aFrameName 'Size)
         ((Small  Little  Tiny) 'Light)
         ((Large  Big  Huge) 'Heavy)
         (("NOTKNOWN") "NOTKNOWN"))))
```

Remember that 'NOTKNOWN' is returned by the toolbox whenever it is unable to establish a slot's value.

The following *WhatIs* function will now implement a simple block recognition procedure.

```
(define WhatIs
 (lambda initialAttributes

  (define satisfiesAttribute
    (lambda (aFrameList anAttribute)
    ; return only those frames in aFrameList that satisfy anAttribute
    (let ((attrname (car anAttribute))
         (attrvalue (cadr anAttribute)))
       (do ((returnedList ( ))
            (toTestList aFrameList (cdr toTestList))
            (aFrameName #f))
           ((null? toTestList) returnedList)
           (set! aFrameName (car toTestList))
           (if (not (equal? attrvalue (GETAValue ToyLand
                                                   aFrameName
                                                   attrname)))
```

```
                              #f
                              (set! returnedList (append returnedList
                                                  (list aFrameName))))))))
  ; try and discover what kind of object it might be
  (let ((possibleObjects (FindAllFrameNames ToyLand)))
    (for-each
      (lambda (anAttribute)
        ; reduce the list of candidates using this attribute
        (set! possibleObjects
              (satisfiesAttribute possibleObjects anAttribute)))
      initialAttributes)
    (cond ((null? possibleObjects)
           (DisplayLine "Sorry, no such object is known to me"))
          ((= 1 (length possibleObjects))
           (DisplayLine "It might be a" (car possibleObjects)))
          (else
           ; now keep asking for another attribute to reduce the list
           ; until only one (or none) is left
           (do ((list possibleObjects)
                (newAttribute #f))
               ((or (null? list) (= 1 (length list)))
                (newline)
                (if (null? list)
                    (DisplayLine "Sorry, no such object is known to me")
                    (DisplayLine "It might be a" (car list))))
               (DisplayLine "We've narrowed it down to one of:")
               (DisplayLine list)
               (DisplayLine "Please apply further discrimination")
               (set! newAttribute (read))
               (newline)
               ; try and reduce the list further
               (set! list
                     (satisfiesAttribute list newAttribute))))))))
```

In trying to identify an object this procedure obtains successively more specific information about its properties. These facts are then matched against the frames contained in its memory, the *Toyland* frame network. If matches succeed, the list of candidates, which initially includes all the objects the program knows about, will be shortened. The whole process stops when a frame can be fully matched, or when the list of alternatives has been exhausted. In the first case a solution has been found. It is the object characterized by the frame for which the match was successful. In the second case we have to report that no matching object is known to the program. Note that the program's discriminatory abilities can easily be extended by adding new frames to the network, or by adding new slots to existing ones.

Although this can of course be done solely by using the toolbox functions, the next function offers a 'shortcut'. *AddObject* makes and adds a new frame to *Toyland*. It expects the name of the object's superclass, as well as a series of (attribute, value) lists.

```
(define AddObject
  (lambda (aName parentClass . anAttributeList)
    (let ((aSlotList (map (lambda (anAttribute)
                            (SLOT (car anAttribute)
                                  (VALUE (cadr anAttribute))))
                          anAttributeList)))
      (set! ToyLand
        (AddFrame ToyLand
                  (apply FRAME
                         (cons aName (cons (AKO parentClass)
                                           aSlotList)))))
      (DisplayLine "New object" aName "added to network"))))
```

Show may be used to view any particular frame.

```
(define Show
  ; shows the state of a frame
  (lambda (aName)
    (let ((aFrame (FindFrame ToyLand aName)))
      (if (not aFrame)
          #f
          (PrintFrame aFrame)))))
```

The final set of procedures deals solely with bridges. *NewBridge* defines a new bridge object, as yet without any components, to which we can then add tops and supports (*AddToBridge*).

```
(define NewBridge
  ; this procedure adds an uninstantiated "bridge" object
  (lambda (aName)
    (set! ToyLand
          (AddFrame ToyLand (FRAME aName (AKO 'Bridge))))
    (DisplayLine "New bridge" aName "added to network")))

(define AddToBridge
  ; this procedure lets us "build" bridges incrementally. It expects the
  ; name of an existing bridge, followed by the "position" in which the new
  ; component should go (one of: left, right, top), followed by the name of the
  ; component (which we have to create before we use it).
  (lambda (aBridgeName where anObject)
    (DisplayLine "Adding" anObject "to position"
                 where "of bridge" aBridgeName "of network")
    (set! ToyLand
     (AddAValue ToyLand
                aBridgeName
                (case where ((Left)   'LeftSupport)
```

```
                    ((Right) 'RightSupport)
                    ((Top)   'Top)
                    (else    (DisplayLine
                                "I don't know what kind of"
                                "position' "where
                                "'is supposed to be")
                             (DisplayLine
                                "- let's start at the 'top'")
                             'Top))
          anObject)) #t))
```

When we defined the *Toyland* network you will have noted that we included references to a number of demon procedures for bridges. These are intended to enforce certain constraints on the way bridges are built. For example, it should not be possible to add a top before the supports are in place. Also, we should not be allowed to remove a support from a completed bridge, since such a structure would then collapse. There are a number of other things we might usefully test for, and we leave this as an exercise. Note, for example, that our program will happily let you add the same block as support and top; that is, no checks on 'distinctness' are made.

CheckIfRemovalPossible is to ensure that no block supporting a top is ever removed (by returning #f in that case).

```
(define CheckIfRemovalPossible
  (lambda (aNetwork aFrameName aSlotName aBlock)
   ; prevent removal of Base and First components of a Compound object
   ; (if a top there is present)
   (if (equal? (GetAValue aNetwork aFrameName 'Top)
           "NOTKNOWN")
       aNetwork
       (begin
         (DisplayLine aBlock
                     "supports a bridge -"
                     "since I hate vandalism I won't remove it")
         #f))))
```

CheckIfValidSupport tests whether a given object can in fact support a top. You may wish to check that triangles are not allowed to act as supports in our original example.

```
(define CheckIfValidSupport
  (lambda (aNetwork aFrameName aSlotName anObject)
   ; check whether this object can support others
   (let ((supports (GetAValue aNetwork anObject 'Supports)))
```

```
(if (eq? supports 'CanDo)
    aNetwork
    (begin
      (DisplayLine "Object" anObject "is not fit to support anything")
      #f)))))
```

Finally, we must ensure that both supports are in place before a top is added. *CheckIfHas2Supports* tests for this.

```
(define CheckIfHas2Supports
  (lambda (aNetwork aFrameName aSlotName anObject)
   ; check that this object has both a left and a right support
   (let ((left   (GetAValue ToyLand aFrameName 'LeftSupport))
         (right (GetAValue ToyLand aFrameName 'RightSupport)))
     (if (or (equal? left "NOTKNOWN")
             (equal? right "NOTKNOWN"))
       (begin
         (DisplayLine "Object" anObject
                                   "cannot be placed, since it"
                                   "would be unsupported in this"
                                   aFrameName "structure")
         #f)
       aNetwork))))
```

Figures 3.69 and 3.70 explain how the program may be used. The first shows the process of recognizing an equilateral triangle, while the second explores what may happen when building a bridge. Note that the program refuses to remove the bridge's support, once the top is in place. This is regardless of the fact that we use *square-1* twice, which it doesn't check for. To correct our mistake we would have to demolish the whole structure.

The frame concept is closely associated with the idea of 'informal' reasoning systems, which permit conclusions to be drawn from partial evidence. Frames may be used to encode what is 'relevant' in a given structure, situation or process, and what is to be 'expected' in typical cases. In contrast to logic, frames can also be non-monotonic; that is, we may retract assertions as a result of additional information. Frame-based systems will typically perform some finite amount of processing and then 'jump' to conclusions. The problem of course is to decide what should be seen as 'typical' or 'relevant', and where (that is, which frame in a network, which slot in a frame, as a value, default, or demon, and so on) such information should be attached. An answer to this question strongly depends on the expected patterns of access and cannot be given outside a specific context of problems and purposes.

Another representational schema whose structure is very similar to the frames idea is often referred to as '*scripts*'. *Scripts* were proposed by

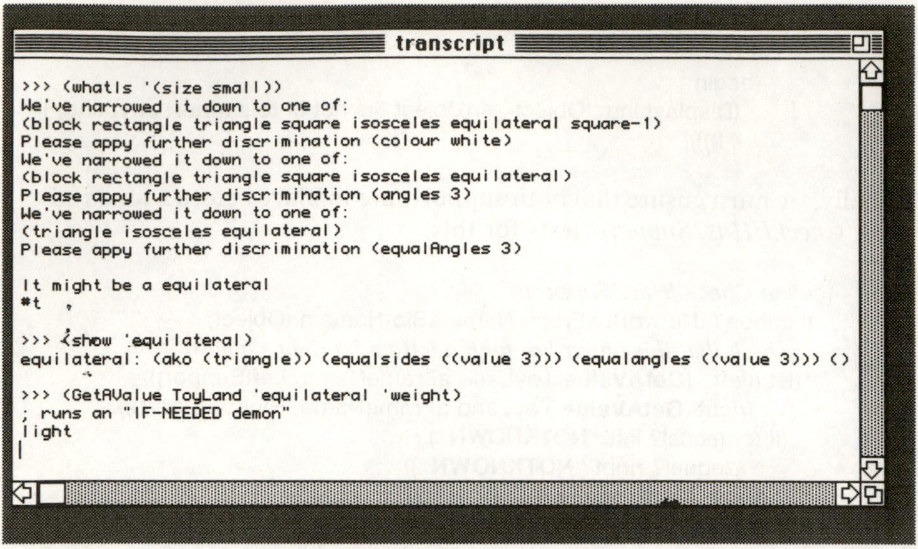

transcript

```
>>> (whatIs '(size small))
We've narrowed it down to one of:
(block rectangle triangle square isosceles equilateral square-1)
Please appy further discrimination (colour white)
We've narrowed it down to one of:
(block rectangle triangle square isosceles equilateral)
Please appy further discrimination (angles 3)
We've narrowed it down to one of:
(triangle isosceles equilateral)
Please appy further discrimination (equalAngles 3)

It might be a equilateral
#t

>>> (show 'equilateral)
equilateral: (ako (triangle)) (equalsides ((value 3))) (equalangles ((value 3))) ()

>>> (GetAValue ToyLand 'equilateral 'weight)
; runs an "IF-NEEDED demon"
light
```

Figure 3.69 What kind of block is it?

Schank and Abelson (1977) in order to represent background information that a program could use in story analysis. Here slots may be filled with data or actions, or with references to other scripts. The primary mechanism of understanding a line in a story is to instantiate one or more of such scenarios and to attempt any matches they suggest. The scenario of actions performed when eating in a restaurant, taking a bath, shopping in a supermarket or using a piggy bank are frequently cited as examples of such stereotyped situations. Figure 3.71 shows a simple script for a dinner party, together with a possible instantiation. As you can see, our instantiation uses both values and procedures to fill the slots of the script. We leave these procedures as an exercise. References to subscripts could also be used.

Although they have served as convenient structuring devices for story understanding programs, scripts have so far been mainly applied to simple children's tales or newspaper articles. It remains to be shown how they could represent less stereotypical information, or stories with unusual twists. A critical aspect of this idea for program organization is the way in which scripts are activated. This will clearly require some type of pattern-matching process. The literature is usually vague in this respect, and special-purpose and fairly *ad hoc* strategies are often used. One area in which scripts have profitably been employed outside the field of story understanding is in models of user behaviour, attached to 'intelligent' help systems. Here they represent theories of classes of users and, when instantiated, give appropriate guidance to the behaviour of the program. This will include the kinds of questions to ask and the type or

transcript

```
>>>(NewBridge 'bonzo)
New bridge bonzo added to network
#t
(FindAllFrameNames ToyLand)
(bridge block rectangle triangle square isosceles equilateral square-1
triangle-1 bonzo)
>>> (AddObject 'square-2 'square '(colour green))
New object square-2 added to network
#t
>>> (show 'square-2)
square-2 :
      (AKO ((square)) )
      (SLOT colour  (VALUE  green ) )
()

; build bonzo, top-down, left to right
>>> (addToBridge 'bonzo 'rightOnTop 'triangle-1)
; fires if added demon - can't do it "top-down"
Adding triangle-1 to position rightontop of bridge bonzo of network
I don't know what kind of position ' rightontop ' is supposed to be
- let's start at the 'top'
Object triangle-1 can not be placed, since it would be unsupported in this
bonzo structure
#t
>>> (addToBridge 'bonzo 'left 'triangle-1)
; fires IF-ADDED demon - fuzzy, won't accept triangles as supports
Adding triangle-1 to position left of bridge bonzo of network
Object triangle-1 is not fit to support anything
#t
>>> (addToBridge 'bonzo 'left 'square-1)
Adding square-1 to position left of bridge bonzo of network
#t
>>> (addToBridge 'bonzo 'right 'square-1)
Adding square-1 to position right of bridge bonzo of network
#t
>>> (addToBridge 'bonzo 'top 'triangle-1)
Adding triangle-1 to position top of bridge bonzo of network
#t
>>> (show 'bonzo)
bonzo :
      (AKO ((bridge)) )
      (SLOT leftsupport  (VALUE  square-1 ) )
      (SLOT rightsupport  (VALUE  square-1 ) )
      (SLOT top  (VALUE  triangle-1 ) )
()

; oops, we used square-1 in 2 places - replace by square-2

>>> (addToBridge 'bonzo 'right 'square-2)
; fires an IF-REMOVED demon, bridge will collapse if support is removed
Adding square-2 to position right of bridge bonzo of network
square-1 supports a bridge - since I hate vandalism I won't remove it
#t

; seems that we need to knock bonzo over to fix this !|
```

Figure 3.70 How *bonzo* was built.

amount of information given; a 'novice' may welcome more guidance than an 'expert'. Script selection may be performed on the basis of error rates or other more complex measures. Computer-aided learning systems in general can profit from this idea.

Since a more detailed account of this research program is beyond the scope of this book, we will refer the interested reader to the references. Schank (1980) gives a good summary.

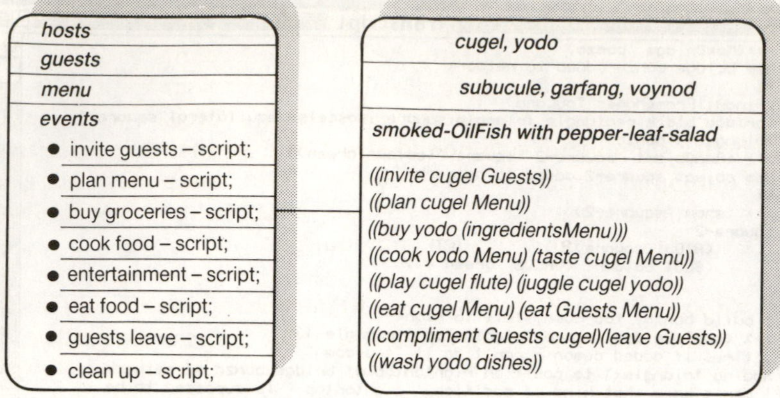

Figure 3.71 A dinner party script and one of its instantiations.

EXERCISES

3.52 Extend the *Habitat* microworld. This will involve defining new creatures and a more detailed network of relationships between them. You may wish to populate the zoo with a variety of animals. These may be put into different surroundings (for example, temperate, tropical, prairie, polar, aquarium, aviary, and so on), which may all be represented by suitable subframes. Demons should enforce constraints on an animal's placement. For example, carnivores should not be placed in the same habitat as herbivores, and only creatures who swim should be put into an aquarium.

3.53 Write frame definitions for all the rooms in your flat or house. To do this you will first need to identify all relevant features and decide whether to store them as values, or whether to expand them into subframes. Relationships between objects should be stored as **AKO** links or demon procedures. Once the frames are defined you should use them to drive a 'room recognition' procedure, reflecting some theory of what one will first look for when entering a new room. Your program should be dialogue driven. It should ask you to locate a particular feature and expect either a positive or negative reply, which will then be used to ask further questions, announce a solution or switch to a different frame.

3.54 Write a program which lets you assemble new frames interactively. You may use patterns to recognize user input.

3.55 Extend the *Toyland* program. Provide a richer query language, define new blocks and attach tighter constraints to bridges. For example, it should not be possible to use the same block twice in different places. An interesting further exercise would involve better support for compound structures, so that any primitive or compound structure may be used as a component of a new compound structure. The recognition procedure could also be extended to deal with such compounds.

3.56 Add a new *CONSTRAINT facet* to the 'Frames' toolbox. This facet should attach logical expressions to a slot. If these return true, then a new value may be added. In implementing this feature you will have to write a small program which parses expressions and generates and attaches **IF-ADDED** demon procedures as a result. The printing routines should also be modified, so that only these expressions and not the 'behind-the-scene' demons are shown. How could you also cater for specifications of value ranges (upper and lower bounds, enumerations of values, and so on)?

3.57 Write a program that acts as a travel agent to determine a customer's air travel requirements and advise him in choosing a suitable flight. Airlines, planes and flight information should be stored in a frame network, and a dialogue could establish the customer's requirements while filling in slots. In order to prevent any superfluous questions you should provide a number of default values and a mechanism that can avoid asking questions whose answers have already been given at some earlier time, either implicitly or explicitly.

Your program should also be able to cope with clients who change their minds and detect any consequent contradictions from user inputs.

3.58 Write frames (for structural description of places, guests, presents, foods, entertainment, and so on) and scripts (to describe typical sequences of events) for a children's birthday party, and then test this program in such an event's simulation.

3.7 Natural language processing and ATNs

'Trurl had once had the misfortune to build an enormous calculating machine that was capable of only one operation, namely the addition of two and two, and that it did incorrectly. . . . From that time on Klapaucius teased Trurl unmercifully, making comments at every opportunity, until Trurl decided to silence him once and for all by building a machine that could write poetry. First Trurl collected eight hundred and twenty tons of books on cybernetics and twelve thousand tons of the finest poetry, then sat down to read it all. Whenever he felt he just couldn't take another chart or equation, he would switch over to verse, and vice versa. After a while it became clear to him that the construction of the machine itself was child's play in comparison with the writing of the program. The program found in the head of the average poet, after all, was written by the poet's civilization, and that civilization was in turn programmed by the civilization that preceded it, and so on to the very Dawn of Time, when those bits of information that concerned the poet-to-be were still swirling about in the primordial chaos of the cosmic deep. Hence in order to program a poetry machine, one would first have to repeat the entire universe from the beginning – or at least a good piece of it.

Anyone else in Trurl's place would have given up then and there, but our intrepid constructor was nothing daunted. He built a machine and fashioned a digital model of the Void, an Electrostatic Spirit to move upon the face of the electrolytic waters, and he introduced the parameter of light, a protogalactic cloud or two, and by degrees worked his way up to the first ice age. Trurl could move at this rate because his machine was able, in one five-billionth of a second, to simulate one hundred septillion events at forty octillion locations simultaneously. And if anyone questions these figures, let him work it out for himself. . . .'

[*Lem (1975), pp. 43–44.*]

3.7.1 General principles and historical perspective

Language is the most important means of communication and its study has been a major interest of philosophers and scientists in all human cultures. Early linguistic analyses reach back as far as the Sanskrit grammarians of more than 2000 years ago, while modern linguistics' distinction between syntax, semantics and pragmatics was first proposed by Morris in 1938.

The term *syntax* is used to refer to purely grammatical analyses without any regard to the 'meaning' of structures. *Semantics*, on the other hand, does concern itself with a structure's denotation, but it avoids consideration of the contexts in which such references occur. The notion of *pragmatics*, finally, must take the whole of the communicative framework into account.

The goal of the syntactic stage of processing language therefore consists of either analyzing the 'grammaticity' of structures, or in the generation of grammatically correct objects. To achieve this goal we require a knowledge base, called a *grammar*, which expresses a language's structural regularities, as well as a program for generation and analysis of instances of such structures. This program is commonly referred to as a *parser*, and it may produce a variety of outputs for further processing (for example, parse trees, tables, and so on). As hinted at in the story of Trurl's plight we quoted at the start of this section, many of the issues involved in natural languages are highly complex. A language is much more than vocabulary and syntax; much of the context of the culture in which a language is used will ultimately be relevant to the way in which its sentences must be processed. Discussion of any pragmatic or semantic aspects of natural language processing is well beyond the scope of this book, but we will briefly look at the process of parsing. Winograd (1983b) and Allen (1988) are excellent references for an in-depth treatment of these and other relevant issues, and computer-based natural language processing in general.

One of the very first applications of computer systems concerned the translation of texts from one language into another, particularly between Russian and English. Since the early 1950s the US military provided large sums of money for this research, but largely without much success. Most of the early programs used a simple-minded dictionary-lookup approach. Each word in a Russian text, for example, would be related to a Russian dictionary, which would provide information about appropriate English equivalents. The main result of these efforts was the realization that human language is extraordinarily complex and that much further research into semantic and pragmatic issues was needed before language translation could successfully be automated.

In the field of linguistics the so-called *generative* approach also emerged in the 1950s, largely due to the work of Chomsky (1957). This framework views language as a mathematical object, and a sentence is perceived to be grammatical if there is some derivation that demonstrates that its structure corresponds to a set of rules. On the basis of this paradigm, Chomsky categorized language into four classes, with increasing expressive power and complexity. Under this scheme, the most powerful grammars are the 'type 0' class which allow any form of production. Most computer languages can be processed by a so-called 'type 2', or context-free grammar (CFG), which permits only a single non-terminal symbol on the left of its productions. A number of efficient parsing techniques are known for this class of grammars, but natural languages exhibit a much more complex structure and are clearly not context free. In English, for example, the form of a verb must be plural when the noun phrase is plural, as demonstrated by the two sentences:

The boy was hungry – singular form
The boys were hungry – plural form

Furthermore, natural language speakers are able to cope with highly ambiguous sentences such as:

I saw the man on the hill with a telescope

often without even being aware that they are ambiguous. This requires contextual knowledge about the world and what interpretations are most likely or possible. It therefore becomes necessary to provide enough understanding of the world, or at least a small relevant part of it, to be able to deal with ambiguity and relativity.

Much of the early work in AI experimented with pattern matchers, similar to the one we discussed in Section 3.3, in order to build simple problem solvers and conversational interfaces. **SIR** [Raphael (1968)] used fixed templates for information retrieval, while **Eliza** [Weizenbaum (1966)] employed a more flexible matching strategy. Winograd's (1972) **SHRDLU** had a major impact on research in natural language processing (**NLP**). This program could converse with a user about a simulated 'blocks world' scenario. It used a syntactic parser producing a syntax tree, which was then processed by a number of so-called 'semantic specialists'. The success of this program was instrumental in persuading many sceptics that computers could indeed be made to 'understand' language, and NLP became a flourishing area for further research. This euphoria was in many ways ill-founded, since many of SHRDLU's strategies were task specific and could not easily be transferred to other domains, and it therefore served to generate over-optimistic expectations.

To date no general-purpose language understanding systems have emerged, although some progress has been made in relatively constrained domains, such as NLP front ends for information retrieval, question answering and computer-aided instruction systems. NLP programs have also been developed to support knowledge acquisition, explanations of chains of deduction and dialogue generation in expert systems, as well as for text analysis (concordances, spelling, style, and so on). The **Lunar** system [Woods (1970)] was one of the most successful question-answering systems based on AI ideas of the early 1970s. It converses about the domain of lunar geology and contains an *Augmented Transition Network* (**ATN**) as a parser module. Since the late 1970s a number of commercial parsers have been developed at Bolt, Beranck and Newman (BBN) using SIR, which can serve as general-purpose front ends to data- or knowledge-based applications. **Ladder** [Hendrix *et al.* (1978)] demonstrates the application of this technology to a database query system.

Based on earlier work by Bobrow and Fraser (1969) and Thorne *et al.* (1968), Woods (1970) introduced a powerful formalism for the definition and parsing of natural language grammars. This metaphor, called augmented transition networks, is currently one of the most common methods of parsing natural language in computer programs.

An ATN is a graph structure consisting of nodes and arcs. One of these nodes must be designated as an initial state and any set of nodes may represent final states. Nodes are joined by arcs, labelled by either word *categories* (such as article, verb, and so on) or the name of another ATN graph. Parsing a sentence with a series of such ATNs begins at the initial state of an initial ATN. Each transition along an arc labelled with a category allows such a word to be matched against the sentence, while each arc labelled by another ATN corresponds to saving the current state of the parse on a stack and recursively passing control to the initial state of the new ATN, where the parsing process continues. When a final state is eventually encountered, parsing can either proceed in the current ATN, if the state has any further arcs, or we may 'pop' control back to a previously stacked ATN. A successful parse corresponds to a valid series of transitions along the arcs, 'consuming' a word at each category arc, and eventually returning from a final state of the initial ATN. At that stage the whole sentence must have been processed.

There are two additional features which increase the power of ATNs as a parsing method. These features allow the construction of parse trees and the enforcement of various context-dependent restrictions. Firstly, a series of *registers* is available, which may be used to store any relevant information gathered during the parse. Actions to manipulate these registers may be associated with any transition, or with 'pops' from a final state. Secondly, any transition or 'pop' from a final state may be controlled by a test, which must be satisfied before that transition is allowed to succeed. Such tests can use any of the previously stored register values.

A simple example is given in Figure 3.72. The grammar described by these ATNs accepts sentences of the general form:

a quick brown fox jumps the lazy dog

where the two noun phrases are separated by a verb, and where each noun phrase can include any number of adjectives. Tests of the form '*TEST (Expression)*' and assignments to registers of the form '*Register* := *Expression*' have been attached to the arcs, in order to ensure that successive adjectives in a noun phrase are distinct, and that the two noun phrases are different. The symbol ** is used to denote the last word processed, or the last value returned from an ATN.

It is well known [Aho and Ullman (1972)] that context-free grammars are unable to describe completely languages such as those of the form $a^n b^m c^n d^m$ (that is, strings containing n a's, then m b's, then the same number of c's as there were a's, then the same number of d's as there

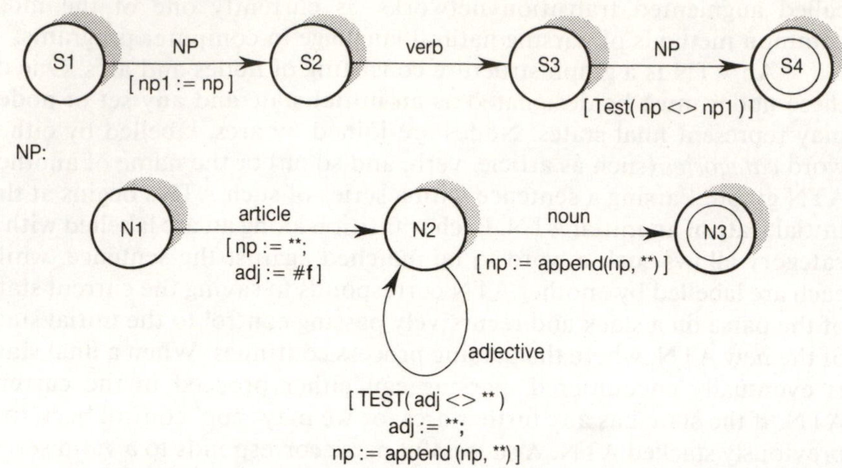

Figure 3.72 ATNs specifying a simple sentence structure.

were b's) where there are restrictions between parts of the strings of the language. It should be clear from the foregoing discussion that such restrictions can be enforced by an ATN and hence that their descriptive power is greater than that of context-free grammars. In fact, their descriptive power corresponds to that of unrestricted 'type 0' grammars, which are computationally equivalent to Turing machines.

In order to parse ATNs, Woods (1970) suggested an adaptation of Early's (1970) algorithm for parsing context-free languages. His strategy considers all of a sentence's words in turn, and it will generate the set of every possible state that could be reached from the initial one by 'consuming' these words one after the other. As more of the sentence is processed, some lines of analysis will terminate, since they have no further arcs to follow. Others will continue to generate valid sentences. After the final word of a sentence has been consumed, the generated set will contain every state that can possibly be reached from the initial state of the initial ATN. If it contains any final states of the initial ATN, then a successful parse has been found. More than a single final state indicates ambiguity.

3.7.2 The 'ATN' toolbox

Our toolbox allows experimentation with ATNs for parsing and generating sentences. The following is just a brief outline of the available routines; the comments and code in Appendix III should be consulted for the full details.

Figure 3.73 lists the top-level functions offered by this toolbox. Clearly some textual notation is needed to describe an ATN's graphical

Routine name	Parameters
	Functions to build ATNs, States and Categories:
MakeATN	any number of states
STATE	aLabel any number of arcs
AddState	anATN aState
MakeCategory	any number of words
	Functions to build Arcs:
CAT	aCategory aTest any number of actions
ANY	aTest any number of actions
PUSH	anATN aTest any number of actions
POP	aTest aForm
	Functions to build Actions:
SETR	aRegister aForm
TO	aLabel
	Functions to build Forms:
GETR	aRegister
*Other valid forms include **, which is equivalent to (GETR '**), #t, #f or any lambda expression which will be invoked with the current state of the RegisterBank as a parameter.*	
	Functions on Registers:
GetRegister	a RegisterBank aRegisterName
	Functions to perform the parse:
Parse	anATN aSentence [optional: TraceFlag]

Figure 3.73 Summary of the *ATN* toolbox interface.

structure and any associated register assignments and tests. Each ATN is constructed with the **MakeATN** function, which accepts any number of states as parameters. These states are constructed by using the **STATE** procedure. **STATE** accepts a label (which is later used to indicate transitions to this state) followed by an arbitrary number of arcs. The first state of an ATN will be its initial state, and the final states will be indicated by the presence of '**POP**' arcs, as described in the following. This explicit encoding of final states allows greater flexibility in controlling the order in which alternatives are investigated. The **AddState** function may be used to construct ATNs incrementally, by adding new states to a previously defined ATN.

Arcs are constructed with **CAT**, **ANY**, **PUSH** and **POP**. Each of these takes a test as a parameter. This may be **#t** to indicate that the arc is always valid, or some predicate function. Predicates will expect a so-called *RegisterBank* as a parameter, which is a data type encapsulating the current state of the registers. The **GetRegister** function can be used to retrieve the value of any register, including the register ** (which holds the last word processed or the last value returned from a 'popped' ATN). **CAT** arcs expect a category constructed with **MakeCategory**, while **PUSH** arcs require a new ATN as a parameter. **ANY** arcs are used in the same way as **CAT**, but they will accept any word rather than only those in a given category. This makes it easier to deal with certain types of constructs, where we do not wish to enumerate all the possible words that will be accepted in a particular position. The *form* in the **POP** arc defines the value to be returned when control returns from the ATN. This value will then be available in the ** register.

The *actions* that appear in the **CAT, ANY** and **PUSH** arcs refer to a series of **SETR** operations, which alter the register values, followed by a final **TO**, which labels the next state (in the current ATN) to which control will be transferred. The *forms* that appear in **SETR** assignments may include **#t**, **#f**, ** (which stores the last word consumed, or the value returned from the last **POP**), **GETR** (which retrieves a value from a register) or an arbitrary lambda expression which accepts the current *RegisterBank* as a parameter.

The ATNs shown in Figure 3.72 may therefore be encoded as follows:

```
(define article (MakeCategory 'a 'the))
(define adjective (MakeCategory 'quick 'brown 'slow 'lazy))
(define verb (MakeCategory 'jumps 'runs))
(define noun (MakeCategory 'fox 'dog))
```

Some predicates are needed to test that the current adjective differs from the previous one and that the two noun phrases are distinct:

```
(define notLast?
  (lambda (aRegisterBank)
    (not (equal? (GetRegister aRegisterBank 'adj)
                 (GetRegister aRegisterBank '**)))))
(define differentNP?
  (lambda (aRegisterBank)
    (not (equal? (GetRegister aRegisterBank 'np)
                 (GetRegister aRegisterBank 'np1)))))
```

To collect the words of the noun phrase into a list that can be maintained in the register 'np' we must add to it.

```
(define addToEnd
  (lambda (aRegisterBank)
    (append (GetRegister aRegisterBank 'np)
            (list (GetRegister aRegisterBank '**)))))
```

The *noun phrase* (*NP*) ATN can now be defined, which will bind register ** to a list of all the words in the phrase.

```
(define NP
  (MakeATN
    (STATE 'N1 (CAT article #t  (SETR 'np #f)
                                (SETR 'adj #f)
                                (SETR 'np addToEnd)
                                (TO 'N2)))
    (STATE 'N2 (CAT adjective notLast?
                                (SETR 'np addToEnd)
                                (SETR 'adj **)
                                (TO 'N2))
               (CAT noun #t     (SETR 'np addToEnd)
                                (TO 'N3)))
    (STATE 'N3 (POP             (GETR 'np) #t))))
```

Finally, the *complete sentence* ATN can be defined:

```
(define SentenceATN
  (MakeATN (STATE 'S1 (PUSH NP #t (SETR 'np1 **)
                                  (TO 'S2)))
           (STATE 'S2 (CAT verb #t (SETR 'verb **)
                                  (TO 'S3)))
           (STATE 'S3 (PUSH NP #t (TO 'S4)))
           (STATE 'S4 (POP #t differentNP?))))
```

The function **Parse** must be called with an initial ATN and a sentence in the form of a list of words. It will then attempt to parse the sentence with that ATN. It is possible to obtain a trace of the parse's progress by setting an optional flag. **Parse** returns the final state of the *RegisterBank*, if the parse succeeds, or #f if it fails. Rather than using the adaptation of the Early parsing algorithm suggested by Woods, our implementation uses a simpler algorithm of following each alternative arc in a depth-first manner. Figure 3.74 offers a brief description. The procedure backtracks to try an alternative arc whenever some line of investigation fails. There is no danger of cycles, since each of the arcs must consume some part of the sentence. The only shortcoming of this simplification is that the testing for alternatives at a node is terminated as soon as a **POP** arc with a valid test is encountered. Subsequent arcs at that node are not investigated if this decision later causes our parse to fail, even though they could possibly have resulted in a successful parse. This defect is not quite as serious as it may seem, however, as it is always possible to put **POP** arcs as the last out of any node, so that they will be tried only after all other alternatives have failed.

```
function Parse ( ATN, Sentence )
    let state = initial state of ATN
    let RB   = an empty register bank
    if ParseAux( ATN, state, RB, Sentence ) fails then
        return #f
    else return register bank of result
;; ParseAux attempts to parse as much of "Sentence" as possible beginning
;; from "state" of "ATN". It returns #f if the sentence cannot be parsed
;; successfully, and otherwise a pair of: (a RegisterBank of bindings, that part of
;; the sentence yet to be parsed)
function ParseAux( ATN state, RegisterBank, Sentence )
    let result = #f
    while there remains an untried arc out of state state of ATN do {
        if result ≠ #f then
            return result
        let newRB = RegisterBank
        let word = #f
        if Sentence is not empty then {
            word ← first word of Sentence
            bind register '**' to word in newRB
        }
        if the test associated with arc is satisfied then
            case form of arc of {
            (CAT Category Test Actions (TO newState) ):
                if Sentence not empty and word in Category then {
                        let newerRB = newRB
                        execute Actions updating bindings of newerRB
                        result ← ParseAux( ATN, newState,
                                        newerRB, cdr(Sentence) )
                }
            (ANY Test Actions (TO newState) ):
                if Sentence not empty then {
                    let newerRB = newRB
                    execute Actions updating bindings of newerRB
                    result ← ParseAux( ATN, newState,
                                    newerRB, cdr(Sentence) )
                }
            (PUSH newATN Test Actions (TO newState) ):
                let initState = initial state of newATN
                result ← ParseAux( newATN, initState,
                                newRB, Sentence)
                if result ≠ #f then {
                    let newerRB = register bank from result
                    let newSentence = sentence from result
                    execute Actions updating bindings of newerRB
                    result ← ParseAux( ATN, newState,
                                    newerRB, newSentence )
                }
            (POP Test Form):
```

```
                let newerRB = evaluate Form using newRB and bind
                                result to register '**'
                result ← pair of (Sentence, newerRB )
            }
}
return result
```

Figure 3.74 Outline of the auxiliary routine used by the parsing algorithm.

The following expressions show some attempts at parsing sentences with the ATNs we used for our example.

```
>>> (Parse SentenceATN '(a quick brown fox jumps a lazy dog))
; parse succeeds and returns a register bank
; ((** #t)
   (np (a lazy dog))
   (adj lazy)
   (verb jumps)
   (np1 (a quick brown fox)))
>>> (Parse SentenceATN '(a quick quick fox jumps a lazy dog))
; ()
>>> (Parse SentenceATN
              '(a quick brown fox jumps a quick brown fox))
; ()
```

3.7.3 The 'JanesGarden' microworld

To give an example for slightly more complicated ATNs, we will use the toolbox to construct a limited natural language interface to another simple microworld. The garden of the wife of one of the authors has been chosen as its setting. Similar task domains abound in the literature, often associated with robot navigation through a 'cluttered' environment. Our variation is closely related to Tanimoto's (1987) *StoneWorld* scenario. *JanesGarden* is populated by a gardener, called Jane, and various other common garden objects: flowers, flower beds, trees, goldfish ponds, gnomes and a watering can. To simplify the display, Jane's garden will be represented by a simple 8×8 grid of locations, 'bent into' a continuous plane. If Jane moves 'off the top' of her garden she will therefore reappear at the bottom, and similar effects occur at the sides. The initial layout of the garden is shown in Figure 3.75 along with the corresponding display provided by our program.

After each action the display will show the new state of the world. Naturally, Jane will obscure anything in her immediate vicinity, so that we need only show at most one object at each location.

The user of our program will be allowed to ask Jane to move about the garden in order to perform various tasks, such as going to the pond to

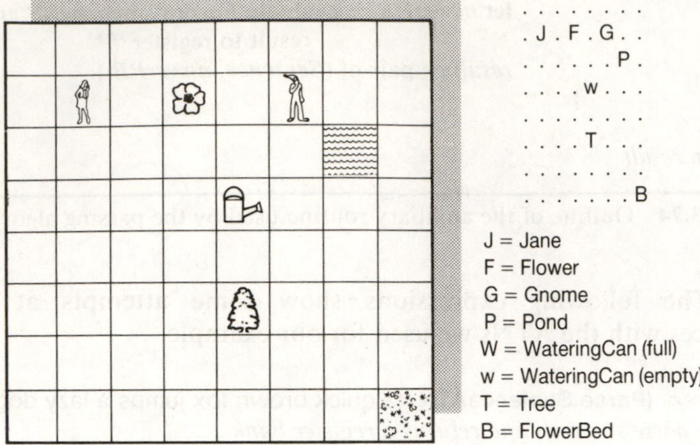

Figure 3.75 The initial state of *JanesGarden*.

fill the watering can, going to the flower bed to water the flowers, picking flowers, and so on. All valid user requests are encoded by the ATNs in Figure 3.76. The following word categories are recognized by these ATNs:

article	a the
objectNoun	tree flower pond gnome flowerbed wateringcan water
dirNoun	north south east west
dirPrep	near beside in from at by to
dirAdverb	up down left right
toVerb	to towards
goVerb	walk go head
pickVerb	pick grab get fill
putVerb	put drop

This grammar allows us to parse sentences such as the following:

(Bye)
(Show)
(Go to the gnome by the pond near the wateringcan)
(Pick up the gnome)
(Drop it in the pond)

The first of these is used to terminate the session. The second request shows all items currently carried by Jane, and the remaining three are commands to direct Jane's movements, the acquisition and the release of objects. In our implementation of Jane's garden we will account for some degree of short-sightedness, and we therefore assume that Jane can only 'see' objects which are no more than three squares away. The *direction*

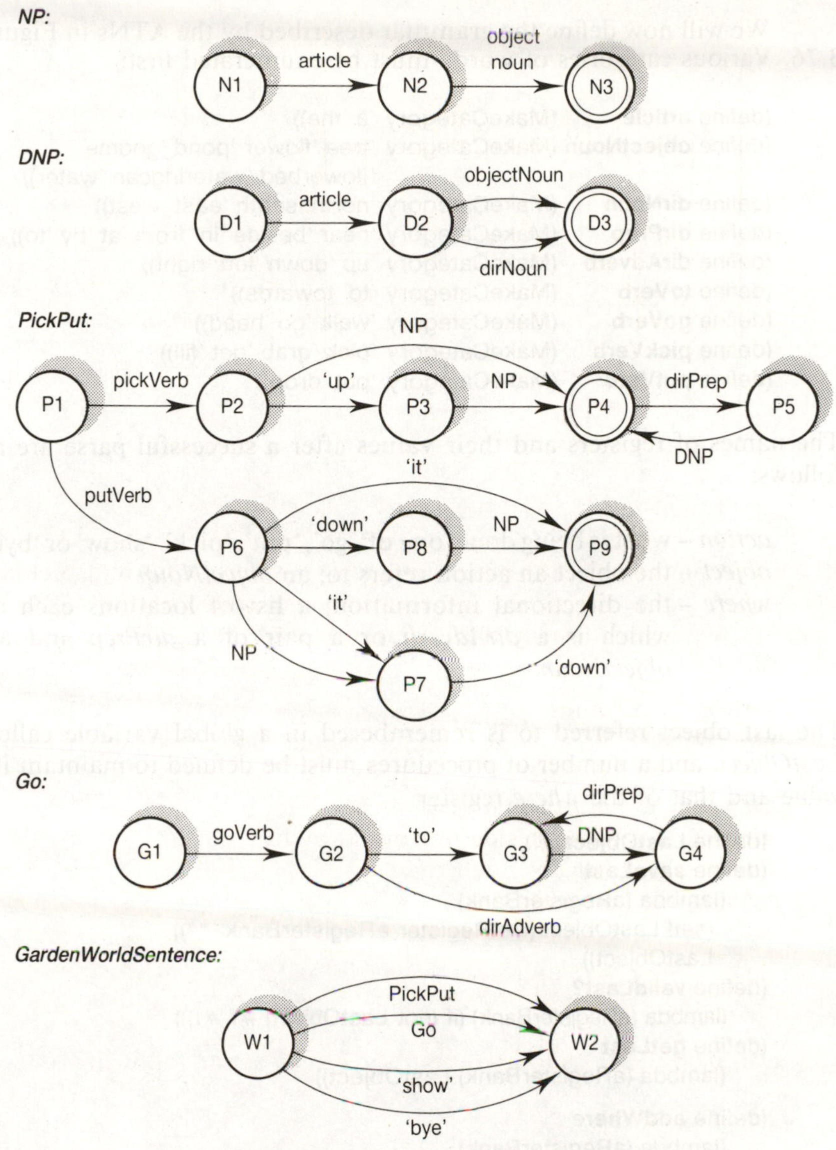

Figure 3.76 ATNs for *JanesGarden*.

preposition 'near' will correspond to 3 squares, 'by' to 2, 'beside' to 1 and all other ones (in, at, from, to) correspond to 0 squares. Only flowers, gnomes and the watering can can be carried, and water can only be picked up when Jane is already holding the watering can. The pond will supply an infinite source of water, while the flower bed is an infinite source of flowers. In line with tradition (and to simplify the programming) we will view Jane's garden as an enchanted, timeless sort of place, in which there are no seasons and things happen instantaneously.

We will now define the grammar described by the ATNs in Figure 3.76. Various categories of words must be enumerated first:

```
(define article      (MakeCategory 'a 'the))
(define objectNoun   (MakeCategory 'tree 'flower 'pond 'gnome
                                   'flowerbed 'wateringcan 'water))
(define dirNoun      (MakeCategory 'north 'south 'east 'west))
(define dirPrep      (MakeCategory 'near 'beside 'in 'from 'at 'by 'to))
(define dirAdverb    (MakeCategory 'up 'down 'left 'right))
(define toVerb       (MakeCategory 'to 'towards))
(define goVerb       (MakeCategory 'walk 'go 'head))
(define pickVerb     (MakeCategory 'pick 'grab 'get 'fill))
(define putVerb      (MakeCategory 'put 'drop))
```

The names of registers and their values after a successful parse are as follows:

action – what is being done; one of: 'go', 'put', 'pick', 'show' or 'bye'
object – the object an action refers to; an *objectNoun*
where – the directional information; a list of locations each of which is a *dirAdverb* or a pair of a *dirPrep* and an *objectNoun.*

The last object referred to is remembered in a global variable called *LastObject*, and a number of procedures must be defined to maintain its value and that of the *where* register:

```
(define LastObject #f)
(define saveLast!
    (lambda (aRegisterBank)
      (set! LastObject (GetRegister aRegisterBank '**))
      LastObject))
(define validLast?
    (lambda (aRegisterBank) (if (not LastObject) #f #t)))
(define getLast
    (lambda (aRegisterBank) LastObject))

(define addWhere
    (lambda (aRegisterBank)
      ; prepend the current value of register '**' to the register 'where'
      (cons (GetRegister aRegisterBank '**)
            (GetRegister aRegisterBank 'where))))

; Noun phrases:
; =======

(define NP
  (MakeATN
    (STATE 'N1 (CAT article #t (TO 'N2)))
    (STATE 'N2 (CAT objectNoun #t (SETR 'object saveLast!)
                                  (TO 'N3)))
    (STATE 'N3 (POP (GETR 'object) #t))))
```

```
(define DNP
  (MakeATN
    (STATE 'D1 (CAT article #t (TO 'D2)))
    (STATE 'D2 (CAT objectNoun #t (SETR 'where addWhere)
                                   (TO 'D3))
               (CAT dirNoun     #t (SETR 'where addWhere)
                                   (TO 'D3)))
    (STATE 'D3 (POP ** #t))))
```

; *Picking and putting*
; ==========

```
(define PickPut
  (MakeATN
    (STATE 'P1 (CAT pickVerb #t (SETR 'action **)
                               (SETR 'where ( ))
                               (TO 'P2))
               (CAT putVerb  #t (SETR 'action **)
                               (SETR 'where ( ))
                               (TO 'P6)))
    (STATE 'P2 (CAT (MakeCategory 'up) #t (TO 'P3))
               (PUSH NP      #t (SETR 'where addWhere)
                               (TO 'P4)))
    (STATE 'P3 (PUSH NP      #t (SETR 'where addWhere)
                               (TO 'P4)))
    (STATE 'P4 (CAT dirPrep  #t (SETR 'where addWhere)
                               (TO 'P5))
               (POP **       #t))
    (STATE 'P5 (PUSH DNP     #t (TO 'P4)))
    (STATE 'P6 (CAT (MakeCategory 'down) #t (TO 'P8))
               (CAT (MakeCategory 'it) validLast?
                               (SETR 'object getLast)
                               (TO 'P7))
               (CAT (MakeCategory 'it) validLast?
                               (SETR 'object getLast)
                               (TO 'P9))
               (PUSH NP      #t (TO 'P7)))
    (STATE 'P7 (CAT (MakeCategory 'down) #t (TO 'P9)))
    (STATE 'P8 (PUSH NP      #t (TO 'P9)))
    (STATE 'P9 (POP **       #t))))
```

; *Going*
; ===

```
(define Go
  (MakeATN
   (STATE 'G1 (CAT goVerb    #t (SETR 'action **)
                               (SETR 'where ( ))
                               (TO 'G2)))
   (STATE 'G2 (CAT toVerb    #t (TO 'G3))
              (CAT dirAdverb #t (SETR 'where addWhere)
                               (TO 'G4)))
   (STATE 'G3 (PUSH DNP      #t (TO 'G4)))
```

```
    (STATE 'G4 (CAT dirPrep    #t (SETR 'where addWhere)
                                  (TO 'G3))
               (POP **         #t))))
; Full sentence structure
; ============
(define GardenWorldSentence
  (MakeATN
    (STATE 'W1 (CAT (MakeCategory 'show) #t (SETR 'action **)
                                            (TO 'W2))
               (CAT (MakeCategory 'bye)  #t (SETR 'action **)
                                            (TO 'W2))
               (PUSH PickPut #t (TO 'W2))
               (PUSH Go      #t (TO 'W2)))
    (STATE 'W2
               (POP **       #t))))
```

A number of further routines are necessary to maintain the display and move Jane around the garden. These procedures use information collected in the *where* register.

```
; Symbols used to represent objects: use "W" for full wateringcan and "w"
; for an empty one. Its state is stored in a global variable 'FullWateringCan?'
(define FullWateringCan? #f)
(define Symbols '( (tree         "T")
                   (flower       "F")
                   (flowerbed    "B")
                   (wateringcan  "W")
                   (gnome        "G")
                   (pond         "P")
                   (empty        ".")))

(define MakePos (lambda (x y) (list x y)))
(define GetX    (lambda (pos)(car pos)))
(define GetY    (lambda (pos)(cadr pos)))

(define GardenWorldGrid #f)
(define MaxX 8)
(define MaxY 8)

(define GetXY
  (lambda (pos)
    (vector-ref (vector-ref GardenWorldGrid (GetY pos))
                (GetX pos))))

(define SetXY!
  (lambda (pos object)
    (vector-set! (vector-ref GardenWorldGrid (GetY pos))
                 (GetX pos)
                 object)))
```

The garden's initial state is 'hard-wired' into the *InitGardenWorld* procedure.

```
(define InitGardenWorld
  (lambda ()
    (set! GardenWorldGrid (make-vector MaxY))
    (do ((y 0 (+ y 1))
         (newrow #f))
        ((>= y MaxY) #f)
        (set! newrow (make-vector MaxX))
        (do ((x 0 (+ x 1)))
            ((>=x MaxX) #f)
            (vector-set! newrow x 'empty))
        (vector-set! GardenWorldGrid y newrow))
    (SetXY! '(3 1) 'flower)
    (SetXY! '(5 1) 'gnome)
    (SetXY! '(6 2) 'pond)
    (SetXY! '(4 3) 'wateringcan)
    (SetXY! '(7 7) 'flowerbed)
    (SetXY! '(4 5) 'tree)
    (Set! FullWateringCan? #f) ; initially empty
    #f))

(define JanesPos (MakePos 1 1))
(define JanesBag ( )) ; initially empty

(define DisplayWorld
  (lambda ()
    (newline)
    (do ((y 0 (+ y 1)))
        ((>= y MaxY) #f)
        (do ((x 0 (+ x 1))
             (pos #f)
             (obj #f))
            ((>= x MaxX) #f)
            (set! pos (MakePos x y))
            (set! obj (GetXY pos))
            (cond ((equal? pos JanesPos) (display "J"))
                  ((equal? obj 'wateringcan)
                   (if FullWateringCan?
                       (display "W")
                       (display "w")))
                  (else (display (cadr (assoc obj Symbols))))))
        (newline))))

; Moving through the world – it "wraps" around at the ends

(define mod
  (lambda (x y)
    (let ((r (remainder x y)))
      (if (negative? r) (+ r y) r))))
```

```
(define +xy
  (lambda (pos nx ny)
    ; add nx to x and ny to y of pos
    (MakePos (mod (+ nx (GetX pos)) MaxX)
             (mod (+ ny (GetY pos)) MaxY))))

(define FindObject
  (lambda (object currPos range)
    ; find nearest example of object to "currPos" that is in range
    (do ((r 0 (+ r 1))
         (newpos #f)
         (found #f))
        ((or found (> r range)) found)
        (do ((y (- 0 r) (+ y 1)))
            ((or found (> y r)) #f)
            (do ((x (- 0 r) (+ x 1)))
                ((or found (> x r)) #f)
                (set! newpos (+ xy currPos x y))
                (if (or (eq? object (GetXY newpos))
                        (and (eq? object 'flower)
                             (eq? (GetXY newpos) 'flowerbed))
                        (and (eq? object 'water)
                             (eq? (GetXY newpos) 'pond)))
                    (set! found newpos)
                    #f))))))

; definitions of ranges

(define eyesight 3)
(define ranges '((near    3)
                 (by      2)
                 (beside  1)
                 (in      0)
                 (at      0)
                 (from    0)
                 (to      0)))

(define MoveJane
  (lambda (where)
    ; try and move Jane according to the instructions in the
    ; "where" register

    (define moveJane
      (lambda (newPos)
        ; move from JanesPos to newPos
        (set! JanesPos newPos)))

    (define moveAux
      (lambda (whereList)
        ; move Jane recursively
        (if (null? whereList)
            #f
```

```
(let ((head (car whereList))
     (tail   (cdr whereList))
     (newPos #f)
     (range eyesight))
  (if (member head dirPrep)
     (begin
        (set! range (cadr (assoc head ranges)))
        (set! head (car tail))
        (set! tail (cdr tail)))
     #f)
  (case head
     ((north up)    (moveJane (+ xy JanesPos 0 -1))
                    (moveAux tail))
     ((south down) (moveJane (+ xy JanesPos 0 +1))
                    (moveAux tail))
     ((east right)  (moveJane (+ xy JanesPos -1 0))
                    (moveAux tail))
     ((west left)   (moveJane (+ xy JanesPos +1 0))
                    (moveAux tail))
     ((tree flower pond gnome flowerbed
       wateringcan water)
                          (set! newPos
                                (FindObject head JanesPos range))
                          (if (null? newPos)
                             (begin (display "Can't find")
                                    (display head))
                             (begin (moveJane newPos)
                                    (moveAux tail))))
     (else (display "Error in where list")))))))

(let ((oldPos JanesPos))
  (moveAux where)
  (if (equal? oldPos JanesPos)
     #f ; hasn't moved so don't redisplay
     (DisplayWorld)))))
```

To chat with Jane and update the world each time she moves, the function *Converse* is defined. It will first initialize the world and will then repeatedly prompt the user for replies, which it expects as sentences in the form of a list. *Parse* will be invoked each time a new sentence is read. If a successful parse can be generated, the appropriate action is performed and the garden's image is updated accordingly. (*bye*) terminates a session.

```
(define Converse
  (lambda ( )
    ; hold a conversation: read sentences, parse, perform action,
    ; update world!
    (InitGardenWorld)
    (DisplayWorld)
```

```
        (do ((sentence #f)
             (result #f)
             (done #f))
            ((equal? sentence '(bye)) #f)
            (newline)
            (display ".> ")
            (set! sentence (read))
            (newline)
            (if (not (pair? sentence))
                (display "Please give your command as a list")
                (begin
                  (set! result (Parse GardenWorldSentence sentence #f))
                  (if (not result)
                      (display "Sorry, I didn't understand that")
                      (UpdateWorld result)))))))
```

Updating the world requires the use of information saved in registers during the parse, in order to make the appropriate changes:

```
(define UpdateWorld
  (lambda (aRegisterBank)
    ; use information in the registers to update the world
    (define remove
      (lambda (object bag)
        ; remove object from bag and return lighter bag
        (cond ((null? bag) #f)
              ((equal? object (car bag)) (cdr bag))
              (else (cons (car bag) (remove object (cdr bag)))))))
    (define doPut
      (lambda (object)
        ; put object at current position, but only if empty or if the object there
        ; is a pond. We may also try to put a flower into a flowerbed or pour
        ; water over it
        (cond ((not (member object JanesBag))
               (display "Jane doesn't have it"))
              ((equal? 'pond (GetXY JanesPos))
               (display "Splash!")
               (set! JanesBag (remove object JanesBag)))
              ((and (equal? 'flowerbed (GetXY JanesPos))
                    (equal? object 'flower))
               (display "Planted flower")
               (set! JanesBag (remove object JanesBag)))
              ((equal? object 'water)
               (display "Watered it")
               (set! JanesBag (remove object JanesBag))
               (set! FullWateringCan? #f))
              ((not (equal? 'empty (GetXY JanesPos)))
               (display "There is already something there"))
              (else
               (SetXY! JanesPos object)
```

```
            (set! JanesBag (remove object JanesBag))
            (if (and (equal? object 'wateringcan)
                     FullWateringCan?)
               (set! JanesBag (remove 'water JanesBag))
               #f)))))

(define doGet
  (lambda (object)
   ; get object from current position, but not unmoveable objects. Only
   ; flowers can be taken from flowerbeds. The wateringcan can only be
   ; filled if Jane has it and if she is at the pond
   (let ((currObject (GetXY JanesPos)))
     (cond ((member object '(tree pond flowerbed)
             (display "Can't take that object"))
            ((and (equal? object 'flower)
                  (equal? currObject 'flowerbed))
             (set! JanesBag (cons object JanesBag)))
            ((and (equal? object 'water)
                  (member 'wateringcan JanesBag)
                  (equal? currObject 'pond))
             (set! FullWateringCan? #t)
             (set! JanesBag (cons object JanesBag)))
            ((equal? currObject object)
             (set! JanesBag (cons object JanesBag))
             (if (and (equal? object 'wateringcan) FullWateringCan?)
                 (set! JanesBag (cons 'water JanesBag))
                 #f)
             (SetXY! JanesPos 'empty))
            (else
             (display "There is no such object here"))))))

(let ((action #f)
      (object #f)
      (where #f))
  (set! action (GetRegister aRegisterBank 'action))
  (case action
    ((show)
     (DisplayLine "Contents of Jane's bag:" JanesBag))
    ((bye)
     (DisplayLine "Thanks for visiting"))
    ((walk go head)
     (set! where (GetRegister aRegisterBank 'where))
     (MoveJane where))
    ((put drop)
     (set! where (GetRegister aRegisterBank 'where))
     (MoveJane where)
     (doPut (GetRegister aRegisterBank 'object)))
    ((pick grab get fill)
     (set! where (GetRegister aRegisterBank 'where))
     (MoveJane where)
     (doGet (GetRegister aRegisterBank 'object)))
    (else (display "illegal action"))))))
```

transcript

```
>>> (Converse)
........
.J.F.G..
......P.
....w...
........
....T...
........
.......B

..> (walk to the tree)
Can't find tree
..> (walk to the wateringCan)
........
...F.G..
......P.
....J...
........
....T...
........
.......B

..> (pick a flower from the flowerBed)
Can't find flowerbed. There is no such object here
..> (go to the tree)
........
...F.G..
......P.
....w...
........
....J...
........
.......B

..> (pick a flower from the flowerBed)
........
...F.G..
......P.
....w...
........
....T...
........
.......J

..> (show)
Contents of Jane's bag:  (flower)

..>
```

Figure 3.77 A walk in *JanesGarden.*

A transcript of possible events in Jane's garden is shown in Figures 3.77 and 3.78.

Here we should note the limiting effects of Jane's vision. She needs to be guided from object to object. There is however the possibility of specifying compound actions in a recursive manner (for example, '*walk to the pond near the watering can near the tree*').

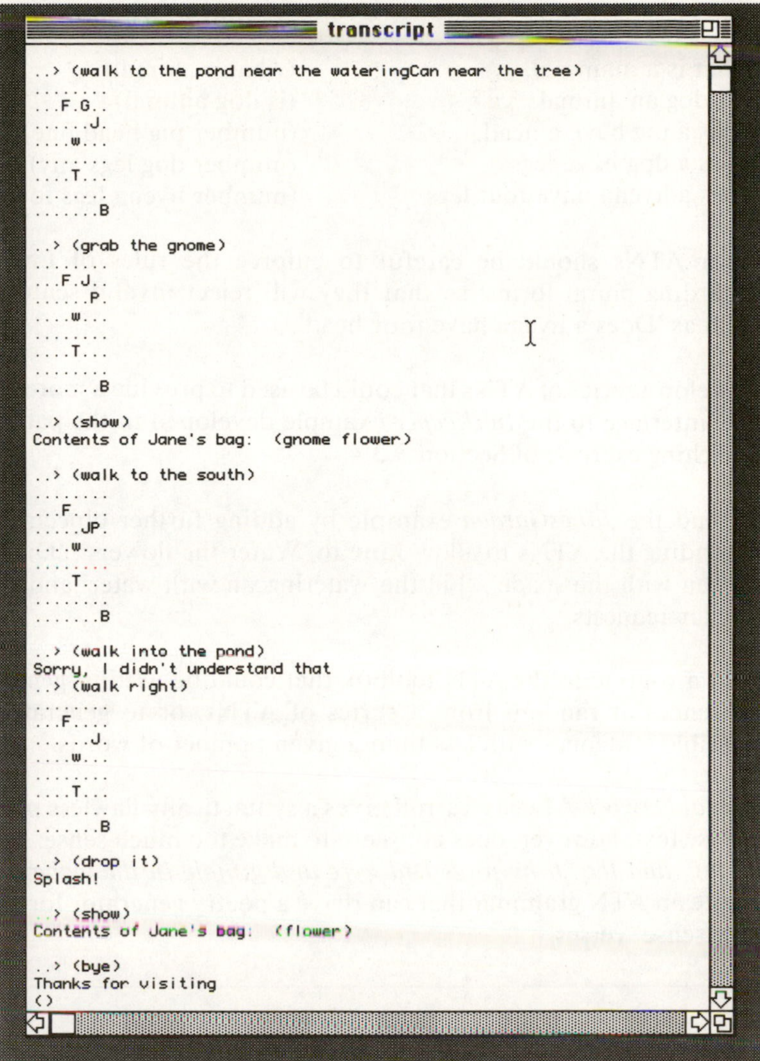

transcript
..> (walk to the pond near the wateringCan near the tree)
....
...F.G..
......J.
....w...
....
....T...
....
.......B
..> (grab the gnome)
....
...F.J..
......P.
....w...
....
....T...
....
.......B
..> (show)
Contents of Jane's bag: (gnome flower)
..> (walk to the south)
....
...F....
.....JP.
....w...
....
....T...
....
.......B
..> (walk into the pond)
Sorry, I didn't understand that
..> (walk right)
....
...F....
......J.
....w...
....
....T...
....
.......B
..> (drop it)
Splash!
..> (show)
Contents of Jane's bag: (flower)
..> (bye)
Thanks for visiting
()

Figure 3.78 Walking further . . . .

EXERCISES

3.59* Construct a series of ATNs with appropriate tests and actions that could be used for a natural language interface to an animal query database. The form of the sentences accepted and the corresponding query constructed should include at least the following:

Sentence	*Resulting query*
What is a mammal.	(what mammal)
Is a dog an animal.	(is dog animal)
Does a pig have a head.	(number pig head one)
Does a dog have legs.	(number dog legs any)
Does a hyena have four legs.	(number hyena legs four)

Your ATNs should be careful to enforce the rules of English regarding plural forms, so that they will reject invalid sentences such as 'Does a hyena have four head'.

3.60 Develop a series of ATNs that could be used to provide a more flexible interface to the *InnKeeper* example developed in the pattern-matching exercise of Section 3.3.4.

3.61 Extend the *JanesGarden* example by adding further objects and extending the ATNs to allow Jane to 'Water the flowers', 'Dig the garden with the spade', 'Fill the wateringcan with water' and fulfil similar requests.

3.62 Add a routine to the ATN toolbox that could be used to **generate** sentences at random from a series of ATNs, or to generate all possible sentences with less than a given number of words.

3.63 In '*Jabberwocky*' Lewis Carroll gives a syntactically flawless poem, whose text, however, does not seem to make too much sense: *Twas brillig, and the slithy toves Did gyre and gimble in the wabe*: . . . . Write an ATN grammar that can drive a poetry generator for such 'nonsense' verses.

3.8 Rodney – a restaurant advisory program

'The world is all which is the case.'
[*Wittgenstein (1922), Tractatus Logico-Philosophicus, Section 1.*]

3.8.1 Combining the toolboxes for a final example

To conclude our discussion of common AI programming metaphors we will now demonstrate how our toolboxes may be combined into 'knowledge-based' systems. We have chosen the problem of giving advice about restaurants as our task domain. The '*Rodney*' program uses a **frame network** to store information about restaurants and their features; a

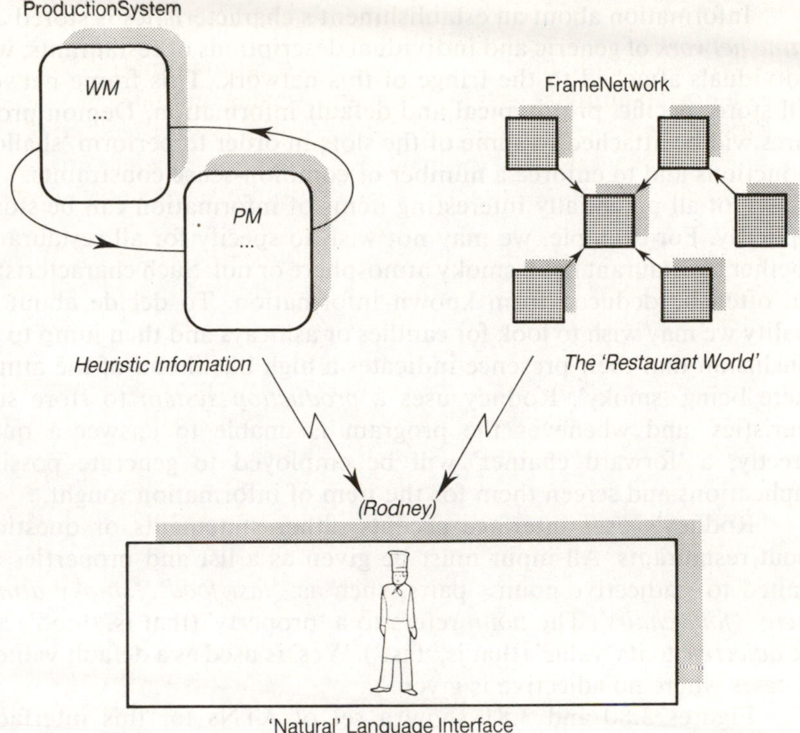

Figure 3.79 *Rodney* – a restaurant advisory program.

production system will be employed to encode heuristics about some properties which have not been directly asserted, and the **ATN** toolbox provides a 'natural' language front end. This design, as shown in Figure 3.79, is therefore based on three of the toolboxes, but since an associative network and a pattern matcher are needed internally by the frame network and the production system interpreter, five of them are effectively involved. This number could increase further if Rodney would also play games or solve puzzles to entertain his clients.

In order to keep the size of the program to a manageable level we have equipped Rodney with only a minimal level of functionality. The structure of the program, however, makes it easy to extend the knowledge bases and patterns of interaction, so that it should serve to convey the flavour of a larger, more realistic system.

The *'natural' language interface* is defined by a simple ATN grammar for processing assertions (for example, '*the PleasureGarden is a ChineseRestaurant*', '*a ChineseRestaurant serves CashewnutChicken*') and queries (for example, '*is the BlueUnicorn a TakeAway?*', '*does the BlueUnicorn serve any AvocadoDip?*', '*do TakeAways have TableCloths?*', '*describe the PinkPlatypus*'). 'Bye' is used to terminate a conversation.

Information about an establishment's characteristics is stored as a *frame network* of generic and individual descriptions of restaurants, with individuals attached to the fringe of this network. This frame network will store specific, prototypical and default information. Demon procedures will be attached to some of the slots in order to perform 'shallow' deductions and to enforce a number of common-sense constraints.

Not all potentially interesting items of information can be stored explicitly. For example, we may not wish to specify for all restaurants, whether a restaurant has a smoky atmosphere or not. Such characteristics can often be deduced from known information. To decide about air quality we may wish to look for candles or ashtrays and then jump to the conclusion that their presence indicates a high likelihood of the atmosphere being 'smoky'. Rodney uses a *production system* to store such heuristics, and whenever the program is unable to answer a query directly, a 'forward chainer' will be employed to generate possible implications and screen them for the item of information sought.

Rodney's user interface accepts either statements or questions about restaurants. All input must be given as a list and properties are limited to <adjective noun> pairs, such as: '*fast food*', '*smoky atmosphere*', '*four chairs*'. The *noun* refers to a 'property' (that is, 'food') and the *adjective* to its 'value' (that is, 'fast'). 'Yes' is used as a default value in all cases where no adjective is given.

Figures 3.80 and 3.81 show a set of ATNs for this interface's grammar.

CLASS may denote a restaurant or a class of restaurants (such as 'Italian', 'DirtyDicks'). It is restricted to a single word and it must be different from any valid keywords, such as: *the*, *a*, *an*, *is*, *has*, *does*, *have*, *own*, *owns*?.

```
(define notKeyWord?
  (lambda (aRegisterBank)
   ; check that the current value of the register '**' is not a valid keyword
   (not (member (GetRegister aRegisterBank '**)
                '(the a an is has does have own owns ?)))))

(define CLASS
  (MakeATN (STATE 'C1 (ANY notKeyWord? (SETR 'class **)
                                       (TO 'C2)))
           (STATE 'C2 (POP (GETR 'class) #t))))
```

The notion of a **taCLASS** includes any valid bindings to **CLASS**, **the CLASS** or **article CLASS** (for example, '*ChezChristophe*', '*the Chez Christophe*', '*all French*').

```
(define article (MakeCategory 'a 'an 'all 'most))

(define taCLASS
  (MakeATN
```

InterfaceATN:

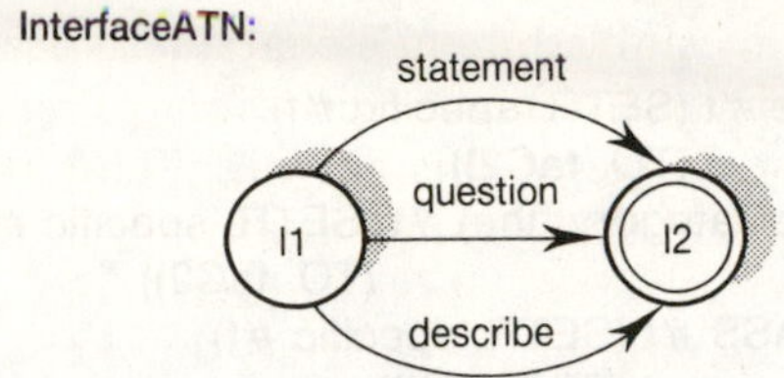

describe:

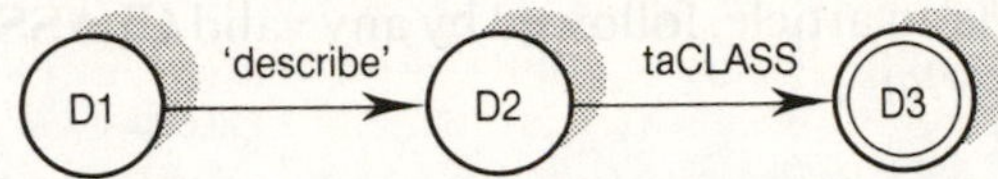

Figure 3.80 ATNs for our *Rodney* NLP interface.

CLASS:
C1 —ANY→ C2

aCLASS:
aC1 —article→ aC2 —CLASS→ aC3

taCLASS:
taC1 —article→ taC2 —CLASS→ taC3
taC1 —'the'→ taC2
taC1 —CLASS→ taC3

PROP:
P1 —ANY (adjective)→ P2 —ANY (noun)→ P3
P1 —ANY (noun)→ P3

statement:
S1 —taCLASS→ S2 —'is'→ S3 —aCLASS→ S4
S2 —hasCategory→ S5 —PROP→ S6

question:
Q1 —'is'→ Q2 —taCLASS→ Q3 —aCLASS→ Q4
Q4 —'?'→ Q4
Q1 —'does, has'→ Q5 —taCLASS→ Q6 —haveCategory→ Q7 —PROP→ Q4

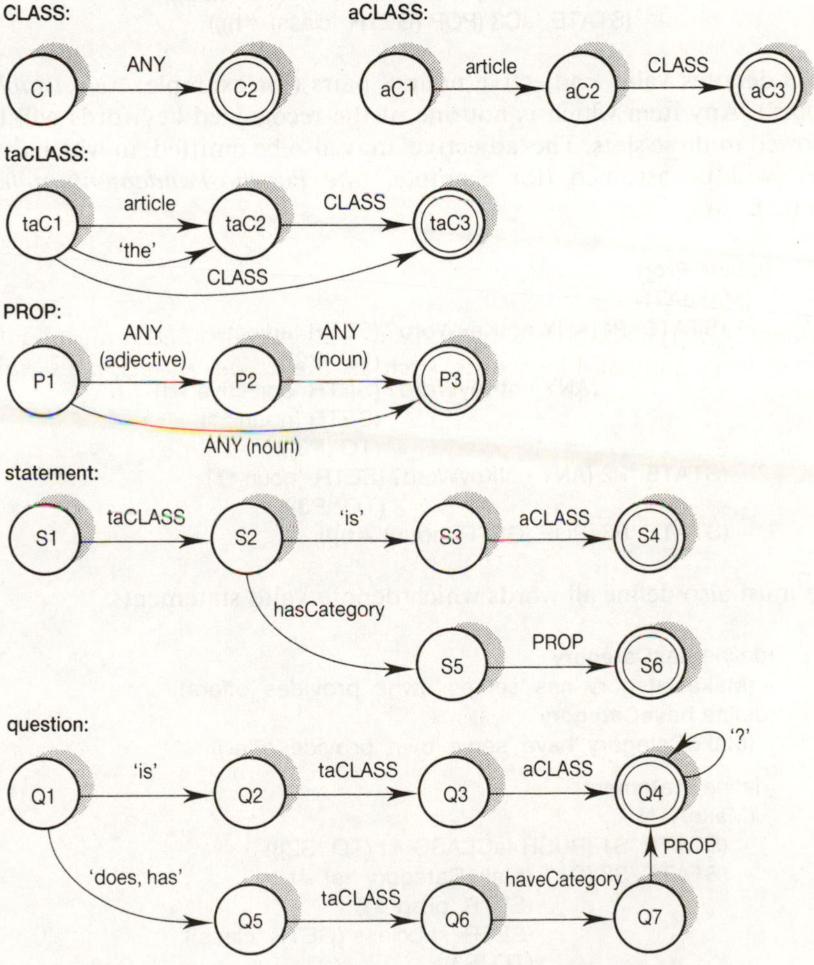

Figure 3.81 Further ATNs for our *Rodney* NLP interface.

```
(STATE 'taC1
        (CAT article #t (SETR 'specific #f)
                        (TO 'taC2))
        (CAT (MakeCategory 'the) #t (SETR 'specific #t)
                                    (TO 'taC2))
        (PUSH CLASS #t (SETR 'specific #t)
                       (TO 'taC3)))
(STATE 'taC2 (PUSH CLASS #t (TO 'taC3)))
(STATE 'taC3 (POP (GETR 'class) #t))))
```

aCLASS represents an article, followed by any valid **CLASS** instance (for example, '*a Vegetarian*').

```
(define aCLASS
  (MakeATN (STATE 'aC1 (CAT article #t (TO 'aC2)))
           (STATE 'aC2 (PUSH CLASS #t (TO 'aC3)))
           (STATE 'aC3 (POP (GETR 'class) #t))))
```

Prop denotes valid <adjective noun> pairs (for example, '*velvet tablecloths*'). Any item which is not one of the recognized keywords will be allowed in these slots. The 'adjective' may also be omitted, in which case 'yes' will be assumed (for example, '*the PanchosPandemonium has music*').

```
(define Prop
  (MakeATN
    (STATE 'P1 (ANY notKeyWord? (SETR 'adjective **)
                                (TO 'P2))
               (ANY notKeyWord? (SETR 'adjective #f)
                                (SETR 'noun **)
                                (TO 'P3)))
    (STATE 'P2 (ANY notKeyWord? (SETR 'noun **)
                                (TO 'P3)))
    (STATE 'P3 (POP (GETR 'noun) #t))))
```

We must also define all words which denote valid statements:

```
(define hasCategory
  (MakeCategory 'has 'serves 'owns 'provides 'offers))
(define haveCategory
  (MakeCategory 'have 'serve 'own 'provide 'offer))

(define statement
  (MakeATN
    (STATE 'S1 (PUSH taCLASS #t (TO 'S2)))
    (STATE 'S2 (CAT (MakeCategory 'is) #t
                    (SETR 'prop #f)
                    (SETR 'subclass (GETR 'class))
                    (TO 'S3))
```

```
                        (CAT hasCalegory #t
                                (SETR 'prop #t)
                                (SETR 'propclass (GETR 'class))
                                (TO 'S5)))
        (STATE 'S3 (PUSH aCLASS #t
                                (SETR 'superclass (GETR 'class))
                                (TO 'S4)))
        (STATE 'S4 (POP #t #t))
        (STATE 'S5 (PUSH Prop #t (TO 'S6)))
        (STATE 'S6 (POP #t #t))))
```

and all valid questions:

```
(define question
  (MakeATN
    (STATE 'Q1 (CAT (MakeCategory 'is) #t (SETR 'prop #f)
                                          (TO 'Q2))
               (CAT (MakeCategory 'does 'has) #t (SETR 'prop #t)
                                                 (TO 'Q5)))
    (STATE 'Q2 (PUSH taCLASS #t
                      (SETR 'subclass (GETR 'class))
                      (TO 'Q3)))
    (STATE 'Q3 (PUSH aCLASS #t
                      (SETR 'superclass (GETR 'class))
                      (TO 'Q4)))
    (STATE 'Q4 (CAT (MakeCategory '?) #t (TO 'Q4))
               (POP #t #t))
    (STATE 'Q5 (PUSH taCLASS #t
                      (SETR 'propclass (GETR 'class))
                      (TO 'Q6)))
    (STATE 'Q6 (CAT haveCategory #t (TO 'Q7)))
    (STATE 'Q7 (PUSH PROP           #t (TO 'Q4)))))
```

describe will list all slots of a frame:

```
(define describe
  (MakeATN
    (STATE 'D1 (CAT (MakeCategory 'Describe) #t (SETR 'prop #f)
                                                (TO 'D2)))
    (STATE 'D2 (PUSH taCLASS #t (TO 'D3)))
    (STATE 'D3 (POP #t #t))))
```

Finally, we define the 'top-level' ATN:

```
(define InterfaceATN
  (MakeATN
    (STATE 'I1 (PUSH statement #t
                       (SETR 'type (lambda (aRB) 'stmt))
                       (TO 'I2))
```

```
        (PUSH question #t (SETR 'type (lambda (aRB) 'quest))
                          (TO 'I2))
        (PUSH describe #t (SETR 'type (lambda (aRB) 'desc))
                          (TO 'I2)))
    (STATE 'I2 (POP (GETR 'type) #t))))
```

The *ReadAndProcessASentence* procedure connects Rodney to the ATN grammar. Any user input (sentence) will be parsed, and appropriate procedures will be invoked if the parse was successful.

```
(define ReadAndProcessASentence
  (lambda ()

   (define invalidSentence?
     ; check that it is a list first. . .
     (lambda (aSentence) (not (pair? aSentence))))

   (newline)
   (display ". . .> ")
   (let ((aSentence (read)))
    (newline)
    (if (invalidSentence? aSentence)
       (begin
          (newline)
          (DisplayLine "Please enter your sentence as a list")
          (ReadAndProcessASentence))
       (if (equal? aSentence '(bye))
          #t
          (let ((registers (Parse InterfaceATN aSentence #f)))
            (if (not registers)
               (DisplayLine "Sentence not understood")
               (ProcessSentence aSentence registers))
            #f))))))
```

After a successful parse the contents of the registers will be as shown in Figure 3.82. The processing of the valid sentence may now be guided by this information.

```
(define ProcessSentence
  (lambda  (aSentence aRegisterBank)
   (let      ((type  (GetAssociationValue 'type aRegisterBank))
              (prop  (GetAssociationValue 'prop aRegisterBank))
              (specific (GetAssociationValue 'specific aRegisterBank)))
    (if prop
      ; question or statement about properties
      (let ((adjective (GetAssociationValue 'adjective aRegisterBank))
            (noun (GetAssociationValue 'noun aRegisterBank))
            (propowner (GetAssociationValue 'propclass
                                                aRegisterBank)))
```

```
(if (eq? type 'stmt)
    (ProcessPropertyStatement specific
                              propowner
                              adjective
                              noun)
    (ProcessPropertyQuestion specific
                             propowner
                             adjective
                             noun)))
(if (eq? type 'desc)
    ; request for a frame description
    (let ((class (GetAssociationValue 'class aRegisterBank)))
      (ProcessDescribe specific class))
    (let ((subclass (GetAssociationValue 'subclass aRegisterBank))
          (superclass (GetAssociationValue 'superclass aRegisterBank)))
      (if (eq? type 'stmt)
          ; "containment" (isa) question or statement
          (ProcessInclusionStatement
              specific subclass superclass)
          (ProcessInclusionQuestion
              specific subclass superclass))))))))
```

Register	"Value"
type	'stmt' if *statement*, 'quest' if *question*, 'desc' if *describe*
prop	#t if a property is involved – e.g. "*large tables*"
specific	#t if the specific "the" rather than a general "a" or "an" clause is encountered
adjective	the adjective describing a property (if prop = #t) – e.g. "*large*" *tables*
noun	the noun used to describe a property (if prop = #t) – e.g. *large* "*tables*"
propowner	the identifier used for the class involved in a property question or statement (if prop = #t) – e.g. '*PleasureGarden*'
subclass	the identifier used for the subclass object in a containment question or statement (if type not 'desc' and prop = #f)
superclass	the identifier used for the superclass object in a containment question or statement (if type not 'desc' and prop = #f)
class	the identifier used for the class object in a *describe* question (type = desc)

Figure 3.82 The register contents after a parse.

Figure 3.83 shows the initial contents of the frame network, to which the user can add information as desired.

Demon procedures are attached to some of the slots. For example, we relate 'variety' to the number of items on a restaurant's menu, and an **'IF-NEEDED'** demon is used to decide on the value of this property whenever it is selected. This has the advantage that there is no need to worry about updates each time a menu is amended or shortened. *BYO* ('bring your own') *restaurants* have no licence to serve alcohol, and they therefore are not allowed to offer a winelist. An **'IF-ADDED'** demon procedure is employed to police this constraint. Reflecting the nature of its clientele, we have also dispatched an **'IF-REMOVED'** demon to the *DirtyDicks* take-away (a quick-service, 'downmarket' type of restaurant).

```
(define CountMenu
  ; IF-NEEDED demon: decides on variety by counting the number of
  ; items on the menu
  (lambda (aFN aFrame aSlot)
   (let ((menu (GetAValue aFN aFrame 'Menu)))
    (if (and (pair? menu) (> (length menu) 2))
        'yes
        'no))))

(define RefuseToAdd
  ; IF-ADDED demon: return #f to stop addition of some item
  (lambda (aFN aFrame aSlot aValue)
   (if (eq? aValue 'yes)
      (begin (DisplayLine "Sorry, but the" aFrame
                           "is not allowed to provide" aSlot)
             #f)
      aFN)))
(define RiotIfRemoved
  ; IF-NEEDED demon: return #f to stop removal of ashtrays
  (lambda (aFN aFrame aSlot aValue)
   (DisplayLine "I can't remove" aSlot "from a" aFrame)
   (DisplayLine "This might start a riot among the clientele")
   #f))
```

The frame network itself, called *RestaurantWorld*, can now be defined:

```
(define RestaurantWorld
  (MakeFN
    (FRAME 'Restaurant
      (SLOT 'Food        (DEFAULT 'edible))
      (SLOT 'Tables      (DEFAULT 'yes))
      (SLOT 'Toilets     (DEFAULT 'yes))
      (SLOT 'Portions    (DEFAULT 'reasonable))
      (SLOT 'Variety     (IF-NEEDED CountMenu)))
```

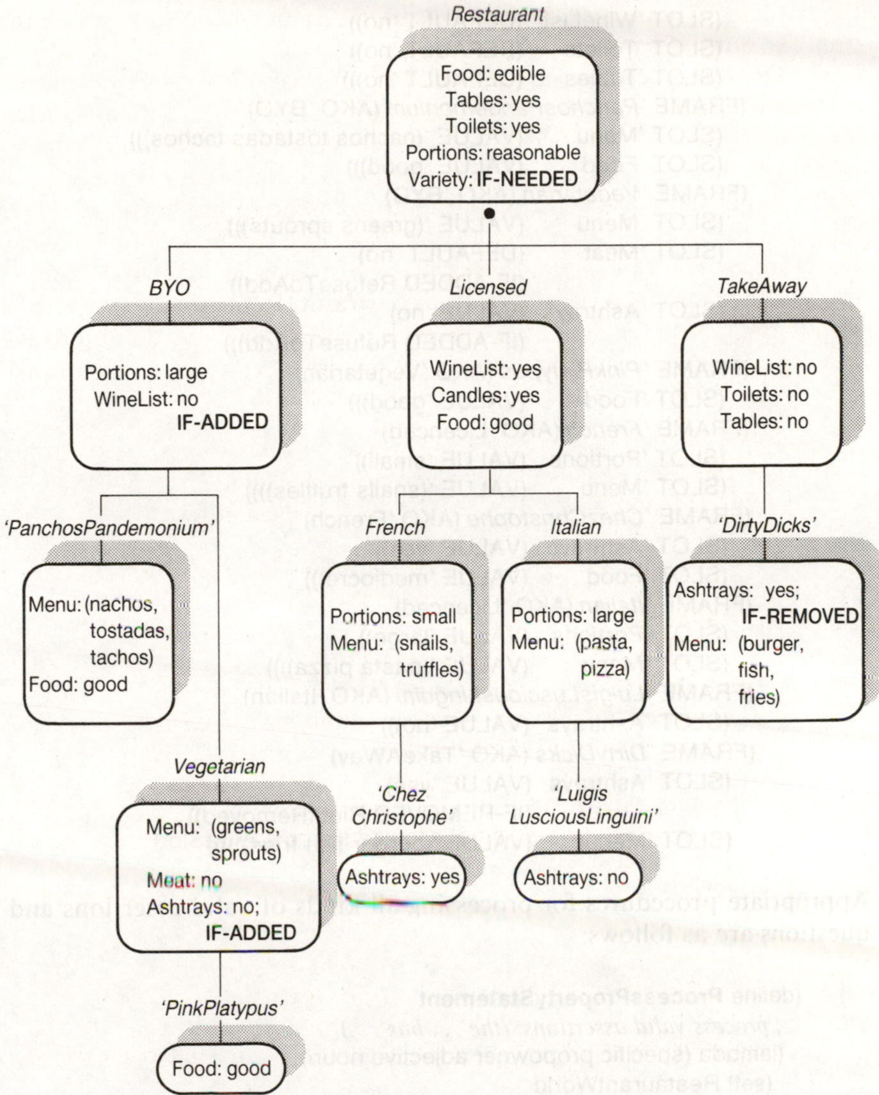

Figure 3.83 The initial frames in Rodney's *RestaurantWorld.*

```
(FRAME 'BYO (AKO 'Restaurant)
   (SLOT 'Portions   (DEFAULT 'large))
   (SLOT 'WineList   (VALUE 'no)
                     (IF-ADDED RefuseToAdd)))
(FRAME 'Licenced (AKO 'Restaurant)
   (SLOT 'WineList   (DEFAULT 'yes))
   (SLOT 'Candles    (DEFAULT 'yes))
   (SLOT 'Food       (DEFAULT 'good)))
(FRAME 'TakeAway (AKO 'Restaurant)
```

```
      (SLOT 'WineList  (DEFAULT 'no))
      (SLOT 'Toilets   (DEFAULT 'no))
      (SLOT 'Tables    (DEFAULT 'no)))
    (FRAME 'PanchosPandemonium (AKO 'BYO)
      (SLOT 'Menu      (VALUE '(nachos tostadas tachos)))
      (SLOT 'Food      (VALUE 'good)))
    (FRAME 'Vegetarian (AKO 'BYO)
      (SLOT 'Menu      (VALUE '(greens sprouts)))
      (SLOT 'Meat      (DEFAULT 'no)
                       (IF-ADDED RefuseToAdd))
      (SLOT 'Ashtrays  (VALUE 'no)
                       (IF-ADDED RefuseToAdd)))
    (FRAME 'PinkPlatypus (AKO 'Vegetarian)
      (SLOT 'Food      (VALUE 'good)))
    (FRAME 'French (AKO 'Licenced)
      (SLOT 'Portions  (VALUE 'small))
      (SLOT 'Menu      (VALUE '(snails truffles))))
    (FRAME 'ChezChristophe (AKO 'French)
      (SLOT 'Ashtrays  (VALUE 'yes))
      (SLOT 'Food      (VALUE 'mediocre)))
    (FRAME 'Italian (AKO 'Licenced)
      (SLOT 'Portions  (VALUE 'large))
      (SLOT 'Menu      (VALUE '(pasta pizza))))
    (FRAME 'LuigisLusciousLinguini (AKO 'Italian)
      (SLOT 'Ashtrays  (VALUE 'no)))
    (FRAME 'DirtyDicks (AKO 'TakeAWay)
      (SLOT 'Ashtrays  (VALUE 'yes)
                       (IF-REMOVED RiotIfRemoved))
      (SLOT 'Menu      (VALUE '(burger fish fries))))))
```

Appropriate procedures for processing all kinds of valid assertions and questions are as follows:

```
(define ProcessPropertyStatement
  ; process valid assertions: (the . . . has . . .)
  (lambda (specific propowner adjective noun)
    (set! RestaurantWorld
        (AddAValue RestaurantWorld
                   propowner
                   noun
                   (if (not adjective) 'yes adjective)))))

(define ProcessPropertyQuestion
  ; process valid queries: (does the . . . have . . . ?)
  (lambda (specific propowner adjective noun)

    (define testForItemOnMenu
      (lambda (item menu)
        (if (pair? menu)
            (member item menu)
```

```
            (equal? item menu))))
    (let ((value (GetAValue RestaurantWorld
                            propowner
                            noun)))
        (cond
          ; test if a particular menu item is asked for
          ((equal? adjective 'any)
           (let ((menu (GetAValue RestaurantWorld
                                  propowner
                                  'menu)))
             (if (testForItemOnMenu noun menu)
                 (DisplayLine "Of course - quite a wide range in fact")
                 (DisplayLine "Unfortunately not, but they do offer"
                              menu))))
          ; test if property is asked for about which no information is stored.
          ; If yes, invoke the forward chainer.
          ((equal? value "NOTKNOWN")
           (TryByInference propowner
                           adjective
                           noun))
          ; if information is given, then it must either be a yes/no
          ; question (e.g. toilets = yes), or a question asking for a
          ; specific property value e.g. toilets = clean). Test for and
          ; process yes/no queries first.
          ((not adjective)
           (cond ((eq? value 'yes)
                  (DisplayLine "Yes, it seems very likely that it has"
                               noun))
                 ((eq? value 'no)
                  (DisplayLine "No, it's unlikely to have much"
                               noun))
                 (else
                  (DisplayLine "Yes it has" value noun))))
          ;- followed by processing of more specific queries
          (else
           (cond ((and (eq? adjective 'no) (eq? value 'yes))
                  (DisplayLine "No, it does have" noun))
                 ((eq? value 'yes)
                  (DisplayLine "Sorry, I know that it will have" noun
                               "but not if they are" adjective))
                 ((equal? value adjective)
                  (DisplayLine "Yes it does"))
                 ((eq? value 'no)
                  (DisplayLine "No, it does not have any" noun))
                 (else
                  (DisplayLine "No, but it does have" value noun)))))))
```

The remaining procedures are much simpler.

```
(define ProcessInclusionStatement
  ; process valid class/subclass assertions: (the . . . is . . .)
  (lambda (specific subclass superclass)
    (set! RestaurantWorld
          (AddAKOLink RestaurantWorld
                      subclass
                      superclass))))

(define ProcessInclusionQuestion
  ; process valid class/subclass queries (is the . . . a . . . ?)
  (lambda (specific subclass superclass)
    (let ((chain (GetAKOChain RestaurantWorld subclass)))
      (if (member superclass chain)
          (DisplayLine "Yes it is")
          (DisplayLine "Not that I know of")))))

(define ProcessDescribe
  ; respond to requests for more information with a "frame dump"
  (lambda (specific class)
    (DisplayLine "Here is all I known about"
                 (if specific "the" " ") class)
    (let ((frame (FindFrame RestaurantWorld class)))
      (if frame
          (PrintFrame frame)
          (DisplayLine "nothing known")))))
```

The forward chainer uses predicate functions to test for the presence of some particularly noteworthy menu items:

```
(define HasSnails?
  ; check if list bound to x contains the symbol "snails"?
  (lambda (anAList)
    (let ((list (GetAssociationValue 'x anAList)))
      (and (pair? list) (member 'snails list)))))

(define HasFries?
  ; check if list bound to x contains the symbol "fries" ?
  (lambda (anAList)
    (let ((list (GetAssociationValue 'x anAList)))
      (and (pair? list) (member 'fries list)))))
```

We assume that the production system's *working memory* is initially empty, but we will enter a number of simple heuristics in the *production memory*. Note that these are very crude 'rules of thumb', sometimes derived from personal experience, and that we cannot accept any responsibility for their accuracy.

```
(define RestaurantPM
  (MakePM
    (RULE 'smokyness?
      (CONDITIONS      (PATTERN 'yes 'ashtrays))
      (CONCLUSIONS     (ASSERT '(smoky atmosphere)
                       (ASSERT '(unhealthy atmosphere))))

    (RULE 'intimacy?
      (CONDITIONS      (PATTERN 'yes 'Candles))
      (CONCLUSIONS     (ASSERT '(smoky atmosphere)
                       (ASSERT '(intimate atmosphere))))

    (RULE 'classiness?
      (CONDITIONS      (PATTERN 'yes 'tables)
                       (PATTERN 'yes 'wineList))
      (CONCLUSIONS     (ASSERT '(yes class))))

    (RULE 'romanticity?
      (CONDITIONS      (PATTERN 'intimate 'atmosphere)
                       (PATTERN 'yes 'class)
                       (PATTERN 'expensive 'bills))
      (CONCLUSIONS     (ASSERT '(yes romantic))))

    (RULE 'Portions->Expense?
      (CONDITIONS      (PATTERN 'small 'portions))
      (CONCLUSIONS     (ASSERT '(expensive bills))))

    (RULE 'Snails->Expense?
      (CONDITIONS      (PATTERN (? 'x HasSnails?) 'menu))
      (CONCLUSIONS     (ASSERT '(expensive bills))))

    (RULE 'cheapness?
      (CONDITIONS      (PATTERN (? 'x HasFries?) 'menu))
      (CONCLUSIONS     (ASSERT '(cheap bills))))

    (RULE 'familyClientele?
      (CONDITIONS      (PATTERN (? 'x HasFries?) 'menu)
                       (PATTERN 'yes 'toilet))
      (CONCLUSIONS     (ASSERT '(family clientele))))

    (RULE 'businessClientele?
      (CONDITIONS      (PATTERN 'expensive 'bills))
      (CONCLUSIONS     (ASSERT '(business clientele))))
```

Unfortunately, we will have to build a new working memory each time the forward chainer is invoked, since our pattern matcher is designed to work with lists of items and not directly with values stored in the frames' property slots, and since these values may change dynamically in response to user requests. In order to do this the *BuildMemory* procedure will 'run' the frame network and assert all known facts about a relevant class of properties.

```
(define BuildMemory
; construct a working memory containing all facts known about
; a relevant class of properties
  (lambda (propowner)
    (let ((chain (GetAKOChain RestaurantWorld propowner))
          (nameList ( ))
          (aWM (MakeWM)))
      ; go through each slot in each frame to build a list of all slot names, and
      ; add them as facts to the working memory
      (for-each
          (lambda (aFrameName)
            (set! aWM
                  (AddFact aWM (list 'CLASS aFrameName)))
            (let ((slots
                    (GetSlots (FindFrame RestaurantWorld
                                         aFrameName))))
              (for-each
                (lambda (aSlot)
                  (let ((aSlotName (GetSlotName aSlot)))
                    (if (or (AKOSlot? aSlot)
                            (member aSlotName nameList))
                        #f
                        (set! nameList (cons aSlotName nameList)))))
              slots)))
        chain)
    ; go through names, getting their value, and add them as facts to aWM
    (for-each
      (lambda (aName)
        (let ((value (GetAValue RestaurantWorld
                                propowner
                                aName)))
          (set! aWM (AddFact aWM (list value aName)))))
      nameList)
    aWM)))
```

TryByInference is invoked whenever no directly asserted fact can be found, in an attempt to answer a query by deduction. Note that in Figure 3.84 we have set the 'verbose flag' in order to trace the flow of deduction. It should probably be reset for 'normal' use.

```
(define TryByInference
  (lambda (propowner adjective noun)
    (DisplayLine "Sorry, I can't remember if"
                 propowner
                 "has"
                 adjective
                 noun)
    (DisplayLine "let me think for a while !")
```

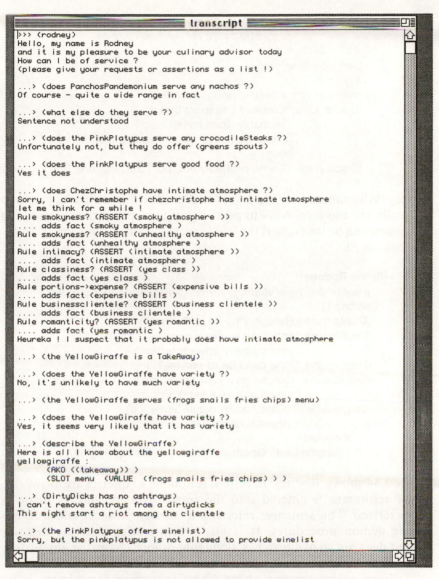

```
transcript
>>> (rodney)
Hello, my name is Rodney
and it is my pleasure to be your culinary advisor today
How can I be of service ?
(please give your requests or assertions as a list !)

...> (does PanchosPandemonium serve any nachos ?)
Of course - quite a wide range in fact

...> (what else do they serve ?)
Sentence not understood

...> (does the PinkPlatypus serve any crocodileSteaks ?)
Unfortunately not, but they do offer (greens spouts)

...> (does the PinkPlatypus serve good food ?)
Yes it does

...> (does ChezChristophe have intimate atmosphere ?)
Sorry, I can't remember if chezchristophe has intimate atmosphere
let me think for a while !
Rule smokyness? (ASSERT (smoky atmosphere ))
.... adds fact (smoky atmosphere )
Rule smokyness? (ASSERT (unhealthy atmosphere ))
.... adds fact (unhealthy atmosphere )
Rule intimacy? (ASSERT (intimate atmosphere ))
.... adds fact (intimate atmosphere )
Rule classiness? (ASSERT (yes class ))
.... adds fact (yes class )
Rule portions->expense? (ASSERT (expensive bills ))
.... adds fact (expensive bills )
Rule businessclientele? (ASSERT (business clientele ))
.... adds fact (business clientele )
Rule romanticity? (ASSERT (yes romantic ))
.... adds fact (yes romantic )
Heureka ! I suspect that it probably does have intimate atmosphere

...> (the YellowGiraffe is a TakeAway)

...> (does the YellowGiraffe have variety ?)
No, it's unlikely to have much variety

...> (the YellowGiraffe serves (frogs snails fries chips) menu)

...> (does the YellowGiraffe have variety ?)
Yes, it seems very likely that it has variety

...> (describe the YellowGiraffe)
Here is all I know about the yellowgiraffe
yellowgiraffe :
     (AKO ((takeaway)) )
     (SLOT menu  (VALUE  (frogs snails fries chips) ) )

...> (DirtyDicks has no ashtrays)
I can't remove ashtrays from a dirtydicks
This might start a riot among the clientele

...> (the PinkPlatypus offers winelist)
Sorry, but the pinkplatypus is not allowed to provide winelist
```

Figure 3.84 A session with 'Rodney'.

```
; We begin by constructing a working memory containing all the facts
; known about "propowner" (recursing through all its ancestors). We
; then find all the facts that may be concluded from this, followed by a
; check on whether the requested property is present in the newly
; constructed working memory
(let ((newWM
       (ForwardChainer Restaurant PM
```

```
                                   (BuildMemory propowner)
                                   #t))) ; turn the 'verbose' flag on
        (if (eq? adjective #f)
            (set! adjective 'yes)
            #f)
        (if (member (list adjective noun) newWM)
            (DisplayLine "Eureka ! I suspect that it"
                         "probably does have"
                         (if (eq? adjective 'yes) " " adjective)
                         noun)
            (DisplayLine "Sorry, probably not, but I am not sure!")))))
```

Rodney is the name of our top-level function. It reads sentences in a loop and 'calls' the top-level ATN to parse them. Sentences are processed if a valid parse can be found, and the whole cycle terminates as soon as '(*bye*)' is encountered.

```
(define Rodney
  ; a polite version of Rodney, the restaurant advisory program
  (lambda ()
    (DisplayLine "Hello, my name is Rodney")
    (DisplayLine "and it is my pleasure to be"
                 "your culinary advisor today")
    (DisplayLine "How can I be of service?")
    (DisplayLine "(please give your requests or"
                 "assertions as a list !)")
    (do ((finished? (ReadAndProcessASentence)
                    (ReadAndProcessASentence)))
        (finished?
          (DisplayLine "Goodbye, thank you for coming")))))
```

Figure 3.84 shows 'Rodney' in action. A number of queries are answered, a new restaurant is entered into the frame network and its menu is characterized. The sentences referring to *variety*, *winelist* and *ashtrays* invoke demon procedures. It is also worth noting that the *describe* request does not spawn searches along inheritance chains, or any further deductions. Only the mentioned frame's slots will be shown.

Since no information about *ChezChristophe*'s atmosphere is directly asserted, Rodney tries to guess. The trace of his line of reasoning is shown because the forward chainer's 'verbose' flag is set to #t. The conclusion is reached that the fact that *ChezChristophe* boasts ashtrays (and candles) makes it highly likely that its atmosphere is smoky, and that a smoky atmosphere implies intimacy. If you argue this point you are invited to provide your own heuristics. The trace also shows that a number of additional inferences can be drawn about the *ChezChristophe.* The facts that it is probably unhealthy (smoke!), classy (winelist), expensive (small portions, snails on the menu), romantic (intimate and classy and expensive) and predominantly visited by business people (expensive) are, however, not relevant in this context. Since our forward chainer will process all information available and deducible for the *ChezChristophe* and because *all* possible deductions will be drawn, it will still produce all of these conclusions. This can obviously be quite an expensive strategy for large knowledge bases.

EXERCISES

There are a large number of contexts in which so-called knowledge-based systems can be applied and where combinations of the toolboxes described in this chapter can profitably be employed. In many cases small modifications should be made to tailor their features to the specific requirements of the task at hand. We will suggest only three such areas, but it should be easy to identify many others according to your special hobbies and interests. As with any other programming project you should start with a simple but flexible design, which you can then expand in line with any growth in your skills and shifts in your interests.

3.64 Write a tax law consultant program. Such a program may be structured quite similarly to 'Rodney'. There should be a frame network for storing relevant facts about entities (forms, cases, and so on), as well as a number of rules for heuristic information (how to fill in a form, legal precedents, and so on). The interface may allow a convenient, 'English-like' style of interaction.

3.65 Extend the travel agent program we referred to in Exercise 3.57 so that it uses heuristic information about popular holiday destinations and customers (for example, *if 'looks scruffy' and 'little money' then 'cheap hotel'*) as well as a more sophisticated user interface.

3.66 Write a program that can act as student adviser. Its knowledge base should (at least) contain information about degrees, courses and departments. Regulations can serve as a rich source for heuristics (for example, '*never enrol for more than 48 credit points in a given year*', '*if you failed COSC111 for the third time you can't do it again*'). Such a system may even be extended to provide a somewhat more knowledgeable 'Eliza-style' computerized therapist.

Chapter 4
The Smalltalk-80 Programming System

'Smalltalk is an exploratory system, in which it is easy to make changes and test prototypes. The goal is to provide an environment in which you can take a fall and get up again faster than you could plan a careful, conservative course of action.'

[*Kaehler and Patterson (1986a).*]

4.1 Historical development

Smalltalk-80 is a much younger programming language than LISP. Its roots reach back to the early 1970s when many of the ideas which later grew into the Smalltalk programming system were first explored in the context of the *Dynabook* project at the Xerox Palo Alto Research Center (Xerox **Parc**). The underlying concepts for such a *Dynabook* were based on the expectation that it would soon be feasible to build inexpensive, notebook-sized personal computers for both adults and children, with the power to handle all their information-related needs. Prior to joining Xerox Parc, Alan Kay, the main advocate of this idea, had been a graduate student at the University of Utah, where he obtained a PhD for work on the **FLEX** programming system [Kay (1969)]. FLEX was a novel design for a flexible simulation- and graphics-oriented language, with many ideas derived from **SIMULA** [Dahl and Nygaard (1966), Birtwistle *et al.* (1973)] and **Sketchpad** [Sutherland (1963)]. When Kay proposed his *Dynabook* concept to the Xerox Corporation, the hardware support for this project was eventually envisaged to provide ample memory and processing power, as well as a flat-screen display sensitive to the touch of a finger. For sound reproduction it was designed to be plugged into a stereo system, and for access to large shared databases there was provision for a connection to telephone lines. Kay firmly believed that *Dynabooks* would soon prove just as revolutionary as the availability of affordable personal books which replaced the handmade texts of the Middle Ages after Gutenberg's invention of the printing press. He envisioned a multitude of uses for such devices, in areas as diverse as the drawing of pictures (for example, for pre-school children), the storage of large quantities of information (for example, for doctors), the instrumentation of pieces of music (for example, for composers), the dynamic simulation and graphical animation of models (for example, for teachers), the representation of objects in three-dimensional space (for example, for architects), or the computation of inventories and cash flows within a company (for example, for businessmen) [Kay (1977), Kay and Goldberg (1977)].

In order to exploit fully the potential for interaction offered by the new medium, some degree of programming knowledge would be required from its users. Existing programming languages, however, were largely designed for specialists, for mainly numerical tasks – exactly those kinds of applications which Kay saw as relatively unimportant for the style in which he expected the *Dynabook* to be used. Development of a new programming system was therefore a high priority. At around the same time, Papert and other researchers at MIT were also working on an interactive and highly graphical computer-based learning environment called **LOGO** [Papert (1980)], which they used to teach programming concepts to children. LOGO was based on Piaget's work in developmental psychology [Piatelli-Palmarini (1980)], and Kay adopted many of its ideas, particularly those concerning expressive communication.

'There was also a realization that children require more computer power than adults were willing to settle for in a time-sharing system. The best outputs that time sharing could provide were crude green-tinted line drawings and square-wave musical tones. Children, however, are used to finger paints, color television and stereophonic records, and they usually find the things that can be accomplished with a low-capacity time-sharing system insufficiently stimulating to maintain their interest.'

[*Kay (1977), p. 232.*]

Classical programming languages were therefore unsuitable, and languages of the LISP family, although they offered the necessary symbol-processing power, were still lacking in constructs for data encapsulation, and did not cater for easy extension by non-specialist users, or for easy ways of constraining the complexities of the resulting artifacts. Programming in procedural languages often requires elaborate combinations of procedures, and the complexity of getting such constructs to work often increases exponentially with the number of components. Since the whole idea of a 'dynamic' personal computing medium was crucially dependent on features for *easy* extension of concepts by non-specialist users, Kay opted for a lego-like building block approach of layered designs, built around the notions of encapsulation and inheritance. As we saw in Chapter 2, this approach encourages representation at multiple levels of organization, with encapsulation acting as a layer of protection against unwelcome operations on objects. This constraint on patterns of interaction reduces complexity and encourages extensibility. It is highly likely that Kay's early involvement with SIMULA was instrumental in his choosing this metaphor, but he carried SIMULA's ideas much further. **Smalltalk** was the programming language which finally emerged. It was the first computer language based entirely on the notions of messages and activities, although Hewitt's *actor* proposal followed shortly thereafter [Hewitt (1977)]. In early Smalltalk both data and procedures were replaced by the idea of 'activities', as entities that exhibit behaviour when receiving a message. The system was highly orthogonal in that every description, transformation, or control structure became part of this paradigm. Each activity belonged to a family of similar activities (flavour, class) and new families could be created by combination and enrichment of 'traits'.

The original *Dynabook* project was never completed, although many of today's most advanced personal workstations (such as Macintosh, Sun) come close to its ideal. Much of the research done at Xerox Parc during the almost 15 years of the project's existence, however, has had a tremendous influence on many areas of computer science and computing in general. On the hardware side, the first experimental systems ran on the *Alto* workstation, a modified Data General NOVA minicomputer. This was later replaced by the *Dorado*, a fast custom-built personal workstation. At the time of their development both these computers were at the cutting edge of technology. The *Dynabook* also pioneered the ideas of memory-mapped black on white graphics and the *Ethernet* architecture for local area networks. On the software side, innovative ideas on the use of window-based, mouse- and menu-driven user interfaces were thoroughly explored over a period of many years. This paradigm is now known as the '*desktop metaphor*' and will be discussed and illustrated in detail in the remainder of this section.

Smalltalk, the programming tool for the *Dynabook*, was originally envisioned as a simple language, suitable for use by children without any prior knowledge of computers. The choice of name reflects this intention.

> 'The very first Smalltalk evaluator was a thousand-line BASIC program, which first evaluated 3+4 in October 1972. It was followed in two months by a NOVA assembly code implementation which became known as the Smalltalk-72 system.
>
> [*Ingalls, in: Krasner, ed. (1983), p. 10.*]

The following discussion of Smalltalk's history is based on Ingalls' (1977, 1983) accounts.

Smalltalk-72 was used for a period of two years, before the first redesign was undertaken in 1974. It was ported to the afore-mentioned Alto computer and a number of experiments in building graphical user interfaces were performed. Applications included turtle graphics, a mouse-driven program editor, a structured graphics editor, an animation system and a music system. Smalltalk-72 also served as a base for experimental programs in teaching object-oriented programming to high-school children. **Smalltalk-74** added better features for bit-mapped graphics (class *BitBlt*) and virtual memory. The improved system was used to implement an information retrieval system and a window-based user interface. Smalltalk-74 evolved into **Smalltalk-76**, which was based on a much cleaner design. Smalltalk-76 also added the idea of inheritance, absent in the two earlier systems. The concept of 'byte codes' as a base for portable implementations was proposed and a micro-coded emulator for this design resulted in much improved performance. Smalltalk-76 was used on a daily basis by more than 20 people for a period of four years, and it also hosted a design for a portable Smalltalk machine, finally taking up the challenge of the original *Dynabook* idea. Ten prototypes of this system were built. A further clean-up of the implementation (**Smalltalk-78**) then resulted in **Smalltalk-80**, the first system which was made available outside Xerox Parc.

During the eight years of Smalltalk's early development occasional publications by members of the 'learning research group' and reports by visiting researchers had caused a considerable amount of interest in the system. Attempts to obtain more detailed information, however, often turned into frustrating experiences until in 1979 and 1980, Xerox finally agreed to the public distribution of Smalltalk-80. The dissemination process was planned in three parts: a series of introductory articles, a book with detailed system specifications and a tape with a portable implementation [Goldberg (1983b)]. The introductory articles were published in a special issue of *BYTE* (August 1981). The plans for the detailed system specification were revised to a series of four books. The first of these [the so-called 'Blue Book' – Goldberg and Robson (1983)] defines the language and its implementation. The second [called the 'Orange Book' – Goldberg (1984)] offers a detailed discussion of Smalltalk's user interface. The third book was meant to describe how to use Smalltalk as a tool for graphical and interactive applications, and the fourth book [the so-called 'Green Book' – Krasner (1983)] was intended as an aid to implementors. Unfortunately to this date the third of these texts has not been published, leaving a major gap in the documentation on the system's usage, particularly with regard to the so-called 'model–view–controller' (MVC) paradigm used to support interaction and graphical applications.

The portable implementation was divided into two major parts, the *Virtual Machine* and the *Virtual Image*. The **Virtual Image (VI)** is the collection of classes encoding Smalltalk's functionality. This includes definitions of basic data structures, basic graphics and text handling, compiler, decompiler, debugger, viewing and user interface support. At the time of its first distribution the Virtual Image contained Smalltalk code for about 10 000 objects. It was machine independent in the sense that all definitions were given in Smalltalk itself, with the compiler producing code in an intermediate language called 'byte codes'. The **Virtual Machine (VM)** formed the machine-dependent part of an implementation, consisting of a byte code interpreter, a storage manager and a number of primitive methods (for example, for basic arithmetic and handlers for I/O devices). Provided an appropriate Virtual Machine implementation was written, Smalltalk could then be ported to any hardware that offered support for bit-mapped graphics and some pointing device. Xerox retained the copyrights to the system and any unauthorized reproduction and distribution was prohibited. In order to test the system's portability before wider distribution was attempted, a decision was made to invite a number of hardware suppliers to develop pilot implementations of the Smalltalk-80 Virtual Image (**VI1**) on suitable equipment. Four of the companies which accepted this invitation eventually produced working implementations: Apple Computers, Digital Equipment, Hewlett-Packard and Tektronix. Of these four, only Tektronix and Apple now offer Smalltalk to customers, but the review process removed a number of errors from the system and in 1983 a new version (**VI2**) was finally distributed to the wider community. In return for their participation in this process each of the four manufacturers received the rights to distribute their own version of Smalltalk for their products. At around the same time, Xerox Parc reached an agreement with the University of California at Berkeley whose computer science department wanted to use Smalltalk in Professor Patterson's graduate seminar on computer architecture. This led to a C-based implementation on VAX and Sun equipment, often referred to as **Berkeley Smalltalk**, which later became very popular among universities. It has also resulted in a thesis on specialized hardware support for Smalltalk: the *SOAR* (Smalltalk on a RISC) chip [Ungar (1987)].

Once the system's distribution had begun, Xerox Parc started to cooperate with Fairchild's laboratory for AI research on an improved design for a Smalltalk implementation for the Motorola 68000 microprocessor. This resulted in a system called **PS Smalltalk**, which forms the base for most of Xerox's current Smalltalk products. Smalltalk projects were also initiated in Japan and Europe, and the efforts by Heeg and Ganzinger at the University of Dortmund, for example, led to implementations for Cadmus and Atari computers. While Hewlett-Packard and Digital Equipment decided not to pursue Smalltalk any further, Tektronix retained a very active interest in the language and now offers a whole range of Smalltalk-based workstations. They also support a group of researchers who have been responsible for many interesting innovations to the system. Apple computers also has always had a strong interest in Smalltalk. In the early 1980s a number of the original members of the learning research group (including Tesler and Ingalls) joined Apple in an effort to design and implement a new computer architecture strongly based on ideas taken from the Smalltalk environment. This project led directly to the *Lisa* and *Macintosh* microcomputers. It should therefore not be surprising that the Macintosh user interface turned out to be very similar to Smalltalk, apart from a small number of simplifications and elaborations. Apple also continued to refine its VI1 Smalltalk interpreter for use on Lisa and Macintosh computers. For a long time these systems have been available for a nominal fee and they deserve much credit for making Smalltalk more widely accessible. Apple has now decided not to market any commercially based and fully supported Smalltalk product. The currently distributed system is based on an older version of the Virtual Machine and there are therefore major differences to current Xerox products. Apple also continues to distribute a stripped-down version of Smalltalk, called **V0**, for use on 512K Macintoshes.

In parallel with these developments, Budd (1987) at the University of Oregon implemented his own version of Smalltalk, called **Little Smalltalk**. This system is targeted at conventional time-sharing machines, and for this reason it lacks an integrated programming environment. GNU Smalltalk is a more recent attempt along similar lines, although an X-windows interface is in preparation. It is available from MIT. Among a number of implementations on IBM equipment, **Smalltalk V** also deserves special mention. Although it restricts itself to a simplified user interface, due largely to hardware restrictions on IBM PCs, it is available for a very reasonable price. It has now also been implemented for Apple Macintoshes and is accompanied by a very readable user manual which can be used as a textbook. Like Apple's Macintosh implementation, Smalltalk V has done much for the language's growing popularity.

Xerox itself has so far reaped few rewards from the Smalltalk project. Some early Smalltalk workstations (Xerox 1100 series) were probably overpriced and sold only in small numbers. The *Star* machine, an advanced office workstation based on ideas from the Smalltalk user interface, was also too highly priced and never became very popular. In 1987 Xerox decided to corporatize its Smalltalk interests. A separate company named **ParcPlace Systems** was founded and is now responsible for further development of the Xerox Smalltalk licences and systems. This new company employs some of the members of the original Smalltalk team and has already released a number of new implementations **(VI2.3** and **VI2.5)** on workstations ranging from Apple Macintoshes to Sun 4 systems. The European distribution has been taken over by G. Heeg Inc., an offshoot of the development group at the University of Dortmund. One of the priorities of the new company is to produce a range of application packages, in order to make the language more attractive to people outside universities and research laboratories. Two major packages have already been released. *Humble* [Piersol (1987)] is a Smalltalk-based expert system shell, and the *Analyst* offers an integrated environment for text processing, data management, graphics and spreadsheets.

Figure 4.1 summarizes some of the more relevant aspects of Smalltalk's history.

Smalltalk is not a 'small' system and requires considerable processor and memory resources. Recent hardware advances and price reductions, however, have made this much less of a concern than it was, and Smalltalk has now become a viable and affordable tool for many users. The *Dynabook* project itself has long since died, although a portable Macintosh-like system with a touch screen or Job's recently unveiled *Next* workstation may come quite close to a first approximation of Kay's original ideas. While its powerful programming environment and the excellent support it offers for graphical applications remain Smalltalk's strongest points, it has lost much of the simplicity which made early versions suitable for teaching programming to schoolchildren. Smalltalk has never claimed to be an artificial intelligence language as such, although it seems eminently suitable for such tasks. However, it is still true that object orientation coupled with Smalltalk's advanced user interface serves to constrain complexity in many applications which would otherwise be notoriously difficult to develop. This claim is confirmed by its popularity as a tool for rapid prototyping of user interfaces. The Smalltalk programming environment was completely

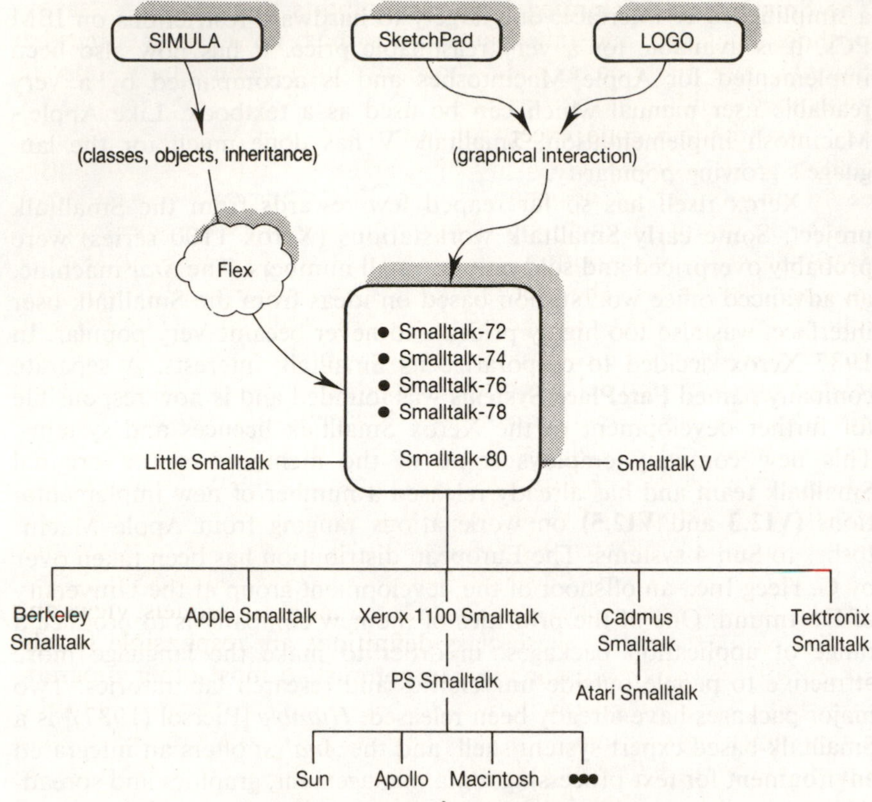

Figure 4.1 The Smalltalk family tree.

developed within the language itself, and must surely be classed as one of the more ambitious programming efforts of the last decade.

The remainder of this chapter will examine the language in more detail. Since we have already discussed the basic philosophy behind object orientation in Section 2.5, we choose not to emphasize this aspect again. After a brief survey of Smalltalk's syntax and functionality we will concentrate instead on the characteristics of desktop-based user environments and the relevant features for writing interactive and graphical applications.

4.2 Of mice, menus and windows – the Smalltalk system and the desktop metaphor

Smalltalk is different from flavour systems in that it offers much more than just an object-oriented programming tool.

Smalltalk = Object-Oriented Programming Language
+ Desktop-Based Programming Environment

The Smalltalk programming language supports the notion of classes, methods, messages and inheritance. Its syntax, however, is somewhat unusual, and there is a wide range of functionality built into its predefined building blocks (classes).

All Smalltalk code, except for expressions involving assignment, is composed of chains of messages sent to objects. Even the programming environment itself is designed around this metaphor. It provides a number of prototypical objects which are manipulated via selection and execution of messages, either through menus or by direct evaluation of message expressions. The user interface's basic functionality is reflected in the so-called **'model–view–controller' (MVC)** metaphor. Here the term *model* refers to those pieces of code which together describe all logically related structural and behavioural properties of a specific application – a 'program' in a conventional sense. A *view* is a particular screen representation of a model. It will typically reside in a window and reflect some of its model's aspects in a textual or graphical form. Those two perspectives are orthogonal in the sense that more than a single view of a model may be active at any given point in time. *Controller* entities, finally, provide a means of user interaction. The Smalltalk system offers a number of standard implementations for 'off the shelf' models, views and controllers. Collectively these class definitions are responsible for the system's impressive functionality. In contrast to most other programming tools, all of the system is always accessible to browsing and change, a fact which makes Smalltalk an extremely malleable system which is easy to customize according to one's own preferences. There are a few so-called 'primitives', but this is only attributable to the fact that for efficiency reasons some operations are implemented directly in machine code. Typically this applies to basic arithmetic, graphics and other I/O operations, making up less than 5% of a particular Smalltalk system's code. Even these primitives are not immutable, however, since their definition may be overridden if one is willing to pay the performance penalty.

To a beginning Smalltalk programmer the distinction between models, views and controllers may well remain hidden for quite some time. Although it is possible to write specialized view and controller objects, there are enough standard components to suit most purposes. In fact, good Smalltalk programming style strongly encourages judicious modification of existing code in preference to the creation of new programs. This requires code-reading skills and a context in which class descriptions and their documentation are readily accessible for browsing and modification. Smalltalk provides such an environment, and, although the concepts of object orientation and programming environments are usually considered in isolation, there are good reasons to suspect that synergistic benefits are gained from combining these two ideas. Object orientation typically leads to large numbers of relatively short definitions for classes and methods within these classes. Through the notion of inheritance it also encourages the sharing of code. The importance of proper tools for organizing and accessing class definitions should therefore be apparent. Traditional manuals and help systems may well be insufficient to provide the required degree of support and there is a growing recognition that so-called 'code browsers', as pioneered by Smalltalk, may well be a necessity rather than a luxury for the effective use of object-oriented programming.

The **desktop metaphor** has shaped the way in which Smalltalk offers access to programs. The workstyle associated with desk-based environments has been evolved and refined over many centuries. It can cope with large numbers of documents, in various stages of completion, containing both text and graphics. The user is free to shuffle things around and even stack them on top of each other. Documents are accessed through spatial selection and will thus be brought to the forefront of our attention. The user also has a large number of tools at his disposal (pens, scissors, glue, staplers, a telephone, and so on) and may switch among different activities at will. When we return to a previously interrupted task we expect it to be in the state we last left it in. Another key aspect of the desktop environment is that it makes changes in objects directly and immediately visible. The notion that tasks may be temporarily interrupted to divert attention to some other activity is also a crucial ingredient. The flexibility inherent in this workstyle may well be an essential component of creative behaviour and Smalltalk's interface therefore makes direct interaction with objects an integral part of the programming process. Objects are represented in windows on a display screen, and mouse-driven selection is used to activate them. The system supports pseudo-concurrency through time slicing and there may therefore be more than one active process, although only the currently selected view will be shown in the foreground. Foreground views are framed in windows which may be scrolled, and their contents may be manipulated through mouse-driven activities. In line with the desktop idea, windows may be expanded, collapsed, resized and moved around the screen. They may overlap or even cover each other. A window is brought to the foreground by pointing and clicking the mouse. Each window presents a view of a process, which may display itself in a number of prototypical frames: *workspaces*, *transcripts*, *inspectors*, *browsers*, *notifiers*, *debuggers* and others. The conceptual power of this environment for program development and exploration can only be truly appreciated through practical experience. In the following sections we will discuss Smalltalk's syntax, as well as the interface's major components. We will also demonstrate its use through some simple examples. A more thorough treatment, and in particular any attempt at completeness in surveying the built-in functionality (class libraries) of the system, is beyond the scope of this book. Goldberg and Robson (1983) and

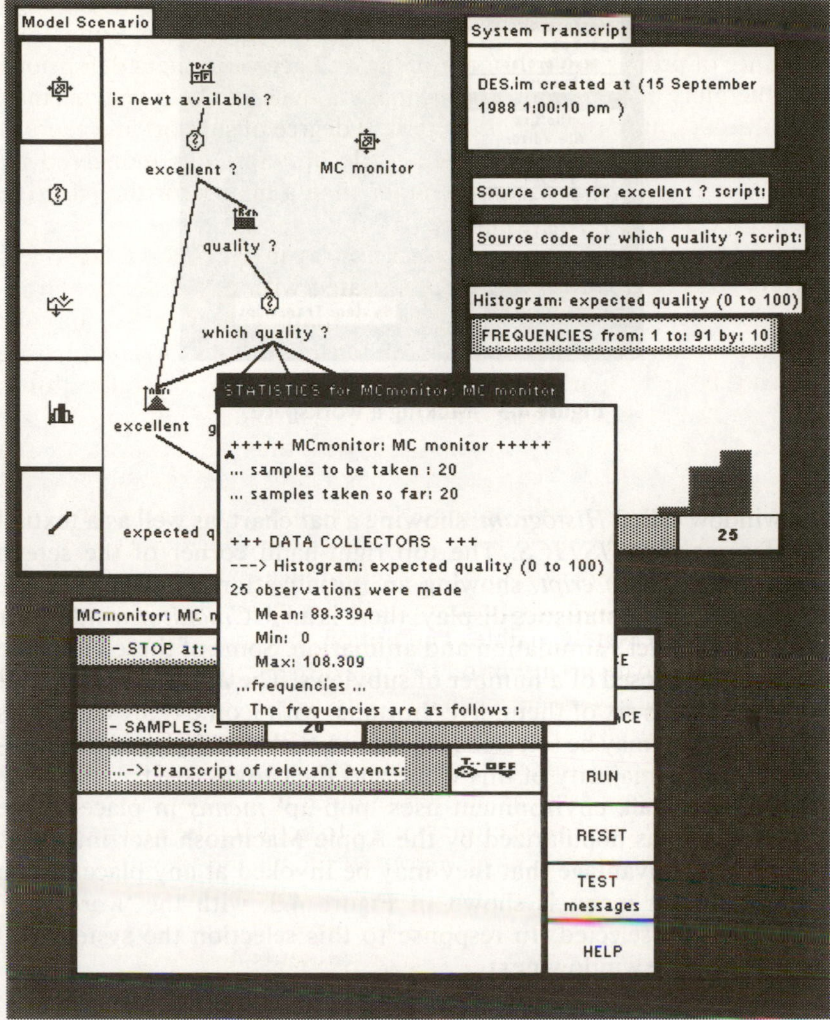

Figure 4.2 The Smalltalk 'desktop'.

Goldberg (1984) are the standard technical references, with Wiener and Pinson (1988) and Lalonde and Pugh (1989) as alternative sources.

Figure 4.2 shows a 'snapshot' of a Smalltalk desktop for a typical project. Seven views are visible on this screen. Two of these, *Source code for excellent?* and *Source code for which quality?* are currently collapsed and positioned in the right-hand corner of the screen. The other five are framed in appropriate windows. There is a *Model Scenario*, showing a graphical representation of a simple Monte Carlo simulation. There is

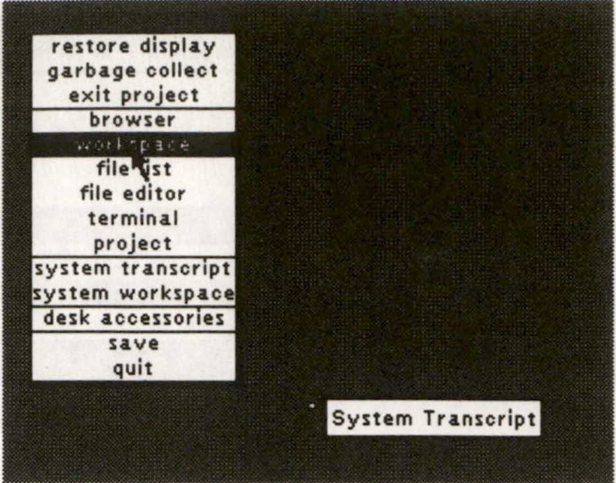

Figure 4.3 Making a workspace.

also a window called *Histogram:* showing a bar chart, as well as a textual view of some *STATISTICS*. The top right-hand corner of the screen holds a *System Transcript*, showing an initialization message. Finally, partly hidden by the statistics display, there is an *MCmonitor* window for controlling a model's simulation and animation. Some of these views are themselves composed of a number of subviews. The *Model Scenario*, for example, contains six of them: five 'buttons' with iconic representations for objects which may be selected (via mouse clicks) and placed on a canvas covering the majority of this view, and the canvas itself.

The Smalltalk environment uses 'pop-up' *menus* in place of the 'pull-down' menus popularized by the Apple Macintosh user interface. They have the advantage that they may be invoked at any place on the screen. One such menu is shown in Figure 4.3, with the '*workspace*' option currently selected. In response to this selection the system will open a *workspace* window next.

Smalltalk requires a pointing device for system/user interaction; preferably a three-button *mouse* (Figure 4.4). The three mouse buttons are labelled 'yellow', 'red' and 'blue', following the terminology of the original Alto implementation. Figure 4.4 shows their functions. If a three-button mouse is not available to a particular implementation, it must be simulated, via mouse button/control key combinations or in some other way. Apple's version uses a one-button mouse whose function is determined by context; that is, the menus it invokes depend on the cursor's position. The 'red' button is used to select information, while the 'yellow' button invokes menus for operations on a view's contents (such as cut, paste, evaluate expressions, format, and so on). The 'blue' button menu suggests transformations on windows themselves (such as resize, move, collapse, expand, and so on). While the 'blue' button choices are fixed, the specific contents of menus associated with the 'yellow' mouse

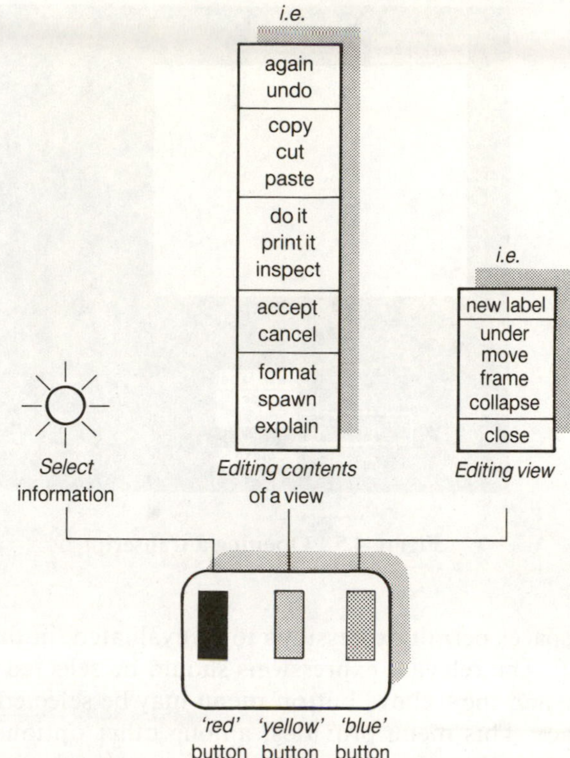

Figure 4.4 Smalltalk's three-button mouse (VI1 menus).

button largely depend on the cursor's position. Figure 4.3 shows the *system menu*, which is invoked by pushing this button while the cursor is located in the grey screen area. Here we are just about to create a workspace window, an operation whose results are reflected in Figure 4.5.

Workspaces offer a simple view of some piece of Smalltalk text. They are associated with a Macintosh-like 'cut and paste' editor and are often employed as a temporary 'scratchpad', to enter and evaluate expressions during the process of testing new class and method definitions. In common with any other Smalltalk window, workspaces own a label and a body, which in this case is just a white area for entering text. Figure 4.5 also illustrates how the 'blue' button menu may be used to open a collapsed *transcript* window. This menu contains other operations applicable to all standard system views and their effects should be easy to visualize.

Transcript windows are simple text collectors, to which requests to display information may be sent. The *System Transcript* is a predefined entity used to display various system messages. The global name 'Transcript' is permanently associated with this object.

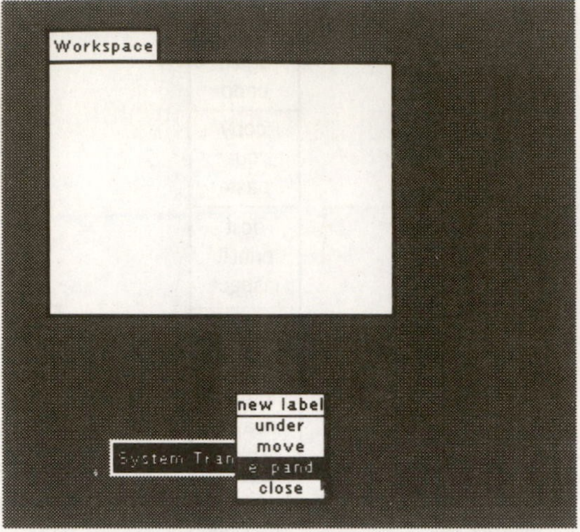

Figure 4.5 Opening a transcript.

Workspaces permit expressions to be evaluated, in the way shown in Figure 4.6. The relevant expressions should be selected by using the 'red' button, and the 'yellow' button menu may be selected from within the workspace. This menu provides, among other options, two operations which trigger evaluation. **doIt** will simply send messages to the objects involved, while **printIt** will also show the returned value. All Smalltalk code will return some value. If not otherwise specified this will be the receiver of the last message. Here we send the message +, with an argument of '2', to the number '2'. The resulting value (4) is shown in reverse video.

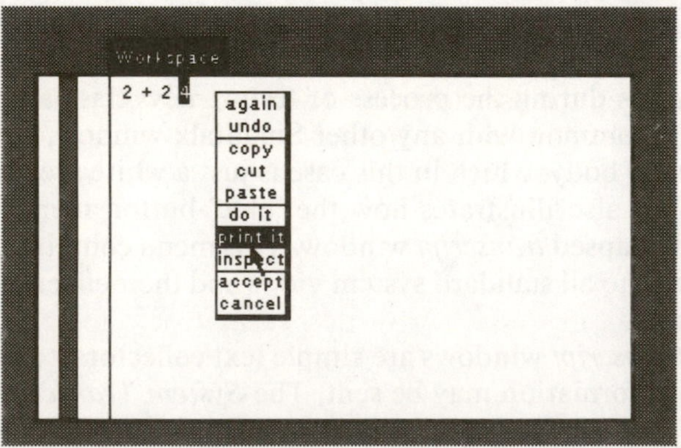

Figure 4.6 Evaluating a message expression.

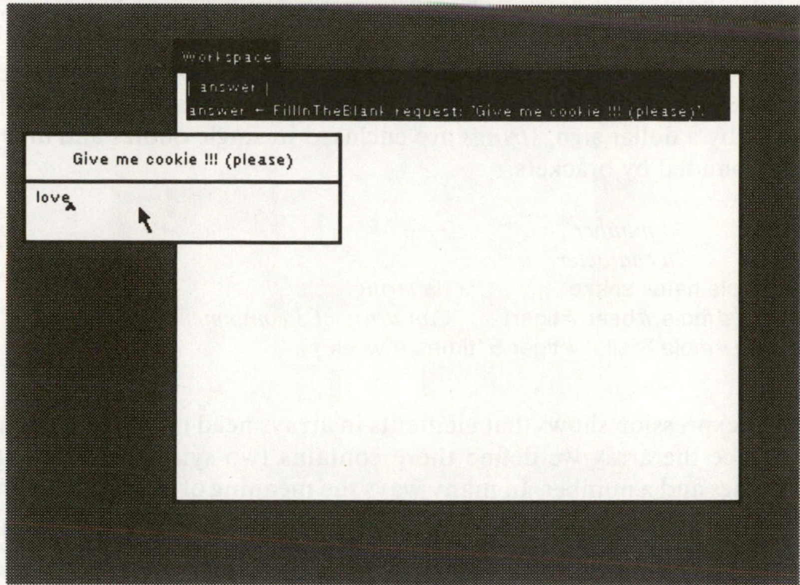

Figure 4.7 A **FillInTheBlank** request.

Workspaces and the transcript will suffice for a brief summary of Smalltalk's syntax, and we will later return to discuss the user interface's other components.

4.3 A glance at basic syntax, data structures, operations and control structures

Like flavour systems and any other object-oriented programming languages Smalltalk is built around the notions of classes, methods and messages. The system itself is composed of a large collection of predefined classes, whose functionality may be invoked through message passing. Even the user interface itself is designed in this style, so that we can open views by evaluating an appropriate message expression, instead of selecting it from the system menu. For example:

```
answer ← FillInTheBlank request: 'Give me cookie !!! (please)'.
```

is a message expression in which **request:** is sent to object **FillInThe-Blank**. This is a class in the Smalltalk library, which, in response, will create a 'query box' and show it on the screen. The user must then give a reply. In this example the answer will be bound to a local variable, *answer*, provided this variable has previously been declared. Figure 4.7 shows the effect.

Smalltalk supports numbers, characters, strings, symbols, arrays, classes and objects among its basic primitives. *Comments* may occur at any place in our code, as long as they are enclosed by double quotes. *Numbers* are written in the conventional fashion. *Characters* must be prefixed by a dollar sign, *strings* are enclosed in single quotes and *arrays* are surrounded by brackets.

```
42      "a number"
$x      "a character"
'mole hates snake'          "a string"
# (#mole #bear #tiger)      "an array of 3 components"
# (#mole 'visits' #tiger 5 'times a week')
```

The last expression shows that elements in arrays need not be of the same type, since the array we define there contains two symbolic constants, two strings and a number. In many ways the meaning of the # character is similar to Scheme's **quote** operator. It will inhibit evaluation of identifiers. In Figure 4.8 reference to **cugel** results in an 'undeclared identifier' response, with a menu of possible options to resolve this situation, while the previous use of **#cugel** simply referred to the symbol itself. In interpreting this figure it should be apparent that **show:** and **cr** messages sent to the transcript cause a display of their arguments and a carriage return respectively.

Smalltalk **identifiers** may be any sequence of letters and digits, beginning with a letter. No other symbols are allowed. Smalltalk draws a syntactic distinction between local and global variables. All **global** identifiers must start with an upper-case letter, while **local** ones will always begin in lower case. Class names are globals and must therefore always start with an upper-case letter. Smalltalk is a 'dynamically typed' language. Any object may therefore be bound to any identifier and type specifications are not required when variables are declared. However, all variables must still be defined prior to reference. Local variables may be bound as instance variables to an object, or they may be temporarily declared. *Temporary variables* are enclosed by vertical bars and separated by spaces.

```
|littleBear littleTiger happyMole|
```

declares three temporary variables. Note that the Smalltalk interpreter enforces the afore-mentioned naming conventions and would refuse to accept this definition if any of the identifiers had started with a capital. There is also an object called **Smalltalk**, holding references to all globally declared variables. Smalltalk contains references to all system constants and classes and we may also use **at:put:** messages to make some appropriate entries.

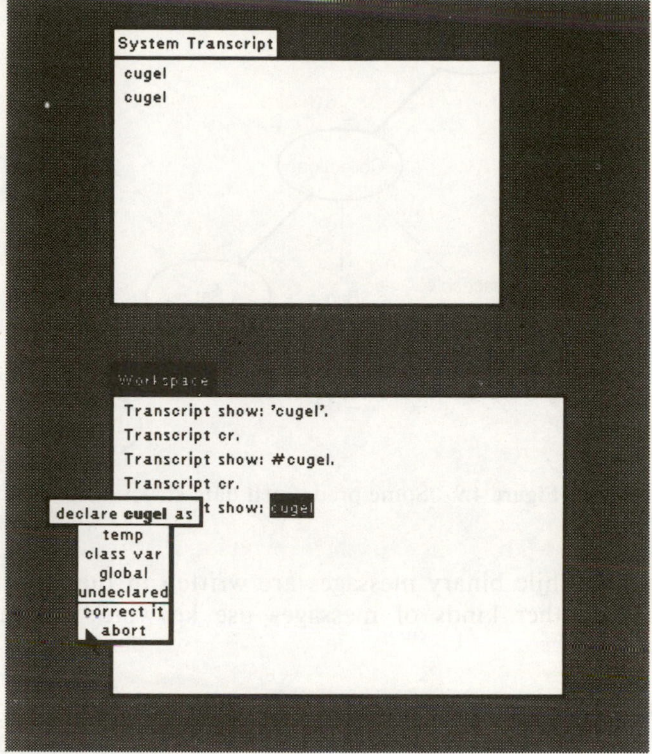

Figure 4.8 Writing into a *Transcript*.

Smalltalk **at:** #MeaningOfLife **put:** 42.
Smalltalk **at:** #Cugel **put:** nil.
Smalltalk **at:** #Sadlark **put:** nil.

The ← symbol assigns names to objects.

|littleBear|
littleBear ← Bear new.

creates a new instance of class *Bear* and binds it to an identifier, after which we may start to send messages to it.

Message expressions are sequences of messages sent to objects, separated by periods. *Messages* name the type of reaction desired. They consist of selectors followed by any arguments. Unary messages require

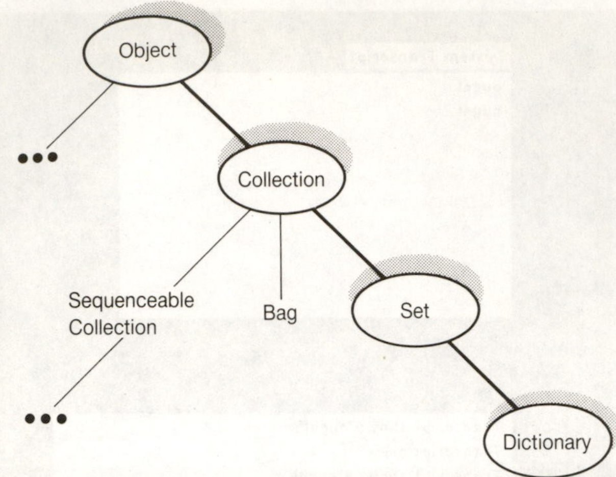

Figure 4.9 Some predefined data structures.

no argument, while binary messages are written in the familiar 'infix' notation. All other kinds of messages use keywords to name their arguments.

> *"unary message to a class: returns a newly created instance of class CookieMonster"*
> CookieMonster **new**.
>
> *"binary message to an instance: returns an instance of class integer"*
> 7 + 7.
>
> *"keyword message: prompts object Cugel to perform a nefarious deed"*
> Cugel **steal**: #Jewel **from**: Sadlark **at**: 12.

Messages sent to the same receiver can be 'cascaded', using semicolons, so that:

> bear **center**; **show**; **dance**.

would be interpreted as a request for sending a sequence of messages to class instance *bear*; that is, first causing her to centre herself on the screen, then to display herself and then to engage in some dancing activity.

All of Smalltalk's *data structures* are represented as objects, and a rich repertoire of these is available in its class library. As with all objects, valid operations are implemented by methods encapsulated within their scope. Computation must therefore be initiated by message passing, through evaluation of message expressions. Figure 4.9 shows a small excerpt from Smalltalk's class library.

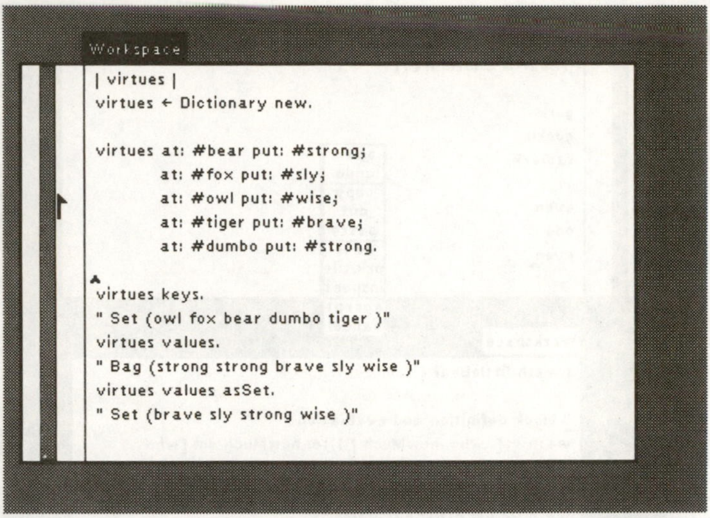

```
Workspace
| virtues |
virtues ← Dictionary new.

virtues at: #bear put: #strong;
        at: #fox put: #sly;
        at: #owl put: #wise;
        at: #tiger put: #brave;
        at: #dumbo put: #strong.

virtues keys.
" Set (owl fox bear dumbo tiger )"
virtues values.
" Bag (strong strong brave sly wise )"
virtues values asSet.
" Set (brave sly strong wise )"
```

Figure 4.10 Some experiments with a dictionary.

Object is the root of the system library, offering some basic functionality common to all objects. Class *Collection* is among class *Object*'s many subclasses, and may itself be further specialized into a whole range of data structures. *Sets* are just one of these, with *Dictionaries* as a subclass. *Dictionaries* represent associations between objects. Figure 4.10 shows the use of these data structures in a simple example. First a dictionary is defined, associating some of our old friends with a particular selection of virtues. Messages are then sent to this object, selecting its *keys* and *values*. Finally the effect of an '*asSet*' transformation is shown. '*virtues values*' results in a newly constructed *bag* object, which in response to this message produces a set of unique virtues in which 'strong' appears only once.

The Smalltalk system subscribes to a fairly radical interpretation of object orientation. Even *control structures* are implemented as message patterns. Selection among alternative paths of execution is supported through **ifTrue:**, **ifFalse:** and **ifFalse:ifTrue:** messages. Loops may be specified with **whileTrue:**, **whileFalse:**, **timesRepeat:**, **do:**, **to:do:**, **collect:** or via recursion. Smalltalk uses the notion of blocks to defer evaluation until some decision is made. *Blocks* may take arguments and are used to encapsulate code which may later be evaluated. They may be bound to identifiers and the **value** message forces their execution. Among other things blocks are commonly used as arguments to control messages.

The workspace in Figure 4.11 shows three examples. In the first case a block with two arguments is defined and assigned to a local variable. Note that colons are used to prefix the names of block

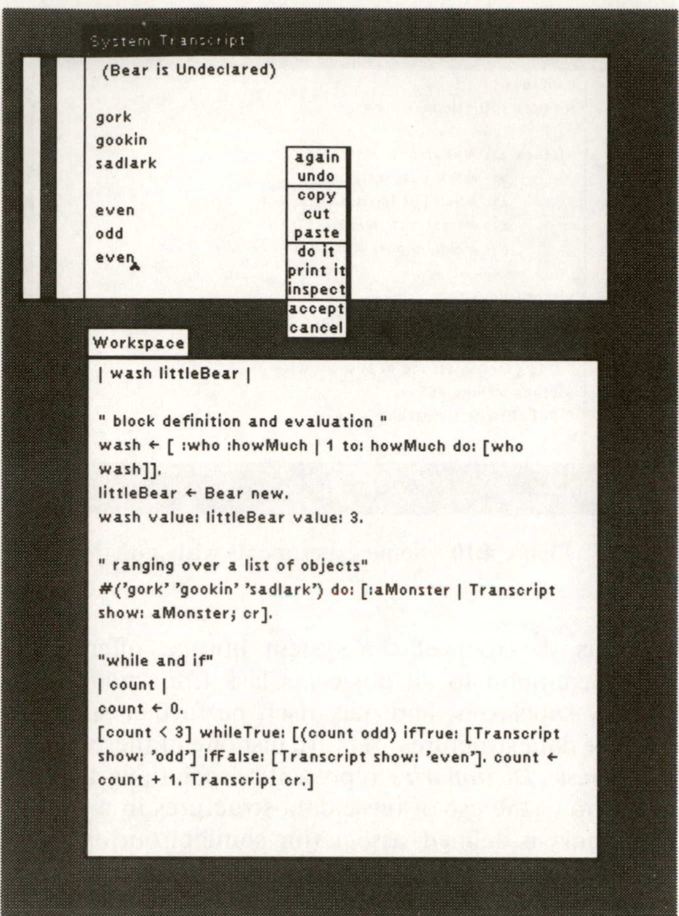

Figure 4.11 Some experiments with control structures.

arguments, which are separated from the block body by a vertical bar. Receiving **value:value:** should then force the stored block's evaluation with the two specified arguments. Our first attempt to create *littleBear*, however, is doomed to fail, since there is currently no class *Bear* in the system. The second example processes a sequence of strings, by listing them in the transcript window. Finally we show a slightly more complex example involving **while True**: and **if**: messages. The task is to increment and test a number inside a loop. If the number is even, 'even' is shown, and if it is odd, then 'odd' should be printed. Here we restrict ourselves to numbers smaller than three, so that 0, 1 and 2 will be tested. Note that Smalltalk code, if not properly formatted, may become quite hard to read. The system provides assistance for this on demand, and we will use this feature in the remainder of this chapter.

Recursive structures may be defined by objects sending messages to themselves. We will see some examples for this later. Smalltalk's strong object orientation also permits additional control structures to be defined in an elegant way, as methods attached to the class of objects which direct their execution. For example, if we intend a numeric value to control a selection or loop, then an appropriate method should be attached to class *Number*. We will later give an example of how to use this idea to provide a Pascal-like 'case' statement.

4.4 Defining a simple application – classes, properties, methods – browsers, inspectors and debuggers

Smalltalk has a special syntax for *class descriptions*, which is shown in the lower pane of browser windows. Such specifications require a superclass, instance and class variables (if any), as well as instance and class methods (if any) as summarized in Figure 4.12. The notions of instance variables and methods are similar to the corresponding concepts in flavour systems. Class variables and methods are used to attach properties and operations to classes instead of individuals. The fact that the life expectancy of all humans lies somewhere between 0 and 120, or the number of currently active instances of a class, are examples of the kind of information which should not be directly associated with individual objects but rather be stored with a class as a whole. Methods for creating instances (for example, *new*) must obviously also be attached to classes and not to their instances.

Smalltalk's environment uses so-called browser windows to define classes. Each class definition effectively functions as an interpreter for a command language of its own. This functionality is defined through its *message protocol*; that is, the set of all messages it can respond to.

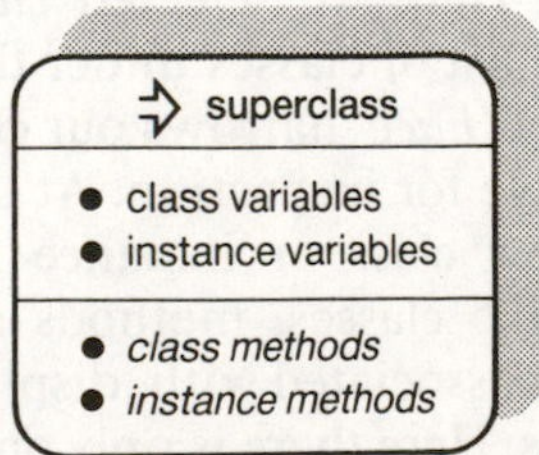

Figure 4.12 A shell for Smalltalk's classes.

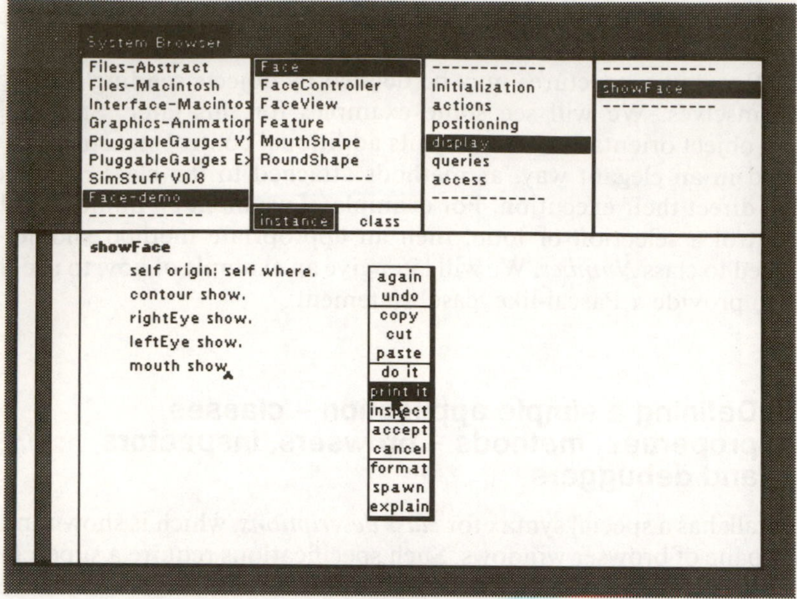

Figure 4.13 A browser.

Messages may refer to methods defined within a given class as well as to those inherited from superclasses. 'Officially' Smalltalk only supports a hierarchical scheme for inheritance, although 'hooks' to implement multiple inheritance are available within the system.

Various categories of so-called browser objects play a very important role in Smalltalk. **Browsers** are used to access definitions for all the classes and methods, both system defined and user defined, that Smalltalk knows about. They are also used to define new classes and methods. Figure 4.13 shows a typical *System Browser*, whose display may be selected from the system menu. System browsers are shown in windows of five panes. The four upper ones are used for navigating a 'path' through the space of definitions, while the lower one views the selected definition itself. For this purpose all of Smalltalk's classes are grouped into categories. Here we selected *class category Face-demo*, which caused a scrollable list of classes under that category to appear in the next pane. Selection of '*Face*' narrows our choice to this class, whose methods are now accessible for inspection. At this stage we must decide whether we want to view class or instance methods. Here *instance* methods are selected. Like classes, methods are categorized, and we decide to inspect methods associated with 'display' activities. This finally produces a list of methods. Here there is only one. *showFace* may now be selected and its code is then shown in the lower window pane. Each of the five panes has its own 'yellow' button menu, offering various messages

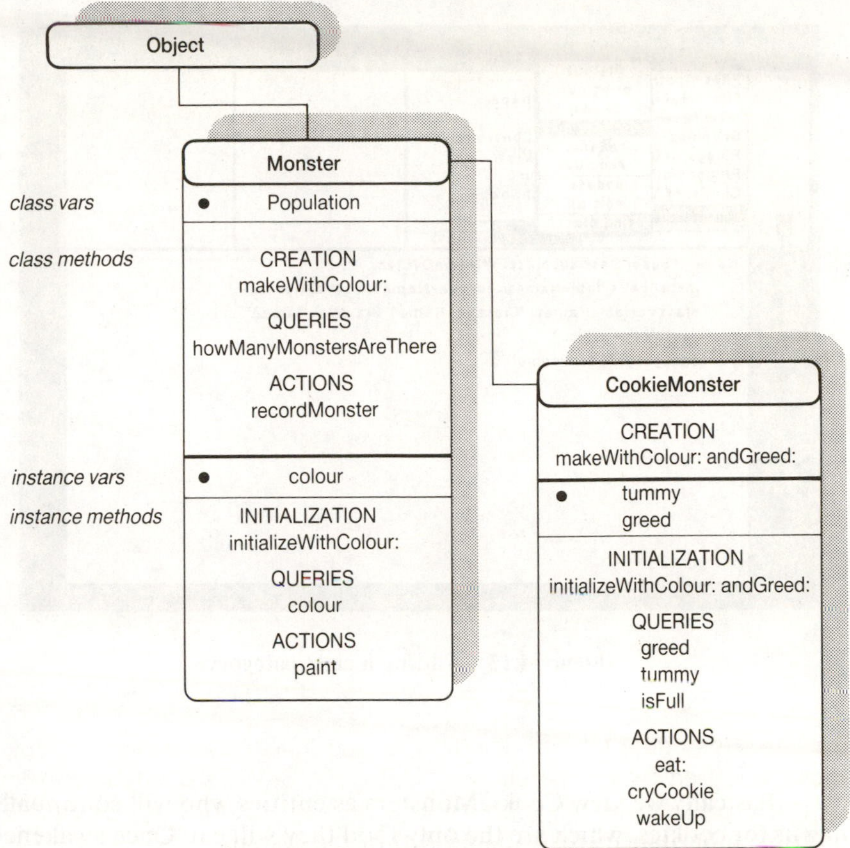

Figure 4.14 *Monster* and *CookieMonster* – structure and functionality.

which can be sent to class categories, classes, method categories or methods. The menu for the lower pane is also shown in the figure. The various options could now be applied to all or any selected part of the code.

From this discussion it should be apparent that browsers offer a powerful tool for viewing and accessing code. All of the Smalltalk system is uniformly accessible for inspection and modification in this way. Let us now look at the procedure in which we define a new application. For this we assume that we wish to describe a small segment of **Sesame Street**, a well-known urban neighbourhood populated by monsters of various kinds. To keep things simple we will concentrate on two classes only: Monsters and CookieMonsters. Monsters are used to demonstrate the concept of subclassing, and a number of properties and methods which may be considered common to any brand of monster will therefore make up their description. CookieMonsters are a subclass of Monster, and Figure 4.14 shows those of their properties which we may consider as relevant in this context.

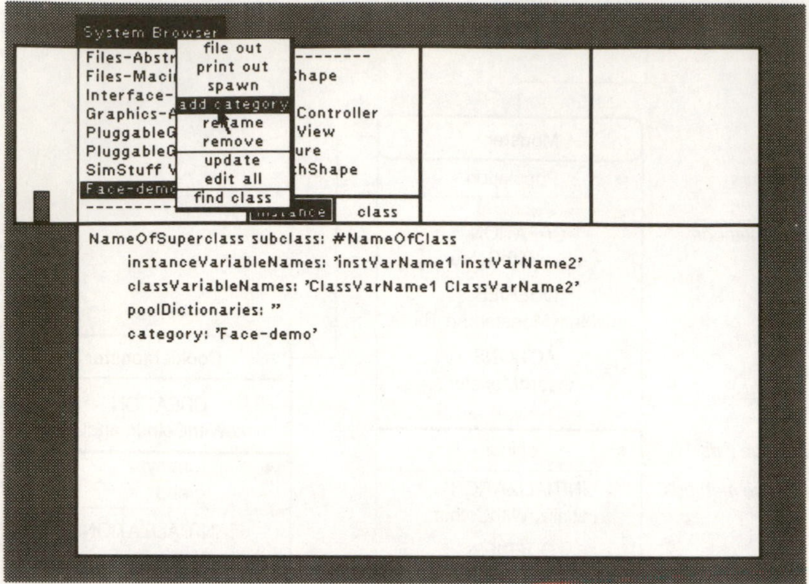

Figure 4.15 Adding a class category.

Basically we view CookieMonsters as entities who will continually nag us for cookies, which are the only food they will eat. Once awakened they can only be silenced once their greed has been filled. Monsters own a class variable (*Population*) for keeping track of the number of monsters which have been created. Appropriate class methods will be provided to make new monsters and to access this information. There is also an instance variable for storing a monster's *colour* and appropriate instance methods categorized as initializations, queries and actions. CookieMonsters specialize this protocol further. No additional class variables are defined, but two new instance variables, *tummy* and *greed*, are introduced. We also add a number of appropriately categorized methods.

To implement this scenario in Smalltalk we must first make a new class category, *SesameStreet*, add the *Monster* and *CookieMonster* classes, and then define and test all class and instance methods. All these definitions can be made within a browser, while workspaces and a new type of view, called *inspectors*, may be employed for testing purposes. Figure 4.15 shows how to add a new class category.

The yellow button menu of the first browser pane offers an 'add category' command, which brings up a dialogue box in which the name of the new category can be entered. Classes can be defined once the new category has been added to the system. The lower browser pane shows a

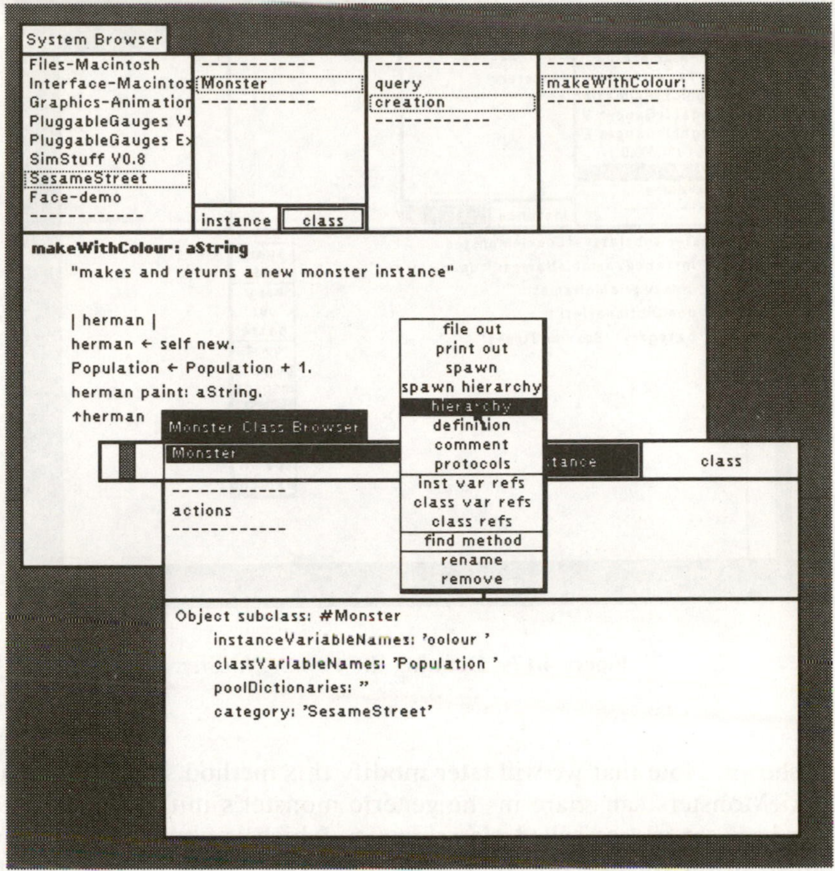

Figure 4.16 Once the Monster is defined.

template for class definition, which the user may fill with detail. Let us assume that we have proceeded to define all class and instance methods for Monsters, and that the state of the model is now reflected by Figure 4.16.

Figure 4.16 demonstrates that more than one browser may be viewed simultaneously. In fact the number of views (of the same or different categories) on the desktop is limited only by the available memory. Multiple browsers are often useful to view different aspects of code simultaneously, eliminating the need for constant scrolling back and forth. By cutting and pasting, information may also be transferred between views. The upper browser in Figure 4.16 views the class methods currently defined for *Monster*. The *makeWithColour:* method is selected

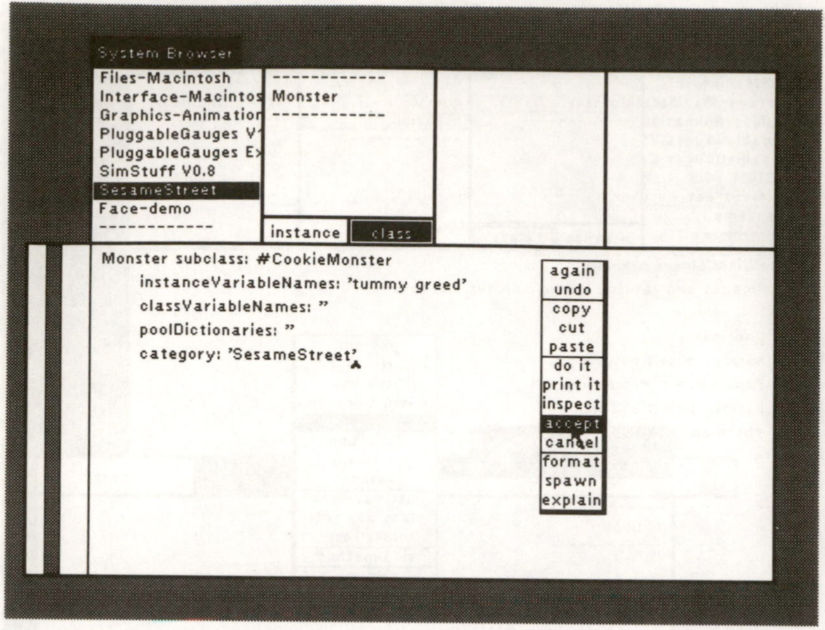

Figure 4.17 Defining the *CookieMonster*.

and shown. Note that we will later modify this method slightly, so that CookieMonsters can share in the generic monster's initialization. The lower browser is a so-called *class browser*, which is obtained from the yellow button menu associated with the second pane of the system browser. Class browsers restrict selection to the specified class. Its yellow button menus are the same as those of the last three panes of the system browser. Here the class browser is used to show a Monster's class definition. This description was obtained from the yellow button menu shown in the picture (selecting 'definition'), and the shown selection will cause a display of the class hierarchy (Object -> Monster) next (which is not shown). Note that the class description contains an item called 'poolDictionaries'. This feature can be used to share state among groups of classes. Since the concept is peripheral to most of Smalltalk's functionality we will not discuss it any further.

We will now proceed to add the CookieMonster's definition. Figure 4.17 shows the filled-in template for class *CookieMonster*.

Choosing 'accept' from the yellow button menu will compile this definition into the system. What remains to be done is to specify all the class and instance methods. Smalltalk aids the programmer in this task through dialogue boxes for specifying the method categories. Once a (class or instance) category is selected it will then display a template for method definitions. (See Figure 4.18.) We will not trace the whole

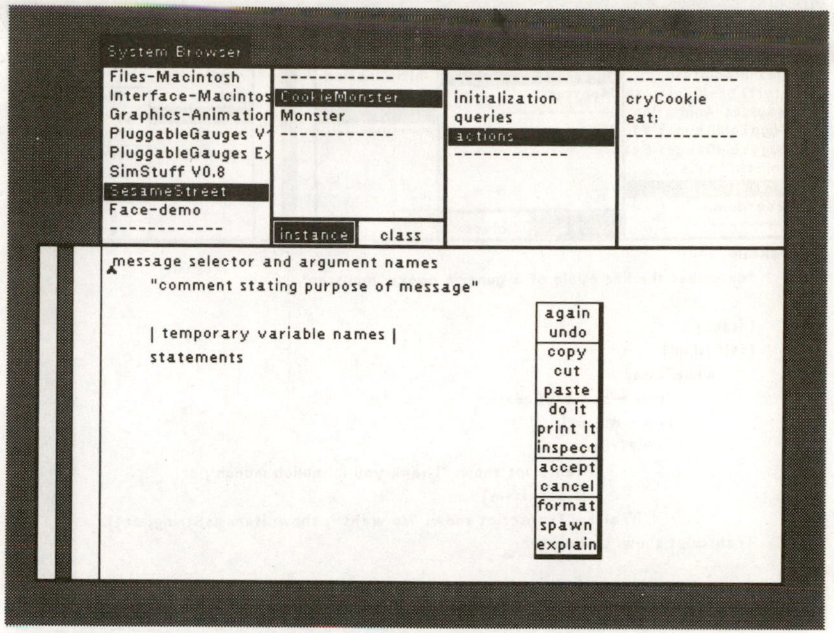

Figure 4.18 Prior to *wakeUp*'s definition.

process in detail, but will instead look at the state of the system again at the time the CookieMonster's *wakeUp* method is defined.

Filling the template and choosing 'accept' will add a method to the class. Figure 4.19 reflects this situation. In an object-oriented framework, messages separate functionality from implementation. Message protocols are used to describe a class's functionality by associating messages with methods. *Methods* are pieces of Smalltalk code, encapsulated within the body of class definitions, describing the details of data manipulation. Unlike conventional procedures, however, methods cannot directly 'call' other methods. An appropriate message must be sent instead. Two pseudo-variables, *self* and *super*, are provided to facilitate this. ***self*** always refers to the current context of execution; it may therefore be used by objects to send messages to themselves. ***super*** can be employed to access methods whose definition in one of an object's superclasses is 'shadowed' by a more local method of the same name. An up-arrow (↑) is used to indicate what value should be returned from a method. If this is not explicitly prescribed, the method returns the receiver of the message by which it was activated (that is, the object 'itself').

The *wakeUp* method shown in Figure 4.19 contains a **while** loop, guarded by a test on the contents of a CookieMonster's *tummy*. This loop repeatedly asks for a 'cookie'. If one is offered, a thank-you note is shown

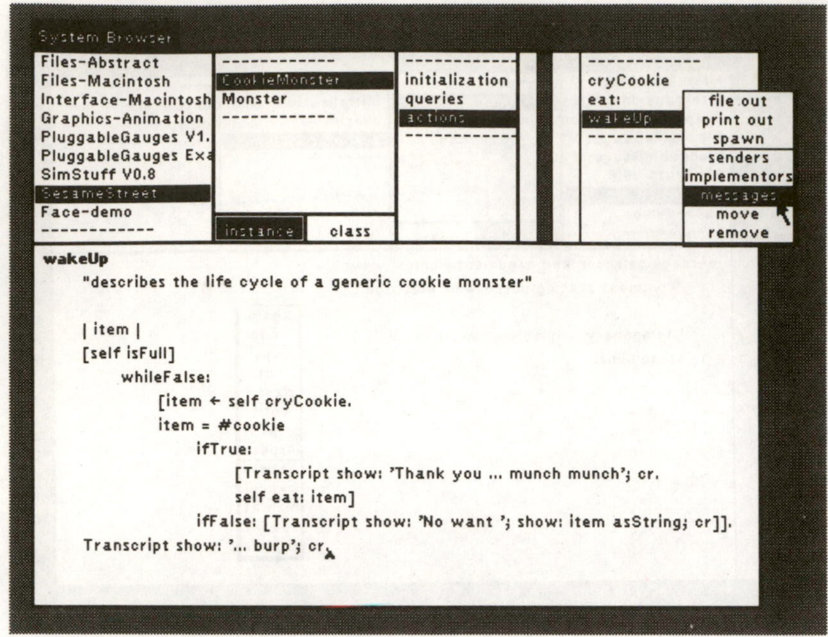

Figure 4.19 Defining the *wakeUp* method.

in the transcript, and only then is the cookie eaten (these are polite creatures). Any other item will be refused. This cycle will only terminate once the monster is 'full'. For the sake of completeness Figure 4.19 also shows the fourth pane's yellow button menu. Here we request to view all messages sent in this method definition although the resulting list is not shown. The menu also offers messages to browse all methods which send or implement a selected method. This functionality can often be very useful – for instance, if changes to the method header should necessitate modification of messages sent somewhere else in the system, it is easy to locate all these places.

We have now defined class *CookieMonster* and can start testing its responses. In a real application it would have been better to test each method as soon as it was written, but space limitations have prevented us from using such an approach. Let us look at the completed code before we proceed any further.

The class definition for *Monster*:

```
Object subclass: #Monster
       instanceVariableNames: 'colour'
       classVariableNames: 'Population'
       poolDictionaries:''
       category: 'SesameStreet'
```

Monster's class methods:

```
recordMonster
"count the number of monsters"
      Population isNil
            ifTrue: [Population ← 0]
            ifFalse: [Population ← Population + 1]

howManyMonstersAreThere
"return value of class variable Population"
      ↑ Population

makeWithColour: aString
"make and return a new monster instance"
|herman|
      herman ← self new.
      self recordMonster.
      ↑ herman
```

and its instance methods:

```
initializeWithColour: aString
"initialize instance variables of monster"
      colour ← aString.

colour
"show the beast's colour"
      ↑ colour

paint: aString
"assign a new value to colour"
      colour ← aString
```

The class definition for *CookieMonster*:

```
Monster subclass: #CookieMonster
   instanceVariableNames: 'tummy greed'
   classVariableName: ''
   poolDictionaries: ''
   category: 'SesameStreet'
```

CookieMonster has only one class method:

```
makeWithColour: aString andGreed: aNumber
"make and return a cookie monster instance"
|clara|
      clara ← self new.
      clara initializeWithColour: aString andGreed: aNumber.
      ↑ clara
```

but quite a number of instance methods:

```
initializeWithColour: aString andGreed: aNumber
"initialize instance variables of cookie monster"
    greed ← aNumber.
    tummy ← Bag new.
    super initializeWithColour: aString

greed
"show the cookie monster's greed"
    ↑ greed

isFull
"is the cookie monster still hungry ?"
    ↑ (tummy size >= greed)

tummy
"show the contents of the cookie monster's tummy"
    ↑ tummy

cryCookie
"keep asking for a cookie and return the item received"
|itemName|
    itemName ← FillInTheBlank
                    request: 'Give me cookie !!!!!! (please)'.
    ↑ itemName

eat: aString
"stuff item into tummy"
    tummy add: aString   "tummy is implemented as a bag"

wakeUp
"describes the life cycle of a generic cookie monster"
|item|
    [self isFull]
        whileFalse: [item ← self cryCookie.
                    item = #cookie
                        ifTrue: [Transcript show:
                                'Thank you . . . munch munch'; cr.
                            self eat: item]
                        ifFalse: [Transcript show: 'No want';
                                    show: item asString; cr]].
    Transcript show: '. . . burp'; cr
```

You will probably have noted that most messages are rather short. In fact, a large proportion of them consists of a comment followed by a single line of code, returning (↑) or assigning (←) some value. This is typical for object-oriented programs and Smalltalk code in particular, since all valid patterns of access to variables from outside an object's own scope must be procedurally defined. In our flavour system we provided the option of generating many such access procedures automatically (via switches:

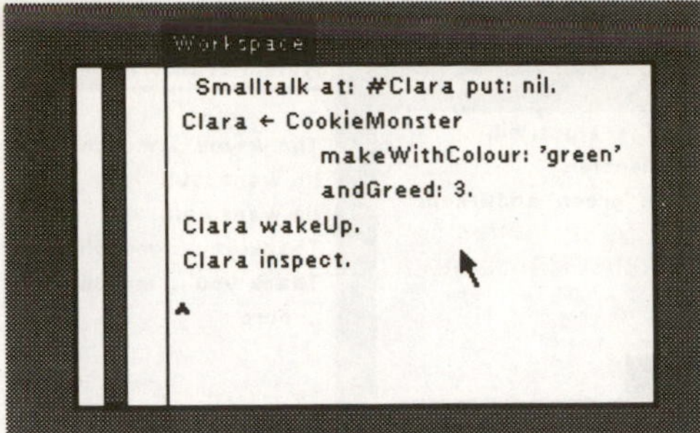

Figure 4.20 Making and waking a *CookieMonster.*

setivars, *getivars*, *testivars*). The flavour system without *setivars, getivars* and *testivars* would often be tedious to use. In the interest of reliability, however, many state variables should not be accessible at all from outside an object. Smalltalk's approach of requiring explicit method definitions for all 'outside' access to variables is facilitated by its programming environment. Since the browser allows quick definition of such selectors with only a few mouse clicks, modifying an already existing method, this is not particularly bothersome to do and it pays in terms of program reliability. In a traditional listing such method definitions would still clutter the code, but the browser largely eliminates the need for such documents.

We can now proceed to test our CookieMonster's behaviour by sending appropriate messages from a workspace. In Figure 4.20 we declare *Clara* as a global variable and bind it to a newly created green *CookieMonster* who lusts for three cookies. If we now send the *wakeUp* message the scenario shown in Figure 4.21 will unfold. Figure 4.21 shows a 'snapshot' of the message's execution. As we can see from the transcript,

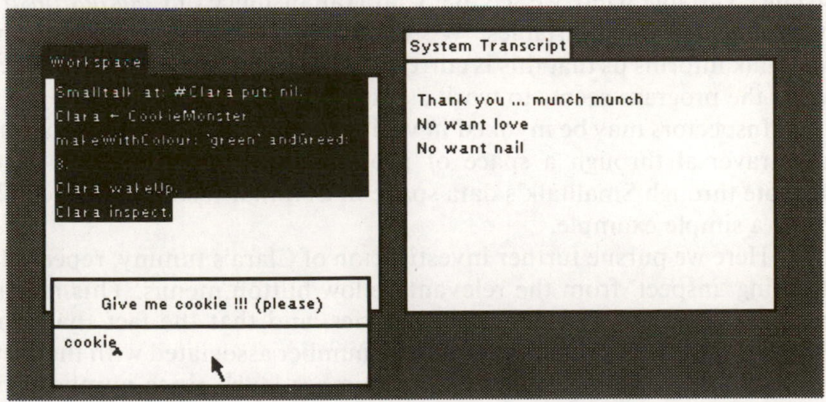

Figure 4.21 Begging for cookies.

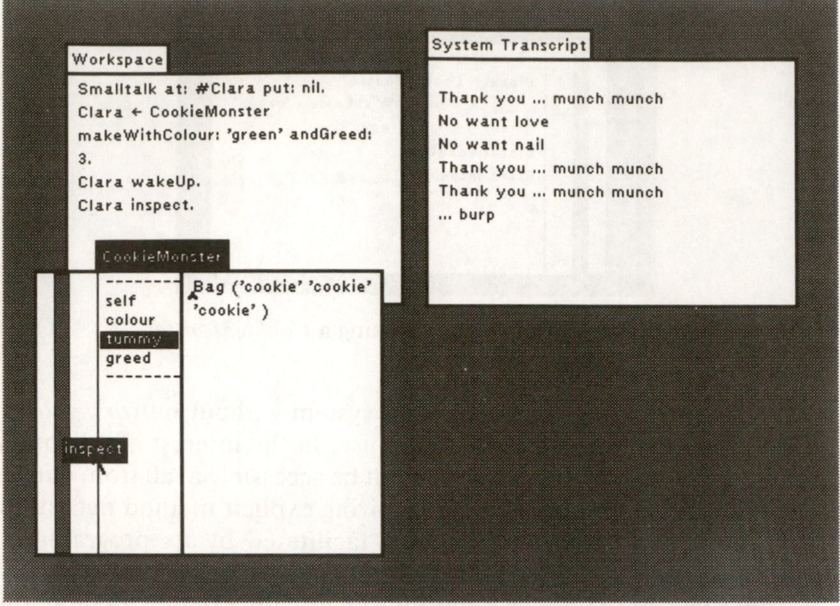

Figure 4.22 A view of *Clara*'s contents.

three items have so far been offered. Two of these, *love* and a *nail*, have been rejected, while the cookie has naturally been eaten. We also note that a second cookie is currently being tendered. After the third cookie is eaten, control will return to the workspace. We can then send an *inspect* message to Clara, in response to which an *inspector* window will be framed, which lets us view Clara's state (Figure 4.22).

Inspectors enable us to view an object's state at any time during a computation. They consist of a list view, with a list of instance variable names, and a text view which displays the current value of the selected instance variable. Here we see that Clara (an instance of *CookieMonster*) owns four instance variables. We choose to inspect her *tummy* and Smalltalk informs us that this is currently bound to a bag of three cookies. So far the program seems to work as expected.

Inspectors may be invoked in various ways. While browsers permit easy traversal through a space of procedures, inspectors allow us to navigate through Smalltalk's data space in a similar fashion. Figure 4.23 shows a simple example.

Here we pursue further investigation of Clara's tummy, repeatedly choosing 'inspect' from the relevant yellow button menus. This reveals that bags are implemented as dictionaries, and that the fact that item 'cookie' occurs three times is stored as a number associated with that key. Inspection then 'bottoms out' at the number level, since numbers are

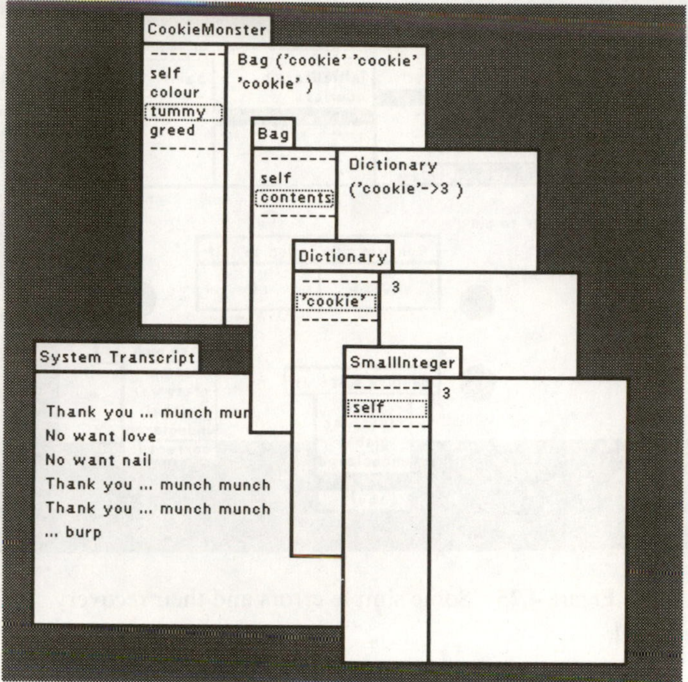

Figure 4.23 Inspection is recursive.

represented literally and cannot be inspected any further. Since *Clara* is globally defined, her state remains open for further inspection. We should also remember that we declared *Population* as a class variable of class *Monster*, and that we defined an access method for it. Sending *howManyMonstersAreThere* to *Clara*'s class reveals that there is currently only one, *Clara* herself (Figure 4.24).

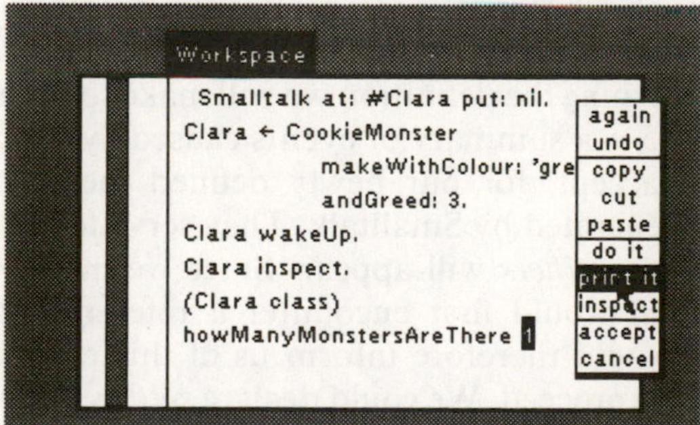

Figure 4.24 How many monsters are there?

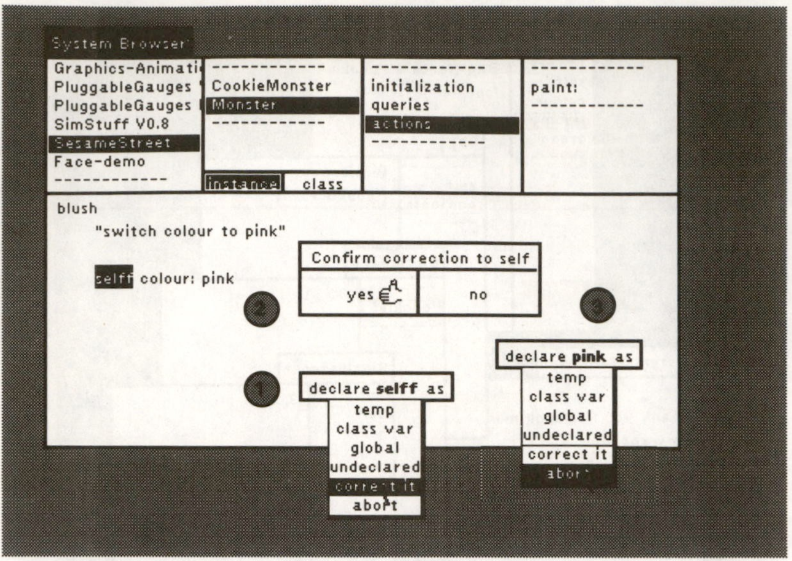

Figure 4.25 Some simple errors and their recovery.

One of the attractions of Smalltalk is its high degree of support for *error tracing* and *debugging*. The strong data encapsulation encouraged by the object-oriented programming style already provides for a considerable degree of robustness and reliability, since neither instance nor class variables can be 'fiddled with' directly. Although Smalltalk does not require variables to be typed, it performs a number of other checks. For instance, it will notify the programmer of all references to variables or methods which have not yet been declared, and it will make a reasonable attempt at spelling correction.

Let us assume that we would like to add a *blush* method to a *Monster's* protocol, so that the monster turns pink whenever it is embarrassed (such as when it has to decline a cookie if it is already 'full'). We can easily add such a method to class *Monster's action* protocol. However, while typing the definition we will make some simple mistakes.

Figure 4.25 is a summary of events caused by choosing the yellow button option 'accept' for our newly defined method. The numbers circled are not generated by Smalltalk. They serve to sequence the order in which various *notifiers* will appear. Since we mistyped '*selff colour: pink*', the system would first encounter a reference to an undefined object, *selff*. It would therefore inform us of this event and offer some options on how to proceed. We could declare *selff* as a new variable of the respective categories, we could abort the evaluation (for instance, to think for a while!) or we could ask the system to offer a suggestion on how

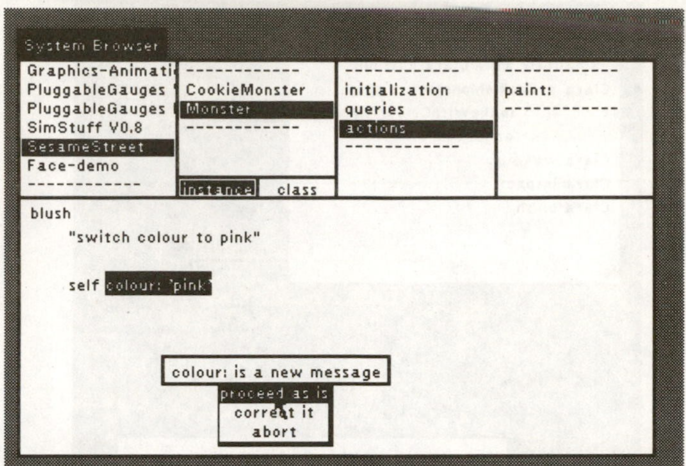

Figure 4.26 An unknown message selector is encountered.

the problem might be resolved. Here we chose the last option and Smalltalk's built-in spelling corrector suggests *self* as a plausible correction (2). This is of course what we intended to type all along, and we confirm this choice. Evaluation would therefore continue and *pink* would be encountered as an undeclared object. We immediately see that we forgot the enclosing apostrophes and, since it seems highly unlikely that the system would be 'intelligent' enough to suggest this correction, we abort execution, 'manually' change the code in the browser and choose 'accept' again. Not all is well, however, and a further error is encountered, a situation which is reflected by Figure 4.26.

colour: is an unknown message selector. Of course, we should have used *paint:* instead, but for argument's sake let us assume that we confirm *colour:* as a valid message, for which we intend to define a method later (by choosing 'proceed as is'). Let us also forget to do this. We may now try to test *blush* by sending it to *Clara*, our *CookieMonster*. A notifier will again appear (Figure 4.27). This time a run-time error has been encountered.

The notifier informs us that a message was sent to a CookieMonster which is not part of its protocol, or any of the protocols of its superclasses. '*Message not understood:*' is by far the most common execution-time error ever encountered in Smalltalk programs (others may include '*divide by zero*'). The notifier window shows a partial trace of the last few messages which were sent before the error occurred. Here we see that other than a few system-specific messages directed to the contents of the workspace and the compiler, a **doIt** message was sent. This is of course what we selected from the workspace's yellow button menu.

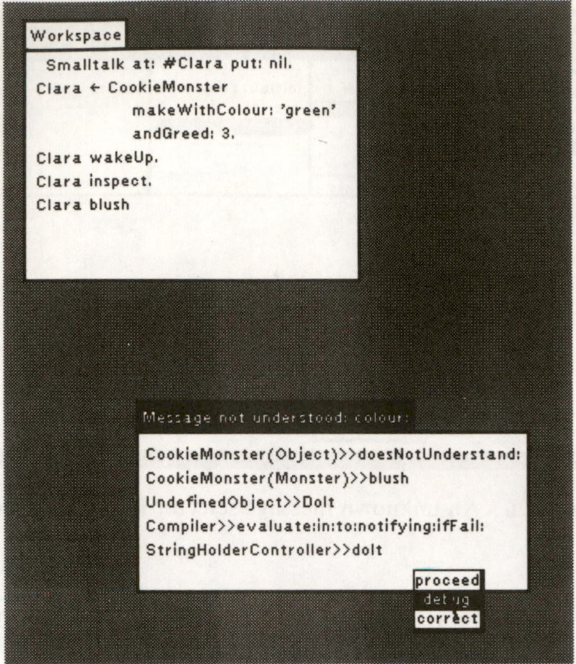

Figure 4.27 An unknown message has been received.

blush was then sent to *Clara*, a *CookieMonster*, and an implementation for this message was found in its superclass, *Monster*. An error must then have occurred somewhere in *blush*, since from there a *doesNotUnderstand* message was eventually sent to class *Object* (the root of Smalltalk's inheritance network), in response to which the notifier was created and scheduled. To trace this error the notifier's yellow button menu now offers three options; we choose 'debug'. A debugger window, as shown in Figure 4.28, will appear as a result.

Smalltalk's *debuggers* are composed of four panes, each with a different yellow button menu of options. The topmost pane allows us to scroll through the sequence of messages sent before the error occurred. The associated menu offers references to senders and implementors of selected messages and other useful information. Selecting a message in this context will display its definition in the large middle pane. The offending message and its receiver are highlighted. The middle pane's yellow button menu will now allow all the standard cutting, pasting and evaluation activities to be performed within the context of the selected message execution. The two lower panes offer inspectors on the receiver of the selected message and the context in which the message was sent (for example, the values of arguments if any). Each selected item may then be further inspected.

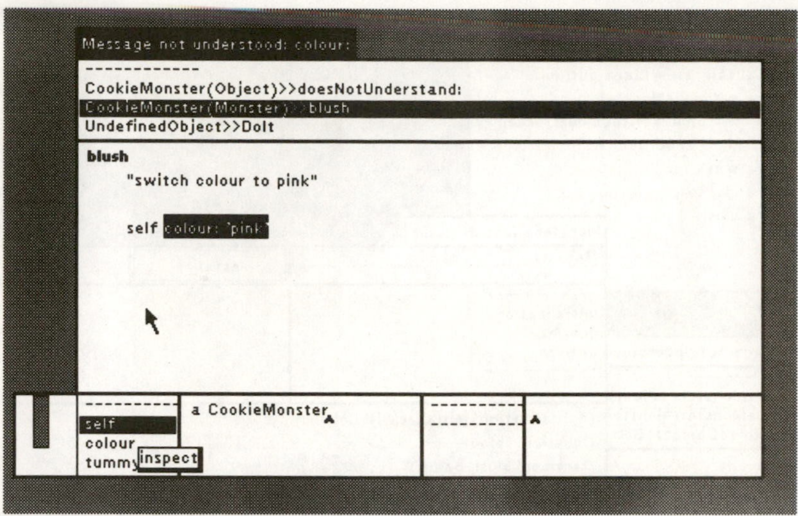

Figure 4.28 A debugger window.

Figure 4.29 shows our screen with a number of selections. We have viewed the *blush* message and noted that *colour:* was sent, but apparently not understood. Since it should have been defined either in class *Monster* or *CookieMonster* we have opened browsers on these two classes. From the yellow button menu of the *Monster* browser we have selected to view its 'instance protocols' (that is, the names of all methods in all the categories defined for this class). Inspection reveals that *colour:* is not among this list of valid method identifiers. Choosing *findMethod* from the yellow button menu of *CookieMonster* produces a menu of methods known to that class. Again, *colour:* is not among them. This should lead us to the conclusion that *colour:* was indeed not declared and we may perhaps remember that we intended, but forgot to define it. The 'bug' could easily be fixed by changing *colour:* to *paint:* and then compiling the method. This change could be made and accepted from within the middle pane of the debugger window, and 'proceed' could then be chosen from its top pane's yellow button menu. This should suffice to make *Clara* blush.

Although this example is admittedly somewhat contrived and simplistic, it may serve to convey some taste of the power and flexibility of Smalltalk's error detection and recovery tools. The important thing is that the whole system is always open for investigation. We may follow chains of messages that have been sent, and explore the contexts in which each was evaluated. Additionally we may inspect the state of any object, once some appropriate 'handle' has been obtained. The debugger makes it easy to access such handles, either by selecting information from what is listed in the two lower panes, or by selecting and evaluating message expressions in the middle one.

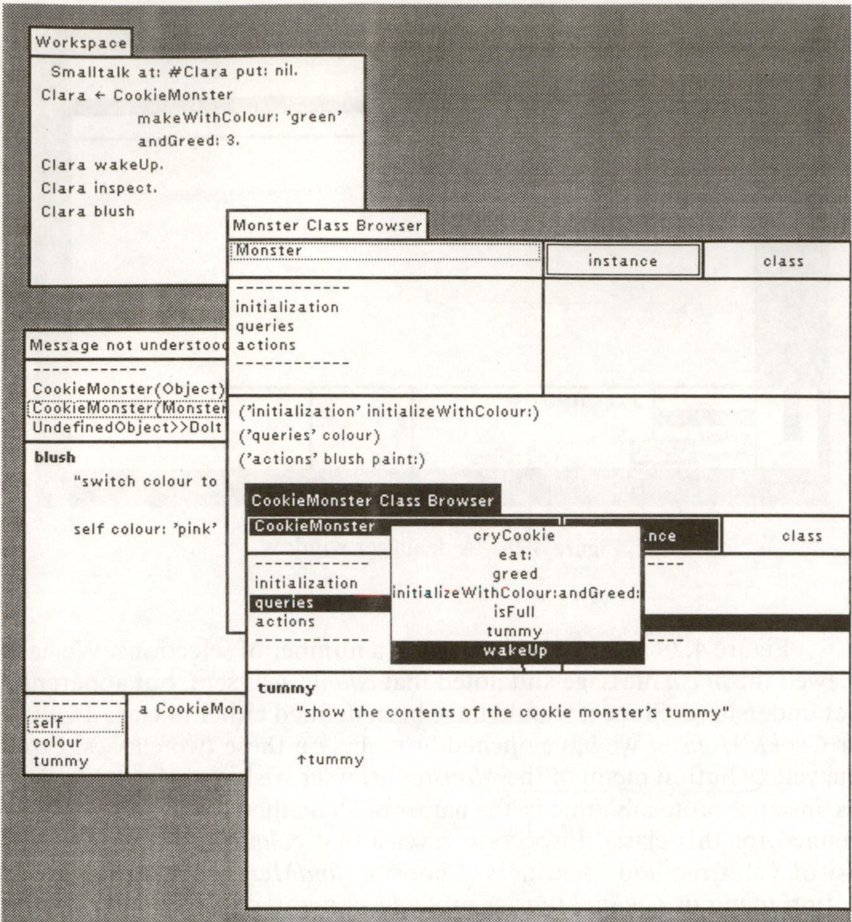

Figure 4.29 The debugger and two class browsers.

This concludes our discussion on how to write a simple Smalltalk application, a task in which browsers, workspaces, transcripts, inspectors, notifiers and debuggers all have a major role to play. Figure 4.30 summarizes this process.

A novice Smalltalk programmer may for a while be quite happy to explore the system and to build such simple programs. The exercises at the end of this chapter suggest a few examples. The reason why, from this point on, Smalltalk's learning curve is comparatively steep is because one must now become well acquainted with the functionality encoded in Smalltalk's large collection of predefined classes. This necessitates a period of frequent browsing, code reading and experimentation, after

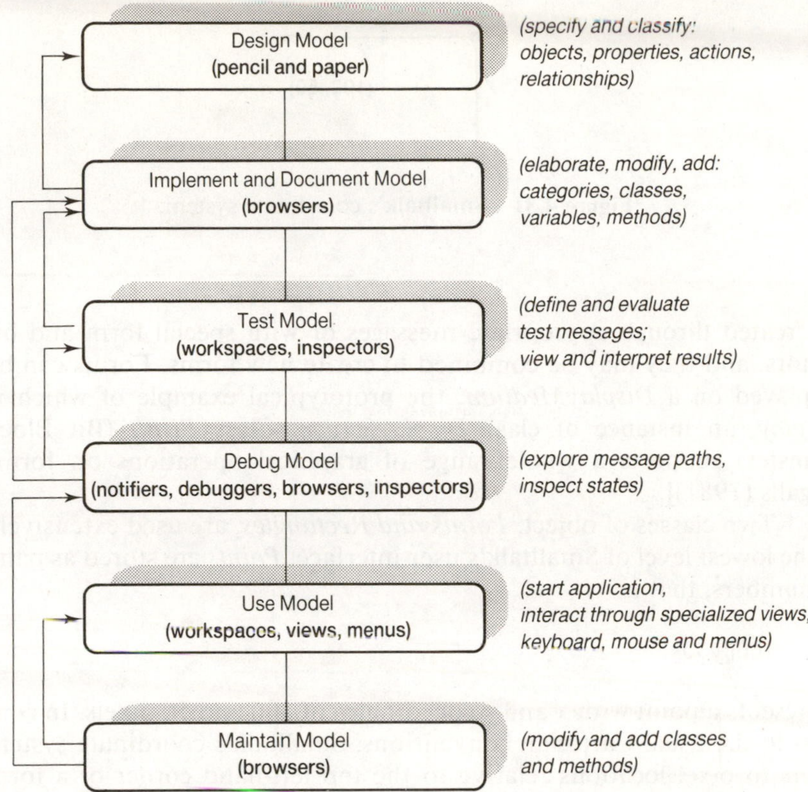

Figure 4.30 The Smalltalk development cycle.

which the programmer will have become confident enough to include and modify this code in his own programs. This process can be compared to the task of mastering large application libraries in a 'classical' language. Although Smalltalk's excellent support of object orientation and exploratory programming alone would make it an invaluable tool for complex software development tasks, such as the rapid prototyping of AI and modelling applications, much further functionality is offered. It is in graphical applications and for frameworks in which windows, menus and mouse-based user interaction are required that Smalltalk really shines. The next two sections will attempt to convey some of the flavour of such applications.

4.5 Some simple graphics – classes Pen and Form

Smalltalk's graphics system is built around a model of bit-mapped displays in which each pixel may be turned to black or white (1 or 0). Images are stored as *Forms*, which represent such bit-maps. **Forms** may

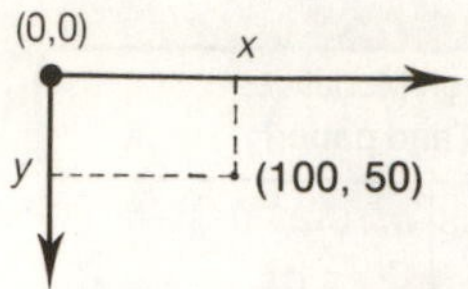

Figure 4.31 Smalltalk's coordinate system.

be created through appropriate messages or with special form and bit editors, and they may be combined to create new forms. Forms can be displayed on a *DisplayMedium*, the prototypical example of which is *Display*, an instance of class *DisplayScreen*. Class *BitBlt* (Bit Block Transfer) supports a whole range of graphical operations on forms [Ingalls (1981)].

Two classes of object, *Points and Rectangles*, are used extensively at the lowest level of Smalltalk's user interface. *Points* are stored as pairs of numbers, that is:

```
100@50
```

represents a point with *x* and *y* coordinates of 100 and 50 pixels. In contrast to the usual Cartesian conventions, Smalltalk's coordinate system refers to pixel locations relative to the top left-hand corner of a form (Figure 4.31). Values for *x* coordinates increase to the right (that is, they label columns), while values for *y* coordinates increase downwards (rows). Class *Point*'s message protocol offers a rich collection of transformations on points.

Rectangles are specified by giving two points, corresponding to their top left- and bottom right-hand corners. They represent rectangular areas of pixels and their message protocol contains a number of actions for scaling, translating, filling and other basic graphical operations.

Forms are a kind of display object with some width, some height and a relative coordinate system of their own (starting at 0@0). Complex images may be represented as single forms or as a structure of many forms together with rules for combining and repeating them. Two interactive editors for forms are provided: a *form editor* and a *bit editor*. We will soon see an example of how the bit editor may be used. There are three subclasses of *DisplayObject*: *DisplayMedium*, *DisplayText* and *Path*. *DisplayMedium* represents images which may be filled and bordered, *DisplayText* stores textual information in different styles and fonts, and *Path* is the superclass of all objects that represent image sequences. As with any other display object, forms can be copied, scaled and translated. Forms are the only subclass of *DisplayMedium*, but there are actually two other categories of forms, class *InfiniteForm* for describing repeating patterns and class *OpaqueForm*, in which part of the background image remains visible underneath a transparent part.

Smalltalk provides two further subclasses of *Form*, *Cursor* and *DisplayScreen*. Instances of class *Cursor* are defined as an area of 16 by 16 pixels, and a large number of such predefined symbols are used by the system to indicate different activities. In this way the user gets an immediate visual feedback on the task which is currently being performed. During time-consuming processes this can be very reassuring. For example, the cursor will show a blinking dot or hourglass during activities requiring a major amount of processing time, a vertical bar during garbage collection, a pair of spectacles while reading a file, a pen shape while writing a file, and so forth. Since a cursor is a special kind of form, it can be edited – by sending a message **edit** or **bitEdit** to it.

There is usually only one instance of *DisplayScreen* in the system, referred to by the global variable *Display*. The only case in which multiple instances may be convenient applies to graphical animations, where they may serve as hidden buffers to prepare new images while the current one is being displayed. Animations, however, will rarely require the whole of the screen. Typically they use only some smaller subarea, in which case any form can be displayed in the background.

Since forms are a fairly 'low-level' concept, and a novice Smalltalk programmer will often find it somewhat difficult to use them properly, Smalltalk also provides support for 'higher-level' drawing operations. Although straight lines, curves, arcs and circles are defined as subclasses of *Paths*, there is an easier way to draw simple pictures. Class **Pen** has been modelled on LOGO's turtle graphics [Abelson and diSessa (1981)]. It is a subclass of *BitBlt* which allows users to 'scribble' on the screen.

Figure 4.32 shows a *Pen*'s instance variables and categories of instance messages. This figure also demonstrates a feature for finding class definitions quickly. The number of classes in the Smalltalk system is very large, and it is often difficult to remember under which category a particular class may be found. There is a 'find class' option in the first browser pane's yellow button menu, which queries a user for a name or pattern and will then set the browser to show the relevant class's definition (if it exists). Here we detect that class *Pen* is categorized as a *Graphics-Primitive*. *Pens* have properties of *source* and *destination*, represented as forms. The destination form is usually associated with a display screen (normally the *Display*), while the source form describes what should be applied to this 'surface'. Following the original metaphor, one may view the source as the tip of the pen, and the destination as the writing surface. Apart from source and destination, pens also need a position (a point) and direction. Drawings may be created by moving pens to different screen locations and copying their source forms on to the destination form. In fact, knowledge of only a few messages suffices for simple pictures. **down** and **up** start and stop the copying process (that is, they put the pen on to and lift it off the form). Initially pens are located

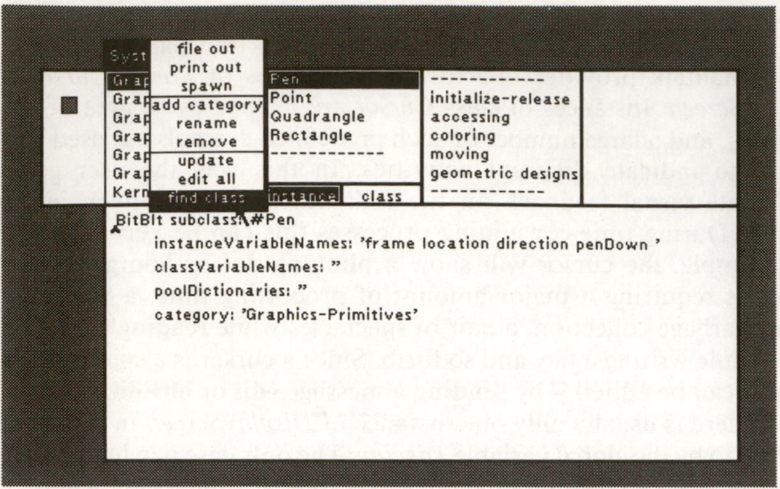

Figure 4.32 class *Pen*.

in the centre of the screen and point to the 'north'. **turn:** *a0to360number* will change this orientation, while **go:** *aNumberOfPixels* will move the pen in the currently indicated direction. One may also steer pens to a specified point, using **goTo:** *aPoint*. The source form is referred to as a pen's 'nib', which defaults to a dot of 1 black pixel. Erasers can easily be simulated by pens drawing with the screen's background colour (usually 'lightGray').

Smalltalk also supports a concept under which arrays of pens may be coordinated. This is referred to as a pen *Commander*, and Smalltalk contains a number of examples on how these can be employed to generate visually pleasing designs (such as polygons, spirals, dragon curves, Hilbert curves).

Let us look at two examples for drawing simple flower pictures. We will take some liberty with botany and propose a geometrical and abstract shape for a flower's presentation.

In our first example we will use pens to define flowers *algorithmically*. Under this interpretation a flower consists of a stem and any number of round petals. We must also insist that the stem is perfectly straight and we won't tolerate any distracting leaves. To draw such flowers we will first declare a number of auxiliary objects as temporary variables. Alternatively we could have defined *Flower* as a class, in which case these definitions should be encapsulated as instance variables.

First we need an area to draw in. This could be just any area on the screen, but we will get a better display if we frame a grey rectangle as its background. *canvas* will refer to such a region. Within this area we will next have to indicate where the flower should grow. *origin* will hold the coordinates of this position. *stemLength*, *petals* and *petalSize* characterize the prospective flower in terms of its properties, while *pen* and *petal* will be used to facilitate the drawing process.

```
"---------- draw a flower with circular petals ----------"
 |canvas origin stemLength petals petalSize
  pen petal|
```

The first actions of our program will be to initialize these variables. We therefore create a *canvas*, as an instance of class *Quadrangle*. *Quadrangle*s 'own' a rectangular *region* which may be filled with a pattern. We could have defined the region through absolute or relative (to the canvas) coordinate values, but it is often more convenient to indicate points and rectangles by using the mouse. '*Rectangle fromUser*' sends the *fromUser* class message to class *Rectangle*. In response the system will prompt us for a new rectangle's upper left-hand and lower right-hand corners. We indicate these through mouse clicks and framing the rectangle's image. The resulting area will now be assigned to *canvas*, after which we may fill it with a grey background. The flower's growing position can be determined in a similar way. '*Sensor waitButton*' will wait until the red mouse button is pressed and return the cursor's position at that moment.

```
"where to draw it ?"
canvas ← Quadrangle new.
canvas region: Rectangle fromUser.
canvas insideColour: Form lightGray.
canvas display.
origin ← Sensor waitButton.
"initialize sizes"
stemLength ← 70. petals ← 5. petalSize ← 20.
```

Now that background and planting position are defined, we may proceed to draw a stem. To do this we make a black source form. The default destination form is always set to *Display*, so that we do not need to worry about this aspect. Since we want the stem nice and lush we will set the pen's tip (nib) to a width of 4 pixels. Thereafter we move it to the growing position without drawing, and then start the drawing process itself.

```
"draw the stem"
pen ← (Pen new) mask: Form black; defaultNib: 4.
pen up; goto: origin; down; north; go:stemLength.
```

Note that the last expression is a 'cascade' (separated by semicolons) of five messages which are all sent to the pen. Since we wish to take a perfectionist stance and assume perfectly round petals, we may show petals as circles. To draw them we must tell the pen to run through their centres,

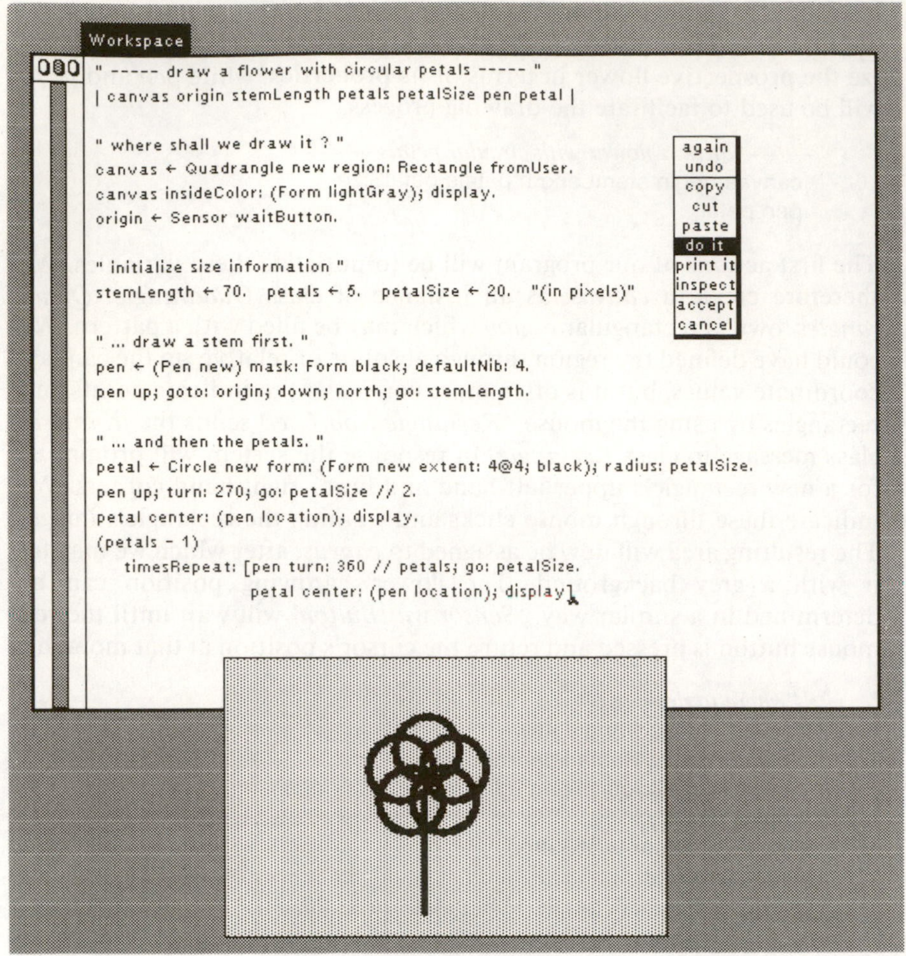
Workspace
" ----- draw a flower with circular petals ----- "
| canvas origin stemLength petals petalSize pen petal |
" where shall we draw it ? "
canvas ← Quadrangle new region: Rectangle fromUser.
canvas insideColor: (Form lightGray); display.
origin ← Sensor waitButton.
" initialize size information "
stemLength ← 70. petals ← 5. petalSize ← 20. "(in pixels)"
" ... draw a stem first. "
pen ← (Pen new) mask: Form black; defaultNib: 4.
pen up; goto: origin; down; north; go: stemLength.
" ... and then the petals. "
petal ← Circle new form: (Form new extent: 4@4; black); radius: petalSize.
pen up; turn: 270; go: petalSize // 2.
petal center: (pen location); display.
(petals - 1)
timesRepeat: [pen turn: 360 // petals; go: petalSize.
petal center: (pen location); display]
again
undo
copy
cut
paste
do it
print it
inspect
accept
cancel

Figure 4.33 Drawing a flower.

without actually drawing anything, and to draw a new circle every *petalSize* pixels. The following procedure shows how to do this. // indicates integer division.

```
"now draw the petals"
petal ← Circle new
        form: (Form new extent: 4@4; black);
        radius: petalSize.
pen up; turn: 270; go: petalSize // 2.
petal center: (pen location); display.
(petals – 1) timesRepeat: [pen turn: 360 // petals; go: petalSize.
                           petal center: (pen location); display]
```

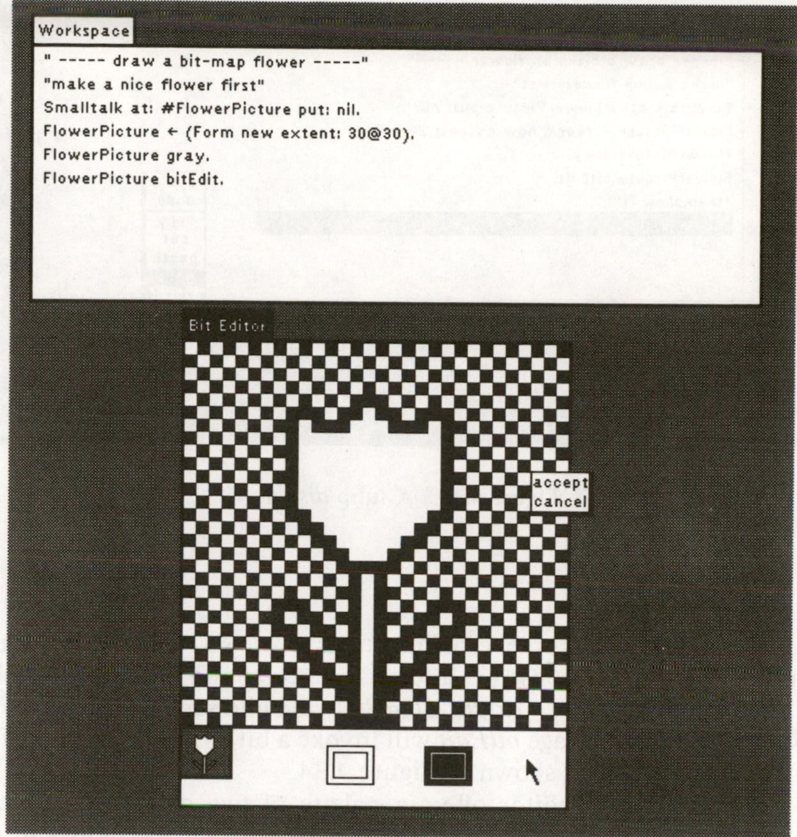

Figure 4.34 A *Form* for a tulip.

Observe that a petal is stored as an instance of a *Circle* of the right radius and a 4*4 black rim. Figure 4.33 shows how a five-petalled flower with these measurements will present itself. Although this picture would swell many a father's breast in pride, it would probably not win any prizes as an entry in a flower show. Smalltalk, however, offers alternative ways to paint objects. Forms may be read (for instance, as digitized images) and edited directly as bitmaps, using a form or a bit editor. Smalltalk's **form editor** is a precursor of the well-known *MacPaint* program and offers a subset of this program's features for working with the 'brush and paint' metaphor. By turning individual bits 'on' or 'off', the **bit editor** allows more fine-grained picture construction. Let us use it to draw a slightly less regular flower. Since the authors' drawing skills are somewhat limited, we opt for drawing a tulip, which is comparatively easy. This time we will provide leaves (two in fact), and we could also cater for other

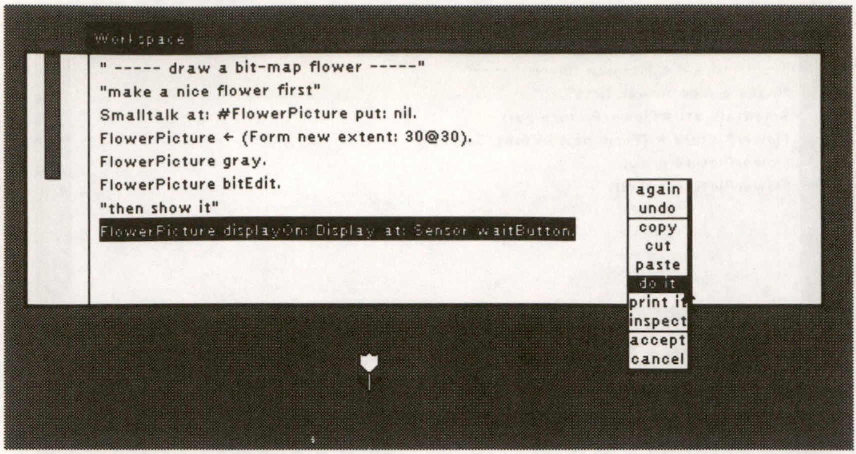

Figure 4.35 A tulip *display.*

imperfections (for example, crooked stems) if we so wished. To achieve our objective we will construct a form for a tulip and bind it to a global *FlowerPicture.* '*Form new extent: 30@30*' will build such a form (30 by 30 pixels wide), and message *bitEdit* will invoke a bit editor on it. The effect of these invocations is shown in Figure 4.34.

Smalltalk's bit editor offers a palette of two colours, black and white. Bits can be turned black or white, by clicking the mouse in the main area. The little insert in Figure 4.34 shows how a picture will look on the screen. Note that the background is coloured in a chessboard pattern. The reason is that we requested a *gray* form before the editor was invoked, and that this is the way in which a *gray* background is simulated in Smalltalk. Now that we have defined our tulip we would like to display it on the screen. '*FlowerPicture displayOn: Display at: Sensor waitButton*' will prompt for a location and show it there (Figure 4.35). Note that the grey form blends in nicely with the screen's background colour.

We can now replicate or animate our flower. Figure 4.36 shows how to grow a 'path' of five flowers in a row. We simply define a starting location, create a *Path* object of *FlowerPictures* and shift this image by 25 pixels to the right five times, adding these images to the path. *add:* expects a point as an argument. '+' sent to a point will add it to another one, so that the first tulip will grow at a point defined by the origin's x coordinate + 25 and the origin's y coordinate + 0. We could easily extend this example to a true animation, by telling Smalltalk to restore the background once a new path image has been shown. Since real tulips can't walk, however, we will refrain from having them do so here.

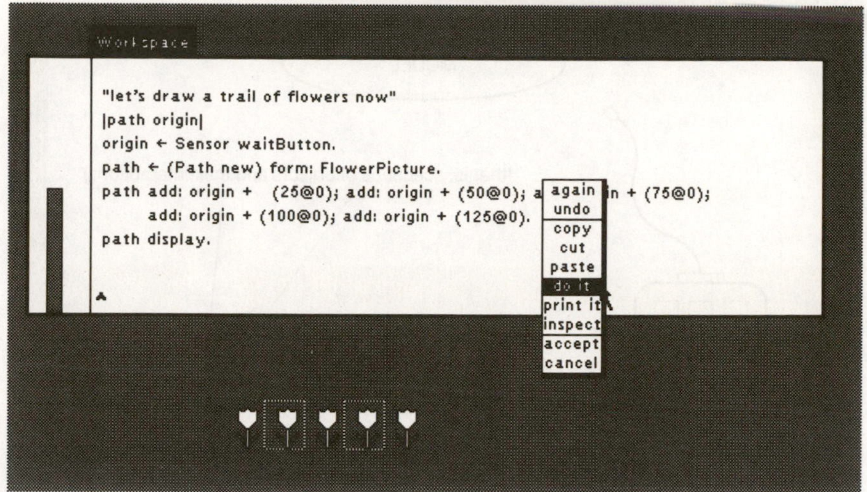

Figure 4.36 A garden *Path*.

Any more detailed discussion of form manipulation is beyond the scope of this book. Goldberg and Robson (1983) contains some information on this, but in the end browsing and experimentation with the code for the relevant classes is unavoidable. What should be appreciated is the rich functionality offered by Smalltalk's graphics framework, which provides support for a wide range of tasks, from drawing simple pictures to complex animations.

4.6 FaceWorld – an example of the model–view–controller (MVC) metaphor

One of the key features of the Smalltalk-80 system is its highly interactive and multi-window user interface. The examples we have explored so far have been very limited in their style of output presentation and user interaction. In *SesameStreet*, all output went to the *Transcript* and input was only obtained from a query box. The *flower* examples simply scribbled on the screen and accepted some input from mouse clicks. We even need to invoke 'restore display' from the top-level yellow button menu to get rid of our artwork. Although we provide a canvas as a background form for our program to draw on, this area is simply a filled rectangle, in a fixed position on the screen, not a window which can be collapsed, closed or moved. We have previously mentioned that Smalltalk provides an excellent framework for building graphical animations and interactive user interfaces, and a number of applications give

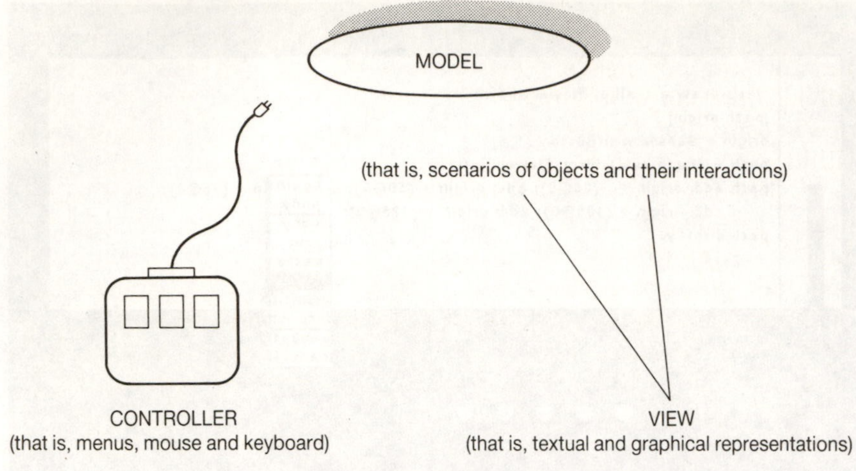

Figure 4.37 The model–view–controller (MVC) metaphor.

evidence for this claim – for example, *SimulationKit* [Goldberg and Robson (1979)], *ThingLab* [Borning (1981)], *Animus* [London and Duisberg (1985)], *Humble* [Piersol (1987)], *PluggableGauges* [Adams (1987)], *Ollie* [Kubitzsch and Strauch (1987)], *ThinkerToy* [Gutfreund (1987)] and others. What is surely minimally required for such applications is some means by which windows can be used for textual and graphical output, and also some way in which menu- and mouse-driven input can be supported.

The central concepts behind the way in which a Smalltalk program can build such interfaces are referred to as the so-called *model–view–controller* (**MVC**) **metaphor**. To use this idea effectively one must first understand how these three components interact (Figure 4.37).

To make full use of this framework's conceptual power one must also learn about the many prepackaged subclasses of *view* and *controller*, which offer a ready-made starting point for many typical applications.

Smalltalk separates three aspects of a program. The term *model* refers to the data and functionality contained in all classes which are relevant to a particular task domain. A *view* presents textual and graphical information on the screen, and a *controller* interprets mouse or keyboard inputs from the user. The objects representing the model will typically respond to requests for information about their state (from a view) and to instructions to change it (from a controller).

In many simple applications this separation of tasks need not concern the programmer at all. The controller will notify all dependent views of changes resulting from user requests, which may then poll their models to update the representation of their state. Using standard components for view and controller, the model may remain unaware of the other two components' existence. Sometimes, however, the model will need to change in response to messages other than those sent by the view or controller. In this case the views depending on any of those values will have to be notified. Models often do not own direct links to their views, which could be used to propagate such information. There is instead a global dictionary, which records all such dependencies and enters this information when a new view for a model is built. The 'updating' protocol of class *Object* provides the necessary functionality for model/view communication. The message '**changed**' may be sent when such a change of state has occurred. In response, an *update:* message is sent to all that model's dependents, and propagated to all of their dependents in turn, and so forth until the 'bottom' level is reached. The argument of the *update:* will be the changed model itself. Most standard views will have some protocol to redisplay themselves appropriately in response to *update:* messages.

Of course, an object can have more than a single active view in which case all of these would be informed. Views, however, act as intermediaries between particular classes of objects and the display. They must therefore be uniquely bound to a single model and a single controller. The same restriction also applies to controllers. Those two objects therefore need to 'own' instance variables with pointers to their respective partners (*model*, *view* in controllers, *controller* in views). Views take the initiative for instantiating the links between the three components of an MVC structure. Upon receipt of a **model:controller:** message they will register themselves as a model's dependent, set their *controller* variables and pass a message '*view: self*' to the controller so that object can set its variable accordingly. Since it is often the case that views wish to contain subviews that contain subviews, . . ., class *View* supports this idea and Smalltalk's user environment itself makes good use of it. The system browser, for example, is composed of five subviews. The standard coordinate transformations to support such a framework are handled automatically. *StandardSystemViews*, a subclass of *View*, represent generic window behaviour. Instances of this class have a location and extent on the screen, and they may be moved and transformed according to the options provided by their blue button menus. An application designer may subclass it to add special functionality needed for his application, or he may use it as a top view for some structured collection of subviews.

As for views, a number of predefined controllers are provided as part of the Smalltalk system and can be used 'off the shelf' or subclassed appropriately. Most of these will be a subclass of the prototypical *MouseMenuController*, whose instance variables refer to red, blue and yellow button messages and methods. All top-level controllers are

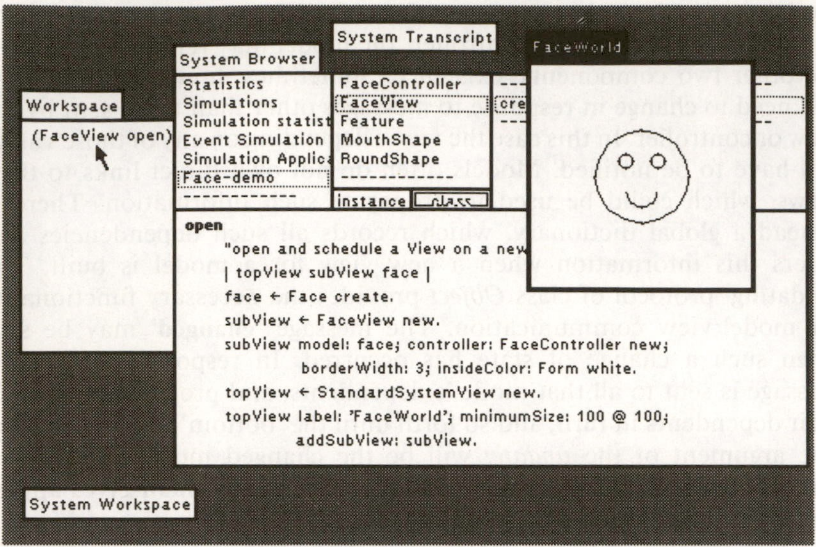

Figure 4.38 A *FaceWorld* window.

instances of class *StandardSystemController*, a subclass of *MouseMenuController* which manages the standard blue button menu for navigating windows across the screen. In a typical case a controller will use the standard blue button menu at the top level and implement its own menu of yellow button activities. The *FaceWorld* example will demonstrate this.

Let us now look at what is involved in writing a simple, window-based graphical application. This time we will choose **FaceWorld** as our task domain. To keep the model simple we constrain our efforts to the construction of cartoon-like pictures of faces on the screen. The faces themselves should be easy enough to draw, but we will also require that they reside in a movable and resizeable window. In addition we wish to define a few transformations on faces, such as *happy*, *sad* and *wink*, which should be selected from menus. When our program starts up it will query for characteristics of a face's four components: a contour, two eyes and a mouth. It will then build an appropriate view, in which the face will be centred and drawn. Figure 4.38 shows an example.

The application was started from the partly obscured workspace, by evaluating the message expression '*FaceView open*'. Figure 4.38 also shows a browser in which various classes in *FaceWorld* are visible, together with the definition of the '**open**' message. FaceWorld's model is represented by class *Face*, which owns a contour, two eyes and a mouth.

It also holds a reference to an *activeView*, although this is not strictly required in view of our discussion.

```
Object subclass: #Face
    instanceVariableNames: 'activeView
   origin contour leftEye rightEye mouth'
   classVariableNames: ''
   poolDictionaries: ''
   category: 'Face-demo'
```

"The Face class serves as the 'model' for this example. Faces are composed of a contour of circular shape, two eyes and a mouth. The 'origin' of the face is located in the centre of its 'activeView' and is updated by the 'showFace' method prior to its display, which is triggered automatically by the 'displayView' method of the FaceView object each time the view is moved."

There is a class method for making a face:

```
create
|fred|
  fred ← self new.
  fred makeContour.
  fred addDetails.
  ↑ fred
```

and a number of instance methods of various categories:

```
Face methodsFor: 'initialization'

addDetails
"fill in the missing parts"
   rightEye ← EyeShape create.
   rightEye owner: self; orientation: 'right'.
   leftEye ← EyeShape create.
   leftEye owner: self; orientation: 'left'.
   mouth ← MouthShape create.
   mouth owner: self

makeContour
   contour ← RoundShape create.
   contour owner: self

Face methodsFor: 'actions'

happy
  mouth showHappy

sad
  mouth showSad
```

```
wink
|numberOfTimes|
  numberOfTimes ←
   (FillInTheBlank request:
     'How many winks would you like to see ?') asNumber.
  leftEye flipToBlack: numberOfTimes
```

Face methodsFor: 'positioning'

```
where
  ↑ activeView where
```

Face methodsFor: 'display'

```
showFace
  self origin: self where.
  contour show.
  rightEye show.
  leftEye show.
  mouth show
```

Face methodsFor: 'queries'

```
isHappy
  ↑ mouth mood = 'happy'

isSad
  ↑ self isHappy not
```

Face methodsFor: 'access'

```
activeView
  ↑ activeView

activeView: aView
  activeView ← aView

contour
  ↑ contour

contour: aShape
  contour ← aShape

origin
  ↑ origin

origin: aPoint
  origin ← aPoint
```

Class *Feature* will be used to combine aspects common to all facial features. *owner* and *size* are two of those. Individual features (for example, eyes, mouth) may then be described by subclassing.

```
Object subclass: #Feature
    instanceVariableNames: 'owner size'
    classVariableNames: ''
    poolDictionaries: ''
    category: 'Face-demo'
```

"This class represents some common functionality of facial features. Its 'create' method is used by all of the feature classes. There are two instance variables. 'owner' provides a link to the face instance a feature instance is associated with (this is needed to obtain a reference to its current centre) and 'size' stores the extent of a feature (normally its radius in the case of eyes and mouths)."

Again there is a class method for feature creation:

```
create
|fred|
fred ← self new.
fred initialize.
↑ fred
```

and appropriate instance methods:

Feature methodsFor: 'initialization'

```
initialize
  size ← (FillIn TheBlank request:
            'What is the size of this feature ?') asNumber
```

Feature methodsFor: 'access'

```
owner
  ↑ owner

owner: anObject
  owner ← anObject

size
  ↑ size

size: aNumber
  size ← aNumber
```

Feature's subclasses include *RoundShape* (for contour and eyes):

```
Feature subclass: #RoundShape
    instanceVariableNames: ''
    classVariableNames: ''
    poolDictionaries: ''
    category: 'Face-demo'
```

"This class represents and displays round shapes as 'empty' circles. In this example it is used to instantiate a face's contour"

Here there are no further class methods and only a couple of instance methods. The *show* method is the interesting one. It makes an appropriate circle and shows it on the screen:

RoundShape methodsFor: 'positioning'

```
where
    ↑ owner where
```

RoundShape methodsFor: 'display'

```
show
|form circle|
    form ← Form new extent: 1 @ 1.
    form black.
    circle ← Circle new.
    circle form: form.
    circle radius: size.
    circle center: (self where).
    circle display
```

EyeShape inherits from *RoundShape.* Eyes will have an orientation, depending on whether they have been instantiated as a left or a right eye. The *isWhere* method is of special interest, since it defines the eye's position relative to the centre of the view in which it is displayed. 'Winking' is implemented by turning an eye to an eye-sized black dot any specified number of times, with an appropriate delay (0.1 seconds) between each wink.

```
Feature subclass: #EyeShape
    instanceVariableNames: 'orientation'
    classVariablenames:''
    poolDictionaries:''
    category: 'Face-demo'
```

"This class defines the shape of an eye as a round shape (a white circle or a black dot). It is a subclass of 'Feature' and adds an instance variable called 'orientation', which is either 'left' or 'right'. This variable is needed by the 'isWhere: . . .' method to determine its position within a face's contour."

Again, there are no class methods.

EyeShape methodsFor: 'positioning'

```
isWhere: anOrientation
|viewCenter coordinates|
 viewCenter ← owner where.
 anOrientation = 'right'
   ifTrue:
    [coordinates ←
                  (viewCenter x − (owner contour size / 3)) @
                  (viewCenter y − (owner contour size / 3))]
   ifFalse:
    [coordinates ←
                  (viewCenter x + (owner contour size / 3)) @
                  (viewCenter y − (owner contour size / 3))]
 ↑ coordinates
```

EyeShape methodsFor: 'display'

```
eraseBlackForm
  (Form dotOfSize: self size * 2 + 1) white;
     displayAt: (self isWhere: orientation)

flipToBlack: aNumberOfTimes
  aNumberOfTimes timesRepeat: [self showBlackForm.
                               (Delay forSeconds: 0.1) wait.
                               self eraseBlackForm.
                               self show]

show
|form circle|
   form ← Form new extent: 1 @ 1.
   form black.
   circle ← Circle new.
   circle form: form; radius: size; center: (self isWhere: orientation).
   circle display

showBlackForm
   (Form dotOfSize: self size * 2 + 1)
      displayAt: (self isWhere: orientation)
```

EyeShape methodsFor: 'access'

```
orientation
   ↑ orientation

orientation: aString
   orientation ← aString
```

MouthShape is an example of 'non-round' features. Mouths are represented as two arcs (quarter-circles). Depending on *mood*, mouths may be happy or sad. If they are asked to redisplay themselves after a change in mood they must first erase their 'old' image. This is accomplished by redrawing the shape with a white pen.

```
Feature subclass: #MouthShape
    instanceVariableNames: 'mood'
    classVariableNames: ''
    poolDictionaries: ''
    category: 'Face-demo'
```

"This class displays a mouth as 2 circular arcs. It is a subclass of 'Feature' and adds one new instance variable, 'mood'. This variable is used by its 'show' method to determine whether a 'happy' or 'sad' face is to be drawn. Note that the old path must be erased before it can be redrawn in a new shape. This happens in the two private 'erase . . .' methods."

Again there are no additional class methods.

MouthShape methodsFor: 'private'

```
eraseDownBend
|form|
  form ← Form new extent: 1 @ 1.
  form white.
  self showBendWithFirstQ: 1
              andSecondQ: 2
                 andForm: form

eraseUpBend
|form|
  form ← Form new extent: 1 @ 1.
  form white.
  self showBendWithFirstQ: 4
              andSecondQ: 3
                 andForm: form

showBendWithFirstQ: a1to4
        andSecondQ: another1to4
           andForm: aForm
|arc position|
  arc ← Arc new.
  position ← self where.
  arc form: aForm; radius: size; center: position;
     quadrant: a1to4.
  arc display.
  arc ← Arc new.
  arc form: aForm; radius: size; center: position;
     quadrant: another1to4.
  arc display
```

MouthShape methodsFor: 'display'

```
show
  self owner isHappy
     ifTrue: [self showHappy]
     ifFalse: [self showSad]
```

```
showHappy
|form|
  mood ← 'happy'.
  self eraseDownBend.
  form ← Form new extent: 1 @ 1.
  form black.
  self where y: self where y − size.
  self showBendWithFirstQ: 3
            and SecondQ: 4
                andForm: form

showSad
|form|
  mood ← 'sad'.
  self eraseUpBend.
  form ← Form new extent: 1 @ 1.
  form black.
  self where y: self where y + size.
  self showBendWithFirstQ: 2
            and SecondQ: 1
                andForm: form
```

MouthShape methodsFor: 'initialization'

```
initialize
"Mouths are always initialized in the 'Up' position !!"
  super initialize.
  mood ← 'happy'
```

MouthShape methodsFor: 'positioning'

```
where
| viewCenter offset |
 viewCenter ← owner where.
  self owner isHappy
    ifTrue: [offset ← (owner contour size / 3)]
    ifFalse: [offset ← (owner contour size / 3)].
 ↑ viewCenter x @ (viewCenter y + offset)
```

MouthShape methodsFor: 'access'

```
mood
   ↑ mood

mood: aString
   mood ← aString
```

The following definitions of view and controller entities are the most interesting parts of this program. The 'view' represents the window in which a face will display itself. We will call our view a *FaceView*, and we will make it a subclass of *View*. *FaceView* has three components, a top view, a subview and a model of the face itself. When it is 'opened' it will first create a new *Face* (the 'model') and an instance of itself as a 'subview'. *FaceView* then sends appropriate messages to its top view and subviews in order to install its dependency relationships (their links to a model and controller) in the global *DependentFields* dictionary. Since this application has no particularly special requirement we may just use an instance of *StandardSystemView* as our 'top view', to which we add the face's image as a subview. This has the advantage that the *StandardSystemView* protocol will automatically ensure that our window will follow all of the standard Smalltalk user interface conventions – that is, for selection, movement, resizing, and so on. To this we will then add a new yellow button menu for the *FaceView* subview, associated with the appropriate methods for computing any of those actions which faces are willing to perform. While we may delegate the window handling itself to the default controller for *StandardSystemView*, which is associated with our top view, we will have to define our own *MouseMenuController* to control the selection of facial expressions.

```
View subclass: #FaceView
    instanceVariableNames: ''
    classVariableNames: ''
    poolDictionaries: ''
    category: 'Face-demo'
```

"This class is used to provide a 'View' of our model (face). When 'opened' it creates a new face as its 'model', and a 'StandardSystemView' as a labelled, movable and collapsible window (assembled in local variable 'topView') for its view of the face (assembled in local variable 'subview'). The controller for the 'topView' shows the standard 'blue' button behaviour, while a new FaceController is associated with the 'subView' to cater for a special menu obtained through the 'yellow' mouse button (defined in class 'FaceController')."

open is the name of the class method which creates and schedules this view.

FaceView class methodsFor: 'creation'

```
open
  "open and schedule a View on a new face"
|topView subView face|
  face ← Face create.
  subView ← self new.
  subView model: face;
      controller: FaceController new;
      borderWidth: 3;
      insideColor: Form white.
  topView ← StandardSystemView new.
  topView label: 'FaceWorld'; minimumSize: 100 @ 100;
           addSubView: subView.
  topView controller open
```

There are also a number of instance methods, for displaying the view, updating it after each change and determining the centre of the window's new position after it has been moved. The *update:* message is a crucial component in this. Each time a change has occurred, it will automatically be sent by a view to each of its registered dependents. The *activeView:* message provides a handle of the view to the model, so that the position of the window's new centre is known. Smalltalk actually lets you work with relative coordinates, while performing the necessary transformations in the background. Using this feature, we can 'get rid of' the need for explicit reference to the *activeView* instance variable, while making our program more flexible. We will leave this modification as an exercise in preparation for which you may like to browse through class *View's display transformation* methods.

```
FaceView methodsFor: 'display'

displayView
"show a face - this message is sent automatically by 'update: . . .' "
    model activeView: self.
    model showFace

update: aParameter
"this method is sent automatically each time the view's position is changed
or if a 'changed' message is received by the view's model. The parameter
may be used to transmit information about a change's reason. It is not used
in this example."
    self display

FaceView methodsFor: 'positioning'

where
"use the coordinates of the view's bounding box to compute the absolute
coordinates at which the model will draw itself"
    ↑ self insetDisplayBox center x @ self insetDisplayBox center y
```

Finally, we need to define a *FaceController*, to handle the menu of actions associated with the face transformations themselves. We will make it a subclass of *MouseMenuController*, and an instance of such a controller is attached to the view's subview (the face's image) during the view's opening ceremony. This subview will only respond to our customized yellow button menu. While in its range the blue mouse button will be disabled. There are, however, applications where control of mouse activity through selection (red button) is vital – for instance, by pointing to and selecting an object through clicking on its symbol, typing text or drawing pictures, and so on. Schmucker (1986a) shows an example of a Smalltalk program to handle a 'microworld' in which a range of geometrical shapes may be drawn and selected using a mouse controller attached to an appropriately defined subview. Some of the exercises at the end of this chapter will also give some hints on how to explore such scenarios. If this type of interaction was asked for, then this would need to be specified here, and the controller would be responsible for informing the model of such events.

```
MouseMenuController subclass: #FaceController
    instanceVariableNames: ''
    classVariableNames: ''
    poolDictionaries: ''
    category: 'Face-demo'
```

"This class provides a 'Controller' for the subview in which the model will be displayed. Functionality to interact with the model is provided by a customized 'yellow' button menu. The 'blue' button is disabled via the standard 'isControlActive' method provided as part of the 'control defaults' protocol. (Note, however, that the 'blue' button of the surrounding 'topView' offers normal blue button functionality for the view as a whole !!!!). The new 'yellow' button messages and associated actions are defined by 'initialize' and the 'menu messages' protocol."

FaceControllers can be created using the standard *new* message, and no other class methods need to be defined. Instance methods elaborate on the responses to menu options, which they simply dispatch to the model. Since there are three menu options, there are also three such messages. There is a method for disabling any blue button activity while the cursor is in this view (*isControlActive*). Red button activity will select the view, but will otherwise be ignored.

FaceController methodsFor: 'menu messages'

```
makeHappy
    self model happy

makeSad
    self model sad

makeWink
    self model wink
```

FaceController methodsFor: 'control defaults'

```
isControlActive
"inherits control from its superclass. Within the view the 'blue' mouse
button should be disabled (returns 'false' if the blue button is pressed)"
    ↑ super isControlActive & sensor blueButtonPressed not
```

The *FaceController's initialize* method is the 'place' where the menus are defined and associated with messages. It will first delegate all tasks for standard *MouseMenuController* initializations to its superclass. Then the menu's screen appearance and its methods are described and bound to *menu* and *messageList*. As is normally the case, the controller's *menu* is

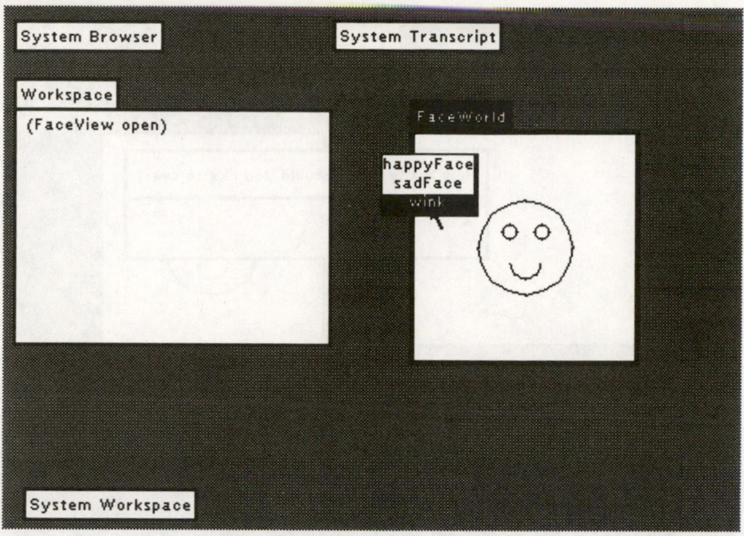

Figure 4.39 Asking for a wink.

instantiated to a *PopUpMenu* here. One could, however, attach it to other types of menus, if that was desired. The *lines:* message is used to request lines to separate groups of menu options. It expects an array of index numbers as its argument. Here there will be a line after the second menu item. The *messageList* is bound to an array of the previously mentioned methods, and then the new yellow button menu is installed, using the *yellowButtonMenu:yellowButtonMessages:* message defined as part of class *MouseMenuController.*

```
FaceController methodsFor: 'initialization'

initialize
"sets up menu items and their associated messages"
|menu messageList|
   super initialize.
   menu ← PopUpMenu labels: ('happyFace\sadFace\wink') withCRs
                              lines: # (2).
   messageList ← # (makeHappy makeSad makeWink).
   self yellowButtonMenu: menu
          yellowButtonMessages: messageList
```

This concludes our excursion into window-based applications. The *FaceView* created in this application will now behave as any other standard Smalltalk view. It appears in a labelled, rectangular window, with a white background. It may be activated by clicking the red mouse button while the cursor is within its boundaries. Its blue mouse button

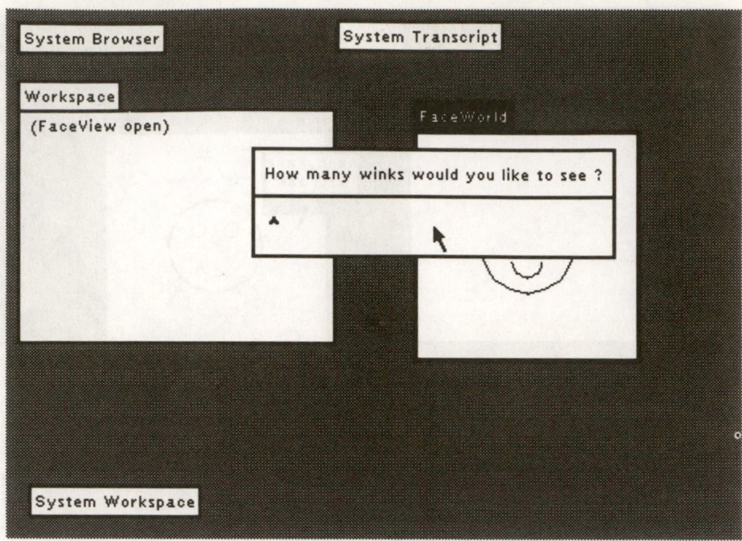

Figure 4.40 How many winks do you want?

menu will allow us to open and close, resize, move, collapse and expand it at will. At each new position the face's image will automatically redraw itself in the view's centre. The necessity for this process may be avoided by 'cacheing' the face in a form attached to an appropriately declared instance variable, which may then be displayed at a new location. Since this is much faster than repeated redrawing we recommend such a modification as a further exercise.

To start a new 'FaceWorld' we must evaluate '*FaceView open*', which will display the view after querying about the size of the face, its eyes and mouth. **30**, **5**, **5** and **10** are good values to use for dimensions. By exploring the yellow button menu in the view's subview we may ask faces to be happy or sad, or to wink a specified number of times. Figures 4.39 to 4.41 show how the 'wink' action may be requested and will be performed by the face we created in Figure 4.38. Note that we have opted for a left-lidded kind of wink.

It should be obvious how different reactions, additional facial features and further menu items could easily be added to this framework. Permitting feature manipulation (such as stretching, by clicking on 'handles' and dragging them into a new position) will be a slightly more challenging task, which suggests a range of additional exercises. Although this example has been particularly simple, it should serve to convey the flavour of how Smalltalk's predefined building blocks may be

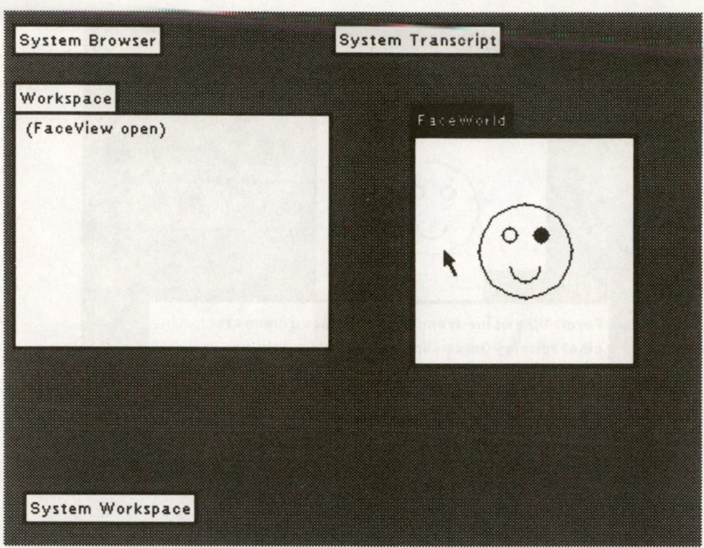

Figure 4.41 A single wink's frame. *(Run the program to view its full glory!)*

employed to attach a fairly sophisticated user interface to an application. As long as the required functionality follows the general 'style' of the Smalltalk user interface, this may be done with a surprisingly minimal amount of effort, and Smalltalk proves therefore an excellent tool for rapid prototyping of graphical and window-based frameworks for user/program interaction. Remember that one of the most important advantages in object-oriented programming lies in constraining complexity; that is, removing from consideration as many things as possible so that you need not concern yourself with them. In our examples we did not need to understand exactly how *StandardSystemViews* and *MouseMenuControllers* are implemented and how they communicate. We only needed to know the basic structure of MVC applications, as well as these components' functionality and part of their message protocol. This information is quickly and easily gleaned by using the browser and by performing some experimentation, and these classes can then be used as 'closed' building blocks. Although this has not been demonstrated, it is just as easy to customize a browser or inspector for your particular application, and this is in fact a very common technique in 'real' Smalltalk programs. Goldberg (1984, pp. 300–349) gives a discussion on how special browsers may be defined.

For debugging purposes, Smalltalk offers a customized view for browsing all three components of a 'model–view–controller' ensemble.

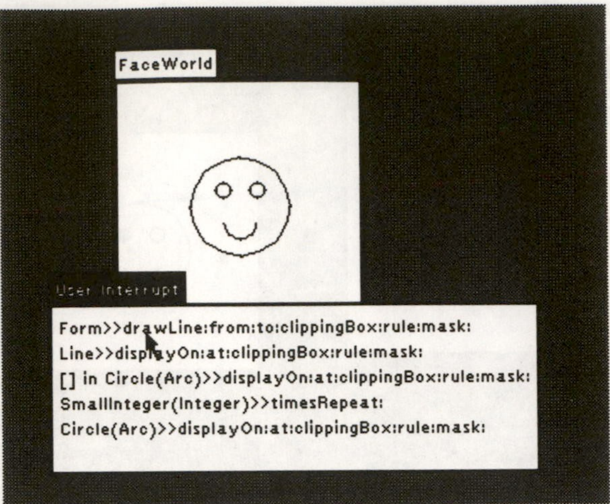

Figure 4.42 A *user interrupt*.

This is called an **MVC inspector**, and instances can be created by sending *inspect* to a view. To create such a creature we therefore need a 'handle' on the view in which our program resides. This can be obtained in various ways. Unfortunately the *FaceWorld* view is not directly accessible to us, since it is not globally named and was anonymously created by *open* sent to class *FaceWorld*. We could capture it there, but this requires a patch to our *open* message. Another possibility is to interrupt our program during execution, using '**Ctrl-C**', which brings up a notifier with an invitation to frame a debugger (Figure 4.42). This is only one of the many ways in which interrupts can be forced; they may also be explicitly requested from within a method by sending '*self halt: aMessage*' or '*self error: aMessage*'. The way in which objects handle these messages is inherited from class *Object*.

We may now decide to choose 'debug' from the yellow button menu. This will create a debugger window, in which we may browse until we find a reference to the view we wish to inspect. In Figure 4.43 we scroll to a message sent to *FaceController*, which of course owns a pointer to the view it is associated with. Choosing *inspect* opens the desired *MVC inspector*. It is framed in a view of three subviews. The first of these allows access to the state of the model, while the other two refer to the view and controller. As in any other inspector we may opt to view information and we can choose to inspect objects further. To demonstrate this we selected the instance variable *leftEye* in the model inspector and chose *inspect* from its yellow button menu. As expected an inspector on that object appears, and we may browse through its attributes. Further inspection would reveal further details.

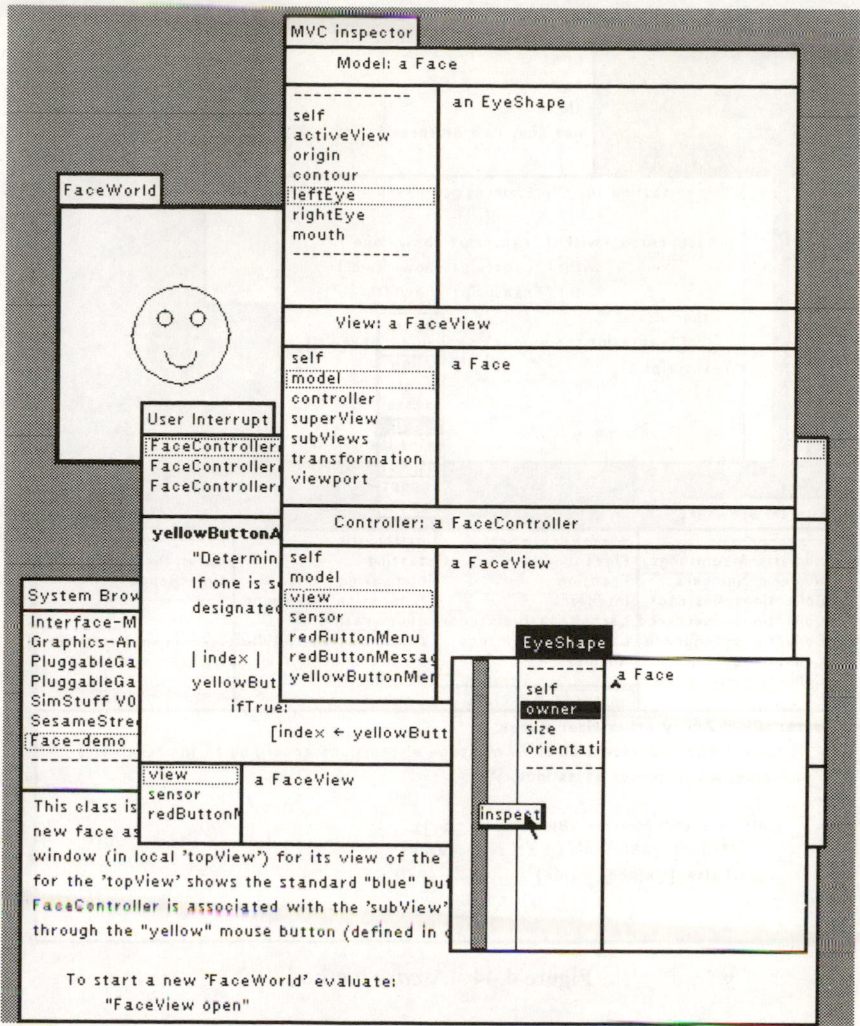

Figure 4.43 An *MVC inspector.*

4.7 Control structures as message patterns and Smalltalk's view of pseudo-concurrency

As we have mentioned before, Smalltalk subscribes to a very clean interpretation of object orientation. Every data structure is viewed as an object, every operation is triggered through message passing, and even all of Smalltalk's control structures are implemented as message patterns. One of the advantages of this orthogonality is that it becomes easy to

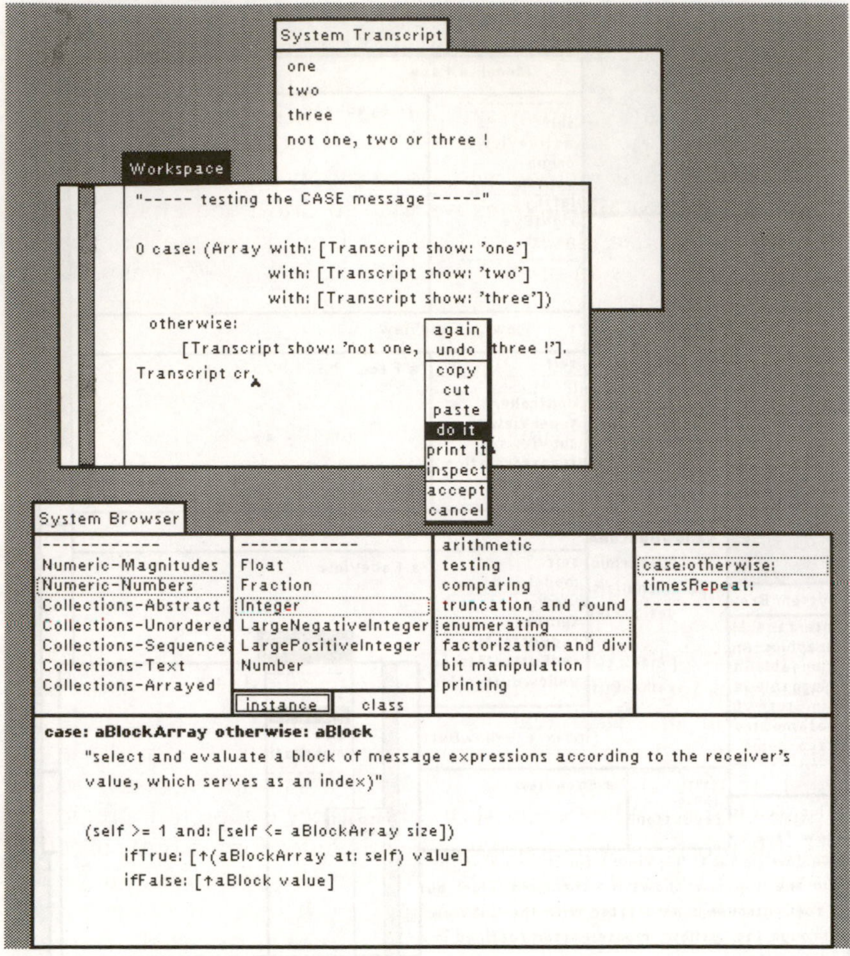

Figure 4.44 A *case* method.

redefine things. Declaring a new data type reduces to a class definition, and new operations and control structures may both be provided as methods attached to appropriate classes. Very few other languages make it so easy to extend their features. To illustrate this, let us assume that we harbour a nostalgic attachment to Pascal's **case** statement. Since Smalltalk does not support such a message, we decide to define it ourselves. This can in fact very easily be accomplished by 'patching' the message protocol of class *Number* [Deutsch (1981)]. Let us categorize *case* as an *enumeration* message, where it keeps good company with *timesRepeat:*. Figure 4.44 shows how it may then be defined. We will use the value of the receiver (a number) as an index into an array of blocks of message expressions. Once a particular block is selected, we will force its evaluation by sending *value* to it. This strategy corresponds to the behaviour of a case statement with 'lazy' evaluation. We may even wish to cater for an 'otherwise' clause. Observe that message *size* returns the number of elements in an array, and that *self* refers to the message's receiver (a number).

To use this new method we need to supply an array of blocks, one for each of the case distinctions we wish to draw, and attach another block to the *otherwise:* clause. *with:* sent to *Array* returns an array object. The workspace shows an invocation at the stage where '0' was tested as the *case* message's receiver. 1, 2 and 3 have previously also been used in this role, as testified by the text in the transcript window.

What should be appreciated is the ease with which such new functionality may be added to the system. As in Scheme there is no need to worry about reserved symbols or cumbersome syntactic conventions, and the new message has just the same structure as any of the system-defined ones.

It has often been claimed that object orientation provides a good framework for the description of *parallelism* in hardware and software. In fact, at MIT, so-called actor languages have long been used as tools for research into concurrency issues. Although the idea of data and process encapsulation leads to a high degree of modularity, with associated opportunities for parallel execution, Smalltalk has not yet explored this potential. For historical reasons it was designed for a uniprocessor environment, and concurrency issues have only been addressed in the context of time slicing among different views and processes at the software level. Smalltalk's model of concurrency is therefore predicated on a single processor, which needs to be scheduled for use by a collection of processes. The user can quite easily spawn new processes and request that they are administered by the scheduler. It should be pointed out, however, that this kind of parallelism is defined at the block level, and not among objects themselves.

Blocks may specify concurrently executing processes. Incidentally, each method's execution also results in a *BlockContext* which can be used in this fashion. It is the user's responsibility to schedule blocks and to arrange for their proper synchronization. *Semaphores* are the basic building blocks of all synchronization schemes, and they also provide synchronous communication with asynchronous hardware devices. *SharedQueues* offer a protocol for safe transfer of objects between independent processes, and *Delays* allow synchronization with the system clock.

Smalltalk's functionality for concurrent execution is localized in three classes: *Process*, *ProcessScheduler* and *Semaphore*. A *Process* is a sequence of actions describing some logically connected, state-changing and time-consuming chain of activities. Many of the processes in the Smalltalk system monitor asynchronous devices (such as the keyboard, mouse, clock) and the views framed on the user's desktop. Although it provides for pseudo-concurrency, Smalltalk will always maintain a single thread of execution, coordinated by the cooperation of a hierarchy of controllers attached to various activities. At the root of this structure is the global *ScheduledControllers* object. It owns a collection of top-level controllers, one for each active window. In addition to this there is also a controller for managing the top-level menu. Each of the top views may then contain additional controllers, an idea that extends naturally in a hierarchical fashion. The proper functioning of this scheme relies on rather well-behaved controllers, which are regularly polled, but are expected to refuse control unless the cursor is currently positioned in their view. Modifying this scheme for sharing control among a range of activities is a subtle task, and it therefore should not be attempted without a sound knowledge of the underlying architecture and adequate safeguards against system crashes. Fortunately, however, most applications will not have to invent new controllers from scratch and subclassing will normally suffice.

New **Processes** may be created by sending a *fork* message to blocks. In response a process instance will be created and the processor will be scheduled to execute the expressions it contains. There are a number of scheduling priorities available for selection. It is advisable that user processes be given a priority that is below that of any of the system controllers – that is, those processes handling hardware devices, interrupts and the various system views. Level 4, the *ProcessorScheduler's UserSchedulingPriority*, is often a good choice [Adams (1988)]. If no priority is given, then the new process will run at the same level as the process by which it was created. A process's priority can be changed by sending *priority:* to it. There is also a *newProcess* message, which will create a process, but will refrain from scheduling it. Suspended processes can be *resumed*, and all processes can be *suspended* or *terminated.* Process may have arguments, in which case they should be created by *newProcessWith:*.

A *ProcessorScheduler*, of which there is a single instance called *Processor*, keeps track of all active processes. It responds to messages *activeProcess* and *terminateActive. ProcessorScheduler*s also react to *yield*, suspending the currently active process and filing it at the tail of the scheduling list for processes with the same priority.

Semaphores are the only safe mechanism for interaction between processes. They respond to messages *wait* and *signal.* All processes waiting for a semaphore will be handled in a first in, first out fashion. Various patterns of process synchronization can be defined on top of semaphores. To ensure mutual exclusion from capacity-constrained resources, for example, each process must *wait* for a semaphore and *signal* to it after completion.

Class *Delay* models Smalltalk's clock and processes may be suspended by sending *wait:* to it. We have already used this feature to delay our left eye's closing during *FaceWorld*'s 'winking' activity.

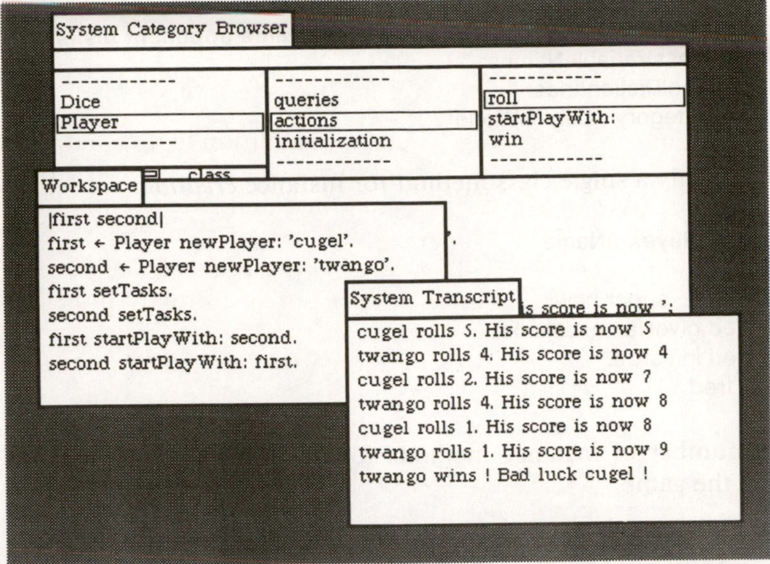

Figure 4.45 A game of chance.

Let us consider a simple example of how processes may be used. Assume that we wish to monitor a friendly game of dice between two obscure characters, *cugel* and *twango*. Fortunately the game's rules are extremely simple. Each player owns his own dice and they will take turns in rolling them. Whoever first reaches a score of '9' or higher wins some delectable prize. Figure 4.45 shows a game in progress.

To implement this game in Smalltalk we need to define a class *Player*, as seen in the browser. We may then create *cugel* and *twango* as instances, taking care not to start playing until they are both ready. The *startPlayWith:* message will link them together, so that they will resume from their opponent after each move. The transcript reflects the game's progress. Note that we must assume a strict code of honour, since players bring their own dice, cugel's announcements are made by cugel and twango's announcements are made by twango. That is, there is no umpire and the winner also announces himself.

Let us now look at the 'program' encapsulated by this class definition. We assume that a *RandInt* class of distributions, similar to the one we defined for the flavour system, is available. Although drawing of random numbers is catered for, Smalltalk does not directly include such an object. It is, however, often distributed as part of a 'goodies' toolbox, and a listing of such a class is given in Goldberg and Robson (1983). You may wish to try to define your own (*see* Section 2.5.2).

Players own five instance variables, for remembering their dice, score, an opponent's name, his 'body' and their own tasks.

```
Object subclass: #Player
    instanceVariableNames: 'dice score name opponent tasks'
    classVariableNames: ''
    poolDictionaries: ''
    category: 'CugelsWorld'
```

We need only a single class method for instance *creation*:

```
newPlayer: aName
|fred|
fred ← super new.
fred giveName: aName.
fred initialize.
↑ fred
```

and a number of instance methods for initialization, queries and for playing the game:

```
Player methodsFor: 'initialization'

giveName: aName
  name ← aName

initialize
  score ← 0.
  dice ← RandInt from: 1 to: 6

setOpponent: aPlayer
  opponent ← aPlayer
```

The next method defines and creates a new process. It is a block which represents a player's 'life cycle', and it will need to be scheduled whenever a new game begins. Note that this process contains a loop guarded by a test on whether the opponent has already won. This clause protects us against 'stubbornness' on the part of a player who may not accept that he's lost. As soon as a player has won, he will announce it and terminate both his and his opponent's *tasks*. Observe that the expression '*Processor yield*' is essential. The poor opponent would otherwise never get a chance to have a roll!

```
setTasks
  tasks ←
    [[opponent won not]
        whileTrue: [self roll.
                    Processor yield]] newProcess

Player methodsFor: 'queries'

name
 ↑ name
```

```
opponent
  ↑ opponent

score
  ↑ score

tasks
  ↑ tasks

won
   (self score >= 9) ifTrue: [↑ true]
                      ifFalse: [↑ false]
```

Player methodsFor: 'actions'

```
roll
|eyes|
  Transcript show: name; show: ' rolls '.
  eyes ← dice next.
  score ← score + eyes.
  Transcript show: eyes printString;
             show: '. His score is now ';
             show: score printString; cr.
  self won ifTrue: [self win]
```

startPlayWith: activates a player and starts the *tasks* process, which was previously created by the *setTasks* method. Note also that a player's win will immediately terminate the game. The player's *tasks* are terminated and his opponent is forced to resign.

```
startPlayWith: aPlayer
  self setOpponent: aPlayer.
  tasks resume

win
   Transcript show: (self name);
              show: ' wins !! Bad luck ';
              show: (self opponent) name;
              show: ' !!'; cr.
   (opponent tasks) terminate.
   (self     tasks) terminate
```

4.8 Files and other miscellaneous features

It was the intention of this book to demonstrate the flavour of object-oriented programming and within this context we have put particular emphasis on a discussion of Smalltalk's user interface. The Smalltalk programming environment is rich in functionality and we have demonstrated only a few of its features, a selection which was made on the basis of what we perceive as important in order to convey an appreciation of the power of good programming environments. There are many further aspects of Smalltalk we have not mentioned, and we recommend that you consult an appropriate textbook to learn about them. Like any practical programming tool, Smalltalk offers a file system. This is built around classes *File*, *FileDirectory* and *FileStream*. Files can be created, opened, read, written, renamed and deleted from within a Smalltalk session. There is a special browser for viewing files and their contents. Class categories, classes, method categories and methods can be written to and reinstantiated from files by selecting appropriate yellow menu options. A suffix '*.st*' is usually attached to such files. They are written in a format which allows them to be read into any standard Smalltalk image, and they can also be manipulated as a text file. The listings of our example programs are formatted versions of such text files (with all control characters removed). Smalltalk offers a very comprehensive selection of code management and error recovery tools. Each user will have his own image, which may be structured into different 'projects' each of which owns its own desktop. Code may be shared with others, and there is extensive support for interactive documentation and version management. The so-called '*changes*' file keeps an audit trail of all of a user's actions, so that the state of the system can be completely recovered after a crash. There is also a special browser to facilitate this process. Since the '*changes*' file can grow quite large, it will need to be pruned at regular intervals.

Smalltalk's implementation is uniformly object oriented. A class is therefore an object itself, which means that it is an instance of class *Class*. Class *Class* describes the general nature of classes which are themselves instances of the so-called *MetaClass*. That is where the recursion ends. This 'level crossing' is sometimes a bit confusing, but it may in fact be safely ignored in most contexts.

4.9 Some comments on style

Most of the basic issues concerning well-structured object-oriented programs, many of them fairly obvious, were already addressed in Section 2.5. Rochat (1986) offers some more specific guidance on Smalltalk style. Some recommendations are worth restating here.

The general principles of classification and reusable code should be applied to any program and object orientation offers excellent support for this strategy. You should therefore always design your classes so that they may become reusable in future applications. It is often tempting to attach new classes to *Object*, and then to proceed to construct their descriptions from scratch. It is, however, much more sensible and in keeping with Smalltalk's philosophy consciously to make good use of the functionality encoded in the system's existing classes and factor common aspects into ***class/subclass structures***. In such inheritance networks, subclasses should share some of the functionality of their superclasses. They may respond to additional messages, restrict the use of certain messages or implement some messages differently. A *method* should have a single purpose. If it performs more than a single function, these should probably be decomposed into separate methods. Method placement should be carefully scrutinized. It may be better to attach methods to a different class, if *self*, instance or class variables are never accessed and no new class instances are created. The ***textual layout of methods*** should reflect their flow of control and proper indentation should be used to highlight this. The yellow button *format* option gives some assistance here, although some form of aesthetic judgement is often still required. There should be a ***comment*** describing a method's general purpose, if this is not already obvious from the choice of name. In Smalltalk it is customary that such comments also provide an expression for testing the message. This should be given at the beginning, so that it may be found immediately. Although a method's layout should reflect its structure, it should not appear cluttered by unnecessary brackets or assignments to intermediate variables. Invoke the formatter when in doubt about parsing order. It will remove all unnecessary parentheses. Direct access to internal variables may often be dangerous, since it short-circuits an object's ability to protect itself against invalid operations and parameter values. Sending a message, even within the same object, will often be more appropriate.

Before a new layer of objects is built, the *message* ***protocol*** of all classes at the current level should have been thoroughly tested. In the context of a simulator, such as the one we discussed in Section 2.5, this may mean that the protocol of all data collection classes should be verified before any of the distribution classes are defined. This may be accomplished by sending messages with parameters reflecting the typical cases as well as all boundary values. In Smalltalk this may conveniently be done using the yellow button option *printIt*, or by evaluating '<tested object> <message name> *inspect*' from a workspace.

Smalltalk is a dynamically typed language, in which any value may be bound to any variable at execution time. It is, however, good practice to choose argument ***names*** so that they reflect the type of values we expect to provide. For example, it would be better to use:

```
to: aBag add: someObject.
```

than:

```
to: x add: y.
```

Identifiers should be prudently chosen for their mnemonic value. Smalltalk enforces further restrictions, in that globals and class names must start with an upper-case letter, while locals and instance variables must begin in lower case. Method names should usually also start in lower case. When an identifier is composed of more than a single word, which happens frequently, the generally accepted convention requires that all words but the first should begin with a capital letter – for example, *isEmpty*. It is not customary to start selectors or keywords with capitals: '*steal: from: At:*' should therefore be written as '*steal: from: at:*'.

Many of the foregoing recommendations are applicable to any object-oriented system. The question of good Smalltalk style, however, is a somewhat wider issue than this. Smalltalk is an interactive system, and special considerations arise. Rochat (1986) again offers some guidance. Except for some books and a fairly basic manual, the code is the system's only documentation. The usual conventions for indentation and placement of white space do not always transfer very well to this context. Classes and methods should be categorized, and ***method categories*** should follow standard conventions (for example, *initialization*, *queries*, *access*, *display*, and so on) and ordering (for example, *initialization* at the beginning and *private* at the end). Programmers are often encouraged to use lots of ***white space*** to improve readability. However, Smalltalk methods are typically much shorter than their procedural counterparts and they are predominantly viewed in the bottom pane of a *browser*. This often forces a restriction of at most 40 lines which are simultaneously visible. Brackets on lines by themselves waste space and result in other code being hidden from view. If longer methods need blank lines to separate sections of code there is a danger that these may fall at the bottom of a window, and it may be easy to assume that the method ends at this break. Using blank lines often means that a method is doing more than it should and would profit from being split into separate parts.

Since it is such a malleable system, embedded in a highly interactive and visually oriented environment, Smalltalk style also has to address the question of ***how to interact with the users*** of a program. How to reflect objects in windows is a difficult problem and any attempt at an answer is well beyond the scope of this book. Texts on how to design man/computer interfaces offer some guidance [for example, Foley and van Dam (1983)], but the whole area is still in a considerable state of flux.

Another responsibility derives from the fact that Smalltalk places the entire system on the same level, where we may change any of its aspects and we may even eventually come to share such changes with others. Beck (1987) comments that such ***sharing of whole problem-solving styles*** is different from the sharing of code in conventional languages. If someone offered you a C program that worked and turned out to be useful, you would most likely use it without too much concern about the style in which it was written. The worst you may expect is that it might occasionally crash. If a Smalltalk programmer, however, received an image that changes kernel classes gratuitously, doesn't follow conventions on naming or indentation, or uses unfamiliar and unpleasant styles of interaction, it is quite likely that he won't use it, even if it worked well [Beck (1987), p. 10]. Just as there are the Apple user interface guidelines that permeate the Macintosh world, there are some tacit agreements among Smalltalk programmers about which styles are acceptable and which are not.

Complex embedded systems like Smalltalk go beyond being isolated tools, which one may use interchangeably, in combination with others. More than other programming languages they encourage the development of a 'culture', in which stylistic considerations play a prominent role. To become a proficient Smalltalk programmer one must therefore progress beyond the stage where one is merely confident in using the language as a tool. From there on one must submerge oneself in its 'cultural' aspects, by studying typical metaphors, styles and applications, thereby acquiring some appropriate sense of aesthetics. This state is only achievable through practise and critical appraisal of other people's work.

4.10 Summary and perspective

> 'Beyond this I must add that programming in Smalltalk is fun. On the one hand, the act of assembling expressions into statements and then into methods is not very different from conventional programming. On the other hand, the experience is totally different, for the objects which populate and traverse the code are active entities, and writing expressions feels like organizing trained animals rather than pushing boxes around.'
>
> [*Ingalls (1977).*]

SIMULA pioneered the notion that no part of a complex system should depend on the internal details of any other part; flavour systems provided an implementation of this idea in the more flexible environment of an interactive and interpreted language, and Smalltalk has added the concept of a 'desktop style' environment in which such activities may occur. The salient characteristic of Smalltalk is that all objects are 'active', that they are able to present themselves to a user in a meaningful way and that they can be manipulated at any time. Since pictures are themselves manipulable objects and can easily be animated, graphical displays and interaction become a natural part of this programming metaphor.

The authors believe that one needs an interface that makes direct interaction with objects a part of the programmer's experience in order to teach, learn and use object-oriented programming well. Changes in an object's state should be directly and immediately visible. Smalltalk provides such an environment. Although it is true that one can almost always write better programs in a language one is familiar with, than in one which one knows only poorly, some languages are superior to others if they are used for the tasks for which they were designed. From its beginnings, Smalltalk was designed for personal workstations with a high-resolution display, keyboard and pointing device – a context which is now becoming more and more common. Smalltalk offers a complete development environment based on a simple and consistent metaphor. There is no arbitrary distinction between functions allocated to 'user interface', 'programming language' or 'operating system'. The user can customize his environment at will, the notion of overlapping windows allows tasks to be suspended and resumed whenever convenient, and the whole system's state can be explored through inspectors and browser.

Although at this point in time use of Smalltalk is still largely confined to the academic environment, there are indications that Smalltalk has a commercial future as well. Tesler (1986) reports on a survey of object-oriented programming in large-scale programming applications, while London and Duisberg (1985) and Diederich and Milton (1987) relate personal experiences with Smalltalk as a tool for sizeable projects. Many of the general advantages and disadvantages of object-oriented approaches to program design have already been discussed. To these Smalltalk adds some additional requirements of its own. As a substantial system in its own right, which does not normally make use of virtual memory techniques and will generate many transient objects at execution time, Smalltalk needs adequate memory space to perform satisfactorily. Provision of at least 4 Megabytes of memory seems to be a conservative requirement for any 'serious' work. As with other object-oriented programming systems, Smalltalk is also processor intensive. Dynamic binding and the long chains of indirect references created by multi-level interpretation are largely responsible for this. Because of the system's rich functionality the learning curve for novice programmers may be quite steep. The programmer has to become familiar with the class library, get acquainted with object orientation and its basic principles of design, as well as assimilating Smalltalk's unusual syntax. Although simple programs can be written fairly quickly, mastering the class library is ultimately essential, since one of Smalltalk's greatest strengths lies in the ease with which one may use and modify other people's code for one's own purposes. Finally, many people view Smalltalk's lack of data typing as a serious disadvantage, the same argument which is often also used against the LISP family of languages. Although it must be accepted that data typing may increase the potential for writing reliable programs, and that it can offer a base for establishing a program's correctness, many often-cited advantages of data typing disappear in an interactive context. In compiled languages and for large programs the notorious '*edit*, *compile*, *link*, *load*, *execute*' cycle becomes so tedious that early error detection is indispensable. This is not the case in an exploratory environment. If a Smalltalk object encounters a message it cannot understand, the user may simply invoke a debugger and the complete state of the system, including all processes' history, is open for inspection. While type declarations serve to document programs, a similar effect may be achieved by well-chosen identifiers and comments. Lastly, the argument that type declarations enable compilers to optimize code is certainly a valid one and Smalltalk's method compiler could use some such declarations to good effect. The associated loss in flexibility, however, is such that most programmers would probably resist its introduction on the strength of that argument alone. What remains is the view of a program as an object about whose properties one may reason and whose correctness one may try to establish formally. Although this is certainly an important area of research, which has yielded interesting results in analyzing simple programs, it remains difficult to see how such techniques may be transferred to the exceedingly complex task domains in which Smalltalk is normally used. Smalltalk applications are typically interactive and of a highly dynamic nature. Given the state of the art in program proving and its likely advances in the foreseeable future, type declarations' benefits for correctness proofs are currently not of concern to the practising Smalltalk programmer. There is, however, a different criticism whose validity is hard to dispute. Smalltalk is a highly individualistic system, which, coupled with the often *ad hoc* nature of exploratory programming styles, makes it difficult to manage programming teams in a disciplined fashion. What is required is a high degree of self-discipline and a comprehensive set of guidelines. The functionality of how to organize projects, communicate and distribute code among small groups of programmers is already part of Smalltalk. Coordinating and monitoring the progress of large groups of programmers remains an important area for further research.

References to the small body of literature on philosophy, principles and practice of object-oriented programming were given in Section 2.5. As yet Smalltalk itself has not been the subject of many textbooks. The classical texts are the language definition in the 'Blue' Book [Goldberg and Robson (1983)], the user interface specification in the 'Orange' Book [Goldberg (1983)] and some implementation experiences recorded in the 'Green' Book [Krasner (1983)]. At the time of writing, the fourth volume in this series, on how to use the MVC paradigm, has long been waited for, and Pugh and Lalonde (1990) have only recently filled this gap. Although these books are indispensable reference material, they are not particularly well suited for learning the language from scratch. The brief text by Kaehler and Patterson (1986a) currently fills that role, and recent books by Pinson and Wiener (1988) may also well become popular for this purpose. Kaehler and Patterson (1986a) is written with Apple computer's restricted VI1 version in mind, and as such is accessible to a hobbyist with an inexpensive machine. Pinson and Wiener (1988) is predicated on Tektronix's enhanced VI2 version. There is also the Smalltalk V reference manual [Digitalk (1988)], which offers a good tutorial on that dialect's use on Macintoshes and IBM PC compatibles. Budd (1987) describes his 'Little Smalltalk' implementation. Although user interface issues are not relevant here, Budd's book contains many useful descriptions of some of Smalltalk's system classes. A simple Smalltalk introduction by Mevel and Gueguen (1987) has recently been translated from French, and the August 1981, May 1985 and August 1986 issues of *BYTE* magazine are also still well worth reading. The articles contained in these special issues contain some of the most accessible and understandable discussions of many of Smalltalk's less well-documented aspects.

EXERCISES

Further to the exercises listed here, many of those given for Scheme, PROLOG and flavours, as well as those for the toolboxes in Chapter 3, are also suitable material for a Smalltalk implementation.

4.1 Kaehler and Patterson's (1986a) introductory text on Smalltalk programming uses the well-known '*Towers of Hanoi*' problem as its paradigmatic example. In a subsequent paper [Kaehler and Patterson (1986b)] they also discuss how to implement '*animal guessing*' in Smalltalk. This game involves communication with users who are asked to think of some animal, whose identity we then have to guess. A simple program for playing the game may easily be written by a novice Smalltalk programmer. It will have to store some knowledge about typical animals and their characteristics, for example, as a decision tree. This tree structure and the different types of animals themselves can all be represented as appropriately classified objects. User interaction may involve both binary (yes/no) and 'FillInTheBlank' query boxes. An expansion of this theme may involve augmenting the program with some capacity for 'learning by being told' about new animals and their characteristics. This could even happen 'automatically' in all cases in which the program 'lost' because it could not make the correct guess.

4.2 Smalltalk is also a good vehicle for studying the run-time performance of *graph algorithms* [*see*, for example, Even (1979)], and

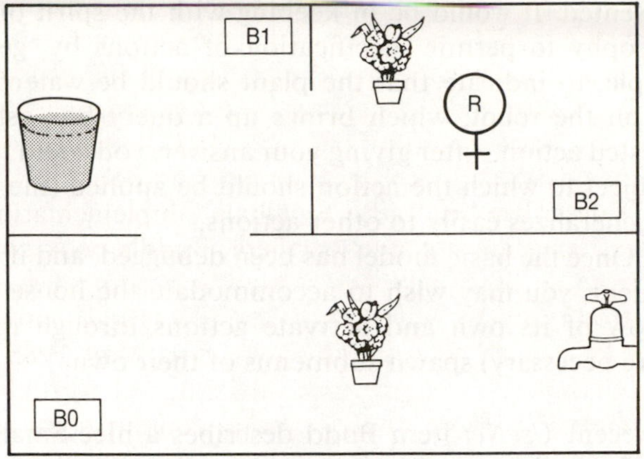

Figure 4.46 A domestic robot's simple habitat.

various types of displays may be designed to view *animations* of their execution. In the simplest case a graph can be plotted as a network of connected nodes, and blinking an object (that is, using the *reverse* message of class *Form*) may indicate the progress in exploration. Select a simple algorithm and write such a Smalltalk animation.

4.3 Extend the ideas for making pictures demonstrated in our *Garden-Path* example by writing a Smalltalk program to *simulate moving a small domestic robot around* the house. The 'world' of the robot should be a white form representing the house – for example, as shown in Figure 4.46. In this figure, R symbolizes the robot while B1 and B2 represent *box* objects. The robot can accomplish actions that change the world. For example, it can move around, push or carry movable objects from one place to another, fill the pail with water, water the plants, and so on. Each of these actions requires that certain conditions hold. Watering a plant, for example, can only be accomplished if the robot holds a pail filled with water, and if it is also next to the plant. Also, only dry plants should be watered.

Use a form or bit editor to draw the respective objects, which may then be placed by using the mouse. Mobile objects should be attached to a pen, which can move them around. You need not provide smooth animation, but you should be careful to erase an old picture before the new one is drawn. Use your artistic imagination to define appropriate actions and how they may be represented. It would be in keeping with the spirit of Smalltalk's philosophy to permit specification of actions by 'gestures'. For example, to indicate that the plant should be watered, you may click on the robot, which brings up a query box asking for the requested action. After giving your answer, you could then click on the object to which the action should be applied (the plant). This idea generalizes easily to other actions.

Once the basic model has been debugged, and if you still feel confident, you may wish to accommodate the house picture in a window of its own and activate actions through menus which (where necessary) spawn submenus of their own.

4.4* In a recent *UseNet* item Budd describes a nice Smalltalk assignment for building a *simple graphics editor*, similar to *MacPaint*. Although this may sound difficult to do, in Smalltalk it is actually surprisingly easy. You may wish to start with pens drawing on the screen, in different sizes. Initially you should not worry at all about windows, but simply provide a white box as a canvas. You may also want to constrain the pens' movements to within this rectangle; classes *Rectangle* and *Pen* offer appropriate methods. Making a pen follow the cursor while a button is pressed should be simple (browse through the *Pen*'s message protocol), and you should also cater for the notion of an 'eraser'. Selecting line width and switching between drawing and erasing may be achieved by clicking the mouse on a symbol. Define appropriate forms and place them on a palette beside the canvas. Many extensions to this basic scenario suggest themselves.

Add brushes, rulers, replication, scrolling, different 'colours' (for instance, grey) and geometric shapes (such as rectangles, circles, and so on). Selecting an action can also be done from a pop-up menu, and, finally, you may wish to retain your picture in a proper window.

The project can be extended with a view to construct simple 'object-oriented' drawing tools, similar to *MacDraw*. It should then be possible to designate, replicate, colour and move a picture's components as objects. Collections of objects may be grouped as well as ungrouped, so that pictures can be built in terms of a hierarchy of layers. Objects should be able to partially obscure each other and it should be possible to send them to the background or foreground. A multitude of extensions to such a basic scenario suggest themselves.

4.5 In this chapter we have discussed the problem of drawing a simple face picture, in order to demonstrate Smalltalk's features for writing window-based and menu-driven applications. Extend *FaceWorld* to cater for faces with demonic (supply two horns) and angelic (supply a halo) aspects and add other useful features (such as a nose, ears, hair). Dewdney (1986) reports an interesting argument on how a few basic transformations of features may serve uniquely to capture a person's personality. Read this article and add the required functionality to your classes and menus. As a more ambitious exercise you may wish to consider direct interaction with a face's components. For example, change the width and 'tilt' of a mouth by dragging with the mouse, a concept which obviously generalizes to other features as well.

4.6 Schmucker (1986a) discusses *QuadWorld*, a scenario which uses the mouse and a set of menus to define and select basic geometric objects, like rectangles, triangles and circles. Write such a program, attach it to its own window and add some transformations (like grow, shrink, colour, rotate, spin, and so on) as menu commands.

4.7 In their 1981 article Goldberg and Ross describe an experiment in designing a simple Smalltalk-based *animation kit*, called '*DanceWorld*'. They invite you to imagine that you are a choreographer, able to direct the movements of a dancer on the stage. As the dancer follows your instructions and you see the effects, you may modify them, to realize more closely your intentions and to explore new creative ideas.

Write a Smalltalk program to support such animations, set in a window-based, menu-driven environment. The dancer herself may be drawn as a 'stick figure', with commands to move a limb (face, arm, leg), move the whole body (up, down, right, left), create a pause and to demand repetitions of some pattern of movement. Also, the speed at which such actions may be performed should be dynamically adjustable. This basic framework should suffice to act as a platform for defining 'higher-level' concepts, like kicks, pirouettes, jumps, glides, slides, and so forth. You may also wish to generalize this idea so that dancing objects can easily be replaced by any figure which can be decomposed into the relevant limbs – using elephants, turtles, robots or other figures. Storing such animations (dances) as 'scripts' (sequences of commands) would be an interesting extension of this basic scenario.

4.8 Smalltalk can easily be used to *plot mathematical functions*. Define your own classes for function evaluation and their graphical presentation. You should provide a query box for a function's definition (as Smalltalk code or in some more convenient format), and then parse and evaluate it for a specified number of data points. Plotting a function should take place in a separate graphics window. Mevel and Gueguen (1987) describe such an expression evaluator.

4.9 Write a Smalltalk-based pattern matcher, according to the ideas presented in Section 3.3. This project may be extended to provide a production system interpreter, with forward and backward chaining, and this may eventually even grow into a full-fledged Smalltalk-based expert system shell, similar to *Opus* [Laursen and Atkinson (1987)] or *Humble* [Piersol (1987)].

4.10 Smalltalk's graphics capabilities make it an excellent tool for the representation and exploration of *conceptual networks* and similar classification structures. Drawing on concepts discussed in Section 3.4, implement such an application. A network should be plotted, and selection and modification of nodes and links should be permitted. This project offers an interesting setting for exploration of graphical means of interaction (for instance, drag a link to a new node, click on a node to inspect and change values) and the segmentation of large pictures (such as scrolling versus a hierarchy of layers, where we may 'zoom' into a node which expands into a subnetwork). Integration with the idea of using frames and scripts for concept representation (*see* Section 3.6) suggests itself, and this may even be combined with the production system suggested in Exercise 4.9.

4.11 Smalltalk's graphics capabilities also make it a particularly attractive tool for *exploring and animating game playing and search algorithms*, a theme we already mentioned in Exercise 4.2. Write Smalltalk implementations for some of the examples and exercises in Section 3.2.

4.12 Write a Smalltalk-based *ATN parser*, according to the ideas presented in Section 3.7. It may be instructive to browse through the functionality offered by Smalltalk's built-in classes for parsing and compilation. A challenging aspect of this project is finding a convenient (that is, graphical) formalism for grammar design.

4.13 Smalltalk can also be an appropriate tool for data or *document retrieval systems.* A frame for a small, memory-based relational database can easily be defined, and specialized inspection and browsing support may be provided. As an example, implement a simple application for document storage and retrieval. Short documents may be stored as text files or character strings, and your system should offer a query language for retrieval by keyword expressions (you may use a pattern matcher (Exercise 4.9) or ATN parser (Exercise 4.12)), as well as a customized browser for viewing the documents.

4.14 Write a *graphical interface* to support the definition of and to animate the execution of *simulation models*. This is a substantial and open-ended project, which will involve porting a simulator, defining appropriate symbol systems and writing the relevant animation primitives. For simple event-oriented stochastic simulations our flavour-based simulator could serve as a starting point. Kreutzer (1986) discusses block diagrams and so-called 'activity cycle diagrams', which may provide appropriate symbol systems, and Adams (1988) offers a brief survey of how Smalltalk's multitasking facilities may be used to write time-slicing simulators.

Chapter 5
Summary and Future Perspectives

> 'By great good fortune, and just in time, we have to hand a device that can rescue us from the mass of complexity. That device is the computer. The computer will be to the organization revolution what steam power was to the industrial revolution. . . . Of course we have to ensure that the result is more human rather than less human. Similarly we have to use the computer to reduce complexity rather than to increase complexity, by making it possible to cope with increased complexity.'
>
> [*DeBono (1979).*]

Perception of external 'reality' is largely determined by our conceptual framework, as a set of purposes, concepts, prejudices, procedures and models which we acquire during a lifetime of experience. Models are abstractions of reality. 'Objective' reality remains an attractive but elusive myth, which we nevertheless strive to uncover. People understand worlds by building mental models of structures (extended in space) and events (extended in time). 'Recognition' of structures and events is largely determined by the theories, methodologies and metaphors we subscribe to. There is no 'unbiased' problem analysis without some methodological frame to guide us. The importance of appropriate frames of reference and structuring tools can therefore hardly be overstated. Programming languages and metaphors provide such contexts, and a sufficiently 'deep' understanding of a rich repertoire of tools with different orientations offers the best chance for less biased approaches to problem solving. It has been the purpose of this book to lay such a foundation for knowledge-based system development.

Managing the complexity inherent in the programming process has been a recurrent theme throughout the previous four chapters. Three crucial components of computer-based tools for program development were identified at the start of Chapter 2, namely *languages*, *metaphors* and *environments*. There are many close interconnections among these three aspects of a programming culture and study of any of them in isolation will often result in insufficient depth of understanding. This book has surveyed, discussed and demonstrated prototypical styles of AI programming from three different **language perspectives:** *procedural programming* in LISP, *declarative programming* in PROLOG and *object-oriented programming* styles in the context of flavour systems and Smalltalk. The choice of these languages was motivated by a desire to study essential aspects of AI programming and reflects the fact that artificial intelligence has made many contributions to programming technology which had a significant impact on the complexity issue, and that tools and metaphors supporting such strategies have now begun to penetrate other, more traditional areas of computing.

Although typical **programming metaphors** were discussed in all the three frameworks, the Scheme language was singled out for particular attention in Chapter 3. Selecting Scheme as a representative for the LISP family of languages was justified in terms of its didactic merits and the conceptual elegance of its features. LISP has for a long time served as the main programming tool for AI applications, and it is still filling this role today. The Scheme toolboxes in Chapter 3 have therefore been used to highlight the programming styles and structures of many typical AI applications.

The third aspect of the 'languages–metaphors–environments' triad was covered in Chapter 4, where the Smalltalk system served to demonstrate some essential features of a powerful exploratory **programming environment**. Smalltalk's desktop metaphor was discussed with regard to the way in which rapid prototyping of multi-window and graphics-based applications may be supported in a rich, tool-oriented environment.

Recent shifts in cost/performance ratios have combined with advances in hardware and software technology to offer unprecedented opportunities for computer-based tools which support powerful problem-solving styles, instead of particular computer architectures to which they were often dedicated in the past. This background, together with the evolution of the personal computer, has elevated symbolic programming, exploratory styles of system development, and graphical and user-friendly environments from the realm of technological possibilities to the status of economically viable propositions. Relatively inexpensive workstations with large memory spaces, high processor speeds, large screen displays, mouse- and menu-driven graphical interfaces will replace the monolithic time-sharing systems and dedicated AI computers of the past. Linked into local and wide-area networks they will offer the potential for true 'information utilities', at a fraction of the cost formerly thought possible. As an example, one may now augment the Macintosh II, a

Motorola 68020-based workstation, with many Megabytes of memory and a special chip which implements all the functionality of the TI Explorer LISP machine. Combined with a large bit-mapped colour screen and the wide range of software available for the Macintosh and Explorer environments this makes the power of formerly very expensive high-end AI workstations available to a large number of individuals at a fraction of the previous cost. Much of this processing power and memory space will be consumed by improvements in user interfaces, which will offer complete environments for computer-aided software design. Our discussion of the Smalltalk environment has tried to convey some of the flavour of such a context. Combined with object-oriented styles of system development and other appropriate metaphors for particular task domains, these developments will reduce the complexity of the programming process, and result in a significant reduction in an individual programmer's cognitive load. Together with the increased processing power of new generations of highly parallel computer systems, this may eventually enable us to tackle problems which are currently beyond the reach of technology. In this way the dream of 'intelligent' machines may still at least partially come true.

Historically, artificial intelligence has moved from inflated expectations almost to the status of a 'black' art, followed by the sudden surge in popularity attributable to the knowledge-based approach. The 'first generation's' quest for power, generality and simulation of human performance has been replaced by a quest for expert performance in specific task domains [Hayes-Roth (1984)], which may be achieved by any means. In terms of economics this shift in emphasis has proved extremely beneficial, but it has also resulted in a situation where the philosophical and methodological foundations of the field remain comparatively weak. What is somewhat alarming are the number of overly optimistic claims and expectations, which, if they remain unmoderated, may eventually lead to under-achievement and a new period of disenchantment with the research program as a whole [Bobrow *et al.* (1986)].

Instead of directly addressing particular achievements of artificial intelligence as such, this book has concentrated on AI's contributions to programming technology. In our opinion, interactive and exploratory styles of program development are a very effective metaphor for complex situations and tasks. The merits of viewing programming as an empirical, inductive and essentially experimental activity are still somewhat controversial. Our emphasis on exploratory programming should not be taken as a claim that 'classical' styles of program development, where a program's implementation is seen as deduction from well-defined specifications and the programming activity itself as a task closely related to theorem proving, are unimportant. On the contrary, there are many contexts in which this approach is the most appropriate way to proceed. There are, however, also many situations in which insufficient pre-understanding and a lack of theoretical foundations requires an empirical approach. Many of the problems of concern to artificial intelligence and system-modelling applications fall into this category. These two approaches, however, are not mutually exclusive. They can be combined, in that exploratory styles may be used to derive the precise and stable specifications the classical style is predicated upon. Implementation will then benefit from an improved understanding of what is 'relevant' and 'important', and we may thus reap the rewards of improved reliability and efficiency in a more rigorous context.

We also feel that *symbolic languages* are superior tools for tasks which are mainly concerned with symbol transformation. Historically, computing has concentrated on predominantly numerical applications, and most programming languages still reflect this heritage. While complex numerical computations are still required in many contexts, their importance is now increasingly overshadowed by essentially non-numerical symbol-processing tasks. This trend will accelerate as increased processing power causes us to expand the limits of our ambition, and we come to view computing as a symbol-processing instead of a calculating activity. Many, or even most, challenging problems force a more direct mapping between some slice of the world and its programmed representation than is achievable through the use of numbers. 'In theory' we can always 'Gödelize' such models and map them into some abstract, numeric representation. This is, however, often very ill advised 'in practice', since it widens the conceptual distance between real-world entities and their representation, and thereby increases the cognitive load on the programmer who must mentally map between these two levels.

LISP and PROLOG will continue to coexist as tools for symbolic programming. LISP will probably remain dominant in practical applications, unless there is some major breakthrough in the use of parallel hardware which will significantly reduce the performance penalty of PROLOG programs. COMMON LISP will remain the main workhorse for commercial applications, although smaller and more structured dialects like Scheme and T may dominate education and research. Smalltalk has played a major role as a tool for prototyping desktop-style user interfaces and graphical applications, and a continuing fall in hardware prices will enable it to further penetrate the commercial and hobbyist markets.

Issues about knowledge and its relationship with the world have been debated by philosophers and scientists since the dawn of civilization. A large number of formalisms have been invented for knowledge representation, and appropriate reasoning procedures have been associated with them. Since representation can never be completely separated from usage, all of these formalisms must offer frameworks for both structural description and interpretative processes. The ultimate purpose of knowledge representation as a computational formalism lies in a program whose behaviour reflects a user's conceptual framework, and therefore his perception of 'reality', in some relevant way. Over the past few years the label '*knowledge-based system*' has become a fashionable buzz-word. This term is often considered to be coextensive with 'expert system', which has some rather unfortunate connotations. A distinction between 'knowledge' and 'data' may well be made, such as that which has been suggested by Wiederhold (1984, p. 63), according to whom databases should be viewed as large collections of facts, updated in fixed intervals, and typically maintained for operational purposes. The predominant form of interaction is through predefined transaction processing and report-generation programs. Knowledge bases, on the other hand, store information at a higher level of aggregation and abstraction. They are often significantly smaller and have a less predefined structure. Interaction occurs in more direct and immediate ways, and on a more personal level, so that the main way in which they differ from conventional computing techniques is in the flexibility they offer their users.

The toolboxes we discussed in Chapter 3 can serve as building blocks for knowledge-based systems, and Figure 5.1 summarizes their role in the problem-solving process.

Space and time are the two fundamental dimensions in which reasoning occurs, and there have been recurring arguments about the relative merits of declarative and procedural formalisms. *Declarative representations* are closely associated with structural descriptions and the concept of space. This approach views knowledge as a collection of facts that can be encoded by logical propositions or graph structures. Since the notion of 'change' is absent from this view, such descriptions are often easy to understand, and they can be formally analyzed because of the many independent assumptions which can safely be made. *Procedural representations*, on the other hand,

> '. . . allow "quick and dirty" solutions when theoretical issues are still unresolved. As theory progresses more of the knowledge can be removed from procedures and put into declarative form.'
>
> [*Sowa (1984), p. 24.*]

Many aspects of the world are best described as processes, and require explicit recognition of the concept of 'change' and the time-dependent nature of objects. Procedures can easily handle exceptions and '*ad hoc*' patches that a more rigorous, declarative approach finds difficult to deal

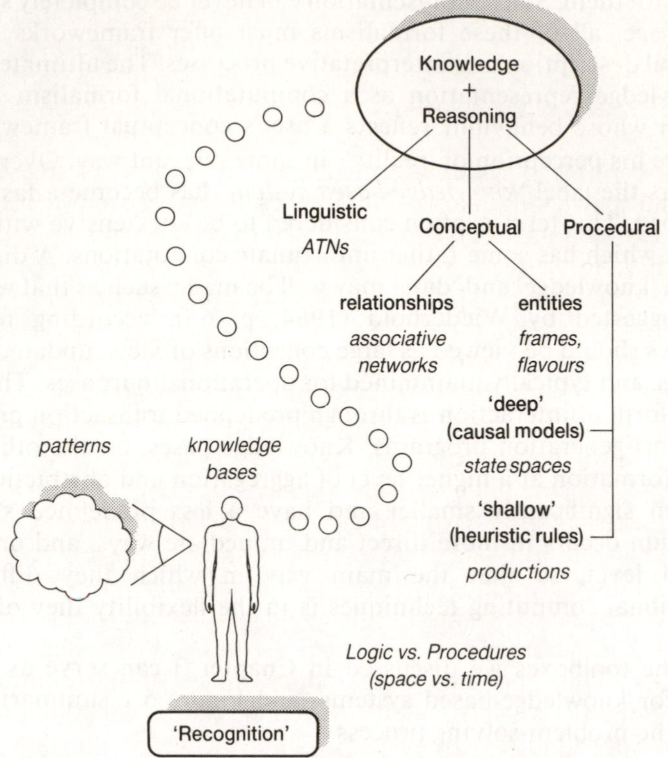

Figure 5.1 Problem recognition, representation and reasoning.

with. Logic is the classical vehicle for declarative specifications, while procedural programming languages may serve as prototypical examples for the opposite end of the representational spectrum.

The schemes that are used most often in practice are neither purely declarative nor procedural. Frames and object-oriented languages, for example, strive for a compromise and attempt to combine advantages of both approaches. They offer the modularity and the ease of structural understanding normally associated with declarative notations, as well as the conceptual power and flexibility of procedural frameworks for process specification.

The history of search in state spaces has been a long one. Search is an area which is most susceptible to mathematical analyses, and many algorithms exist for which there are solid theoretical foundations. Our discussion in Section 3.2 could only convey a relatively shallow view of the field. Pearl (1984) is a good source for a more in-depth treatment. During the early years of AI it was almost felt that intelligence *was* search, and many problem-solving systems were built on that basis. This is no longer a commonly held view, the paradigm shift of the 1970s towards a more knowledge-based approach had in fact almost removed search from the forefront of AI research altogether. Currently, however, search is enjoying a renaissance, driven by the realization that some sort of 'deep' reasoning is probably inevitable if one is to equip programs with the capacity to adapt to unusual or novel situations. All search problems are highly susceptible to 'combinatorial explosion', and search trees can grow wildly and spawn long chains of inferences. Effective pruning is crucial to any successful application of search techniques, and the use of heuristic information to increase search efficiency has therefore been studied extensively in both AI [Newell (1981), Lenat (1982)] and operations research.

Sometimes a path to a solution is more important than the solution itself. For example, a monkey may wish to find the shortest sequence of actions by which he may obtain a banana. In such cases it may be better to think of problems in terms of searching a 'planning space', where we may wish to execute the best of these plans later. The final result of such planning activity is a strategy in which the original goal has been recursively split into simpler subgoals, which have eventually been reduced to a set of elementary actions. The main advantage of planning over search is that we may use problem decomposition graphs (*see* Figure 3.6) and build compound operators as 'canned' sequences of state transitions. This approach may reduce much of the computational expense normally associated with searching, but its effective implementation usually requires some 'deeper' knowledge of the task domain. Nilsson (1980) gives a good summary of the basic principles and problems underlying the construction of planning systems. In this book we have chosen not to stress planning, although simple planning programs may easily be defined on top of the 'Search' toolbox. The General Problem Solver (GPS) [Newell and Simon (1972)] is a famous example of an early forward chaining planning system with backtracking. Its central ideas are the notions of subgoals and a strategy called 'means–ends analysis'. At each step in a problem-solving cycle GPS tries to select the operator which will reduce the 'distance' between the current state and the goal state by the largest amount (in terms of some predefined measure). This will frequently require producing new subgoals, to create the conditions under which that operator may eventually be applied. Initially GPS generated great enthusiasm for this style of problem reduction, but as with many other general techniques it could not avoid the pitfalls of combinatorial explosion, which is always associated with reasoning from first principles. GPS's ideas have been further explored and extended in STRIPS [Fikes and Nilsson (1971)] and ABSTRIPS [Sacerdoti (1974)], and planning is now a very active research area. Warplan [Warren (1974)] is a well-known example of a PROLOG-based planning system, a simple implementation of which is described by Coelho (1980).

Puzzles, games and *chess*, in particular, have fascinated many researchers interested in problem-solving strategies, and the first chess-playing programs were written as early as the 1950s. The *minimax* procedure we discussed in Section 3.2 was first proposed by C. Shannon in 1950, for a chess-playing program. The famous *checkers* program by Samuel (1959) already contained ideas such as *alpha-beta* search and the use of *evaluation functions*. While simple games like checkers, *reversi*, and so on have easily succumbed to computer analysis, many others have proved to be less easy to tackle. *Go* and *chess* are the two most prominent of these. The first chess-playing program of some repute was developed by R. Greenblatt early in 1967. It was called *MACHAC*, in honour of MIT's project MAC. In 1968 a number of well-known AI people made a bet with D. Levy (an international chess master) that within ten years a chess program would emerge that could beat him, and the first annual ACM computer chess tournament was held in 1970. The 1976 winner, *Chess 4.5*, played D. Levy in a 1977 challenge match, and lost. In general it is probably fair to say that, as in many other areas of AI, progress has been much slower than was initially hoped for, and many promising techniques have proved to be inapplicable to realistically large state spaces. There have been many attempts at emulating the strategies used by human players, but implementation has so far proved elusive. What seems to be true is that abstraction and stored patterns play a much larger role in human play than in a typical computer program. Progress is most likely to be made by skilful combination of different techniques, rather than by a single revolutionary new approach. *Belle*, a recent winner of the computer chess championship, may serve as an example. It uses *alphabeta* techniques for pruning the search tree, a fixed cutoff to limit the depth of the search, special case analyses and heuristics for ordering alternative moves, a knowledge base of well-known openings, and parallel hardware to speed up move generation and evaluation.

The history, strengths and limitations of pattern matching, production systems, associative networks, frames and ATNs have already been discussed in Chapter 3. Together with logic- and flavour-based notations these metaphors represent some of the historically most important and popular approaches to knowledge representation, but this list is by no means exhaustive. A number of specialized schemes have been used for special problems (for example, analogical representations), and two particularly interesting metaphors have emerged more recently.

So-called *constraint languages* [Leler (1988), Borning and Duisberg (1987)] share logic's view of programming as a declarative task. The programmer states a set of relations among objects and a '*constraint-satisfaction system*' attempts to find a solution that will satisfy them. Constraint-based systems are not new. They are closely related to structural description by use of equations, a common practice in the physical and engineering sciences. As in a PROLOG program, equations are 'non-directional' in that they only restrict the space of potential solutions, and do not prescribe any computational processes. A separate procedure (the 'constraint-satisfaction system') is required somehow to generate candidate solutions. Spreadsheets have emerged as a well-known example of a constraint-based metaphor within the field of computing. Although there are still some performance problems, other constraint-based systems have already proved their usefulness in a variety of applications, including layout problems, simulation and user interface design. Abelson *et al.* (1985) discuss a simple Scheme-based implementation of a constraint-satisfaction system. To some extent the demon procedures of Section 3.6 may be employed to attach constraints to a variable's values. Particular implementations of this idea are often referred to as '*active values*' or '*access-driven computation*'. Such a technique is especially convenient for automatic updating of multiple-screen representations of models, and Smalltalk's MVC metaphor thereby also supports this style of system description.

Another approach which is quickly gaining in popularity is the view of computation as a cooperative activity among a number of so-called '*knowledge sources*'. This idea is similar to that of actors, flavours and other object-oriented approaches. It was first proposed by Minsky, and Kornfeld and Hewitt [Minsky (1980, 1987), Kornfeld and Hewitt (1981)]. Minsky called his idea the '*society of minds*', while Kornfeld and Hewitt referred to it as the '*scientific community metaphor*'. Both proposals stress the importance of parallelism for the design of 'intelligent' software, although they make no commitment on implementation and either software (co-routines) or hardware (multi-tasking) concurrency may be employed. Figure 5.2 sketches a possible architecture.

Each knowledge source is an autonomous 'program' (object), with some well-defined purpose (acting, for example, as servant, critic, censor, witness). It communicates with other programs via some global database. Since these entities must share limited resources (such as memory and processor cycles), there must also be some scheduling system, and various schemes for synchronization between such 'actors' have been explored. One interesting idea uses the concept of 'bids'. Each knowledge source will initially be allocated some credit for resource usage, which it can then spend in any way it desires. Knowledge sources may make bids for resources (the highest bidder wins) and they can invite bids for tasks they would like other knowledge sources to perform. All this activity occurs through the global database, and such a system therefore shares many of the properties of so-called 'blackboard systems'.

Blackboard systems [Nii (1986), Engelmore and Morgan (1988)] originated in the Hearsay-II speech-understanding system [Erman *et al.* (1980)], developed between 1971 and 1976. They offer an early example of a programming metaphor using autonomous knowledge sources. In the blackboard model a problem space is partitioned into knowledge

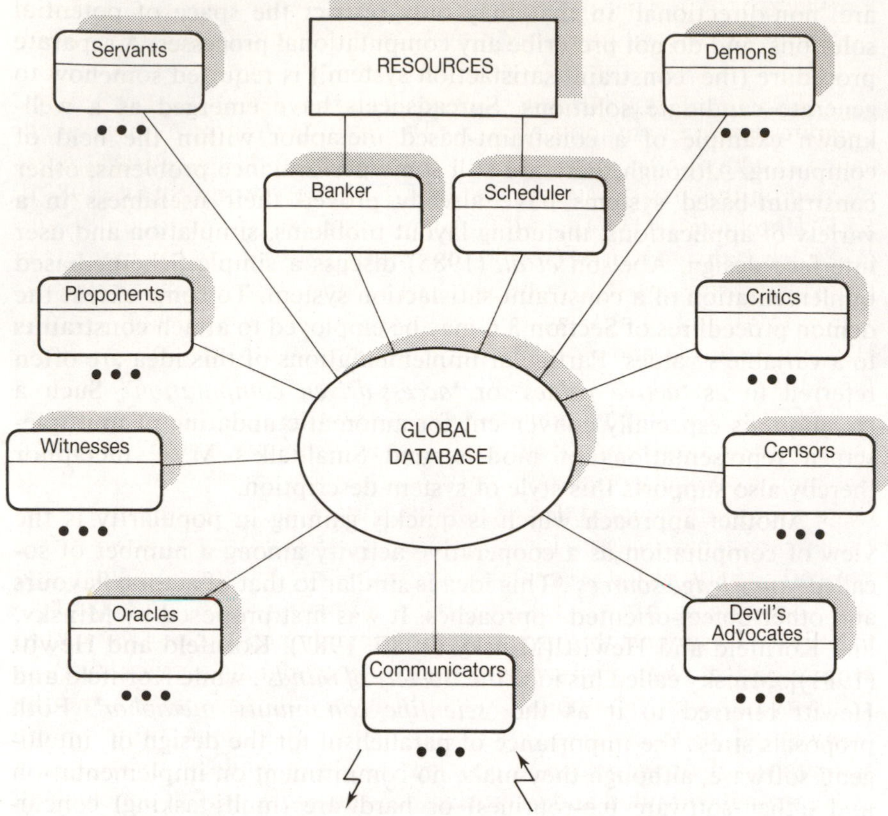

Figure 5.2 A 'society of minds'.

modules. These modules engage in what has been referred to as 'opportunistic' problem solving, in which pieces of knowledge are applied, in either forward or backward chaining fashion, at the most 'opportune' time. Modules communicate via a shared data structure (the 'blackboard'), and a choice of which module to execute may be based on the module's past contributions (for example, its latest additions to and deletions from the blackboard) as well as the existence of modules believed to be capable of improving the state of a solution. Many variations of this metaphor have been proposed and implemented, but the basic technology has not changed much over the last decade. The reason why very few 'pure' blackboard systems have been reported may be because of the high communication overhead and the associated hardware requirements. The similarity to the 'society of minds' and 'scientific community' metaphors should be obvious. Smalltalk and our concurrent flavour system would offer a good framework for implementing this idea, and we recommend experimentation with blackboards and knowledge sources as an exercise. The knowledge-base and pattern-matching facilities of our other toolboxes should encourage exploration of different schemes for process interaction.

Desktop-style interfaces to collections of conventional LISP-based program development tools already abound in AI. A large number of so-called *expert system development tools* have been designed and implemented on this basis. Systems like **LOOPS** [Bobrow and Stefik (1983)], **KEE** [Intellicorp (1984)], **ART**, **KnowledgeCraft** [Pepper and Kahn (1986)] or **Babylon** [GMD (1987)] offer such programming environments for AI workstations (for example, TI Explorer, Symbolics, Tektronix, Xerox 1100, and so on), engineering workstations (such as Sun, Apollo, Hewlett-Packard) and even microcomputers (like Macintosh II, IBM PC AT).

Chapter 4's brief discussion of Smalltalk gave an appreciation of the nature of most of the features of a good programming environment. The merits of object-oriented programming styles have begun to become more widely appreciated. Eventually object-oriented programming may evolve into a 'bandwagon' like structured programming was in the 1970s and early 1980s. What it is important to stress is that methodology and environment may not be as easily separable as some people have been led to believe. To support this programming metaphor effectively, some kind of interactive code-browser and source-level debugging tools are a necessity rather than a luxury, due to the highly dynamic nature and the many small methods associated with objects. Although some of the advantages of object-oriented programming can well be enjoyed in a conventional compiled and line-oriented framework, its full benefits will only become apparent in an appropriate interactive and reactive environment.

Although object-oriented programming holds great promise as a way of organizing complex programming systems, it will not be the only metaphor a programmer needs to be familiar with. In the authors' opinion the quest for a penultimate single metaphor, tool or language for all classes of applications is a mistaken endeavour which is doomed to fail. There is no 'good' notation independent of use, and there will always be a need for different tools for different purposes. This perception is corroborated by history, and it may also be validated in practical terms by studying the evolution of programming styles. So-called *multiparadigm languages* [Halpern (1986), Takeuchi *et al.* (1986)] set in desktop-style environments with graphics support will prevail in AI and will eventually migrate into main-stream computing. All of the more sophisticated expert system development tools offer more than a single programming paradigm, usually bound into a common, LISP-based context. Object-oriented, logic- or rule-based, and constraint-oriented programming styles are often supported, with object orientation used typically at the 'top level'. Together with a distributed approach based on knowledge sources, these techniques are also most likely to continue to provide the most important organizing frames for the programming activity in the short- and mid-term future.

Finally, harnessing the potential of highly parallel systems has become one of the main challenges for AI. Highly parallel hardware already exists and is continuing to drop in price. At this stage it is still difficult to utilize such systems effectively. Most of our programming tools have been designed for sequential program execution, and more research into concurrency is sorely needed. Effective use of parallelism for numerical computation is often much easier to achieve than for symbol-processing applications, where many basic issues are still unresolved. Logic- and object-based metaphors promise improvements in this respect, but there is currently no consensus on details about what features must be restricted or which are still missing.

In the long run massive concurrency may well be the only way in which 'true' intelligence may ever be achieved. Although knowledge-based systems have been very successful in narrow task domains, our programs can still not even begin to approach the common sense and sensory abilities of a young child. Although quite successful in many structured problem-solving tasks, research programs based on the symbol-processing metaphor do not appear to close this gap in any significant way. Some vital element seems to be missing. Fahlman and Hinton (1987), in arguing for so-called 'connectionist architectures', claim that massive amounts of associative memory as well as effective and robust pattern matching in the presence of 'noisy' and distorted data may well make a crucial difference. They propose a less structured, very processor-intensive approach based on very large numbers (millions) of very simple processors operating in parallel and communicating via self-organizing conceptual networks of direct connections. Gallant (1988) presents similar arguments for machine learning. Fahlman's (1979) NETL system is probably the earliest proposal for a connectionist architecture. Connectionism is quite different in style from any of the traditional approaches, and it is still somewhat controversial in the AI community. Quite a number of researchers, however, are now working in this direction. Some connectionist schemes use discrete representations, while others explore more analogical approaches. The recent renewed interest in 'genetic algorithms' [Goldberg (1989)] and 'neural networks' [Grossberg (1988), Pao (1989)] should be viewed from a similar perspective.

Appendix I
AI Programming – An Annotated Bibliography

This bibliography is selective and 'completeness' of coverage has not been attempted for any of its sub-areas. It contains only references with which the authors are familiar and offers some personal opinions on these. The reference section will often contain additional relevant material, which is referred to in the main text.

I.1 Artificial intelligence – history and philosophy

[McCorduck (1979)]
Machines Who Think
An extremely well-written and entertaining account of AI's intellectual roots and its historical evolution. The book is based on a series of interviews with many of the best-known pioneers of the field. A wealth of personal, often humorous, anecdotes offers valuable insights and succeeds in holding the reader's interest.

[Gardner (1985)]
The Mind's New Science – A History of the Cognitive Revolution
Gardner's book describes AI's history from a psychologist's viewpoint, with particular emphasis on the development of cognitive science.

[Sloman (1978)]
The Computer Revolution in Philosophy
Sloman's book offers a philosophical perspective on the notion of 'intelligence' and how computers may be employed to aid philosophical analysis of this concept. It is well written and contains valuable insights.

[Ringle, M. D. (ed.) (1979)]
Philosophical Perspectives of Artificial Intelligence
This book contains a collection of interesting articles on various philosophical aspects of AI. It would be useful as a first orientation about basic issues and contains numerous references to more specialized, in-depth discussion.

[Minsky (1985)]
'Communication with alien intelligences.' *BYTE*, April 1985
Some intriguing speculations on the nature of 'intelligence' by one of the leading researchers in AI.

[Dreyfus (1972), and Dreyfus and Dreyfus (1986)]
What Computers Can't Do: A Critique of Artificial Intelligence and *Mind Over Machine – The Power of Human Intuition and Expertise in the Era of the Computer*
These two books offer probably the most eloquent accounts of many criticisms which can be directed at AI's main research programs from a philosophical perspective. They are written from a hermeneutical point of view and seek to establish why discrete computational processes can never model human intelligence in any 'true' sense. In the early 1970s, the first of these two books caused a particularly heated and emotional discussion of the adequacy of the symbol-processing model of intelligence, while the second argues about various shortcomings of the currently fashionable knowledge-based systems approach. Well worth reading.

[Weizenbaum (1976)]
Computer Power and Human Reason
Another interesting and influential critical appraisal of AI's goals and aspirations. This book is largely written from a humanistic perspective and presents cogent arguments for why certain tasks, even if technologically possible, should not be performed by machines.

[Hofstadter (1979 and 1985)]
Gödel, Escher, Bach: The Eternal Golden Braid and
Meta-Magical Themas: Questing for the Essence of Mind and Pattern
Although not primarily dedicated to AI as such, both these books offer many tantalizing glimpses and original perspectives on the problem of 'intelligence' from a computational point of view. The first book in particular contains a brilliant discussion of the potential and limitations of formal systems and should be compulsory reading for any computer scientist.

[Simon (1969 and 1981)]
The Sciences of the Artificial (first and second editions)
Simon and Newell, at Carnegie-Mellon University, have been two of the most influential researchers for much of the early work in AI and cognitive science. This collection of essays gives an excellent summary of Simon's more 'philosophical' views about the essence of intelligence, and the 'symbol-processing metaphor' in particular. The essay on 'The Architecture of Complexity' is particularly relevant.

[Simon (1983)]
'Search and reasoning in problem solving.' *Artificial Intelligence* **21**
A more detailed justification of the 'symbol-processing metaphor' as a suitable model for human intelligence.

[Wittgenstein (1922, 1953 and 1956)]
Tractatus Logico-Philosophicus,
Philosophical Investigations and
Remarks on the Foundations of Mathematics
Wittgenstein's work has much relevance to many of the most general problems involved in modelling 'intelligent' behaviour, and the study of natural language in particular. He demonstrates convincingly that some of these issues can never be completely resolved, an insight which might have served to guide and shorten many fruitless discussions of 'fundamental' issues (for example, the famous 'procedural' vs 'declarative' debate) if it had been more widely known within AI. Wittgenstein's notion of 'language games' also offers many insights into the problems and inherent limitations associated with the prescription of semantics to formal systems.

I.2 Artificial intelligence – general introductory textbooks

[Barr *et al.* (eds) (1981)]
The Handbook of Artificial Intelligence (3 volumes)
This handbook offers a good selection of summaries on various relevant topics. Although somewhat uneven in their coverage, these summaries may collectively provide a good introduction to the field, or, alternatively, they may individually give a brief first overview of some topic including relevant references for further study.

[Shapiro (ed.) (1987)]
Encyclopedia of Artificial Intelligence (2 volumes)
This encyclopaedia provides a more recent perspective of most of AI's relevant aspects. Such books are intended to be used as a reference tool, not a textbook. As appropriate for an encyclopaedia, each of the entries is shorter than the summaries given in Barr *et al.* (1981), but the coverage is both wider and more specific. A valuable resource for the serious researcher.

[Nilsson (1971 and 1980)]
Problem-Solving Methods in Artificial Intelligence and
Principles of Artificial Intelligence
Nilsson, at the Stanford Research Institute, is one of the leading proponents of a 'formal' approach to AI. Both books concentrate on

search-based planning and problem-solving techniques, although other topics are also treated. The second book emphasizes the use of 'logic' as a description language.

[Rich (1983)]
Artificial Intelligence
This is a general textbook, giving a wide-ranging overview of AI techniques and applications, with many examples. It is largely pragmatic in outlook and not programming oriented, although some attention is given to a description of properties of LISP as an implementation vehicle for many of the systems discussed in the text.

[Winston (1984)]
Artificial Intelligence (second edition)
A 'classic' text, which offers a good overview and illustration of principles of AI and their applications from an MIT perspective. Although there is no dependence on any particular programming vehicle, the book is somewhat 'LISPy' in outlook and is intended to be used in conjunction with Winston and Horn (1984).

[Charniak and McDermott (1985)]
Introduction to Artificial Intelligence
This is a somewhat more demanding introductory textbook, which is less pragmatic in its approach than the one by Winston. It emphasizes the use of logic as the most appropriate description language, although LISP is used as an implementation vehicle and the text contains a good one-chapter LISP introduction.

[Tanimoto (1987)]
The Elements of Artificial Intelligence – An Introduction Using LISP
This text offers a more programming-oriented introduction to AI. It contains a discussion of the most important AI techniques, illustrated by microworlds patterned after well-known AI systems. There is a particular emphasis on vision and language understanding.

[Sowa (1984)]
Conceptual Structures – Information Processing in Mind and Machine
This is a somewhat unusual introduction to AI. It centres on the use of conceptual graphs as a descriptive vehicle for intelligent systems and offers particularly interesting insights on philosophical foundations and natural language processing. The book is probably most effective as a second text, to be read after some more general introduction to the field.

[Boden (1977)]
Artificial Intelligence and Natural Man
A very well-written survey of AI's principles and systems, from a psychologist's perspective. The book contains much interesting historical detail and will serve very well as a relatively non-technical, but theoretically sound introduction to the field.

[Hayes (1978)]
Cognitive Psychology – Thinking and Creating
A very readable introduction to cognitive psychology with somewhat more emphasis on computational aspects than other texts in that area.

I.3 Expert systems

[Stefik (1982)]
'The organization of expert systems. A tutorial.' *Artificial Intelligence,* **18**
This article gives a good, brief introduction and summary of basic principles.

[Hayes-Roth (1984)]
'The knowledge-based expert system: A tutorial.' *IEEE Computer*, September 1984
Another good introductory article, with more reference to existing programs.

[Hayes-Roth *et al.* (eds) (1983)]
Building Expert Systems
A somewhat uneven collection of articles on expert system theory, design, tools, implementation and evaluation. Contains a case study of an expert system for managing toxic waste emergencies.

[Bobrow *et al.* (1986)]
'Expert systems: perils and promise.' *Communications of the ACM*, **29**
This article offers an excellent critical appraisal of strengths and weaknesses of knowledge-based systems.

I.4 Artificial intelligence programming

[Bobrow (1985)]
'If PROLOG is the answer, what is the question? *or* What it takes to support AI programming paradigms.' *IEEE Transactions on Software Engineering,* **SE-11**
An excellent, brief discussion of basic requirements related to programming AI applications and how they may be met.

[Sheil (1983)]
'Power tools for programmers.' *Datamation*, February 1983
An excellent, brief article which explains and justifies 'exploratory programming' as an alternative approach to program development.

[Charniak *et al.* (1980)]
Artificial Intelligence Programming
A summary of advanced programming techniques in LISP. Discrimination nets, search, backtracking, co-routines, unification, slot and filler

databases and ATNs are also covered. To use this book effectively some basic competence in LISP programming must be highly recommended. UCI LISP was used originally, but a new edition based on COMMON LISP has just been published.

[Burton and Shadbolt (1987)]
POP-11 Programming for Artificial Intelligence
This book offers a brief introduction to the Pop-11 language, and a discussion of some simple programming techniques for problem solving, planning, knowledge representation and natural language processing. The text seems most suitable for undergraduates with little prior computing experience and evolved from a course given to psychology students.

[Bundy (ed.) (1984)]
Catalogue of Artificial Intelligence Tools
Useful listing of profiles and of various AI software tools, together with references and addresses from which they may be obtained. Slightly outdated, but a new edition has been announced.

I.5 Programming in LISP

[Allen (1978)]
The Anatomy of LISP
Excellent, 'serious' introduction to LISP. Proposes a 'layered' approach to program design and contains much useful detail on implementation, including a nice example of the notorious 'LISP interpreter written in LISP'.

[Winston and Horn (1984)]
LISP (second edition)
A standard text. Nice, readable introduction with many examples and projects from AI applications. The first part of the text introduces basic LISP concepts, while the second closely follows the treatment of AI systems given in Winston (1984). MACLISP was originally used, but a COMMON LISP edition is now available.

[Hofstadter (1983)]
(1) 'LISP: atoms and lists', (2) 'LISP: lists and recursion', (3) 'LISP: recursion and generality'. *Scientific American*, **Feb.-April, 1983**
A series of three *Scientific American* articles, which give a humorous and lucid description of LISP's main characteristics and provides an excellent answer to the perennial 'Why LISP?' questions. These articles may be most effective as a first exposure to the language, before starting to work through a 'conventional' introductory textbook.

[Hasemer (1984)]
A Beginner's Guide to LISP
A particularly easy to read, 'gentle' introduction, largely targeted at micro-based implementations and computer hobbyists. The book introduces a minimal subset of the language and shows how to extend this to the 'normal' repertoire of functions. The book is suitable for novices with little programming experience.

[Touretzki (1984)]
LISP – A Gentle Introduction to Symbolic Computation
Another 'gentle' LISP introduction for novice programmers. The text is easy to read and written in a humorous style. It offers a particularly nice treatment of recursion and many interesting and stimulating exercises with solutions. A slightly enhanced version of MACLISP is used, but hints on how to map it on to other dialects are given in appendices.

[Wilensky (1984)]
LISPCraft and *COMMON LISPCraft*
A fairly technical introduction, with lots of detail on programming techniques. The book was originally specifically oriented towards Franz-LISP, for which it still is the only easily accessible reference. A 'COMMON LISPCraft' version has now also been published.

[Steele (1984)]
COMMON LISP: The Language
This is the official COMMON LISP definition. Indispensable reference to the practising COMMON LISP programmer, but not particularly suitable as light 'bed-time' reading.

I.6 Programming in Scheme

[Abelson *et al.* (1985)]
Structure and Interpretation of Computer Programs
Excellent introductory computer science textbook. Should be compulsory reading. The text forms the core of MIT's programming course for undergraduate electrical engineering students. It introduces and uses the Scheme language as a programming vehicle. Many examples are taken from a large variety of numeric and non-numeric applications, with no particular emphasis on AI. The book offers a wealth of exercises and projects, but no sample solutions. The first three chapters are still the most suitable introduction to Scheme for the inexperienced programmer.

[Dybvig (1987)]
The Scheme Programming Language
This is a more technical introductory text, which should appeal to experienced programmers. Large parts of the book also double as a

reference manual for the 'Chez Scheme' implementation marketed by the book's author.

[Rees and Clinger (eds) (1986)]
'Revised^3 report on the algorithmic language scheme.' *ACM SIGPLAN Notices*, **21**
Although highly unexpected and unusual for an 'official' language definition, the Scheme report is itself a very readable document, which experienced programmers may well find suitable as a study guide for learning the language.

[Springer and Friedman (1989)]
Scheme and the Art of Programming
An excellent introductory computer science text based on Scheme. Less wide-ranging than Abelson and Sussman's book, it stresses abstraction and covers both functional and imperative programming styles.

I.7 Logic programming and PROLOG

[Kowalski (1979a)]
Logic for Problem Solving
A 'classic' textbook on basic principles of logic programming. Contains good discussions of many foundational issues. This is not a PROLOG textbook.

[Clocksin and Mellish (1981)]
Programming in PROLOG
The first (and for a long time only) textbook on PROLOG. Written with the beginning programmer in mind. Defines the Edinburgh *de facto* standard representation.

[Rogers (1986)]
A PROLOG Primer
Excellent brief introduction to 'basic' PROLOG. Suitable for both inexperienced and experienced programmers.

[Bratko (1986)]
PROLOG Programming for Artificial Intelligence
An excellent PROLOG introduction for experienced programmers. The second part of the book shows how to implement simple AI systems in PROLOG.

[Malpas (1987)]
PROLOG – A Relational Language and Its Applications
Good, readable introductory textbook for the 'intermediate' programmer. It contains a particularly nice discussion of the history and philosophical foundations of logic.

[Sterling and Shapiro (1986)]
The Art of PROLOG
A textbook with a more 'formal' approach. It offers an excellent treatment of foundational issues and advanced PROLOG programming techniques. Suitable for experienced programmers and as a 'second' PROLOG text, in particular.

[Walker *et al.* (1987)]
Knowledge Systems and PROLOG
This text is based on IBM PROLOG. Apart from an introduction to the language and some basic programming techniques, it offers a fairly detailed discussion on how to build expert and natural language understanding systems. The text is probably most suitable for the experienced programmer working with IBM PROLOG, or as a reference for PROLOG applications in the two areas mentioned above.

[Clark and McCabe (eds) (1984)]
Micro-PROLOG: Programming in Logic
An introductory text based on the popular micro-PROLOG implementation of the language, using the so-called 'simple' syntax. Two separate chapters cover applications to combinatorial problem solving and expert systems.

[Townsend (1987)]
Introduction to Turbo PROLOG
An introduction to this particular PROLOG implementation. Mainly aimed at computer hobbyists.

[Coelho (1980)]
How to Solve It in PROLOG
A large and useful collation of example programs in areas such as AI and others. Suitable for experienced PROLOG programmers, since the structure of the programs is not described and they are typically only sparsely commented upon. A new, much improved and more accessible edition (published by Springer) has just appeared.

I.8 Object-oriented programming, actors and flavour systems

[Robson (1981)]
'Object-oriented software systems.' *BYTE*, August 1981
This article offers an 'easily readable' introduction to the essence of object orientation.

[Stefik and Bobrow (1985)]
'Object-oriented programming: themes and variations.' *The AI Magazine*, 1985
An excellent summary of the key ideas of object-oriented programming.

[Cardelli and Wegener (1986)]
'On understanding types, data abstraction and polymorphism.' *ACM Computing Surveys*, **17**
A more 'formal' discussion of object orientation from the viewpoint of data abstraction.

[Cox (1986)]
Object-Oriented Programming – An Evolutionary Approach
A brief introduction to object-oriented programming from the viewpoint of large software projects. The rest of the text describes and discusses the use of the 'Objective C' programming language.

[Schmucker (1986a)]
Object-Oriented Programming for the Macintosh
A good survey of object-oriented programming techniques, exemplified by a number of software systems available for the Apple Macintosh, including Smalltalk, Object Pascal and MacApp.

[Tesler (1986)]
'Programming experiences.' *BYTE*, August 1986
This article reports on experiences made while using object-oriented programming tools in some large-scale applications.

[Hewitt (1977)]
'Viewing control structures as patterns of passing messages.' *Artificial Intelligence*, **8**
The original paper describing Hewitt's 'actor' idea.

[Agha (1986)]
Actors: A Model of Concurrent Computations in Distributed Systems
A comprehensive discussion of history and principles of actor systems.

[Hewitt and Agha (1989)]
Concurrent Systems for Knowledge Processing. An Actor Perspective
A thorough discussion and analysis of the actor metaphor of knowledge representation. This book provides a historical perspective as well as a survey of languages and speculation on future developments.

[Yonezawa and Tokoro (eds) (1986)]
Object-Oriented Concurrent Programming
This collection of articles presents a good view of the current state of research in exploiting object orientation's potential for parallelism. Most of this discussion is centred on the actor model.

I.9 Smalltalk and programming environments

[Kaehler and Patterson (1986b)]
'A small taste of Smalltalk.' *BYTE*, August 1986
Simple, very accessible and readable introduction. Suitable for a first whiff of Smalltalk's flavour.

[Kaehler and Patterson (1986a)]
A Taste of Smalltalk
An excellent brief tutorial for beginners. The book demonstrates the use of the language and programming environment by showing, in a step-by-step fashion, how various versions of a graphical display for a 'Tower of Hanoi' program can be built. Uses no features which are not part of the Apple Macintosh 'level 0' subset.

[Goldberg and Robson (1983)]
Smalltalk-80 – The Language and Its Implementation
The 'Blue' Book. Doubles as textbook and a complete language specification. It also includes the definition of Smalltalk's virtual machine (in Smalltalk). This text is best approached after working through some simpler introduction [such as the article and book by Kaehler and Patterson (1986a and 1986b)].

[Diederich and Milton (1987)]
'Experimental Prototyping in Smalltalk.' *IEEE Software*, May 1987
This short article gives a good demonstration and summary of various strengths and weaknesses of object orientation in general, and Smalltalk's highly interactive programming style in particular.

[Sandewall (1978)]
'Programming in the interactive environment: the LISP experience.' *Computing Surveys*, **10**
A 'classic' summary of the LISP-style program development cycle. Uses the InterLISP software tools and programming environments to illustrate the advantages of exploratory programming.

[Tesler (1981)]
'The Smalltalk environment.' *BYTE*, August 1981
This article discusses the basic philosophy behind the so-called 'desktop metaphor'. After working with Smalltalk for many years, Tesler has also been one of the key implementors of the Apple Lisa/Macintosh line of personal workstations.

[Goldberg (1984)]
Smalltalk-80 – The Interactive Programming Environment
The 'Orange' Book. It shows how to use and explore the Smalltalk programming environment. An essential companion to Goldberg and Robson (1983).

[Pinson and Wiener (1988)]
Object Oriented Programming and Smalltalk
Pinson and Wiener have written a good textbook, covering most aspects of Smalltalk programming. Their treatment of many issues is more accessible than [Goldberg and Robson (1983)] and more complete than [Kaehler and Patterson (1986a)]. This book also contains a chapter on

the use of the MVC metaphor to write graphical and interactive applications. Note that Pinson and Wiener employ the Tektronix dialect of Smalltalk, which differs slightly from the 'standard' Xerox version. These differences are unfortunately not emphasized in the text.

[Budd (1987)]
A Little Smalltalk
This textbook describes Budd's Little Smalltalk implementation for time-sharing systems. Although this version makes no assumptions about user interfaces, the basic syntax and some of the class libraries are identical to 'normal' Smalltalk, and the first part of this book may therefore be useful for a first look at Smalltalk. The second part contains implementation details which are only relevant to Little Smalltalk.

I.10 Problem solving

[Korf (1980)]
'Towards a model of representation changes.' *Artificial Intelligence*, **14**
This article offers a good discussion of the importance of appropriate representations in problem solving.

[Wickelgren (1974)]
How to Solve Problems
An excellent discussion of various classes of representations and problem-solving heuristics by a psychologist.

[Rubinstein (1975)]
Patterns of Problem Solving
An interesting survey and demonstration of principles of problem-solving techniques, as applied to the engineering sciences.

I.11 Search puzzles, games and heuristics

[Amarel (1968)]
'On representation of problems of reasoning about actions.' In *Machine Intelligence 3* (Michie, D., ed.)
This 'classical' article describes the state space model and uses the 'missionaries and cannibals' problem as a paradigmatic example.

[Nilsson (1971)]
Problem-Solving Methods in Artificial Intelligence
The 'classical' text on search methods and heuristics.

[Banerji (1980)]
Artificial Intelligence – A Theoretical Approach
This text introduces a formal model of problem-solving heuristics and puts particular emphasis on concept 'learning'.

[Pearl (1984)]
Heuristics – Intelligent Search Strategies for Computer Problem Solving
A modern, formal and fairly 'complete' discussion of heuristic search techniques. An indispensable reference for any serious work in this area.

[Berlekamp, Conway and Guy (1982)]
Winning Ways for Your Mathematical Plays (2 volumes)
This is a beautiful book which discusses and analyses a multitude of puzzles and games from a mathematical perspective. It is a virtual goldmine of information on this area and should be owned by anyone who is seriously interested in games or mathematical puzzles and problem solving.

I.12 Pattern matching, associative databases and production systems

[Davis and King (1977)]
'An overview of production systems.' In *Machine Intelligence 8* (Elcock, E. W. and Michie, D., eds)
An excellent, still relevant summary article on the basic principles, properties, advantages and disadvantages of production systems.

[Waterman and Hayes-Roth (eds) (1978)]
Pattern-Directed Inference Systems
A collection of highly relevant discussions of important aspects of production system architectures.

[Brownston, Farrell, Kant and Martin (1985)]
Programming Expert Systems in OPS5. An Introduction to Rule-based Programming
This introduction to the OPS5 programming system, which is still the most paradigmatic tool for the development of rule-based programs, also discusses other important aspects of production systems.

I.13 Semantic networks, frames and scripts

[Findler (ed.) (1971)]
Associative Networks – Representation and Use of Knowledge by Computers
An important collection of articles on the use of semantic networks and related formalisms.

[Minsky (1975)]
'A framework for representing knowledge.' In *The Psychology of Computer Vision* (Winston, P., ed.)
The 'original' paper proposing the use of frame-based knowledge representations in the context of vision systems.

[Schank and Abelson (1977)]
Scripts, Plans, Goals and Understanding
A discussion on how to use scripts in story-understanding programs with examples.

I.14 Natural language processing and ATNs

[Winograd (1983)]
Language as a Cognitive Process – Syntax (volume 1)
This text offers a comprehensive treatment of grammars and parsing. Augmented transition networks (ATNs) are covered in detail.

[Allen (1988)]
Natural Language Understanding
An excellent and very readable introduction to the rapidly growing field of computational linguistics. Not as thorough, but wider ranging and more complete than [Winograd (1983)]. Many examples and implementations for important algorithms are given.

Appendix II
A Simple Discrete Event Simulator

The following code uses the C-Flavour system. It will therefore work on an Apple Macintosh with sufficient memory (>= 1MB) and the flavour package installed. A number of issues, including the implementation of co-routines, would need to be resolved in order to 'port' it to a different environment and/or flavour system.

Only a minimal set of sampling and data collection objects is given. This can easily be extended according to the recommendations in Section 2.5. More detailed advice can be found in Kreutzer (1986) or some other book on simulation programming.

II.1 Data collection devices

```
(defFlavour DataCollector (ako Vanilla) (ivars name obs)
  testivars getivars setivars)

; ----- a Counter -----
(defFlavour Count (ako DataCollector) (ivars counter)
  setivars getivars testivars)

(defMethod (update! Count) (aValue)
  (if (self 'counter?)
     (self 'counter! (+ (self 'counter) aValue) )
     (self 'counter! aValue) )
  (if (self 'obs?)
     (self 'obs! (+ (self 'obs) 1) )
     (self 'obs! 1) ) )

(defMethod (reset! Count) ( ) (self 'obs! 0) (self 'counter! 0))

(defMethod (show Count) ( )
  (if (self 'obs?)
     (begin (DisplayLine "--- counter:" (self 'name) )
            (DisplayLine (self 'obs) "observations were made.")
            (DisplayLine " The value of this count is:"
                         (self 'counter) ) )
     (DisplayLine "*** this counter has not been updated !") ) )
```

```
; ----- a Tally -----
(defFlavour Tally (ako DataCollector) (ivars sum min max)
  setivars getivars testivars)

(defMethod (update! Tally) (aValue)
  (if (self 'obs?)
      (set! obs (+ 1 (self 'obs) ) )
      (set! obs 1) )
  (if (self 'sum?)
      (set! sum (+ aValue sum) )
      (set! sum aValue) )
  (if (or (not (self 'min?) ) (<? aValue min) )
      (set! min aValue) )
  (if (or (not (self 'max?) ) (>? aValue max) )
      (set! max aValue) ) )

(defMethod (reset! tally) ()
  (set! obs 0) (set! sum 0) (set! min 0) (set! max 0) )

(defMethod (show Tally) ()
  (if (self 'obs?)
      (begin (DisplayLine "--- tally:" (self 'name) )
             (DisplayLine (self 'obs)
                          "observations were made.")
             (DisplayLine "      Mean:"
                          (if (not (zero? (self 'obs) ) )
                              (/ sum (self 'obs) )
                              "0") )
             (DisplayLine "   Min : " min)
             (DisplayLine "   Max : " max) ) ) )
```

II.2 Probability distributions

```
; --- the MacScheme "random" function is used ---
; if necessary this may be replaced by the "MyRandom" procedure
; in our "Systems" toolbox

(defFlavour Distribution (ako Vanilla) (ivars name sampleTally)
  setivars getivars testivars)

(defMethod (reset! Distribution) () (sampleTally 'reset!) )

(defMethod (show Distribution) ()
  (DisplayLine "===" (self 'flavourName) ":" name)
  (if (self 'sampleTally?)
      (sampleTally 'show)
      (DisplayLine "No samples were taken !") ) )

(defMethod (update Tally! Distribution) (aValue)
  (if (not (self 'sample Tally?) )
      (set! sampleTally (Tally 'new) ) )
  (sampleTally 'update! aValue) )
```

```
; ----- Boolean Distribution -----
(defFlavour DrawDist (ako Distribution) (ivars %true)
  setivars getivars testivars)

(defMethod (sample DrawDist) ()
  (define tORf (>? (* %true 100) (random 100) ) )
  (define value (if tORf 1 0) )
  (self 'updateTally! value)
  tORf)

; ----- Integer Uniform Distribution -----
(defFlavour RandIntDist (ako Distribution) (ivars lower upper)
  setivars getivars testivars)

(defMethod (sample RandIntDist) ()
  (define sampleInt 0)
  (define range (- upper lower) )
  (set! sampleInt (+ lower (random (+ 1 range) ) ) )
  (self 'updateTally! sampleInt)
  sampleInt)
```

II.3 A discrete event simulator

```
; ----- a MONITOR flavour -----

(defFlavour Monitor (ako Actor)
  (ivars clockTime agenda simTime dataCollectors distributions tracing?)
  setivars getivars testivars)

; <clockTime> holds the model's current clock time (a real number)
; <agenda>    is an object of flavour "SequencingSet"
; <simTime>   limits a simulation's duration
; <dataCollectors> and <distributions> are lists of entities -
; used by reset! and report!
(defMethod (simulate! Monitor) (aTimeLimit)
  (set! tracing? #f)
  (set! clockTime 0)
  (set! simTime aTimeLimit)
  (if (not (self 'agenda?) ) (set! agenda (SequencingSet 'new ) ) )
  #t )

(defMethod (addDataCollectors! Monitor) anEntityList
  (for-each (lambda (anEntity)
              (self 'dataCollectors!
                    (if (pair? dataCollectors)
                        (cons anEntity dataCollectors)
                        (list anEntity) ) ) )
            anEntityList) )
```

```
(defMethod (addDistributions! Monitor) anEntityList
  (for-each
    (lambda (anEntity)
      (self 'distributions!
        (if (pair? distributions)
            (cons anEntity distributions)
            (list anEntity) ) ) )
    anEntityList) )

(defMethod (startUp! Monitor) ()
  (if (>? simTime clockTime)
    (self 'continue 'resumeProcesses)
    (DisplayLine "time limit too low – no simulation started !!!") ) )

(defMethod (schedule! Monitor) (anObject aMethodName aTime)
  (if (self 'tracing?)
    (begin (DisplayLine "* MONITOR: at:" clockTime "another"
                        aMethodName
                        "event scheduled for:" aTime) ) )
  (if (<? aTime clockTime)
    (error "clocks can't run backwards !!!" aClockTime)
    (agenda 'noteEvent! aTime anObject aMethodName) ) )

(defCoroutine (resumeProcesses Monitor) ()
  (let ((next nil) )
    (while (not (self 'finished?) ) ; may be replaced by "do"
        (begin
          ; get first event on the agenda
          (set! next (agenda 'nextEvent!) )
          ; update the clock to this event
          (set! clockTime (next 'timeOfOccurrence) )
          ; execute event
          (if (<=? clockTime simTime)
                (begin (if (self 'tracing?)
                           (begin (DisplayLine "* MONITOR: --- executing ---")
                                  (next 'show) ) )
                       ; else transfer control to the appropriate process
                       ; (coroutine) of the relevant actor
                      (self 'resume (next 'actorRef)
                                    (next 'processName) ) ) ) ) )
    (DisplayLine "*** simulation stops at:" clockTime) ) )

(defMethod (finished? Monitor) ()
  (or (agenda 'empty?) (>? clockTime simTime) ) )

(defMethod (reset! Monitor) ()
  (set! tracing? #f)
  (set! clockTime 0)
  (agenda 'clear!)
  (for-each (lambda (anEntity) (anEntity 'reset!) ) dataCollectors)
  (for-each (lambda (anEntity) (anEntity 'reset!) ) distributions)
  #t)
```

```
(defMethod (show Monitor) ()
  (define toGo (if (or (<=? simTime 0) (<=? clockTime 0) )
                   0
                   (- simTime clockTime) ) )
  (DisplayLine "+++++ Monitor STATE +++++")
  (DisplayLine "... Clock Time:" clockTime "...")
  (DisplayLine "->" (if (>? toGo 0) toGo 0) "to go !")
  (agenda 'show) )

(defMethod (report Monitor) ()
  (self 'show) (newline)
  (DisplayLine "+++ data collectors:")
  (for-each (lambda (anEntity) (anEntity 'show) (newline) )
            dataCollectors)
  (DisplayLine "+++ distributions:")
  (for-each (lambda (anEntity) (anEntity 'show) (newline) )
            distributions) )

; ----- flavour SequencingSet -----

(defFlavour SequencingSet (ako Vanilla) (ivars contents)
  setivars getivars testivars)

; Sequencing sets contain a list of event notices.
; Event notices are sorted, so that the "next imminent event"
; will always be at the head of this list.

(defMethod (empty? SequencingSet) () (not (self 'contents?) ) )

(defMethod (clear! SequencingSet) () (self 'contents! nil) )

(defMethod (noteEvent! SequencingSet) (aTime anObject aMethodName)

  (define notice (EventNotice 'new) )
  (define AgendaSearchedSoFar nil)
  ; this is used to remember the head of the agenda while "cdr-ing"
  ; down its tail

  (define (insert! anEventNotice aSequencingSet)

    (define nextEvent (car aSequencingSet) )
    (if (not (null? aSequencingSet) )
        ; then look for the right place to insert it !
        (begin
          (if (>? (nextEvent 'timeOfOccurrence)
                  (anEventNotice 'timeOfOccurrence) )
              ; insert here, by appending to the tail of the list, and appending
              ; this structure to the unchanged head
              (set! AgendaSearchedSoFar
                    (append AgendaSearchedSoFar
                            (append (list anEventNotice) aSequencingSet) ) )
              ; keep on looking in the list's cdr - remembering what we
              ; chopped off (in "AgendaSearchedSoFar")
              (begin (set! AgendaSearchedSoFar
```

```
                    (append AgendaSearchedSoFar
                        (list nextEvent) ) )
                    (insert! anEventNotice
                                (cdr aSequencingSet) ) ) ) )
        ; else put it at the end
        (set! AgendaSearchedSoFar
              (append AgendaSearchedSoFar
                          (list anEventNotice) ) ) )
        AgendaSearchedSoFar)

    (notice 'timeOfOccurrence! aTime)
    (notice 'actorRef!          anObject)
    (notice 'processName!       aMethodName)
    ; now insert "notice" at its proper place in the agenda
    ; - "insert!" will return an updated SequencingSet
    (self 'contents! (insert! notice (self 'contents) ) )
    #f)

(defMethod (nextEvent! SequencingSet) ()
    (define next nil)
    (if (self 'empty?)
        (DisplayLine "no more events in system !!!")
        (begin (set! next        (car contents) )
               (set! contents (cdr contents) ) ) )
    next)

(defMethod (show SequencingSet) ()
    (if (self 'empty?)
        (DisplayLine "----- no events in system -----")
        (begin (displayLine "---- scheduled for execution -----")
               (for-each (lambda (anEvent) (anEvent 'show) )
                         (self 'contents) ) ) ) )

; ----- flavour EventNotice -----

(defFlavour EventNotice (ako Vanilla)
    (ivars timeOfOccurrence actorRef processName)
    setivars getivars testivars)

; Event notices encapsulate all information relevant to a particular event – its
; nature (defined by a process attached to an actor object), and the clock
; time at which it is about to occur.

(defMethod (show EventNotice) ()
    (DisplayLine ". at:" (self 'timeOfOccurrence) "a"
                (self 'processName) "event.") )

; ----- flavour Process -----

; Processes define objects with life cycles

(defFlavour Process (ako Actor) (ivars name monitor)
    setivars getivars testivars)
```

```
(defMethod (hold Process) (aMethodName aDuration)
  (monitor 'schedule! self aMethodName
                        (+ (monitor 'clockTime) aDuration) )
  (self 'resume monitor 'resumeProcesses) )

(defMethod (show Process) ()
  (displayLine "+" name ", a Process of flavour" (self 'flavourName) ) )
```

Appendix III
Toolbox Sources

III.1 System Toolbox

```
;;;
;;; S Y S T E M   T O O L B O X
;;; = = = = = = =   = = = = = = = =
;;;
;;; System Dependent Toolbox
;;;
;;; This toolbox localizes those calls to routines that are specific
;;; to a particular implementation.
;;;
;;; This version is specific to MacScheme
;;;

(define *SchemeVersion* "MacScheme")

; The following is the most negative/positive fixnum. They are used
; for example as the value of a state in the search toolbox of
; little/great relevance.

(define NEG-INFINITY -536870911)
(define INFINITY     +536870911)

; Output
; ----------
; Allow multiple argument form of display with and without final newline

(define DisplayLine
  (lambda someArgs
    (for-each (lambda (arg)
                (display arg) (display " "))
              someArgs)
    (newline)))

(define DisplayList
  (lambda someArgs
    (for-each (lambda (arg)
```

```
                (display arg) (display " "))
            someArgs)))

; Error handling
; ------------------
; All detected errors in the toolboxes call Fatal-Error with a
; message describing the error. If a routine named Error-Continuation
; has been defined it is called instead of the system debugger

(define Error-Continuation #f)

(define Fatal-Error
  (lambda aMessageList
    (display "TOOLBOX ERROR: ")
    (for-each (lambda (aMessage)
                (display " ")
                (display aMessage))
              aMessageList)
    (newline)
    (if Error-Continuation
        (Error-Continuation "ERROR-VALUE")
        (error "TOOLBOX ERROR: "))))

; Testing
; ----------
; The following routines are only called in the testing routines so that
; it is not necessary that they be defined to use the toolbox. The
; functions 'eval' and 'pretty-print' are not part of standard R3
; schema but they are available in many implementations.

(define EvalExp (lambda (anExp) (eval anExp)))

(define MyPrettyPrint (lambda (anExp) (pretty-print anExp)))

; Random Numbers
; ------------------------
; The following routine is called in places such as where a move is
; to be chosen at random from a list of equally suitable candidates.
; This function is suitable only for non-critical uses.

(define MyRandom
  (lambda (n)
    ; Returns a pseudo-random non-negative integer less than a
    ; positive integer n.
    ; (random n)))

; Mac Graphics (specific to MacScheme)
; ------------------
; Allow the use of graphics. Set up the graphics window and set
; variable AllowGraphics to notify display routines

(define AllowGraphics #f)

(define BeginGraphics (lambda () (set! AllowGraphics #t) (start-graphics 'half)))

(define EndGraphics (lambda () (set! AllowGraphics #f) (end-graphics)))
```

III.2 Search Toolbox

```
;;;
;;; S E A R C H    T O O L B O X
;;; = = = = = =    = = = = = = =
;;;
;;; Depends on the following other toolboxes:
;;;     Systems
;;;
;;; This toolbox provides the tools to define and explore a
;;; search space.
;;;
;;;  STATE            - a list of symbols encoding a state description
;;;  STATETRIPLE      - a vector of <status value (state)> triples
;;;  PATH             - a list of statetriples
;;;  SEARCHLEVEL      - a list of (partially) explored paths of
;;;                     the same length (<depth> <path> . . .)
;;;  STATESPACE       - a list of searchlevels
;;;  ACTIONLIST       - a list of function names
;;;  SEARCH-PROBLEM - a vector of variables controlling a search
;;;                     problem.
;;;

;;; = = = = = operations on SEARCHPROBLEMS = = = = =

;
; A search problem is represented by a vector whose elements
; store information about a search.
;  traceFlag       - determines the amount of information
;                    displayed during the search
;  announceFlag - determines the amount of information
;                    displayed after the search
;  count           - number of moves performed to date
;  initialState    - state in state space from which the search began
;  printStateFN    - a procedure used to display a state
;  evalFN          - a function that provides a measure of
;                    closeness to a goal state. The closer the
;                    state the larger the returned value.
;  goalFN          - a function that tests for goal states
;  actions         - a list of transformer functions that generate a new
;                    state from an old state. An action returns #f if
;                    it cannot be applied to the state.
;  sameStateFN? - a procedure used to compare states for equality.
;

(define *traceIndex        0)
(define *announceIndex     1)
(define *countIndex        2)
(define *stateIndex        3)
(define *printStateIndex   4)
(define *evalIndex         5)
```

```
(define *goalIndex           6)
(define *actionIndex         7)
(define *sameStateIndex 8)

(define *lengthSearchVector 9)
(define MakeSearchProblem
  (lambda (aState aGoalFN anEvalFN someActions)
  (let ((aProblem (make-vector *lengthSearchVector)))
    (vector-set! aProblem *traceIndex          #f)
    (vector-set! aProblem *announceIndex #f)
    (vector-set! aProblem *countIndex          0)
    (vector-set! aProblem *stateIndex          aState)
    (vector-set! aProblem *printStateIndex display)
    (vector-set! aProblem *evalIndex           anEvalFN)
    (vector-set! aProblem *goalIndex           aGoalFN)
    (vector-set! aProblem *actionIndex         someActions)
    (vector-set! aProblem *sameStateIndex equal?)
    aProblem)))

(define ZeroCount!
  (lambda (aSearchProblem)
    (vector-set! aSearchProblem *countIndex 0)))

(define GetCount
  (lambda (aSearchProblem)
    (vector-ref aSearchProblem *countIndex)))

(define IncCount!
  (lambda (aSearchProblem)
    (vector-set! aSearchProblem
                 *countIndex
                 (+ (vector-ref aSearchProblem *countIndex) 1))))

(define GetInitialState
  (lambda (aSearchProblem)
    (vector-ref aSearchProblem *stateIndex)))

(define PrintState
  (lambda (aState aSearchProblem)
    ((vector-ref aSearchProblem *printStateIndex) aState)))

(define SetPrintState!
  (lambda (aSearchProblem aValue)
    (vector-set! aSearchProblem *printStateIndex aValue)))

(define GetEvalFN
  (lambda (aSearchProblem)
    (vector-ref aSearchProblem *evalIndex)))

(define GetGoalFN
  (lambda (aSearchProblem)
    (vector-ref aSearchProblem *goalIndex)))
```

```
(define GetActions
  (lambda (aSearchProblem)
    (vector-ref aSearchProblem *actionIndex)))

(define SameState?
  (lambda (aState1 aState2 aSearchProblem)
    ((vector-ref aSearchProblem *sameStateIndex) aState1 aState2)))

(define SetSameState!
  (lambda (aSearchProblem aValue)
    (vector-set! aSearchProblem *sameStateIndex aValue)))

(define GetAnnounceFlag
  (lambda (aSearchProblem)
    (vector-ref aSearchProblem *announceIndex)))

(define SetAnnounceFlag!
  (lambda (aSearchProblem)
    (vector-set! aSearchProblem *announceIndex #t)))

(define ResetAnnounceFlag!
  (lambda (aSearchProblem)
    (vector-set! aSearchProblem *announceIndex #f)))

(define GetTraceFlag
  (lambda (aSearchProblem)
    (vector-ref aSearchProblem *traceIndex)))

(define SetTraceFlag!
  (lambda (aSearchProblem)
    (vector-set! aSearchProblem *traceIndex #t)))

(define ResetTraceFlag!
  (lambda (aSearchProblem)
    (vector-set! aSearchProblem *traceIndex #f)))

(define PrintSearchProblem
  (lambda (aSearchProblem)
    (newline)
    (display "Initial state: ")
    (PrintState (GetInitialState aSearchProblem) aSearchProblem)
    (newline)
    (DisplayLine "Move(s)        :" (GetCount aSearchProblem))
    (DisplayLine "Goal function:" (GetGoalFN aSearchProblem))
    (DisplayLine "Eval function :" (GetEvalFN aSearchProblem))
    (DisplayLine "Action(s)      :" (GetActions aSearchProblem))
    (DisplayLine "Tracing        :"
                 (if (GetTraceFlag aSearchProblem) "on" "off"))
    (DisplayLine "Announcing  :"
                 (if (GetAnnounceFlag aSearchProblem) "on" "off"))))
```

```
; ===== fns on STATES =====
; These functions may be of use to the user if a state
; consists of a simple list of symbols.

(define FirstElement
  (lambda (aState) (car aState)))

(define RestOfElements
  (lambda (aState) (cdr aState)))

(define EmptyState?
  (lambda (aState) (null? aState)))

(define FindSymbolInSlot
  (lambda (aSlotNumber aState)
    (if (EmptyState? aState)
        (Fatal-Error "FindSymbolInSlot:" "Slot-Index in State out of Range")
        (if (eq? aSlotNumber 1)
            (FirstElement aState)
            (FindSymbolInSlot (- aSlotNumber 1)
                              (RestOfElements aState))))))

(define FindFirstSlotOfSymbol
  (lambda (aSymbol aState)
    (let ((subList (memq aSymbol aState)))
      (if (null? subList)
          (Fatal-Error "FindFirstSlotOfSymbol:"
                       "No symbol" aSymbol "in state" aState)
          (- (length aState) (length (RestOfElements subList)))))))

(define FillSlot
  (lambda (aSlotNumber aSymbol aState)
    (cond ((or (<= aSlotNumber 0) (EmptyState? aState))
           (Fatal-Error "FillSlot:" "Slot-Index in State out of Range"))
          ((eq? aSlotNumber 1)
           (cons aSymbol (RestOfElements aState)))
          (else
           (cons (FirstElement aState)
                 (FillSlot (- aSlotNumber 1)
                           aSymbol
                           (RestOfElements aState)))))))

; ===== fns on ACTIONLISTS =====
; (lists of function names)

(define MakeActionList (lambda aList aList))

(define FirstAction (lambda (anActionList) (car anActionList)))

(define RestOfActions (lambda (anActionList) (cdr anActionList)))

(define EmptyActions? (lambda (anActionList) (null? anActionList)))

(define PrintActionList (lambda (anActionList) (display anActionList)))
```

```
; ===== fns on STATETRIPLES =====
; Vectors of <status> <value> <state>
; - The "status" slot will record the fact that a state is "ok", has
;   been "seen-before" or has some other reason for being invalid;
; - The "value" slot records the state's score according to
;   some user-defined EvalFN. It defaults to NEG-INFINITY, a large
;   negative score representing a state of little relevance.
; - The "state" slot holds a list of symbols encoding the
;   state's instantiation.

(define *statusSlot 0)
(define *valueSlot  1)
(define *stateSlot  2)

(define MakeTriple
  (lambda (aState aStatus) (vector aStatus NEG-INFINITY aState)))

(define GetTripleStatus
  (lambda (aStateTriple) (vector-ref aStateTriple *statusSlot)))

(define SetTripleStatus!
  (lambda (aStateTriple aStatus)
    (vector-set! aStateTriple *statusSlot aStatus)
    aStateTriple))

(define ValidTripleState?
  (lambda (aStateTriple) (eq? 'ok (GetTripleStatus aStateTriple))))

(define InvalidTripleState?
  (lambda (aStateTriple) (not (ValidTripleState? aStateTriple))))

(define GetTripleValue
  (lambda (aStateTriple)
    ; return -INFINITY if state not 'ok'
    (if (ValidTripleState? aStateTriple)
      (vector-ref aStateTriple *valueSlot)
      NEG-INFINITY)))

(define SetTripleValue!
  (lambda (aStateTriple aValue)
    (vector-set! aStateTriple *valueSlot aValue)
    aStateTriple))

(define ScoreTripleValue!
  (lambda (aStateTriple anEvalFN)
    (if (or (null? anEvalFN) (InvalidTripleState? aStateTriple))
      NEG-INFINITY
      (let* ((state (GetTripleState aStateTriple))
             (value (apply anEvalFN (list state))))
        (SetTripleValue! aStateTriple value)
        value))))

(define GetTripleState
  (lambda (aStateTriple) (vector-ref aStateTriple *stateSlot)))
```

```
(define EmptyTriple?
  (lambda (aStateTriple) (null? aStateTriple)))

(define SameTriple?
  (lambda (aTriple 1 aTriple2 aSearchProblem)
    (if (EmptyTriple? aTriple1)
        (EmptyTriple? aTriple2)
        (SameState? (GetTripleState aTriple1)
                    (GetTripleState aTriple2)
                    aSearchProblem))))

(define PrintTriple
  (lambda (aStateTriple aSearchProblem)
    (if (EmptyTriple? aStateTriple)
        (display "empty triple")
        (begin
          (DisplayList "#<" (GetTripleStatus aStateTriple)
                       (let ((val (GetTripleValue aStateTriple)))
                         (if (= val NEG-INFINITY) "-INF" val)))
        (PrintState (GetTripleState aStateTriple) aSearchProblem)
        (display ">")))))

(define ExploreAll
  (lambda (aStateTriple aSearchProblem)
    ; Return a new search-level (list of all successors of a given statetriple),
    ; obtained by applying all transformations described in "anActionList"

    (define exploreTriple
      (lambda (anAction)
        ; Return a new statetriple, by applying a specified
        ; transformation to the current triple
        (if (or (EmptyTriple? aStateTriple) (null? anAction))
            (Fatal-Error "ExploreAll:"
                         "Unable to Explore state triple" aStateTriple
            (let* ((oldState (GetTripleState aStateTriple))
                   (newState (apply anAction (list oldState))))
             (if (EmptyState? newState)
                 (MakeTriple #f 'invalid-state)
                 (MakeTriple newState 'ok))))))

    (define exploreAllAux
      (lambda (anActionList)
        (if (EmptyActions? anActionList)
            #f
            (begin (IncCount! aSearchProblem)
                   (cons (exploreTriple (FirstAction anActionList))
                         (exploreAllAux (RestOfActions anActionList)))))))

    (cond ((EmptyTriple? aStateTriple)
           (Fatal-Error "ExploreAll: Illegal empty triple"))
          ((EmptyActions? (GetActions aSearchProblem))
           #f)
          (else (exploreAllAux (GetActions aSearchProblem))))))
```

```
; ===== fns on PATHS =====
; A list of statetriples giving the path from the initial
; state. The first triple of the path is the current triple
; and the remaining are ancestors of the current triple
(define MakePath
  (lambda aStateTriple aStateTriple))

(define CurrentTriple (lambda (aPath) (car aPath)))

(define AncestorTriples (lambda (aPath) (cdr aPath)))

(define PathLength (lambda (aPath) (length aPath)))

(define EmptyPath? (lambda (aPath) (null? aPath)))

(define ValidPath?
  (lambda (aPath)
    (equal? (GetTripleStatus (CurrentTriple aPath)) 'ok)))

(define InvalidPath? (lambda (aPath) (not (ValidPath? aPath))))

(define PrintPath
  (lambda (aPath aSearchProblem)

    (define printPathAux
      (lambda (aPath)
        (if (EmptyPath? aPath)
            #f
            (begin (PrintTriple (CurrentTriple aPath)
                                aSearchProblem)
                   (display "")
                   (printPathAux (AncestorTriples aPath))))))

    (cond ((EmptyPath? aPath) (display "Empty path !"))
          ((InvalidPath? aPath) (display "Invalid path: ")
                                (printPathAux aPath))
          (else (printPathAux aPath)))))

(define SpawnSearchLevel
  (lambda (aPath aSearchProblem aDepth)
    ; Return a new search-level by building a list of valid,
    ; partially explored state sequences (paths). This is achieved
    ; by finding all successors of the state at the end of a given
    ; path and deleting all cycles (those sequences leading to states
    ; which were previously encountered on the same path). This
    ; function returns #f if "aPath" is invalid or a list of new
    ; alternative paths (with next nodes tacked on). "cycle" is stored
    ; in the terminal path node if that path leads to a cycle and can
    ; therefore not be extended any further.

    (define FlagCyclicPaths
      (lambda (aPath)
        ; If aPath contains a cycle then return aPath with
        ; the status of the head node as "cycle",
        ; otherwise return the original path.
```

```
        (define containsTriple?
          (lambda (aTriple aPath)
            ; Does path contain triple?
            (cond ((EmptyPath? aPath)
                   #f)
                  ((SameTriple? aTriple (CurrentTriple aPath
                                            aSearchProblem)
                   #t)
                  (else
                   (containsTriple? aTriple
                                    (AncestorTriples aPath))))))
      (if (EmptyPath? aPath)
          #f
          (if (containsTriple? (CurrentTriple aPath)
                               (AncestorTriples aPath))
            (cons (SetTripleStatus! (CurrentTriple aPath) 'cycle)
                  (AncestorTriples aPath))
            aPath))))
(let ((newPath aPath))
  (if (InvalidPath? newPath) ; if 'status' is not 'ok' collapse path to #f
      #f
      (MakeSearchLevel
       aDepth
       (map (lambda (newState)
              (FlagCyclicPaths (cons newState newPath)))
            (ExploreAll (CurrentTriple newPath) aSearchProblem))))))

; ===== fns on SEARCHLEVELS =====
; (a list of <depth> <path> . . .)

(define MakeSearchLevel
  (lambda (aLevelNo aPathList) (cons aLevelNo aPathList)))

(define GetLevelDepth (lambda (aSearchLevel) (car aSearchLevel)))

(define GetPathList (lambda (aSearchLevel) (cdr aSearchLevel)))

(define EmptySearchLevel? (lambda (aSearchLevel) (null? aSearchLevel)))

(define CurrentPath
  (lambda (aSearchLevel)
    (if (not (EmptySearchLevel? aSearchLevel))
        (car (GetPathList aSearchLevel))
        #f)))

(define RestOfPaths
  (lambda (aSearchLevel)
    (if (EmptySearchLevel? aSearchLevel)
        (Fatal-Error ''RestOfPaths: Illegal empty search level'')
        (cdr (GetPathList aSearchLevel)))))
```

```
(define RestOfSearchLevel
  (lambda (aSearchLevel)
    (if (or (EmptySearchLevel? aSearchLevel)
            (null? (RestOfPaths aSearchLevel)))
        #f
        (MakeSearchLevel (GetLevelDepth aSearchLevel)
                         (RestOfPaths aSearchLevel)))))

(define PrintSearchLevel
  (lambda (aSearchLevel aSearchProblem)

    (define printSearchLevelAux
      (lambda (aPathList)
        (if (null? aPathList)
            #f
            (begin (display "....")
                   (PrintPath (car aPathList) aSearchProblem)
                   (newline)
                   (printSearchLevelAux (cdr aPathList))))))

    (if (EmptySearchLevel? aSearchLevel)
        (DisplayLine "Empty search level")
        (begin (DisplayLine "Level at depth"
                            (GetLevelDepth aSearchLevel)
                            "contains"
                            (length (GetPathList aSearchLevel))
                            "path(s):")
               (printSearchLevelAux (GetPathList aSearchLevel))))
    #f))

; ===== fns on STATESPACES =====
; (list of search-levels)

(define MakeStateSpace
  (lambda someSearchLevels someSearchLevels))

(define CurrentSearchLevel (lambda (aStateSpace) (car aStateSpace)))

(define OldSearchLevels (lambda (aStateSpace) (cdr aStateSpace)))

(define EmptyStateSpace? (lambda (aStateSpace) (null? aStateSpace)))

(define PrintStateSpace
  (lambda (aStateSpace aSearchProblem)
    (if (EmptyStateSpace? aStateProblem)
        #f
        (begin (PrintSearchLevel (CurrentSearchLevel aStateSpace)
                                 aSearchProblem
               (PrintStateSpace (OldSearchLevels aStateSpace)
                                aSearchProblem)))))
```

```
; ===== fns to control search of a SearchProblem =====

(define Search
  (lambda (aSearchProblem aSearchMethod evalInitial?)
    ; attempt to find a solution to aSearchProblem using aSearchMethod
    ; to control the generation of new state spaces. If evalInitial?
    ; is #t then it is necessary to score the initial state

    (define failSearch
      (lambda (aStateSpace)
        (if (GetAnnounceFlag aSearchProblem)
            (begin (DisplayLine "Search failed after"
                                (GetCount aSearchProblem)
                                "move(s) ")
                   (if aStateSpace
                       (begin
                         (display "State space at failure: ")
                         (PrintStateSpace aStateSpace aSearchProblem)
                         (newline))
                       #f))
            #f)))

    (define announceSolution
      (lambda (aStateSpace)
        (let* ((finalLevel (CurrentSearchLevel aStateSpace))
               (finalPath  (CurrentPath finalLevel))
               (depth      (GetLevelDepth finalLevel))
               (result (list depth
                             (GetCount aSearchProblem)
                             finalPath)))
          (if (GetAnnounceFlag aSearchProblem)
              (begin (DisplayLine "Solution found after"
                                  (GetCount aSearchProblem)
                                  "move(s) at depth"
                                  depth)
                     (DisplayLine "Successful path (length"
                                  (PathLength finalPath) ") is:")
                     (PrintPath finalPath aSearchProblem)
                     (newline))
              #f)
          result)))

    (define searchAux
      (lambda (aStateSpace tracing?)
        ; Look for a solution to aSearchProblem using aSearchMethod to
        ; control the generation of new state spaces. The search
        ; fails if aStateSpace contains no search levels. If the
        ; current search level is empty it is stripped from the state
        ; space and the search is continued, else the procedure
        ; aSearchMethod is called to generate a new state space.
```

```
        (define finished?
          (lambda (aStateTriple)
             (apply (GetGoalFN aSearchProblem)
                   (list (GetTripleState aStateTriple)))))
        (define foundSolution?
          (lambda ()
             (let ((currLevel (CurrentSearchLevel aStateSpace)))
                (cond ((EmptySearchLevel? currLevel) #f)
                      ((InvalidPath? (CurrentPath currLevel)) #f)
                      ((finished? (CurrentTriple (CurrentPath currLevel))) #t)
                      (else #f)))))
        (define pruneTopLevel
          (lambda ()
             (if (GetTraceFlag aSearchProblem)
                (DisplayLine ''PruneTopLevel pruning empty''
                             ''level in state space!!'')
                #f)
             (OldSearchLevels aStateSpace)))
        (define makeNewStateSpace
          (lambda ()
             (if (EmptySearchLevel? (CurrentSearchLevel aStateSpace))
                (pruneTopLevel)
                (apply aSearchMethod (list aStateSpace aSearchProblem)))))
        (if tracing?
           (begin (newline)
                  (DisplayLine ''*** After''
                               (GetCount aSearchProblem)
                               ''moves the state space is:'')
                  (PrintStateSpace aStateSpace aSearchProblem))
              #f)
        (cond ((EmptyStateSpace? aStateSpace)
               (failSearch aStateSpace))
              ((foundSolution?)
               (announceSolution aStateSpace))
              (else
               (searchAux (makeNewStateSpace) tracing?)))))
  (ZeroCount! aSearchProblem)
  (let ((initialTriple (MakeTriple (GetInitialState aSearchProblem) 'ok)))
    (if evalInitial?
       (ScoreTripleValue! initialTriple (GetEvalFN aSearchProblem))
       #f)
  (let* ((initialPath (MakePath initialTriple))
       (initialLevel (MakeSearchLevel 1 (list initialPath)))
       (initialStateSpace (MakeStateSpace initialLevel)))
    (searchAux initialStateSpace (GetTraceFlag aSearchProblem))))))
```

```
; ======================================
; ********************** S E A R C H   M E T H O D S *******
; ======================================

; ===== Depth-First Search =====
; Method to generate a newStateSpace is as follows: at each node all
; successor nodes are expanded and the first of these is always selected for
; further exploration, pushing a search path deeply into the state-action
; tree. Backtracking occurs whenever a node terminates in a dead-end
; or a specified maximum level of recursion (aMaxDepth) has been
; reached. This strategy makes no attempt to classify states into more or
; less 'promising' ones. Its effectiveness largely depends on the 'intel-
; ligent' ordering of action-functions in 'Actions'. If no constraint on
; the search depth is made the strategy may 'lose itself' in an infinite
; search space and may not terminate, even if solutions might be found
; at quite shallow levels of the state-action tree.

(define DFSearch
  (lambda (aSearchProblem aMaxDepth)
    ; The following method is used to generate a new state space by
    ; expanding the first node if the current depth is less than the
    ; max depth to be explored. If this is not the case then the first
    ; node is removed from the state space

    (define aDFMethod
      (lambda (aStateSpace aSearchProblem)
        (let* ((currLevel (CurrentSearchLevel aStateSpace))
               (currDepth (GetLevelDepth currLevel)))
          (append (if (= currDepth aMaxDepth)
                      (list (RestOfSearchLevel currLevel))
                      (list (SpawnSearchLevel (CurrentPath currLevel)
                                              aSearchProblem
                                              (+ currDepth 1))
                            (RestOfSearchLevel currLevel)))
                  (OldSearchLevels aStateSpace)))))

    (Search aSearchProblem aDFMethod #f)))

; ===== Breadth-First Search =====
; Method to generate a newStateSpace is as follows: this is (like depth-first
; search) another ''uninformed'' search strategy. Instead of growing
; a search path downwards into a state/action tree (as is done for
; depth-first search), it first explores ALL alternatives at a given
; level. This is guaranteed to find any possible solution eventually, but it can
; be VERY slow if this is hidden deeply inside the tree. Its effectiveness
; can again be influenced by the order in which ''Actions'' are evaluated.

(define BFSearch
  (lambda (aSearchProblem)
    ; The following method is used to generate a newStateSpace by deal-
    ; ing with a new level only if the top level is empty. The first path
    ; of the top level is taken and any new levels spawned by it are
    ; added to the end of all the remaining partially explored paths.
```

```
(define appendLevel
  (lambda (aStateSpace aLevel)
    ; Add aLevel to end of aStateSpace and merge with the
    ; last level if they are of the same depth

    (define appendLevelAux
      (lambda (aStateSpace aLevel)
        (let ((head (CurrentSearchLevel aStateSpace))
              (tail    (OldSearchLevels aStateSpace)))
          (if (EmptyStateSpace? tail)
              (if (and (not (EmptySearchLevel? head))
                       (not (EmptySearchLevel? aLevel))
                       (= (GetLevelDepth head)
                          (GetLevelDepth aLevel)))
                  (list (cons (GetLevelDepth head)
                              (append (GetPathList head)
                                      (GetPathList aLevel))))
                  (list head aLevel))
              (cons head (appendLevelAux tail aLevel))))))

    (if (EmptyStateSpace? aStateSpace)
        (list aLevel)
        (appendLevelAux aStateSpace aLevel))))

(define aBFMethod
  (lambda (aStateSpace aSearchProblem)
    (let ((currLevel (CurrentSearchLevel aStateSpace)))
      (if (EmptySearchLevel? currLevel)
          (OldSearchLevels aStateSpace)
          (append (list (RestOfSearchLevel currLevel))
                  (appendLevel
                      (OldSearchLevels aStateSpace)
                      (SpawnSearchLevel (CurrentPath currLevel)
                                        aSearchProblem
                                        (+ (GetLevelDepth currLevel)
                                           1))))))))

(Search aSearchProblem aBFMethod #f)))
; ===== Hill Climbing Search =====
; Method to generate a newStateSpace is as follows:
; this strategy introduces the idea of a 'scoring function' which is
; used to rank states according to their expected distance from a
; solution. A hill climbing search will always select the 'next'
; alternative on a search path (essentially 'depth first') as long as
; its value is non-descreasing. As soon as it encounters a 'downhill'
; path, this node is pruned from the tree and the next alternative
; is selected, backtracking whenever a search-level has been exhausted.
; Effectiveness of this strategy is strongly dependent on the 'quality'
; of the scoring function. It may not always find a (pruned) solution
; even though one exists. For well-behaved search spaces it may,
; however, quite quickly converge to a goal state.
```

```
(define HillSearch
  (lambda (aSearchProblem aMaxDepth)
    ; The following method is used to generate a newStateSpace by
    ; expanding the first node only if the current depth is less than
    ; the max depth. Paths produced by this node are pruned if their
    ; scores are less than the score of the expanded node.

    (define aHillMethod
      (lambda (aStateSpace aSearchProblem)

        (define pruneDownhillPaths
          (lambda (aSearchLevel aScore)
            (if (EmptySearchLevel? aSearchLevel)
                aSearchLevel
                (let ((aDepth    (GetLevelDepth aSearchLevel))
                      (oldPaths  (GetPathList aSearchLevel))
                      (newPaths  #f))
                  (for-each
                    (lambda (aPath)
                      (if (>= (ScoreTripleValue!
                                (CurrentTriple aPath)
                                (GetEvalFN aSearchProblem))
                              aScore)
                          (set! newPaths (append new Paths list aPath)))
                          #f))
                    oldPaths)
                  (if (null? newPaths)
                      #f
                      (MakeSearchLevel aDepth newPaths))))))

        (let* ((currLevel   (CurrentSearchLevel aStateSpace))
               (currDepth  (GetLevelDepth currLevel))
               (nodeScore (GetTripleValue  (CurrentTriple
                                              (CurrentPath currLevel)))))
          (append
            (if (= currDepth aMaxDepth)
                (list (RestOfSearchLevel currLevel))
                (list (pruneDownhillPaths (SpawnSearchLevel
                                             (CurrentPath currLevel)
                                             aSearchProblem
                                             (+ currDepth 1))
                                           nodeScore)
                      (RestOfSearchLevel currLevel)))
            (OldSearchLevels aStateSpace)))))

    (Search aSearchProblem aHillMethod #t)))

; ===== Steepest Ascent Search =====
; Method to generate a newStateSpace is as follows:
; this strategy carries the idea of scoring states even further. As
; each node is expanded the whole list of its successors can be
; scanned for their scores. At each level, therefore, the 'best'
```

```
; alternative is always chosen next. This approach suffers from the
; same difficulty as the 'hill climbing' approach, in as much as its
; performance is very sensitive to the predictions made by the
; evaluation function. It may converge more quickly to a solution,
; but the additional computational effort of scoring and finding the
; 'best' alternative of all the successors of a state may be
; significant.

(define SteepestSearch
  (lambda (aSearchProblem)
    ; The following method is used to generate a newStateSpace. The
    ; state space will consist of only a single level and a single
    ; "best" path. This path is expanded and then the next level
    ; constructed by selecting the best from those paths that result.

    (define aSteepestMethod
      (lambda (aStateSpace aSearchProblem)

        (define findBestPath
          (lambda (aPathList bestValue bestPath)
            (if (null? aPathList)
                bestPath
                (let* ((head      (car aPathList))
                       (tail      (cdr aPathList))
                       (currValue (ScoreTripleValue!
                                    (CurrentTriple head)
                                    (GetEvalFN aSearchProblem))))
                  ; Note the next line is >= rather than > to ensure that even if all
                  ; paths have a value of NEG-INFINITY then one will be chosen.
                  (if (>= currValue bestValue)
                      (findBestPath tail currValue head)
                      (findBestPath tail bestValue bestPath))))))

        (let* ((currLevel (CurrentSearchLevel aStateSpace))
               (currPath (CurrentPath currLevel)))
          (if (EmptyPath? currPath)
              ( ) ; return empty state space; i.e. failure
              (let*
                ((newDepth (+ (GetLevelDepth currLevel) 1))
                 (newLevel (SpawnSearchLevel currPath
                                             aSearchProblem
                                             newDepth)))
                (if (EmptySearchLevel? newLevel)
                    #f
                    (MakeStateSpace (MakeSearchLevel
                                      newDepth
                                        (list (findBestPath
                                                (GetPathList newLevel)
                                                NEG-INFINITY
                                                #f)))))))))))

    (Search aSearchProblem aSteepestMethod #t)))
```

III.3 Games Toolbox

```
;;;
;;;   G A M E S    T O O L B O X
;;;   = = = = =    = = = = = = =
;;;
;;;
;;; Depends on the following other toolboxes:
;;;      Systems
;;;      Search

; This toolbox is built upon the lower levels of the search toolbox.
; It provides routines to select the best move from the
; current game position for the machine and it also provides a framework
; to play a game with the user. The game tree is an AND/OR tree to be
; evaluated to a particular ply level. It assumes the existence of an
; 'evaluation' function that can be used to rate each game position
; from the machine's perspective. The higher the value, the
; better the position (as far as the machine is concerned).

; ===== operations on Game Problems =====
;
; A game problem shares some of the structure of a Search Problem.
; The tracing, announcing, count, initial state and evaluation slots
; are used in the same way except that the evaluation function is now
; passed a second parameter, which is #t if the next move from the
; state is the machine's. The goal function slot is now used to hold a
; user function that detects special states such as won, lost or
; drawn states, or states in which the game allows an extra move to the
; last player. It is passed both the state and a flag indicating who moves next
; (#t for machine). It should return one of the following:
;
; "machine"  - This state is a won position for the machine.
; "opponent" - This state is a won position for the opponent.
; "draw"     - This state is a draw position.
; "again"    - This state is one which allows an extra move for the
;              last player.
; #f         - There is nothing special about this state.
; The actions are split into two sets, the machine's moves and the opponent's
; moves. A slot is used to hold an optional function to accept moves from
; the user, check their validity and then return the state produced after
; a move (which may be the same state if a pass is allowed) or #f to indicate
; resignation. If no such function is supplied, a simple interface to request
; a new move is used.

(define *specialStateIndex      6)
(define *machineActionsIndex    7)
(define *opponentActionsIndex   8)
(define *getAMoveIndex          9)

(define *lengthGameVector      10)

(define MakeGameProblem
```

```
(lambda (aState aSpecialStateFN anEvalFN
         machineActions opponentActions)
  let ((aProblem (make-vector *lengthGameVector)))
    (vector-set! aProblem *traceIndex              #f)
    (vector-set! aProblem *announceIndex           #f)
    (vector-set! aProblem *countIndex              0)
    (vector-set! aProblem *stateIndex              aState)
    (vector-set! aProblem *printStateIndex         display)
    (vector-set! aProblem *evalIndex               anEvalFN)
    (vector-set! aProblem *specialStateIndex       aSpecialStateFN)
    (vector-set! aProblem *machineActionsIndex     machineActions)
    (vector-set! aProblem *opponentActionsIndex    opponentActions)
    (vector-set! aProblem *getAMoveIndex           #f)
    aProblem)))

(define SpecialState
  (lambda (aState aGameProblem machineMove?)
    ((vector-ref aGameProblem *specialStateIndex)
     aState machineMove?)))

(define GetMachineActions
  (lambda (aGameProblem)
    (vector-ref aGameProblem *machineActionsIndex)))

(define GetOpponentActions
  (lambda (aGameProblem)
    (vector-ref aGameProblem *opponentActionsIndex)))

(define SetGetAMove!
  (lambda (aGameProblem aUserFN)
    (vector-set! aGameProblem *getAMoveIndex aUserFN)))

(define GetGetAMove
  (lambda (aGameProblem)
    (vector-ref aGameProblem *getAMoveIndex)))

(define PrintGameProblem
  (lambda (aGameProblem)
    (newline) (display "Initial State         : ")
    (PrintState (GetInitialState aGameProblem) aGameProblem)
    (newline)
    (DisplayLine "Move(s)                : " (GetCount aGameProblem))
    (DisplayLine "Eval function          : " (GetEvalFN aGameProblem))
    (DisplayLine "Machine Action(s)  : "
                 (GetMachineActions aGameProblem))
    (DisplayLine "Opponent Action(s) : "
                 (GetOpponentActions aGameProblem))
    (DisplayLine "GetAMove function : " (GetGetAMove aGameProblem))
    (if (GetTraceFlag aGameProblem)
      (DisplayLine "Tracing              : on")
      (DisplayLine "Tracing              : off"))
    (if (GetAnnounceFlag aGameProblem)
```

```
      (DisplayLine "Announcing            : on")
      (DisplayLine "Announcing            : off"))))

; ===== operations on GAMELEVELS =====
; A list of (score move . . .)

(define MakeGameLevel
  (lambda (aScore aMoveList)
    (if (null? aMoveList) #f (cons aScore aMoveList))))

(define GetLevelScore
  (lambda (aGameLevel) (car aGameLevel)))

(define GetLevelMoves
  (lambda (aGameLevel) (cdr aGameLevel)))

(define EmptyGameLevel?
  (lambda (aGameLevel) (null? aGameLevel)))

(define DisplayScore
  (lambda (score)
    (display (cond ((= score NEG-INFINITY) "-INF")
                   ((= score INFINITY)     "+INF")
                   (else                   score)))))

(define ChooseRandomMove
  (lambda (aLevel aGameProblem)
    ; Return one of the moves at random
    (newline)
    (DisplayList "Move chosen from among"
                 (length (GetLevelMoves aLevel))
                 "of value")
    (DisplayScore (GetLevelScore aLevel))
    (DisplayList " after generating" (GetCount aGameProblem))
    (list-ref (GetLevelMoves aLevel)
              (MyRandom (length (GetLevelMoves aLevel))))))

(define PrintGameLevel
  (lambda (aGameLevel aGameProblem)

    (define printGameLevelAux
      (lambda (aMoveList)
        (if (null? aMoveList)
            #f
            (begin (PrintState (car aMoveList) aGameProblem)
                   (display "   ")
                   (printGameLevelAux (cdr aMoveList))))))

    (if (EmptyGameLevel? aGameLevel)
        (display "Empty game level")
        (begin (display "Best score: ")
               (DisplayScore (GetLevelScore aGameLevel))
               (DisplayLine " Best moves:")
               (printGameLevelAux (GetLevelMoves aGameLevel))))))

; ===== fns to control playing of a GameProblem =====
```

```
(define MakeStateGenerator
  (lambda (aState aGameProblem machineMove?)
    ; Return a function that will return successor states of 'aState'
    ; using the machine or opponent's actions of aGameProblem. After
    ; the last state has been produced the function returns #f.
    (let ((remainingActions (if machineMove?
                                (GetMachineActions aGameProblem)
                                (GetOpponentActions aGameProblem))))
      (lambda ()
        (do ((nextState #f))
            ((or (EmptyActions? remainingActions) nextState)
             (if nextState
                 (IncCount! aGameProblem)
                 #f)
             nextState)
            (set! nextState ((FirstAction remainingActions) aState))
            (set! remainingActions (RestOfActions remainingActions)))))))

(define FindBestMachineMove
  (lambda (aState aGameProblem alphabeta? aPly)
    ; Return the best moves for the machine from 'aState' expanding
    ; the game tree to level 'aPly'. If 'alphabeta' is #t then apply
    ; alpha-beta pruning.

    (define scoreState
      (lambda (aState aDepth machineMove? alpha beta tracing?)
        ; Return the value of this position.
        ; The value of 'aDepth' gives the current number of levels
        ; from the bottom of the 'aPly' game tree. 'machineMove?' is
        ; #t if the next move is to be made by the machine. The values
        ; alpha and beta are used by the alpha-beta method and simply
        ; hold NEG-INFINITY and INFINITY for the minimax method.
        (let ((result 0)
              (pruneRest #f)
              (status (SpecialState aState aGameProblem machineMove?)))
          (if tracing?
              (begin (DisplayList "Enter scoreState"
                                  (if machineMove? "(MAX)" "(MIN)")
                                  "state =" aState
                                  "depth =" aDepth)
                     (if aphabeta?
                         (begin (display " alpha=") (DisplayScore alpha)
                                (display " beta=") (DisplayScore beta))
                         #f)
                     (newline))
              #f)
          (cond ((and status (string=? status "machine"))
                 (set! result INFINITY))
                ((and status (string=? status "opponent"))
                 (set! result NEG-INFINITY))
                ((and status (string=? status "draw"))
                 (set! result 0))
```

```
((and (not status) (zero? aDepth))
 (set! result
       ((GetEvalFN aGameProblem) aState
                                 machineMove?)))
(else
  ; At interior node of tree. Build new set of states
  ; and then call this function recursively to evaluate
  ; them and return the best score. If status was
  ; 'again' then swap move and do not decrement
  ; depth.
  (let ((stateGenerator #f)
        (newDepth 0))
     (if status
        (begin
         (if (string=? status "again")
             #f
             (Fatal-Error "FindBestMachineMove:"
                          "Unexpected value"
                          status
                          "returned from user fn"))
         (set! machineMove? (not machineMove?))
         (set! newDepth aDepth))
       (set! newDepth (- aDepth 1)))
(set! stateGenerator
      (MakeStateGenerator aState
                          aGameProblem
                          machineMove?))
(do ((nextState (stateGenerator) (stateGenerator))
     (nextScore 0)
     (bestScore (if machineMove? alpha beta)))
    ((or pruneRest (EmptyState? nextState))
     (set! result bestScore))
    (set! nextScore (scoreState nextState
                                newDepth
                                (not machineMove?)
                                alpha
                                beta
                                tracing?))
    (if machineMove?
        (begin ; MAX level
         (set! bestScore (max bestScore nextScore))
         (if alphabeta?
             (begin
              (set! alpha bestScore)
              (if (>= alpha beta)
                  (begin (set! bestScore beta)
                         (set! pruneRest #t))
```

```
                                        #f))
                                    #f))
                              (begin ; MIN level
                               (set! bestScore (min bestScore nextScore))
                               (if alphabeta?
                                   (begin
                                    (set! beta bestScore)
                                    (if (>= alpha beta)
                                        (begin (set! bestScore alpha)
                                               (set! pruneRest #t))
                                        #f))
                                   #f)))))))
      (if tracing?
          (begin (DisplayList "Exit scoreState"
                              (if machineMove? "(MAX)" "(MIN)")
                              (if pruneRest "(PRUNED)" " ")
                              "state=" aState "depth=" aDepth
                              "-> ")
                 (DisplayScore result)
                 (newline))
          #f)
      result)))
(define announceMoves
  (lambda (aGameLevel)
    (DisplayLine "Best moves for machine from state:")
    (PrintState aState aGameProblem)
    (DisplayLine " found after trying"
                 (GetCount aGameProblem)
                 "moves at" aPly "ply.")
    (PrintGameLevel aGameLevel aGameProblem)
    (newline)))
(ZeroCount! aGameProblem)
(let ((stateGenerator (MakeStateGenerator aState aGameProblem #t))
      (resultLevel #f))
  (do ((nextState (stateGenerator) (stateGenerator))
       (nextScore 0)
       (bestScore NEG-INFINITY)
       (bestMoves #f))
      ((EmptyState? nextState)
       (set! resultLevel (MakeGameLevel bestScore bestMoves)))
      (set! nextScore
            (scoreState nextState
                        (- aPly 1)
                        #f
                        (if (and alphabeta?
                                 (not (= bestScore NEG-INFINITY)))
                            (- bestScore 1)
```

```
                                  NEG-INFINITY)
                                INFINITY
                                (GetTraceFlag aGameProblem)))
        (cond ((> nextScore bestScore)
                (set! bestScore nextScore)
                (set! bestMoves (list nextState)))
               ((= nextScore bestScore)
                (set! bestMoves (cons next State bestMoves)))))
    (if (GetAnnounceFlag aGameProblem)
      (announceMoves resultLevel)
      #f)
    resultLevel)))

(define GetAMove
  (lambda (aState aGameProblem)
    ; Get a move from the user. Use the user-supplied function if one
    ; is produced, otherwise just request the state of the game after
    ; the move.
    (let ((userFN (GetGetAMove aGameProblem))
          (newState #f))
      (newline)
      (if userFN
        (set! newState (userFN aState))
        (begin
          (DisplayLine "Enter the board state after your move.")
          (DisplayLine "(#f if resign, same state if pass):" aState)
          (set! newState (read))))
      newState)))

(define PlayGame
  (lambda (aGameProblem)
    ; Play the game defined by 'aGameProblem' with the user.
    ; Request the ply level, who is to move first, and whether
    ; alpha-beta pruning is requested.

    (define announceEnd
      (lambda (aState status)
        (newline)
        (cond ((string=? status "machine")
               (DisplayLine "Machine wins. Bad luck!"))
              ((string=? status "resign")
               (DisplayLine "You resign, machine wins. Bad luck!"))
              ((string=? status "opponent")
               (DisplayLine "You win. Well done!"))
              ((string=? status "draw")
               (DisplayLine "Game is draw. Good game!"))
              (else
               (Fatal-Error "PlayGame:"
                            "Unexpected value"
                            status
                            "returned from user fn")))
```

```
        (if (EmptyState? aState)
            #f
            (begin (DisplayLine ''Final state of game is:'')
                   (PrintState aState aGameProblem)))))
    (let ((aPly (do ((n 0))
                    ((and (number? n) (positive? n)) n)
                    (newline)
                    (DisplayLine ''Give ply level (>0) :'')
                    (set! n (read))))
          (alphabeta? (do ((reply ''invalid''))
                          ((boolean? reply) reply)
                          (newline)
                          (DisplayLine ''Use alpha-beta pruning? (y/n) :'')
                          (set! reply (read))
                          (cond ((eq? reply 'y) (set! reply #t))
                                ((eq? reply 'n) (set! reply #f)))))
          (machineMove? (do ((reply ''invalid''))
                            ((boolean? reply) reply)
                            (newline)
                            (DisplayLine ''Is machine to move first? (y/n) :'')
                            (set! reply (read))
                            (cond ((eq? reply 'y) (set! reply #t))
                                  ((eq? reply 'n) (set! reply #f)))))
          (state (GetInitialState aGameProblem)))
  (do ((stateStatus #f)
       (gameOver #f))
      (gameOver (announceEnd state stateStatus))
      (newline)
      (DisplayLine ''Current game state (''
                   (if machineMove? ''Machine's'' ''Your'')
                   ''move) :'')
      (PrintState state aGameProblem)
      (newline)
      ; get machine or user to make a move
      (set! state
            (if machineMove?
                (ChooseRandomMove (FindBestMachineMove
                                    state
                                    aGameProblem
                                    alphabeta?
                                    aPly) aGameProblem)
                (GetAMove state aGameProblem)))
      ; ensure next move is next player's
      (set! machineMove? (not machineMove?))
      ; is it a special state?
      (set! stateStatus
            (if (EmptyState? state)
                ''resign''
                (SpecialState state aGameProblem machineMove?)))
```

```
; look for end of game or repeated move
(if stateStatus
    (cond ((or (string=? stateStatus "machine")
               (string=? stateStatus "resign")
               (string=? stateStatus "opponent")
               (string=? stateStatus "draw"))
           (set! gameOver #t))
          ((string=? stateStatus "again")
           (set! machineMove? (not machineMove?))))
    #f)))))
```

III.4 Patterns Toolbox

```
;;;
;;;  P A T T E R N S   T O O L B O X
;;;  = = = = = = = = =   = = = = = = =
;;;
;;; Depends on the following other toolboxes:
;;;     Systems
;;;
;;; This toolbox contains routines to match patterns. The patterns
;;; may contain elements that match any single atom/list or a
;;; sequence of atoms/lists. It is possible to bind such a part of
;;; the matching string to a variable. It is also possible to provide
;;; additional restrictions that must be fulfilled for a match to
;;; succeed.
;;;
; User interface:
; ========
;
;       (Match pattern string)
; or
;       (Match pattern string AList)
;
; where pattern consists of a list of atoms, lists or matching
; elements; string is a list which will be tested for conformance
; with the pattern. Match with only two parameters uses an initially
; empty AList. However, optionally a third parameter AList may be
; supplied to provide initial variable bindings. This AList may have
; for example been returned from a previous call to Match. Both
; functions return #f if the match fails and #t or an AList if the
; match succeeds. If the pattern specified bindings then an
; association list (alist) giving the binding will be returned on
; success rather than #t. If an initial AList was supplied to Match
; then the returned AList also includes these initial bindings.
;
; The form of the matching elements are:
;
```

```
; ?          match any single atom or list
; ?+         match any number of atoms and/or lists
; (?   var) match any single atom or list and bind it to
;            var in the returned AList
; (?+ var) match any sequence of atoms and/or lists and
;            append them to any existing list bound to var
;            or create a new list and bind to var in the
;            returned AList
; (<-? var) match against the value (atom or list) bound
;            to var by a previous matching
; (?    var predicate1? predicate2? . . .)
; (?+  var predicate1? predicate2? . . .)
; (<-? var predicate1? predicate2? . . .)
;            match and bind as above but also require that
;            none of the expressions
;            (predicate1? var), (predicate2? var), . . .
;            evaluate to #f for the match to succeed.
;            Each predicate is called with the current
;            association list as a parameter
;
; Examples
; =====
;
; (Match (PATTERN "xxx" 123 'a)
;          '("xxx" 123 a))                ==> #t
; (Match (PATTERN "xxx" 123 'a)
;          '("xxx" 124 a))                ==> #f
; (Match (PATTERN "xxx" ? 'a)
;          '("xxx" 123 a))                ==> #t
; (Match (PATTERN "xxx" ?+)
;          '("xxx" 123 a))                ==> #t
; (Match (PATTERN "xxx" (? 'x) 'a)
;          '("xxx" 123 a))                ==> ((x 123))
; (Match (PATTERN "xxx" (? 'x) (? 'y))
;          '("xxx" 123 a))                ==> ((x 123) (y a))
; (Match (PATTERN "xxx" (?+ 'x))
;          '("xxx" 123 a))                ==> ((x (123 a)))
; (Match (PATTERN "xxx" (? 'x) (<-? 'x))
;          '("xxx" 123 123))              ==> ((x 123))
; (Match (PATTERN "xxx" (?+ 'x) (<-? 'x))
;          '("xxx" 123 124 123 124))  ==> ((x (123 124)))
; (Match (PATTERN "xxx" (? 'x isxnumber? isxpositive?))
;          '("xxx" 123))                  ==> ((x 123))
; (Match (PATTERN "xxx" (? 'x isxnumber? isxpositive?))
;          '("xxx" -123))                 ==> #f
; (Match (PATTERN "xxx" (PATTERN 1 (? 'x)) (? 'y))
;          '("xxx" (1 3) 123))            ==> ((x 3) (y 123))
; (Match (PATTERN "xxx" (<-? 'x))
```

```
;          '("xxx" 123)
;          '((x 123)))         ==> ((x 123))

; Data Structures
; ========
;
;    STRING                    - a list of symbols (atoms or lists)
;    ASSOCIATION               - a <name value> list, where atoms or
;                                lists may be used as values
;    ALIST                     - a list of ASSOCIATIONs
;    PATTERN                   - a list of symbols, including
;                                matching elements
;    MATCHING-ELEMENT - an (indicator var predicate) list
;
; ===== fns on STRINGs =====
; list of symbols (atoms or lists)
;
; implemented through the usual list processing functions

; ===== fns on ASSOCIATIONs =====
; (symbol value) lists

(define MakeAssoc
  (lambda (aSymbol aValue) (list aSymbol aValue)))

(define GetSymbol
  (lambda (anAssociation) (car anAssociation)))

(define GetValue
  (lambda (anAssociation) (cadr anAssociation)))

; ===== fns on ALISTs =====
; lists of ASSOCIATIONs

(define MakeAList (lambda anAssocList anAssocList))

(define GetNextAssoc (lambda (anAList) (car anAList)))

(define GetRestOfAssocs (lambda (anAList) (cdr anAList)))

(define StoreAssocAsItem
  (lambda (aSymbol anItem anAlist)
    ; used for "(? var . . .)" matches
    (append anAlist (list (MakeAssoc aSymbol anItem)))))

(define StoreAssocAsList
  (lambda (aSymbol anItem anAlist)
    ; used for "(?+ var . . .)" matches
    (cond ((null? anAlist)
           ; no binding for symbol yet - make new entry
           (MakeAList (MakeAssoc aSymbol (list anItem))))
          ((equal? aSymbol (GetSymbol (GetNextAssoc anAlist)))
           ; old binding already on the list - if association is a list append new
           ; values else make a fresh list
```

```
        (cons (MakeAssoc
                  aSymbol
                  (if (pair? (GetValue (GetNextAssoc anAlist)))
                      (append (GetValue (GetNextAssoc anAlist)) (list anItem))
                      (list anItem)))
              (GetRestOfAssoc anAlist)))
        (else (cons (GetNextAssoc anAlist)
                    ; remember first association and keep looking
                    (StoreAssocAsList aSymbol
                                      anItem
                                      (GetRestOfAssocs anAlist)))))))

(define GetAssociation
  (lambda (aPatternVariable anAlist)
    ; retrieves binding for "aPatternVariable" (if any)
    (assoc aPatternVariable anAlist)))

(define GetAssociationValue
  (lambda (aPatternVariable anAlist)
    ; retrieves value for "aPatternVariable" giving error if none
    (let ((association (GetAssociation aPatternVariable anAlist)))
      (if (null? association)
          (Fatal-Error "GetAssociationValue:"
                       "no previous binding for"
                       aPatternVariable)
          (GetValue association)))))

; ===== fns on PATTERNs =====
; lists of symbols, some of which are interpreted as
; MATCHING-ELEMENTs

(define PATTERN (lambda symbols symbols))

(define BuildNewPattern
  ; used for "(<-? var . . .)" elements. If old binding is a list
  ; prepend all the previous sequence to pattern (to be matched again)
  (lambda (anItemOrList aPattern)
    (if (pair? anItemOrList)
        (append anItemOrList aPattern)
        (cons anItemOrList aPattern))))

(define ? (lambda (var . predicates) (list ? var predicates)))

(define ?+ (lambda (var . predicates) (list ?+ var predicates)))

(define <-? (lambda (var . predicates) (list <-? var predicates)))

(define ?Symbol? (lambda (aSymbol) (equal? aSymbol ?)))

(define ?+Symbol? (lambda (aSymbol) (equal? aSymbol ?+)))

(define <-?Symbol? (lambda (aSymbol) (equal? aSymbol <-?)))

(define IsMatchingOperator?
  (lambda (anOperator)
```

```
    (or (?Symbol? anOperator)
        (?+ Symbol? anOperator)
        (<-?Symbol? anOperator))))

(define PrintMatchingOperator
  (lambda (anOperator)
    (cond ((?Symbol? anOperator)    (display "?"))
          ((?+Symbol? anOperator) (display "?+"))
          ((<-?Symbol? anOperator) (display "<-?")))))

(define PrintPattern
  (lambda (aPattern)

    (define printPatternAux
      (lambda (aPattern)

        (define printPatternElement
          (lambda (aPatternElement)
            (cond ((IsMatchingOperator? aPatternElement)
                   (PrintMatchingOperator aPatternElement))
                  ((IsMatchingElement? aPatternElement)
                   (PrintMatchingElement aPatternElement))
                  ((pair? aPatternElement)
                   (PrintPattern aPatternElement))
                  (else (display aPatternElement)))))

        (if (null? aPattern)
            #f
            (begin (printPatternElement (car aPattern))
                   (display " ")
                   (printPatternAux (cdr aPattern))))))

    (display "(")
    (printPatternAux aPattern)
    (display ")")))

(define MakeVariableSubst
  (lambda (aPattern anAList)
    ; replace all (<-? var) elements in pattern with the
    ; value bound to the variable in anAList
    (if (null? aPattern)
        (PATTERN)
        (let ((element (car aPattern)))
          (cons (if (and (IsMatchingElement? element)
                         (<-?Symbol? (MatchingOperator element)))
                    (GetAssociationValue (MatchingVariable element) anAList)
                    element)
                (MakeVariableSubst (cdr aPattern) anAList))))))

; ===== fns on MATCHING-ELEMENTs =====

; (indicator variable) or (indicator variable predicatelist) lists;
; where indicator is one of: ?, ?+, <-?, or <-?+.
```

```
(define MatchingOperator
  (lambda (aMatchingElement) (car aMatchingElement)))

(define MatchingVariable
  (lambda (aMatchingElement) (cadr aMatchingElement)))

(define MatchingPredicateList
  (lambda (aMatchingElement) (caddr aMatchingElement)))

(define IsMatchingElement?
  (lambda (aMatchingElement)
    (and (pair? aMatchingElement)
         (>= (length aMatchingElement) 2)
         (IsMatchingOperator? (MatchingOperator aMatchingElement)))))

(define SatisfiesPredicates?
  (lambda (anAList aPredicateList)
    ; returns the (boolean) result of applying ALL
    ; restricting fns to the restricted symbol
    (cond ((null? aPredicateList) #t)
          (((car aPredicateList) anAList)
           (SatisfiesPredicates? anAList (cdr aPredicateList)))
          (else #f))))

(define PrintMatchingElement
  (lambda (aMatchingElement)

    (define printPredicateList
      (lambda (aPredicateList)
        (if (null? aPredicateList)
            #f
            (begin (display (car aPredicateList))
                   (printPredicateList (cdr aPredicateList))))))

    (display "(")
    (PrintMatchingOperator (car aMatchingElement))
    (display " ")
    (display (cadr aMatchingElement))
    (if (caddr aMatchingElement)
        (begin (display " ")
               (printPredicateList (caddr aMatchingElement)))
        #f)
    (display ")")))

(define ProcessMatchingElement
  (lambda (aPattern aString anAList)

    (let* ((patternElement (car aPattern))
           (operator       (MatchingOperator patternElement))
           (variable       (MatchingVariable patternElement))
           (predicateList  (MatchingPredicateList patternElement))
           (restPattern    (cdr aPattern))
           (stringElement  (car aString))
```

```
        (restString          (cdr aString))
        (newAList            anAList))
    ; build new ALIST if (? . . .) of (?+ . . .)
    (cond ((?Symbol? operator)
           (set! newAList (StoreAssocAsItem variable
                                            stringElement
                                            anAList)))
          ((?+Symbol? operator)
           (set! newAList (StoreAssocAsList variable
                                            stringElement
                                            anAList)))
          (else #f))
    ; check predicates first and then attempt match
    (if (or (null? predicateList)
            (SatisfiesPredicates? newAList predicateList))
      (cond ((?Symbol? operator)
             ; matches and binds any SINGLE symbol to the pattern variable
             (MatchWithAList restPattern restString newAList))
            ((?+ Symbol? operator)
             ; matches and binds any SEQUENCE of symbols
             (or (MatchWithAList restPattern
                                 restString
                                 newAList)
                 (MatchWithAList aPattern
                                 restString
                                 newAList)))
            ((<-?Symbol? operator)
             ; retrieves a previous binding for the pattern
             ; variable and THEN tries to match that VALUE
             ; against the current symbol.
             (MatchWithAList (BuildNewPattern
                               (GetAssociationValue variable anAList)
                               restPattern)
                             aString
                             newAList)))
      #f))))

; ===== fns for control of pattern matching =====

(define MatchWithAList
  (lambda (aPattern aString anAList)
    ; scans a string for correspondence with a pattern using initial
    ; bindings given by anAList. If match is successful, it will
    ; return #t or a list of associations (bindings for pattern variables)

    (define ReportSuccess
      (lambda (anAList)
        ; indicates a successful match, returning variable bindings (if any)
        (if anAList anAList #t)))
```

```
(define ReportFailure (lambda () #f))

(cond ((and (null? aPattern) (null? aString))
       (ReportSuccess anAList))
      ((or (null? aPattern) (null? aString))
       (ReportFailure))
      ((?Symbol? (car aPattern))
       ; match against any SINGLE symbol
       (MatchWithAList (cdr aPattern) (cdr aString) anAList))
      ((?+ Symbol? (car aPattern))
       ; match against any SEQUENCE of symbols
       (or (MatchWithAList (cdr aPattern) (cdr aString) anAList)
           (MatchWithAList aPattern (cdr aString) anAList)))
      ((IsMatchingElement? (car aPattern))
       (ProcessMatchingElement aPattern aString anAList))
      ((and (pair? (car aString)) (pair? (car aPattern)))
       ; try matching sublist recursively
       (let ((newAList (MatchWithAList (car aPattern)
                                       (car aString)
                                       anAList)))
         (if newAList (MatchWithAList (cdr aPattern)
                                      (cdr aString)
                                      newAList)
                      (ReportFailure))))
      ; test if elements are equal?
      ((equal? (car aPattern) (car aString))
       (MatchWithAList (cdr aPattern) (cdr aString) anAList))
      (else (ReportFailure)))))

(define Match
  (lambda (aPattern aString . optionalAList)
    ; scans a string for correspondence with a pattern. If optionalAList is not
    ; supplied then no initial bindings are used. If match is successful, it
    ; will return #t or a list of associations (bindings for pattern variables)
    ; including any initial bindings if the optionalAList was supplied
    (cond ((null? optionalAList)
           (MatchWithAList aPattern aString (MakeAList)))
          ((null? (cdr optionalAList))
           (MatchWithAList aPattern aString (car optionalAList)))
          (else (Fatal-Error "Match:"
                             "Too many args"
                             (+ 2 (length optionalAList)))))))
```

III.5 KnowledgeBases Toolbox

```
;;;
;;;   K N O W L E D G E   B A S E S   T O O L B O X
;;;   = = = = = = = = =   = = = = =   = = = = = = =
;;;
;;; Depends on the following other toolboxes:
```

```
;;;      Systems
;;;      Patterns
;;;
;;; This toolbox contains routines to search an associative knowledge
;;; base for entries that contain a match for a given pattern. It is built on top of the
;;; pattern-matching toolbox.

; Data Structures
; ========
;
; FACT                  - arbitrary item. Some part of the FACT will
;                         contain either a STRING or a PATTERN in the
;                         pattern-matching toolbox sense
; KB                    - a list of FACTs
; RETRIEVED-ELEMENT - a list of the form (aFact anAList)
; RETRIEVED-LIST        - a list of RETRIEVED-ELEMENTs

; ===== fns on FACTs =====
; Not defined by this toolbox. The usual list-processing functions
; can be used to build and manipulate these

; ===== fns on KBs =====
; a KB is a list of FACTs.

(define MakeKB (lambda initialFacts initialFacts))

(define EmptyKB? (lambda (aKB) (null? aKB)))

(define FirstInKB (lambda (aKB) (car aKB)))

(define RestOfKB (lambda (aKB) (cdr aKB)))

(define KnownFact? (lambda (aFact aKB) (member aFact aKB)))

(define AddFact
  (lambda (aKB aFact)
    ; add a new fact to end of KB if not already present
    (if (KnownFact? aFact aKB)
      aKB
      (append aKB (list aFact)))))

(define RemoveFact
  (lambda (aKB aFact)
    ; remove a fact from the KB
    (cond ((null? aKB) #f)
          ((equal? (FirstInKB aKB) aFact) (RestOfKB aKB))
          (else (cons (FirstInKB aKB)
                      (RemoveFact (RestOfKB aKB) aFact))))))

(define PrintKB
  (lambda (aKB aDisplayProcedure)
      (if (null? aKB)
          #f
          (begin (aDisplayProcedure (FirstInKB aKB))
                 (newline)
                 (PrintKB (RestOfKB aKB) aDisplayProcedure)))))
```

```
; ===== fns on RETRIEVED-ELEMENTs =====
; a list of the form (fact aList)

(define MakeRetrievedElement
  (lambda (aFact anAList)
   (if (null? anAList)
       #f
       (list aFact anAList))))

(define GetFact
  (lambda (aRetrievedElement) (car aRetrievedElement)))

(define GetAList
  (lambda (aRetrievedElement) (cadr aRetrievedElement)))

; ===== fns on RETRIEVED-LISTs =====
; lists of RETRIEVED-ELEMENTs

(define MakeRetrievedList
  (lambda aRetrievedList aRetrievedList))

(define EmptyRetrievedList?
  (lambda (aRetrievedList) (null? aRetrievedList)))

(define CurrentRetrievedElement
  (lambda (aRetrievedList) (car aRetrievedList)))

(define RestOfRetrievedList
  (lambda (aRetrievedList) (cdr aRetrievedList)))

(define AddRetrievedElement
  (lambda (aRetrievedElement aRetrievedList)
   ; if aRetrievedElement is not empty append it to aRetrievedList
   (if (null? aRetrievedElement)
       aRetrievedList
       (append aRetrievedList (MakeRetrievedList aRetrievedElement)))))

(define CombineRetrievedLists
  (lambda (aRetrievedList1 aRetrievedList2)
   (cond ((EmptyRetrievedList? aRetrievedList1) aRetrievedList2)
         ((EmptyRetrievedList? aRetrievedList2) aRetrievedList1)
         (else (append aRetrievedList1 aRetrievedList2)))))

; ===== matching fns on KBs =====
; Each of these retrieving functions may optionally contain a selector
; function that can be applied to a FACT in the KB to extract either
; a STRING (for RetrieveByPattern or RetrieveAllByPattern) or a
; PATTERN (for RetrieveByString or RetrieveAllByString). If none is
; supplied then the whole FACT is used. There may also be an
; optionally supplied initial AList which will be used as a
; parameter to Match. If none is provided then it defaults to #f.
; The distinction between these two optional parameters is achieved
; by using the 'procedure?' predicate function.

(define SelectWholeFact (lambda (aFact) aFact))
```

```
(define RetrieveByPattern
  (lambda (aKB aPattern . optionalArguments )
    (let ((aSelectorFN SelectWholeFact)
          (anAList #f))

      ; Find first fact in 'aKB' that matches 'aPattern'. Only the
      ; part of the fact selected by 'aSelectorFN' is involved in the
      ; match. The list 'anAList' is passed to each call of Match
      ; Returns #f or a RETRIEVED-ELEMENT

      (define retrieveAux
        (lambda (aKB)
          (if (EmptyKB? aKB)
              #f
              (let* ((fact (FirstInKB aKB))
                     (string (aSelectorFN fact))
                     (result (Match aPattern string anAList)))
                (if result
                    (MakeRetrievedElement fact result)
                    (retrieveAux (RestOfKB aKB)))))))

      (if (> (length optionalArguments) 2)
          (Fatal-Error ''RetrieveByPattern:''
                       ''Too many optional arguments''
                       optionalArguments)
          #f)

      (do ((args optionalArguments (cdr args))
           (arg #f))
          ((null? args) #f)
          (set! arg (car args))
          (if (procedure? arg)
              (set! aSelectorFN arg)
              (set! anAList arg)))
      (retrieveAux aKB))))

(define RetrieveAllByPattern
  (lambda (aKB aPattern . optionalArguments )
    (let ((aSelectorFN SelectWholeFact)
          (anAList #f))
      ; Find all facts in 'aKB' that matches 'aPattern'. Only the
      ; part of the fact selected by 'aSelectorFN' is involved in the
      ; match. The list 'anAList' is passed to each call of Match
      ; Returns #f or a RETRIEVED-LIST

      (define retrieveAux
        (lambda (remainingKB prevResults)
          (if (EmptyKB? remainingKB)
              prevResults
              (let* ((fact (FirstInKB remainingKB))
                     (string (aSelectorFN fact))
                     (result (Match aPattern string anAList)))
```

```
            (retrieveAux (RestOfKB remainingKB)
                         (AddRetrievedElement
                          (MakeRetrievedElement fact result)
                         prevResults))))))
   (if (> (length optionalArguments) 2)
     (Fatal-Error "RetrieveByPattern:"
                  "Too many optional arguments"
                  optionalArguments)
     #f)
   (do ((args optionalArguments (cdr args))
        (arg #f))
       ((null? args) #f)
       (set! arg) (car args))
       (if (procedure? arg)
          (set! aSelectorFN arg)
          (set! anAList arg)))
   (retrieveAux aKB (MakeRetrievedList)))))

(define RetrieveByString
  (lambda (aKB aString . optionalArguments )
   (let ((aSelectorFN SelectWholeFact)
         (anAList #f))
    ; find first fact in 'aKB' with a pattern that matches 'aString'.
    ; Only the part of the fact selected by 'aSelectorFN' is
    ; involved in the match. The list 'anAList' is passed to each
    ; call of Match. Returns #f or a RETRIEVED-ELEMENT

    (define retrieveAux
      (lambda (aKB)
        (if (EmptyKB? aKB)
            #f
            (let* ((fact      (FirstInKB aKB))
                   (pattern (aSelectorFN fact))
                   (result    (Match pattern aString anAList)))
              (if result
                  (MakeRetrievedElement fact result)
                  (retrieveAux (RestOfKB aKB)))))))

    (if (> (length optionalArguments) 2)
      (Fatal-Error "RetrieveByPattern:"
                   "Too many optional arguments"
                   optionalArguments)
      #f)
    (do ((args optionalArguments (cdr args))
         (arg #f))
        ((null? args) #f)
        (set! arg (car args))
        (if (procedure? arg)
            (set! aSelectorFN arg)
```

```
          (set! anAList arg)))
    (retrieveAux aKB))))

(define RetrieveAllByString
  (lambda (aKB aString . optionalArguments )
    (let ((aSelectorFN SelectWholeFact)
          (anAList #f))
      ; Find all facts in 'aKB' with a pattern that matches 'aString'.
      ; Only the part of the fact selected by 'aSelectorFN' is
      ; involved in the match. The list 'anAList' is passed to each
      ; call of Match Returns #f or a list of RETRIEVED-ELEMENTs

      (define retrieveAux
        (lambda (remainingKB prevResults)
          (if (EmptyKB? remainingKB)
              prevResults
              (let* ((fact (FirstInKB remainingKB))
                     (pattern (aSelectorFN fact))
                     (result (Match pattern aString anAList)))
                (retrieveAux (RestOfKB remainingKB)
                             (AddRetrievedElement
                              (MakeRetrievedElement fact result)
                             prevResults))))))

      (if (> (length optionalArguments) 2)
          (Fatal-Error "RetrieveByPattern:"
                       "Too many optional arguments"
                       optionalArguments)
          #f)
      (do ((args optionalArguments (cdr args))
           (arg #f))
          ((null? args) #f)
          (set! arg (car args))
          (if (procedure? arg)
              (set! aSelectorFN arg)
              (set! anAList arg)))
      (retrieveAux aKB (MakeRetrievedList)))))
```

III.6 Productions Toolbox

```
;;;
;;;     P R O D U C T I O N S   T O O L B O X
;;;     = = = = = = = = = = = =   = = = = = = =
;;;
;;; Depends on the following other toolboxes:
;;;      Systems
;;;      Patterns
;;;      KnowledgeBases
;;;
;;; This toolbox contains routines to implement Production Systems.
```

```
;;; It is built on top of the pattern-matching and KB toolboxes.
;;;
;;; Knowledge-based systems store information as a collection of facts
;;; and rules. The package implements a simple forward chaining
;;; strategy for reasoning with rule-based knowledge bases implemented
;;; through production systems

; Data Structures
; =======
;
;   MEMORY                        - a list of facts ("working memory" WM) or
;                                   rules ("production memory" PM) implemented
;                                   as a KB data type from the KB toolbox
;   FACT                          - a list asserting a state of affairs in some world
;   RULE                          - a list of the form:
;                                   (Identifier aConditionList aConclusionList)
;   NEGATED-CONDITION             - a list of the form (~ PATTERN)
;   CONDITION-ELEMENT             - either a PATTERN or a NEGATED-CONDITION
;   CONDITION-LIST                - a list of CONDITION-ELEMENTs
;   ASSERTION                     - a list (ASSERT fact)
;   RETRACTION                    - a list (RETRACT fact)
;   EXECUTION                     - a list (EXECUTE procedure parameters)
;   RETURN                        - a list (RETURN procedure parameters)
;   CONCLUSION-ELEMENT            - an assertion, retraction, execution or return
;   CONCLUSION-LIST               - a list of CONCLUSION-ELEMENTs

; ===== fns on MEMORY =====
; The WM is a list of facts and the PM is a list of rules. The
; procedures from the KB toolbox can be used to create and manipulate
; these

(define MakeWM MakeKB)

(define MakePM MakeKB)

(define PrintWM (lambda (aWM) (PrintKB aWM PrintFact)))

(define PrintPM (lambda (aPM) (PrintKB aPM PrintRule)))

; ===== fns on FACTs =====
; the facts that make up the WM are lists of unspecified structure

(define PrintFact (lambda (aFact) (DisplayList "Fact:" aFact)))

; ===== fns on RULEs =====
; a list of the form (identifier conditions conclusions)

(define RULE
  (lambda (aName aConditionList aConclusionList)
    (list aName aConditionList aConclusionList)))

(define GetName (lambda (aRule) (car aRule)))

(define GetConditionList (lambda (aRule) (cadr aRule)))
```

```
(define GetConclusionList (lambda (aRule) (caddr aRule)))

(define PrintRule
  (lambda (aRule)
   (DisplayLine "+++ Rule:" (GetName aRule))
   (display " Conditions : ")
   (PrintConditions (GetConditionList aRule)) (newline)
   (display " Conclusions: ")
   (PrintConclusions (GetConclusionList aRule))
   (newline) (newline)))

; ===== fns on NEGATED-CONDITIONs =====
; lists of the form (~ pattern)

(define ~ (lambda (aPattern) (list '~ aPattern)))

(define GetNegatedPattern (lambda (aCondition) (cadr aCondition)))

(define NegatedCondition?
  (lambda (aCondition)
   ; is the condition of the form (~ pattern)?
   (and (not (null? aCondition))
        (eq? (car aCondition) '~))))

; ===== fns on CONDITION-LISTs =====
; lists of condition elements. Each condition element is a pattern
; data type from the pattern toolbox

(define CONDITIONS (lambda conditionList conditionList))

(define CurrentCondition (lambda (aConditionList) (car aConditionList)))

(define RestOfConditions (lambda (aConditionList) (cdr aConditionList)))

(define NoMoreConditions? (lambda (aConditionList) (null? aConditionList)))

(define PrintConditions
  (lambda (aConditionList)
   (if (null? aConditionList)
      #f
      (begin (PrintPattern (car aConditionList))
             (display "  ")
             (PrintConditions (cdr aConditionList))))))

; ===== fns on ASSERTIONs =====
; a list of the form: (ASSERT a-fact)

(define ASSERT (lambda (aFact) (list 'ASSERT aFact)))

(define GetAssertion
  (lambda (anAssertionElement) (cadr anAssertionElement)))

(define PrintAssertion
  (lambda (anAssertion)
   (display "(ASSERT ")
```

```
    (PrintPattern (GetAssertion anAssertion))
    (display ")")))

; ===== fns on RETRACTIONs =====
; a list of the form: (RETRACT a-fact)

(define RETRACT (lambda (aFact) (list 'RETRACT aFact)))

(define GetRetraction
  (lambda (aRetractionElement) (cadr aRetractionElement)))

(define PrintRetraction
  (lambda (aRetraction)
    (display "(RETRACT ")
    (PrintPattern (GetRetraction aRetraction))
    (display ")")))

; ===== fns on EXECUTIONs =====
; a list of the form: (EXECUTE aProc aParameterList)

(define EXECUTE
  (lambda (aProc . aParameterList)
    (list 'EXECUTE aProc aParameterList)))

(define GetProc (lambda (anExecution) (cadr anExecution)))

(define GetParameters (lambda (anExecution) (caddr anExecution)))

(define PrintExecution
  (lambda (anExecution)
    (DisplayList "(EXECUTE"
                 (GetProc anExecution)
                 (GetParameters anExecution)
                 ")")))

; ===== fns on RETURNs =====
; a list of the form: (RETURN aProc aParameterList)

(define RETURN
  (lambda (aProc . aParameterList)
    (list 'RETURN aProc aParameterList)))

(define PrintReturn
  (lambda (aReturn)
    (DisplayList "(RETURN"
                 (GetProc aReturn)
                 (GetParameters aReturn)
                 ")")))

; ===== fns on CONCLUSIONs =====
; either an ASSERTION, a RETRACTION, an EXECUTION or RETURN

(define Assertion?
  (lambda (aConclusionElement)
    (eq? (car aConclusionElement) 'ASSERT)))
```

```
(define Retraction?
  (lambda (aConclusionElement)
    (eq? (car aConclusionElement) 'RETRACT)))

(define Execution?
  (lambda (aConclusionElement)
    (eq? (car aConclusionElement) 'EXECUTE)))

(define Return?
  (lambda (aConclusionElement)
    (eq? (car aConclusionElement) 'RETURN)))

(define PrintConclusion
  (lambda (aConclusionElement)
    (cond ((Assertion? aConclusionElement)
            (PrintAssertion aConclusionElement))
           ((Retraction? aConclusionElement)
            (PrintRetraction aConclusionElement))
           ((Execution? aConclusionElement)
            (PrintExecution aConclusionElement))
           ((Return? aConclusionElement)
            (PrintReturn aConclusionElement))
           (else
              (Fatal-Error "PrintConclusion:"
                           "Bad conclusion"
                           aConclusionElement)))))

; ===== fns on CONCLUSION-LISTs =====
; lists of CONCLUSIONs

(define CONCLUSIONS (lambda conclusionList conclusionList))

(define CurrentConclusion
  (lambda (aConclusionList) (car aConclusionList)))

(define RestOfConclusions
  (lambda (aConclusionList) (cdr aConclusionList)))

(define NoMoreConclusions?
  (lambda (aConclusionList) (null? aConclusionList)))

(define PrintConclusions
  (lambda (aConclusionList)
    (if (null? aConclusionList)
        #f
        (begin (PrintConclusion (car aConclusionList))
               (display "   ")
               (PrintConclusions (cdr aConclusionList))))))

; ===== control fns for the Deduction Machine =====

; The "forward-chaining" problem solver uses the following strategy:
;
; Data structures: WM remembers facts,
;                  PM remembers rules.
```

```
;
; A. FOR EACH rule in PM
;
;    (1) Match the first CONDITION in the rule against all facts
;        in the WM using an initially empty association list to
;        yield RL, a RETRIEVEDLIST of fact/aList pairs, one for
;        each successful match against the pattern.
;    (2) FOR EACH remaining CONDITION in a rule:
;           (a) If RL is empty then this rule doesn't match so
;               try the next rule at step A
;           (b) Set RLNEW to be empty
;           (c) FOR EACH retrievedElement in RL
;                  (i) Match condition against all facts in WM
;                      with aList as the initial association list
;                      extracted from retrievedElement
;                  (ii) Append the resulting RETRIEVEDLIST to
;                      RLNEW.
;           (d) Set RL to be RLNEW
;    (3) FOR EACH conclusion in the rule
;           (a) If the conclusion is an Assertion/Retraction
;               then FOR EACH retrievedElement in RL
;                  (i) Replace all (<-? x) matching elements in
;                      the conclusion using the binding from AList
;                      extracted from retrievedElement
;                  (ii) Add/Remove the fact to/from theWM
;           (b) If the conclusion is an Execution then
;               FOR EACH retrievedElement in RL
;                  (i) Replace all (<-? x) matching elements in
;                      the parameters using the binding from AList
;                      extracted from retrievedElement
;                  (ii) Apply the procedure to the substituted
;                      parameters
;           (c) If the conclusion is a Return then
;               FOR ONLY THE FIRST retrievedElement in RL
;                  (i) Replace all (<-? x) matching elements in
;                      the parameters using the binding from AList
;                      extracted from retrievedElement
;                  (ii) Apply the procedure to a list of aWM plus
;                      the substituted parameters
;
; B. If any of the rules in the above causes an ASSERTION or
;    RETRACTION to change the WM then go back to step A.
;
; C. Return the updated value of WM
;

(define TestCondition
  (lambda (aCondition aWM anAList)
  ; Return a RETRIEVEDLIST of successful matches against aWM of
```

```
; the pattern in aCondition. If aCondition is a NEGATEDCONDITION
; then return a non-empty RETRIEVEDLIST only if there is no match
; against aWM for the pattern in aCondition.
(let ((pattern (if (NegatedCondition? aCondition)
                   (GetNegatedPattern aCondition)
                   aCondition))
      (aRL #f))
  (set! aRL (RetrieveAllByPattern aWM
                                  pattern
                                  (lambda (x) x)
                                  (if (eq? anAList #t)
                                      #f
                                      anAList)))
  (if (NegatedCondition? aCondition)
      (if (EmptyRetrievedList? aRL)
          (MakeRetrievedList
            (MakeRetrievedElement 'NEGATED-FACT (if anAList anAList #t)))
          (MakeRetrievedList))
      aRL))))

(define TestConditions
  (lambda (aConditionList aWM)
    ; If all the conditions in aConditionList are satisfied by the
    ; facts in aWM then return an updated RETRIEVEDLIST containing an
    ; entry for each successful match using the ALISTs obtained from
    ; oldRL. For a NEGATED-CONDITION the match succeeds only if an
    ; empty RETRIEVEDLIST is returned from the match

    (define testConditionsAux
      (lambda (aConditionList oldRL)

        (if (or (NoMoreConditions? aConditionList)
                (EmptyRetrievedList? oldRL))
            oldRL
            (let ((newRL (MakeRetrievedList))
                  (condition (CurrentCondition aConditionList)))
              (do ((restOfRL oldRL (cdr restOfRL))
                   (aList #f))
                  ((EmptyRetrievedList? restOfRL) #f)
                  (set! aList (GetAList (CurrentRetrievedElement restOfRL)))
                  (set! newRL
                        (CombineRetrievedLists
                         newRL
                         (TestCondition condition aWM aList))))
              (testConditionAux (cdr aConditionList) newRL)))))

    ; deal with the first condition as a special case in order to build the initial
    ; RETRIEVEDLIST and then use testConditionsAux to deal with
    ; any further conditions
    (if (NoMoreConditions? aConditionList)
```

```
      (MakeRetrievedList)
      (testConditionsAux (cdr aConditionList)
                          (TestCondition (car aConditionList)
                                         aWM
                                         (MakeAList))))))

(define ForwardChainer
  (lambda (aPM aWM . verboseFlag)
    (call-with-current-continuation
      (lambda (returnContinuation)
        ; Cycle through all the rules in aPM while there are resulting
        ; changes in aWM. If verboseFlag is absent it defaults to #f,
        ; if present with value #t then each deduction, retraction,
        ; execution and return is output. Return updated aWM
        (define performConclusions
          (lambda (ruleName aConclusionList anRL)
            ; return #t if any Assertion in aConclusionList causes
            ; aWM to be altered
            (let ((changedWM? #f))
              (define performAssertion!
                (lambda (anAssertion)
                  ; add fact to aWM for each aList substitution in anRL
                  (do ((restOfRL anRL (cdr restOfRL))
                       (aList #f)
                       (newFact #f))
                      ((EmptyRetrievedList? restOfRL) #f)
                      (set! aList (GetAList (CurrentRetrievedElement restOfRL)))
                      (set! newFact (MakeVariableSubst
                                      (GetAssertion anAssertion)
                                      (if (eq? aList #t) #f aList)))
                      (if (KnownFact? newFact aWM)
                          #f
                          (begin
                            (set! changedWM? #t)
                            (if verboseFlag
                                (begin
                                  (DisplayList "Rule" ruleName)
                                  (PrintAssertion anAssertion) (newline)
                                  (display ". . . adds fact ")
                                  (PrintPattern newFact) (newline))
                                #f)
                            (set! aWM (AddFact aWM newFact)))))))
              (define performRetraction!
                (lambda (aRetraction)
                  ; remove fact from aWM for each aList substitution in anRL
                  (do ((restOfRL anRL (cdr restOfRL))
                       (aList #f)
                       (oldFact #f))
```

```
          ((EmptyRetrievedList? restOfRL) #f)
          (set! aList (GetAList (CurrentRetrievedElement restOfRL)))
          (set! oldFact (MakeVariableSubst
                           (GetRetraction aRetraction)
                          aList))
          (if (not (KnownFact? oldFact aWM))
            #f
            (begin
              (set! changedWM? #t)
              (if verboseFlag
                 (begin
                   (DisplayList "Rule" ruleName)
                   (PrintRetraction aRetraction) (newline)
                   (display ". . . removes fact ")
                   (PrintPattern oldFact) (newline))
                #f)
              (set! aWM (RemoveFact aWM oldFact)))))))

(define substParams
  (lambda (aParamList anAList)
   ; substitute for (<-? x) type elements if possible PATTERNs
   (map (lambda (aParam)
           (if (pair? aParam)
              (MakeVariableSubst aParam anAList)
              aParam))
         aParamList)))

(define performExecution
  (lambda (anExecution)
   ; call the procedure for each AList with substituted
   ; parameters
   (if verboseFlag
      (begin (DisplayList "Rule" ruleName)
             (PrintExecution anExecution) (newline))
        #f)
   (do ((restOfRL anRL (cdr restOfRL))
        (aList #f)
        (newParams #f))
       ((EmptyRetrievedList? restOfRL) #f)
       (set! aList (GetAList (CurrentRetrievedElement restOfRL)))
       (set! newParams
             (substParams
              (GetParameters anExecution)
              (if (eq? aList #t) #f aList)))
       (apply (GetProc anExecution) newParams))))

(define performReturn
  (lambda (aReturn)
   ; call the procedure with parameters aWM and AList as
   ; substituted parameters. Use only the first
```

```
        ; RetrievedElement if there is more than one. Return the
        ; result from ForwardChainer
        ; WARNING: this fn causes a jump out of the ForwardChainer
        (let ((finalResult #f)
              (aList #f)
              (newParams #f))
          (if  verboseFlag
               (begin (DisplayList "Rule" ruleName)
                      (PrintReturn aReturn) (newline))
               #f)
          (set! aList (GetAList (CurrentRetrievedElement anRL)))
          (set! newParams
                (substParams (GetParameters aReturn)
                             (if (eq? aList #t) #f aList)))
          (set! finalResult
                (apply (GetProc aReturn)
                       (append (list aWM) newParams)))
          (returnContinuation finalResult))))

     (do ((restOfConclusions aConclusionList
                             (cdr restOfConclusions))
          (conclusion #f))
         ((NoMoreConclusion? restOfConclusions) changedWM?)
         (set! conclusion (CurrentConclusion restOfConclusions))
         (cond ((Assertion? conclusion)
                (performAssertion! conclusion))
               ((Retraction? conclusion)
                (performRetraction! conclusion))
               ((Execution? conclusion)
                (performExecution conclusion))
               ((Return? conclusion)
                (performReturn conclusion))
               (else
                (Fatal-Error "ForwardChainer:"
                             "Invalid conclusion"
                             conclusion))))
     changedWM?)))
(if  (null? verboseFlag)
     #f
     (set! verboseFlag (car verboseFlag)))
(do ((changedWM? #t))
    ((not changedWM?) aWM)
    (set! changedWM? #f)
    (do ((rulesToTry aPM (RestOfKB rulesToTry))
         (rule #f))
        ((EmptyKB? rulesToTry))
        (let* ((rule          (FirstInKB rulesToTry))
               (name          (GetName rule))
               (conditions    (GetConditionList rule))
```

```
          (conclusions (GetConclusionList rule))
          (RL #f))
    (set! RL (TestConditions conditions aWM))
    (if RL
        (set! changedWM?
              (performConclusions name conclusions RL))
        #f)))))))

(define FireRule
  (lambda (aRule aWM . verboseFlag)
    ; try a single rule by constructing a PM containing the
    ; rule and invoking ForwardChainer with aWM
    (if (null? verboseFlag)
        #f
        (set! verboseFlag (car verboseFlag)))
    (ForwardChainer (MakePM aRule) aWM verboseFlag)))
```

III.7 Associative Networks Toolbox

```
;;;
;;;     A S S O C I A T I V E   N E T W O R K S   T O O L B O X
;;;     = = = = = = = = = = = =   = = = = = = = =   = = = = = = =
;;;
;;; Depends on the following other toolboxes:
;;;         Systems

; This toolbox supports Associative Networks (ANs) among concepts
; which may be linked. Special property inheritance links labelled
; by AKO (A Kind Of) are recognized and other user-defined links may
; also be supplied. These links can be traversed by query functions.
; Simple "certainty" factors may optionally be attached to the user-
; defined links with values ranging from 0.0 (highly improbable) to
; 1.0 (virtually certain). Queries may then supply a threshold
; (value 0.0 to 1.0) specifying a minimum "strength" before which a
; path is considered to be present. Any factor that is not explicitly
; provided defaults to 1.0.

; The following data types are used:

; AKO-SLOT :a list of (AKO aListOfConceptNames)
; SLOT      :a list of (aLinkName aConceptName aCertaintyFactor)
; SLOT-LIST :a list of SLOTs
; CONCEPT   :a list of (aSymbol aSlotList)
; AN        :a list of CONCEPTs

; ===== fns on SLOTs =====
; either an AKO slot, a list of the form:
;         (AKO aConceptList)
; or a user-defined slot, a list of the form:
;         (aLinkName aConceptName aCertaintyFactor)
```

```
; or a list with an implied certainty factor of 1.0 of the form
;        (aLinkName aConceptName)
(define AKO (lambda aConceptList (list 'AKO aConceptList)))

(define LINK
  (lambda (aLinkName aConceptName . aCertaintyFactor)
   ; aCertaintyFactor defaults to 1.0 if not present and is not
   ; stored if 1.0
   (cond ((or (null? aCertaintyFactor) (= (car aCertaintyFactor) 1.0))
          (list aLinkName aConceptName))
         ((and (positive? (car aCertaintyFactor))
               (<= (car aCertaintyFactor) 1.0))
          (list aLinkName aConceptName (car aCertaintyFactor)))
         (else (Fatal-Error "LINK:" "Certainty factor" aCertaintyFactor
                            "not valid")))))

(define GetLinkName (lambda (aSlot) (car aSlot)))

(define AKOSlot?
  (lambda (aSlot)
   (if (pair? aSlot)
      (eq? 'AKO (GetLinkName aSlot))
      (Fatal-Error "AKOSlot?:" "Slot" aSlot "is illegal"))))

(define GetConceptList
  (lambda (anAKOSlot)
   (if (AKOSlot? anAKOSlot)
      (cadr anAKOSlot)
      (Fatal-Error "GetConceptList:" "Slot" anAKOSlot "not an AKO slot"))))

(define GetConceptName
  (lambda (aSlot)
   (if (AKOSlot? aSlot)
      (Fatal-Error "GetConceptName:" "Not valid on AKO slot" aSlot)
      (cadr aSlot))))

(define HasCertaintyFactor? (lambda (aSlot) (not (null? (cddr aSlot)))))

(define GetCertaintyFactor
  (lambda (aSlot)
   ; return 1.0 if it has none
   (cond ((AKOSlot? aSlot)
          (Fatal-Error "GetCertaintyFactor:" "Not valid on AKO slot" aSlot))
         ((HasCertaintyFactor? aSlot)
          (caddr aSlot))
         (else 1.0))))

(define PrintANSlot
  (lambda (aSlot)
   (if (AKOSlot? aSlot)
   (DisplayList "(AKO" (GetConceptList aSlot) ") ")
   (DisplayList "(LINK" (GetLinkName aSlot)
                       (GetConceptName aSlot)
```

```
                              (if (HasCertaintyFactor? aSlot)
                                  (GetCertaintyFactor aSlot)
                                  " ")
                              ")"))))
; ===== fns on SLOT-LISTs =====
; lists of SLOTs
(define NoMoreSlots? (lambda (aSlotList) (null? aSlotList)))
(define FirstSlot (lambda (aSlotList) (car aSlotList)))
(define RestOfSlots (lambda (aSlotList) (cdr aSlotList)))
; ===== fns on CONCEPTs =====
; list of the form (aConceptSymbol aSlotList)
(define CONCEPT
  (lambda (aConceptName . aSlotList) (list aConceptName aSlotList)))
(define MakeConceptWithList
  (lambda (aConceptName aSlotList) (list aConceptName aSlotList)))
(define GetConceptSymbol (lambda (aConcept) (car aConcept)))
(define GetSlots (lambda (aConcept) (cadr aConcept)))
(define PrintConcept
  (lambda (aConcept)
    (display (GetConceptSymbol aConcept)) (display ": ")
    (for-each (lambda (aSlot) (PrintANSlot aSlot) (display " "))
              (GetSlots aConcept))))
; ===== fns on ANs =====
; lists of CONCEPTs
(define MakeAN (lambda aConceptList aConceptList))
(define EmptyAN? (lambda (anAN) (null? anAN)))
(define FirstConcept (lambda (anAN) (car anAN)))
(define RestOfConcepts (lambda (anAN) (cdr anAN)))
(define AddConcept
  (lambda (anAN aConcept)
    (append (RemoveConcept anAN (GetConceptSymbol aConcept))
            (list aConcept))))
(define RemoveConcept
  (lambda (anAN aConceptSymbol)
    (cond ((EmptyAN? anAN) #f)
          ((eq? aConceptSymbol
                (GetConceptSymbol (FirstConcept anAN)))
           (RestOfConcepts anAN))
          (else (cons (FirstConcept anAN)
                      (RemoveConcept (RestOfConcepts anAN)
                                     aConceptSymbol))))))
```

```
(define RemoveLink
  (lambda (anAN aConceptSymbol aLinkSymbol)

    (define removeAux
      (lambda (aSlotList)
        ; remove LINK with name aLinkSymbol from list
        (cond ((null? aSlotList) #f)
              ((eq? aLinkSymbol (GetLinkName (car aSlotList)))
               (cdr aSlotList))
              (else (cons (car aSlotList)
                          (removeAux (cdr aSlotList)))))))

    (let ((aConcept (FindConcept anAN aConceptSymbol)))
      (if (null? aConcept)
          anAN
          (AddConcept anAN
                      (MakeConceptWithList
                        aConceptSymbol
                        (removeAux (GetSlots aConcept))))))))

(define AddLink
  (lambda (anAN aConceptSymbol aLink)
    (let* ((newAN (RemoveLink anAN aConceptSymbol
                              (GetLinkName aLink)))
           (aConcept (FindConcept newAN aConceptSymbol)))
      (AddConcept newAN
                  (MakeConceptWithList aConceptSymbol
                                       (if (null? aConcept)
                                           (list aLink)
                                           (append
                                             (GetSlots aConcept)
                                             (list aLink))))))))

(define RemoveAKOLink
  (lambda (anAN aConceptSymbol superClassConceptSymbol)

    (define removeAux
      (lambda (aConceptNameList)
        ; remove superClassConceptSymbol from list
        (cond ((null? aConceptNameList) #f)
              ((eq? superClassConceptSymbol (car aConceptNameList))
               (cdr aConceptNameList))
              (else (cons (car aConceptNameList)
                          (removeAux (cdr aConceptNameList)))))))

    (let ((oldLinks (GetAKOLinks anAN aConceptSymbol)))
      (AddLink anAN
               aConceptSymbol
               (list 'AKO (removeAux oldLinks))))))

(define AddAKOLink
  (lambda (anAN aConceptSymbol superClassConceptSymbol)
```

```
   (let ((oldLinks (GetAKOLinks anAN aConceptSymbol)))
     (if (member superClassConceptSymbol oldLinks)
         anAN
         (AddLink anAN
                  aConceptSymbol
                  (list 'AKO (append
                               oldLinks
                               (list superClassConceptSymbol))))))))

(define PrintAN
  (lambda (anAN)
   (DisplayLine "*** Associative Network ***")
   (for-each (lambda (aConcept)
              (display " ")
              (PrintConcept aConcept) (newline))
             anAN)
   (newline)))

; ===== query fns on ANs =====

(define RecurseThruLists
  (lambda (anAN nodesToSearch nodesSeen aGeneratorFN aCmpFN)
   ; general searching procedure for finding all nodes linked from an
   ; initial node by some type of links. Initial call is of the form:
   ; (RecurseThruLists (list initialNode)
   ;                   #f
   ;                   aGeneratorFN
   ;                   aCmpFN)
   ; where aGeneratorFN returns a list of nodes immediately linked to
   ; a given node and aCmpFN can be used to test nodes for equality.
   ; Algorithm:
   ;   Repeatedly remove one node N from nodesToSearch, use
   ;   aGeneratorFN to generate a new list NEW and add N to
   ;   nodesSeen. Then for each node in NEW not in nodesSeen
   ;   add it to nodesToSearch. Repeat while there are still
   ;   nodes in nodesToSearch

   (define onList?
    (lambda (aNode aList)
     (cond ((null? aList) #f)
           ((aCmpFN aNode (car aList)) #t)
           (else (onList? aNode (cdr aList))))))

   (if (null? nodesToSearch)
      nodesSeen
      (let* ((n (car nodesToSearch))
             (rest (cdr nodesToSearch))
             (new (aGeneratorFN anAN n)))
       (set! nodesSeen (append nodesSeen (list n)))
       (for-each (lambda (aNode)
```

```
                (if (onList? aNode nodesSeen)
                    #f
                    (set! rest (append rest (list aNode)))))
              new)
    (RecurseThruLists anAN
                     rest
                     nodesSeen
                     aGeneratorFN
                     aCmpFN)))))
```

(define **FindAllConcepts**

```
  (lambda (anAN) (map GetConceptSymbol anAN)))
```

(define **FindAllLinkNames**

```
  (lambda (anAN)
   (let ((result #f))
    (for-each
     (lambda (aConcept)
      (for-each (lambda (aSlot)
                  (if (or (AKOSlot? aSlot)
                          (member (GetLinkName aSlot) result))
                      #f
                      (set! result (cons (GetLinkName aSlot) result))))
                (GetSlots aConcept)))
     anAN)
    result)))
```

(define **FindConcept**

```
  (lambda (anAN aConceptSymbol) (assoc aConceptSymbol anAN)))
```

(define **GetAKOSlot**

```
  (lambda (anAN aConceptSymbol)
   (let ((aConcept (FindConcept anAN aConceptSymbol)))
    (if (null? aConcept)
        #f
        (assoc 'AKO (GetSlots aConcept))))))
```

(define **GetAKOLinks**

```
  (lambda (anAN aConceptSymbol)
   (let ((aSlot (GetAKOSlot anAN aConceptSymbol)))
    (if (null? aSlot)
        #f
        (GetConceptList aSlot)))))
```

(define **GetAKOChain**

```
  (lambda (anAN aConceptSymbol)
   ; return a list of all concepts linked via AKO links
   ; starting from concept aConceptSymbol
   (if (member aConceptSymbol (FindAllConcepts anAN))
     (RecurseThruLists anAN
                      (list aConceptSymbol)
```

```
                                  #f
                                  GetAKOLinks
                                  equal?)
    #f)))

(define GetLinkSymbolSlots
  (lambda (anAN aConceptSymbol aLinkSymbol)

   (define getAux
     (lambda (aSlotList aResultList)
       (if (NoMoreSlots? aSlotList)
           aResultList
           (let ((aSlot (FirstSlot aSlotList)))
             (getAux (RestOfSlots aSlotList)
                     (if (eq? aLinkSymbol (GetLinkName aSlot))
                         (cons aSlot aResultList)
                         aResultList))))))

   ; return all slots of aConceptSymbol labelled with
   ; aConceptSymbol
   (let ((aConcept (FindConcept anAN aConceptSymbol)))
     (if (null? aConcept)
         #f
         (getAux (GetSlots aConcept) #f)))))

(define FindAllLinkedConcepts
  (lambda (anAN aConceptSymbol aLinkSymbol . aThresholdValue)
   ; return a list of all concepts linked via aLinkSymbol links
   ; starting from concept aConceptSymbol that exceed the optional
   ; certainty factor aThresholdValue (which defaults to 1.0 if not
   ; supplied). The nodes during the call to RecurseThruLists are
   ; tuples with the first element either aConceptName derived from
   ; AKO links or slots with a link name of aLinkSymbol and the
   ; second element is the current multiplicative weight.

   (define makeTuple (lambda (anElement aWeight) (list anElement aWeight)))
   (define getElement (lambda (aNode) (car aNode)))
   (define getWeight (lambda (aNode) (cadr aNode)))

   (define getBothLinks
     (lambda (anAN aNode)

     ; get both AKO and all aLinkSymbol links
     (let* ((anElement      (getElement aNode))
            (aWeight        (getWeight aNode))
            (aConceptSymbol (if (pair? anElement)
                                (GetConceptName anElement)
                                anElement))
            (akoLinks (GetAKOLinks anAN aConceptSymbol))
            (symbolLinks (GetLinkSymbolSlots anAN
                                              aConceptSymbol
                                              aLinkSymbol)))
```

```
        (append (map (lambda (akoElement)
                          (makeTuple akoElement aWeight))
                        akoLinks)
                    (map (lambda (symbolElement)
                          (makeTuple symbolElement
                                     (* aWeight
                                        (GetCertaintyFactor symbolElement))))
                        symbolLinks)))))

(define cmpNodes
  (lambda (aNode1 aNode2)
    ; decide if aNode1 is different from aNode2 and should
    ; be added to the list of links. Return #f only if they
    ; are different and it should be added.
    ; Don't add it if it has a weight less than the threshold.
    (let* ((element1 (getElement aNode1))
           (element2 (getElement aNode2))
           (aConceptSymbol1 (if (pair? element1)
                                (GetConceptName element1)
                                element1))
           (aConceptSymbol2 (if (pair? element2)
                                (GetConceptName element2)
                                element2))
           (aWeight1 (getWeight aNode1))
           (aWeight2 (getWeight aNode2)))
      (or (< aWeight1 aThresholdValue)
          (and (eq? aConceptSymbol1 aConceptSymbol2)
               (= aWeight1 aWeight2))))))

(define removeExtraneousSymbols
  (lambda (aList)
    ; remove concept symbols and if their weight is above
    ; aThresholdValue use this weight for link symbol elements
    (cond ((null? aList) #f)
          ((or (not (pair? (getElement (car aList))))
               (< (getWeight (car aList)) aThresholdValue))
           (removeExtraneousSymbols (cdr aList)))
          (else
           (let ((element (getElement (car aList))))
             (cons (LINK (GetLinkName element)
                         (GetConceptName element)
                         (getWeight (car aList)))
                   (removeExtraneousSymbols (cdr aList))))))))

(set! aThresholdValue
      (if (null? aThresholdValue) 1.0 (car aThresholdValue)))
(removeExtraneousSymbols
 (RecurseThruLists anAN
                   (list (makeTuple aConceptSymbol 1.0))
```

```
                        #f
                        getBothLinks
                        cmpNodes))))

(define FindAllLinks
  (lambda (anAN aConceptSymbol1 aConceptSymbol2 . aThresholdValue)
    ; return a list of all possible links that can connect the two
    ; symbols in the sense of the function FindAllLinkedConcepts.
    ; If there are pure AKO links connecting them then AKO is
    ; also prepended to the list.
    ; The optional certainty factor aThresholdValue defaults to
    ; 1.0 if not supplied.

    (define filterOnConceptSymbol2
      (lambda (aConceptList)
        ; remove those without aConceptSymbol2 as their concept name
        (cond ((null? aConceptList) #f)
              ((eq? (GetConceptName (car aConceptList)) aConceptSymbol2)
               (cons (car aConceptList)
                     (filterOnConceptSymbol2 (cdr aConceptList))))
              (else (filterOnConceptSymbol2 (cdr aConceptList))))))

    (set! aThresholdValue
          (if (null? aThresholdValue) 1.0 (car aThresholdValue)))
    (let ((result #f))
      (for-each
       (lambda (aLinkSymbol)
         (set! result
               (append result
                       (filterOnConceptSymbol2
                        (FindAllLinkedConcepts anAN
                                               aConceptSymbol1
                                               aLinkSymbol
                                               aThresholdValue)))))

       (FindAllLinkNames anAN))
      (if (member aConceptSymbol2 (GetAKOChain anAN aConceptSymbol1))
          (cons 'AKO result)
          result))))

(define Linked?
  (lambda (anAN aConceptSymbol1 aConceptSymbol2 . aThresholdValue)
    ; Are there any possible link symbols that can connect the two
    ; symbols in the sense of the functions FindAllLinkedConcepts
    ; The optional certainty factor aThresholdValue defaults to
    ; 1.0 if not supplied.
    (set! aThresholdValue
          (if (null? aThresholdValue) 1.0 (car aThresholdValue)))
    (not (null? (FindAllLinks anAN
                              aConceptSymbol1
                              aConceptSymbol2
                              aThresholdValue)))))
```

III.8 Frames Toolbox

```
;;;
;;;   F R A M E S   T O O L B O X
;;;   = = = = = =   = = = = = = =
;;;
;;; Depends on the following other toolboxes:
;;;      Systems
;;;      AssociativeNetworks

; This toolbox supports a simple framework catering for property
; inheritance, defaults and demon procedures. It is built
; upon the AN toolbox using the property inheritance links labelled by
; AKO to provide the inheritance, and the user-defined links are used
; to hold the user-defined slots for the frame. Such a user-defined
; frame contains a list of facets enabling the default and demon
; procedures to be specified via the following standard facet types:

; VALUE         - supply a specific value
; DEFAULT       - supply a default value in the absence of any other value
; IF-NEEDED     - a demon procedure to be called to supply a value if one
;                    is requested but not stored
; IF-ADDED      - a demon procedure to be called if a value is added to
;                    the frame
; IF-REMOVED - a demon procedure to be called if a value is deleted
;                    from the frame

; The following data types are used:

; FACET          :a list of <aType aValueList> where aType is one of the
;                      standard facet types
; FACET-LIST :a list of FACETs
; AKO-SLOT   :a list of (AKO aListOfFrameNames)
; SLOT           :a list of (aSlotName aFacetList)
; SLOT-LIST  :a list of SLOTs including up to one AKO-SLOT
; FRAME        :a list of (aSymbol aSlotList)
; FN              :a list of FRAMEs

; ===== fns on FACETs =====
; a list of (aType aValueList) where aType is one of the standard
; facet types: VALUE, DEFAULT, IF-NEEDED, IF-ADDED, IF-REMOVED

(define MakeFacet (lambda (aType ValueList) (list aType aValueList)))

(define GetFacetType (lambda (aFacet) (car aFacet)))

(define GetValueList (lambda (aFacet) (cadr aFacet)))

(define VALUE (lambda (aValue) (list 'VALUE aValue)))

(define ValueFacet?
  (lambda (aFacet) (eq? 'VALUE (GetFacetType aFacet))))

(define DEFAULT (lambda (aValue) (list 'DEFAULT aValue)))
```

```
(define DefaultFacet?
  (lambda (aFacet) (eq? 'DEFAULT (GetFacetType aFacet))))

(define IF-NEEDED
  (lambda (aDemonProc) (list 'IF-NEEDED aDemonProc)))

(define IF-NEEDEDFacet?
  (lambda (aFacet) (eq? 'IF-NEEDED (GetFacetType aFacet))))

(define IF-ADDED
  (lambda (aDemonProc) (list 'IF-ADDED aDemonProc)))

(define IF-ADDEDFacet?
  (lambda (aFacet) (eq? 'IF-ADDED (GetFacetType aFacet))))

(define IF-REMOVED
  (lambda (aDemonProc) (list 'IF-REMOVED aDemonProc)))

(define IF-REMOVEDFacet?
  (lambda (aFacet) (eq? 'IF-REMOVED (GetFacetType aFacet))))

(define DemonFacet?
  (lambda (aFacet)
   (or (IF-NEEDEDFacet? aFacet)
       (IF-ADDEDFacet? aFacet)
       (IF-REMOVEDFacet? aFacet))))

(define GetDemonProc (lambda (aDemonFacet) (cadr aDemonFacet)))

(define InvokeDemon
  (lambda (aDemonFacet . optionalArgs)
   (apply (GetDemonProc aDemonFacet) optionalArgs)))

(define PrintFacet
  (lambda (aFacet)
    (DisplayList
        (cond ((ValueFacet? aFacet)           "(VALUE ")
              ((DefaultFacet? aFacet)         "(DEFAULT ")
              ((IF-NEEDEDFacet? aFacet)       "(IF-NEEDED ")
              ((IF-ADDEDFacet? aFacet)        "(IF-ADDED ")
              ((IF-REMOVEDFacet? aFacet)      "(IF-REMOVED "))
        (GetValueList aFacet)
        ") ")))

; ===== fns on FACET-LISTs =====
; lists of FACETs

(define NoMoreFacets? (lambda (aSlotList) (null? aSlotList)))

(define FirstFacet (lambda (aSlotList) (car aSlotList)))

(define RestOfFacets (lambda (aSlotList) (cdr aSlotList)))

; ===== fns on SLOTs =====
; These are different from the AN Toolbox ones except for the
```

```
; ones that act on AKO slots. Either an AKO slot, a list of the form:
;           (AKO aListOfFrameNames)
; or a user-defined slot, a list of the form
;           (aSlotName aFacetList)
;
; AKO            - as for AN Toolbox, use as in (AKO any_number_of_SLOTs)

(define SLOT
  (lambda (aSlotName . aFacetList) (list aSlotName aFacetList)))

(define MakeSlotFromList
  (lambda (aSlotName aFacetList) (list aSlotName aFacetList)))

(define GetSlotName GetLinkName)
;                     from AN Toolbox, use as in
;                     (GetSlotName aSlot)

; AKOSlot?       - as for AN Toolbox, use as in
;                  (AKOSlot? aSlot)

(define GetFrameList
  (lambda (anAKOSlot)
    (if (AKOSlot? anAKOSlot)
        (cdr anAKOSlot)
        (Fatal-Error "GetFrameList:" anAKOSlot
                     "is not an AKO slot"))))

(define GetFacetList
  (lambda (aSlot)
    (if (AKOSlot? aSlot)
        (Fatal-Error "GetFacetList:" "Action not valid on AKO slot" aSlot)
        (cadr aSlot))))

(define PrintSlot
  (lambda (aSlot)
    (if (AKOSlot? aSlot)
        (DisplayList "(AKO" (GetFrameList aSlot) ") ")
        (begin (DisplayList "(SLOT" (GetSlotName aSlot))
               (for-each (lambda (aFacet)
                           (display "   ")
                           (PrintFacet aFacet))
                         (GetFacetList aSlot))
               (display ") ")))))

; ===== fns on SLOT-LISTs =====
; lists of SLOTs

; NoMoreSlots? - as for AN Toolbox, use as in
;                (NoMoreSlots? aSlotList)

; FirstSlot      - as for AN Toolbox, use as in
;                  (FirstSlot aSlotList)

; RestOfSlots    - as for AN Toolbox, use as in
;                  (RestOfSlots aSlotList)
```

```
; ===== fns on FRAMEs =====
; list of the form (aSymbol aSlotList)
; uses the fns on CONCEPTs from our AN Toolbox

(define FRAME CONCEPT)
;                 - from AN Toolbox, use as in
;                   (FRAME aFrameName any_number_of_slots)

(define MakeFrameWithList MakeConceptWithList)
;                 - from AN Toolbox, use as in
;                   (MakeFrameWithList aFrameName aSlotList)

(define GetFrameSymbol GetConceptSymbol)
;                 - from AN Toolbox, use as in
;                   (GetFrameSymbol aFrame)

; GetSlots        - as for AN Toolbox, use as in
;                   (GetSlots aFrame)

(define PrintFrame
  (lambda (aFrame)
    (DisplayLine (GetFrameSymbol aFrame) ":")
    (for-each (lambda (aSlot)
                (display " ")
                (PrintSlot aSlot) (newline))
              (GetSlots aFrame))))


; ===== fns on FNs =====
; lists of FRAMEs - uses the fns on ANs from our AN Toolbox

(define MakeFN MakeAN)
;                 - from AN Toolbox, use as in
;                   (MakeFN any_number_of_frames)

(define EmptyFN? EmptyAN?)
;                 - from AN Toolbox, use as in
;                   (EmptyFN? anFN)

(define FirstFrame FirstConcept)
;                 - from AN Toolbox, use as in
;                   (FirstFrame anFN)

(define RestOfFrames RestOfConcepts)
;                 - from AN Toolbox, use as in
;                   (RestOfFrames anFN)

(define AddFrame AddConcept)
;                 - from AN Toolbox, use as in
;                   (AddFrame anFN aFrame)

(define RemoveFrame RemoveConcept)
;                 - from AN Toolbox, use as in
;                   (RemoveFrame anFN aFrame)
```

```
(define RemoveSlot RemoveLink)
;                     - from AN Toolbox, use as in
;                     (RemoveSlot anFN aFrameSymbol aSlotName)

(define AddSlot AddLink)
;                     - from AN Toolbox, use as in
;                     (AddSlot anFN aFrameSymbol aSlot)

; AddAKOLink       - as for AN Toolbox, use as in
;            (AddAKOLink anFN aFrameSymbol superClassFrameSymbol)

; RemoveAKOLink - as for AN Toolbox, use as in
;            (RemoveAKOLink anFN aFrameSymbol
;                                 superClassFrameSymbol)

(define PrintFN
  (lambda (anFN)
    (DisplayLine "*** Frame Network ***")
    (for-each (lambda (aFrame)
                (display " ")
                (PrintFrame aFrame))
              anFN)
    (newline)))

; ===== query fns on FNs =====

(define FindAllFrameNames FindAllConcepts)
;                     - from AN Toolbox, use as in
;                     (FindAllFrames anFN)

(define FindAllSlotNames FindAllLinkNames)
;                     - from AN Toolbox, use as in
;                     (FindAllSlotNames anFN)

(define FindFrame FindConcept)
;                     - from AN Toolbox, use as in
;                     (FindFrame anFN aFrameSymbol)

(define FindSlot
  (lambda (aFrame aSlotName) (assoc aSlotName (GetSlots aFrame))))

(define FindFacet
  (lambda (aSlot aFacetType) (assoc aFacetType (GetFacetList aSlot))))

; GetAKOSlot    - as for AN Toolbox, use as in
;                 (GetAKOSlot anFN aFrameSymbol)

; GetAKOLinks - as for AN Toolbox, use as in
;                 (GetAKOLinks anFN aFrameSymbol)

; GetAKOChain - as for AN Toolbox, use as in
;                 (GetAKOChain anFN aFrameSymbol)

(define TriggerDemons
  (lambda (anFN aFrameName aSlotName aDemonType aValue)
    ; invoke the demons procedures of type aDemonType contained in the
    ; slots aSlotName on the chain of AKO links back from the
```

```
    ; aFrameName frame. Each demon is called with parameters:
    ;      (demon anFN aFrameName aSlotName aValue)
    ; and returns #f to suppress the addition/deletion in which case
    ; TriggerDemons also returns #f immediately, OR the demon returns a
    ; new FN that will be passed to the next demon etc. If none of the
    ; demons return #f then the FN returned from the last demon is
    ; produced as a value.
    (do ((frames (GetAKOChain anFN aFrameName) (cdr frames))
         (returnedFN anFN))
        ((or (null? returnedFN) (null? frames)) returnedFN)
        (let ((aFrame (FindFrame returnedFN (car frames))))
         (if aFrame
             (let ((aSlot (FindSlot aFrame aSlotName)))
              (if aSlot
                  (let ((demon (FindFacet aSlot aDemonType)))
                   (if demon
                       (set! returnedFN
                             (InvokeDemon demon
                                          returnedFN
                                          aFrameName
                                          aSlotName
                                          aValue))
                       #f))
                  #f))
             #f)))))

(define RemoveFacet
  (lambda (anFN aFrameName aSlotName aFacetName)
    ; remove facet with name aFacetName from slot with name aSlotName
    ; of frame with aFrameName in anFN and return the updated FN. If
    ; aFacetName is a VALUE facet then invoke all IF-REMOVED demon
    ; procedures of this frame and in the AKO chain of super frames of
    ; this frame
    (define removeAux
      (lambda (aFacetList aFaceName)
        (cond ((NoMoreFacets? aFacetList) #f)
              ((eq? aFacetName
                    (GetFacetType (FirstFacet aFacetList)))
               (RestOfFacets aFacetList))
              (else (cons (FirstFacet aFacetList)
                          (removeAux (RestOfFacets aFacetList)
                                     aFacetName))))))

    (let ((frame (FindFrame anFN aFrameName)))
      (if  (null? frame)
           anFN
           (let ((aSlot (FindSlot frame aSlotName)))
             (if (null? aSlot)
```

```
anFN
(let ((facet (FindFacet aSlot aFacetName)))
  (if (null? facet)
      anFN
      (let
         ((newFN (if (eq? 'VALUE aFacetName)
                     (TriggerDemons anFN
                                    aFrameName
                                    aSlotName
                                    'IF-REMOVED
                                    (GetValueList facet))

                     anFN)))
          (if newFN
              (AddSlot newFN
                       aFrameName
                       (MakeSlotFromList
                          aSlotName
                          (removeAux (GetFacetList aSlot)
                                     aFacetName)))

              anFN))))))))))

(define RemoveAValue
  (lambda (anFN aFrameName aSlotName)
    ; remove the value facet from slot with the name aSlotName
    ; from the frame with the name aFrameName from the network
    ; anFN and return the updated network
    (RemoveFacet anFN aFrameName aSlotName 'VALUE)))

(define AddFacet
  (lambda (anFN aFrameName aSlotName aFacet)
     ; add aFacet to slot with aSlotName to frame with aFrameName in
     ; anFN and return the updated FN - if the facet is a VALUE facet
     ; and the slot has an IF-ADDED facet then invoke the demon in this
     ; frame and also all such demons in the AKO chain of super frames
     (let* ((newFN (RemoveFacet anFN
                                aFrameName
                                aSlotName
                                (GetFacetType aFacet)))

            (aFrame (FindFrame newFN aFrameName)))
       (if (null? aFrame)
           (AddSlot newFN aFrameName (SLOT aFacet))
           (let ((aSlot (FindSlot aFrame aSlotName))
                 (newerFN (if (ValueFacet? aFacet)
                              (TriggerDemons newFN
                                             aFrameName
                                             aSlotName
                                             'IF-ADDED
                                             (GetValueList aFacet))

                              newFN)))
```

```
          (if newerFN
             (if (null? aSlot)
                (AddSlot newerFN
                         aFrameName
                         (SLOT aSlotName aFacet))
                (AddSlot newerFN
                         aFrameName
                         (MakeSlotFromList
                            aSlotName
                            (append (GetFacetList aSlot) (list aFacet)))))
          newFN))))))

(define AddAValue
  (lambda (anFN aFrameName aSlotName aValue)
    ; add a value facet (VALUE) to slot with the name
    ; aSlotName of the frame with the name aFrameName in the
    ; network anFN and return the updated network
    (AddFacet anFN aFrameName aSlotName (VALUE aValue))))

(define GetAValue
  (lambda (anFN aFrameName aSlotName)
    ; return the value of the VALUE facet of the slot with the name
    ; aSlotName of the frame with the name aFrameName of the network
    ; anFN. If there is no VALUE facet return the value in the DEFAULT
    ; facet or, if none but there is an IF-NEEDED demon, call that for
    ; the value. If all these fail try each frame on the chain of AKO
    ; super frames for such a slot looking for VALUE, DEFAULT and then
    ; IF-NEEDED facets to supply the value. If all these fail then a
    ; value of ''NOTKNOWN'' is returned
    (do ((nameList (GetAKOChain anFN aFrameName) (cdr nameList))
         (foundValue? #f)
         (returnedValue #f))
        ((or foundValue?
             (null? nameList)) (if foundValue?
                                   returnedValue
                                   ''NOTKNOWN''))
      (let ((frame (FindFrame anFN (car nameList))))
        (if (null? frame)
            #f
            (let ((slot (FindSlot frame aSlotName)))
              (if (null? slot)
                  #f
                  (cond ((FindFacet slot 'VALUE)
                         (set! foundValue? #t)
                         (set! returnedValue (GetValueList
                                                (FindFacet slot 'VALUE))))
                        ((FindFacet slot 'DEFAULT)
                         (set! foundValue? #t)
                         (set! returnedValue (GetValueList
```

```
                        (FindFacet slot 'DEFAULT))))
          ((FindFacet slot 'IF-NEEDED)
           (set! foundValue? #t)
           (set! returnedValue (InvokeDemon
                        (FindFacet slot 'IF-NEEDED)
                        anFN
                        aFrameName
                        aSlotName))))))))))
```

III.9 ATN Toolbox

```
;;;
;;;    A U G M E N T E D   T R A N S I T I O N
;;;    = = = = = = = = =   = = = = = = = = = =
;;;
;;;    N E T W O R K   T O O L B O X
;;;    = = = = = = =   = = = = = = =
;;;
;;; Depends on the following other toolboxes:
;;;     Systems
;;;
;;; Augmented Transition Network (ATN) Toolbox
;;;
;;; This toolbox contains routines to build and use ATNs to
;;; parse natural languages.

; An ATN consists of a finite automaton with states connected by arcs
; where the arcs are labelled by category names (these represent a
; class of words such as verb or noun which must appear in the input
; sentence) or the name of another ATN (in which case that ATN is
; called recursively). Also arcs can have tests that must be satisfied
; before an arc is followed and actions can be performed. There is
; a set of registers that can store information about the parse
; and be referred to by the tests.
;
; The following data structures are used:
;
; REGISTERBANKs - association list of register value pairs
; PARSEPAIRs    - list of the form (aSentence aRegisterBank)
; TESTS         - either #t or a boolean procedure
; FORMs         - one of #t, #f, **, (GETR . . .) or lambda
; ACTIONs       - either (SETR . . .) or (TO . . .)
; ARCs          - one of (CAT . . .), (ANY . . .), (PUSH . . .) or (POP . . .)
; ARCLISTs      - a list of ARCs
; STATEs        - a list of the form (label anArcList)
; ATNs          - a list of states

; ===== fns on REGISTERBANKs =====
```

```
; The registers are stored in register banks as association lists.
(define MakeRegisterBank (lambda () #f))

(define SetRegister
  (lambda (aRegisterBank aRegister aValue)

    (define removeAux
      (lambda (aList aKey)
        (cond ((null? aList) #f)
              ((eq? aKey (caar aList)) (cdr aList))
              (else (cons (car aList) (removeAux (cdr aList) aKey))))))

    (cons (list aRegister aValue)
          (removeAux aRegisterBank aRegister))))

(define KnownRegister?
  (lambda (aRegisterBank aRegister)
    (if (assoc aRegister aRegisterBank) #t #f)))

(define GetRegister
  (lambda  (aRegisterBank aRegister)
    (let ((pair (assoc aRegister aRegisterBank)))
      (if (null? pair)
          (Fatal-Error "GetRegister:" "No such register as" aRegister)
          (cadr pair)))))

(define UpdateRegisters
  (lambda (anActionList aRegisterBank)
    (if (EmptyActions? anActionList)
        aRegisterBank
        (let ((action (FirstAction anActionList)))
          (if (SETR? action)
              (UpdateRegisters (RestOfActions anActionList)
                               (SetRegister aRegisterBank
                                            (GetActionRegister action)
                                            (EvalForm (GetActionForm
                                                       action)
                                                      aRegisterBank)))

              (Fatal-Error "UpdateRegisters:" "illegal action" action))))))

; ===== fns on PARSEPAIRs =====
; list of the form (aSentence aRegisterBank)

(define MakeParsePair
  (lambda (aSentence aRegisterBank) (list aSentence aRegisterBank)))

(define GetSentence (lambda (aParsePair) (car aParsePair)))

(define GetRegisterBank (lambda (aParsePair) (cadr aParsePair)))

; ===== fns on TESTs =====
; Either #t or a boolean procedure
```

```
(define CheckTest?
  (lambda (aTest aRegisterBank)
    (cond ((eq? aTest #t) #t)
          ((procedure? aTest) (aTest aRegisterBank))
          (else (Fatal-Error ''CheckTest:'' ''invalid test'' aTest)))))

; ===== fns on FORMs =====
; one of the following:
;       (GETR aRegister)
;       **
;       #t
;       #f
; or an arbitrary lambda expression

(define GETR (lambda (aRegister) (list 'GETR aRegister)))

(define GETR? (lambda (aForm) (and (pair? aForm) (eq? 'GETR (car aForm)))))

(define GetFormRegister (lambda (aForm) (cadr aForm)))

(define ** '**)

(define **? (lambda (aForm) (eq? '** aForm)))

(define EvalForm
  (lambda (aForm aRegisterBank)
    (cond ((GETR? aForm)
           (GetRegister aRegisterBank (GetFormRegister aForm)))
          ((**? aForm)
           (GetRegister aRegisterBank '**))
          ((eq? aForm #t) #t)
          ((eq? aForm #f) #f)
          ((procedure? aForm) (aForm aRegisterBank))
          (else (Fatal-Error ''EvalForm: illegal form'')))))

; ===== fns on ACTIONs =====
; one of the following:
;       (SETR aREGISTER aFORM)
;       (TO     label)
;
; (define FirstAction         - See Search Toolbox
;
; (define RestOfActions       - See Search Toolbox
;
; (define EmptyActions?       - See Search Toolbox

(define ActionType (lambda (anAction) (car anAction)))

(define SETR (lambda (aRegister aForm) (list 'SETR aRegister aForm)))

(define SETR? (lambda (anAction) (eq? 'SETR (ActionType anAction))))

(define GetActionRegister (lambda (anAction (cadr anAction)))

(define GetActionForm (lambda (anAction) (caddr anAction)))
```

```
(define TO (lambda (aLabel) (list 'TO aLabel)))

(define TO? (lambda (anAction) (eq? 'TO (ActionType anAction))))

(define CheckActions
  (lambda (anActionList)
    ; check that the last action is (TO . .) and return a list
    ; of the form (otherActions (TO label))

    (define checkActions Aux
        (lambda (anActionList otherActions)
            (let ((head (FirstAction anActionList))
                  (tail    (RestOfActions anActionList)))
              (cond ((EmptyActions? tail)
                     (if (TO? head)
                       (list otherActions head)
                       (Fatal-Error "CheckActions: last action not TO")))
                    ((SETR? head)
                     (checkActionsAux tail
                                      (append otherActions (list head))))
                    (else
                     (Fatal-Error "CheckActions:" "illegal action" head))))))

    (if (null? anActionList)
      (Fatal-Error "CheckActions:"
                   "there must be at least one action")
      (checkActionsAux anActionList #f))))

; ===== fns on ARCs =====
; one of the following lists:
;     (CAT   aCATEGORY test actions (TO aLabel))
;     (ANY             test actions (TO aLabel))
;     (PUSH anATN      test actions (TO aLabel))
;     (POP   aFORM     test)

(define ArcType (lambda (anArc) (car anArc)))

(define CAT
  (lambda (aCategory aTest . anActionList)
    (append (list 'CAT aCategory aTest)
            (CheckActions anActionList))))

(define CAT? (lambda (anArc) (eq? 'CAT (ArcType anArc))))

(define MakeCategory (lambda aWordList aWordList))

(define GetCategory
  (lambda (anArc)
    (if (CAT? anArc)
      (cadr anArc)
      (Fatal-Error "GetCategory:" "Arc" anArc "not a CATegory"))))

(define InCategory?
  (lambda (aWord aCategory) (if (member aWord aCategory) #t #f)))
```

```
(define ANY
  (lambda (aTest . anActionList)
    (append (list 'ANY aTest) (CheckActions anActionList))))

(define ANY?
  (lambda (anArc) (eq? 'ANY (ArcType anArc))))

(define PUSH
  (lambda (anATN aTest . anActionList)
    (append (list 'PUSH anATN aTest) (CheckActions anActionList))))

(define PUSH? (lambda (anArc) (eq? 'PUSH (ArcType anArc))))

(define GetATN
  (lambda (anArc)
    (if (PUSH? anArc)
        (cadr anArc)
        (Fatal-Error "GetATN:" "Arc" anArc "not a PUSH"))))

(define POP (lambda (aForm aTest) (list 'POP aForm aTest)))

(define POP? (lambda (anArc) (eq? 'POP (ArcType anArc))))

(define GetForm
  (lambda (anArc)
    (if (POP? anArc)
        (cadr anArc)
        (Fatal-Error "GetForm:" "Arc" anArc "not a POP"))))

(define GetTest
  (lambda (anArc)
    (if (ANY? anArc)
        (cadr anArc)
        (caddr anArc))))

(define GetArcActions
  (lambda (anArc)
    (cond ((POP? anArc)
           (Fatal-Error "GetArcActions:"
                        "there are no actions for a POP arc"))
          ((ANY? anArc)
           (caddr anArc))
          (else
           (cadddr anArc)))))

(define GetNextState
  (lambda (anArc)
    (if (POP? anArc)
        (Fatal-Error "GetNextState:"
                     "there is no next state for a POP arc")
        (let ((toarc (if (ANY? anArc)
                         (car (cdddr anArc))
                         (car (cddddr anArc)))))
          (if (TO? toarc)
```

```
            (cadr toarc)
            (Fatal-Error "GetNextState:" "bad TO arc" toarc))))))
; ===== fns on ARCLISTs =====
; a list of ARCs

(define CurrentArc (lambda (anArcList) (car anArcList)))

(define RestOfArcs (lambda (anArcList) (cdr anArcList)))

(define EmptyArcList? (lambda (anArcList (null? anArcList)))

; ===== fns on STATEs =====
; a list of the form (label ARCLIST)

(define STATE
  (lambda (aStateLabel . anArcList) (cons aStateLabel anArcList)))

(define GetStateLabel (lambda (aState) (car aState)))

(define GetArcs (lambda (aState) (cdr aState)))

; ===== fns on ATNs =====
; an ATN is a list of states.

(define MakeATN (lambda aStateList aStateList))

(define AddState
  (lambda (anATN aState) (append anATN (list aState))))

(define InitialState (lambda (anATN) (car anATN)))

(define FindState
  (lambda (anATN aStateLabel)
    (cond ((null? anATN) #f)
          ((eq? aStateLabel (GetStateLabel (car anATN))) (car anATN))
          (else (FindState (cdr anATN) aStateLabel)))))

; ===== fns for Parsing sentences =====
; To parse ATNs in general a form of Early's parsing method is
; needed which follows all possible parses of the sentence in a
; breadth-first manner. The following routines use a simpler recursive
; descent with backtracking method. This is possible because we have
; disallowed arcs with tests only, so that a word is
; consumed or an ATN called recursively as every arc is followed. Each
; call to the parsing routines will follow each arc in turn for as far
; as possible until either a node with no valid arcs is found
; (failure) or a POP arc is found (success). This differs from the
; general Early algorithm that would also look at the arcs that
; appear AFTER the successful POP arc for further matches. Some
; measure of control over this is available to the user as the arcs
; are considered in the order they are defined - this suggests that
; POP arcs should normally appear last.

(define ParseAux
  (lambda (anATN aState aRegisterBank restOfSentence aTraceFlag)
    ; Attempts to parse the 'restOfSentence' beginning from 'aState' of
```

```
; 'anATN' with the current register values given in
; 'aRegisterBank'. Arcs with successful tests are followed by
; calling ParseAux recursively with updated register values. When
; a node with no valid arcs is encountered the routine returns #f.
; When a valid POP is encountered a PARSEPAIR is returned.
(if aTraceFlag
  (DisplayLine "PauseAux: state=" (GetStateLabel aState)
               "sentence=" restOfSentence)
  #f)
(do ((arcs (GetArcs aState) (RestOfArcs arcs))
    (arc #f)
    (newRegisterBank #f)
    (newerRegisterBank #f)
    (word #f)
    (actions #f)
    (result #f))
   ((or (EmptyArcList? arcs)
      result) (if aTraceFlag
               (DisplayLine "PauseAux: state="
                            (GetStateLabel aState)
                            "-->"
                            result)
               #f)
             result)
   (set! arc (CurrentArc arcs))
   (if (null? restOfSentence)
      (begin (set! word #f)
             (set! newRegisterBank aRegisterBank))
      (begin (set! word (car restOfSentence))
             (set! newRegisterBank
                (SetRegister aRegisterBank '** word))))
   (if (CheckTest? (GetTest arc) newRegisterBank)
     (cond ((CAT? arc)
           (if (and restOfSentence
                    (InCategory? word (GetCategory arc)))
               (begin
                (set! newerRegisterBank
                   (UpdateRegisters (GetArcActions arc)
                                    newRegisterBank))
                (set! result
                   (ParseAux anATN
                             (FindState anATN (GetNextState arc))
                             newerRegisterBank
                             (cdr restOfSentence)
                             aTraceFlag)))
               #f))
          ((ANY? arc)
           (if restOfSentence
               (begin
```

```
                    (set! newerRegisterBank
                          (UpdateRegisters (GetArcActions arc)
                                           newRegisterBank))
                    (set! result
                          (ParseAux anATN
                                    (FindState anATN (GetNextState arc))
                                    newerRegisterBank
                                    (cdr restOfSentence)
                                    aTraceFlag)))
                  #f))
            ((PUSH? arc)
             (set! result
                   (ParseAux (GetATN arc)
                             (InitialState (GetATN arc))
                             newRegisterBank
                             restOfSentence
                             aTraceFlag))
             (if result
                 (begin
                  (set! newerRegisterBank
                        (UpdateRegisters (GetArcActions arc)
                                         (GetRegisterBank result)))
                  (set! result
                        (ParseAux anATN
                                  (FindState anATN (GetNextState arc))
                                  newerRegisterBank
                                  (GetSentence result)
                                  aTraceFlag)))
                 #f)
            ((POP? arc)
             (set! result
                   (MakeParsePair
                   restOfSentence
                   (SetRegister newRegisterBank
                                '**
                                (EvalForm (GetForm arc)
                                          newRegisterBank)))))
            (else (Fatal-Error ''ParseAux:'' ''illegal arc type'' arc)))

       #f))))

(define Parse
  (lambda (anATN aSentence . aTraceFlag)
    ; Return #f if parse fails. If it succeeds then return the
    ; register bank. If not supplied aTraceFlag defaults to #f
    (let ((result (ParseAux anATN
                            (InitialState anATN)
                            (MakeRegisterBank)
```

```
                    aSentence
                    (if (null? aTraceFlag)
                        #f
                        (car aTraceFlag)))))
(if (or (null? result)
        (not (null? (GetSentence result))))
    #f
    (GetRegisterBank result)))))
```

Appendix IV
Software Tools – Some Useful Addresses and Profiles

The following list offers pointers to sources for a range of language processors implemented on a variety of machines. Selection is based on personal experience by the authors and no claim for completeness is being made.

IV.1 Some Scheme implementations

MIT-Scheme

There are currently two implementations, one of which is portable to any machine with a C-compiler. The portable version has substantial memory requirements and is not particularly efficient, but there is a commitment to continuing improvements. The system includes an EMACS-style editor and may be obtained for a nominal charge.

Contact: Scheme Team c/o Prof. H. Abelson
MIT
545 Technology Square, Rm 410
Cambridge, MA 02139, USA
e-mail: INFO-CSCHEME%MIT-OZ@MIT-MC

Chez Scheme

Chez Scheme claims to be an efficient implementation of the language. This version was originally developed by K. Dybvig at the University of Indiana. It is based on an incremental optimizing compiler and offers most of the Scheme standard's optional features. Multi-tasking ('engines') and syntactic extensions are also supported, and some environmental assistance for error tracing is provided. The textbook by Dybvig (1987) is based on this version. Our toolbox programs have been successfully tested for compatibility with Chez Scheme, running on a

VAX 750. The system has grown into a commercial implementation for VAX (UNIX, VMS), Sun and Apollo computers, and further details may be obtained from:

Contact: Cadence Research Systems
620 Park Ridge Rd
Bloomington, IN 47401, USA
e-mail: dyb@cs.indiana.edu

T

T is a new programming language for use in education, systems and AI programming. It was designed and implemented at Yale University. T is based on an extension of Scheme, and it also offers a subset environment which corresponds to the Scheme standard given by Rees and Clinger (1986). Slagle (1987) describes the T-specific extensions. Our toolbox programs have been successfully tested under T on a Sun 3/60. The T system is available for UNIX-based VAXes or MC 68000-based workstations (Sun, Apollo, HP), and may be obtained for a nominal charge.

Contact: T Project
Yale University, Dept. of Computer Science
P.O. Box 2158 Yale Station
New Haven, CT 06520, USA
e-mail: t-project@yale.edu

MacScheme

MacScheme is an efficient, incrementally compiling Scheme implementation for the Apple Macintosh family. It offers a complete editing, execution and debugging environment, following the usual Macintosh conventions. All standard and most of the optional features described in Rees and Clinger (1986) are provided, as well as some simple graphics routines. The editor is mouse- and syntax-driven, and the system supports multiple windows and a limited form of multi-tasking. There is a 'Toolbox' version, which adds high-level support for interactive menus, windows and editors, as well as interface procedures for all Macintosh toolbox traps. 'Double clickable' heap images can be built and the 'Toolbox' version allows the construction of stand-alone applications. All our Scheme examples and toolbox programs were originally implemented and tested under this version. MacScheme was written by W. Clinger and others, and is now distributed as a low-priced commercial implementation.

Contact: Lightspeed Software
P.O. Box 1636
Beaverton, OR 97005, USA

PC Scheme

PC Scheme is a fast and compact Scheme version for the TI Professional and IBM PC-compatible personal computers. It was developed at Texas Instruments, runs under MS-DOS and requires a minimum of 320K, dual floppy system. PC Scheme is based on an incremental compiler and offers all essential and most optional features of Scheme, as described by Rees and Clinger (1986). It also provides extensive run-time support, a display-oriented editor (*Edwin*), multi-tasking with engines and a flavour system (*SCOOPS*). Our toolbox programs have been successfully tested in the PC Scheme environment. This language implementation has been extensively used for education and for developing AI software at Texas Instruments' Digital Systems group. It is available for a low price (TI part no. #2537900-0001).

Contact: Texas Instruments
12501 Research Blvd, MS 2151
Austin, TX 78759, USA
e-mail: Oxley@TI-CSL

XScheme

Based on the popular *XLisp* [Betz (1985)], this is a public-domain Scheme version which has lately been widely distributed through mail groups and electronic bulletin boards. XScheme implements most of the features of the Scheme standard, with a few exceptions and a number of extensions (such as some additional support for object-oriented programming). In order to test our toolbox programs under XScheme we needed to add some macros, since, for example, the *do* procedure was not implemented in the version we had available to us. We include these compatibility procedures in our software distribution.

Contact: D. Betz
114 Davenport Av.
Manchester, NH 03103, USA
(or the Lisp-group at your favourite electronic bulletin board)

Scheme in COMMON LISP

PseudoScheme is an experimental preprocessor for a Scheme subset embedded in COMMON LISP. The system was originally written by J. Rees at MIT and runs under any COMMON LISP implementation. All essential features described in Rees and Clinger (1986) other than continuations and number exactness are supported. PseudoScheme may be obtained free of charge via e-mail or FTP.

Contact: J. Rees
MIT AI Laboratory
545 Technology Square
Cambridge, MA 02139, USA
e-mail: JAR@AI.AI.MIT.EDU

IV.2 Some PROLOG implementations

There is now such a multitude of PROLOG implementations for both main frames and personal workstations that a comprehensive survey of even the most important of these is beyond the scope of this book. The following list gives only a small selection.

C-PROLOG

An inexpensive PROLOG interpreter, popular among universities. C-PROLOG follows the Edinburgh syntax. It offers no aid to program development other than some debugging support.

Contact (UK): Edinburgh University
Department of Architecture
Forest Hill Rd
Edinburgh EH1 1GZ, Great Britain
(US): SRI International
333 Ravenswood Ave
Menlo Park, CA 94025, USA

Micro-PROLOG

An efficient PROLOG implementation for a variety of personal computers, including IBM PCs and Apple Macintoshes. Our example programs were developed and tested under the Macintosh version. Micro-PROLOG offers three different syntaxes: Edinburgh, 'simple' and list-based. An optimizing compiler is available as an option.

Contact: Logic Programming Associates
Studio 4, The Royal Victoria Patriotic Building
Trinity Rd
London SW18 6SX, Great Britain

Quintus PROLOG

An advanced and efficient, but somewhat expensive commercial PROLOG system with an integrated program development environment and a large variety of tools and library procedures. A compiler to generate stand-alone applications is offered, as well as interfaces to 'foreign' languages. This PROLOG version claims a particular strength for development of AI applications. Implementations exist for DEC VAXes (VMS and UNIX) and a range of workstations (Apollo, Sun, Xerox, IBM 6150).

Contact: Artificial Intelligence Ltd
Intelligence House, Merton Rd
Watford, Herts. WD1 7BY, Great Britain

Turbo PROLOG

A very fast, compact and inexpensive implementation for IBM PCs and compatible personal computers. A number of restrictions ensure compiler efficiency at some cost to descriptive flexibility. These modifications make Turbo PROLOG a distinctly separate dialect, with a particular strength in deductive database applications. Many typical AI problems, however, seem to be less well supported. The distribution includes a completely self-contained environment for program development and testing.

Contact: Borland International
4585 Scotts Valley Drive
Scotts Valley, CA 95066, USA

AAIS PROLOG

A fast and inexpensive PROLOG implementation for Apple Macintosh computers. AAIS PROLOG supports both Edinburgh standard syntax and an alternative with some advanced features. It offers multi-window program development support according to the standard Macintosh conventions, and provides good debugging facilities.

Contact: Advanced AI Systems
P.O. Box 39-0360
Mountain View, CA 94039-0360, USA

IV.3 Two Scheme-based flavour systems

SCOOPS

A Scheme-based flavour system, supporting classes, objects and multiple inheritance. SCOOPS was developed at Texas Instruments and can be obtained free of charge. It is also part of the standard PC Scheme distribution (see earlier). SCOOPS has also been ported to MacScheme.

Contact: J. Ulrich
Lightspeed Software
P.O. Box 1636
Beaverton, OR 97005, USA
(*or your local TI representative*)

C-Flavours

A Scheme-based flavour system, with support for objects, multiple inheritance and co-routine-based concurrency. C-Flavours was developed at the University of Canterbury for writing simulation software. An implementation in MacScheme is available as part of the toolbox code referred to in the Preface (see p. vii).

IV.4 Some Smalltalk implementations

Apart from those mentioned below, there are additional implementations for IBM PCs, Ataris, Cadmus and some other workstations. Information about these may be obtained from ParcPlace Systems.

ParcPlace Systems

ParcPlace Systems, a newly founded company, has taken over all distribution of Xerox Parc's Smalltalk systems. Currently there are a number of implementations for Xerox 1100 workstations, Suns, Apollos and Macintosh computers. Smalltalk needs a hard disk and a considerable amount of memory in order to run on a Macintosh (in excess of 2MB). A basic system and a developers' flavour of the version 2 release of the Smalltalk virtual image are available.

Contact: ParcPlace Systems
1550 Plymouth Street
Mountain View, CA 94043, USA
Info@ParcPlace.COM

Tektronix

Tektronix offers a particularly efficient version 2 Smalltalk implementation with a variety of extensions and utilities. Tektronix Smalltalk runs on the Tektronix 4400 family of engineering workstations.

Contact: Tektronix Inc.
P.O. Box 1700
Beaverton, OR 97075, USA

Apple

Apple Computers offers a Macintosh implementation for the version 1 dialect of Smalltalk. This is currently distributed for a nominal charge and runs on a basic 1MB Macintosh, although the space for applications is severely limited under such a configuration. A more usable system requires a hard disk and additional memory. Apple also offers an older, severely pruned version (version 0), which may be used to run simple examples on 512K machines. The discussion in Kaehler and Patterson (1986a) is based on this subset. In 1989 Apple's commercial Smalltalk development was discontinued in response to the ParcPlace and Digitalk implementations on Macintoshes.

Contact: Apple Programmer's and Developer's Association (APDA)
APDA Product # KMSST4
Apple Computers
20525 Mariani Ave., MS: 336
Cupertino, CA 95014, USA

Digitalk (Smalltalk V)

Digitalk offers a very efficient and inexpensive version of Smalltalk for IBM PCs and compatible MS-DOS machines with a minimum of 512K RAM. A mouse and graphics controller are also required. Smalltalk V's user interface is a simplified variant of the 'normal' Smalltalk environment. Although not 'proper' Smalltalk, this system is very well suited for initial experimentation. It comes with a good introductory manual, which may also serve as a textbook. An Apple Macintosh version of Smalltalk V has recently been released and has been well received.

Contact: Digitalk Inc.
9841 Airport Boulevard
Los Angeles, CA 90045, USA

Little Smalltalk

Little Smalltalk is an implementation of the Smalltalk language kernel without its user interface. This offers an object-oriented framework for conventional time-sharing systems, but it does not provide Smalltalk's graphical, desktop-based environment, and there is no support for exploratory software development. Use of the system is described in Budd (1987). The software has been ported to many UNIX varieties on a wide range of machines and may be obtained for the cost of distribution.

Contact: Smalltalk Distribution
Department of Computer Science
Oregon State University
Corvallis, OR 97331, USA
e-mail: budd@cs.orst.edu
(*or the Smalltalk group at your favourite electronic bulletin board*)

GNU Smalltalk

GNU Smalltalk is an attempt at providing a portable public domain Smalltalk implementation, along similar lines as Little Smalltalk. There is currently no integrated user interface, although an X-windows implementation is in preparation. GNU Smalltalk is currently available from E. Vielmetti at MIT's AI-lab. (see p. 586) by anonymous FTP from prep.ai.mit.edu as pub/gnu/smalltalk-1.0.tav.Z. It is written in C and runs on Sun, Next, DecStation, Atari ST, and other machines.

IV.5 The Scheme-based toolboxes

The toolbox programs described and exemplified in this text may be obtained for a nominal charge to cover the cost of media, handling and distribution. This includes the programs themselves, together with a number of examples and solutions to exercises. The Macintosh distribution will also include the C-Flavour system, a simulator, and all the Scheme, PROLOG and Smalltalk examples and sample solutions. Prices and ordering instructions are given on p. viii of this book.

Appendix V
Solutions to Starred (*) Exercises

A few programs for solving end-of-chapter exercises are given here. The toolbox disk also contains a variety of additional sample solutions.

V.1 Scheme

A 'Maze' program (Section 2.3.5, Ex. 2.3)

```
; a maze is an association list of exits and other objects
(define Maze '((entry     (north exit)     (east exit)
                          (south pit)      (west dungeon))
               (exit      (north #f)       (east #f)
                          (south entry)    (west entry))
               (dungeon   (north entry)    (east #f)
                          (south pit)      (west #f)
                          (monster troll)  (treasure jewel))
               (pit       (north #f)       (east #f)
                          (south #f)       (west dungeon))))

; adventurers are bound to a list of their properties (name-value pairs), including
; "position" (see definition of "room" below)
(define Adventurer (list (list 'position (room Maze 'entry))) )

; 0: return an adventurer in a new location
(define changeLocation
  (lambda (anAdventurer aRoom)
    (map
      (lambda (aPropertyPair)
        (if (equal? (car aPropertyPair) 'position)
            (list 'position aRoom)
            aPropertyPair))
      anAdventurer)))

; 1: Maze description
(define displayMaze
```

```
  (lambda (aMaze)
  (display "*** Maze ***") (newline)
  (for-each (lambda (aDescription)
              (display "  ") (display (car aDescription))
              (display ":") (newline)
              (for-each (lambda (aProperty) (display aProperty))
                        (cdr aDescription))
              (newline))
              Maze)
  (newline)))
; 2: Adventurer position (returns a room)
(define where
  (lambda (anAdventurer) (cadr (assoc 'position anAdventurer))))
; 3a: find a room in a maze (by name)
(define room
  (lambda (aMaze aRoomName) (assoc aRoomName aMaze)))
; 3b: inspect an association and test if it describes an exit
(define exit?
  (lambda (anAssociation)
    (and (member (car anAssociation) '(north east south west))
         (not (null? (cadr anAssociation)))) ))
; 3c: inspect a room and return all exits . . .
(define exits
  (lambda (aRoom)
    (define associations (cdr aRoom))
    (map (lambda (anAssociation)
           (if (exit? anAssociation) anAssociation))
         associations)))
; 4: return the next room (if any) in a maze, given a direction
(define next
  (lambda (aMaze aRoom aDirectionName)
    (define directionAssoc (assoc aDirectionName (cdr aRoom)))
    (if (exit? directionAssoc)
      (room aMaze (cadr directionAssoc))) ))
; 5: change an adventurer's location by walking in a given
;    direction (if there is an exit that way) - returns a "new" adventurer
(define walk
  (lambda (aMaze anAdventurer aDirectionName)
    (define destination
            (next aMaze (where anAdventurer) aDirectionName))
    (if (not (null? destination))
      (changeLocation anAdventurer destination)
    (begin (display "ouch .. (there's a wall here) @#!!") (newline)
           anAdventurer))))
; . . . {and so forth} . . .
```

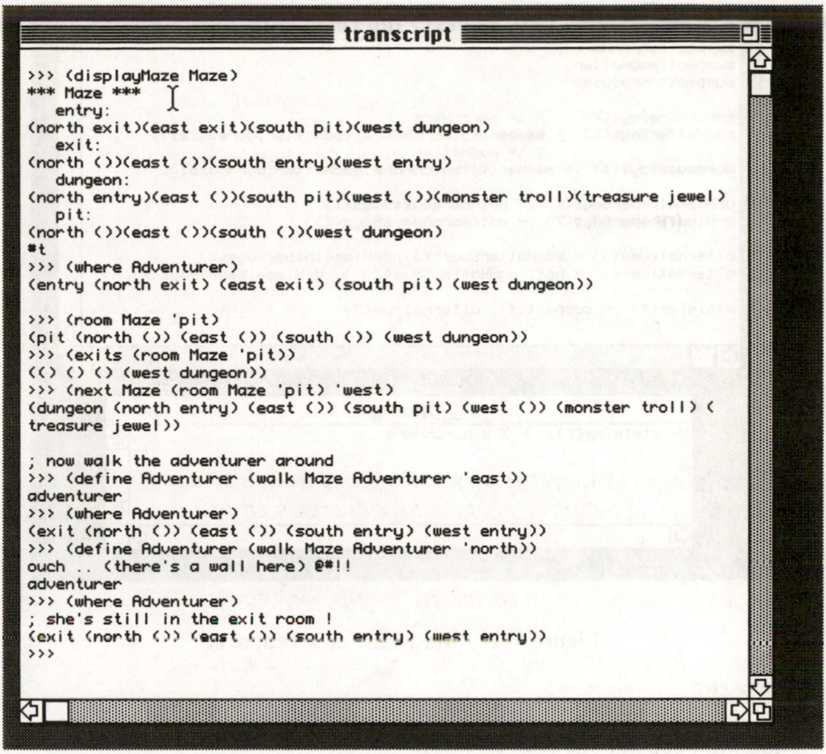

```
>>> (displayMaze Maze)
*** Maze ***
   entry:
(north exit)(east exit)(south pit)(west dungeon)
   exit:
(north ())(east ())(south entry)(west entry)
   dungeon:
(north entry)(east ())(south pit)(west ())(monster troll)(treasure jewel)
   pit:
(north ())(east ())(south ())(west dungeon)
#t
>>> (where Adventurer)
(entry (north exit) (east exit) (south pit) (west dungeon))

>>> (room Maze 'pit)
(pit (north ()) (east ()) (south ()) (west dungeon))
>>> (exits (room Maze 'pit))
(() () () (west dungeon))
>>> (next Maze (room Maze 'pit) 'west)
(dungeon (north entry) (east ()) (south pit) (west ()) (monster troll) (
treasure jewel))

; now walk the adventurer around
>>> (define Adventurer (walk Maze Adventurer 'east))
adventurer
>>> (where Adventurer)
(exit (north ()) (east ()) (south entry) (west entry))
>>> (define Adventurer (walk Maze Adventurer 'north))
ouch .. (there's a wall here) @#!!
adventurer
>>> (where Adventurer)
; she's still in the exit room !
(exit (north ()) (east ()) (south entry) (west entry))
>>>
```

Figure V.1 'Maze'.

V.2 PROLOG

The 'Mad Hatter's Teaparty' (Section 2.4.5, Ex. 2.12)

```
/* this program is executed through query '?- stolejam (X).'   */
/* It will respond with a list of all reasonable suspects      */

/* list all potential suspects first                           */

suspect (marchHare).
suspect (madHatter).
suspect (dormouse).

/* now represent each person's statement:                      */
/* each rule succeeds if X is instantiated to a suspect who    */
/* could have logically stolen the jam                         */

/* 1. the March Hare said that he didn't do it                 */
marchHareSays (X) :- X \= marchHare.
```

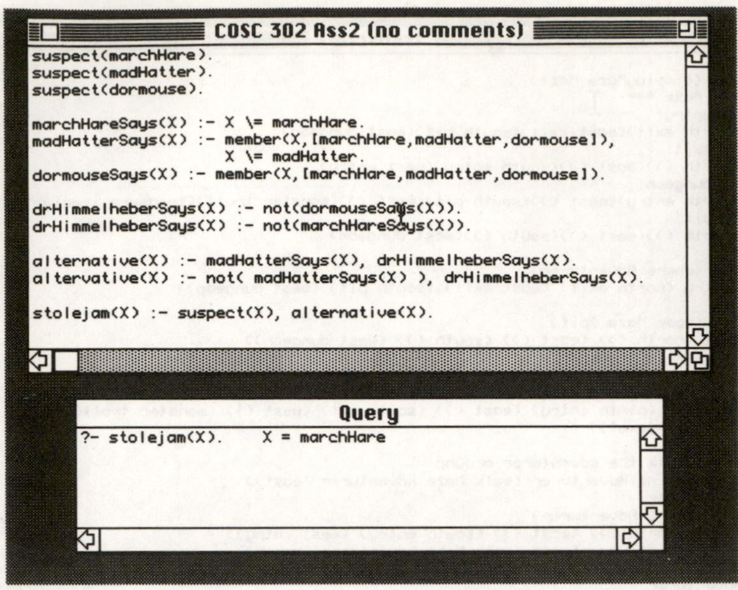

Figure V.2 'Mad Hatter's Teaparty'.

```
/* 2. the Mad Hatter said that one of them did it, but he didn't        */
madHatterSays (X) :- member (X, [marchHare, madHatter, dormouse]),
                     X \= madHatter.

/* 3. the dormouse said that one of them did it                          */
dormouseSays (X) :- member (X, [marchHare, madHatter, dormouse]).

/* 4. Dr. Himmelheber's investigation revealed that the                  */
/*    Dormouse and the March Hare could not both have                    */
/*    spoken the truth                                                   */

drHimmelheberSays (X) :- not dormouseSays (X).
drHimmelheberSays (X) :- not marchHareSays (X).

/* 5. this leaves us with the two alternatives that either               */
/*    the Mad Hatter is telling the truth; or he isn't !                 */

alternative (X) :- madHatterSays (X), drHimmelheberSays (X).
alternative (X):- not madHatterSays (X), drHimmelheberSays (X).

/* 6. X stole the jam iff he/she is a suspect and one of                 */
/*    the above alternatives holds.                                      */

stolejam (X) :- suspect (X), alternative (X).
```

V.3 Flavours

An 'Embassy Party' (Section 2.5.5, Ex. 2.24)

```
(define EmbassyParty
  (lambda (ambassadors)
      (define next (vector-ref ambassadors 1))
      (while (<? 1 (random 9))
          ; 20% chance that there's no caviar left
          ; try to continue with the next talker on the agenda
          (if (not (next 'terminated? 'talk))
              (next 'continue 'talk))
          (set! next (next 'nextTalker)) )
      (display "Horror! – No caviar left, let's all go home.")
      (newline)))

(defflavour Ambassador (ako Actor) (ivars nextTalker number)
  setivars getivars testivars)

(defcoroutine (talk Ambassador) ()
      (while (<? 1 (random 9))
            ; number drawn from 0 to 9 – 20% for #f
            (display "ambassador ") (display number)
            (display " says, mumble . . .") (newline)
            ; back to the party
            (self 'detach))
      (display "That is all ambassador ") (display number)
      (display " can eat !!") (newline) )

(define setupParty
; . . . some tedious code to set up and link the list of ambassadors
  (lambda (noOfParticipants)
      (define crowd (make-vector noOfParticipants))
      (define maxIndex (– noOfParticipants 1))
      (define lastOne nil)
      ; first create the right number of ambassadors
      (do ((index 0 (+ 1 index)))
          ((> index maxIndex) #t)
          (vector-set! crowd index (Ambassador 'new)))
      ; now let them mingle, so that they find their partners
      (set! lastOne (vector-ref crowd maxIndex))
      (do ((index 0 (+ 1 index)))
          ((> index (– maxIndex 1)) #t)
          ((vector-ref crowd index)
                'nextTalker!
                (vector-ref crowd (+ 1 index)))
          ((vector-ref crowd index) 'number! index))
      ; close the chain into a circle !
      (lastOne 'nextTalker! (vector-ref crowd 0))
      (lastOne 'number! maxIndex)
```

```
transcript

>>> (EmbassyParty (setUpParty 3))

ambassador 1 says, mumble ...
That is all ambassador 2 can eat !!
ambassador 0 says, mumble ...
ambassador 1 says, mumble ...
ambassador 0 says, mumble ...
ambassador 1 says, mumble ...
ambassador 0 says, mumble ...
That is all ambassador 1 can eat !!
Horror ! - No caviar left, let's all go home.
#t
>>>
```

Figure V.3 'Embassy Party'.

```
    ; return the whole setUp
    crowd))
```

V.4 Toolboxes

V.4.1 'Lineland' (Section 3.2.3, Ex. 3.1)

```
; ********** The "Lineland" microworld **********

; This is a problem of reverse discrimination within a 7 seat bus containing
; 3 students and 3 lecturers. Initially all the lecturers are in front of the
; students and the empty seat is at the front of the bus. The goal is to
; reverse the situation so that all students are in front of all lecturers
; (with no regard to where the empty seat occurs). Valid moves for any
; lecturer or student are:
;
; (1) Move one position in either direction into the adjacent empty seat
; (2) Jump over one person in either direction into the empty seat

(define LL-SearchProblem #f)

(define SetUpLineland
  (lambda ()

    ; represent bus state as in (e l l s s) where 'e', 'l'
    ; and 's' are the empty seat, a lecturer or student
    ; respectively. Thus the initial state is:
```

```
(define initialState '(e l l s s))

; the goal is to reach the state (s s l l) when the
; position of the empty seat is ignored

(define removeEmptySeat
  (lambda (aState)
    (if (EmptyState? aState)
      ()
      (if (eq? 'e (FirstElement aState))
        (removeEmptySeat (RestOfElements aState))
        (cons (FirstElement aState)
              (removeEmptySeat
               (RestOfElements aState)))))))

(define goalFN
  (lambda (aState) (equal? '(s s l l) (removeEmptySeat aState))))

; the actions are easier to deal with if we assume that the
; empty seat moves 1 or 2 places in either direction.

(define moveEmpty
  (lambda (n)
   ; return a function that will move the empty seat n
   ; to left if n is negative, and n to right if positive
   (lambda (aState)
     (let* ((origin      (FindFirstSlotOfSymbol 'e aState))
            (destination (+ origin n)))
      (cond ((or (<= origin 0)
                 (> origin (length aState))
                 (<= destination 0)
                 (> destination (length aState))) #f)
            (else
             (let ((destSym
                    (FindSymbolInSlot destination aState)))
              (FillSlot destination
                        'e
                        (FillSlot origin destSym aState)))))))))

; a measure of closeness to the solution is obtained by accumulating
; a penalty score over all lecturers for each student that is behind the
; lecturer. This is improved by weighting each student's contribution
; by 1 for the first lecturer and 2 for the second lecturer and also
; including the number of seats the student is behind the lecturer.
; This gives a penalty of zero for the goal states and a negative value
; for others. The initial state yields a value of -11 with a contribution
; of -5 for the first lecturer (students 2 and 3 seats behind) and a
; contribution of -6 (-2*3) for the second lecturer (students 1 and 2
; seats behind).

(define computePenalty
  (lambda (aState)
```

transcript

```
>>> (load "LineLand.scm")

>>> (SetUpLineland)
#(() () 0 (e l l s s) #<PROCEDURE display> #<PROCEDURE computepenalty>
#<PROCEDURE goalfn> (#<PROCEDURE> #<PROCEDURE> #<PROCEDURE> #<PROCEDURE>)
#<PROCEDURE equal?>)

>>> (DFSearch LL-SearchProblem 2) ; not deep enough
#f
>>> (DFSearch LL-SearchProblem 8) ;  148 moves
(8 148 (#(ok NEG-INFINITY (s s l e l)) #(ok NEG-INFINITY (s e l s l))
        #(ok NEG-INFINITY (e s l s l)) #(ok NEG-INFINITY (l s e s l))
        #(ok NEG-INFINITY (l s l s e)) #(ok NEG-INFINITY (l s l e s))
        #(ok NEG-INFINITY (l e l s s)) #(ok NEG-INFINITY (e l l s s))))
>>> (BFSearch LL-SearchProblem)   ;  440 moves
(8 440 (#(ok NEG-INFINITY (s s l e l)) #(ok NEG-INFINITY (s e l s l))
        #(ok NEG-INFINITY (e s l s l)) #(ok NEG-INFINITY (l s e s l))
        #(ok NEG-INFINITY (l s l s e)) #(ok NEG-INFINITY (l s l e s))
        #(ok NEG-INFINITY (l e l s s)) #(ok NEG-INFINITY (e l l s s))))

; other search strategies fail to find this shortest solution
>>> (HillSearch LL-SearchProblem 99)  ;  72 moves
(10 72 (#(ok   0 (s e s l l)) #(ok  -1 (s l s e l)) #(ok  -1 (s l s l e))
        #(ok  -4 (s l e l s)) #(ok  -6 (e l s l s)) #(ok  -6 (l e s l s))
        #(ok -11 (l l s e s)) #(ok -11 (l l e s s)) #(ok -11 (l e l s s))
        #(ok -11 (e l l s s))))
>>> (HillSearch LL-SearchProblem 99)  ;  56 moves
(13 56 (#(ok   0 (s s l e l)) #(ok  -1 (s e l s l)) #(ok  -1 (s l e s l))
        #(ok  -4 (s l l s e)) #(ok  -4 (s l l e s)) #(ok  -4 (s e l l s))
        #(ok  -4 (s l e l s)) #(ok  -6 (e l s l s)) #(ok  -6 (l e s l s))
        #(ok -11 (l l s e s)) #(ok -11 (l l e s s)) #(ok -11 (l e l s s))
        #(ok -11 (e l l s s))))
>>> (SteepestSearch LL-SearchProblem) ;  only 44 moves
(12 44 (#(ok   0 (s s l e l)) #(ok  -1 (s e l s l)) #(ok  -1 (e s l s l))
        #(ok  -3 (l s e s l)) #(ok  -3 (l s s e l)) #(ok  -3 (l s s l e))
        #(ok  -6 (l s e l s)) #(ok  -6 (l e s l s)) #(ok -11 (l l s e s))
        #(ok -11 (l l s s e)) #(ok -11 (l l e s s)) #(ok -11 (e l l s s))))
```

Figure V.4 'Lineland'.

```
(do ((score 0)
     (lecturerNumber 1 (+ lecturerNumber 1))
     (section (member 'l (removeEmptySeat aState))
              (member 'l section)))
    ((not section) score)
    (do ((relPos 0 (+ relPos 1))
         (subSection section (cdr subSection))
         (lecturerScore 0))
        ((null? subSection)
         (set! score (+ score lecturerScore)))
        (if (eq? 's (car subSection))
            (set! lecturerScore
                  (- lecturerScore (* lecturerNumber relPos)))
            #f))
   (set! section (cdr section)))))

; Now set up the Search Problem
```

```
        (set ! LL-SearchProblem
              (MakeSearchProblem initialState
                                 goalFN
                                 computePenalty
                                 (MakeActionList
                                   (moveEmpty -2)
                                   (moveEmpty -1)
                                   (moveEmpty +1)
                                   (moveEmpty +2))))))
(begin (SetUpLineland) #t)
```

V.4.2 'Kalah' (Section 3.2.3, Ex. 3.16)

```
; ***** K A L A H *****
;
; This game is for two players, with each player having 6 pits
; each containing 6 stones and a Kalah. These are arranged as
; follows:
;    Player 1:   kalah  pit6  pit5  pit4  pit3  pit2  pit1
;    stones:              6     6     6     6     6     6
;
;    Player 2:          pit1  pit2  pit3  pit4  pit5  pit6 kalah
;    stones:              6     6     6     6     6     6
;
; Each move involves taking all the stones out of one of your
; pits and then dropping one in each of your own pits, your
; kalah and your opponent's pit (but skipping their kalah) in a
; counter-clockwise direction. E.g. if the stones come from
; player 2, pit 3 and there were 11 stones then one stone
; would be dropped in each of: player 2 pits 4, 5, 6 - player
; 2 kalah - player 1 pit 1, 2, 3, 4, 5, 6 and the last stone
; would go into player 2, pit 1.
;
; There are three possible outcomes:
;      1) if the last stone lands in the player's own kalah he or
;         she can make a further move
;      2) if the last stone lands in an empty pit owned by the
;         player and the opponent's hole directly opposite
;         contains stones, then the last stone plus all the
;         stones in the opponent's pit are dropped in the
;         player's kalah
;      3) otherwise the player's turn ends.
;
; The game ends when one player's pits are all empty or more than half
; the stones are in one of the kalahs. The winner is the player with
; the most stones in their kalah at the end of the game.
;
```

```
(define KalahGameProblem #f)

(define SetUpKalah
  (lambda ()
; The state of the board will be represented as a 14 element
; vector of first the machines pits plus kalah and then the
; opponent's pits plus kalah. An additional element (the last)
; will be used to indicate that this state is one that allows
; another move to a player. It will be #f for no extra move,
; "machine" if the machine gets another move and "opponent" if
; the opponent gets another move. Hence the initial state is:

    (define initial
      (vector 6 6 6 6 6 6  0     6 6 6 6 6 6  0 #f))
    ; The following functions are used to select and set the
    ; values in the state

    (define machinePits      0)
    (define machinePit1      0)
    (define machinePit2      1)
    (define machinePit3      2)
    (define machinePit4      3)
    (define machinePit5      4)
    (define machinePit6      5)
    (define machineKalah     6)
    (define opponentPits     7)
    (define opponentPit1     7)
    (define opponentPit2     8)
    (define opponentPit3     9)
    (define opponentPit4     10)
    (define opponentPit5     11)
    (define opponentPit6     12)
    (define opponentKalah    13)
    (define lastPit          13)
    (define numberPits       14)
    (define extraMove?       14)

    (define getStones
      (lambda (aState whichPit) (vector-ref aState whichPit)))

    (define setStones!
      (lambda (aState whichPit stones)
        (vector-set! aState whichPit stones)))

    (define getExtra
      (lambda (aState) (vector-ref aState extraMove?)))

    (define setExtra!
      (lambda (aState) (vector-set! aState extraMove? #t)))

    (define resetExtra!
      (lambda (aState) (vector-set! aState extraMove? #f)))
```

```
(define copyState
  (lambda (aState)
  ; return a new vector with same contents and extra move cleared
   (let ((result (list->vector (vector->list aState))))
     (resetExtra! result)
     result)))

(define nextPit
  (lambda (aPit machine?)
    ; wrap around end and skip opponent's kalah
    (let ((n (+ aPit 1)))
      (cond ((> n lastPit) 0)
            ((and (= n machineKalah) (not machine?))
             opponentPit1)
            ((and (= n opponentKalah) machine?)
             machinePit1)
            (else n)))))

 ; Evaluation function – return the difference between
 ; number of stones in machine's and opponent's kalah.

 (define evalFN
   (lambda (aState machineMove?)
     (let* ((machine (getStones aState machineKalah))
            (opponent (getStones aState opponentKalah)))
       (– machine opponent))))

 ; Winning positions are if all of a player's pits are empty or one
 ; kalah has more than half the stones

 (define status
   (lambda (aState machineMove?)

     (define moreThanHalf? (lambda (n) (> n 36)))

     (define nostones?
       (lambda (aPlayer)

         (do ((number 0)
              (pit aPlayer (+ pit 1))
              (i 6 (– i 1)))
             ((zero? i) (zero? number))
             (set! number (+ number (getStones aState pit))))))

      (define playerWithMost
        (lambda ()
          (cond ((> (getStones aState machineKalah)
                    (getStones aState opponentKalah))
                 ''machine'')
                ((< (getStones aState machineKalah)
                    (getStones aState opponentKalah))
                 ''opponent'')
                (else ''draw''))))
```

```
    (cond ((moreThanHalf? (getStones aState machineKalah))
           ''machine'')
          ((moreThanHalf? (getStones aState opponentKalah))
           ''opponent'')
          ((or (noStones? machinePits)
               (noStones? opponentPits)) (playerWithMost))
          ((getExtra aState) ''again'')
          (else #f))))

(define checkForExtraTurn!
  (lambda (newState machine? lastPit)
    ; if last move is into own kalah then set extra move
    ; if last move is into pit opposite a non-empty pit then transfer
    ; stones to kalah
    (define oppositePit
      (lambda (aPit)
        (vector-ref (vector 12 11 10 9 8 7 #f 5 4 3 2 1 0 #f)
                    aPit)))
    (cond ((or   (= lastPit machineKalah)
                 (= lastPit opponentKalah)) (setExtra! newState))
          ((and machine?
                (< lastPit machineKalah)
                (=1 (getStones newState lastPit))
                (positive? (getStones newState
                                      (oppositePit lastPit))))
           (begin (setStones! newState
                              machineKalah
                              (+ (getStones newState
                                            machineKalah)
                                 (+ (getStones newState
                                               (oppositePit lastPit))
                                    1)))
                  (setStones! newState (oppositePit lastPit) 0)
                  (setStones! newState lastPit 0)
                  newState))
          ((and (not machine?)
                (>= lastPit opponentPits)
                (=1 (getStones newState lastPit))
                (positive? (getStones newState
                                      (oppositePit lastPit))))
           (begin (setStones! newState
                              opponentKalah
                              (+ (getStones newState opponentKalah)
                                 (+ (getStones newState
                                               (oppositePit lastPit))
                                    1)))
```

```
            (setStones! newState (oppositePit lastPit) 0)
            (setStones! newState lastPit 0)
            newState)))))

(define moveStones
  (lambda (aPit machine?)
  ; Return a function that moves the stones from a given
  ; pit. Machine? is #t if it is a machine move.
    (lambda (aState)
      (let ((n (getStones aState aPit)))
        (if (zero? n)
            #f
            ; construct a new state with stones in 'aPit'
            ; redistributed
            (let ((newState (copyState aState))
                  (lastPit 0))
              (setStones! newState aPit 0)
              (do ((pit (nextPit aPit machine?)
                         (nextPit pit machine?)))
                  ((zero? n))
                  (setStones! newState
                              pit
                              (+ 1 (getStones newState pit)))
                  (set! n (- n 1))
                  (set! lastPit pit))
              (checkForExtraTurn! newState
                                  machine?
                                  lastPit)
              newState))))))

(define printKalah
  (lambda (aState)
    ; arrange display in two facing rows. e.g.:
    ; K  6  5  4  3  2  1
    ; 0  6  6  6  6  6  6
    ; ====================
    ;    6  6  6  6  6  6  0
    ;    1  2  3  4  5  6  K

    (define myDisplay
      (lambda (n)
        (if (< n 10)
            (display " ")
            #f)
        (display n) (display " ")))

    (newline)
    (display "K  6  5  4  3  2  1") (newline)
    (myDisplay (getStones aState opponentKalah))
    (do ((i OpponentPit6 (- i 1)))
```

```
transcript

(load "Kalah.scm")
kalahgameproblem
setupkalah
#t
#t
(SetUpKalah)
#(() () 0 #(6 6 6 6 6 6 0 6 6 6 6 6 6 0 ()) #<PROCEDURE printkalah> #<PROCEDURE
evalfn> #<PROCEDURE status> (#<PROCEDURE> #<PROCEDURE> #<PROCEDURE> #<PROCEDURE>
#<PROCEDURE> #<PROCEDURE>) (#<PROCEDURE> #<PROCEDURE> #<PROCEDURE> #<PROCEDURE>
#<PROCEDURE> #<PROCEDURE>) #<PROCEDURE getmove>)
Type (PlayGame KalahGameProblem) to play Kalah
#t
#t

>>> (FindBestMachineMove (vector 6 6 6 6 6 6 0 6 6 6 6 6 6 0 #f)
                         KalahGameProblem
                         #f  ; no alpha/beta pruning
                         3)  ; 3 ply
(2 #(0 7 7 7 7 7 1 6 6 6 6 6 6 0 #t))
>>> (GetCount KalahGameProblem)
401 ; the program tried 401 moves
>>>
```

Figure V.5 'Kalah': making a move.

```
         ((= i machineKalah))
         (myDisplay (getStones aState i)))
    (newline)
    (display) "=========================" )(newline)
    (display "   ")
    (do ((i machinePit1 (+ i 1)))
         ((= i machineKalah))
         (myDisplay (getStones aState i)))
    (myDisplay (getStones aState machineKalah)) (newline)
    (display "          1  2  3  4  5  6  K")))

(define getMove
  (lambda (aState)
    (let ((which 0))
      (if (getExtra aState)
        (begin (newline) (display "Have an extra move!"))
        #f)
      (set! which
           (do ((pos -1))
                ((and (number? pos)
                       (<= 0 pos)
                       (<= pos 6)
                       (positive? (getStones aState (+ pos machineKalah))))
                  pos)
                 (newline)
```

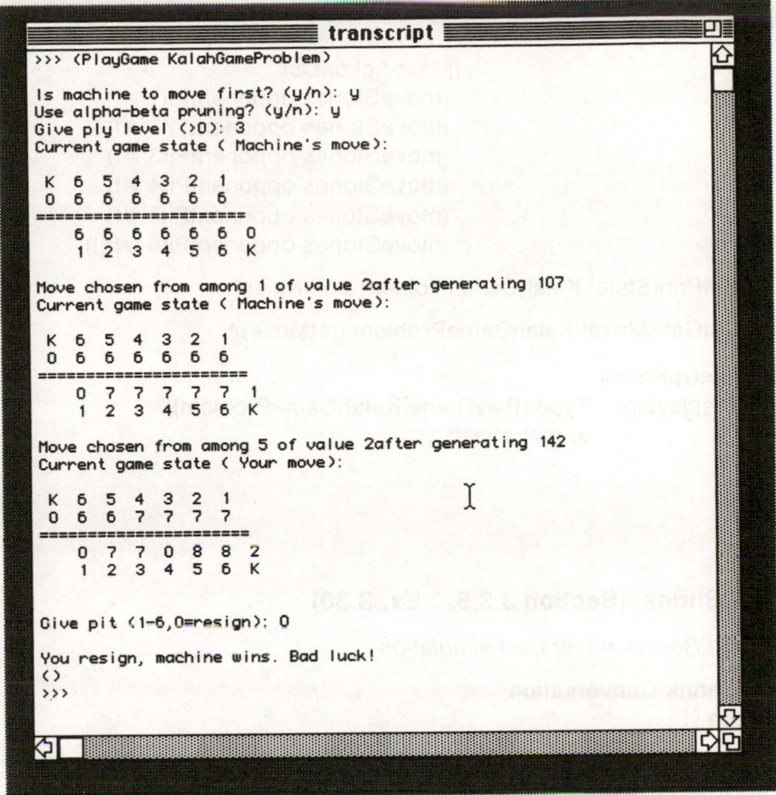
```
transcript
>>> (PlayGame KalahGameProblem)

Is machine to move first? (y/n): y
Use alpha-beta pruning? (y/n): y
Give ply level (>0): 3
Current game state ( Machine's move):

 K  6  5  4  3  2  1
 0  6  6  6  6  6  6
=====================
    6  6  6  6  6  6  0
    1  2  3  4  5  6  K

Move chosen from among 1 of value 2after generating 107
Current game state ( Machine's move):

 K  6  5  4  3  2  1
 0  6  6  6  6  6  6
=====================
    0  7  7  7  7  7  1
    1  2  3  4  5  6  K

Move chosen from among 5 of value 2after generating 142
Current game state ( Your move):

 K  6  5  4  3  2  1
 0  6  6  7  7  7  7
=====================
    0  7  7  0  8  8  2
    1  2  3  4  5  6  K


Give pit (1-6,0=resign): 0

You resign, machine wins. Bad luck!
()
>>>
```

Figure V.6 'Kalah': playing a game.

```
                (display "Give pit (1-6, 0=resign): ")
                (newline)
                (set! pos (read))))
   (if (zero? which)
       #f
       ((moveStones (+ which machineKalah) #f) aState)))))

(set! KalahGameProblem
    (MakeGameProblem initial
                     status
                     evalFN
                     (MakeActionList
                       (moveStones machinePit1 #t)
                       (moveStones machinePit2 #t)
                       (moveStones machinePit3 #t)
                       (moveStones machinePit4 #t)
```

```
                                   (moveStones machinePit5 #t)
                                   (moveStones machinePit6 #t))
                                  (MakeActionList
                                   (moveStones opponentPit1 #f)
                                   (moveStones opponentPit2 #f)
                                   (moveStones opponentPit3 #f)
                                   (moveStones opponentPit4 #f)
                                   (moveStones opponentPit5 #f)
                                   (moveStones opponentPit6 #f))))

    (SetPrintState! KalahGameProblem printKalah)

    (SetGetAMove! KalahGameProblem getMove)))

(begin (SetUpKalah)
    (DisplayLine "Type (PlayGame KalahGameProblem)"
                 "to play Kalah"))
```

V.4.3 'Shrink' (Section 3.3.5, Ex. 3.30)

```
; A simple Rogerian therapist simulation

(define Shrink-Conversation
  (lambda ()

    ; the Shrink KB and globals
    (let ((Shrink-KB #f)
          (allDone #f))

      ; store all patterns for a conversation as a pair of the
      ; pattern to match and a procedure to call upon
      ; successful match

      (define makeFact
        (lambda (aPattern aProcedure) (cons aPattern aProcedure)))

      (define selectPattern car)
      (define selectProc cdr)

      ; functions to test for word properties

      (define verb?
        (lambda (anAL)
          ; is the variable 'verb' a verb?
          (member (GetAssociationValue 'verb anAL)
                  '(go have be try eat take help make get jump
                    write type fill put turn compute
                    think drink blink crash crunch add))))
```

```
(define whyWord?
  (lambda (anAL)
    ; is the variable 'why' a why type word?
    (member (GetAssociationValue 'why anAL)
            '(why where when what))))

(define doWord?
  (lambda (anAL)
    ; is the variable 'do' a do type word?
    (member (GetAssociationValue 'do anAL)
            '(do can should would))))

(define iWord?
  (lambda (anAL)
    ; is the variable 'i' an i type word?
    (member (GetAssociationValue 'i anAL) '(i me))))

(define changePerson
  (lambda (aList)
    ; change from 1st to 2nd person and vice versa
    (define 1<->2Person
      (lambda (word)
        (cond ((eq? word 'i)     'you)
              ((eq? word 'me)    'you)
              ((eq? word 'you)   'me)
              ((eq? word 'my)    'your)
              ((eq? word 'your)  'my)
              ((eq? word 'yours) 'mine)
              ((eq? word 'mine)  'yours)
              ((eq? word 'am)    'are)
              (else word))))

    (map 1<->2Person aList)))

(define questionNo 0)
(define questionList '(when why where))
(define question
  (lambda ()
    (set! questionNo (+ 1 questionNo))
    (if (= questionNo (length questionList))
      (set! questionNo 0)
      #f)
    (list-ref questionList questionNo)))

(define replyNo 0)
(define replyList '("Please go on"
                    "Tell me more"
                    "I see"
                    "What does that indicate?"
                    "But why be concerned about that?"
                    "Just tell me how you feel"))
```

```
(define generalReply
  (lambda ()
    (set! replyNo (+ 1 replyNo))
    (if (= replyNo (length replyList))
      (set! replyNo 0)
      #f)
    (list-ref replyList replyNo)))

(define reply
  (lambda aList
    ; display aList without outer brackets or sublists

    (define replyAux
      (lambda (aList)
        (do ((rest aList (cdr rest)))
            ((null? rest))
          (if (pair? (car rest))
              (replyAux (car rest))
              (display (car rest)))
          (display " "))))
    (replyAux aList)))

; build the Knowledge Base

(define initKB
  (lambda ( )
   (set!
   Shrink-KB
   (MakeKB
    (makeFact (PATTERN 'Bye)
              (lambda (al)
                (set! allDone #t)
                (reply "Come back soon. Goodbye")
                (newline)))
    (makeFact (PATTERN 'I 'am ?+)
              (lambda (al)
                (reply "Please tell me" (question) "you are")))
    (makeFact (PATTERN 'I 'have (?+ 'x))
              (lambda (al)
                (reply "How long have you had"
                     (changePerson (GetAssociationValue 'x al)))))
    (makeFact (PATTERN 'I 'feel ?+)
              (lambda (al) (reply "I sometimes feel the same way")))
    (makeFact (PATTERN 'Because ?+)
              (lambda (al) (reply "Is that really the reason?")))
    (makeFact (PATTERN 'Yes ?+)
              (lambda (al) (reply "How can you be so sure?")))
    (makeFact (PATTERN)
              (lambda (al) (reply "Please say something")))
```

```
(makeFact (PATTERN 'You 'are (?+ 'something))
          (lambda (al)
            (reply "O yeah. I am"
              (changePerson (GetAssociationValue 'something al)))))
(makeFact (PATTERN (? 'verb verb?) (?+ 'rest))
          (lambda (al)
            (reply "So you want me to go and"
              (GetAssociationValue 'verb al)
              (changePerson (GetAssociationValue 'rest al)))))
(makeFact (PATTERN (? 'why whyWord?) (?+ 'rest))
          (lambda (al)
            (reply "You tell me"
              (GetAssociationValue 'why al))))
(makeFact (PATTERN (? 'do doWord?) 'you (?+ 'rest))
          (lambda (al)
            (reply "Perhaps I"
              (GetAssociationValue 'do al)
              (changePerson (GetAssociationValue 'rest al)))))
(makeFact (PATTERN (? 'Do 'you 'think ?+)
          (lambda (al)
            (reply "I think you should answer that yourself")))
(makeFact (PATTERN (?+ 'dream ?+)
          (lambda (al)
            (reply "For dream analysis see Freud")))
(makeFact (PATTERN ?+ 'love ?+)
          (lambda (al) (reply "All is fair in love and war")))
(makeFact (PATTERN ?+ 'no ?+)
          (lambda (al) (reply "Don't be so negative")))
(makeFact (PATTERN ?+ 'maybe ?+)
          (lambda (al) (reply "Be more decisive")))
(makeFact (PATTERN (? 'i iWord?) (?+ 'rest))
          (lambda (al)
            (reply "You"
              (changePerson (GetAssociationValue 'rest al)))))
(makeFact (PATTERN ?+)
          (lambda (al)
            (reply (generalReply))))))))

(define readSentence
  (lambda ()
    (let ((sentence #f))
      (newline)
      (display "...> ")
      (set! sentence (read))
      (newline)
      (if (not (pair? sentence))
        (begin (DisplayList "Please give your replies as a list")
```

```
                (readSentence))
        sentence))))

      (initKB)
      (set! allDone #f)
      (display ''Welcome to my sofa'')
      (do ((sentence #f)
            (element #f))
           (allDone #f)
           (set! sentence (readSentence))
           (set! element (RetrieveByString Shrink-KB
                                           sentence
                                           selectPattern))
           ((selectProc (GetFact element))
                (GetAlist element))))))
(begin
  (display ''Type (Shrink-Conversation) to talk to the shrink'') (newline))
```

V.4.4 'AnimalKingdom' (Section 3.5.4, Ex. 3.47)

```
; Animal  Kingdom  Example
; ===   ====   ====

; This is similar to the Bestiary example in Section 3.5.3 except that it adds
; a primitive explanation feature – when asked why something
; is the case it replies that it either knew it originally or
; was told about it by the user. The form of the patterns and the
; original facts are therefore different from the Bestiary example.
;
; This example illustrates the use of the AssociativeNetworks
; toolbox to answer questions about animals. Simple statements
; and questions about animals are recognized using the pattern-
; matching toolbox and an associative network is maintained and
; queried.
; The form that statements about animals can take are:
;       (an invertebrate is an animal)
;       (an animal is an organism)
; The questions that can be answered are of the form:
;       (what is an animal)
;       (is an invertebrate an animal)
;       (why is an invertebrate an animal)

; A few initially known facts about organisms

(define AnimalKingdom
  (MakeAN
   (CONCEPT 'organism      '(is fact))
   (CONCEPT 'plant         (AKO 'organism) '(is fact))
```

```
>>> (load "Shrink.scm")
shrink-conversation
Type (Shrink-Conversation) to talk to the shrink
#t
#t
>>> (Shrink-Conversation)
Welcome to my sofa
...> (I'm depressed today !)
Tell me more
...> (I feel extremely miserable)
I sometimes feel the same way
...> (What can I do ?)
You tell me what
...> (My lecturer hates me)
I see
...> (Why don't you try to be more constructive ?)
You tell me why
...> (Because you haven't got a clue what I'm talking about)
Is that really the reason?
...> (No, I'm just immature)
What does that indicate?
...> (I don't like you any more)
You don't like me any more
...> (No)
But why be concerned about that?
...> (Forget that I ever talked to you at all)
Just tell me how you feel
...> (What do you think ?)
You tell me what
...> (That's it ! I'm going and won't leave a tip)
Please go on
...> (No)
Tell me more
...> (No)
I see
...> (I do too)
You do too
...> (bye)
Come back soon. Goodbye
()
>>>
```

Figure V.7 'Shrink'.

```
    (CONCEPT 'animal        (AKO 'organism) '(is fact))
    (CONCEPT 'invertebrate  (AKO 'animal) '(is fact))))

; facts in the knowledge base are lists of the form
;      (pattern-to-match procedure-to-invoke)

(define MakeFact
  (lambda (aPattern aProcedure) (list aPattern aProcedure)))

(define GetPattern car)
(define GetProc     cadr)

(define xarticle?
  (lambda (anAL)
    ; is xArticle bound to 'a' or 'an'?
    (let ((aWord (GetAssociationValue 'xArticle anAL)))
      (or (eq? aWord 'a) (eq? aWord 'an)))))
```

```
(define yarticle?
  (lambda (anAL)
    ; is yArticle bound to 'a' or 'an'?
    (let ((aWord (GetAssociationValue 'yArticle anAL)))
      (or (eq? aWord 'a) (eq? aWord 'an)))))

(define ValidSentences
  (MakeKB
    (MakeFact (PATTERN (? 'xArticle xarticle?)
                       (? 'x)
                       'is
                       (? 'yArticle yarticle?)
                       (? 'y))
              (lambda (anAL)
                (let ((subclass (GetAssociationValue 'x anAL))
                      (supclass (GetAssociationValue 'y anAL)))
                  (set! AnimalKingdom
                        (AddConcept AnimalKingdom
                                    (CONCEPT subclass
                                             (AKO supclass)
                                             '(is told)))))))
    (MakeFact (PATTERN 'what
                       'is
                       (? 'xArticle xarticle?)
                       (? 'x))
              (lambda (anAL)
                (let ((superClass
                        (GetAKOLinks AnimalKingdom
                                     (GetAssociationValue 'x anAL))))
                  (if superClass
                      (begin
                       (display (GetAssociationValue 'xArticle anAL))
                       (display " ")
                       (display (GetAssociationValue 'x anAL))
                       (display " is a subclass of ")
                       (display (car superClass)))
                      (display "I don't know - you tell me"))
                  (newline))))
    (MakeFact (PATTERN 'is
                       (? 'xArticle xarticle?)
                       (? 'x)
                       (? 'yArticle yarticle?)
                       (? 'y))
              (lambda (anAL)
                (let ((subclass (GetAssociationValue 'x anAL)
                      (supclass (GetAssociationValue 'y anAL)))
                  (if (member supclass
                              (GetAKOChain AnimalKingdom subclass))
                      (display "Yes it is")
                      (display "No it is not")))))
```

```
(MakeFact (PATTERN 'why
                   'is
                   (? 'xArticle xarticle?)
                   (? 'x)
                   (? 'yArticle yarticle?)
                   (? 'y))
          (lambda (anAL)
            (let* ((subclass (GetAssociationValue 'x anAL))
                   (isSlots (GetLinkSymbolSlots AnimalKingdom
                                                subclass
                                                'is))
                   (supclass (GetAssociationValue 'y anAL))
                   (links (GetAKOLinks AnimalKingdom subclass))
                   (chain (GetAKOChain AnimalKingdom subclass)))
              (cond ((eq? supclass subclass)
                     (display "Because they are identical"))
                    ((member supclass links)
                     (cond ((eq? 'fact (cadar isslots))
                            (DisplayList "Because I knew it initially"))
                           ((eq? 'told (cadar isslots))
                            (display "Because you said so"))
                           (else (Fatal-Error "Bad is slots"))))
                    ((member supclass chain)
                     (display "Because ")
                     (display (GetAssociationValue 'xArticle anAL))
                     (display " ")
                     (display subclass)
                     (display " is a ")
                     (display (car links)))
                    (else
                     (display "Sorry - I didn't know it was")))
              (newline))))

; get sentences in a loop

(define AskAboutAnimals
  (lambda ()
    (DisplayLine "Please supply your input as a list"
                 "and use (bye) to terminate conversation")
    (display " >> ")
    (do ((sentence (read))
         (aRL) #f))
        ((equal? sentence '(bye)) #f)
        (newline)
        (set! aRL (RetrieveAllByString ValidSentences
                                       sentence
                                       GetPattern))
        (if (null? aRL)
            (begin (display "Sentence not understood") (newline))
            (let ((fact (GetFact (CurrentRetrievedElement aRL)))
```

```
transcript
>>> (load "AnimalKingdom.scm")
animalkingdom
makefact
getpattern
getproc
xarticle?
yarticle?
validsentences
askaboutanimals
Type (AskAboutAnimals) to converse about animals
#t
#t
>>> (AskAboutAnimals)
Please supply your input as a list and use (bye) to terminate conversation
 >> (what is an animal)
an animal is a subclass of organism

 >> (is an invertebrate an animal)
Yes it is
 >> (why is an invertebrate an animal)
Because I knew it initially

 >> (a human is an animal)

 >> (a lecturer is a human)

 >> (is a lecturer an animal)
Yes it is
 >> (why is a lecturer an animal)
Because a lecturer is a human

 >> (why is a lecturer a human)
Because you said so

 >> (is a lecturer an invertebrate)
No it is not
 >> (why is a lecturer an invertebrate)
Sorry - I didn't know it was

 >> (bye)()
>>>
```

Figure V.8 'AnimalKingdom'.

```
                (anAL (GetAList (CurrentRetrievedElement aRL))))
            ((GetProc fact) anAL)))
        (newline)
        (display " >> ")
        (set! sentence (read)))))
(DisplayLine "Type (AskAboutAnimals) to converse about animals")
```

V.4.5 'AnimalQueries' (Section 3.7.4, Ex. 3.59)

```
; Natural language interface for questions about the
; properties of animals
(define ConstructQuery
```

```
  (lambda (aRegisterBank)
   ; given final register values construct the query
   (let ((q (GetRegister aRegisterBank 'Q))
         (x #f)
         (y #f)
         (number #f))
     (cond ((eq? q 'What)
            (list 'what (GetRegister aRegisterBank 'X)))
           ((eq? q 'Is)
            (list 'is (GetRegister aRegisterBank 'X)
                      (GetRegister aRegisterBank 'Y)))
           ((eq? q 'have)
            (list 'number (GetRegister aRegisterBank 'X)
                          (GetRegister aRegisterBank 'Y)
                          (GetRegister aRegisterBank 'N)))
           (else (Fatal-Error ''bad q''))))))

(define article  (MakeCategory 'a 'an 'the))
(define animal  (MakeCategory 'dog 'cow 'snake 'lizard 'shark 'carp))
(define dog     (MakeCategory 'hyena 'spaniel))
(define class   (MakeCategory 'mammal 'reptile 'fish 'animal))

(define NP
  (MakeATN
    (STATE 'N1 (CAT article  #t (TO 'N2)))
    (STATE 'N2 (CAT animal  #t (SETR 'animal **)
                               (TO 'N3))
               (CAT dog     #t (SETR 'animal **)
                               (TO 'N3))
               (CAT class   #t (SETR 'animal **)
                               (TO 'N3)))
    (STATE 'N3 (POP (GETR 'animal) #t))))

(define numpart (MakeCategory 'eyes 'legs 'arms 'ears 'hairs))
(define onepart (MakeCategory 'head 'mouth 'nose))
(define number (MakeCategory 'two 'three 'four))

(define PROP
  (MakeATN
    (STATE 'P1 (CAT (MakeCategory 'have) #t (SETR 'Q **)
                                           (TO 'P2)))
    (STATE 'P2 (CAT numpart #t (SETR 'Y **)
                               (SETR 'N (lambda (x) 'any))
                               (TO 'P3))
               (CAT article #t (SETR 'N (lambda (x) 'one))
                               (TO 'P4))
               (CAT number  #t (SETR 'N **)
                               (TO 'P6)))
    (STATE 'P3 (POP ** #t))
    (STATE 'P4 (CAT onepart #t (SETR 'Y **)
                               (TO 'P5)))
```

```
    (STATE 'P5 (POP ** #t))
    (STATE 'P6 (CAT numpart #t (SETR 'Y **)
                               (TO 'P3)))))

(define What
  (MakeATN
    (STATE 'W1 (CAT (MakeCategory 'What) #t (SETR 'Q **)
                                              (TO 'W2)))
    (STATE 'W2 (CAT '(is)       #t (TO 'W3)))
    (STATE 'W3 (PUSH NP         #t (SETR 'X **)
                                   (TO 'W4)))
    (STATE 'W4 (POP (GETR **)#t))))

(define Is
  (MakeATN
    (STATE 'I1 (CAT (MakeCategory 'Is) #t (SETR 'Q **)
                                            (TO 'I2)))
    (STATE 'I2 (PUSH NP         #t (SETR 'X **)
                                   (TO 'I3)))
    (STATE 'I3 (PUSH NP         #t (SETR 'Y **)
                                   (TO 'I4)))
    (STATE 'I4 (POP (GETR **) #t))))

(define Does
  (MakeATN
    (STATE 'D1 (CAT (MakeCategory 'Does) #t (TO 'D2)))
    (STATE 'D2 (PUSH NP         #t (SETR 'X **)
                                   (TO 'D3))
    (STATE 'D3 (PUSH PROP       #t (TO 'D4)))
    (STATE 'D4 (POP (GETR **) #t))))

(define Enquire
  (MakeATN
    (STATE 'E1 (PUSH What  #t (TO 'E2))
               (PUSH Is    #t (TO 'E2))
               (PUSH Does  #t (TO 'E2)))
    (STATE 'E2 (POP ConstrucQuery #t))))

(define FormEnquiry
  (lambda (aSentence)
    ; parse sentence and return an appropriate enquiry
    (let ((result (Parse Enquire aSentence #f)))
      (if (not result)
          #f
          (GetRegister result '**)))))
```

V.5 Smalltalk

A simple MacPaint-like graphics editor (Section 4.10, Ex. 4.4)

This sample solution provides a three-action palette with icons, and a movable and collapsible window in which drawing takes place. A first

transcript

```
(load "AnimalQueries.scm")
constructquery
article
animal
dog
class
np
numpart
onepart
number
prop
what
is
does
enquire
formenquiry
#t

>>> (Parse NP '(a cow) #f) ; returns a register bank
((** cow) (animal cow))
>>> (Parse What '(What is a fish) #t) ; trace the derivation
PauseAux: state= w1 sentence= (what is a fish)
PauseAux: state= w2 sentence= (is a fish)
PauseAux: state= w3 sentence= (a fish)
PauseAux: state= n1 sentence= (a fish)
PauseAux: state= n2 sentence= (fish)
PauseAux: state= n3 sentence= ()
PauseAux: state= n3 --> (() ((** fish) (animal fish) (q what)))
PauseAux: state= n2 --> (() ((** fish) (animal fish) (q what)))
PauseAux: state= n1 --> (() ((** fish) (animal fish) (q what)))
PauseAux: state= w4 sentence= ()
PauseAux: state= w4 --> (() ((** fish) (x fish) (animal fish) (q what)))
PauseAux: state= w3 --> (() ((** fish) (x fish) (animal fish) (q what)))
PauseAux: state= w2 --> (() ((** fish) (x fish) (animal fish) (q what)))
PauseAux: state= w1 --> (() ((** fish) (x fish) (animal fish) (q what)))
((** fish) (x fish) (animal fish) (q what))
>>> (Parse Does '(Does a fish have legs) #f)
((** legs) (n any) (y legs) (q have) (x fish) (animal fish))
>>> (Parse enquire '(Does a fish have two heads) #t)
#f
>>> (Parse Enquire '(Does a fish have a head) #f)
((** (number fish head one)) (y head) (n one) (q have) (x fish) (animal fish))

>>> (FormEnquiry '(Does a fish have legs))
(number fish legs any)
>>> (FormEnquiry '(Does a fish have two legs))
(number fish legs two)
>>> (FormEnquiry '(Is a dog a cat))
#f
>>> (FormEnquiry '(Is a dog an animal))
(is dog animal)
>>>
```

Figure V.9 'AnimalQueries'.

attempt at this exercise might have been much simpler, and any extensions to improve functionality should be fairly straightforward.

```
View subclass: #CanvasView
    instanceVariableNames: ''
    classVariableName: ''
    poolDictionaries: ''
    category: 'Exercises'
```

CanvasView comment:
"This class represents a view of the actual drawing surface. In cooperation with a 'CanvasController' it permits the user to scribble on the canvas while the red mouse button is pressed, and responds in accordance to the selected 'mode'. The pen's movements are constrained to the view's current window, although the view remains in control until a 'leftshift/blue mouse button' combination is pressed. The 'picture' is saved on the canvas after drawing is finished. A red mouse button click will restore the canvas's previous contents after the topview's window is manipulated. There is a yellow menu item for 'clearing' the canvas."

CanvasView methods for 'updating':

update
    "restore the canvas (show in view, which may have moved)"

```
self model canvas displayOn: Display
                  at: self displayBox origin
                  clippingBox: self displayBox
                  rule: Form over
                  mask: Form black
```

CanvasView methods for 'drawing':

drawWith: aPen
    "draw in the view while the red button is pressed"

```
    Processor yield.
    [self controller iscontrolActive] while True:
        [aPen place: Sensor waitButton.
            [Sensor redButtonPressed]
                whileTrue:
                    [aPen goto: Sensor cursorPoint]].
    self model canvas: (Form fromDisplay: self displayBox)
```

makePenWithColour: aColour **andWidth:** aWidth
"create a new Pen, with the appropriate colour and width, and constrain its drawing surface to within the view's limits."

```
    | candidate |
    candidate ← Pen new.
    candidate mask: (Form perform: aColour).
    candidate combinationRule: Form over.
    candidate defaultNib: aWidth.
    candidate frame: self displayBox.
    ↑candidate
```

CanvasView methods for 'actions':

```
brush
    "draw with a black pen of adjustable width (query the user)"

    | width myPen |
    width ← (FillInTheBlank request: 'How wide a brush ?')
            asNumber.
    myPen ← self makePenWithColour: #black andWidth: width.
    self drawWith: myPen
erase
    "draw with a white pen (default width of 2)"

    |myPen|
    myPen ← self makePenWithColour: #lightGray andWidth: 2.
    self drawWith: myPen
scribble
    "draw with a black pen"

    |myPen|
    myPen ← self makePenWithColour: #black andWidth: 1.
    self drawWith: myPen

View subclass: #MicroPaintView
    instanceVariableNames: 'canvasView'
    classVariableNames: 'BrushIcon EraseIcon ScribbleIcon '
    poolDictionaries: ''
    category: 'Exercises'
```

MicroPaintView comment:
"This class represents a screen representation for our 'document'. The view is composed of two parts: representing the palette and the canvas itself. The palette consists of three subviews, which are 'buttons' to select one of three drawing modes: scribbling, erasing and brushing. These modes are activated by clicking on these buttons and their 'on' state is highlighted appropriately. The canvas itself is shown in an instance of 'CanvasView'. The 'shapes' of the icons used as button labels are stored as class variables of this view. They should be initialized through 'MicroPaintView initializePalette', each time this application is read from a file, but they may also be changed through the appropriate 'set . . .' class method."

MicroPaintView methods for 'queries':

```
canvasView
    ↑canvasView
```

MicroPaintView methods for 'initialization':

```
canvasView: aView
    canvasView ← aView
```

MicroPaintView class methods for 'creation':

```
createWith: aModel
    "build a view with four subviews (three buttons and the canvas itself)"

    |candidate
     scribbleButton scribbleSwitchView
     eraseButton eraseSwitchView
     brushButton brushSwitchView|
    candidate ← self new.
    candidate canvasView: (CanvasView new model: aModel).
    candidate canvasView controller: CanvasController new initialize.
    candidate canvasView controller model: aModel.
    candidate canvasView controller view: candidate canvasView.
    candidate canvasView insideColor: Form lightGray.
    candidate addSubView: candidate canvasView
              in: (0.2 @ 0 extent: 0.8 @ 1)
              borderWidth: 0.

    scribbleButton ← button newOff.
    scribbleButton onAction: [candidate canvasView scribble].
    scribbleSwitchView ← SwitchView new model: scribbleButton.
    scribbleSwitchView controller: IndicatorOnSwitchController new.
    scribbleSwitchView label: (self scribbleIcon).
    scribbleSwitchView insideColor: Form white.
    candidate addSubView: scribbleSwitchView
              in: (0 @ 0 extent: 0.2 @ (1 / 3))
              borderWidth: (0 @ 0 extent: 2 @ 1).

    eraseButton ← Button newOff.
    eraseButton onAction: [candidate canvasView erase].
    eraseSwitchView ← SwitchView new model: eraseButton.
    eraseSwitchView controller: IndicatorOnSwitchController new.
    eraseSwitchView label: self eraseIcon.
    eraseSwitchView insideColor: Form white.
    candidate addSubView: eraseSwitchView
                          in: (0 @ (1 / 3) extent: 0.2 @ (1 / 3))
                          borderWidth: (0 @ 0 extent: 2 @ 1).

    brushButton ← Button newOff.
    brushButton onAction: [candidate canvasView brush].
    brushSwitchView ← SwitchView new model: brushButton.
```

```
brushSwitchView controller: IndicatorOnSwitchController new.
brushSwitchView label: self brushIcon.
brushSwitchView insideColor: Form white.
candidate addSubView: brushSwitchView
                        in: (0 @ (2 / 3) extent: 0.2 @ (1 / 3))
                        borderWidth: (0 @ 0 extent: 2 @ 1).
↑candidate
```

MicroPaintView class methods for 'set icons':

initializePalette

"set the default icons for labelling the buttons. These bit-maps were obtained from edited forms by: 'MicroPaintView scribbleIcon bits asArray', and so on."

```
ScribbleIcon ← Form
                extent: 30 @ 30
                 fromArray: #(0 0 0 0 0 0 0 0 0 0 0 0 0 0 12288 0
30720 0 64512 I 65024 3 65024 7 64512 I5 63488 31 61440 63 57344 127
49152 255 32768 511 0 510 0 508 0 4088 0 2288 0 6272 0 4224 0 4992 0
7680 0 0 0 0 0 0 0 0 0)
                offset: 0 @ 0.
EraseIcon ← Form
                extent: 30 @ 30
                 fromArray: #(0 0 0 0 0 0 0 0 0 0 7 49152 15
49152 31 49152 63 49152 127 49152 255 49152 511 50176 1023 51200 1023
36864 1023 8192 1022 16384 1020 32768 1017 0 1010 0 4 0 8 0 16 0 32 0
64 0 0 0 0 0 0 0 0 0 0 0 0 0 0 )
                offset: 0 @ 0.
BrushIcon ← Form
                extent: 30 @ 30
                fromArray: #(0 0 0 0 0 0 0 0 0 0 14 0 31 0 63
32768 63 32768 31 0 14 0 14 0 14 0 14 0 14 0 255 49152 511 57344 1023
57344 1023 61440 1023 61440 877 45056 877 45056 877 45056 0 0 0 0 0 0 0
0 0 0 0 0 0 0)
                offset: 0 @ 0
```

setBrushIcon

"edit a form and store it as the new icon for the 'brush' button"

```
BrushIcon ← (Form new extent: 30 @ 30).
BrushIcon bitEdit
```

setEraseIcon

"edit a form and store it as the new icon for the 'erase' button"

```
EraseIcon ← (Form new extent: 30 @ 30).
EraseIcon bitEdit
```

```
setScribbleIcon
    "edit a form and store it as the new icon for the 'scribble' button"
    ScribbleIcon ← (Form new extent: 30 @ 30).
    ScribbleIcon bitEdit
```

MicroPaintView class methods for 'query icons':

```
brushIcon
    ↑BrushIcon

eraseIcon
    ↑EraseIcon

scribbleIcon
    ↑ScribbleIcon

MouseMenuController subclass: #CanvasController
    instanceVariableNames: ''
    classVariableNames: ''
    poolDictionaries: ''
    category: 'Exercises'
```

CanvasController comment:

"This is the controller attached to a 'CanvasView'. It is activated by selecting one of the painting modes and remains in control until a 'left shift/blue mouse button' event occurs. It provides for a simple new yellow button menu, with a single item for 'clearing' the canvas."

CanvasController methods for 'control activity':

```
isControlActive
    "overrides the standard 'isControlActive' behaviour provided by
    'MouseMenuController' (which relinquishes control once the cursor is
    moved outside the associated view)."

    ↑(Sensor leftShiftDown & Sensor blueButtonPressed) not
redButtonActivity
    "restore the canvas's saved contents whenever the red button is pressed"

    self model canvas notNil ifTrue: [self view update]
```

CanvasController methods for 'menu messages':

```
clearCanvas
    self model canvas: nil.
    view clearInside
```

CanvasController methods for 'initialization':

```
initialize
    super initialize.
    self yellowButtonMenu: (PopUpMenu labels: 'clear canvas')
        yellowButtonMessages: #(clearCanvas)
```

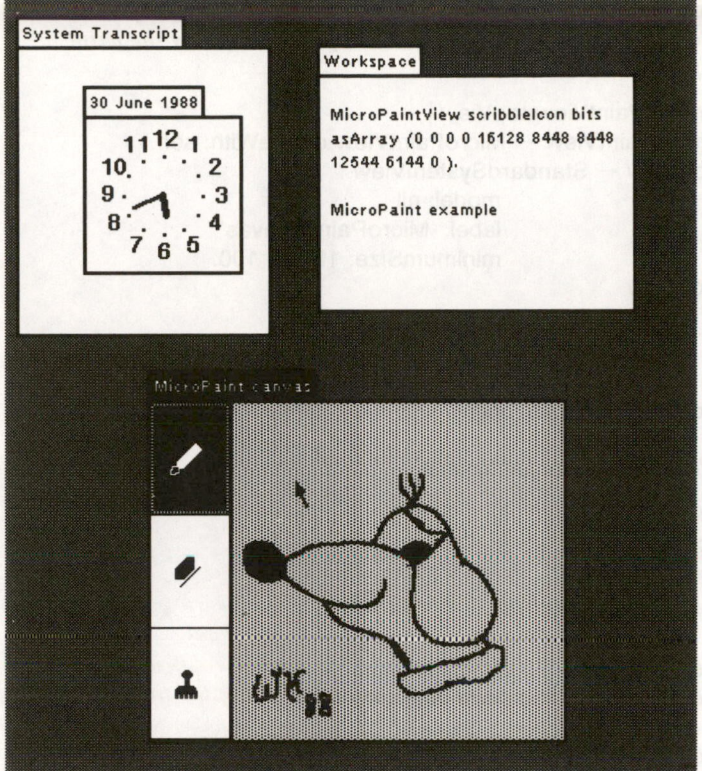

Figure V.10 'MicroPaint'.

```
Object subclass: #MicroPaint
    instanceVariableNames: 'canvas '
    classVariableNames: ''
    poolDictionaries: ''
    category: 'Exercises'
```

MicroPaint comment:
"This class serves as the 'model' for a simple 'paint' application. The user may scribble on the screen, in order to construct a picture stored on a 'canvas'. While the canvas is kept in this class, the painting functionality itself is located in classes 'MicroPaintView' and 'CanvasView', together with their associated controllers. There is a class method to trigger an example."

MicroPaint methods for 'initialization':

```
canvas: aDisplayForm
    canvas ← aDisplayForm
```

```
initialize
    "create and schedule a standard 'topView', to show the paint
    application in"

    | microPaintView topView |
    microPaintView ← MicroPaintView createWith: self.
    topView ← StandardSystemView
                    model: nil
                    label: 'MicroPaint canvas'
                    minimumSize: 100 @ 100.
    topView
        addSubView: microPaintView
        in: (0 @ 0 extent: 1 @ 1)
        borderWidth: 1.
    topView controller open
```

MicroPaint methods for 'query':

```
canvas
    ↑canvas
```

MicroPaint class methods for 'examples':

```
example
    "create and start a paint application"

    self create initialize
```

MicroPaint class methods for 'creation':

```
create
    "create a Paint document (containing a canvas)"

    | candidate |
    candidate ← self new.
    candidate canvas: nil.
    ↑candidate
```

Figure V.10 shows the program in execution.

Appendix VI
Scheme and COMMON LISP – A Comparison

> 'Programming languages should be designed not by piling feature on top of feature, but by removing the weaknesses and restrictions that make additional features appear necessary. Scheme demonstrates that a very small number of rules for forming expressions, with no restrictions on how they are composed, suffice to form a practical and efficient programming language that is flexible enough to support most of the major programming paradigms in use today.'
>
> [*Rees and Clinger (1986), p. 2.*]

> 'COMMON LISP originated in an attempt to focus the work of several implementation groups, each of which was constructing successor implementations of MACLISP for different computers. These implementations had begun to diverge because of the differences in the implementation environments: microcoded personal computers (ZetaLISP, SPICE LISP), commercial time-shared computers (NIL) and supercomputers (S-1, LISP). While the differences among the several implementation environments of necessity will continue to force certain incompatibilities among the implementations, COMMON LISP serves as a common dialect to which each implementation makes any necessary extensions.'
>
> [*Steele (1984), p. 1.*]

The above two quotes from the defining documents for the languages Scheme and COMMON LISP describe the widely different goals of their designers. These goals are clearly reflected in the complexity of the resulting languages and their defining documents. Scheme is a remarkably simple language with few basic concepts but it is designed in such a way that they fit together very closely. Scheme's definition is achieved in a document of just 43 pages [Rees and Clinger (1986)]. COMMON LISP, on the other hand, is an attempt to unify a number of diverging commercial LISP variants and the result has in some cases been a union rather than an intersection of features. Its definition requires a book of 465 pages [Steele (1984)].

VI.1 How to use this appendix

The goal of this appendix is to provide some help to the reader who knows Scheme, but wishes to apply some of the programming techniques learnt in this book to COMMON LISP. It is outside its scope to give anything more than a gentle introduction to this conversion by indicating the (approximately) equivalent COMMON LISP concepts and functions, and giving a brief outline of features in one of the languages which are not directly available in the other. Further information can be obtained from articles such as Touretzky (1988) which contains a discussion on how LISP has evolved into COMMON LISP, while a somewhat critical look at its design is provided by Allen (1987).

Our approach will follow approximately the order of the Scheme report, comparing features in each language. A further section will introduce concepts of COMMON LISP which have no direct equivalent in Scheme. Finally, a table of Scheme procedures will be presented (Table VI.1), which shows their COMMON LISP equivalents. This table should be useful during the early stages of any conversion, pointing the reader to the appropriate function definition in the COMMON LISP report.

V1.2 Comparison of concepts

VI.2.1 Lexical conventions and basic concepts

Rules for **identifiers** in the two languages are essentially the same, except that the characters !, ? and : are not available in COMMON LISP. The first two of these (! and ?) can be made available within user-defined macros and the last (:) is used as part of the package and keyword naming conventions described later. COMMON LISP uses the same conventions as Scheme for **comments (;), strings ("), lists (())** and **characters (#\c** or **#\name)**. The conventions for **numbers** are also similar (for example, **123**, **#d123**, **#o123**, **#b123**, **#x123**) but COMMON LISP makes provision for bases other than **2**, **8 10** or **16**, and greater control over precision.

Unlike most other forms of LISP that preceded them, both Scheme and COMMON LISP use **lexical** rather than **dynamic scoping** rules. However, COMMON LISP does have facilities to allow dynamic scoping, a feature which provides compatibility with 'older' programs.

Rather than using **#t** and **#f** for **Boolean** values, COMMON LISP uses the symbols **t** and **nil**.

VI.2.2 Procedure calls and lambda expressions

In Scheme there is just a single form, **define**, for defining both functions and global variables. All such objects have equal, first class status. Once defined, their values can be changed by **set!**. COMMON LISP, on the other hand, requires separate methods of defining functions and global variables. Functions are defined with **defun** as shown in the following example which accepts two integers n and m as parameters and returns their sum (+ n m) as its result:

```
(defun AddInts (n m) (+ n m))
```

A global variable is defined with **defvar** as in:

```
(defvar *LargestCount* 35)
```

There are also **defconstant**, **defmacro**, **defstruct** and **deftype** forms for defining constants, macros, structures and types. The result of all this is that functions, for example, are no longer first class objects (as in Scheme) and the programmer must be aware of this when **lambda** expressions are manipulated. In particular, any lambda expression being returned from a function must be quoted with the special form **function** (which may be abbreviated as #′ just as **quote** can be abbreviated as ′), and it must be called with the functions **funcall** or **apply** rather than the normal Cambridge prefix form. To demonstrate this we shall use our 'procedure returning procedure' example from Section 2.3.2.

```
(defun GenericMagicLamp (noOfWishes)
  (let ((count 0))
  ; the returned lambda is quoted with #′
  #′ (lambda ()
       (if (< count noOfWishes)
         ; ''progn'' is like ''begin'' in Scheme
         (progn (setq count (+ count 1)) ′Granted)
         ''you've had all you're going to get!''))))
```

To create an instance of this object we can now request:

```
(defvar AladdinsLamp (GenericMagicLamp 3))
```

And to invoke it:

```
(funcall AladdinsLamp)
; 'Granted
(funcall AladdinsLamp)
; 'Granted
(funcall AladdinsLamp)
; 'Granted
(funcall AladdinsLamp)
; "you've had all you're going to get!"
```

Some of the consequences of the treatment of function identifiers being kept distinct from that of other identifiers are elaborated in greater detail in Gabriel and Pitman [1988].

The mechanism in COMMON LISP for dealing with optional and arbitrary numbers of parameters is quite different from the one provided by Scheme. When a function's parameters are declared (in either a **defun** or **lambda**), keywords such as **&optional** or **&rest** may precede them. There is also an additional feature of allowing keyword parameters whose presence is indicated by an occurrence of the keyword when the procedure is called. All such optional arguments can be given default values if no expression is supplied at invocation time.

VI.2.3 Conditionals

As in Scheme, COMMON LISP provides **if**, **cond** and **case**. For the purposes of tests in these contexts **nil** or the empty list corresponds to false and all other values to true. Rather than offering an **else** clause for a **cond** or **case**, COMMON LISP uses **t** in **cond** and either **t** or **otherwise** in **case**. Functions **and**, **or** and **not** are also available.

VI.2.4 Assignments

In Scheme, assignment to objects of most types uses **set!**, although there are specialized **vector-set!**, **vector-fill!**, **string-set!** and **string-fill!** functions for assigning to elements of vectors or strings. COMMON LISP provides the special form **setq** for assigning to simple variables, and the general form **setf**, which takes two arguments: an accessing form to indicate the object to change and the new value of that object. The first element of a list bound to variable x could thus be changed to the value 12 by:

```
(setf (car x) 12)
```

There are also specialized assignment functions for **sequences** (a generic class of types including lists, vectors or strings) such as **fill**, **remove**, **replace**, as well as specialized increment (**incf**) and decrement (**decf**) functions.

VI.2.5 Binding constructs and iterators

The Scheme syntactic forms **let** and **let*** are also available in COMMON LISP, although there is no equivalent to the **letrec** form. As mentioned earlier, since static binding determines the default environment, variables are not available outside the scope of the defining **let** or **let*** form and could be hidden by nested redefinitions.

A **begin** form can encompass a sequence of expressions in Scheme, with the value of the last expression being returned. In COMMON LISP there is a variety of such forms: **prog1**, **prog2** and **progn**. They differ solely in the value returned; **progn** is the form which is equivalent to Scheme's **begin**.

COMMON LISP has a richer set of iteration-type constructs than Scheme. As well as the **do** of Scheme, it has a **do*** (where the variables are bound in a way analogous to **let***), a simple **loop** for infinite repetitions (with various methods of exit), as well as **dolist** and **dotimes** to iterate over the elements of a list or a sequence of integers.

VI.2.6 Predicates and lists

In Scheme all predefined predicate functions have names that end in ?. In COMMON LISP such predicates usually have names that end in **p**, although for historical reasons there are some that do not. The predicates for testing general objects for equality come in the three forms **equal**, **eql** and **eq**, which are similar to the Scheme functions **equal?**, **eqv?** and **eq?**. They test for successively weaker forms of equality.

Scheme has three distinct procedures (**assoc**, **assv** and **assq**), for dealing with association lists and three others (**member**, **memv** and **memq**), for membership tests. These differ only in the form of equality they test for. COMMON LISP supports only **assoc** and **member**, but it allows the test to be supplied as a keyword parameter which defaults to the **equal** function.

List construction and manipulation are very similar in both languages with functions such as **car**, **cdr**, **c. . .r**, **cons**, **list**, **append**, **reverse**, and so on. Differences include the predicates **consp** rather than **pair?** for testing for 'pairness' ('listhood'), and **endp** or **null** rather than **null?** for testing for the end of a list. The functions for retrieving an element or the remainder of a list are called **nth** and **nthcdr** rather than **list-ref** and **list-tail**.

The Scheme functions **map** and **for-each** which apply a function to each element of a list are also available in COMMON LISP and are identified by the names **mapcar** and **mapc**.

VI.2.7 Symbols and numbers

Symbols in the two languages have very similar properties and uses. COMMON LISP symbols have a **property list** associating a name (indicator) with a value (property). This idea is equivalent to association lists but properties are attached to a symbol itself. The list is accessed with the function **get** and altered with **setf**.

In contrast to many older LISP variants, both Scheme and COMMON LISP have a very rich set of number types and functions, although COMMON LISP offers a greater range. They both have integer, real, rational (called 'ratio' in COMMON LISP) and complex types. A complete list of equivalent functions can be found in the table in the last section. A general **coerce** function is further provided to convert a given type into another.

VI.2.8 Characters and strings

Character constants take the same form as in Scheme but they may also contain extra attributes, such as the font (for example, italics) and control bits (for example, control, meta, super and hyper) of the character. Conversion between integers and characters is achieved with **char-int** and **int-char**.

Strings are regarded as a special type of vector and hence inherit all the properties of vectors and sequences. Thus many of the functions that are specific to strings in Scheme such as **string-length** and **string-append** are replaced by more generic functions such as **length** and **concatenate**. There are also functions that are specific to strings, such as **make-string** for constructing new strings, **char** for retrieving a character and **string-trim** for extracting substrings.

VI.2.9 Vectors

COMMON LISP has multi-dimensional array types, with vectors simply being the one-dimensional subtype of this class. Arrays in general are constructed using the function **make-array**, and initial values can be provided by means of the keyword **:initial-contents**. Elements are accessed with the form **aref** and assignments use **setf**. Further procedures are available to compute properties such as the rank and dimensions of an array object.

VI.2.10 Input and output

The primitive Scheme functions **read**, **display** and **newline** map on to the COMMON LISP functions **read**, **write** and **terpri**. There is a **load** function but also a sophisticated *package* facility described in Section VI.3.1 COMMON LISP provides numerous interfaces to the external file system and a multitude of procedures controlling the formatting of output and the reading of input in minute detail.

VI.2.11 Continuations

The Scheme function **call-with-current-continuation** that can be used to implement various control features such as co-routines and exit facilities has no equivalent in COMMON LISP. There are however the special forms **catch** and **throw**, which can be used to handle some of these, such as the exit-type use of continuations. **Catch** allows a series of forms to be evaluated and if any call to **throw** with a matching tag is made, evaluation of the corresponding catch forms is aborted. This allows dynamic non-local exits. It is also possible to protect a series of forms with **unwind-protect** so that if a throw aborts their execution, some clean-up action can be taken.

VI.3 Facilities not available in Scheme

Some of these have already been mentioned but there are some that have no equivalent in Scheme. This section only points to their existence and gives some indication of their use.

VI.3.1 Packages

The package feature of COMMON LISP is an attempt to address the difficulties of having a single, large name space for symbols. This is a problem particularly in large programs, or when there are a number of modules involved, possibly written by different programmers. For example, the names of the functions from the toolboxes of Chapter 3 all inhabit the same global name space and care is needed to avoid accidental redefinition of identifiers.

To overcome this, programmers are able to confine names to packages and use the name of the package to qualify the name. For example, if a package named *Games* contained the game-playing toolbox routines, we could refer to the *PlayGame* routine as *Games:PlayGame*. This would still allow us to have different *PlayGame* routines in other modules, which could be referred to in similar ways. Facilities are also provided for referring to the symbols defined within a package in such a way that their names need not be qualified by the package name. Appropriate procedures are available for creating, loading and performing numerous other operations on packages.

VI.3.2 Macros

Macros allow programmers to define arbitrary functions that convert certain LISP forms into a different representation prior to evaluation. For example, a **while** macro might be defined to transform the expression:

```
(while expression
      form1
      form2
      . . .
      formn)
```

into the do expression:

```
(do ()
    (expression ())
    form1
    form2
    . . .
    formn)
```

It should be apparent that it is not possible to write **while** as a normal function, since the **expression** and **form** parameters would normally be evaluated before **while** is called. Macros allow us to circumvent this problem.

Many versions of Scheme do in fact have some sort of macro facility, but it is *not* defined as part of the Scheme definition and programs using these facilities are therefore not portable. COMMON LISP offers macros as part of its standard environment, so a *while* macro could be written as:

```
(defmacro while (expression &rest body)
      `(do ()
          (, expression ())
          , body)
```

The text within the backquote (`) is returned but with those variables which are preceded by commas (,) replaced by arguments bound to the corresponding parameters.

Macros are a powerful and extremely useful facility, but unless they are written carefully they are vulnerable to a number of difficulties. There is an interesting discussion in the Scheme report [Rees and Clinger (1986), p. 37] on why they were not included in standard Scheme.

VI.3.3 Structures

Structures offer a facility for creating named record structures with named components, much like those in conventional languages such as Pascal or C. A study of the toolboxes of Chapter 3 will reveal that quite a large number of functions are concerned with constructing (for example, **MakeSearchProblem**), accessing (for example, **GetCount**) or updating (for example, **IncCount!**) objects whose internal structure is (partially) hidden from the user of the toolbox. Using structures, the definition, construction, accessing and updating of an object is greatly simplified. The (non-portable) C-Flavour System uses macros to automatically construct access and predicate functions of objects.

The following COMMON LISP code defines a new structure which is to represent a point with an x and y value:

```
(defstruct point x-pos y-pos)
```

This automatically creates functions for constructing, accessing and updating points, and the following expressions indicate their use:

(**make-point**)	returns a new uninitialized point.
(**make-point** :y-pos 0 :x-pos 0)	returns a new initialized point.
#S(**point** x-pos 0 y-pos 0)	also returns a new initialized point.
(**copy-point** aPoint)	returns a copy of aPoint.
(**point-p** aPoint)	returns t if aPoint is an object of type point.
(**point-x-pos** aPoint)	returns the x-pos slot of aPoint.
(**point-y-pos** aPoint)	returns the y-pos slot of aPoint.
(**setf** (**point-x-pos** aPoint) 5)	assigns the value 5 to the x-pos slot of the structure aPoint.

There are further facilities for printing structures, for specifying default initial values for slots of the structure and for other useful operations.

VI.3.4 Hash tables

Hash tables are objects that allow the programmer efficiently to map a given LISP object on to some other LISP object. Rather than using association-type structures with search times linear in the length of the list, hash tables can often locate objects within times that are independent of the number of objects in the table.

New hash tables are created with **make-hash-table**, a key is retrieved using the function **gethash**, new keys are added with **setf** in conjunction with **gethash** and entries are removed by **remhash**.

VI.3.5 Multiple values

Functions in COMMON LISP can return more than a single value by using a form (**values** ...). When the function is invoked the multiple values returned can be bound to a number of variables using **multiple-value-bind** rather than **let**. In Scheme a function would have to package such return values as a list or vector and then extract the individual items later.

VI.4 Table of approximately equivalent functions

Table VI.1 gives COMMON LISP functions which are approximately equivalent to each of the standard Scheme procedures. Refer to the COMMON LISP standard [Steele (1984)] for detailed explanations.

Table VI.1 Approximately equivalent procedures in Scheme and COMMON LISP.

Scheme	*COMMON LISP*
'	'
*	*
+	+
−	−
/	/
<	<
<=	<=
=	=
=>	=>
>	>
>=	>=
abs	abs
acos	acos
and	and

Table VI.1 (cont.)

Scheme	*COMMON LISP*
angle	phase
append	append
apply	apply
asin	asin
assoc	assoc
assq	assoc
assv	assoc
atan	atan
begin	begin
boolean?	*No equivalent*
caar	caar
caddr	caddr
cadr	cadr
call-with-current-continuation	*No equivalent* (*see* catch, throw)
call-with-input-file	with-open-file
call-with-output-file	with-open-file
car	car
case	case
cddar	cddar
cddddr	cddddr
cdr	cdr
ceiling	ceiling
char->integer	char-int
char-alphabetic?	alpha-char-p
char-ci<=?	*No equivalent*
char-ci<?	*No equivalent*
char-ci=?	*No equivalent*
char-ci=>?	*No equivalent*
char-ci>?	*No equivalent*
char-ci>=?	*No equivalent*
char-downcase	char-downcase
char-lower-case?	lower-case-p
char-numeric?	digit-char-p
char-ready?	listen
char-upcase	char-upcase
char-upper-case?	upper-case-p

Table VI.1 (cont.)

Scheme	*COMMON LISP*
char-whitespace?	*No equivalent*
char<=?	char<=
char<?	char<
char=?	char=
char=>?	char=>
char>?	char>
char>=?	char>=
char?	characterp
close-input-port	close
close-output-port	close
complex?	complexp
cond	cond
cons	cons
cos	cos
current-input-port	*standard-input*
current-output-port	*standard-output*
define	defun, defvar
delay	*No equivalent*
denominator	denominator
display	write
do	do
eof-object?	*No equivalent* (*see* read)
eq?	eq
equal?	equal
eqv?	eql
even?	evenp
exact-inexact	*No equivalent*
exact?	*No equivalent*
exactness	format
exp	exp
expt	expt
#f	nil
fix	format
flo	format
floor	floor
for-each	mapc

Table VI.1 (cont.)

Scheme	*COMMON LISP*
force	*No equivalent*
gcd	gcd
heur	format
if	if
imag-part	imagpart
inexact-exact	*No equivalent*
inexact?	*No equivalent*
input-port?	input-stream-p
int	format
integer->char	int-char
integer?	integerp
lambda	lambda
last-pair	last
lcm	lcm
length	list-length, length
let	let
let*	let*
letrec	*No equivalent*
list	list
list->string	coerce
list->vector	coerce
list-ref	nth
list-tail	nthcdr
load	load
log	log
magnitude	abs
make-polar	*No equivalent*
make-rectangular	complex
make-string	make-string
make-vector	make-array
map	mapcar
max	max
member	member
memq	member
memv	member
min	min

Table VI.1 (cont.)

Scheme	*COMMON LISP*
modulo	mod
negative?	minusp
newline	terpri
nil	nil
not	not
null?	null, endp
number->string	write-to-string
number?	numberp
numerator	numerator
odd?	oddp
open-input-file	open
open-output-file	open
or	or
output-port?	output-stream-p
pair?	consp
polar	format
positive?	plusp
procedure?	functionp
quasiquote	\`
quote	quote,'
quotient	*No equivalent*
radix	format
rat	format
rational?	rationalp
rationalize	coerce
read	read
read-char	read-char
real-part	realpart
real?	floatp
rect	format
remainder	rem
reverse	reverse
round	round
sci	format
set!	setq, setf

Table VI.1 (cont.)

Scheme	*COMMON LISP*
set-car!	rplaca
set-cdr!	rplacd
sin	sin
sqrt	sqrt
string->list	coerce
string->number	read-from-string
string->symbol	make-symbol
string-append	concatenate
string-ci<=?	*No equivalent*
string-ci<?	*No equivalent*
string-ci=?	*No equivalent*
string-ci=>?	*No equivalent*
string-ci>?	*No equivalent*
string-ci>=?	*No equivalent*
string-copy	copy-seq
string-fill!	fill
string-length	length
string-ref	char
string-set!	substitute
string<=?	string<=
string<?	string<
string=?	string=
string=>?	string=>
string>?	string>
string>=?	string>=
string?	stringp
substring	string-trim
symbol->string	symbol-name
symbol?	symbolp
#t	t
t	t
tan	tan
transcript-off	*No equivalent*
transcript-on	*No equivalent*
truncate	truncate

Table VI.1 (cont.)

Scheme	*COMMON LISP*
unquote	,
unquote-splicing	,@
vector	make-array
vector->list	coerce
vector-fill!	fill
vector-length	length
vector-ref	aref
vector-set!	setf (+ aref)
vector?	arrayp
with-input-from-file	*No equivalent*
with-output-to-file	*No equivalent*
write	prin1
write-char	write-char
zero?	zerop

References

Abelson H., diSessa A. (1981). *Turtle Geometry: The Computer as a Medium for Exploring Mathematics.* Cambridge MA: MIT Press

Abelson H., Sussman G. J. (1988). LISP: a language for stratified design. *BYTE* (Feb. 1988), 207–218

Abelson H., Sussman J., Sussman J. (1985). *Structure and Interpretation of Computer Programs.* Cambridge MA: MIT Press

Adams S. S. (1987). *Pluggable Gauges – User Manual.* Knowledge Systems Corporation

Adams S. S. (1988). Meta-methods. *HOOPLA* (Jan. 1988), 9–15

Agha G. A. (1986a). An overview of actor languages. In: *SigPlan* 49–57

Agha G. A. (1986b). *Actors: A Model of Concurrent Computations in Distributed Systems.* Cambridge MA: MIT Press

Aho A., Ullman J. (1972). *The Theory of Parsing, Translation and Compiling.* Vol. 1: Parsing. Englewood Cliffs NJ: Prentice-Hall

Allen E. M. (1983). *YAPS: Yet Another Production System.* Technical Report TR–1146, University of Maryland MD

Allen E. M., Trigg R. H., Wood R. J. (1984). *The Maryland Artificial Intelligence Group FranzLISP Environment – Variation 2.7.* Technical Report, University of Maryland MD

Allen J. (1978). *The Anatomy of LISP.* New York: McGraw-Hill

Allen J. R. (1987). The death of creativity: is COMMON LISP a LISP-like language? *AI Expert* (Feb. 1987), 48–61

Allen J. (1988). *Natural Language Understanding.* Reading MA: Addison-Wesley

Allison L. (1983). Stable marriages by coroutines. *Information Processing Letters,* **16**, 61–65

Althoff J. C. Jr. (1981). Building data structures in the Smalltalk-80 system. *BYTE* (Aug. 1981), 230–278

Amarel S. (1968). On representation of problems of reasoning about actions. In: Michie, D. (ed.) *Machine Intelligence 3.* Edinburgh: Edinburgh University Press

Amarel S. (1971). Representations and modelling in problems of program formation. In: Meltzer B. and Michie D. (eds.) *Machine Intelligence 6.* Edinburgh: Edinburgh University Press

Anderson J. R. (1980). *Cognitive Psychology and its Implications.* San Francisco CA: Freeman

Andrews G. R., Schneider, F. B. (1983). Concepts and notations for concurrent programming. *ACM Computing Surveys*, **15**, 3–44

Banerji R. B. (1980). *Artificial Intelligence – A Theoretical Approach.* New York NY: North Holland-Elsevier

Barr A., Cohen P. R., Feigenbaum E. A. (eds.) (1981). *The Handbook of Artificial Intelligence* Vols 1–3. Los Altos CA: Tioga Press

Barron D. W. (1975). *Recursive Techniques in Programming* (second edition). New York NY: Elsevier

Bartley D. H., Jensen J. C. (1986). The implementation of PC Scheme. In: *Proceedings of the 1986 ACM Conference on Lisp and Functional Programming.* New York NY: ACM, pp. 86–93

Batali J., Goodhue E., Hanson C., Shrobe H., Stallman R. M., Sussman G. J. (1982). The Scheme-81 architecture – system and chip. In: *Proceedings, Conference on Advanced Research in VLSI.* Dedham(Ma.): Artech House, pp. 69–77

Beck K. (1987). Smalltalk style. *HOOPLA* (Nov. 1987), 9–10

Berlekamp E. R., Conway J. H., Guy R. K. (1982). *Winning Ways for Your Mathematical Plays – 2 Vols.* New York NY: Academic Press

Berman M. (1981). *The Re-enchantment of the World.* Ithaca: Cornell University Press

Betz D. (1985). An XLISP tutorial. *BYTE* (Mar. 1985), 221–236

Bezivin J., Hullot J. M., Cointe P., Lieberman H. (eds.) (1987). *ECOOP '87. European Conference on Object-Oriented Programming.* Lecture Notes in Computer Science 276. Berlin: Springer

Birtwistle G. M., Dahl O. J., Myhrhaug B., Nygaard K. (1973). *SIMULA BEGIN.* Philadelphia: Auerbach/Studentliteratur

Birtwistle G. M. (1979). *Discrete Event Modelling on SIMULA.* London: MacMillan

Bobrow D. (1968). Natural language input for a computer problem solving system. In: *[Minsky (1968)]*

Bobrow D. G. (1985). If Prolog is the answer, what is the question? *or* What it takes to support AI programming paradigms. *IEEE Transactions on Software Engineering*, **SE-11**, 1401–1408

Bobrow D. G., Fraser J. B. (1969). An augmented state transition network analysis procedure. *Proceedings Int. Joint Conference on Artificial Intelligence.* Washington, pp. 557–567

Bobrow D. G., Raphael B. (1974). New programming languages for artificial intelligence research. *ACM Computing Surveys*, **6**, 153–173

Bobrow D., Collins A. (eds.) (1975). *Representation and Understanding.* New York NY: Academic Press

Bobrow D. G., Winograd T. (1977). An Overview of KRL, a knowledge representation language. *Cognitive Science*, **1**, 3–46

Bobrow D. G., Stefik M. (1983). *The LOOPS Manual – Preliminary Version.* Palo Alto CA: Xerox PARC

Bobrow D. G., Stefik M. J. (1986). Perspectives on artificial intelligence programming. *SCIENCE*, **231**, 951–957

Bobrow D. G., Hayes P. J. (eds.) (1985). Artificial Intelligence – where are we? *Artificial Intelligence*, **25**, 375–415.

Bobrow D. G., Kahn K., Kiczales G., Masinter L., Stefik M., Zdybel F. (1985). CommonLoops: merging Common Lisp and object oriented programming. *Technical Report ISL-85-8*. Palo Alto CA: Xerox PARC

Bobrow D. G., Mittal S., Stefik M. (1986). Expert systems: perils and promise. *Communications of the ACM*, **29**, 880–894

Bobrow D. G., Winograd T. (1977). An overview of KRL, a knowledge representation language. *Cognitive Science*, **1**, 3–46

Bobrow D. G., Winograd T. (1979). KRL – another perspective. *Cognitive Science*, **3**, 29–42

Boden M. A. (1977). *Artificial Intelligence and Natural Man*. New York NY: Basic Books

Borges J. L. (1969). *The Book of Imaginary Beings*. New York

Borning A. H. (1979). THINGLAB – a constraint-oriented simulation laboratory. *Report SSL-79-3*. Palo Alto CA: Xerox PARC

Borning A. (1981). The programming language aspects of ThingLab. A constraint-oriented simulation laboratory. *ACM Transactions on Programming Languages and Systems*, **3**, 353–387

Borning A. H., Ingalls D. H. H. (1982). Multiple Inheritance in SMALLTALK-80. *Proceedings AAAI-82*. pp. 234–237

Borning A., Duisberg R. (1986). Constraint-based tools for building user interfaces. *ACM Transactions on Graphics*, **5**, 345–374

Brachman R. J. (1979). On the epistemological status of semantic networks. In: *[Findler (1979), 3–50]*

Brachman R. J. (1983). What IS-A is and isn't: An analysis of taxonomic links in semantic networks. *IEEE Computer* (Oct. 1983), 30–36

Brachman R. J. (1985). "I lied about the trees" or, defaults and definitions in knowledge representation. *AI Magazine* (Fall 1985), 80–93

Brachman R. J., Smith B. C. (eds.) (1980). Special issue knowledge representation. *ACM SIGART Newsletter*, **70**

Brachman R. J., Schmolze J. G. (1985). An overview of the KL-ONE knowledge representation system. *Cognitive Science*, **9**, 171–216

Bramer M. A. (ed.) (1983). *Computer Game Playing: Theory and Practice*. Chichester: Ellis Horwood

Bratko I. (1986). *PROLOG Programming for Artificial Intelligence*. Wokingham: Addison-Wesley

Brooking A. G. (1984). The fifth generation game. In: *[Forsyth (1984)*, pp. *18–35]*

Brooks R. A., Gabriel R. (1984). A critique of Common Lisp. In: *Proceedings of the 1984 Conference on LISP and Functional Languages*. New York NY: ACM, pp. 1–8

Brown H. I. (1977). *Perception, Theory and Commitment. The New Philosophy of Science*. Chicago: University of Chicago Press

Brown M. H., Sedgewick R. (1985). Techniques for algorithm animation. *IEEE Software* (Jan. 1985), 28–39

Brown F. M. (ed.) (1987). *The Frame Problem in Artificial Intelligence: Proceedings of the 1987 Workshop*. New York NY: ACM

Brownston L., Farrell R., Kant E., Martin N. (1985). *Programming Expert Systems in OPS5. An Introduction to Rule-based Programming*. Reading MA: Addison-Wesley

Bruner J. S. (1983). *In Search of Mind*. New York NY: Harper & Row

Buchanan B. G., Feigenbaum E. A. (1978). DENDRAL and Meta-DENDRAL: their application dimension. *Artificial Intelligence*, **11**, 5–24

Budd T. (1987). *A Little Smalltalk*. Reading MA: Addison-Wesley
Bundy A. (ed.) (1978). *Artificial Intelligence – An Introductory Course*. New York NY: North Holland
Bundy A. (1982). What is the well-dressed AI-educator wearing now? *AI Magazine*, **3**, 13–14
Bundy A. (ed.) (1984). *Catalogue of Artificial Intelligence Tools*. Berlin: Springer
Burbeck S. (1987). How to use model-view-controller. *Technical Report*. Softsmarts Inc.
Burge W. H. (1975). *Recursive Programming Techniques*. Reading MA: Addison-Wesley
Burnham W. D., Hall A. R. (1985). *Prolog Programming and Applications*. London: MacMillan
Burstall R. M., Collins D., Popplestone R. (1971). *Programming in POP-2*. Edinburgh: Edinburgh University Press
Burton A. M., Shadbolt N. R. (1987). *POP-11 Programming for Artificial Intelligence*. Wokingham: Addison-Wesley
Carbonell J. A. (1970). AI in CAI: an artificial intelligence approach to computer-assisted instruction. *IEEE Transactions on Systems, Man and Cybernetics*, **3**
Carbonell J. A. (1981). *Subjective Understanding: Computer Models of Belief Systems*. Ann Arbor MI: UMI Research Press
Cardelli L., Wegener P. (1986). On understanding types, data abstraction and polymorphism. *ACM Computing Surveys*, **17**, 471–523
Carnap R. (1928). *Scheinprobleme in der Philosophie. Das Fremdpsychische und der Realismusstreit*. Berlin
Casimir R. J. (1987). Prolog puzzles. *SigPlan Notices*, **22**, 33–37
Chandy, K. M., Misra, J. (1984). The drinking philosophers problem. *ACM Transactions on Programming Languages and Systems*, **6**, 632–646
Charniak E., Wilks Y. (eds.) (1976). *Computational Semantics*. Amsterdam: North Holland
Charniak E., Riesbeck C., McDermott D. (1980). *Artificial Intelligence Programming*. Hillsdale NJ: Lawrence Erlbaum
Charniak E., McDermott D. (1985). *Introduction to Artificial Intelligence*. Reading MA: Addison-Wesley
Chomsky N. (1957). *Syntactic Structures*. The Hague: Mouton
Clark K. L., McCabe F. G. (1979). The control facilities of IC-Prolog. In: Michie D. (ed.). *Expert Systems in the Microelectronic Age*. Edinburgh: University of Edinburgh Press, pp. 153–167
Clark K. L., McCabe F. G. (eds.) (1984). *Micro-PROLOG: Programming in Logic*. Englewood Cliffs NJ: Prentice-Hall
Clinger W. (1984). The Scheme 311 compiler: an exercise in denotational semantics. In: *Conference Record of the 1984 Symposium on Lisp and Functional Programming*. New York: ACM, pp. 356–364
Clinger W. (1987). The Scheme environment: continuations. *Lisp Pointers*, **1**, I-2.22–28
Clinger W. (1988a). The scheme of things: the June 1987 Meeting. *Lisp Pointers*, **1(5)**, 25–27
Clinger W. (1988b). Semantics of Scheme. *BYTE* (Feb. 1988), 221–227
Clocksin W. F., Mellish C. S. (1981). *Programming in PROLOG*. Berlin: Springer

Coelho H. (1980). *How to Solve It in PROLOG* (second edition). *Technical Report*. Lissabon: Laboratorio Nacional de Engenharia Civil (republished by Springer Verlag)

Computing Surveys (1974). Special issue: Structured Programming. *Computing Surveys*, **6**(4)

Conlon T. (1985). *Start Problem-Solving with Prolog.* Wokingham: Addison-Wesley

Conway M. E. (1963). Design of a separable transition diagram compiler. *Communications of the ACM*

Coral Software Inc. (1987). *Allegro Common Lisp for the MacIntosh.* Cambridge MA: Coral Inc.

Corlett R. A. (1986). Features of artificial intelligence languages and their environments. *Software Engineering Journal*, **1**, 159–164

Cox B. J. (1984). Message/object programming: an evolutionary change in programming technology. *IEEE Software* (Jan. 1984), 50–60

Cox B. J. (1986). *Object-Oriented Programming – An Evolutionary Approach.* Reading MA: Addison-Wesley

Creative Computing (1980). Symposium on actor languages. *Creative Computing* (Oct. 1980), 61–94

Cuadrado C. L., Cuadrado J. L. (1985). PROLOG goes to Work. *BYTE* (Aug. 1985), 151–158

Dahl V. (1983). Logic programming as a representation of knowledge. *IEEE Computer* (Oct. 1983), 106–110

Dahl V., Nygaard K. (1966). SIMULA – an ALGOL-based simulation language. *CACM*, **9**(9), 671–678

Dart S. A., Ellison R. J., Feiler P. H., Haberman A. N. (1987). Software development environments. *IEEE Computer* (Nov. 87), 18–28

Davies D., Julian M. (1973). Popler 1.5 Reference Manual. *TPU Report No. 1*, University of Edinburgh

Davis P., King J. (1977). An overview of production systems. In: Elcock E. W., Michie D. (eds.) *Machine Intelligence 8.* Edinburgh: Edinburgh University Press, pp. 300–334

Davis R. (1979). Interactive transfer of expertise: acquisition of new inference rules. *Artificial Intelligence*, **12**, 121–157

Davis R. (1985). Logic programming and Prolog: a tutorial. *IEEE Software,* **2**(5), 53–62

de Bono E. (1969). *The Five-Day Course in Thinking.* Harmondsworth: Penguin

de Bono E. (1979). *Future Positive.* London: Maurice Temple Smith

Deering M., Faletti J., Wilensky R. (1981). PEARL – a package for efficient access to representations in Lisp. In: *Proceedings of the International Joint Conference in AI.* New York: ACM, pp. 930–932

Delliyanni A., Kowalski R. A. (1979). Logic and semantic networks. *Communications of the ACM*, **22**, 184–192

DeMichiel L. G., Gabriel R. P. (1987). The Common Lisp Object System: an overview. In: *[Bezivin et al. (1987), 151–170]*

Deutsch L. P. (1981). Building control structures in the Smalltalk-80 system. *BYTE* (Aug. 1981), 322–346

Dewdney A. K. (1985). Artificial insanity: when a schizophrenic program meets a computerized analyst. *Scientific American – Computer Recreations* (Jan.

1985), 10–13

Dewdney A. K. (1986). The compleat computer caricaturist and a whimsical tour of face space. *Scientific American – Computer Recreations* (Oct. 1986), 20–27

Dewdney A. K. (1985). Five easy pieces for a DO loop and a random number generator. *Scientific American – Computer Recreations* (April 1985), 12–16

Dewdney A. K. (1987). Diverse personalities search for social equilibrium at a computer party. *Scientific American – Computer Recreations* (Sept. 1987), 104–107

Diederich J., Milton J. (1987). Experimental prototyping in Smalltalk. *IEEE Software* (May 1987), 50–64

Digitalk (1988). *Smalltalk V Reference Manual.* Los Angeles (CA): Digitalk Inc.

di Primio F., Christaller T. (1983). A poor man's flavor system – Part 1. *Working Paper No.* **47**, Institut dalle Molle ISSCO. Geneva: Université de Génève

Dijkstra E. W. (1976). *A Discipline of Programming.* Englewood Cliffs NJ: Prentice-Hall

Dodd L. (1983). *Hairy MacLary from Donaldson's Dairy.* Wellington: Mallinson Rendel Publ.

Doyle J. (1985). Expert systems and the 'myth' of symbolic reasoning. *IEEE Transactions on Software Engineering*, **SE-11**, 1387–1390

Doyle K. (1986). Pascal procedures – introduction to object Pascal. *MacTutor* (Dec. 1986), 49–58

Drege J. P. (1981). Clefs des songes de Tuoeng-Houang. In: Nouvel Contributions aux Etudes de Toueng-Houang. *Centre des Recherches d'Histoire et de Philosophie*, Geneva: Librairie Droz, pp. 205–249

Drescher G. L. (1985). *The ObjectLisp User Manual (preliminary).* Cambridge MA: LMI Corporation

Dreyfus H. L. (1972). *What Computers Can't Do: A Critique of Artificial Intelligence.* New York: Harper & Row

Dreyfus H. L., Dreyfus S. E. (1986). *Mind Over Machine – The Power of Human Intuition and Expertise in the Era of the Computer.* New York NY: Free Press

Duda R. O., Gaschnig J. G., Hart P. E. (1979). Model design in the PROSPECTOR consultant system for mineral exploration. In: Michie D. (ed.) *Expert systems in the Micro-electronic Age.* Edinburgh: Edinburgh University Press, pp. 153–167

Duff C. B. (1986). Designing an efficient language. *BYTE* (Aug. 1986), 211–224

Dybvig R. K. (1987). *The Scheme Programming Language.* Englewood Cliffs NJ: Prentice-Hall

Dybvig R. K., Smith B. T. (1985). *Chez Scheme Reference Manual – Version 1.0.* Bloomington IN: Cadence Research Systems

Early J. (1970). An efficient context-free parsing algorithm. *Communications of the ACM*, **13**(2), 94–102

Eisenberg M. (1987). *Programming in Scheme.* Redwood City CA: Scientific Press

Engelmore R. S., Morgan A. J. (eds.) (1988). *Blackboard Systems.* Wokingham: Addison-Wesley

Erman L. D., Hayes-Roth F., Lesser V., Reddy D. (1980). The HEARSAY-II speech understanding system: integrating knowledge to resolve uncertainty. *Computing Surveys*, **12**, 213–253

Ernst G., Newell A. (1969). *GPS: A Case Study in Generality and Problem Solving.* New York NY: Academic Press

Even S. (1979). *GPS: Graph Algorithms.* Potomac MD: Computer Science Press

Fahlman S. E. (1979). *NETL: A System for Representing and Using Real-World Knowledge.* Cambridge MA: MIT Press

Fahlman S. E., Hinton G. E. (1987). Connectionist architectures for artificial intelligence. *IEEE Computer* (Jan. 1987), 101

Feigenbaum E., and McCorduck P. (1984). *The Fifth Generation.* New York NY: Signet

Feldman J. A., Rovner P. D. (1969). An Algol-based associative language. *Communications of the ACM*, **12**, 439–449

Felleisen M., Friedman D., Kohlbecker E., Duda B. (1986). Reasoning with continuations. In: *Proceedings of Symposium on Logic in Computer Science.* Washington: IEEE Press, pp. 131–141

Field A. J., Harrison P. G. (1988). *Functional Programming.* Wokingham: Addison-Wesley

Fikes R. E., Nilsson N. J. (1971). STRIPS: a new approach to the application of theorem proving to problem solving. *Artificial Intelligence*, **2**, 189–208

Findler N. V. (ed.) (1971). *Associative Networks – Representation and Use of Knowledge by Computers.* New York NY: Academic Press

Flood M. M. (1985). Mastermind strategy. *Journal of Recreational Mathematics*, **18**, 194–202

Floyd R. (1979). The paradigms of programming. *Communications of the ACM*, **22**, 455–460

Foderaro J. K. (1979). *The FRANZLISP Manual.* Berkeley CA: University of California

Foley J. D., van Dam A. (1983). *Fundamentals of Interactive Computer Graphics.* Reading MA: Addison-Wesley

Forgy C. L. (1981). OPS5 user's manual. *Report CMU-CS-81-135.* Pittsburgh: Carnegie-Mellon University

Forsyth R. (1984). *Expert Systems. Principles and Case Studies.* London: Chapman & Hall

Frank R. (1979). The Clocks of Klotz and Klutz. *J. Recreational Mathematics*, **12**(1), 53–54

Frege G. (1960). *Translations from the Philosophical Writings of G. Frege* (eds: Geach P. and Black M.), Oxford: Blackwell

Friedman D., Haynes C., Kohlbecker E., Wand M. (1984). Scheme 84 interim reference manual. *Technical Report 153.* Computer Science Department. Bloomington IN: Indiana University

Futo I., Szeredi J. (1982). A very high level discrete simulation system: T-PROLOG. *Computational Linguistics and Computer Languages*, **XV**, 111–131

Gabriel R. P., Pitman K. M. (1988). Technical issues of separation in function cells and value cells. *Lisp and Symbolic Computation*, **1**, 81–101

Gaines B. R. (1976). System identification, approximation, and complexity. *International Journal of General Systems*, **3**, 145–174

Gallant S. I. (1988). Connectionist expert systems. *CACM*, **31**, 152–169

Gale D., Shapley L. S. (1962). College admissions and the stability of marriage. *American Mathematics Monthly*, **69**, 9–15

Gans G. (1972). *Die Ducks – Psychogramm einer Sippe.* Hamburg: Rowohlt

Gardner H. (1985). *The Mind's New Science – A History of the Cognitive Revolution.* New York NY: Basic Books

Gardner M. (1959). *Mathematical Puzzles and Diversions.* Harmondsworth: Penguin

Gardner M. (1962). *More Mathematical Puzzles and Diversions.* Harmondsworth: Penguin

Gardner M. (1969). *Further Mathematical Puzzles and Diversions.* Harmondsworth: Penguin

Gardner M. (1981). *Puzzles from Other Worlds.* New York NY: Vintage Books

Gardner M. (1984). *Wheels, Life and Other Mathematical Amusements.* San Francisco CA: W. H. Freeman

Genesereth M. R., Nilsson N. J. (1987). *The Logical Foundations of Artificial Intelligence.* Palo Alto CA: Tioga Press

Giannesini F., Kanoui H., Pasero R., van Caneghem M. (1986). *PROLOG.* Wokingham: Addison-Wesley

GMD (1987). *Babylon – Benutzerhandbuch V.1.1/2.* Gesellschaft fuer Mathematik und Datenverarbeitung (GMD) – Forschungsgruppe Expertensysteme Bonn: GMD

Goldberg A. (1984). *Smalltalk-80 – The Interactive Programming Environment.* Reading MA: Addison-Wesley

Goldberg A., Robson D. (1979). A metaphor for user interface design. In: *Proceedings 12th Hawaii International Conference on System Sciences* **6**, pp. 148–157

Goldberg A., Ross J. (1981). Is the Smalltalk-80 system for children? *BYTE* (Aug. 1981), 348–368

Goldberg A., Robson D. (1983). *Smalltalk-80 – The Language and Its Implementation.* Reading MA: Addison-Wesley

Goldberg D. E. (1989). *Genetic Algorithms in Search, Optimization and Machine Learning.* Reading MA: Addison-Wesley

Gondran M. (1983). *An Introduction to Expert Systems.* New York NY: McGraw Hill

Green T. R., Sime M. E., Fitter M. J. (1980). The art of notation. In: *[Smith and Green (1980), 221–251]*

Greif I., Hewitt C. (1975). Actor semantics of Planner-73. In: *Proceedings ACM SignPlan-SigAct Conference on Programming Language Issues in Artificial Intelligence.* Palo Alto: ACM, pp. 67–77

Griss M. L., Morrison B. (1981). The portable Standard LISP users manual. *Technical Report TR-10.* Dept of Computer Science. Salt Lake City: University of Utah

Grossberg S. (ed.) (1988). *Neural Networks and Natural Intelligence.* Cambridge MA: MIT Press

Gutfreund S. (1987). Manipulable Icons in ThinkerToy. In: *[SigPlan (1987)]*

Gyllenskog J. H. (1976). Konane as a vehicle for teaching AI. *ACM SigArt Newsletter* (Feb. 1976), 5–6

Hall R. P., Kibler D. F. (1985). Differing methodological perspectives in artificial intelligence research. *The AI Magazine* (Fall 1985), 166–178

Halpern B. (ed.) (1986). Multiparadigm languages and environments – special issue. *IEEE Software* (Jan. 1986)

Halstead R. H. Jr. (1984). MultiLisp: a language for concurrent symbolic computation. *ACM Transactions on Programming Languages and Systems*, 7, 501–538

Hardy S. (1984). A new software environment for list-processing and logic programming. In: *[O'Shea and Eisenstadt (1984), 110–136]*

Hart P. E., Nilsson N. J., Raphael B. (1968). A formal basis for the heuristic determination of minimum cost paths. *IEEE Transactions on Systems, Science and Cybernetics*, **4**, 100–107

Hartheimer A. (1987). Lisp listener – Scheme does windows! *MacTutor* (Jan. 1987), 42–48

Hasemer T. (1984). *A Beginner's Guide to LISP.* Wokingham: Addison-Wesley

Hasemer T., Domingue J. (1989). *Common Lisp Programming for Artificial Intelligence.* Wokingham: Addison-Wesley

Hayes B. (1986). Scissors, paper, stone: A tournament of schemes. *Computer Languages* (Dec. 1986), 19–30

Hayes B. (1987). Mutant languages from the LISP lab. *Computer Languages* (April 1987), 23–26

Hayes J. R. (1978). *Cognitive Psychology – Thinking and Creating.* Homewood, IL: The Dorsey Press

Hayes J. R., Simon H. A. (1976). The understanding process: problem isomorphs. *Cognitive Psychology*, **8**

Hayes C. T., Friedman D. P. (1984). Engines build process abstractions. In: *Proceedings of the 1984 Conference on Lisp and Functional Languages.* New York: ACM, pp. 18–24

Hayes C. T., Friedman D. P., Wand M. (1986). Obtaining co-routines with continuations. *Computer Languages*, **11**, 143–152

Hayes C. T., Friedman D. P. (1987). Embedding continuations in procedural objects. *ACM Transactions on Programming Languages and Systems*, **9**, 582–598

Hayes-Roth F. (1984). The knowledge-based expert system: a tutorial. *IEEE Computer* (Sept. 1984), 11–28

Hayes-Roth F. (1985). Rule-based systems. *Communications of the ACM*, **28**, 921–932

Hayes-Roth F., Waterman D., Lenat D. (eds.) (1983). *Building Expert Systems.* Reading MA: Addison-Wesley

Heidorn G. E. (1974). English as a very high-level language for simulation programming. In: *Proceedings Symposium on Very High-Level Languages – SigPlan Notices*, **9**, 91–100

Heidorn G. E. (1975). Augmented phrase structure grammar. In: Schank R. C. and Nash-Webber B. (eds.) (1975) *Theoretical Issues in Natural Language Processing.* Association for Computational Linguistics

Henderson P. (1980). *Functional Programming – Application and Implementation.* Englewood Cliffs NJ: Prentice-Hall

Hendrix G. G. (1979). Encoding knowledge in partitioned networks. In: *[Findler (1979), 51–92]*

Hendrix G. G., Sacerdoti E. D., Sagalowicz D., Slocum J. (1978). Developing a natural language interface to complex data. *ACM Transactions on Database systems*, **8**

Hewitt C. (1972). Description and theoretical analysis (using schemata) of Planner: a language for proving theorems and manipulating models in a robot. *AI Memo No. 251.* Cambridge MA: MIT Project MAC

Hewitt C. (1977). Viewing control structures as patterns of passing messages. *Artificial Intelligence*, **8**, 323–384

Hewitt C. (1980). The Apiary network architecture for knowledgeable systems. *Conference Record of the 1980 Lisp Conference.* New York: ACM, pp. 107–117

Hewitt C. (1985). The challenge of open systems. *BYTE* (Apr. 1985), 223–242

Hewitt C., Agha G. A. (1989). *Concurrent Systems for Knowledge Processing. An Actor Perspective.* Cambridge MA: MIT Press

Hewitt C., Attardi G., Simi M. (1980). Knowledge embedding in the description system Omega. In: *Proceedings of the First National Conference on AI at Stanford University*. Palo Alto: AAAI

Hilton A. M. (1963). *Logic, Computing Machines, and Automation.* New York NY: World Publishing

Hodgson J. P. E. (1986). Interactive problem solving. *ACM SigArt Newsletter* (Oct. 1986), 22–24

Hofstadter D. R. (1979). *Gödel, Escher, Bach: The Eternal Golden Braid.* New York NY: Basic Books

Hofstadter D. R. (1983). (1) Lisp: atoms and lists, (2) Lisp: lists and recursion, (3) Lisp: recursion and generality. *Scientific American – Metamagical Themas*, February, March, April

Hofstadter D. R. (1985). *Meta-Magical Themas: Questing for the Essence of Mind and Pattern.* New York NY: Viking Penguin

Hofstadter D. R. (1985). On viral sentences and self-replicating structures. In: *[Hofstadter (1985), 49–69]*

Hofstadter D. R. (1985). Parquet deformations: a subtle, intricate art form. In: *[Hofstadter (1985), 191–212]*

Hogger C. J. (1984). *Introduction to Logic Programming.* New York NY: Academic Press

Horowitz E. (1983). *Fundamentals of Programming Languages.* Berlin: Springer

Ingalls D. H. (1977). The Smalltalk-76 programming system. Design and implementation. In: *Proceedings Fifth Annual ACM Symposium on Principles of Programming Languages.* New York: ACM, pp. 9–15

Ingalls D. H. (1981). The Smalltalk graphics kernel. *BYTE* (Aug. 1981), 168–194

Ingalls D. H. (1983). The evolution of the Smalltalk virtual machine. In: *[Krasner (1983), 9–28]*

Intellicorp (1984). Knowledge Engineering Environment (KEE) – user manual. Menlo Park CA: Intellicorp

Itoga S. (1978). The upper bound for the stable marriage problem. *Journal Operations Res. Society*, **29**, 811–814

Itoga S. (1981). A generalization of the stable marriage problem. *Journal Operations Res. Society*, **32**, 1069–1074

Itoga S. (1983). A probabilistic version of the stable marriage problem. *BIT*, **23**, 161–169

Jeffries R., Polson P. G., Razran L. (1977). A process model for missionaries-cannibals and other river-crossing problems. *Cognitive Psychology*, **9**, 412–440

Kaehler T., Patterson D. (1986a). *A Taste of Smalltalk*. New York NY: Norton

Kaehler T., Patterson D. (1986b). A small taste of Smalltalk. *BYTE* (Aug. 1986), 145–159

Kahan S. (1987). Alphametics and solutions. *Journal of Recreational Mathematics*, **19**, 64–68

Kaisler S. H. (1987). *INTERLISP The Language and Its Usage*. New York NY: J. Wiley

Kay A. (1969). *The Reactive Engine*. PhD. thesis. Salt Lake City: University of Utah

Kay A. (1977). Microelectronics and the personal computer. *Scientific American*, **237**, 230–244

Kay A., Goldberg A. (1977). Personal dynamic media. *IEEE Computer* (March 1977), 31–40

Kempf R., Stelzner M. (1987). Teaching object-oriented programming with the KEE system. In: *[SigPlan (1987), 11–25]*

Kernighan B. W., Plauger P. J. (1974). *The Elements of Programming Style*. New York NY: McGraw-Hill

Klir G. J. (ed.) (1972). *Trends in General Systems Theory*. New York NY: J. Wiley

Knuth D. E. (1969). *The Art of Computer Programming. Vol. II: Seminumerical Algorithms*. Reading MA: Addison-Wesley

Korf R. E. (1980). Towards a model of representation changes. *Artificial Intelligence*, **14**, 41–78

Korf R. E. (1985). Depth-first iterative deepening: an optimal admissible tree search. *Artificial Intelligence*, **27**, 97–109

Kornfeld W. A., Hewitt C. E. (1981). The scientific community metaphor. *IEEE Transactions on Systems, Man, and Cybernetics*, **SMC-11**, pp. 1–10

Kornman B. D. (1983). Pattern-matching and pattern-directed invocation in systems programming languages. *The Journal of Systems and Software*, **3**, 95–102

Kowalski R. (1979a). *Logic for Problem Solving*. New York NY: American Elsevier

Kowalski R. (1979b). Algorithm = logic + control. *Communications of the ACM*, **22**, 424–436

Kowalski R. (1985). The origins of logic programming. *BYTE* (Aug. 1985), 192–193

Kowalski R. (1988). The early years of logic programming. *Communications of the ACM*, **31**, 38–43

Krasner G. (ed.) (1983). *SMALLTALK-80: Bits of History, Words of Advice*. Reading MA: Addison-Wesley

Kreutzer W. (1986) *System Simulation: Programming Styles and Languages*. Wokingham: Addison-Wesley

Kreutzer W., Stairmand M. (1989). Concurrent flavour systems – a model based approach to AI and simulation. *Tech. Report* #1/89. University of Canterbury, New Zealand, Dept of Computer Science

Kubitsch P., Strauch W. (1987). *Strukturierter Entwurf und Simulation von Praedikat/Transitionsnetzen*. Dip. Inf. Thesis. Dortmund(FRG): Univ. of

Dortmund, Computer Science Dptm.

Kuhn T. S. (1970). *The Structure of Scientific Revolutions* (second edition). Chicago IL: Chicago University Press

Kulken K. (1983). *Kerry Kulken's Witch Tips on Love, Sex and the Stars.* Melbourne: TNPL Books

Kurzweil R. (1985). What is artificial intelligence anyway? *American Scientist* (May-June 1985), 258–264

Ladkin P. (1987). Logical time pieces. *AI Expert* (Aug. 1987), 58–68

Lakatos I. (1970). Falsification and the methodology of scientific research programmes. In: *[Lakatos & Musgrave (1970), 91–196]*

Lakatos I., Musgrave A. (eds.) (1970). *Criticism and the Growth of Knowledge.* Cambridge: Cambridge University Press

Lalonde W. R., Pugh J. R. (1989). *Inside Smalltalk.* Englewood Cliffs NJ: Prentice-Hall

Laursen J., Atkinson R. (1987). Opus: a Smalltalk production system. In: *[SigPlan (1987), 377–387]*

Leblanc R. (1977). Specification and rationale of Telos, a Pascal-based artificial intelligence programming language. *PhD thesis – Technical Report No. 49.* Academic Computing Center. Madison: The University of Wisconsin

Ledgard H. F. (1975). *Programming Proverbs.* Rochelle Park NJ: Hayden

Le Faivre R. A. (1974). Fuzzy problem solving. *PhD thesis – Technical Report No. 37.* Academic Computing Center. Madison: The University of Wisconsin

Leith P. (1985). An IKBS implementation. *SOFTWARE – Practice and Experience*, **15**, 65–86

Leler W. (1988). *Constraint Programming Languages.* Reading MA: Addison-Wesley

Lem S. (1974). *The Cyberiad – Fables for the Cybernetic Age.* Translated from the Polish by: M. Kandel. London: Secker & Warburg

Lenat D. B. (1976). AM: an artificial intelligence approach to discovery in mathematics as heuristic search. *Technical Report STAN-CS-76-570*, Stanford University

Lenat D. B. (1982). The nature of heuristics. *Artificial Intelligence*, **19**, 189–249

Lloyd J. W. (1984). *Foundations of Logic Programming.* Berlin: Springer

Loefgren L. (1977). Complexity of descriptions of systems: a foundational study. *Intl Journal of General Systems*, **3**, 197–214

Logic Programming Associates (1986). *LPA MacProlog Reference Manual.* London: LPA

London R. L., Duisberg R. A. (1985). Animating programs using Smalltalk. *IEEE Computer* (Aug. 1985), 61–71

MacLennan B. J. (1982). Values and objects in programming languages. *ACM SigPlan Notices*, **17**, 70–79

MacLennan B. J. (1983). *Principles of Programming Languages: Design, Evaluation & Implementation.* New York NY: Holt, Rinehart & Winston

Malpas J. (1987). *PROLOG – A Relational Language and Its Applications.* Englewood Cliffs NJ: Prentice-Hall

Marcoussis (1986). Lore – an object-oriented programming environment – a survey. *Technical Report.* Marcoussis(France): Laboratoires de Marcoussis GEC Research Center

Marlin C. (1980). Coroutines: a programming methodology, a language design and an implementation. *Lecture Notes in Computer Science*, **95**, Berlin: Springer

Martin W. A., Fateman R. J. (1971). The MACSYMA system. In: *Proceedings ACM 2nd Symposium on Symbolic and Algebraic Manipulation*, Los Angeles, pp. 23–25

Martin W. A. (1978). Descriptions and the specialization of concepts. *Techn. Report TM-101.* Laboratory of Computer Science, MIT. Cambridge MA: MIT and in: Winston P. H. and Brown H. (eds.) (1979). *Artificial Intelligence: an MIT Perspective.* Cambridge MA: MIT, 375–419

Masterman M. (1970). The nature of a paradigm. In: *[Lakatos and Musgrave (1970), 159–90]*

Mayer M. (1978). *Little Monster's Counting Book.* New York NY: Golden Press

McCarthy J. (1959). LISP: A programming language for manipulating symbolic expressions. *Annual Meeting ACM.* Cambridge MA: MIT

McCarthy J. (1960). Recursive functions of symbolic expressions and their computation by machine. *Communications of the ACM*, **1**, 184–195

McCarthy J. (1978). Lisp. In: Wexelblat R. L. (ed.). *Proceedings ACM SigPlan History of Programming Languages Conference.* New York: ACM, pp. 217–224

McCarthy J., Abrahams P. W., Edwards D. J., Hart T. P., Levin M. I. (1962). *Lisp 1.5 Programmers Manual.* Cambridge MA: MIT – Computation Center

McCorduck P. (1979). *Machines Who Think.* San Francisco CA: W. H. Freeman

McDermott D. (1980). The Prolog phenomenon. *SigArt Newletter*, 72, 16–20

McDermott D. (1981). R1: The formative years. *AI Magazine*, **2**, 21–29

McDermott D. (1982a). Nonmonotonic logic II: nonmonotonic modal theories. *Journal of the ACM*, **29**, 33–57

McDermott D. (1982b). A temporal logic for reasoning about processes and plans. *Cognitive Science*, **6**, 101–155

McDermott D., Sussman G. J. (1972). The Conniver Reference Manual. *AI Memo No. 259.* MIT Project MAC. Cambridge MA: MIT

McDermott D., Doyle J. (1980). Non-monotonic logic I. *Artificial Intelligence*, **13**, 41–72

McGregor J. D. (1987). Object oriented programming with SCOOPS. *Computer Language* (July 1987), 49–56

McMillan C. (1975). *Mathematical Programming* (second edition). New York NY: J. Wiley

McVitie D. G., Wilson L. B. (1969). Three procedures for the stable marriage problem. Algorithm 411. *Collected Algorithms.* New York NY: ACM

McVitie D. G., Wilson L. B. (1970). Stable marriage assignment for unequal sets. *BIT*, **10**, 295–309

Meehan J. (1979). *New UCI LISP Manual.* Hillsdale NJ: Lawrence Erlbaum

Mevel A., Gueguen T. (1987). *Smalltalk-80.* London: MacMillan

Meyer B. (1987). Reusability: the case for object-oriented design. *IEEE-Software* (March 1987), 50–64

Michaelson G. (1989). *An Introduction to Functional Programming through Lambda Calculus.* Wokingham: Addison-Wesley

Michalski R. S., Carbonell J. G., Mitchell T. M. (1985). *Machine Learning.* Palo Alto CA: Tioga

Mitchell T. M. (1982). Generalization as search. *Artificial Intelligence*, **18**, 203–226

Minsky M. (ed.) (1968). *Semantic Information Processing*. Cambridge MA: MIT Press

Minsky M. (1975). A framework for representing knowledge. In: Winston P. (ed.). *The Psychology of Computer Vision*. New York NY: McGraw-Hill

Minsky M. (1980). K-Lines: a theory of memory. *Cognitive Science*, **4**, 117–133

Minsky M. (1985). Communication with alien intelligence. *BYTE* (April 1985), 127–138

MIT (1984). *Scheme Manual* (seventh edition). Dept of Electrical Engineering and Computer Science. Cambridge MA: MIT

Moon D. (1974 – revised 1978). *MacLisp Reference Manual*. Artificial Intelligence Lab. MIT Project MAC. Cambridge MA: MIT

Moses J. (1967). Symbolic integration. *Technical Report MAC-TR-47*, Cambridge MA: MIT

Munakata T. (1986). Procedurally oriented programming techniques in Prolog. *IEEE Expert* (Summer 1986), 41–47

Mylopoulos J., Badler N., Melli L., Roussopoulos N. (1973). 1.PAK: a SNOBOL-based programming language for artificial intelligence applications. In: *3rd Joint Conference on Artificial Intelligence*. New York: ACM, pp. 691–696

Nau D. (1983). Expert computer systems. *IEEE Computer* (Feb. 1983), 63–84

Nebel B. (1985). How well does a vanilla loop fit into a frame? *Data & Knowledge Engineering*, **1**, 181–194

Newell A. (1973). Artificial intelligence and the concept of mind. In: *[Schank & Colby (1973), 1–60]*

Newell A. (1980). Physical symbol systems. *Cognitive Science*, **4**, 135–183

Newell A. (1981). The heuristic of George Polya and its relation to artificial intelligence. In: Groner, Groner, Bischoof (eds.). *Methods of Heuristics*. Hillsdale NJ: Lawrence Erlbaum

Newell A. (1982). The knowledge level. *Artificial Intelligence*, **18**, 87–127

Newell A., Simon H. A. (1956). The logic theory machine: a complex information processing system. *I.R.E. Transactions on Information Theory*, **2**, 61–79

Newell A., Shaw J., Simon H. (1957). Empirical explorations of the logic theory machine. In: *Proc. West. Joint Computer Conf.*, **15**, pp. 218–239

Newell A., Simon H. A. (1972). *Human Problem Solving*. Englewood Cliffs NJ: Prentice-Hall

Newell A., Simon H. A. (1976). Computer science as empirical inquiry: symbols and search. *Communications of the ACM*, **19**, 113–126

Nii P. (1986a). Blackboard systems: the blackboard model of problem solving and the evolution of blackboard architectures. *The AI Magazine* (Summer 1986), 38–53

Nii P. (1986b). Blackboard systems: blackboard application systems, blackboard systems from a knowledge engineering perspective. *The AI Magazine* (Aug. 1986), 82–106

Nilsson N. J. (1971). *Problem-Solving Methods in Artificial Intelligence*. New York NY: McGraw-Hill

Nilsson N. J. (1980). *Principles of Artificial Intelligence*. Palo Alto CA: Tioga & Berlin: Springer

Norvig P. (1984). Playing Mastermind optimally. *ACM SigArt Newsletter* (Oct. 1984), 33–34

Novak G. S. Jr. (1983). Data abstraction in GLISP. In: *Proceedings ACM Conference on Principles of Programming Languages*. New York: ACM, pp. 170–177

Nygaard K., Dahl O. J. (1978). The development of the SIMULA languages. In: 'Preprints of the Conference on History of Programming Languages'. *ACM SigPlan Notices*, **13**

O'Shea T., Eisenstadt M. (eds.) (1984). *Artificial Intelligence – Tools, Techniques, and Applications.* New York NY: Harper & Row

Organick E. I. (1973). *Computer System Organization – The B5700/B6700 Series.* New York NY: Academic Press

Ortoni A., Wilks Y. (1980). Cognitive science vs. artificial intelligence? *SigArt Newsletter* (Jan. 1980), 14–15

Pao Yoh-Han (1989). *Adaptive Pattern Recognition and Neural-Nets Implementation.* Reading MA: Addison-Wesley

Papert S. (1980). *Mindstorms: Children, Computers, and Powerful Ideas.* New York NY: Basic Books

Paroli F. (1983). A fine adventure. *ACM SigArt Newsletter* (April 1983).

Pascoe G. A. (1986). Elements of object-oriented programming. *BYTE* (Aug. 1986), 139–144

Pearl J. (1984). *Heuristics – Intelligent Search Strategies for Computer Problem Solving.* Reading MA: Addison-Wesley

Pepper J., Kahn G. (1986). KnowledgeCraft: an environment for rapid prototyping of expert systems. In: *Proceedings Artificial Intelligence for the Automotive Industry*. Detroit (MI): Society of Manufacturing Engineers, pp. 1–8

Piatelli-Palmarini M. (ed.) (1980). *Language and Learning. The Debate between Jean Piaget and Noam Chomsky.* Cambridge MA: Harvard University Press

Piersol K. (1987). *Humble Reference Manual.* Pasadena CA: Xerox Special Information Systems

Pinson L. J., Wiener R. S. (1988). *An Introduction to Object-Oriented Programming and Smalltalk.* Reading MA: Addison-Wesley

Polya G. (1957). *How to Solve It.* Princeton: Princeton University Press

Polya G. (1962). *Mathematical Discovery Vols. 1 & 2.* New York NY: Wiley

Post E. L. (1943). Formal reduction of the general combinatorial decision problem. *American Journal of Mathematics*, **65**, 197–268

Pountain D. (1986). Object-oriented Forth. *BYTE* (Aug. 1986), 227–233

Pugh J. R. (1984). Actors – the stage is set. *ACM SigPlan Notices*, **19**, 61–65

Pugh, J. R., Lalonde, W. R. (1990). *Inside Smalltalk.* Englewood Cliffs NJ: Prentice-Hall

Pylyshyn Z. (1984). *Computation and Cognition.* Cambridge MA: MIT Press

Quarterman J. S., Silberschatz A., Peterson J. L. (1985). 4.2BSD and 4.3BSD as examples of the UNIX system. *ACM Computing Surveys*, **17**, 379–418

Quillian (1968). Semantic memory. In: *[Minsky (1968), 227–70]*

Racter (1984). *The Policeman's Beard is Half-Constructed.* New York NY: Warner Books

Ramamoorthy C. V., Shekhar S., Garg V. (1987). Software development support for AI programs. *IEEE Computer* (Jan. 1987), 30–40

Raphael B. (1968). SIR: semantic information retrieval. In: *[Minsky (1968)]*

Raphael B. (1976). *The Thinking Computer.* San Francisco CA: Freeman

Ramsdell J. (1987). *Poem.* Contributed to: Scheme electronic mailing list at MIT. Cambridge MA: UUCP

Rathke C. (1984). *ObjTalk Primer.* Technical Report – Project Inform. Department of Computer Science. Stuttgart (FRG): University of Stuttgart

Rauch-Hindin W. B. (1987). *Artificial Intelligence in Business, Science and Industry – Vol. I: Fundamentals, Vol. II: Applications.* Englewood Cliffs NJ: Prentice-Hall

Reade C. (1989). *Elements of Functional Programming.* Wokingham: Addison-Wesley

Reenskaug T. (1981). User-oriented descriptions of Smalltalk systems. *BYTE* (Aug. 1981), 148–166

Rees J. A., Adams N. I. (1982). T: A dialect of Lisp or, lambda: the ultimate software tool. In: *Conference Record of the 1982 ACM Symposium on Lisp and Functional Programming.* New York: ACM, pp. 114–122

Rees J. A., Adams N. I., Meehan R. (1984). *The T manual* (fourth edition). Computer Science Dptm. New Haven CT: Yale University

Rees J. A., Clinger W. (eds.) (1986). Revised^3 report on the algorithmic language Scheme. *ACM SigPlan Notices,* **21**, 37–79

Rentsch T. (1982). Object oriented programming. *ACM SigPlan Notices,* **17**, 51–57

Rich E. (1983). *Artificial Intelligence.* New York NY: McGraw-Hill

Rieger C., Rosenberg J., Samet H. (1979). Artificial intelligence programming languages for computer aided manufacturing. *IEEE Transactions on Systems, Man, and Cybernetics,* **SMC-9**, 205–226

Ringle M. D. (ed.) (1979). *Philosophical Perspectives of Artificial Intelligence.* Hassocks: Harvester Press

Ringwood G. A. (1988). PARLOG86 and the dining logicians. *Communications of the ACM,* **31**, 10–15

Roberts E. S. (1986). *Thinking Recursively.* New York NY: Wiley

Roberts I., Goldstein R. (1977). The FRL primer. *AI Memo #408.* Cambridge MA: MIT

Roberts N., Andersen D., Deal R., Garet M., Shaffer W. (1983). *Introduction to Computer Simulation – A System Dynamics Modeling Approach.* Reading MA: Addison-Wesley

Robinson J. A. (1965). A machine-oriented logic based on the resolution principle. *Journal of the ACM,* **12**(1), 23–41

Robinson J. A. (1979). *Logic: Form and Function. The Mechanization of Deductive Reasoning.* New York NY: American Elsevier

Robson D. (1981). Object-oriented software systems. *BYTE* (Aug. 1981), 75–86

Rochat R. (1986). In search of good Smalltalk programming style. *Technical Report CR-86-19.* Tektronix Computer Research Laboratory. Beaverton OR: Tektronix Inc.

Rogers J. (1986). *A PROLOG Primer.* Reading MA: Addison-Wesley

Rosenfeld A. (1979). *Picture Languages.* New York NY: Academic Press

Rosenholtz I. (1984). Tackling a ticklish type of Tic-Tac-Toe (or the case of the (almost) total tactics) II. *Journal of Recreational Mathematics,* **17**, 81–90

Rowe N. C. (1988). *Artificial intelligence through PROLOG.* Englewood Cliffs NJ: Prentice-Hall

Rubin F. (1980). The clocks of Klotz and Klutz. *Journal of Recreational Mathematics,* **12**, 53–54

Rubinstein M. F. (1975). *Patterns of Problem Solving.* Englewood Cliffs NJ: Prentice-Hall

Rulifson J. F., Waldinger R. J., Derksen J. A. (1973). QA4: a procedural calculus for intuitive reasoning. *Techn. Note 73.* Palo Alto CA: Stanford Res. Institute

Russell B. (1923). Vagueness. *Australian Journal of Philosophy*, **1**, 84–92

Rychener M. D. (1976). Production systems as a programming language for artificial intelligence applications. *PhD thesis, Dept of Computer Science.* Pittsburgh: Carnegie-Mellon University

Sacerdoti E. D. (1974). Planning in a hierarchy of abstraction spaces. *Artificial Intelligence*, **5**, 115–135

Sacerdoti E. D. (1977). *A Structure for Plans and Behaviour.* New York NY: Elsevier

Sacerdoti E. D., Fikes R. E., Reboh R., Sagalowicz D., Waldinger R. J., Wilber B. M. (1976). QLISP: a language for the interactive development of complex systems. *Techn. Note 120.* Palo Alto CA: Stanford Research Institute

Sammut C. A., Sammut R. A. (1983). The implementation of UNSW-Prolog. *Australian Computer Journal*, **15**(2), 58–64

Samuel A. L. (1959). Some studies in machine learning using the game of checkers. *IBM Journal of Research & Development*, **3**, 211–229

Sandewall E. (1978). Programming in the interactive environment: the LISP experience. *Computing Surveys*, **10**, 35–72

Savage C. W. (ed.) (1978). *Perception and Cognition Issues in the Foundation of Psychology.* Minneapolis: Minnesota Studies in the Philosophy of Science, Vol. IX

Schank R. C. (1980). Language and memory. *Cognitive Science*, **4**, 243–284

Schank R. C., Colby K. M. (eds.) (1973). *Computer Models of Thought and Language.* San Francisco CA: Freeman

Schank R., Abelson R. (1977). *Scripts, Plans, Goals and Understanding.* Hillsdale NJ: Lawrence Erlbaum

Schank R. C., Riesbeck C. K. (eds.) (1981). *Inside Computer Understanding: Five Programs Plus Miniatures.* Hillsdale NJ: Lawrence Erlbaum

Schmucker K. (1986a). *Object-Oriented Programming for the Macintosh.* Hasbrouk Heights NJ: Hayden

Schmucker K. (1986b). MacApp: an application framework. *BYTE* (Aug. 1986), 189–193

Sedgewick R. (1983). *Algorithms.* Reading MA: Addison-Wesley

Semantic Microsystems (1986). *MacScheme Reference Manual.* Portland OR: Semantic Microsystems

Shalit A. (1986). LISP listener – simple graphics objects. *MacTutor* (Nov. 1986), 69–72

Shapiro E. (1986). Concurrent Prolog: a progress report. *IEEE Computer* (Aug. 1986), 44–58

Shapiro S. C. (1979). The SNePS semantic network processing system. In: *[Findler (1979), 179–203]*

Shapiro S. C. (ed.) (1987). *Encyclopedia of Artificial Intelligence* – 2 vols. New York NY: Wiley

Sheil B. A. (1981). The psychological study of programming – special issue. *ACM Computing Surveys*, **13**, 101–120

Sheil B. A. (1983). Power tools for programmers. *Datamation* (Feb. 1983),

131–144
Shortliffe E. H. (1976). *Computer-Based Medical Consultation: MYCIN.* New York NY: American Elsevier
SigPlan (1977). Proceedings of the Symposium on Artificial Intelligence and Programming Languages. *ACM SigPlan Notices,* **12**
SigPlan (1985). Proceedings of the ACM SigPlan 85 Symposium on Language Issues in Programming Environments. *ACM SigPlan Notices,* **20**
SigPlan (1986a). Proceedings Object-Oriented Programming Workshop. *ACM SigPlan Notices,* **21**
SigPlan (1986b). *OOPSLA '86 Conference Proceedings.* New York NY: ACM
SigPlan (1987). *OOPSLA '87 Conference Proceedings.* New York NY: ACM
Siklossy L. (1976). *Let's Talk LISP.* Englewood Cliffs NJ: Prentice-Hall
Simon H. A. (1962). The architecture of complexity. In: *Proceedings of the American Philosophical Society* **106**, pp. 467–482. Reprinted in: *[Simon (1969)]*
Simon H. A. (1969). *The Sciences of the Artificial.* Cambridge MA: MIT Press (2nd edition (1981)
Simon H. A. (1983). Search and reasoning in problem solving. *Artificial Intelligence,* **21**, 7–29
Simon H. A., Feigenbaum E. A. (1964). An information processing theory of some effects of similarity, familiarization, and meaningfulness in verbal learning. *Journal of Verbal Learning and Verbal Behaviour,* **3**, 385–396
Slagle J. R. (1963). A heuristic program that solves symbolic integration problems in freshman calculus. *Journal of the ACM,* **10**, 507–520
Slagle S. (1987). *The T Programming Language: A Dialect of Lisp.* Englewood Cliffs NJ: Prentice-Hall
Sloman A. (1971). Interactions between philosophy and artificial intelligence: the role of intuition and non-logical reasoning in intelligence. *Artificial Intelligence,* **2**, 209–225
Sloman A. (1978). *The Computer Revolution in Philosophy.* Hassocks: Harvester
Smith H. T., Green T. R. G. (eds.) (1980). *Human Interaction with Computers.* New York NY: Academic Press
Smith D. C. (1970). MLISP. *Memo AIM-135.* Palo Alto: Stanford AI Project
Smullyan R. (1984). *Alice in Puzzle-Land.* Harmondsworth: Penguin
Snyder A. (1985). Object-oriented proposal for Common Lisp. *Technical Report ATC-85-1.* Palo Alto CA: Hewlett Packard Laboratories
Sowa J. A. (1984). *Conceptual Structures – Information Processing in Mind and Machine.* Reading MA: Addison-Wesley
Springer, G., Friedman, D.P. (1989). *Scheme and the Art of Programming.* New York: McGraw-Hill
Steele D. (1989). *Lisp Programming for AI.* Wokingham: Addison-Wesley
Steele G. L. Jr. (1984). *COMMON LISP: The Language.* Bedford MA: Digital Press
Steele G. L., Sussman G. J. (1978). The revised report on Scheme: a dialect of Lisp. *AI Memo No. 452.* MIT Project MAC. Cambridge MA: MIT
Stefik M. (1979). An examination of a frame structured representation system. In: *Proceedings Int. Joint Conference on Artificial Intelligence* **1979**. New York NY: ACM, pp. 845–852
Stefik M. (1982). The organization of expert systems. A tutorial. *Artificial Intelligence,* **18**, 135–173

Stefik M., Bobrow D. G. (1985). Object-oriented programming: themes and variations. *The AI Magazine*, 40–62

Sterling L., Shapiro E. (1986). *The Art of PROLOG*. Cambridge MA: MIT Press

Stoyan H. (1980). *LISP – Anwendungsgebiete, Grundbegriffe, Geschichte*. Berlin: Akademie Verlag

Stoyan H., Goerz G. (1984). *LISP* (in German). Berlin: Springer

Stroustrup B. (1986). An overview of C++. In: *[SigPlan (1986), 7–18]*

Stroustrup B. (1985). *The C++ Programming Language*. Reading MA: Addison-Wesley

Sussman G. J. (1975). *A Computer Model of Skill Acquisition*. New York NY: Elsevier

Sussman G. J., Winograd T. (1970). Micro-Planner reference manual. *AI Memo No. 203*. MIT Project MAC. Cambridge MA: MIT

Sussman G. J., McDermott D. V. (1972). Why conniving is better than planning. *AI Memo No. 255A*. MIT Project MAC. Cambridge MA: MIT

Sussman G. J., Steele G. L. Jr. (1975). Scheme: an interpreter for extended lambda calculus. *AI Memo No. 349*. MIT Project MAC. Cambridge MA: MIT

Sussman G. J., Holloway J., Steele G. J. Jr., Bell A. (1981). Scheme 79 – Lisp on a chip. *IEEE Computer*, **14**, 10–21

Sutherland I. E. (1963). SKETCHPAD: a man-machine graphical communication system. In: *Proceedings Spring Joint Computer Conference*. New York NY: ACM, pp. 329

Tanimoto S. L. (1987). *The Elements of Artificial Intelligence – An Introduction Using LISP*. Rockville: Computer Science Press

Teitelman W. (1974 – revised 1978). *INTERLISP Reference Manual*. Palo Alto CA: Xerox Palo Alto Research Center, and Cambridge MA: Bolt, Beranek and Newman

Teitelman W., Masinter L. (1981). The Interlisp programming environment. *IEEE Computer* (April 1981), 25–33

Tesler L. (1981). The Smalltalk environment. *BYTE* (Aug. 1981), 90–141

Tesler L. (1986). Programming experiences. *BYTE* (Aug. 1986), 195–206

Texas Instruments (1985). *Scheme Language Reference Manual – SCOOPS*. Texas Instruments

Theriault D. (1982a). A primer for the ACT-1 language. *AI-Memo No. 672*. MIT Project MAC. Cambridge MA: MIT

Theriault D. (1982b). Issues in the design and implementation of Act 2. *AI-Memo No. 728*. MIT Project MAC. Cambridge MA: MIT

Thomas J. C., Carroll J. M. (1981). Human factors in communications. *IBM Systems Journal*, **20**, 237–263

Thorne J., Bratley P., Dewar H. (1968). The syntactic analysis of English by machine. In: Michie D. (ed.) *Machine Intelligence 3*. New York NY: American Elsevier

Tokoro M., Ishikawa Y. (1986). Concurrent programming on Orient 84/K: an object-oriented knowledge representation language. In: *[SigPlan (1986), 39–48]*

Touretzki D. S. (1984). *LISP – A Gentle Introduction to Symbolic Computation*. New York NY: Harper & Row

Touretzki D. S. (1988). How Lisp has changed. *BYTE* (Feb. 1988), 229–234

Townsend C. (1987). *Introduction to Turbo PROLOG*. Berkeley: Sybex

Turing A. (1936). On computable numbers, with an application to the Entscheidungsproblem. In: *Proceedings of the London Mathematical Society*. Series 2, **42**, 230–265

Turing A. (1950). Computing machinery and intelligence. *Mind*, **59**, 433–460

Turner D. A. (ed.) (1989). *Declarative Programming*. Reading MA: Addison-Wesley

Turner R. (1984). *Logics for Artificial Intelligence*. Chichester: Ellis Horwood

Ungar D., Patterson D. (1987). What price Smalltalk? *IEEE Computer* (Jan. 1987), 67–74

Vance J. (1972). *The Eyes of the Overworld*. London: Granada Publ.

Vance J. (1983). *Cugel's Saga*. New York NY: Simon & Schuster

van Emden M. (1982). Warren's doctrine on the slash. *Logic Programming Newsletter* (Oct. 1982)

Vasak T. (1986). A survey of control facilities in logic programming. *The Australian Computer Journal*, **18**, 136–145

Vaucher J. G., Duval P. (1975). A comparison of simulation event list algorithms. *CACM*, **18**(4), 223–230

Von Neumann J. (1958). *The Computer and the Brain*. New Haven CT: Yale University Press

Waismann F. (1967). *Wittgenstein und der Wiener Kreis (Conversations recorded by Waismann)*. Oxford: Basil Blackwell

Walker A., McCord M., Sowa J. F., Wilson W. G. (1987). *Knowledge Systems and PROLOG*. Reading MA: Addison-Wesley

Waltz D. (1975). Understanding line drawings of scenes with shadows. In: Winston P. H. (ed.) *The Psychology of Computer Vision*. New York NY: McGraw-Hill

Wand M. (1980). Continuation-based multiprocessing. In: *Proceedings of the 1980 LISP Conference*. New York NY: ACM, pp. 19–27

Warren D. H. (1974). WARPLAN: a system for generating plans. *Memo 76* Dept of Computational Logic, School of Artificial Intelligence. University of Edinburgh

Waterman R., Hayes-Roth F. (eds.) (1978). *Pattern-Directed Inference Systems*. New York NY: Academic Press

Wegner P. (1986). Classification in object-oriented systems. In: *[SigPlan (1986), 173–182]*

Wegner P. (1987). Dimensions of object-based language design. In: *[SigPlan (1987), 168–182]*

Wegner P., Shriver B. (eds.) (1986). Proceedings of an Object-Oriented Programming Workshop. *ACM SigPlan Notices*, **21**

Weinberg G. M. (1972). A computer approach to general systems theory. In: *[Klir (1972), 98–141]*

Weinreb D., Moon D. A. (1980). Flavors: message passing in the Lisp machine. *AI Memo No. 602*. MIT Project MAC. Cambridge MA: MIT

Weinreb D., Moon D. A. (1981). *LISP Machine LISP Manual* (fourth edition). Cambridge MA: MIT

Weizenbaum J. (1966). ELIZA – a computer program for the study of natural language communication between man and machine. *Communications of the ACM*, **9**, 36–45

Weizenbaum J. (1976). *Computer Power and Human Reason*. San Francisco CA: W. H. Freeman

Weyrhauch R. W. (1980). Prolegomena to a theory of mechanized formal reasoning. *Artificial Intelligence*, **13**

White A. R. (1975). Conceptual analysis. In: Bontempo C. L. and Odell S. J. (eds.) *The Owl of Minerva.* New York NY: McGraw-Hill, pp. 103–117

Whitehead A. N. (1925). *Science and the Modern World.* London: MacMillan

Whitehead A. N., Russell B. (1910–1913). *Principia Mathematica.* Cambridge: Cambridge University Press

Wickelgren W. A. (1974). *How to Solve Problems.* New York NY: W.H. Freeman

Wiederhold G. (1984). Knowledge and database management. *IEEE Software* (Jan. 1984), 63–73

Wiener N. (1948). *Cybernetics, or Control and Communication in the Animal and the Machine.* MIT Press 1961 (original work published in 1948)

Wiener R. S., Pinson L. J. (1988). *An Introduction to Object-Oriented Programming and C++.* Reading MA: Addison-Wesley

Wilensky R. (1984). *LISPCraft and COMMON LISPCraft.* New York NY: Norton

Wilson L. B. (1972). An analysis of the stable marriage assignment algorithm. *BIT*, **12**, 569–575

Winograd T. (1972). *Understanding Natural Language.* New York NY: Academic Press

Winograd T. (1975). Frame representations and the declarative-procedural controversy. In: *[Bobrow and Collins (1975), 185–210]*

Winograd T. (1980). Extended inference modes in reasoning by computer systems. *Artificial Intelligence*, **13**, 5–26

Winograd T. (1983a). Programming issues for the 1980s (panel discussion). In: SigPlan '83: Symposium on Programming Language Issues in Software Systems – reprinted in: *ACM SigPlan Notices*, **19**, 51–61

Winograd T. (1983b). *Language as a Cognitive Process – Syntax* (volume 1). Reading MA: Addison-Wesley

Winston P. H. (1980). Learning and reasoning by analogy. *Communications of the ACM*, **23**, 689–703

Winston P. H. (1984). *Artificial Intelligence* (second edition). Reading MA: Addison-Wesley

Winston P. H. (1985). The Lisp revolution. *BYTE* (April 1985), 209–218

Winston P. H., Horn K. P. (1984). *LISP* (second edition). Reading MA: Addison-Wesley

Wirth N. (1971). Program development by stepwise refinement. *Communications of the ACM*, **14**, 221–227

Wise M. J. (1986). *Prolog Multiprocessors.* Englewood Cliffs NJ: Prentice-Hall

Wittgenstein L. (1922). *Tractatus Logico-Philosophicus.* London: Routledge & Kegan Paul

Wittgenstein L. (1953). *Philosophical Investigations.* Oxford: Blackwell

Wittgenstein L. (1956). *Remarks on the Foundations of Mathematics.* Oxford: Blackwell

Wong W. G. (1987). PC Scheme: a lexical Lisp. *BYTE* (March 1987), 223–226

Woods W. A. (1970). Transition network grammars for natural language analysis. *Communications of the ACM*, **13**, 591–606

Woods W. A. (1977). Lunar rocks in natural English: explorations in natural language question answering. In: Zamponi A. (ed.) *Linguistic Structures Processing.* New York NY: Elsevier–North Holland

Wulf W. A., Shaw M., Hilfinger P. N., Flon L. (1981). *Fundamental Structures of Computer Science.* Reading MA: Addison-Wesley

Yonezawa A., Tokoro M. (eds.) (1986). *Object-Oriented Concurrent Programming.* Cambridge MA: MIT Press

Yonezawa A., Shibayama E., Honda Y., Takada T. (1986). Modelling and programming in a concurrent object-oriented language ABCL/1. In: *[Yonezawa & Tokoro (1986)]*

Zadeh L. A. (1979). A theory of approximate reasoning. In: Hayes J. E., Michie D., Mikulich L. I. (eds.). *Machine Intelligence 9.* New York NY: J. Wiley, pp. 149–194

Zadeh L. A. (1986). A simple view of the Dempster-Shafer theory of evidence and its implication for the rule of combination. *The AI Magazine* (Summer 1986), 85–90

Index

1 General terms

2 Toolbox procedures

3 Programs